SUPERVISION

A Skill-Building Approach

"He makes me so mad I could scream!" exclaimed Kay Hanson. "A charge nurse's job is tough enough, but Walt Fallon doesn't make it any easier." Kay had just asked Walt to help one of the nurses on her floor move a patient. Walt, an orderly, came back with, "Get somebody else who isn't a shop steward; I've got important union business I'm in the middle of." Kay complained that Walt had to be available for work, "Since that's what you were hired to do."

"My contract says that I can spend a reasonable amount of time doing union business since I'm a steward. I think the 15 hours a week I spend is reasonable."

"Well, I don't!" replied Kay. "And I'm going to see to it that you are more help around here."

Two days later, Walt had filed a grievance that ultimately went all the way to arbitration. The process cost both the hospital and the union a great deal in time and money. What could either side have done to prevent all this?

I. Unions

Before you read about unions, let's define labor relations. **Labor relations** *are the interactions between management and unionized employees.* Labor relations are also called *union-management relations* or *industrial relations.* A recent study revealed that better labor relations can have an effect on productivity three times greater than either a capital investment (including robots) or a change in labor methods.[1]

There are many more organizations without unions than there are with unions. As a supervisor, you may not work for a unionized organization. However, there is a good chance that you will have to interact with organizations that do have unions. The more you know about labor relations, the better are your chances of dealing effectively with unions and their employees.

The **union** *is an organization that represents employees in collective bargaining with the employer.* The union is typically associated with the blue-collar worker. Salaried and professional employees do not tend to associate themselves with unions. They are more likely to form or join an *employee association* to gain collective bargaining power. About 40 percent of the public employees in the United States belong to employee associations. These are the largest:

- National Education Association.
- New York State Employee Association.
- American Nurses Associations.
- Fraternal Order of Police.

A major difference between unions and employee associations is that unions have the legal right to strike. Employee associations have been known to strike, however. In 1981, 11,000 air traffic controllers illegally went on strike. The strike resulted in President Reagan's firing them. Throughout this chapter, when I use the term *union* it will include employee associations as well.

A Brief History of Unions

In the late 18th century, skilled workers such as shoemakers, tailors, printers, bakers, and carpenters organized into trade unions. In those early days, the unions did not bargain collectively as they do today. Instead, members posted the prices and conditions under which they would work. If an employer would not meet these terms, the skilled craftspeople would not work. Although these workers did occasionally band together to demand wage increases, the association usually ended when the demands were met.

The first permanent national union was the Knights of Labor, founded in 1869. By 1886 it had over 700,000 members. Internal difficulties and lack of success in a few major strikes hurt the union. Within a few years it was defunct. The Knights of Labor was ultimately replaced by the American Federation of Labor (AFL), founded in 1886. Under the leadership of its president, Samuel Gompers, the AFL became a craft union representing skilled workers such as printers, carpenters, plumbers, and so on. Three-fourths of the skilled workers in this country had joined the AFL by 1920. In order to continue to grow, in 1935 the AFL offered membership to unskilled workers who were not eligible previously. These unskilled workers were represented by the Congress of Industrial Organizations (CIO). Despite certain conflicts, in 1955 the two merged to form the AFL-CIO, which is by far the largest union in this country, representing about 80 percent of all union members.

Why Employees Join Unions

There are several advantages to union membership:

Increased Wages and Benefits: Employees who want higher wages, better benefits, or both often join unions. In 1985 union workers enjoyed substantially higher median earnings than nonunion workers.[2] For a comparison of wage differences, see Exhibit 16–1.

Job Security: It is generally more difficult to fire a union employee. Labor unions tend to have seniority provisions to protect workers with longer service to the organization from being laid off temporarily or permanently. A union helps prevent management from getting rid of highly paid, experienced employees while keeping lower paid employees to save money. With the decrease in the number of employees in the manufacturing sector, job security is a major concern of unions.[3]

Uniform Treatment: Unions usually require uniform treatment of members on issues such as seniority.[4] Unions often provide all employees with the same wage increase. They fear that merit raises will not be given equitably. Uniform treatment helps protect the employee from an unfair supervisor. Supervisors must be careful to treat all employees alike or they may have a conflict with the union.

Strength in Numbers: If one employee is dissatisfied and complains to management, he or she may not be heard. But if the union complains, management is likely to listen and take corrective action. Dissatisfaction is a major reason why employees join unions. They believe they will get better treatment from management if they are unionized.

Social Benefits: Unions provide members with social activities that help meet their affiliation needs. Unions have meetings that members can attend, and they offer social functions as well.

Employment: In some situations, you cannot get or retain certain jobs unless you belong to the appropriate union.

There is a direct relationship between the reasons why employees join unions, and motivation, discussed in Chapter 11. In other words, people join unions to meet their needs.

Why Employees Do Not Join Unions

As the foregoing discussion indicates, there are many advantages to joining a union. However, they do not appeal to some employees for the following reasons:

Satisfaction with Management: Employees who are satisfied with their pay and the way management treats them are often unwilling to join a union. They do not believe that a union will make the situation any better. In fact, some employees believe things will be worse with a union representing them.

Cost: Union membership costs money. Initial fees are usually less than $100; however, some are considerably higher. The average employee must work one to two hours per month to pay union dues. An employee who earns $15,000 annually will pay an average of $300 per year in dues.[5] Many employees do not think the cost is worth the benefits of union membership.

Social Pressure: Some people are against unions and pressure others not to join them. This is particularly the case in white-collar and professional jobs where unions are traditionally thought of as being for blue-collar workers.

Union Membership

Union membership has been on the decline since 1953. Between 1983 and 1989, membership dropped from 17.7 to 16.9 million. After three decades of decline, the union share of total employment leveled at 16.1 percent in 1991.[6] In the private sector, union membership shrank to 11.9 percent, from about 40 percent in the

EXHIBIT 16-1   TABLE NO. 697. UNION MEMBERS, BY SELECTED CHARACTERISTICS; 1983 AND 1989

[Annual averages of monthly data. Covers employed wage and salary workers 16 years old and over. Excludes self-employed workers whose businesses are incorporated although they technically qualify as wage and salary workers. Based on Current Population Survey, see text, section 1 and Appendix III]

| CHARACTERISTIC | Employed Wage and Salary Workers | | | | | | | | | | Median Usual Weekly Earnings[3] (dollars) | | | | | | | |
| | Total (1,000) | | Union Members[1] (1,000) | | Represented by Unions[2] (1,000) | | Percentage Union Members | | Percentage Represented by Union | | Total | | Union Members[1] | | Represented by Unions[2] | | Not Represented by Unions | |
	1983	1989	1983	1989	1983	1989	1983	1989	1983	1989	1983	1989	1983	1989	1983	1989	1983	1989
Total	88,290	103,480	17,717	16,960	20,532	19,198	20.1	16.4	23.3	18.6	313	399	388	497	383	494	288	372
16-24 years	19,305	19,154	1,749	1,203	2,145	1,424	9.1	6.3	11.1	7.4	210	259	281	335	275	331	203	252
25-34 years	25,978	31,210	5,097	4,471	5,990	5,150	19.6	14.3	23.1	16.5	321	394	382	473	376	466	304	378
35-44 years	18,722	25,316	4,648	5,292	5,362	5,975	24.8	20.9	28.6	23.6	369	472	411	519	407	518	339	438
45-54 years	13,150	16,233	3,554	3,719	4,014	4,134	27.0	22.9	30.5	25.5	366	472	404	523	402	523	335	431
55-64 years	9,301	9,302	2,474	2,056	2,788	2,372	26.9	22.1	30.3	24.4	346	431	392	504	390	504	316	401
65 years and over	1,934	2,265	196	220	234	243	10.1	9.7	12.1	10.7	260	334	338	478	330	470	238	306
Men	47,856	54,789	11,809	10,820	13,270	11,955	24.7	19.7	27.7	21.8	378	468	416	527	414	524	349	430
Women	40,433	48,691	5,906	6,141	7,262	7,243	14.6	12.6	18.0	14.9	252	328	309	417	307	416	237	312
White	77,046	88,622	14,844	13,894	17,182	15,689	19.3	15.7	22.3	17.7	319	409	396	506	391	503	295	384
Men	42,168	47,410	10,134	9,140	11,364	10,055	24.0	19.3	26.9	21.2	387	482	423	589	421	537	362	452
Women	34,877	41,212	4,710	4,754	5,818	5,634	13.5	11.5	16.7	13.7	254	334	314	427	313	423	240	317
Black	8,979	11,470	2,440	2,549	2,850	2,912	27.2	22.2	31.7	25.4	261	319	331	425	324	423	222	290
Men	4,477	5,597	1,420	1,387	1,615	1,566	31.7	24.8	36.1	28.0	293	348	366	478	360	470	244	305
Women	4,502	5,873	1,020	1,162	1,235	1,345	22.7	19.8	27.4	22.9	231	301	292	385	287	390	209	276
Hispanic[4]	(NA)	7,894	(NA)	1,196	(NA)	1,330	(NA)	15.2	(NA)	16.8	(NA)	298	(NA)	420	(NA)	417	(NA)	276
Men	(NA)	4,710	(NA)	793	(NA)	870	(NA)	16.8	(NA)	18.5	(NA)	315	(NA)	457	(NA)	451	(NA)	291
Women	(NA)	3,184	(NA)	403	(NA)	460	(NA)	12.6	(NA)	14.5	(NA)	269	(NA)	369	(NA)	368	(NA)	255
Full-time workers	70,976	84,553	16,271	15,701	18,745	17,683	22.9	18.6	26.4	20.9	313	399	388	497	383	494	288	372
Part-time workers	17,314	18,926	1,446	1,259	1,787	1,515	8.4	6.7	10.3	8.0	(X)	(X)	(X)	(X)	(X)	(X)	(X)	(X)
Managerial and professional specialty	19,657	25,357	3,354	3,739	4,307	4,606	17.1	14.7	21.9	15.2	437	583	423	584	421	581	446	584
Technical sales, and admin. support	28,024	32,633	3,377	3,299	4,199	3,932	12.1	10.1	15.0	12.1	281	359	350	439	341	431	270	346
Service occupations	12,875	14,410	1,971	1,948	2,306	2,172	15.3	13.5	17.9	15.1	205	253	305	411	299	406	182	226
Precision, production, craft, and repair	10,542	11,906	3,466	3,134	3,760	3,355	32.9	26.3	35.7	28.2	377	454	456	574	450	568	322	405
Operators, fabricators, and laborers	15,416	17,399	5,452	4,774	5,839	5,050	35.4	27.4	37.9	29.0	275	323	366	455	361	448	226	287
Farming, forestry, and fishing	1,775	1,774	98	67	122	82	5.5	3.8	6.0	4.6	196	246	292	393	287	379	189	259
Agricultural wage and salary workers	1,446	1,499	49	18	55	31	3.4	1.2	3.8	2.1	196	249	(B)	(B)	(B)	(B)	195	246
Private nonagri. wage and salary workers	71,225	84,504	11,953	10,520	13,369	11,556	16.8	12.4	18.8	13.7	307	387	389	489	385	485	286	368
Mining	869	664	180	117	201	131	20.7	17.5	23.1	19.7	481	565	470	572	470	572	488	561
Construction	4,109	5,322	1,131	1,145	1,207	1,203	27.5	21.5	29.4	22.6	348	431	518	642	510	634	296	393
Manufacturing	19,066	20,690	5,303	4,467	5,812	4,779	27.8	21.6	30.5	23.1	335	415	370	460	368	458	315	400
Transportation and public utilities	5,142	6,109	2,182	1,927	2,376	2,083	42.4	31.6	46.2	34.1	417	502	449	567	445	561	386	458
Wholesale and retail trade, total	18,061	21,136	1,568	1,321	1,775	1,478	8.7	6.3	9.8	7.0	252	305	353	407	348	402	242	298
Finance, insurance, and real estate	5,559	6,851	160	155	228	209	2.9	2.3	4.1	3.1	296	406	284	400	285	399	297	407
Services	18,400	23,731	1,410	1,388	1,770	1,673	7.7	5.8	9.6	7.0	272	357	303	398	303	402	268	352
Government	15,618	17,476	5,735	6,422	7,109	7,611	36.7	36.7	45.5	43.6	351	472	386	509	381	506	316	419

B Data not shown where base is less than 50,000.

NA Not available.

X Not applicable.

[1] Members of a labor union or an employee association similar to a labor union.

[2] Members of a labor union or an employee association similar to a union as well as workers who report no union affiliation but whose jobs are covered by a union or an employee association contract.

[3] For full-time employed wage and salary workers; 1983 revised since originally published.

[4] Persons of Hispanic origin may be of any race.

Source: U.S. Bureau of Labor Statistics, Employment and Earnings, January issues. in Statistical Abstracts,

mid-1950s.[7] The government sector has the largest percentage of union membership at 36.9 percent, followed by the transportation and public utilities sector with 31.6 percent. For a more detailed analysis of union membership by various characteristics, see Exhibit 16–1.

Why Has Union Membership Decreased?

Many people have speculated on the reasons for the decline in union membership. Stepina and Fiorito conducted research to verify these assumptions.[8] I will now list common assumptions followed by Stepina and Fiorito's research findings to support or refute the claims.

Wages: When unions gain significant wage increases, membership increases. This is supported by research. However, in recent years, unions have not gained wage increases. In addition, many organizations are giving similar increases to prevent unions from organizing.

Prices: During inflationary periods people are more apt to join a union to protect their standard of living. Research concludes that this is not always the case.

Unemployment: When unemployment is low, there is a greater opportunity for unionization. Research shows that this is true to some extent. However, with government programs, unemployment does not have the impact it once did.

Business Failures: When the number of business failures is high, there is less chance of unionization. Research shows that this changes with time.

Legislation: Research substantiates that federal legislation, such as the acts we will discuss in the next section, affect union membership.

Wars: Some believe that union membership increases during wars. Research shows that wars improve labor's image but do not affect membership.

It has also been suggested that global competition, deregulation, increased management participation by employees, and the growth of the service sector, which is traditionally not unionized, have all contributed to union decreases.[9]

As we can see, there is no simple answer to why union membership has declined. If there were, unions would solve the problem and continue to grow.

Union Trends

According to one expert, unions are dying. By the year 2000 they will play a small role as bargaining units. They will still exist, but as fraternal organizations offering their members services such as low-interest credit cards and counseling.[10]

Union leaders disagree. They believe unions will come back. To do so, unions are recruiting minorities, women, and the service sector to increase membership.[11] Unions are also fighting on a new battleground. They are trying to expand by redefining their role. Union membership is now also community membership. Unions are trying to change their image. They are exerting pressure on the community, not at the traditional bargaining table, to get what they want. The union is now involved in lawsuits, public hearings, and government appeals. Unions have had some success, and officials say the trend will continue.[12]

LEARNING OBJECTIVE

1. Discuss the history of unions, and present and future trends in labor organization.

CONNECTIONS

1. Name a specific organization and identify the union or unions that represent its employees.
2. Do you believe union membership will continue to decline, level off, or increase? Explain your answer.

II. Labor Legislation

As mentioned, federal legislation has significantly affected union membership. Initially, there was a great deal of opposition to labor's attempts at organizing. For example, the Sherman Antitrust Act was passed in 1890 to control monopolies in restraint of trade. Although the act was originally aimed at business, courts took the position that unions were also a monopoly and that collective bargaining interfered with the free market mechanism. Unions were subject to antitrust legislation until 1914, when the Clayton Act was passed. In addition, until 1932, employers could require a *yellow dog contract* as a condition of employment. This contract stipulated that the employee would not join a union or engage in union activities. If the employee did later join a union, it was considered a breach of contract, and the employee was fired. Legislation in the 1930s did much to establish the rights of workers to organize. We will look at two of the major pieces of legislation, as well as subsequent acts limiting union activities.

The Norris-LaGuardia Act

In 1932 the Norris-LaGuardia Act did away with yellow dog contracts and restricted employers' use of court orders (injunctions). Until this act was passed, employers could easily get injunctions if unions interrupted production.

However, employers were still not required to recognize unions. And they could still fire employees for union activities. In fact, employers blacklisted union activists, preventing them from gaining employment anywhere. Employers could also use lockouts, refusing to let employees work (or get paid) until they agreed not to unionize. During lockouts, employers could easily outlast employees.

The Wagner Act

The Wagner Act of 1935, also known as the National Labor Relations Act, gave employees the right to unionize without fear of prosecution. Section 7 states,

Employees shall have the right to self-organization, to form, join or assist labor organizations, to bargain collectively through representatives of their own choosing, and to engage in concerted activities for the purpose of collective bargaining or other mutual aid or protection.

The act also lists the following employer practices as unfair:

1. Interfering with employees involved in organizing or collective bargaining.
2. Interfering with union administration or providing financial support to that administration.
3. Discrimination against employees for union affiliation.
4. Punishment of union members for reporting any violations of this act.
5. Refusal to bargain in good faith with a duly elected union.

The Wagner Act established the National Labor Relations Board (NLRB). The purposes of the NLRB are to enforce the provisions of the Wagner Act and to conduct elections to determine whether employees will unionize and who will be their representative in collective bargaining.

Given these rights, unions developed several mechanisms for protecting their interest within an organization:

- The *closed shop* makes union membership a requirement for employment.
- The *union shop* requires employees to join the union—usually within 30 days—to maintain employment.

- The *agency shop* requires all employees to pay union dues regardless of membership.
- The *maintenance of membership clause* requires all employees who join to remain members of the union as a condition of employment.

One of the union's most powerful tools is the strike. During 1986 there was a great deal of strike activity in the manufacturing sector. Manufacturers lost nearly 5.8 million worker days to strikes, up 68 percent over 1985 and up 135 percent over 1984.[13]

Taft-Hartley Act

Union membership grew from 4 million in 1932 to over 15 million by 1947. Unions had become very powerful—so powerful, in fact, that the Taft-Hartley Act was passed in 1947 to offset some of the imbalance of power between labor and management. It amended the Wagner Act to include a list of unfair union practices:

1. Workers could not be forced to join or be kept from joining unions.
2. The closed shop was prohibited.
3. Employees must authorize union deductions from their pay.
4. Complex restrictions were placed on certain types of strikes and boycotts.
5. Unions could not charge excessive initiation fees.
6. *Featherbedding* (making employers pay for work not performed) was prohibited.
7. *Certification elections* (a vote for unionization) could not be held more than once a year.
8. Employees could get rid of a union through decertification elections.
9. Unions must bargain in good faith.

In addition, states were given the right to pass laws prohibiting the union shop. These *right-to-work* laws give employees the right to refuse to join a union and still keep their jobs. As shown in Exhibit 16–2, 21 states have passed these laws.

Landrum-Griffin Act

The Landrum-Griffin Act, also known as the Labor Management Reporting and Disclosure Act, was passed in 1959 to protect members from corrupt or discriminatory union activities. The act was designed to regulate internal union affairs. It contains the following provisions:

1. Equality of rights for union members in nomination and voting in elections.
2. Controls over increases in union dues.
3. Controls over the suspension and fining of union members.
4. Elections every three years for local offices and every five years for national or international offices.
5. A definition of the type of person who can hold union office.
6. The requirement of filing annual reports with the Secretary of Labor.

The Future

Congress and the president have the power to affect union activities. The Reagan and Bush administrations was considered promanagement. For example, presidents Reagan and Bush helped to keep unions from getting the tariff protection they

EXHIBIT 16–2   **STATES WITH RIGHT-TO-WORK LAWS**

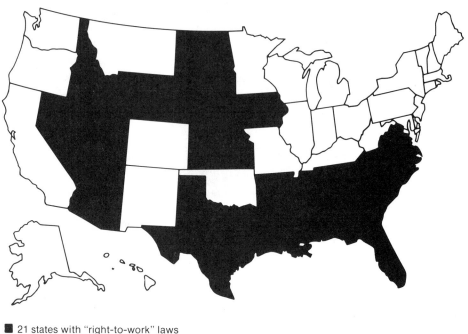

■ 21 states with "right-to-work" laws

LEARNING
OBJECTIVE

2. Describe how the
Norris-LaGuardia,
Wagner, Taft-Hartley,
and Landrum-Griffin acts
have affected union-
management relations.

sought. Labor unions are pleased that the Clinton Administration is more pro-labor. Among the legislation that labor favors are controls on trade and imports that would protect American-made products from cheaper imports and an increasing minimum wage. Unions believe that the country is shifting politically in labor's direction.[14] Will unions gain more power in the future? Time will tell.

CONNECTIONS

3. Should right-to-work laws be required in all states, be repealed, or be left up to the individual states? Explain your answer.

III. The Union Organizing Process

There are typically five stages in forming a union: (1) initial organizing activities, (2) signing authorization cards, (3) determining the bargaining unit, (4) the election, and (5) certification. This process is called *organizing*.

Initial Organizing Activities

The process may begin with employees contacting a union and asking its representatives to come and help them organize, or the union may come to the firm. Union organizers are professionals. They have been well trained to use the most effective techniques in gaining support for the union. Union organizers assist in distributing materials promoting the union, contact individual workers, and hold mass meetings.

During the union drive a supervisor can do the following:[15]

- Keep outside organizers off company premises.
- Prohibit unionization activities during working hours.
- State the disadvantages of unions, such as dues and membership requirements.
- Compare present wages and benefits to those of other firms.
- Inform employees of any untrue or misleading statements made by the organizers.

There are also certain things a supervisor cannot do as a union attempts to organize:[16]

- Coerce employees to vote against the union.
- Promise or give benefits for voting against the union.
- Ask employees either whether they have signed authorization cards or how they plan to vote.
- Attend union meetings.
- Threaten to close, move, or curtail operations, or reduce employee benefits.

Consultants offer services designed to help the firm avoid any unfair labor practices during organizing drives; these help keep unions out.

Signing Authorization Cards

For the union to be recognized, a minimum of 30 percent of the employees must sign authorization cards stating an interest in union representation. To get employees to sign authorization cards, unions generally offer the benefits listed in section I of this chapter.

Relations between a supervisor and employees will influence employees' decision about signing the authorization cards. Employees who are satisfied with their supervisor are less likely to sign. However, when employees sign authorization cards or elect a union, this is not always a sign of poor supervision. In addition, an employee's decision about joining a union does not reflect his or her commitment to the organization. Employees can be committed to both the firm and the union.[17]

Determining the Bargaining Unit

The **bargaining unit** *is the specific group the union represents in collective bargaining.* The NLRB usually defines the bargaining unit using a number of criteria. If more than one union seeks recognition, the NLRB must resolve the issue. More than one union can be placed on the ballot.

The Election

The NLRB usually conducts representation elections. In recent years the NLRB has conducted about 8,000 annual elections. Unions have won about 45 percent of the elections, down from 55 percent in 1969. A secret ballot may be used. The ballot is a simple vote for or against union representation. In order to win union representation, over 50 percent of the voting employees must vote for unionization. Management is responsible for seeing that employees who do not want a union vote against it, rather than simply abstaining.

If more than one union is seeking representation, employees must make a choice. To gain certification, one union must get a majority of the votes. If no union gets a majority, a runoff is held between the two unions with the most votes.

If the majority of employees vote "no union," another unionization election cannot be held for one year.

Certification

The NLRB must certify the election. This means that the union is recognized as the bargaining unit of the employees it represents. Certification requires that the employer bargain in good faith with the union over conditions of employment.

Decertification

LEARNING OBJECTIVE

3. List and explain the five steps of forming a union.

Certification may end if the employees vote to change unions or to get rid of the union. This is called a *decertification election*. The 8,000 annual elections include decertification elections.

Recent studies support the notion that members are generally loyal to their unions.[18] Often they do not have a dual commitment to both the organization and the union. Commitment depends on management-labor relations.

CONNECTIONS

4. As a supervisor, if a union tried to organize at your firm, would you be neutral, positive, or negative? Why? What would you do and say to indicate your stance toward unionization?

IV. Collective Bargaining

Collective bargaining *is the negotiation process resulting in a contract that covers wages, hours, and working conditions.* With the decrease in union membership, the number of collective bargaining agreements has also declined. Between 1980 and 1985, they dropped from 22.5 million to 19.4 million; in other words, the number of employees covered by collective bargaining units has declined from 25.7 percent to 20.5 percent of all employees.[19]

Collective Bargaining Negotiations

Negotiations usually begin with the management and labor teams determining their respective demands. Each side typically has three identifiable positions: the initial demand, the target point, and the resistance point.[20] For example, in negotiating wages, the union has an initial demand point, which is more than it believes it will get ($9.00). It also sets a target point, which is what it believes it can get ($8.50), and a resistance point, which is the least it will accept ($8.00). Management has an initial offer, which is less than it expects to pay ($7.75). It also has a target point, which it expects to pay ($8.25), and a resistance point, which is the most it is willing to pay ($8.75). The initial demand or offer is almost always rejected because both sides ask for more or less than they believe they can get or pay. From this point, both sides generally compromise at a figure in the settlement range between each team's resistance point (union, $8.00; management, $8.75).

EXHIBIT 16 – 3

CONTRACT PROVISIONS

Contract length	Management prerogatives
Union recognition	Wages
Fringe benefits	Work hours
Working conditions	Rest periods
Vacations and holidays	Overtime
Production standards	Discharge and layoffs
Seniority	Discipline procedures
Grievance procedures	Work clothes
Subcontracting	Renewal options
Arbitration and mediation	Dues checkoff
Rules	No-strike clause

The teams may be willing to exchange wage concessions for other demands. Exhibit 16–3 lists some of the typical items in a contract. As the list suggests, the number of items covered by the negotiation can make the negotiating process quite complex.

Unions may threaten to strike, management may threaten a lockout (refusing to let employees work), or both, if a contract is not negotiated by a set time. Thus, as the deadline comes closer, both sides are usually more willing to compromise to avoid a strike or lockout. Less than 2 percent of all contract negotiations result in a strike.

To avoid a strike or lockout, collective bargainers sometimes agree to use neutral third parties, called mediators, from the Federal Mediation and Conciliation Service (FMCS). A **mediator** *is a neutral party who helps management and labor settle their disagreements.* In cases where management and labor are not willing to compromise but do not want to call a strike or lockout, they may call in an arbitrator. An **arbitrator** *is different from a mediator in that the arbitrator makes a binding decision for management and labor.* The arbitrator's decision must be followed. The services of an arbitrator are more commonly used to settle grievances than to deal with impasses in collective bargaining.

The Supervisor's Role in Collective Bargaining

The actual negotiation is best left to experts in this field. Therefore, supervisors are usually not members of management's negotiation team. However, they are often kept informed of the progress of the negotiations. In organizations that recognize the value of supervisory input, higher management may consult with supervisors. There are two major ways in which the supervisor can give input to collective bargaining:

Provide Feedback: The supervisor has the primary responsibility for implementing the contract on a day-to-day basis. He or she therefore knows how existing contract provisions have worked out. The supervisor should also understand what does and does not help in performing the job. The information provided should be documented. Records of grievances, discipline, production, and so forth should be presented.

Recommend Changes: The supervisor should describe ways in which the new contract can be improved. Unions tend to restrict the freedom of supervisors in deciding how the job will be done.[21] A supervisor should defend his or her own need for flexibility in running the departments for the betterment of both management and labor.

Negotiations usually occur every one, two, or three years and can last for days, weeks, or even months. During contract negotiations, emotions may run high. This is why negotiations are often held off the firm's premises. Negotiations may produce an "us against them" attitude. An adversarial relationship is best kept confined to the negotiation table. During negotiations, it is important for the supervisor to maintain good relations with employees. This is often difficult. Discussing the union's demands with employees will not help the department. Such discussions often end in an argument. If employees ask for the supervisor's views, it is usually wise to make a statement such as, "Let's leave the negotiations to the experts; we will live with the contract," or "Let's concentrate on our jobs and let the negotiators develop the contract."

Changes in Collective Bargaining

With global competition increasing, many U.S. companies are seeking salvation through a partnership with employees.[22] The example of Japan and other countries has made top managers realize that a cooperative approach is superior to an adversarial approach. A trusting, cooperative relationship is difficult to achieve, but the results are well worth the effort.[23]

In collective bargaining there is currently too much emphasis on wages and benefits and changing archaic work rules. The focus needs to change to negotiating a contract around common objectives such as profits, jobs, and industrial competitiveness. It would be helpful to have neutral task forces review contracts and point out counterproductive features to both sides in an attempt to develop a better contract for all.[24]

As with most things today, collective bargaining is changing. In 1987 the focus of collective bargaining was on local and plant issues rather than national contracts. Management is pressing for changes in work rules, job classifications, and pay for performance. Unions are balking but may accept some changes in exchange for increased job security.[25] General Motors told the United Auto Workers that wages and job security should depend on the performance of individual plants. This is a sharp break from traditional labor practices.[26]

LEARNING OBJECTIVE

4. Describe the collective bargaining process and the supervisor's role in it.

CONNECTIONS

5. If you have worked for a unionized organization, identify the firm and the provisions of the union contract. (See Exhibit 16–3 for examples.) If you have never worked for a unionized organization, contact one and find out what its contract covers.

6. Do you believe that management and labor should negotiate in a cooperative way or continue with the traditional adversarial approach? Explain your answer.

V. Contract Administration

Collective bargaining ends with a written contract, often called a *labor agreement*. The contract is a legal document that must be administered as specified. Violation of the contract can result in litigation.

The Supervisor's Role in Contract Administration

The supervisor is at the management level to carry out the contract on a day-to-day basis. It is very important that the supervisor study the contract in order to implement it effectively. It is the supervisor who makes the contract become a living document.

The contract serves the same basic purpose as the organization's standing plans. It provides policies, procedures, and rules that the supervisor must follow.

Policies: Contracts often contain broad statements that are open to interpretation by the supervisor. For example, the contract might say that the supervisor cannot discipline an employee without "just cause." What is just cause? It is not stated in the contract. In such situations, it is important that the supervisor uses good judgment in interpreting the contract. If the union perceives that supervisors are taking advantage of general statements, it will require more specific rules during the next negotiation. More specific wording leaves supervisors with less flexibility in running their departments. When interpreting the contract, the supervisor must also be careful to treat employees uniformly.[27]

Procedures: Many contracts require the supervisor to follow specific step-by-step procedures in handling issues such as discipline (Chapter 14) and grievances (discussed in the next section). If the supervisor does not proceed as the contract stipulates, the union may file a complaint. In cases where a supervisor makes a decision, such as to fire an employee, without following procedures, the decision is usually overruled. Either situation is damaging to both a supervisor's career and relations with employees.

Rules: The rules should clearly state what the supervisor and employees can and cannot do. For example, the contract may state that the supervisor must give a set amount of advance notice before requiring overtime.

Labor agreements often produce limited job descriptions.[28] Supervisors are not supposed to ask employees to do things that are not specified in the job description. For example, if a machine is not working, the employee is not supposed to fix it, even if the repair is minor and will only take a few minutes. If the supervisor orders the employee to fix it and the employee refuses, the supervisor will ultimately lose in almost all cases.

As we can see, a union does influence the way a supervisor performs the job. However, the supervisor needs the same skills and performs the same five functions of supervision in a union setting. A supervisor should not be intimidated by the presence of a union. When supervisors act within the authority of the contract, they must do as they deem fit. It is very important to enforce the contract as specified. For example, if the contract calls for a 30-minute lunch period, the supervisor should see to it that the employees do not take longer.

The Supervisor and the Union Steward

The **union steward** *is a full-time employee elected or appointed by the union as its representative.* The union steward, often called the *shop steward,* has a dual role. Stewards are employees who are subject to the organization's standing plans, and the union's voice to management at the work site. Stewards usually are given some time off to conduct union business such as recruiting members, communicating about union activities, and so forth. Like the supervisor, they are caught in the middle; however, shop stewards must deal with employees, management, and union officials.

Duties and Responsibilities

The union steward's duties and responsibilities include these:

- Knowing and enforcing the labor contract. Like supervisors, the union stewards must abide by the contract. They, too, must interpret the contract.

- Protecting the welfare of union members. They must protect the rights of the union members even when they feel or know the member is in the wrong. Like a lawyer, the steward defends members to the best of his or her ability.

- Serving as a spokesperson for the union and its members. When union stewards believe that management is not living up to the contract agreement, they must speak up for the union's rights.
- Settling grievances fairly, within the guidelines of the contract. This is one of their most important jobs. When employees are dissatisfied, they tend to go to the union steward for help. Some contracts stipulate that the union steward must be present during specific steps in the discipline and grievance process.
- Maintaining working relationships with supervisors. In order to expedite the handling of problems, the supervisor and union steward must work together to meet the needs of all parties.
- Keeping supervisors informed about union positions and possible sources of trouble. Both management and labor can work together to eliminate possible problems before they grow serious.

Supervisor-Steward Relationships

The supervisor is in charge of the department. Therefore, the union steward cannot tell the supervisor what to do outside of the specific provisions of the contract. The union steward may also be the supervisor's employee, making the relationship more complex. The union steward's position is not that of a co-manager. However, this does not mean that the supervisor should not be cooperative and have good relations with the union steward. An adversarial position will only make it more difficult for supervisors to get what they want done. The supervisor should work with the union steward to find solutions that will satisfy both parties.[29]

Like supervisors, union stewards will use a variety of styles. Some will be cooperative, and some will not. In any case, the supervisor should take the initiative to develop good relations with the steward. The supervisor and union steward have similar jobs. The better they get along, the easier it will be to get those jobs done.

A union does not eliminate the need for good relations with employees. If the supervisor does not take an interest in employees and look out for their welfare, they will turn to the union steward for leadership. The better the supervisor's relations with employees, the less need there is for settling grievances and other problems.

LEARNING OBJECTIVE

5. Discuss the supervisor's role in contract administration.

CONNECTIONS

7. Do you prefer working as a supervisor in a unionized or nonunionized organization? Explain your preference.
8. Why is it important for a supervisor to be fair in following the contract?

VI. Complaints and Grievances

Formal systems that resolve complaints and grievances have proven to increase morale and communication between management and labor.[30] However, only about one-third of U.S. organizations have such formal systems.[31] Organizations that do not have formal systems run a higher risk of employees' filing lawsuits.[32] One lawsuit, regardless of who wins, can cost substantially more than the price of establishing and implementing a system.

Complaints versus Grievances

A **complaint** *is job-related dissatisfaction expressed to management.* It is common for employees who are not satisfied to go to their supervisor or another manager to complain. A **grievance** *is a complaint filed by management or a union representative.* The formal grievance procedure is a provision of most labor contracts. Therefore, the grievance process is an extension of collective bargaining.[33] When either management or labor believes the other party has violated the contract provisions, a grievance may be filed.

Most grievances are filed by union stewards on behalf of the union member or members claiming the violation. A complaint is usually an informal oral expression of dissatisfaction, whereas the grievance is usually a formal written statement. If a complaint is not resolved to the employee's satisfaction, he or she can either drop the complaint or appeal the decision through the formal grievance procedure. If an organization does not have a formal complaint system, this step may cause more problems than it solves.

Another option in handling complaints or grievances is legal action. In a unionized organization, employees may go to the union steward for help in overruling a supervisor's decision. In some cases, employees go directly to the union steward rather than the supervisor. In any case, the supervisor is almost always involved at some point in a complaint or grievance.

Wages, hours, overtime assignments, job duties, vacation times, promotions, discipline, seniority, discharge, working conditions, broken promises, personal harassment, sexual harassment, unsafe conditions, and employee conflicts all may cause filing of complaints or grievances.

Handling Complaints

As a supervisor, you should use the open-door policy.[34] If your employees do not feel as though they can come to you with a complaint, you may wind up with unhappy, unproductive employees.[35] It is much better to get issues out in the open and try to resolve them than it is to have your employees going around complaining to everyone else. Fair treatment of complaints builds good relations.[36]

You can use the complaint model to help resolve problems in a union or nonunion organization. The **complaint model** *involves four steps: listen to the complaint and paraphrase it; have the complainer recommend a solution; schedule time to get all the facts and make a decision; and develop and implement a plan and follow up.*

Step 1. Listen to the Complaint and Paraphrase It

This is probably the most important step. Listen to the full story without interruptions, and paraphrase it to ensure accuracy.[37] When employees come to you with a complaint, try not to take it personally; even the best supervisors have to deal with complaints. Do not become defensive and try to talk the employee out of the complaint.

Paraphrasing is very important because employees may not know the exact nature of the complaint they have. They often talk about one issue when there is something else causing the problem. It is the supervisor's job to determine the cause of the complaint. If you can state the complaint in your own words, and the complainer agrees with it, you have a chance of settling it; if you cannot paraphrase the complaint, you probably cannot resolve it. Paraphrasing also helps to ensure that you do listen and do not jump to conclusions.

When listening to the complaint, distinguish facts from opinions. There will be times when employees think they know the facts when, in reality, they do not. For example, an employee may have heard that a less experienced worker earns the same wages as he or she does. The experienced employee may complain. When the supervisor states the facts, for example, the experienced worker *is* paid more (it may be best not to state the specific amount), the complaint may be dropped immediately. Identify the person's feelings about the complaint. Try to determine the employee's motives for the complaint.

Step 2. Have the Complainer Recommend a Solution

After the supervisor has paraphrased the complaint, and the employee has agreed with the paraphrasing, the supervisor should ask the complainer to recommend a solution. This does not mean that the supervisor has to implement the suggestion.

In some cases, the recommended solution may not solve the problem, or may not be fair to others. There may be recommendations that are not possible for the supervisor to implement. In such cases, the supervisor should let the employee know that the solution is not possible, and explain why.

Step 3. Schedule Time to Get All the Facts and Make a Decision

Employee complaints often involve other people. It may be necessary to check records to talk to others. It is helpful to talk to your boss or peers who may have had a similar complaint; they may be able to offer you some good advice on how best to resolve the complaint. Even when you have all the facts, it is usually advisable to take some time to weigh them before making a decision.

Set a schedule for when you will make a decision. This does not have to be long in many cases. Generally, the more quickly a complaint is resolved, the fewer the negative side effects. Too many supervisors simply say, "I'll get back to you on this," without specifying when. This is very frustrating to the employee. Some supervisors are purposely vague because they have no intention of getting back to the employee. They are hoping the employee will forget about the complaint. This tactic may get the employee to stop complaining, but it may also cause productivity and turnover problems.

Step 4. Develop and Implement a Plan and Follow Up

After getting all the necessary facts and advice from others, the supervisor should develop a plan. The plan may simply be the complainer's solution. However, when a supervisor does not agree with the complainer's solution, he or she should explain why and either work with the complainer to find an alternative or present his or her own plan. The level of employee participation depends on the capability level.

In cases where supervisors decide not to take any action to resolve the complaint, they should clearly explain why. They should also state that if employees are not satisfied, they can appeal the decision to another level. The complainer should be told how to appeal the decision. In a nonunion organization, the usual step is to go to the supervisor's boss. In a union organization, the next step is often to go to the steward.

As with all plans, it is important for the supervisor to follow up and make sure that the solution is implemented. It may be appropriate to set a follow-up meeting. It is also advisable to keep a record of all meetings and action in your critical incident file (Chapter 12).

These four steps discussed are listed in Model 16–1.

Handling Grievances

A study conducted between 1976 and 1982 revealed that the greater the number of grievances filed, the lower the productivity level of the organization.[38] The

---

MODEL 16–1

HANDLING COMPLAINTS

Step 1. Listen to the complaint and paraphrase it.

Step 2. Have the complainer recommend a solution.

Step 3. Schedule time to get all the facts and make a decision.

Step 4. Develop and implement a plan, and follow up.

supervisor should encourage union members to make a complaint before filing a grievance. Experts say that up to 90 percent of all employee problems can be settled as complaints or at the first stage of the grievance procedure. Most contracts state the specific steps in settling a grievance, which vary from organization to organization, but usually involve from three to five stages.[39] The number usually reflects the size of the organization. Large organizations tend to have the five levels described here.

Level 1. The Complainer, Union Steward, and Supervisor Meet: The union steward gets involved when an employee is dissatisfied with the way a complaint was handled or when the complaint was not dealt with. The union steward files a grievance and meets with the employee and supervisor to try to resolve the grievance. The supervisor may consult with a specialist to determine whether the original decision should be changed. If the supervisor believes there should not be a change, the union steward may appeal to the next level.

Level 2. The Supervisor's Boss, a Labor Relations Specialist, or Both Meet with the Chief Steward: The *chief steward* is the middle manager of stewards. All union stewards report to the chief steward. The chief steward meets with the labor relations specialist, the boss, or both to try to resolve the grievance. If they cannot, it goes to the next level.

Level 3: The Division Manager, a Labor Relations Director, or Both Meet with Union Committee Members: The committee members include local union representatives, the chief steward, and possibly other stewards. Both sides try to keep the grievances from going beyond this level. However, if they cannot agree on a resolution, the grievance does go on.

Level 4. Members of Top Management Meet with National or International Union Representatives: These high-level officials try to resolve the grievance. If they cannot, it goes to the final stage.

Level 5. Mediation or Arbitration: The final step is usually to call in an arbitrator to make a binding decision for management and labor to abide by. The American Arbitration Association (AAA) and Federal Mediation and Conciliation Service (FMCS) process about 2,300 grievances a year.

Rather than turn to outside sources such as the AAA and FMCS, some organizations are setting up their own systems for making a binding decision. One such technique, which is growing in popularity, is the peer review panel. It is used because, during the grievance process described above, union members may feel as though management is ganging up on them. With a peer review panel, they are judged by their own peers, as well. Peer reviews increase commitment, improve relations, and result in better resolution of conflicts.[40] Harvey Caras developed a peer review panel while working at General Electric in a nonunion plant. It worked so well that he set up similar systems in dozens of other GE plants and subsequently in over 20 other organizations.[41] The panel consists of three employees and two managers. Despite the two-to-three split, the panels have upheld management decisions over 80 percent of the time. All panel members are volunteers who receive 12 hours of training on how to make sound, impartial decisions.[42]

LEARNING OBJECTIVES

6. List and explain the four steps in handling complaints and use the model.

7. List and explain the five levels of handling grievances.

CONNECTIONS

9. Identify a complaint you brought to a supervisor. If you have never filed a complaint, interview someone who has. Describe the complaint and identify the steps the supervisor did or did not follow in the complaint model.

REVIEW

Select one or more methods: (1) fill in the missing key terms from memory;
(2) match the key terms from the end of the review with their definitions below;
(3) copy the key terms in order from the key terms at the beginning of the chapter.

_____ are the interactions between management and
unionized employees.

The _____ is an organization that represents employees
in collective bargaining with the employer. Reasons employees join unions
include increased wages and benefits, job security, uniform treatment, strength
in numbers, social benefits, and employment. In recent years union membership
has been dropping. Unions are now focusing on recruiting women, minorities,
and employees in the service sector; reaching out more to the community; and
getting involved in more lawsuits.

Major legislation affecting organized labor includes the Norris-LaGuardia Act,
the Wagner Act, the Taft-Hartley Act, and the Landrum-Griffin Act.

The steps in organizing a union include initial organizing activities, signing
authorization cards, determining the _____ (a specific
group the union represents in collective bargaining), the election, and
certification.

_____ is the negotiation process resulting in a contract
that covers wages, hours, and working conditions. When management and labor
cannot agree they often call in a _____ , a neutral party
who helps management and labor settle their differences; or an
_____ , a neutral party who makes a binding decision for
management and labor. The supervisor's major role in collective bargaining is
usually to provide feedback on how the existing contract provisions have worked
out and to recommend changes in the new contract.

The supervisor has the primary responsibility for administering the
negotiated contract on a day-to-day basis. Supervisors must understand the
contract. The _____ is a full-time employee elected or
appointed by the union as its representative. The supervisor and the union
steward should work closely to ensure that the contract is administered as
intended. A cooperative effort, rather than an adversarial stance, is more
productive for supervisors who want to get things done.

_____ is job-related dissatisfaction expressed to
management. A _____ is a complaint filed by management
or a union representative. The _____ includes four steps:
listen to the complaint and paraphrase it; have the complainer recommend a

solution; schedule time to get all the facts and make a decision; develop and implement a plan, and follow up. The procedure for handling a grievance is usually stated in the collective bargaining contract. The process has from three to five steps involving progressively higher levels of management and labor representatives, and ending with mediation or arbitration.

KEY TERMS

arbitrator   grievance
bargaining unit   labor relations
collective bargaining   mediator
complaint   union
complaint model   union steward

REFERENCES

1. "Labor Relations: Don't Lose Unions," *Industry Week,* October 27, 1986, p. 22.

2. "Union Membership of Employed Wage and Salary Workers, 1985," *Monthly Labor Review,* May 1986, p. 46.

3. Maria Recio, Douglas Harbreht, and Aaron Bernstein, "Labor's Long Winter May Be Coming to an End," *Business Week,* February 23, 1987, p. 140.

4. Sandra Kirmeyer and Arie Shirom, "Perceived Job Autonomy in the Manufacturing Sector: Effects of Unions, Gender, and Substantive Complexity," *Academy of Management Journal,* December 1986, p. 832.

5. Paul Timm, *Supervision* (St. Paul, MN: West Publishing, 1984), pp. 363–64.

6. "End of the Tunnel," *The Wall Street Journal,* March 3, 1992, p. 1.

7. Ron Suskind, "Tough Vote," *The Wall Street Journal,* July 28, 1992, p. 1.

8. Lee Stepina and Jack Fiorito, "Toward a Comprehensive Theory of Union Growth and Decline," *Industrial Relations,* Fall 1986, pp. 248–64.

9. Donald Thompson, "New Role for Labor Unions," *Industry Week,* February 9, 1987, p. 31.

10. Ibid., p. 38.

11. Thompson, "New Role for Labor Unions," p. 30.

12. Michael Verespei, "Unions: The New Battleground," *Industry Week,* April 6, 1987, pp. 40–41.

13. "Strike Activity Surged," *The Wall Street Journal,* April 14, 1987, p. 1.

14. Recio, Harbreht, and Bernstein, "Labor's Long Winter," pp. 140, 145.

15. Robert Mathis and John Jackson, *Personnel: Human Resource Management* (St. Paul, MN: West Publishing, 1985), p. 576.

16. Ibid.

17. Edward Conlon and Daniel Gallagher, "Commitment to Employer and Union: Effects of Membership Status," *Academy of Management Journal,* March 1987, p. 160.

18. Ibid., p. 151.

19. "Union Membership of Employed Wage and Salary Workers," p. 44.

20. Randal Schuler, *Personnel and Human Resource Management* (St. Paul, MN: West Publishing, 1984), pp. 556–59.

21. Kirmeyer and Shirom, "Perceived Job Autonomy," p. 832.

22. Thompson, "New Role for Labor Unions," p. 30.

23. Stephen Smits, "A Lesson in Employee Involvement," *Management Solutions,* January 1987, p. 23.

24. Thomas Raleigh, "It's Time to Revise Collective Bargaining Agreements," *Industry Week,* October 27, 1986, p. 14.

25. "Labor Bargaining," *The Wall Street Journal,* August 4, 1987, p. 1.

26. "General Motors," *The Wall Street Journal,* August 13, 1987, p. 1.

27. Kirmeyer and Shirom, "Perceived Job Autonomy," p. 832.

28. Ibid.

29. Perry Pascarella, "If My Boss Would Only," *Industry Week,* June 23, 1986, p. 9.

30. Roger Madsen and Barbara Knudson-Fields, "Employee-Employer Relationships: When They Have Cause to Complain," *Management Solutions,* April 1987, p. 44.

31. M. P. Rowe and M. Baker, "Are You Hearing Enough Employee Concerns?" *Harvard Business Review,* May–June 1984, p. 130.

32. Madsen and Knudson-Fields, "Employee-Employer Relationships," p. 39.

33. Thomas Knight, "Feedback and Grievance Resolution," *Industrial and Labor Relations Review,* July 1986, p. 586.

34. Madsen and Knudson-Fields, "Employee-Employer Relationships," p. 40.

35. Edward Roseman, *Managing the Problem Employee* (New York: AMACOM, 1982), p. 93.

36. Barry Baroni, "A Complaint Process System that Will Work for Your Business," *Management Solutions,* July 1986, pp. 22, 26.

37. Ibid., p. 24.

38. Casy Inhniowski, "The Effects of Grievances Activity on Productivity," *Industrial Labor Relations Review,* October 1986, p. 75.

39. Knight, "Feedback and Grievance Resolution," p. 586.

40. George Mauer and Jeanne Flores, "From Adversary to Advocate," *Personnel Administrator,* June 1986, p. 53.

41. Thomas Rohan, "Employee Relations: Workers Check Bosses," *Industry Week,* October 27, 1986, p. 33.

42. John Tasini and Patrick Houston, "Letting Workers Help Handle Workers' Gripes," *Business Week,* September 15, 1986, p. 82.

APPLICATION SITUATIONS

Why Employees Join Unions

AS 16–1

Identify the reason for joining a union represented by each statement that follows:

a. increased wages   *d.* a voice to management

b. job security   *e.* social organization

c. uniform treatment   *f.* gain employment

_____ 1. "I joined the union because all my friends did."

_____ 2. "I figure a union will help stop these political appointments."

_____ 3. "I work in a union shop."

_____ 4. "The union looks out for us guys with seniority."

_____ 5. "Looking at Exhibit 16–1 will tell you why I joined."

Labor Legislation

AS 16–2

Identify the legislative acts described.

a. Norris-LaGuardia   *b.* Wagner   *c.* Taft-Hartley   *d.* Landrum-Griffin

_____ 6. The act that outlawed the closed shop.

_____ 7. The act that gave employees the right to unionize without fear of prosecution.

_____ 8. The act that controlled increases in union dues.

_____ 9. The act that established the National Labor Relations Board.

_____ 10. The act that outlawed the yellow dog contract.

Union Organization

AS 16–3

Identify whether each action taken by the supervisor during the unionization process was

a. legal   *b.* illegal

_____ 11. Telling employees how much workers make at unionized competitor firms.

_____ 12. Requiring union officials to get off company property.

_____ 13. Going to union meetings.

_____ 14. Asking to see authorization cards.

_____ 15. Stating why he or she does not like unions.

Grievance Procedures

AS 16–4

Identify each statement by its level in the grievance process:

a. 1   *d.* 4

b. 2   *e.* 5

c. 3

———— 16. "We are here because the supervisor and steward could not come to an agreement."

———— 17. "You do realize that whatever I decide must be done."

———— 18. "Okay, supervisor, I'll be back to see you with the union steward to get what I want done."

———— 19. "I'm from the local union. I'm here to discuss a grievance."

———— 20. "As the chief executive officer, I'm busy. I wish meeting with union representatives was not part of my responsibility."

OBJECTIVE CASE 16

Brad's Complaint

The following conversation took place between Brad, a union employee, and Herman, his supervisor.

HERMAN: Brad, what's the matter now?

BRAD: I want to discuss your preferential treatment of the nonunion members of this department.

HERMAN: You union guys are always crying about something. I don't think it's fair for the nonunion employees to have to pay the same union dues, and you don't see them complaining about it. Well, that is a different story. What is the specific accusation?

BRAD: You play favorites when it comes to assigning jobs and overtime. The union guys get most of the hard jobs and less overtime. There is a law against doing that. It's also the major reason I joined the union, to get protection from supervisors like you who play favorites.

HERMAN: If unions are so great, why did they have to pass legislation to protect you union members from your own leaders?

BRAD: That's the third negative thing you've said about unions since I've been in here. I guess the talk going around about you is true.

HERMAN: What talk?

BRAD: Some of the union guys said you have been recommending that the nonunion employees try to get a decertification election.

HERMAN: Which is your complaint, preferential treatment or my recommending decertification?

BRAD: Like I said, preferential treatment.

HERMAN: Well I disagree. Get back to work now.

BRAD: This is not the last you will hear of this.

HERMAN: Go run to the union, it won't help you.

Answer the following questions, supporting your answers in the space between questions.

_____   1. Brad joined the union for what reason?
           a. increased wages   *d.* a voice to management
           b. job security   *e.* social reasons
           c. uniform treatment

_____   2. Brad claims that Herman's preferential treatment to nonunion members is in violation of the _____ Act.
           a. Norris-LaGuardia   *c.* Taft-Hartley
           b. Wagner   *d.* Landrum-Griffin

_____   3. This organization _____ in a state with right-to-work laws.
           a. is   *b.* is not

_____   4. This organization has a(an) _____ shop.
           a. closed   *b.* union   *c.* agency

_____ 5. The _____ Act made it legal to decertify
unions.
     a. Norris-LaGuardia   *c.* Taft-Hartley
     b. Wagner   *d.* Landrum-Griffin

_____ 6. The law protecting union members that Herman referred to is
the _____ Act.
     a. Norris-LaGuardia   *c.* Taft-Hartley
     b. Wagner   *d.* Landrum-Griffin

_____ 7. Brad's last comment makes it sound like he will now go to the
     a. national union   *b.* local union   *c.* union steward

_____ 8. This grievance will be going to the _____ level.
     a. first   *d.* fourth
     b. second   *e.* fifth
     c. third

_____ 9. Which step in the complaint model did Herman use?
     a. 1   *c.* 3
     b. 2   *d.* 4

_____ 10. If this grievance goes all the way, it will end with top management
deciding who is correct.
     a. true   *b.* false

11. If you were in Herman's position, how would you have handled this situation?

Handling Complaints

SB 16–1

During class you will be given the opportunity to role-play handling a complaint. Select a complaint. It may be one you brought to a supervisor, one that was brought to you, one you heard about, or one you made up. Fill in the information below for the person who will role-play bringing you a complaint to resolve.

Explain the situation and complaint.

List pertinent information about the other party that will help him or her play the role of the complainer (relationship with supervisor, knowledge, years of service, background, age, values, and so on).

Review Model 16–1 and think about what you will say and do when you handle this complaint.

Handling Complaints

SB 16–1

Objective: To experience and develop skills in resolving complaints.

Experience: You will initiate, respond to, and observe a complaint. Then you will evaluate the effectiveness of its resolution.

Material: The preparation for Exercise 16–1.

Procedure 1
(2–3 minutes)

Break into as many groups of three as possible. (You do not have to be with members of your permanent team.) Make some groups of two as necessary. Each member selects a number 1, 2, or 3. Number 1 will be the supervisor, and then 2, followed by 3.

Procedure 2
(8–15 minutes)

a. Number 1 gives his or her preparation to number 2 (the complainer) to read. Once number 2 understands, role-play (step *b*). Number 3 is the observer.

b. Role-play the complaint. Put yourself in this person's situation; ad-lib. The observer writes his or her comments on the observer form at the end of this exercise.

c. Integration. When the role play is over, the observer leads a discussion on the effectiveness of the conflict resolution. All members should discuss the effectiveness. This is not a lecture.
Do not go on until you are told to do so.

Procedure 3
(8–15 minutes)

Same as procedure 2, but number 2 is now the supervisor, number 3 is now the complainer, and number 1 is the observer.

Procedure 4
(8–15 minutes)

Same as procedure 2, but 3 is the supervisor, number 1 is the complainer, and number 2 is the observer.

Conclusion: The instructor leads a class discussion and makes concluding remarks.

Application (2–4 minutes): What did I learn from this experience? How will I use this knowledge in the future?

Sharing: Volunteers give their answers to the application section.

IN-CLASS SKILL-BUILDING EXERCISE

Arbitration

SB 16–2

Objective: To experience handling a grievance by arbitration.

Experience: Three people will role-play a grievance. The class acts as arbitrators, asks them questions, and makes a decision on the grievance.

Materials: None needed.

Situation

A supervisor claims to have seen one of the grievants punch two time cards. The penalty for punching someone else's time card is a one-month suspension for both people. The grievants were suspended. However, the defendants claim innocence and say that they are being harassed by the supervisor. The grievants want pay for the week of work they missed and want the charge dropped and their records cleared.

Procedure 1
(5–10 minutes)

Two people volunteer to play the role of the defendants, and one person volunteers to play the role of the supervisor. They will receive additional information from the instructor to prepare for the arbitration hearing. While they are preparing, the arbitrators (the rest of the class members) think of questions they will ask each side. Write them below and on the top of the next page.

Procedure 2
(15–30 minutes)

   a. The grievant accused of punching two time cards gives his or her version of the story to the arbitrators, who may ask questions.

   b. The grievant accused of letting someone else punch his or her time card gives his or her version of the story to the arbitrators, who may ask questions.

   c. The supervisor gives his or her version of the story to the arbitrators, who may ask questions.

Procedure 3
(3–5 minutes)

The arbitrators vote for the grievants (they receive back pay and are put back to work without the suspension on their records) or the supervisor (the grievants remain suspended). The instructor records the vote.

Conclusion (6–12 minutes): The instructor reads the actual situation to the class and leads a discussion on how the grievants and supervisor could have done a better job of presenting their case. Discuss grievances in general.

Application (2–4 minutes): What did I learn from this experience? How will I use this knowledge in the future?

Sharing: Volunteers give their answers to the application section.

Observer Form

During the role play, observe the handling of the complaint. Determine whether the supervisor followed the steps below, and how well. Try to have positive comments and recommend areas for improvement for each step in the complaint model. Be specific and descriptive and suggest an alternative for every area where the supervisor could improve.

Step 1. How well did the supervisor listen? Was the supervisor open to the complaint? Did the supervisor try to talk the employee out of the complaint? Was the supervisor defensive? Did the supervisor get the full story without interrruptions? Did the supervisor paraphrase the complaint?

Step 2. Did the supervisor have the complainer recommend a solution? How well did the supervisor react to the solution? If the solution could not be used, did the supervisor explain why?

Step 3: Did the supervisor schedule time to get all the facts and make a decision? Was a specific date given? Was it a reasonable length of time?

Step 4. Did the supervisor develop and implement a plan, and schedule a follow-up? (This step may not have been appropriate at this time.)

Contract Negotiations

SB 16–3

During class you will role-play contract negotiations. Think about which side (management or labor) you want to be on, and then read the following information and come up with some demands for your team's new contract. *Note:* actual negotiation preparation and bargaining can take months. The issues in this exercise are limited.

Background: The company is a toy manufacturer that employs around 2,500 workers. Of this number, about 70 percent, or 1,750 belong to the union. The nonunion members get the same pay and benefits as the union members. The seniority is as follows:

Years	Percentage of Employees
0–9	50
10–20	30
20+	20

Owing to the drop in the population and increased competition, sales have been down in recent years; however, the firm's financial situation is relatively good. Below is a copy of last year's income statement.

Sales	$130,000,000
Cost of goods sold	52,000,000
Gross profit	78,000,000
Labor wages	62,500,000
Other expenses	12,500,000
Net income	$ 3,000,000

Wages: The average salary is $12.00 per hour, $481 per week, or $25,000 per year. ($25,000 × 2,500 employees = $62,500,000 total labor wages). The last raise was $.90 per hour over the three-year life of the contract, with no cost-of-living adjustment (COLA). The length of the new contract can be for any number of years.

Benefits and Hours: There is a pension plan that is 90 percent paid by the company. The medical plan is 80 percent paid by the company. The workers get paid holidays, one week of vacation after one year of employment, and two weeks after five years. The workers get two 10-minute breaks, a 30-minute lunch, and a 10-minute washup before quitting time. They work seven hours a day and get paid for eight hours. This amounts to one hour per day of paid time for not working. Management has complained about the cost (2,500 × $12.00 = $30,000) and has tried to eliminate it. Labor has always won. Five years ago the company employed 3,000 workers. In other words, 20 percent have lost their jobs. At the present time 100 workers are laid off. The company does not provide any benefits, and their unemployment benefits will run out soon. Management has not made a decision to rehire these 100 workers. This layoff could result in termination of these 100 jobs.

Seniority: The present contract states that all layoffs must be by seniority. If a person from one department is laid off, he or she can bump a person from another department with less seniority, if he or she can do the job. Management does not like the seniority clause because it feels that several good workers get laid off while several poor workers keep their jobs. Management also feels that for a temporary layoff, seniority should not be considered.

Union Security: The union is an open shop. It would like to have a union or agency shop. Right-to-work laws are not in effect in this state. List your demands below:

IN-CLASS SKILL-BUILDING EXERCISE

Contract Negotiations

SB 16–3

Objective: To gain a better understanding of collective bargaining through negotiating a contract.

Experience: You will be assigned to a labor or management negotiation team to begin collective bargaining.

Materials: The completed list of demands from the preparation exercise.

Procedure 1
(3–4 minutes)

All the students who want to be on a management team stand on the right of the class; students who want to be on the union team stand on the left. The teams' numbers can be unequal (five on management, three on union, and so on). There should be between 6 and 10 members per set of management-union negotiating teams.

Procedure 2
(5–10 minutes)

Labor and management teams select a chairperson to lead the group and, if time permits, report to the class on the results of the negotiations. Labor writes out a list of demands it wants to achieve; management may write out a list if it wishes to do so. Try not to let other teams hear your discussion and list.

Procedure 3
(4–7 minutes)

Management and labor teams meet. Try not to overhear other teams. The union team presents, defends, and explains it demands. Management explains its position and what it wants to achieve. Do not negotiate yet.

Procedure 4
(5–10 minutes)

All team members should speak during negotiations. During your preparation, assign issues to members and agree on your stance.

Procedure 5
(20 minutes)

Management and union teams negotiate. Try not to let other teams hear your discussion. Stick to the time limit. If you do not settle, the union goes out on strike. You may take time to separate and discuss your position, then regroup to continue negotiations.

Procedure 6
(5–10 minutes)

The chairpeople report to the class on whether there is a strike or a settlement.

Conclusion (2–10 minutes): The instructor may make concluding remarks.

Application (2–4 minutes): What did I learn from this experience? How will I use this knowledge in the future?

Sharing: Volunteers may give their answers to the application section.

PART

V

Supervising Yourself

17
Managing Your Time, Stress, and Career

17

Managing Your Time, Stress, and Career

Learning Objectives

1. Explain how to analyze your time.

2. List and explain the three time management steps and use the time management system.

3. List and explain the three steps of the controlling stress plan and control your stress.

4. Describe the four career stages.

5. List and explain the five steps of career planning and use the model to develop your career plan.

Key Terms

To achieve our objectives in this chapter, it is important that you understand the following 10 key terms. They are presented in the order in which they appear in the chapter. The list of key terms also appears in alphabetical order in the end-of-chapter review.

time management	**burnout**	**career development**
stress	**controlling stress plan**	**career plan model**
stressors	**career planning**	**career path**
type A personality		

Whitney and Shane were on coffee break, talking. Whitney was complaining about all the tasks she had to get done. She had all kinds of pressure deadlines to meet. Whitney was a nervous wreck as she listed the many tasks. After a while, Shane interrupted to say that he used to be in the same situation until he took a time and stress management workshop that taught him to get more done in less time with better results. Shane gave Whitney the details so that she could take the course. In return, Whitney told Shane about a career development course she took. It helped her to get the job she has now, and Whitney knows what she wants to accomplish in the future. Have you ever felt as though you have more to do than the time you have to do it in? Do you ever feel stressed out? Do you ever wonder about your career? If you answered yes to any of these questions, this chapter can help you.

The title of this chapter may sound like we will be covering three unrelated topics. This is not the case. Time is one of a supervisor's most valuable resources.[1] Supervisors are usually expected to get more done than can actually be accomplished in a normal working day. When supervisors work hard to meet deadlines, they exert pressure on their minds, nerves, and body. This pressure is popularly called *stress*. When supervisors are stressed, their ability to function effectively may decrease. Therefore, supervisors who are poor time managers feel stress, their performance declines, and they are reviewed less favorably by bosses. On the other hand, supervisors who are good time managers feel less stress, are more efficient, and have greater chances at career advancement.

I. Time Management

Analyzing Time Use

The first step to successful time management is to determine how you currently spend your time.[2] Working long hours is often a sign of poor time management.[3] An analysis of how you use your time will indicate areas for improvement.

The Time Log

The time log is a daily diary that tracks your activities and enables you to determine how you spend your time. You use one time log for each day. An example is given in Exhibit 17–1. It is recommended that you keep track of your time every day over a period of one or two typical weeks. Try to keep the time log with you throughout the day. Fill in each 15 minute time slot, if possible, describing what you did.

Analyzing Time Logs: After keeping time logs for 5 to 10 working days, you can analyze the information recorded as follows:

1. Review the time logs to determine how much time you are spending on your primary responsibilities. How do you spend most of your time?

2. Identify areas where you are spending too much time.

3. Identify areas where you are not spending enough time.

4. Identify major interruptions that keep you from doing what you want to get done. How can you eliminate them?

5. Identify tasks you are performing that you do not have to be involved with. Look for nonsupervisory tasks. To whom can you delegate these tasks? (See Chapter 3 for a discussion of delegation.)

6. How much time is controlled by your boss? How much time is controlled by your employees? How much time is controlled by others outside your department? How much time do you actually control? How can you gain more control of your own time?

7. Look for crisis situations. Were they caused by something you did or did not do? Do you have recurring crises? How can you plan to help eliminate recurring crises?

8. Look for habits, patterns, and tendencies. Do they help or hurt you get the job done? How can you change them to your advantage?

9. List three to five of your biggest time wasters. What can you do to help eliminate them?

10. Ask yourself, "How can I manage my time more efficiently?"

Through the remainder of this section I will give you ideas to help you answer these 10 questions.

A Time Management System

Time management *refers to techniques designed to allow the supervisor to get more done in less time with better results.* The time management system described has a proven record of success with thousands of supervisors. Supervisors should try it for three weeks. After that time, they may adjust it to meet their own needs.

The problem supervisors face is not a shortage of time, but effective use of their time. Could you use an extra two hours every day? Experts say that most people waste at least this much time every day. The average supervisor could improve time use by 20 percent.[4]

There are four major parts to the time management system.

1. *Priorities.* Priorities should be determined in terms of the supervisor's major responsibilities. To determine priorities the supervisor should ask three ques-

EXHIBIT 17 – 1 **TIME LOG**

Date _____

8:00	
8:15	
8:30	
8:45	
9:00	
9:15	
9:30	
9:45	
10:00	
10:15	
10:30	
10:45	
11:00	
11:15	
11:30	
11:45	
12:00	
12:15	
12:30	
12:45	
1:00	
1:15	
1:30	
1:45	
2:00	
2:15	
2:30	
2:45	
3:00	
3:15	
3:30	
3:45	
4:00	
4:15	
4:30	
4:45	
5:00	
5:15	
5:30	
5:45	

TIME LOG

tions: (1) Do I need to be personally involved? (2) Is the task my responsibility—will it affect the department's performance or financial situation? (3) Is quick action needed? These three questions are on the to-do list in Chapter 3 and in Application Situation 3–3. The to-do list helps increase performance.[5] The supervisor should use the list as a time management tool.

2. *Objectives.* Objectives are *what* we want to accomplish within a given period of time. The supervisor should set weekly objectives following the guidelines stated in Chapter 2.[6]

3. *Plans.* Plans state *how* we will achieve our objectives. They list the activities that must be performed. The supervisor should develop plans following the guidelines stated in Chapter 2.

4. *Schedules.* Schedules state *when* the activities or plans will be carried out. The supervisor should schedule each workday.

There are three steps in the time management system.

Step 1. Plan Each Week: On the last day of each week, plan the coming week. Do this each and every week. Using your to-do list and the previous week's plan and departmental objectives, fill in a plan for the week sheet such as the one in Exhibit 17–2. Start by listing the objectives you want to accomplish during the week. These should not be routine tasks you perform weekly or daily but nonroutine items. For example, if an employee's annual review is due, plan for it.

After setting a few major objectives, list the activities necessary to accomplish each objective. To continue our example, you will need to make an appointment with the employee and complete the performance review form.

The next two columns to fill in are the time needed and day to schedule. To continue our example, assume it will take you 10 minutes to schedule the performance appraisal and about one hour to prepare for it. The day to schedule would be on Tuesday, your relatively quiet day. With experience, you will learn how much you can plan for and accomplish in one week. Planning too much is frustrating when you cannot get it all done. On the other hand, if you do not plan enough activities, you will end up wasting time and missing deadlines.

Step 2. Schedule Each Week: You may make a schedule for the week while you plan it or after, whichever you prefer. Planning and scheduling the week should take about 30 minutes. Exhibit 17–3 gives an example of a weekly schedule. Make copies of Exhibits 17–2 and 17–3 for use on the job. When scheduling your plans for the week, select times when you do not already have commitments such as meetings. Most supervisors should leave about 50 percent of the week unscheduled to accommodate unexpected events. Your job may require more or less unscheduled time. With practice, you will perfect weekly planning and scheduling.

Step 3. Schedule Each Day: Successful managers have daily schedules.[7] At the end of each day, you should schedule the next day. Or write each day's schedule first thing in the morning. This should take 15 minutes or less. Base the day's schedule on your plan and schedule for the week and your to-do list, using the form in Exhibit 17–4. Make copies of it as needed.

Begin by scheduling the activities over which you have no control, such as meetings you must attend. Leave your daily schedule flexible.[8] As stated previously, most supervisors need about 50 percent of their time unscheduled to handle unexpected events.

Don't be too optimistic; schedule enough time to do each task. Many supervisors, including the author, find that estimating the time something will take, and then doubling it, works well. With practice, you should improve.

Schedule high-priority items during your "prime time," when you perform at your best. For most people it is early in the morning. However, some people are slow starters and perform better later. Determine your prime time and schedule the tasks that need your full attention. Do routine things, such as checking your mail, at other times.

EXHIBIT 17–2 **WEEKLY PLANNING SHEET**

Plan for the week of _____

Objectives: (What is to be done by when) (Infinitive + action verb + single behavior
result + target data.)

Activities	Priority	Time Needed	Day to Schedule
Total time for the week			

EXHIBIT 17–3 **WEEKLY SCHEDULE**

Schedule for week of _____

	Mon	Tue	Wed	Th	Fri
8:00					
8:15					
8:30					
8:45					
9:00					
9:15					
9:30					
9:45					
10:00					
10:15					
10:30					
10:45					
11:00					
11:15					
11:30					
11:45					
12:00					
12:15					
12:30					
12:45					
1:00					
1:15					
1:30					
1:45					
2:00					
2:15					
2:30					
2:45					
3:00					
3:15					
3:30					
3:45					
4:00					
4:15					
4:30					
4:45					
5:00					
5:15					
5:30					
5:45					

DAILY SCHEDULE

Schedule for day _____

8:00	
8:15	
8:30	
8:45	
9:00	
9:15	
9:30	
9:45	
10:00	
10:15	
10:30	
10:45	
11:00	
11:15	
11:30	
11:45	
12:00	
12:15	
12:30	
12:45	
1:00	
1:15	
1:30	
1:45	
2:00	
2:15	
2:30	
2:45	
3:00	
3:15	
3:30	
3:45	
4:00	
4:15	
4:30	
4:45	
5:00	
5:15	
5:30	
5:45	

DAILY SCHEDULE

Try to schedule a time for unexpected events. Tell employees to see you with routine matters during a set time, such as 3 P.M. Have people call you, and call them, during this set time.

Do not do an unscheduled task before determining its priority. If you are working on a high-priority item and a medium-priority matter is brought to you, let it wait. Often even the so-called urgent matters can wait.

Keep your daily schedule and to-do list with you. Review and prioritize the "should" column. Select at least your top priority item (more items, if you like) now and each week to work on. Write it (them) on your to do list, and schedule if appropriate. Once you have completed the should column, work on the "could" column. Then go back to the "does not apply" column and be sure these items do not apply to you.

CONNECTIONS

1. Why are time management skills important to supervisors?

2. With or without the use of a time log, identify your three biggest time wasters. How can you cut down or eliminate these time wasters?

3. From the 68 techniques listed, chose the three most important techniques you "should" be using. Explain how you will implement each technique.

II. Managing Stress

What Is Stress?

Stress *is an emotional or physical reaction (or both) to environmental activities and events.* Stress is developed internally rather than externally.[9] Some stress improves performance. It helps challenge and motivate us. Many people perform best under some pressure. When deadlines are approaching, their adrenaline flows and they rise to the occasion with top performance. To meet deadlines, supervisors often have to apply pressure to themselves and their employees. However, too much stress too often is harmful to the individual and the organization.[10]

Situations in which too much pressure exists are known as stressors. **Stressors** *are situations in which people feel anxiety, tension, and pressure.* Too much stress over an extended period of time can have negative consequences, which will be discussed next.

Problems Associated with Stress

Stress was labeled the illness of the 80s.[11] The annual cost of stress is estimated to be between $50 and $75 billion, or about $750 per worker in the United States.[12] Too much stress causes poor performance.[13] To be more specific, stress is the major cause of low productivity, high absenteeism, poor decisions, bad judgment, and low morale.[14]

Stress causes physical illness. It has been linked to heart problems, ulcers, asthma, diabetes, multiple sclerosis, cancer, and other maladies. Three-fourths of all visits to family doctors are due to stress. Stress leads to alcohol and drug problems. It may also be the cause of suicide.[15]

Causes of Stress

Stress is an individual matter. In a given situation, one person may be very comfortable and another may feel stress. There are four common work stressors:

TIME MANAGEMENT TECHNIQUES

Following is a list of 68 ideas that can be used to improve your time management skills. Check off the appropriate box for each item.

(1) I should do this   (3) I could do this

(2) I do this now   (4) Does not apply to me

	Should (1)	Do (2)	Could (3)	N/A (4)
Planning and Controlling				
1. Set objectives—long and short term.				
2. Plan your week; how you will achieve your objectives.				
3. Use a to-do list—write all assignments on it.				
4. Prioritize the items on your to-do list. Do the important things rather than urgent things.				
5. Get an early productive start on your top priority items.				
6. During your best working hours—prime time—only do high-priority items.				
7. Don't spend time performing unproductive activities to avoid or escape job-related anxiety. It doesn't really work.				
8. Throughout the day ask yourself, "Should I be doing this—now?"				
9. Plan before you act.				
10. Plan for recurring crises, and plan to eliminate crises.				
11. Make decisions. It is better to make a wrong decision than none at all.				
12. Have a schedule for the day. Don't let your day be planned by the unexpected.				
13. Schedule the next day before you leave work.				
14. Schedule unpleasant or difficult tasks during prime time.				
15. Schedule enough time to do the job right the first time. Don't be too optimistic on the length of time to do a job.				
16. Schedule a quiet hour. Be interrupted only by true emergencies. Have someone take a message or ask people to call you back during this time.				
17. Establish a quiet time for the entire organization or department. The first hour of the day is usually the best time.				
18. Schedule large blocks of uninterrupted (emergencies only) time for projects and so forth. If this doesn't work, hide somewhere.				
19. Break large (long) projects into parts (time periods).				
20. If you don't follow your schedule, ask the *priority question:* Is the unscheduled event more important than the scheduled event?				
21. Schedule a time for doing similar activities (for example, make and return calls, write letters and memos).				
22. Keep your schedule flexible—allow $x\%$ of time for unexpected events.				
23. Schedule unexpected event time and answer mail, and do routine things in between events.				
24. Ask people to see or call you during your scheduled unexpected time only, unless it's an emergency.				
25. If staff members ask to see you—"Got a minute?"—tell them you're busy and ask whether it can wait until x o'clock (scheduled unexpected time).				
26. Set a schedule time, agenda, and time limit for all visitors, and keep on topic.				
27. Control your time. Cut down on the time controlled by the boss, organization, and your subordinates.				
Organizing				
28. Keep a clean desk.				
29. Rearrange your desk for increased productivity. (See "Your Desk" section for how to.)				
30. All non-work-related or distracting objects should be removed from your desk.				
31. Do one task at a time.				
32. With paperwork, make a decision at once. Don't read it again later and decide.				

TIME MANAGEMENT TECHNIQUES (*continued*)

Following is a list of 68 ideas that can be used to improve your time management skills. Check off the appropriate box for each item.

(1) I should do this (3) I could do this

(2) I do this now   (4) Does not apply to me

	Should (1)	Do (2)	Could (3)	N/A (4)
33. Keep files well arranged and labeled.				
34. Have an active and inactive file section.				
35. If you file an item, put a destruction date on it.				
36. Call rather than write, when appropriate.				
37. Delegate someone else to write letters, memos, and so forth.				
38. Dictate rather than write letters, memos, and so forth.				
39. Use form letters and form paragraphs.				
40. Answer letters (memos) on the letter itself.				
41. Have someone read and summarize things for you.				
42. Divide reading requirements with others and share summaries.				
43. Have calls screened to be sure the right person handles it.				
44. Plan before calling. Have an agenda and all necessary information ready—take notes on agenda.				
45. Ask people to call you back during your scheduled time (unexpected). Ask when is the best time to call them.				
46. Have a specific objective or purpose for every meeting.				
47. For meetings, invite only the necessary participants and keep them only as long as they are needed.				
48. Always have an agenda for a meeting and stick to it. Start and end as scheduled.				
49. Conclude each meeting with a summary, and get a commitment on who will do what by when.				
50. Call rather than visit, if possible.				
51. Set objectives for travel. List everyone you will meet with. Send (call) them agendas and have a file folder for each with all necessary data for your meeting.				
52. Combine and modify activities to save time.				
Leading and Staffing				
53. Set clear objectives for subordinates with accountability—give them feedback and evaluate results often.				
54. Use your subordinates' time well. Do you make subordinates wait idly for decisions, instructions, or materials, or in meetings?				
55. Communicate well. Do you wait for a convenient time, rather than interrupt your subordinates and waste their time?				
56. Train your subordinates. Don't do their work for them.				
57. Delegate activities in which you do not need to be personally involved.				
58. Delegate nonmanagement functions.				
59. Set deadlines when delegating.				
60. Set deadlines that are earlier than the actual deadline.				
61. Use the input of your staff. Don't reinvent the wheel.				
62. Teach time management skills to your subordinates.				
63. Don't procrastinate; do it.				
64. Don't be a perfectionist—define acceptable and stop there.				
65. Learn to stay calm. Getting emotional only causes more problems.				
66. Reduce socializing without causing antisocialism.				
67. Identify your time wasters and work to minimize them.				
68. If you have other ideas that are not listed, add them here.				

personality type, organizational climate, management effectiveness, and job satis-faction.[16] Before we begin our discussion of each stressor, complete the question-naire in Self-Learning Exercise 17–1. It will help you determine your personality type as it relates to stress.

The higher your score, the more characteristic you are of the type A stress personality. The lower your score, the more characteristic you are of the type B stress personality. An explanation of these two stress personality types appears below.

SELF-LEARNING EXERCISE 17 – 1

Stress Personality Types

Twenty statements follow. Identify how frequently each item applies to you.

5. usually	4. often	3. occasionally	2. seldom	1. rarely

Place the number 1, 2, 3, 4, or 5 on the line to the left of each statement.

_____ 1. I work at a fast pace.

_____ 2. I work on days off.

_____ 3. I set short deadlines for myself.

_____ 4. I enjoy work or school more than other activities.

_____ 5. I talk and walk fast.

_____ 6. I set high standards for myself, and work hard to meet them.

_____ 7. I enjoy competition; I work or play to win; I do not like to lose.

_____ 8. I skip lunch or eat it fast when there is work to do.

_____ 9. I'm in a hurry.

_____ 10. I do more than one thing at a time.

_____ 11. I'm angry and upset.

_____ 12. I get nervous or anxious when I have to wait.

_____ 13. I measure progress in terms of time and performance.

_____ 14. I push myself to the point of getting tired.

_____ 15. I take on more work when I already have plenty to do.

_____ 16. I take criticism as a personal putdown of my ability.

_____ 17. I try to out perform my co-workers or classmates.

_____ 18. I get upset when my routine has to be changed.

_____ 19. I try to get more done in less time.

_____ 20. I compare my accomplishments with others who are very highly productive.

_____ Total. Add up the numbers you have for all 20 items. Your score will range from 100 to 20. Place an "X" on the scale below.

Type A 100 . . . . .80 . . . . .60 . . . . .40 . . . . .20 Type B

            A   A-   B+   B

Personality Type

The major stressor is our personality type. The **type A personality** *is characterized as fast-moving, hard-driving, time conscious, competitive, impatient, and preoccupied with work.* The type B personality is just the opposite. The 20 statements in Self-Learning Exercise 17–1 relate to these personality styles. The number 5 (usually) represents type A behavior, and the number 1 (rarely) represents type B behavior. People with type A personalities place themselves under stress. They have six times as many heart attacks as people with type B personalities.[17] If you scored 60 or above, you have an A type personality, and stress could be a problem for you. You could end up with some of the problems associated with stress. In the next two parts of this section we will discuss how to identify the signs of stress and how to control it. For now, let's return to the other three stressors.

Organizational Climate   The level of cooperation, motivation, and morale affect stress. The more positive the organizational climate, the less stress there is.

Management Effectiveness   The better the managers supervise employees, the less stress there is. Calm, participative supervisory styles are less stressful. Tight control and the autocratic supervisory style tend to create more stress.[18]

Job Satisfaction   People who have jobs that they enjoy and derive satisfaction from handle stress better than those who do not. In some cases, changing jobs is a wise move that can lower or rid you of stress.

Signs of Stress

Mild signs include an increase in breathing rate and increased perspiration.

When you continually look at the clock or calendar and feel pressured and fear that you will not meet the deadline, you are experiencing stress.[19]

When stress continues for a period of time, it leads to disillusionment, irritability, headaches and other body tension, the feeling of exhaustion, and stomach problems. When people drink, take drugs, eat, or sleep more than usual, this is often a means of escaping stress.[20]

When people lose interest and motivation to do their work, this is often due to stress. If stress is constant, chronic, and severe it can lead to burnout over a period of time. **Burnout** *is the constant lack of interest in and motivation to perform one's job, caused by stress.* People sometimes experience temporary burnout during busy periods, such as exams for students and Christmas for retailers. However, when things slow down again, the interest and motivation come back. When the interest and motivation do not return, burnout is permanent.

Stress and burnout can often be avoided through the use of stress-controlling techniques.

Controlling Stress

Ideally, we should identify what causes stress in our lives and eliminate it or decrease it.[21] We can do this by following a three-stage plan. The **controlling stress plan** *includes three steps: identify stressors; determine their causes and consequences; and plan to eliminate or decrease the stress.* Next we will discuss five ways in which you can eliminate or decrease stress.[22]

Exercise   Physical exercise is an excellent way to release tension. Many supervisors find that exercising helps increase their endurance in handling the job. In a survey by *American Health Magazine,* 76 percent of adult men and 63 percent of adult women said they do some exercise each week.[23]

Aerobic exercise in which you increase your heart rate and maintain that rate for 20 to 30 minutes three or more days per week is generally considered the best type of exercise. Exercises such as fast walking or jogging, swimming, and aerobic dance or exercise fall in this category. Other exercises that increase your heart rate but do not maintain the rate for 20 or more minutes include sports such as racquetball, tennis, and basketball, which are also beneficial.

Before starting an exercise program, you should check with a doctor to make sure you can do so safely. Start gradually and work your way up to 20 to 30 minutes slowly. We often feel fine while exercising; it's later in the day or the next morning that we feel the aftereffects.

Nutrition

Good health is essential to supervisors and nutrition is a major factor in health.[24] Being overweight is stressful. Watch how you eat and what you eat.

How You Eat: Breakfast is considered the most important meal of the day. A good breakfast gets you off to a good start. When you eat, take your time. Rushing is stressful and can cause stomach upset.

What You Eat: Try to minimize your intake of junk food containing high levels of salt and sugar. Consume less fat, salt, caffeine (coffee, tea, cola), alcohol, and drugs.[25]

Relaxation

Get enough rest and sleep. Slow down and enjoy yourself. Have some off-the-job interests that are relaxing. Have some fun and laugh.[26] Some of the things you can do to relax include praying, meditating, listening to music, reading, watching TV and movies, and working on hobbies.[27]

When you feel stress, you can perform some simple relaxation exercises. One of the most popular and simplest is deep breathing. Simply take a deep breath, hold for a few seconds (you may count to five), and then let it out slowly. If you feel tension in one muscle you may do a specific relaxation exercise, or you may relax your entire body going from head to toe or vice versa. A list of relaxation exercises that can be done almost anywhere is given in Exhibit 17–5.

Positive Thinking

Be optimistic. Make statements to yourself in the affirmative, such as "I will do it." Be patient, honest, and realistic. No one is perfect. Admit your mistakes and learn from them; don't let them get you down.[28] Have self-confidence. Develop your time management skills. Don't procrastinate or be a perfectionist.[29]

Support System

LEARNING OBJECTIVE

3. List and explain the three steps of the controlling stress plan and control your stress.

We all need people to depend on. Have family and friends you can go to for help with your problems. Having someone to talk to can be very helpful. But don't take advantage of others and use stress to get attention.[30]

If you try all of the stress controlling techniques and none of them works, you should seriously consider getting out of the situation. If you are experiencing permanent burnout, you should ask yourself two questions: (1) Am I worth it? (2) Is it worth dying for?[31] If you answer yes to question 1 and no to question 2, changing situations or jobs is advisable.

EXHIBIT 17–5   **RELAXATION EXERCISES**

Muscles	Tensing Method
Forehead	Wrinkle forehead. Try to make your eyebrows touch your hairline for five seconds. Relax.
Eyes and nose	Close your eyes as tightly as you can for five seconds. Relax.
Lips, cheeks, jaw	Draw corners of your mouth back and grimace for five seconds. Relax.
Neck	Rotate your head slowly tensing your neck for five seconds. Relax.
Hands	Extend arms in front of you; clench fists tightly for five seconds. Relax.
Forearms	Extend arms out against an invisible wall and push forward with hands for five seconds. Relax.
Upper arms	Bend elbows. Tense biceps for five seconds. Relax.
Shoulders	Shrug shoulders up to your ears for five seconds. Relax.
Back	Arch your back off the floor or bed for five seconds. Relax.
Stomach	Tighten your stomach muscles for five seconds. Relax.
Hips, buttocks	Tighten buttocks for five seconds. Relax.
Thighs	Tighten thigh muscles by pressing legs together as tightly as you can for five seconds. Relax.
Feet	Bend ankles toward your body as far as you can for five seconds. Relax.
Toes	Curl toes under as tightly as you can for five seconds. Relax.

CONNECTIONS

4. Why is stress management important to the supervisor?

5. State your personality type and score from Self-Learning Exercise 17–1. Do you need to work at changing your personality type? Explain why or why not.

6. Identify your major stressor. Determine its cause and consequences. Develop a plan to eliminate or decrease the stress.

7. Of the five ways to eliminate or decrease stress, which do you do best? Which needs the most improvement? Why? What will you do to improve in this area?

III. Career Management

If you want to be a successful supervisor, you must take the responsibility and manage your department. The same holds true for your career; you must take the responsibility for managing your career.[32] In this section you will learn how to do this successfully.

Career Stages

Before planning your career, you must determine what stage you are in. We will focus on career stages by age.[33] As we get older, our needs will change.

The 20s

This is the time when managers are just getting started. The challenge is to prove that you have what it takes to get the job done well—and on time. There is a lot of pressure to be the best. Women who seek advancement in a world dominated by men tend to feel personal pressure to try harder. At this stage, you must develop the job skills needed to do the present job and to prepare for advancement. Initiative is needed; young managers often work long, hard hours to get ahead.

Today's young managers have high expectations.[34] They are impatient as they feel the pressure for quick advancement up the corporate ladder, which is shaky at best.

The 30s

This decade is the time when managers develop expertise and show their strengths as bosses. They try to gain visibility with top management. In their 30s, people often question their careers. Where am I going? Should I be here? Am I secure in my position?

The 40s and 50s

By age 45, most managers have weathered a failure or two and know whether they have a shot at higher management jobs. The majority don't make it and must accept that the race is over. In the past, people at this stage would settle into a secure middle management job. However, times have changed. Many organizations continue to cut back the number of middle manager positions. People in their 40s and 50s are sometimes forced to seek new employers—or new careers. This can be difficult when trying to cope with growing older. As a means of getting rid of middle managers, some organizations are forcing people to take early retirement.

The 60s and 70s

LEARNING OBJECTIVE
4. Describe the four career stages.

At this stage, people begin to prepare for retirement. They can pass along what they have learned and provide continuity. As people live longer the need to provide retirement counseling increases. Many large organizations have full-time staffs to help employees plan for and make the transition to retirement.

Career Planning and Development

There is a difference between career planning and career development. **Career planning** *is the process of setting career objectives and determining how to accomplish them.* **Career development** *is the process of gaining skill, experience, and education to achieve career objectives.*

Most colleges and large organizations offer career planning and development services. It is usually the individual's responsibility to go to them and take advantage of what they provide. A career-planning counselor's role is not to find jobs for people; it is to help them set realistic career objectives and plans. Many colleges also offer career placement services designed to help students find jobs. But it is the student's responsibility to obtain the job offer.

The career planning model can help you develop your own career plan. The steps in the **career planning model** *are performing self-assessment; determining career preferences and exploration; setting objectives; developing plans; and controlling.*

Step 1. Perform Self-Assessment

The starting point in career planning is the self-assessment inventory.[35] Who are you? What are your interests, values, needs, skills, and experience?[36] What do you do well? What do you enjoy doing? What do you want to do during your career?

The preparation for Skill-Building Exercise 17–3 will help you determine your strong and weak areas.

Step 2. Determine Career Preferences and Exploration

Others can help you get a job, but you are responsible for selecting your career and its progression.[37] Based on who you are (self-assessment), you must decide what you want from your job and career, and prioritize these desires. You are responsible for your own job satisfaction.[38]

Career planning is not just a determination of what you want to do. It is important to determine why you want to do these things. What motivates you? And how much do you want it? What is your commitment?[39] Without the appropriate motivation and commitment to career plans, you will not be successful at attaining them.

You should consider the following career aspects:

- *Industry.* What industry do you want to work for? Would you like to work in insurance, automotive, government? Getting into a growing industry gives you better opportunity for advancement.

- *Size.* What size organization do you want to work for? About one-half of the nation's private sector labor force works for small business. Between 1979 and 1985 most new jobs came from small business. Big companies are not as secure as they used to be.[40]

- *Job.* What type of job or jobs do you want in your career? If you want to be a supervisor, what department do you want to manage? Which functional areas interest you? Production or operations, marketing, finance, human resources?

- *Location.* What city, state, or country do you want to work in? People who are willing to relocate often find more opportunities.

Once you have answered these types of questions, talk to people in career planning and to people who hold the types of jobs you are interested in. Determine the requirements and qualifications you need to get a job in the career that interests you. Getting an internship, field work, a cooperative job, a part-time job, or a summer job in your field of interest can help you land the job you want after graduation. In the long run, it is often more profitable to take a job that pays less but gives you experience that will help you in your career progression.

Step 3. Set Objectives

Set short- and long-range objectives using the guidelines from Chapter 2.[41] Objectives should not simply be a listing of the next jobs.[42] Examples of objectives for someone graduating from college in May 19XX would include the following:

- To attain a sales position with a large insurance company by June 30, 19XX.
- To become a sales manager in the insurance industry by June 30, 19XX.
- To attain a starting first-year income of $25,000.
- To attain a salary of $35,000 by June 30, 19XX.
- To attain my MBA by June 30, 19XX.

Step 4. Develop Plans

Develop plans that will enable you to attain your objectives. This is where career development fits in. You must determine what skills, experience, and education you need to get to where it is you want to go, and plan to develop as needed. Talking to others can help you develop a career plan, but you must take responsibility for

MODEL 17–1   **CAREER PLANNING MODEL**

Step 1. Perform self-assessment.

Step 2. Determine career preferences and exploration.

Step 3. Set objectives.

Step 4. Develop plans.

Step 5. Control.

---

its implementation.[43] You may find it helpful to use the operational planning sheet from Chapter 2. A copy appears in Skill-Building Exercise 17–2.

You should have a written career plan, but this does not mean that it cannot be changed. You should be open to unplanned opportunities and take advantage of them when it is in your best interest.

Step 5. Control

Plans are useless unless they are implemented. It is your responsibility to achieve your objectives. You may have to take corrective action. Review your objectives and check your progress at least once a year; change and develop new objectives and plans. Update your résumé at the same time.

Model 17–1 lists the steps in career planning.

Getting a Supervisory Management Job

Through at least the early 1990s, competition for careers in supervisory management will be intense. However, there will be opportunities for those with sound career plans.

A college education is not a prerequisite for all management positions, but the trend toward selecting only college graduates is increasing. A college degree opens doors and offers personal and job satisfaction derived from a higher status and prestige. In the early 1980s, according to the U.S. Bureau of the Census, a bachelor's degree was worth more than $300,000 in extra lifetime earnings for young men and $142,000 for young women.[44] The percentage of jobs requiring a college degree will continue to grow.

It has been said that getting a good job is a job in itself. To obtain any good job, it is advisable to develop a career plan, résumé, and cover letter; conduct research; and prepare for the interview.

Career Plan

Before you begin to look for a job, you should have developed a career plan. Interviewers are turned off by candidates who have no idea of what they want in a job and career. On the other hand, they are usually impressed by candidates with realistic career plans. Having a good career plan gives you a competitive advantage over those who do not. Doing the Preparation for Skill-Building Exercise 17–2 will help you prepare a career plan.

Résumé and Cover Letter

The author was once told by a recruiting executive at Xerox that the résumé is given about 40 percent of the weight in getting a job. Your résumé and the cover letter that accompanies it are your introduction to the organization you wish to work for. If they are not neat and contain errors and mistakes, you may not get an interview. Recruiters tend to believe that a sloppy résumé comes from a sloppy person.

The cover letter should be short, one page. Its purpose is to introduce your résumé and to request an interview. The résumé should also be short; one page is recommended unless you have extensive education and experience. The résumé's primary purpose is to get you an interview. Exhibit 17–6 gives guidelines you can follow when developing your résumé.

The résumé guidelines are designed for a recent graduate with limited work experience. If you have full-time work experience related to the job you seek, list the experience before the education section and be less concerned about internships, honors, and activities. In addition, if you have special training, certifications, and so on, you can add another section to your résumé.

After writing your résumé have someone proofread it to make sure that it contains no spelling or grammatical errors. It should be typed on a high-quality bond paper. Copies should also be made on high-quality paper and should look

---

E X H I B I T   1 7 – 6   **RÉSUMÉ GUIDELINES**

Name

Address

City, State, ZIP

Telephone Number and Area Code

Objective

If you have a specific objective, include it here. If your objective is general or covers several areas, omit this section, and, in a cover letter, tailor the objectives to the job you are applying for.

Education

Degree/Major	College name, address, city, state, ZIP, and telephone number. Date of graduation. Minor area (if any). Grade-point average (if you are proud of it).
Internship (if any)	List organization name, address, city, state, ZIP, telephone. State department and specific work activities; state areas of responsibility and other relevant information. Include dates. Organization supervisor's name and title.
Honors or activities (if any)	List any sports, clubs, or other extracurricular activities. Be sure to state any offices held, honors received, and skills, such as leadership, that you developed.

Experience

Title	List any full-time, summer, part-time, or volunteer jobs held. Give organization name, address, city, state, ZIP, telephone number. List responsibilities and any skills developed, particularly any that relate to the job you are applying for. List dates employed and your supervisor's name and title.
Title	Same as above.
Title	Same as above.

References

Furnished upon request. (Get approval before giving names. You may be able to file references with your college placement department; check with them.)

like originals. Many printing and copying companies offer reasonable package deals that include typesetting the résumé to give it eye appeal; making copies; and including matching personalized stationery for cover letters. This investment can impress a recruiter and get you an interview over other equal candidates with homemade résumés.

Research

Research is needed to determine where to send your résumé. Many colleges offer seminars in job search strategies. There are also a number of articles and books on the subject.

Some people take the attitude that they want to make it on their own. It's an honorable thought, but contacts can help you land the job you are looking for. A lead and recommendation from a friend or relative does not guarantee that you will get the job, however. You still must go through the interview and land the job yourself.

If you are looking for a job with a small organization, career days, campus interviews, and advertisements in newspapers will not be of much help. Small organizations tend to find their managers through suppliers, distributors, and other business contacts.[45] Get to know people in the organization and contact them directly. Some people also say that the personnel department is not the best place to find a job. Making contacts within the department you want to work for can help you get the job you want. People are often hired because they know someone or someone knows them.[46]

Once you have an interview set, you should do research on the organization. You want to know as much about the organization as you can. For example, you should know which products and services it offers, be familiar with the industry and its trends, and know about the organization's profits and future plans. For publicly owned organizations, the annual report has much of this information. If you know people who work for the organization, talk to them about these issues.

Also, as part of your research, you should develop a list of questions you want to ask the interviewer during or at the end of the interview. Asking questions is a sign of intelligence and shows interest in the organization. Two good areas to ask questions about are job responsibilities and career opportunities.

The Interview

The interview is given the most weight in job decisions in most cases—about 60 percent, according to the Xerox recruiter mentioned previously. References and the résumé will get you an interview, but how you perform during the interview usually determines whether you get the job.

Many college career placement services offer workshops on job interviews. Some offer mock interviews on camera that allow you to see how you conduct yourself. If this service is available, take advantage of it.

Be sure to dress appropriately. A conservative suit or dress gives a good impression.

Be a few minutes early. Try not to rush to get to the interview on time. The interview itself is stressful enough. Bring a pen and extra copies of your résumé. Be prepared to discuss your career plans and to ask your questions.

During the interview, answer all questions fully. Pause to think and plan your answers to complex questions.

At the end of the interview, thank the interviewer for the opportunity to discuss your qualifications. If it was not stated, find out when you will hear from the interviewer.

After the interview, evaluate how well you did. Make some notes on what you did and did not do well. If you want the job, send a thank-you letter afterward, adding anything you forgot to say, stating your interest in the job, and saying that you look forward to hearing from the interviewer. Enclose a copy of your résumé.

Getting Raises and Promotions

Following are 10 ways to enhance your chances of getting raises and promotions:

- Be a top performer at your present job. If you are not successful at your present job, you are not a likely candidate for a raise or promotion.
- Finish assignments early. When your boss delegates a task, get it done before the deadline. This shows initiative.
- Volunteer for extra assignments. If you can handle additional work, you should get paid more, and you show your ability to take on a new position.
- Keep up with the latest technology. Request the opportunity for training. Take the time to learn to use the latest technology. Use the computer and MIS (management information systems) to full capability. Read publications that pertain to your field.
- Develop good relations with the important people in the organization. (Follow the ideas in Chapter 6.)
- Know when to approach your boss. Make requests when your boss is in a good mood; stay clear when the boss is in a bad mood unless you can help resolve the reason for the mood.
- Be polite. Say thank you both verbally and in writing. Sending a thank-you note keeps your name in front of people. Saying please, pardon me, and so forth shows concern for others.
- Never say anything negative about anyone. You never know who will find out what you've said. Even a "nobody" may be a good friend of an important person.
- Be approachable. Smile; go out of your way to say "hi" to people. Take time to talk to people who want your help.
- Make effective presentations. If you are not effective at speaking before people, get training. Join Toastmasters International or a similar organization.[47]

Career Paths

A **career path** *is a sequence of job assignments that leads to more responsibility, with raises and promotions.* Some organizations have defined career paths. This makes it easier to develop a career plan, because in a sense that's what the career path is. In the fast-food industry, career paths are common. For example, management trainees start out by going to a formal training program for a few weeks, then they are assigned to a store as a trainee for six months, then they go to a different store as an assistant store manager for a year, and then they become a store manager. After one year they can be promoted to a larger store. After being a store manager for five years they are eligible for regional management positions.

Getting a Raise or Promotion

It is very important to understand what your job responsibilities are and how you are evaluated by your boss, both formally and informally.[48] Be aware of your boss's expectations and try to exceed them; meet them at the very least. Do what needs to be done to get a high evaluation. If you don't get a good performance appraisal, your chances of getting a raise or promotion are lower.

In Chapter 12 we discussed keeping a critical incident file of the good and poor performances of your employees. In reality, most bosses probably don't keep a record, or only record the negative. If you want a raise or promotion, it's your responsibility to prove that you deserve one. The way to prove it is through self-documentation.[49] Keep a critical incident file of every positive thing you do that is not generally required but that helps the organization. Keeping the boss appraised of your success on a regular basis is not bragging. Some things to include are as follows:

- Any additional work you now perform.
- Times when you volunteered or cooperated to help other departments.
- Ideas you suggested that help the organization.
- Any increases in the performance of your department. Be specific. For example, productivity was up by 5 percent last year, absenteeism was down 10 percent last year, returns were down by 100 units this period, or sales increased by $5,000 this quarter.
- If, during the last performance appraisal, you were told about areas that need improvement, gather evidence to show how you have improved.

If you plan to ask for a raise, have a specific amount to state. Check to find out what other supervisors are getting for raises and what other organizations pay their supervisors for similar jobs. If your boss is a negotiator, start with a request for a higher raise than you expect to get. This way, you can compromise and still get what you feel you deserve.

Asking for a Raise or Promotion: Don't catch your boss by surprise. The best time to ask for the raise is usually during the performance appraisal. Present your critical incidents to help you get a good review and raise.

Requests for promotion should be made before a specific position is open. Your boss and the personnel department should know about your career plan. Ask them where you stand, what the chances of promotions are, and when they may come.[50] Have the boss and personnel department help prepare you for a promotion.

Changing Organizations

LEARNING OBJECTIVE

5. List and explain the five steps of career planning and use the model to develop your career plan.

Should you stay with one organization or change organizations to progress in your career? A survey was conducted to determine which route managers recommended. Of the respondents, 50 percent recommend taking successively better positions with different companies, 30 percent recommend growth with one company, 11 percent were not sure, and 9 percent said that either route is valid.[51] The trend is toward changing organizations. In the early 1970s, managers held three or four jobs in a lifetime; soon managers will hold seven to ten jobs.[52]

The choice will be yours. If you are satisfied that you are meeting your career plan with one organization, stay with it; if not, search out new opportunities elsewhere.

CONNECTIONS

8. Which career stage are you in? Does the information given about career stage relate to your career? Explain.

9. What career development efforts are you making?

10. Write a résumé following the chapter guidelines. Bring your résumé to class.

11. Which of the 10 tips for getting ahead need the most and least conscious effort on your part? Explain your answer.

REVIEW

Select one or more methods: (1) fill in the missing key terms from memory; (2) match the key terms from the end of the review with their definitions below; (3) copy the key terms in order from the list at the beginning of the chapter.

_____ refers to techniques designed to allow the supervisor to get more done in less time with better results. Analyzing your time log reveals how you use your time. It serves as the basis for determining how to improve your time management. The four parts of the time management system are priorities, objectives, plans, and schedules. The three steps in a time management system are as follows: plan each week; schedule each week; and schedule each day.

_____ is an emotional or physical reaction (or both) to environmental activities and events. _____ are situations in which people feel anxiety, tension, and pressure. Stress has been proven to be related to a variety of illnesses. There are four common work stressors. (1) Personality types: the _____ is characterized as fast-moving, hard-driving, time conscious, competitive, impatient, and preoccupied with work; the type B personality is the opposite. Type A personalities impose more stress on themselves, which can be dangerous to their health, than do type B personalities. (2) Organizational climate: a cooperative climate is less stressful. (3) Management effectiveness: the better you supervise the less stress there is. (4) Job satisfaction: the more you enjoy your job, the less stressful it tends to be. _____ is the constant lack of interest and motivation to perform one's job caused by stress. The _____ includes identifying stressors; determining their causes and consequences; and planning to eliminate or decrease the stress. There are five ways to help eliminate or decrease stress: exercise, nutrition, relaxation, positive thinking, and the support system.

As we age, we go through different career stages. _____ is the process of setting career objectives and determining how to accomplish them. _____ is the process of gaining skill, experience, and education to achieve career objectives. The _____ steps are as follows: perform self-assessment; determine career preferences and exploration; set objectives; develop plans; and control. To attain a supervisory management job, it is recommended that you develop a career plan, résumé, and cover letter; conduct research; and prepare for the interview. Some organizations offer _____ , a sequence of job assignments that lead to more responsibility, with raises and promotions. Before asking for a raise or promotion, you should prepare yourself by developing a critical incident file of all the positive contributions you make to the organization.

KEY TERMS

burnout	controlling stress plan
career development	stress
career path	stressors
career plan model	time management
career planning	type A personality

REFERENCES

1. H. Kent Baker and Philip Morgan, "Building a Professional Image: Dealing with Time Problems," *Supervisory Management*, October 1985, p. 42.

2. Ibid., p. 37.

3. John Byrne, "Don't Let Time Management Be a Waste of Time," *Business Week*, May 4, 1987, p. 144.

4. Arthur Sondak, "The Multiplier of Good Time Management," *Supervisory Management*, April 1985, p. 35.

5. R. Alex Mackenzie, "The 'To-Do' List is Obsolete," *Supervisory Management*, September 1985, p. 41.

6. Kenneth Wexley and Timothy Baldwin, "Posttraining Strategies for Facilitating Positive Transfer: An Empirical Exploration," *Academy of Management Journal*, September 1986, p. 512.

7. "Spending Time Wisely," *Management Review*, February 1987, p. 9.

8. Byrne, "Don't Let Time Management Be a Waste of Time," p. 144.

9. Robert Eckles, "Stress—Making Friends with the Enemy," *Business Horizons*, March–April 1987, p. 74.

10. Kenneth Hall and Lawson Savery, "Tight Rein, More Stress," *Harvard Business Review*, January–February 1986, p. 160.

11. Eckles, "Stress—Making Friends with the Enemy," p. 74.

12. Jessica Jenner, "On the Way to Stress Resistance," *Training and Development Journal*, May 1986, p. 112.

13. Hall and Savery, "Tight Rein, More Stress," p. 161.

14. Eckles, "Stress—Making Friends with the Enemy," p. 74.

15. Ibid.

16. Ibid., p. 75.

17. Ibid.

18. Hall and Savery, "Tight Rein, More Stress," p. 163.

19. Richard Bauman, "Packaged Stress," *Supervision*, February 1987, p. 14.

20. Eckles, "Stress—Making Friends with the Enemy," p. 74.

21. Bob Curran, "It's a Matter of Stress," *Supervision*, October 1986, p. 13.

22. Jenner, "On the Way to Stress Resistance," p. 113.

23. "No Pain, No Gain," *The Wall Street Journal*, June 22, 1987, p. 31.

24. Janet Barnard, "Leadership Is a Survival Skill," *Administrative Management*, January 1987, p. 56.

25. Carolyn Hines and Wesley Wilson, "A No-Nonsense Guide to Being Stressed," *Management Solutions*, October 1986, pp. 27–28.

26. Ibid.

27. Jenner, "On the Way to Stress Resistance," p. 113.

28. Allan Halcrow, "Galileo, Lincoln, and Stress Management," *Personnel Journal*, April 1986, p. 12.

29. Hines and Wilson, "A No-Nonsense Guide to Being Stressed," p. 28.

30. Halcrow, "Galileo, Lincoln, and Stress Management," p. 12.

31. Ibid.

32. Buck Blessing, "Career Planning: Five Fatal Assumptions," *Training and Development Journal*, September 1986, p. 50.

33. Carol Hymowitz, "Stable Cycles of Executive Careers Shattered by Upheaval in Business," *The Wall Street Journal*, May 26, 1987, p. 35.

34. "Career Development Comes of Age," *Training and Development Journal*, November 1986, p. 16.

35. Donna Christensen, "Organizational Involvement: The Key to Employee Career Development," *Management Solutions*, May 1987, p. 40.

36. Walter Kiechel, "Your New Employment Contract," *Fortune*, July 6, 1987, p. 109.

37. Kevin Nilan, Sally Walls, Sandra Davis, and Mary Lund, "Creating a Hierarchical Career Progression Network," *Personnel Administrator*, June 1987, p. 169.

38. Kiechel, "Your New Employment Contract," p. 109.

39. Blessing, "Career Planning: Five Fatal Assumptions," p. 51.

40. Richard Greene, "Can You Handle Chaos?" *Forbes*, June 16, 1986, p. 156.

41. Peggy Simonsen, "Concepts of Career Development," *Training and Development Journal*, November 1986, p. 70.

42. Blessing, "Career Planning: Five Fatal Assumptions," p. 49.

43. Simonsen, "Concepts of Career Development," p. 74.

44. "How Much Is a Degree Worth? $329,000," *Tulsa World*, March 14, 1983, p. B6.

45. Greene, "Can You Handle Chaos?" p. 158.

46. "Personnel Departments Are No Place to Look for a Job," *The Wall Street Journal*, April 7, 1987, p. 1.

47. Don Bagin, "Career Advice: 15 Tips to Help You Get Ahead!" *BNAC Communicator*, Spring 1987, p. 10.

48. Nilan et al., "Creating a Hierarchical Career Progression Network," p. 183.

49. J. H. Foegen, "The Case for Positive Documentation," *Business Horizons*, September–October 1986, p. 61.

50. Kiechel, "Your New Employment Contract," p. 110.

51. "Which Route?" *The Wall Street Journal*, September 29, 1987, p. 41.

52. "One-Company Executives Lose Favor with Prospective Employers," *The Wall Street Journal*, May 19, 1987, p. 1.

APPLICATION SITUATIONS

Time Management

AS 17−1

Identify each time management statement as applying to one of the following:

a. priorities   *d.* schedule for the week

b. objectives   *e.* schedule for the day

c. plans

_____ 1. I set up my appointments for May 5.

_____ 2. I know what I want to accomplish.

_____ 3. I've decided how to get the work done.

_____ 4. I know my major responsibilities.

_____ 5. I've planned my week; now I'm going to. . . .

Stressors

AS 17−2

Identify each stressor as being one of the following:

a. personality type   *c.* management effectiveness

b. organizational climate   *d.* job satisfaction

_____ 6. The morale in our department is poor.

_____ 7. This job is okay, I guess.

_____ 8. I'm always racing against the clock.

_____ 9. Our priorities keep changing from week to week; it's very confusing when you're not sure what's expected of you.

_____ 10. I work at a comfortable pace.

Controlling Stress

AS 17−3

Identify each statement by the way it helps eliminate stress:

a. exercise   *d.* positive thinking

b. nutrition   *e.* support system

c. relaxation

_____ 11. "I pray every day."

_____ 12. "I have a few close friends that I can count on."

_____ 13. "I don't drink much coffee or tea; thanks anyway."

_____ 14. "I'm joining the bowling league."

_____ 15. "I can have this job done by the deadline; no problem."

Career Planning Steps

AS 17–4

Identify each statement by its step in career planning:

a. 1   *b.* 2   *c.* 3   *d.* 4   *e.* 5

_____ 16. "First, I have to get my degree; then I'll apply for a management trainee position with the major banks in the Midwest."

_____ 17. "I'm very good in math and computers."

_____ 18. "I want to be a partner in a CPA firm within seven years."

_____ 19. "Once a year I sit down and reassess who I am and where I'm going."

_____ 20. "I want to get into the co-op program because I'm not sure what I want to do when I graduate. I figure it will help me decide."

OBJECTIVE   CASE   17

Overworked?

In the following discussion Iris is a middle manager and Peggy is the first-line supervisor.

IRIS: Peggy, I've called you in my office to speak to you about your report; it's late again.

PEGGY: I know. But I'm so busy getting the work out that I don't have time to do it. I'm always the first to arrive for work and the last to go home. I push hard to get the job done. Sometimes I end up redoing employees' work because it's not done properly. I often get headaches and stomach cramps from working so intensely.

IRIS: I know you do. Maybe the problem lies in your time management ability. What do you usually do each day?

PEGGY: Most of each day is spent putting out fires. My employees constantly need me to help them with their work. The days just seem to speed by. Other than putting out fires, I don't do much.

IRIS: So you can't get the reports done on time because of the number of fires. What is your approach to getting the reports done on time?

PEGGY: I just wait until there are no fires to put out, and then I do them. Sometimes it's after the deadline.

IRIS: You are going to have to make some definite changes if you are going to be a successful supervisor. Do you enjoy being a supervisor?

PEGGY: For the most part I do. I think I might like to move up the ladder some day. But I like the hands-on stuff; I'm not too thrilled about doing paperwork.

IRIS: If you develop your time management skills, I believe you will find that you can get the job done on time with less stress. On Monday the company is offering a time management workshop. I took the course myself; it's excellent. It really helped me a lot when I was in your position, and today. It teaches you a three-step approach. [*It covers the to-do list and the information covered in this chapter.*] Do you want to attend?

PEGGY: Yes, but what about the work in my department?

IRIS: I'll cover for you. On Tuesday, I want you to come see me first thing in the morning so that we can discuss what you learned and how you are going to apply it on the job.

Answer the following questions supporting your answers in the space between questions.

_____ 1. Keeping a time log and using a to-do list would be helpful to Peggy.
   a. true   *b.* false

_____ 2. Peggy seems to be effective at setting priorities.
   a. true   *b.* false

_____ 3. Setting weekly objectives, plans, and schedules would help Peggy get the reports done on time.
   a. true   *b.* false

_____ 4. Peggy stated experiencing _____ reactions to stress.

      a. emotional   *b.* physical

_____ 5. Peggy seems to be a _____ personality.

      a. type A   *b.* type B

_____ 6. Peggy's stress is coming primarily from _____ .

      a. organizational climate   *c.* job satisfaction
      b. management effectiveness

_____ 7. Peggy should use _____ to help her control stress.

      a. exercise   *d.* positive thinking
      b. nutrition   *e.* support system
      c. relaxation   *f.* any or all of these

_____ 8. Peggy has a career plan.

      a. true   *b.* false

_____ 9. The time management workshop is best classified as _____ .

      a. career planning   *c.* career plan model
      b. career development   *d.* career path

_____ 10. From the case information, we can assume that this company has career paths.

      a. true   *b.* false

11. How would you conduct the Tuesday morning session with Peggy?

PREPARATION FOR IN-CLASS SKILL-BUILDING EXERCISE

**Time Management
System**

SB 17−1

For this exercise you will need copies of Exhibits 17−1 through 17−4. Before using the time management system, it is helpful, but not necessary, to keep a time log for one or two typical weeks.

Step 1. Plan Your Week: Using Exhibit 17−2, develop a plan for the rest of this week. Begin with today.

Step 2. Schedule Your Week: Using Exhibit 17−3, schedule the rest of this week. Be sure to schedule a 30-minute period to plan and schedule next week, preferably on the last day of this week.

Step 3. Schedule Your Day: Using Exhibit 17−4, schedule each day. Do this for every day at least until the class period for which this exercise is assigned.

Be sure to bring your plans and schedules to class.

IN-CLASS SKILL-BUILDING EXERCISE

**Time Management
System**

SB 17−1

Objective: To understand how to use the time management system to enable you to get more done in less time with better results.

Experience: You will share and discuss your plans and schedules for the week and your daily schedules.

Material: You need your completed plans and schedules.

*Procedure 1
(5−10 minutes)*

Break into groups of five or six and share and discuss your plans and schedules. Pass them around so that you can make comparisons. The comparisons serve as a guide to improving future plans and schedules.

Conclusion: The instructor leads a class discussion and makes concluding remarks.

Application (2−4 minutes): What did I learn from this experience? How will I use this knowledge in the future?

Sharing: Volunteers give their answers to the application section.

PREPARATION FOR IN-CLASS SKILL-BUILDING EXERCISE

Career Planning

SB 17−2

Answering the following questions will help you develop a career plan. Do not reveal anything about yourself that you prefer not to share with classmates during the in-class exercise.

Step 1. Self-Assessment   *a.* List two or three statements that answer the question "Who am I?"

b. Think about two or three of your major accomplishments. (They can be in school, work, sports, hobbies, and so forth.) List the skills it took to achieve them.

c. Identify skills and abilities you already possess that you can use in your career (for example, planning, organizing, communicating, leading). Do the preparation for Skill-Building Exercise 17–3.

Step 2. Career Preferences and Exploration

a. What type of industry would you like to work in? (You may list more than one.)

b. What type and size of organization do you want to work for?

c. List by priority the five factors that will most influence your job or career decisions (opportunity for advancement, challenge, security, salary, hours, location of job, travel involved, educational opportunities, recognition, prestige, environment, co-workers, boss, responsibility, variety of tasks, and so forth).

d. Describe the perfect job.

e. What type of job or jobs do you want during your career (marketing, finance, operations, personnel, and so forth)? After selecting a field, select a specific job—salesperson, manager, accountant, and so on.

Step 3. Career Objectives

a. What are your short-range objectives for the first year after graduation?

b. What are your intermediate objectives for the second through fifth years after graduation?

c. What are your long-range objectives?

Step 4. Planning Sheet

Use this form to develop an action plan to help you achieve your objectives:

Objective:

Starting date _____   Due date _____

Priority _____   Control checkpoints

Steps (What, where, how, resources, etc.—subobjectives)	When	
	Start	End

Career Planning

SB 17–2

Objective: To experience career planning; to develop a career plan.

Experience: You will share your career plan with one or two classmates to help make improvements in it.

Material: You will need the completed preparation, which serves as your career plan.

Procedure 1
(10–20 minutes)

Break into teams of two or three. One at a time, go through your career plan while the others ask questions and make recommendations to help you improve your career plan.

Conclusion: The instructor leads a class discussion and makes concluding remarks.

Application (2–4 minutes): What did I learn from this experience? How will I use this knowledge in the future?

Sharing: Volunteers give their answers to the application section.

PREPARATION FOR IN-CLASS SKILL-BUILDING EXERCISE

Course Objectives—Part II

SB 17–3

Part 1

Following are 34 statements. Select the number that best describes your level of skill for each statement or situation using the scale below.

1	2	3	4	5	6	7
Not skilled			Somewhat skilled			Very skilled

_____ 1. Writing effective objectives.

_____ 2. Developing plans to achieve objectives.

_____ 3. Organizing work to get it done.

_____ 4. Assigning work to others.

_____ 5. Establishing methods to ensure work gets done on time.

_____ 6. Following work through to its completion on time.

_____ 7. Solving problems and making decisions.

_____ 8. Knowing when to use a group to make decisions.

_____ 9. Working with people in your department.

_____ 10. Working with people in other departments and organizations.

_____ 11. Communicating with others.

_____ 12. Changing your communication style to meet the situation.

_____ 13. Getting others to change.

_____ 14. Resolving conflicts between yourself and others, and between others as a mediator.

_____ 15. Performing a job analysis and writing a job description.

_____ 16. Conducting a job interview.

_____ 17. Getting people started on a job.

_____ 18. Teaching people how to do things.

_____ 19. Motivating people to do a good job.

_____ 20. Improving productivity.

_____ 21. Evaluating how well people perform.

_____ 22. Conducting a performance appraisal.

_____ 23. Influencing others to meet objectives.

_____ 24. Gaining and using power.

_____ 25. Getting people with problems to do their work.

_____ 26. Disciplining a person for not meeting requirements.

_____ 27. Getting people to work together as a team.

_____ 28. Knowing when and when not to use other's input on the job, and using the input appropriately.

_____ 29. Dealing with union members.

_____ 30. Handling grievances.

_____ 31. Managing your time.

_____ 32. Handling stressful situations.

_____ 33. Planning your career.

_____ 34. Overall ability to manage as a situational supervisor.

Part 2

Complete the profile form in Skill-Building Exercise 17–3 by placing an X in the box that represents your answer to each of the statements. Each statement refers to the topics (skills) we covered in this course. They are grouped by the parts in the book. To the right of your answers are the chapter numbers and titles where the topic of each statement was covered.

Part 3

Turn back to the Preparation for Skill-Building Exercise 2–1. Compare your present answers to the ones in Chapter 2 and answer the following questions.

1. Did your profile numbers get higher at the end of the course?

2. Review your objectives from Chapter 2. Did you meet them? Why or why not?

3. What are your strongest areas of supervision (high numbers on your profile form)?

4. What are your weakest areas of supervision (lowest numbers on your profile form)?

5. What will you do to improve your weakest areas of supervision in the future?

6. What are the most important skills you have developed and things you have learned through this course?

**Course Objectives—
Part II**

SB 17-3

Objectives: To determine whether you met your course objectives; to determine the most important skill you developed and what you learned during this course.

Experience: This exercise is discussion oriented.

Material: You need the completed preparation for this exercise.

*Procedure 1
(5–10 minutes)*

Break into groups of five or six and share your answers to Part 3 of the preparation. You may also look at each other's profiles if you wish to.

Sharing: Volunteers give their answer to question 6 in Part 3. What are the most important skills you have developed and things you learned through this course?

Conclusion: The instructor may lead a class discussion and make concluding remarks.

PROFILE FORM

	1	2	3	4	5	6	7	**Part 1. The Supervisory Process**
1 2								Ch. 2. Planning the Work
3 4								Ch. 3. Organizing and Delegating Work
5 6								Ch. 4. Controlling Quality Work
								Part 2. Supervisory Skills
7 8								Ch. 5. Problem Solving and Decision Making
9 10								Ch. 6. Human Relations
11 12								Ch. 7. Communicating with Others
13 14								Ch. 8. Managing Change and Conflict
								Part 3. Developing Employees
15 16								Ch. 9. Hiring Employees
17 18								Ch. 10. Orienting and Training Employees
19 20								Ch. 11. Improving Productivity
21 22								Ch. 12. Evaluating and Compensating Employees
								Part 4. Supervising Employees
23 24								Ch. 13. Leading Employees

25 26								Ch. 14. Supervising Problem Employees
27 28								Ch. 15. Supervising Groups
29 30								Ch. 16. Labor Relations
								Part 5. Supervising Yourself
31 32 33								Ch. 17. Managing Your Time, Stress, and Career
34								Ch. 1–17

Index

Supervision
A Skill-Building Approach

SECOND EDITION

Robert N. Lussier

Springfield College

IRWIN

Chicago • Bogotá • Boston • Buenos Aires • Caracas
London • Madrid • Mexico City • Sydney • Toronto

© RICHARD D. IRWIN, INC., 1989 and 1994

Senior sponsoring editor: Kurt L. Strand
Editorial assistant: Michele Dooley
Marketing manager: Kurt Messersmith
Project editor: Jean Lou Hess
Production manager: Diane Palmer
Art coordinator: Heather Burbridge
Art studio: Mary Jo Szymerski
Compositor: Carlisle Communications
Typeface: 10/12 Baskerville
Printer: Malloy Lithographing, Inc.

Library of Congress Cataloging-in-Publication Data
Lussier, Robert N.
     Supervision : a skill-building approach / Robert N. Lussier.–
2nd ed.
          p.   cm.
     Includes bibliographical references and index.
     ISBN 0-256-09050-5 (acid-free paper)
     1. Supervision of employees.   I. Title
HF5549. 12.L87   1994   93–10673
658.3'02—dc20

Printed in the United States of America
  2 3 4 5 6 7 8 9 0   ML   0 9 8 7 6

I would like to dedicate this book to my wife Marie, and to thank her for her patience and support as I worked for about 1,900 hours on this book and total package.

Preface

Changes in This Edition

The second edition of *Supervision: A Skill-Building Approach* reflects a number of improvements from the previous edition.

- The learning objectives are listed in the margins following the material needed to meet the objective. This reinforces the student's achievement of learning objectives.

- The questions (now called Connections) are no longer at the end of the chapter. They now appear in the body of the text in boxes following the material needed to answer the questions. This format makes the relationship between the theory and its application immediate, creating an interactive, rather than passive, book.

- Eleven of the chapter opening cases have been changed and are referred to in the body of text to illustrate the application of the theory to an actual situation.

- The number of exhibits has been increased. Several of the chapters now have exhibits that put more than one theory together to better show similarities and differences between theories.

- Two additional skill-building exercises (37 total) are included.

- Three new self-learning exercises have been added.

- Chapter 4 is now entitled "Controlling Quality Work." The chapter includes a new section on total quality management.

- The title of Chapter 6 has been expanded to include the subtitle "Power, Politics, and Ethics"—the major focus of the chapter. The coverage of politics is expanded, and ethics coverage is new.

- The material in Chapter 7 has been reorganized to better follow the communication process steps. The coverage of listening skills has been expanded.

- Chapter 11 has several new exhibits. There is a new section, "Do Motivational Theories Apply Globally?"

- Chapter 13 has several new exhibits and a new section, "Substitutes for Leadership."

Specific changes for each chapter are discussed in the instructor's manual, making the transition to the second edition easier for those who used the first edition.

Using This Book

The following is an explanation of the major features and contents of *Supervision: A Skill-Building Approach.*

Chapter Overview: Each chapter begins with an overview consisting of four parts:

- The Learning Objectives state what you should be able to do after completing the chapter.
- The Key Terms are listed in the order in which they appear in the chapter.
- The Chapter Outline enables you to see the major topics covered in the chapter to get the big picture.
- The Chapter Opening introductory case situation illustrates the topics that will be covered in the chapter. About half of these cases simply introduce the topics; the others are referred to throughout the chapter to illustrate how the concepts are applied to a given situation.

Key Terms: The key terms are the most important concepts in each chapter. They can be found easily in the body of the text because they are in **bold type** with their definitions in *italics.* A list of key terms also appears at the end of the review, in alphabetical order.

Text: The text is set up like most books with major and minor headings to help you follow the material. I have written the text with you in mind. It is designed to be easy to read and understand. The text takes a practical "how-to" approach, and focuses on giving you practical information that you can use to be a successful supervisor. If you are not already a supervisor, I recommend keeping this book and using it as a reference manual when you face the many challenging tasks of a supervisor after you begin work.

Self-Learning Exercises: About half of the chapters (10 total) include self-learning exercises in the body of the text. They are designed to help you learn about your own style and preferences. For example, you will perform the following self-assessments:

- In Chapter 1 you will determine whether you have the traits it takes to be a successful supervisor and determine your preferred supervisory style.
- In Chapter 5 you will determine your preferred decision-making style.
- In Chapter 6 you will determine how political you are.
- In Chapter 17 you will determine whether your stress personality type is A or B.

Exhibits: All chapters have around five exhibits (79 total), which are included to help you better understand the material.

Models: The text contains 25 models. Unlike most of the exhibits, which are general guidelines, the models offer step-by-step procedures for handling certain situations. Supervisors who use the models on the job have greater success than those who do not. Serving as a consultant, I designed most of the models for in-house company supervisory training programs.

To help you learn to apply the models, several skill-building exercises are included. For example, in Chapter 1, the situational supervisory model is presented. It can be applied to the 12 situations in the book by doing Skill Building Exercise 1–1, Situational Supervision. Through the use of Skill-Building Exercise 1–1, you should develop your ability to change your supervisory style to meet the needs of different situations.

Review: At the end of each chapter there is a chapter review. It highlights the most important concepts in the chapter. The review may be used in one of at least three ways:

1. *Fill in the blanks.* In the review you will find the definitions of all the key terms. However, the key terms themselves are left out. You will find a blank line on which to write the missing key term. You may fill in the key terms from memory.

2. *Matching.* If you cannot, or prefer not to, fill in the key terms from memory, you may turn to the end of the review and refer to the list of key terms which are in alphabetical order. You may match the key terms to their definitions.

3. *Straight review.* If your instructor does not require you to know the key terms word for word, or if you prefer, you may fill in the missing key terms from the list at the beginning of the chapter. The key terms at the beginning of the chapter are in the same order in which they appear in the chapter and in the review.

Connections: Throughout each chapter there are between 9 and 13 questions called connections (178 total). The questions do not ask you to parrot the text material. The answers to the questions cannot be found verbatim in the text. The connections are designed to allow you to apply the text material to actual situations from your present or past jobs.

Whether or not your instructor requires you to write out the answers to the questions, you will learn more by doing so. Writing the answers gets you to think more clearly and develops your written communication skills, which are helpful to supervisors.

Application Situations: At the end of each chapter there are 20 situations (340 total) for which you are required to select the appropriate text concepts. Application situations test your ability to apply the text concepts to actual situations you may face on the job as a supervisor. Without a thorough reading and understanding of the text concepts, you cannot apply the theory.

Objective Case: Each chapter contains an approximately one-page description of a situation followed by 10 multiple choice objective questions (hence the name "Objective Case"). You are required to apply the correct text concepts. In addition to the objective questions, there are one or two subjective questions. Most subjective questions ask you how you would handle the situation if you were the supervisor in the case. Cases help you apply the text concepts to an actual situation in which you must solve a problem, which is a critical supervisory skill.

Skill-Building Exercises: The book contains 37 skill-building exercises. Chapters 7, 16, and 17 have three skill-building exercises and all other chapters have two. The skill-building exercises simulate actual situations you may face as a supervisor. By completing the skill-building exercises, you should further develop your supervisory skills.

The skill-building exercises are designed for in-class use. However, over half of them require preparation before class. If you do not do the preparation before class, your learning and skill development will be limited.

Of the skill-building exercises, 24 give you a written situation to work with, and 13 allow you to select your own situation.

Coverage of the Book's Contents: The connections, application situations, objective cases, and skill-building exercises are designed for preclass preparation and in-class use. Given the large amount of material and your instructor's preferences, you may not be required to use all the material in the book. However, you can use most of the material on your own, if you wish to do so.

If your instructor elects not to use the connections, application situations, or objective cases, or only selects some of them, you may do the rest on your own.

More than likely your instructor will not require you to do all 37 skill-building exercises. Most of the actual learning and skill building for some of the exercises is in the preparation section. You can do these on your own. However, you will not be able to do some of them yourself. You should check those exercises not required by your instructor to determine which you can do on your own.

Acknowledgments

I would like to thank the following people for their contributions:

- Lowell Lamberton, Central Oregon Community College, for writing the chapter opening cases for Chapters 8, 9, 10, 12, 14, and 16.
- The people at Richard D. Irwin, Inc. Kurt Strand, my editor, for his belief in, and dedication to, this book. Special thanks to Michelle Kachur for all her help with the revisions to this second edition. And to the production people particularly: Jean Lou Hess, project editor; Jeanne Rivera, designer; and Diane Palmer, production manager.
- My mentor, Dr. Joel Corman, director of the MBA program at Suffolk University. And the doctoral faculty of the University of New Haven, especially Drs. Baeder, Bockley, Morris, Mottola, Nadim, Neal, and Tedefalk for their advice, encouragement, and excellent education.
- The following reviewers deserve special credit for their advice that led to the improvement in the book:

  Melvin Jones, Jefferson Community College

  George M. Newland, Jacksonville State University

  William Westphal, Danville Area Community College

  Roy Budd, Thomas Nelson Community College

  James Chester, Cameron University

  Carl Jenks, Purdue University at Calumet

  Lowell Lamberton, Central Oregon Community College

  Roger Lynch, Inver Hills Community College

  Donald Pettite, Suffolk County Community College

Contact Me with Feedback

I wrote this book for you. Let me know what you think of it. Write or call me and tell me what you did and didn't like about it. More specifically, how could it be improved? I will be responsive to your feedback. If I use your suggestions for improvement, your name and college will be listed in the acknowledgment section of the next edition. I sincerely hope that you will develop your supervision skills through this book.

Dr. Robert N. Lussier
156 Saw Mill Road
Springfield, MA 01118
413–783–2241

Contents in Brief

Contents

The Supervisory Process

1

The Supervisor's Role and Situational Supervision

Learning Objectives   *After completing this chapter, you should be able to perform the following tasks:*

1. Describe the supervisor's job and responsibilities.
2. List and explain the three supervisory skills and the reasons that they are important.
3. List and explain the five functions of supervision.
4. Describe the differences among management levels in terms of skills needed and functions performed.
5. Identify the major trends and challenges facing supervisors.
6. Describe how to make the transition from employee to supervisor.
7. State your preferred supervisory style.
8. Explain how to use the situational supervision model and use the model on the job.

Key Terms   To achieve our objectives in this chapter, it is important that you understand the following 15 key terms. They are presented in the order in which they appear in the chapter. The list of key terms also appears in alphabetical order in the end-of-chapter review.

levels of management	supervisory functions	controlling
employees	planning	autocratic style
supervisor	organizing	consultative style
supervisory resources	staffing	participative style
supervisory skills	leading	laissez-faire style

Throughout this book we will be using many important, or key, terms. To ensure that you have a clear understanding of these terms, when a key term first appears it is presented in **bold** letters with its definition in *italicized* letters.

I. What Is Supervision?

In this section you will read an interview with a supervisor, a list of common ideas about the supervisor's job, and a discussion of the three levels of supervision. The supervisor's job and responsibility are also defined.

An Interview with a Supervisor

To help you to better understand what supervisors do, the author interviewed Paul Darcy, a first-line continuity supervisor at Monsanto, an international corporation. Monsanto's primary business is chemicals used in products such as shampoo, car paint, adhesives, and fertilizers manufactured by other companies. Monsanto also owns G. D. Searle, the maker of NutraSweet.

AUTHOR: How long have you been a supervisor, Paul?

PAUL: For 16 years.

AUTHOR: Briefly describe your job.

PAUL: A continuity supervisor has a thorough knowledge of general chemical operations and, in particular, of his or her own department. This includes some working knowledge of the chemistry as well as the mechanics (pumps, valves, and controls). We also need an understanding of union contracts and personnel policies.

In addition to my other duties I help train new production supervisors. My job is to provide the experienced leadership needed to run the process and its people on a day-to-day basis.

In Exhibit 1–1, Paul has described a typical day. If you have never worked in a production facility, you may not fully understand everything Paul does. However, you can see that he's involved in a wide variety of things.

AUTHOR: What's the toughest part of your job?

PAUL: Dealing with the frustration. As a supervisor you are the person in the middle. Employees complain to you and upper-level management implements its plans through you. You need tough skin to be a successful supervisor.

AUTHOR: What advice would you give to a college graduate going into a supervisory position?

PAUL: I find most grads are very knowledgeable about the theory. However, practical experience, especially in relating to others, is usually lacking. Too many times, a young grad comes into a department and tries to do it his or her way. They should listen to the words of experience before they make decisions! A grad shouldn't be impatient. He or she should learn the job completely (following the process, dealing with subordinates, dealing with support groups, controlling cost) before worrying about the next step in his or her career.

What People Are Saying about the Supervisor's Job

The foregoing discussion should give a general idea of what a supervisor does. As you can see, the job is varied and dynamic. As a result, there has recently been a great deal of research on the supervisor's job. In this chapter and throughout the book, I will discuss these current research findings. The comments below are typical of the current literature on supervision.

- A supervisory job is one of the most difficult and demanding jobs there is.[1]
- [Supervision] is . . . one of the most exciting and fulfilling positions within an organization.[2]

EXHIBIT 1–1   **A DAY IN THE LIFE OF A SUPERVISOR**

7:50	Enter department — general scan of area.
8:00	Mark important information on daily log. Check operator logs for problems, breakdowns. a. Unit crashed but restarted OK — electrical? b. Product assay still out of range. c. Pump seal leaking.
8:15	Outside contractors need fire permits for potential spark-producing tools. a. Contact lead operator to do a vapor check at work site. b. Discuss process changes to bring product assay into range following unit crash.
8:30	Survey outside contractor's work area; examine results of vapor check. Talk with contractors; make sure they understand work rules; sign permit.
8:45	Call maintenance supervisor — line up mechanic to work on pump with leaking seal. Call electrical engineer — line up monitoring device for blower that caused unit to crash.
9:00	Check truck-loading operations. Talk with operator. Check his log for overnight problems.
9:15	Contact area coordinator for safety tapes. Will need a videotape on this month's safety topic. Start scheduling safety meeting.
9:30	Lead operator brings up exceptions report (payroll timekeeping record). Call payroll and verify overtime.
9:45	Meet with lead operator. Go over plan for repairing leaky pump.
10:00	Meet with project engineer about timing and work to be done on new piece of equipment.
10:15	Operator has problem with overtime scheduling. Review schedule. Operator still not satisfied and will check with union steward.
10:30	Check on process changes — not self-correcting as expected. Look at other possible sources of problem.
10:45	Another corrective action needs to be taken. Lead operator reports work on pump going OK. He will set up for corrective action.
11:00	Coordinate corrective action.
11:30	Corrective action completed. Electrical engineer and electricians waiting to install monitoring device on blower. Will have to be done carefully so that unit doesn't "wash."
11:45	Return to office. Call on answering machine from customer service in St. Louis. Major customer needs to change assay of product in the next truck out. Call loading operator and control operator to make changes.
12:00	Finally, peace and quiet. Everyone else eating. Finish plans for safety meetings.
12:15	Quick check to see if all is OK in control room. Last truck for major customer not in yet. Call traffic department and find out it was delayed at another customer. Truck will just make it.
12:30	Lunch
1:15	Mechanics finishing work on pump. Outside contractor making progress.
1:30	Check with electricians, monitor on blower will be ready by 2:00 P.M. Late for 1:30 meeting on upcoming shutdown.
1:45	Meeting on shutdown.

3:00	Back from meeting. Truck to major customer gone OK. Product assay improving at last. Pump seal repaired.
3:15	Operators have shift change. Operator 3–11 will need to change his vacation week. Call payroll and make change. Loading operator finds loose pin in loading dock stairs. Call about repair.
3:30	Enter work orders on computer. Discuss operational problems with my boss.
3:40	Alarms sounding. Small unit has "crashed" again.
3:45	Try to restart blower.
3:50	Restarts OK. Call electrician and engineer. Process restarting OK (restarting is touchy operation). Swap product to another storage area. Minimize off-grade.
4:00	Ask lead operator to work overtime to help out on unit restart. Electricians arrive.
4:15	Monitor indicates three possible reasons for tripout of blower. Engineer will check with supplier for more troubleshooting equipment.
4:30	Have to take special corrective action again. Lead operator will set up.
4:45	Start writing instructions for night shifts. Coordinate corrective action.
5:15	Finish corrective action. Two late orders on Telex. Call for a truck to pick up one of them.
5:30	Continue writing instructions for night shift. Alarm rings; liquid levels downstream in the process too high.
5:45	Controller not responding. Instrument mechanics have already gone home. Call to get help back in plant. If we cannot control level, we might have to shut down. Start planning contingencies.
6:00	Instrument help on the way. Return to office — two calls on answering machine. Make note to call in the morning. Finish entering work orders on computer.
6:15	Set up schedule for tomorrow. Make final check of department while waiting for instrument mechanic and first sample of product since restarting unit.
6:30	Instrument mechanic arrives — starts troubleshooting. Product assay out of range, but not bad for this soon after restarting. Set-up operator will swap product flow to original storage when product assay gets into range. Should be another hour or two.
6:45	Instrument mechanic finds problem with controller and is making corrections. Finish writing instructions for night shift.
7:00	Instrument repair completed. Leave word that I'll call to see how things are in two hours. Head for home.

I usually finish by 6:00, but on days like this, I stay until the job is done.

- Organizational success comes from employees, and it is the supervisor who has the greatest impact on their attitude and performance.[3]

- Supervisors and other managers are the key to improving American industrial growth.[4]

- The supervisor will be a key player in tomorrow's successful organization.[5]

- Good supervision is the key to success for any business. Truly good supervision is America's most valuable resource.[6]

- A supervisory survey revealed that 82 percent of the respondents said that they are generally satisfied with their jobs.[7]

The Three Levels of Management

Now let's take a look at where supervisors fit in the corporate hierarchy. There are three **levels of management:** *top, middle, and first line,* as illustrated in Exhibit 1–2. All managers are supervisors, but the term usually refers to first-line management. The three levels relate to each other as described below.

Top Managers: These are executive positions with titles such as chairman of the board, chief executive officer (CEO), president, or vice president. There are relatively few top management positions in most organizations. Top managers are responsible for managing the entire organization or major parts of it. They develop and define the organization's purpose, objectives, strategies, and long-term plans. They report to other executives or boards of directors and supervise the activities of middle managers.

Middle Managers: These positions have titles such as sales manager, branch manager, or department head. Middle managers are responsible for implementing top management's strategy by developing short-term operating plans. They generally report to executives and supervise the work of first-line managers.

First-Line Managers: Employment supervisor, head nurse, office manager, and shift supervisor are examples of the titles at this level. These managers are responsible for implementing middle managers' operational plans. They generally report to middle managers. Unlike those at the other two levels of management, first-line managers do not supervise other managers; they supervise employees. **Employees** *are the workers in an organization who do not hold management positions and who report to supervisors.* Employees are the people who make the products, wait on customers, perform repairs, and so on. For example, in a small branch bank the tellers are the employees and the branch manager is the supervisor.

EXHIBIT 1–2   **THE THREE LEVELS OF MANAGEMENT**

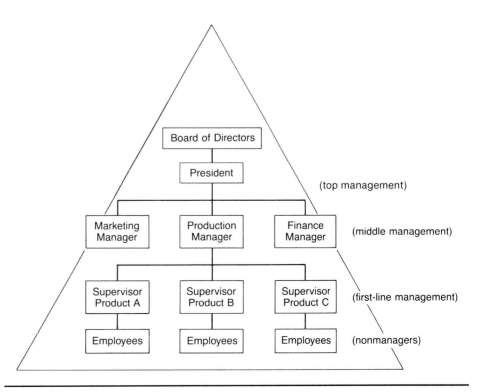

The supervisor is often referred to as the link between the sometimes conflicting demands of upper-level management and the employees.[8] As Paul Darcy mentioned, supervisors sometimes feel as though they are caught in a cross fire.

CONNECTIONS

1. Identify the three levels of management in a specific organization by level and title (give the organization's name).

The Supervisor's Job and Responsibility

A **supervisor** *is a first-line manager responsible for achieving departmental objectives through employees.* A supervisor's primary responsibility is to get the department's work done on time. Upper-level managers evaluate supervisors based on departmental results. As a supervisor, getting the job done should be your highest priority, ultimately taking precedent over the desires and needs of your employees and yourself.[9]

For example, each bank teller is responsible for good customer service, and the branch manager is responsible for the total customer service of the branch. Each teller is responsible for balancing the daily transactions, and the branch manager is responsible for balancing the entire branch's transactions. If deposits increase because of good customer service or decrease because of poor customer service, the branch manager is ultimately responsible.

In accomplishing the department's work, a supervisor has three major resources. **Supervisory resources** *include physical, financial, and human resources.*

Physical Resources: Getting the job done requires efficient use of physical resources. In a production department, this would include the machines and equipment needed to make the product. It also involves the inventory of raw materials and component parts needed during production. Supplies such as chemicals, nails, oil, and so on are needed as well. A supervisor is responsible for keeping the equipment in working condition and for making sure that necessary materials and supplies are available. Having the right physical resources at the right time is critical to the supervisor's success. For example, if a supervisor does not make sure that needed materials are on hand, production might stop, resulting in idle employees and equipment. Deadlines might be missed and future business lost if physical resources are not used properly.

Financial Resources: Most supervisors have a budget stating how much it should cost to operate their department for a set period of time. In other words, it defines the financial resources available. The supervisor is responsible for seeing that the department does not waste money. For example, if a store manager orders too much merchandise, some of it may not be sold. This ties up money and may involve handling and shipping costs if the merchandise is returned.

Human Resources: Employees are the supervisor's human resources. The supervisor is responsible for getting the job done through employees, who are his or her most valuable resource. A supervisor should hire the best people available. These employees must then be trained to use the physical resources to maximize productivity. A supervisor should also motivate employees to do their jobs to the best of their ability. Throughout this book we will be focusing on working with employees to accomplish the department's objectives.

LEARNING OBJECTIVE

1. Describe the supervisor's job and responsibilities.

As we have seen, a supervisor is responsible for, and will be evaluated on, how well he or she gets the work done using the physical, financial, and human resources of the organization. In the section that follows, we'll look at what it takes to do this successfully.

2. Describe the specific resources a supervisor uses. Give the supervisor's job title and department.

II. What Does It Take to Be a Successful Supervisor?

Over the years, numerous studies have attempted to answer the question "What does it take to be a successful supervisor?" A few of the answers follow.

Robert Katz conducted a study over 10 years ago that is still widely quoted today. Katz identified three **supervisory skills**—*technical, human, and conceptual*—that are essential to success.[10] *Technical skills* involve industry and product knowledge. As a supervisor, you must be able to teach employees about their jobs and their department's functions. In fact, most supervisors were promoted to that position primarily because of their technical skills. *Human skills* are necessary to help employees get the job done. Several studies have revealed that 50 to 90 percent of a supervisor's time is spent interacting with people. How well you work and communicate with employees will affect your ability to supervise. A supervisor also needs *conceptual* and *administrative* skills. These enable a supervisor to see how the department contributes to the entire organization and to understand how each task affects the department as a whole. The ease with which you make decisions will also affect your ability to supervise.

The American Telephone and Telegraph Company (AT&T) spent years studying "job content" in order to identify the skills necessary for success as a supervisor. Five emerged: controlling the work, problem solving and decision making, planning the work, informal communications, and communications in general.[11] It is generally believed that these skills are necessary in any organization.

Xerox Learning Systems conducted research that identified six skills as critical for success at the supervisory level: giving feedback, planning, problem solving, assigning and monitoring work, setting standards, and handling performance problems.[12]

Opinion Research Corporation found that successful supervisors are knowledgeable about their jobs and accessible to their employees. These supervisors provide performance feedback and treat employees with respect.[13]

Peters and Waterman conducted eight case studies and found that successful supervisors are cheerleaders, facilitators, and nurturers of "champions." These supervisors create environments in which employees do not fear failure. Organizational goals are clear and are communicated to all employees. Employees trust these managers and feel as though they are part of a team.[14]

Klein and Posey collected performance data on some 75 managers and supervisors. They concluded that successful supervisors are competent, caring, and committed to both the work and the employees. These supervisors push for quality while providing clear direction. Timely feedback is used to motivate employees. A successful supervisor takes responsibility for the actions of the department and their outcome. These supervisors get the right people involved in solving problems.[15]

In a *Wall Street Journal*/Gallup survey, 782 top executives in 282 large corporations were asked, "What are the most important traits for success as a supervisor?"[16] The answers revealed that integrity, industriousness, and the ability to get along with people are the three most important traits for successful supervision. Other traits listed were business knowledge, intelligence, leadership ability, education, sound judgment, ability to communicate, flexibility, and ability to plan and set objectives. The survey also identified seven traits that lead to failure in a supervisor: having a limited viewpoint, not being able to understand others, not being able to work with others, being indecisive, lacking initiative, not assuming responsibility, and lacking integrity. Other failure traits included lack of ability to change, reluctance to think independently, inability to solve problems, and desire for popularity.

Do you possess the traits necessary to be a successful supervisor? Self-Learning Exercise 1–1 lists 15 items related to some of these qualities. Rate yourself on each item on a scale of one to four.

SELF-LEARNING EXERCISE 1–1

Supervisory Traits Questionnaire

1 — The statement is not very descriptive of me.
2 — The statement is somewhat descriptive of me.
3 — The statement is descriptive of me.
4 — The statement is very descriptive of me.

Integrity

_____ 1. I am trustworthy. If I say I will do something by a set time, I do it.

_____ 2. I am loyal. I do not do or say things to intentionally hurt my friends, relatives, or co-workers.

_____ 3. I can take criticism. If people tell me negative things about myself, I give them serious thought and change when appropriate.

_____ 4. I am honest. I do not lie, steal, or cheat.

_____ 5. I am fair. I treat people equally. I don't take advantage of others.

Industriousness

_____ 6. I want to be successful. I do things to the best of my ability to be successful.

_____ 7. I am a self-starter. I get things done without having to be told to do them.

_____ 8. I am a problem solver. If things aren't going the way I want them to, I take corrective action to meet my objectives.

_____ 9. I am self-reliant. I don't need the help of others.

_____ 10. I am hardworking. I enjoy working and getting the job done.

The ability to get along with people

_____ 11. I enjoy working with people. I prefer to work with others rather than working alone.

_____ 12. I can motivate others. I can get people to do things they may not really want to do.

_____ 13. I am well liked. People enjoy working with me.

_____ 14. I am cooperative. I strive to help the team do well, rather than to be the star.

_____ 15. I am a leader. I enjoy teaching, coaching, and instructing people.

To determine your score, add up the ratings you gave each item. Your score will range from 15 to 60. In general, the higher your score, the better your chances of being a successful supervisor. If you are interested in being a supervisor someday, you can work on improving your integrity, industriousness, and ability to get along with people both in this course and in your personal life. As a start, review the list of traits mentioned. Which ones were you strongest and weakest in? Think about how you can improve in the weaker areas or, better yet, write out a plan.

What does it take to be a successful supervisor? According to Kenneth Blanchard, good supervision is based on the ability to get employees committed to doing the job and to work with them.[17] Denova has stated that supervisors must have the skill to obtain, utilize, and motivate employees, and Caskey maintains that the effective supervisor has superVISION, good judgment, analytical skills, and objectivity.[18]

Conclusion

LEARNING OBJECTIVE

2. List and explain the three supervisory skills and the reasons that they are important.

Most of the skills needed for success as a supervisor can be classified as technical, human, or conceptual. All managers must have these skills, but the need for each varies with the level of management. First-line managers need more technical and human skills; middle managers need a good balance of all three; and top management needs more conceptual and human skills.

Good supervisory skills are developed through experience and training in courses like the one you are taking now. The major objective of this book is to help you develop your supervisory skills. The key to success is perseverance through hard work.

CONNECTIONS

3. Identify a specific supervisor, preferably one who was or is your boss, and explain what makes him or her either successful or unsuccessful. Give examples.

4. Identify a specific supervisor, preferably one who was or is your boss, and describe his or her need for technical, human, and conceptual skills.

III. What Do Supervisors Do?

Given the elements for success discussed in the preceding section, you might well ask how the various factors relate to the actual work environment. And that brings us to our next question: What do supervisors do? As stated earlier, supervisors get the job done through employees. A supervisor is paid to plan, organize, staff, lead, and control the work of employees. Regardless of the management level or the organization they work for, all managers perform these five functions. If supervisors run machines, wait on customers, or put up store displays, they are performing nonsupervisory, employee functions.

The five **supervisory functions** are *planning, organizing, staffing, leading, and controlling*. In this section and in later chapters, each function is explained separately. However, you should realize that the five functions are a process; they are interrelated and are often performed simultaneously.

Planning

Planning is typically the starting point in the supervision process. **Planning** *is the process of setting objectives and determining in advance exactly how the objectives will be met.* As a supervisor, you must determine what you want to accomplish with your organizational resources. Supervisors may have to schedule the work, develop and maintain budgets, and develop and enforce policies, procedures, and rules so that employees can perform their jobs. In Chapter 2 planning is discussed in detail.

Organizing

The supervisor must also design and develop an organization that will implement the plans. **Organizing** *is the process of delegating and coordinating tasks and resources with clear authority, responsibility, and accountability.* As a supervisor, you will be responsible for apportioning your department's work among employees. When employee tasks and resources are assigned, plans are put into action. You will also have to coordinate the activities of all your employees to ensure that the work is completed smoothly. In Chapter 3 this is explained in greater detail.

Staffing

As supervisors organize departments, they determine what human resources they need. **Staffing** *is the process of selecting, orienting, training, and evaluating employees.* The supervisor's most valuable asset is human resources, the employees who get the job done. As a supervisor you will be responsible for the development of your employees. Chapters 9 through 12 will teach you how to develop an effective staff.

Leading

In addition to planning, organizing, and staffing, the supervisor must work with employees as they perform their tasks on a daily basis. **Leading** *is the process of influencing employees to work toward achieving objectives.* As a supervisor, you will issue orders, give employees direction, and coach them as they perform their jobs. Communicating and motivating are also part of leading. As we have learned, working with employees is vital to the success of a supervisor. Chapters 6 through 8 and 14 through 16 will help you develop your leadership skills.

Controlling

Planning and controlling are inseparable. When supervisors plan, they should also set controls. **Controlling** *is the process of establishing and implementing mechanisms to ensure that objectives are achieved.* As a supervisor, you should keep track of how your department is progressing toward achieving its objectives. You will set standards of performance and define work methods, select times to measure performance, and compare actual performance to your objectives. If your department is on schedule in meeting its objectives, you should reinforce employee behavior; if it is not, you must take action to get back on schedule. In Chapter 4 you will learn the control process details.

The supervisory functions are not a linear process. Supervisors do not usually plan, then organize, then lead, and then control. The functions are distinct yet interrelated. Supervisors often perform these functions simultaneously, or in any order. For example, when supervisors plan they also establish controls and determine how to organize and lead. A supervisor may be organizing one minute and leading the next. This process is illustrated in Exhibit 1–3. Notice that functions are based on setting and achieving objectives. Some authors list four functions of supervision, making staffing a part of organizing.

LEARNING OBJECTIVE

3. List and explain the five functions of supervision.

CONNECTIONS

5. Identify a specific supervisor, preferably one who was or is your boss, and describe how that person performs each of the five supervisory functions.

EXHIBIT 1–3   **THE FUNCTIONS OF SUPERVISION**

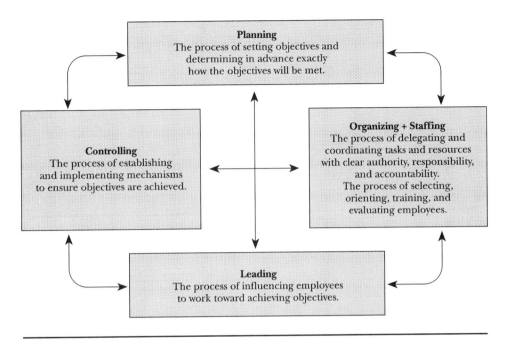

Differences among Managers

LEARNING
OBJECTIVE
4. Describe the differences
among management levels
in terms of skills needed
and functions performed.

All managers perform the five supervisory functions: planning, organizing, staffing, leading, and controlling. However, the time spent on each function varies with the level of management. Studies of the amount of time managers spend on each function have been inconclusive. However, it is generally agreed that supervisors spend more time leading and controlling; that middle-level managers seem to spend equal time on all five functions; and that top managers spend more time planning and organizing. Exhibit 1–4 summarizes this difference in management level as well as the varying skills needed.

IV. Trends and Challenges Facing Supervisors[19]

None of the foregoing discussion is meant to suggest that supervision is a static function. The rate of change has been increasing with each decade. The changes in the work environment directly affect the supervisor's job. Peter Drucker, a leading consultant, writer, and professor, has said that no job in the future is going to change more in the next decade than that of the first-line supervisor. In this section, we will discuss three areas of change—social forces, the workforce, and technology—that pose challenges to supervisors.

The Supervisor's Changing Environment

External Social Forces   Organizations do not operate in a vacuum. What happens in the external environment affects the supervisor's job. Significant environmental forces include the following:

- **Deregulation.** The government's trend toward deregulation has caused major changes in a variety of areas such as the airline and trucking industries.
- **Litigation.** Worker lawsuits, stockholder suits, malpractice suits, injury and damage suits, sexual harassment suits, and other lawsuits are changing supervisory practices. The situation is likely to get worse before it gets better.

EXHIBIT 1–4   **DIFFERENCES AMONG MANAGEMENT LEVELS IN SKILLS NEEDED AND FUNCTIONS PERFORMED**

Management Level	Supervisor	Supervises	Primary Management Function Performed	Primary Skill Needed
Top	Board or executive	Middle/ executive	Planning and organizing	Conceptual and human over technical
Middle	Executive/ top	First-line	All five	All three
First-line	Middle	Employees	Leading and controlling	Human and technical over conceptual
Employees Nonmanagers	First-line	No one	None	Technical

- **A service economy.** Since 1948, the number of employees in the service sector has increased, and the service productivity rate has decreased.[20] America has become a service economy. The service sector accounts for over 73 percent of all jobs and 65 percent of gross national product (GNP). Nearly all of a 25 million increase in nonfarm employment forecast by the Labor Department between 1990 and 2005 will come from service industries, such as health care and retail trade.[21]

- **Quality and productivity.** Organizations have become more quality conscious, and productivity is a major concern. These trends put direct pressure on first-line supervisors for improvements.

- **Global economy.** U.S. companies are moving their manufacturing functions overseas. Big businesses are growing by providing goods and services all over the world. America is moving toward a global economy to compete with foreign businesses. Young managers are being taught global skills by such companies as American Express, Colgate-Palmolive, General Electric, PepsiCo, and Raychem. Honda of America has sent about 42 U.S. supervisors and managers to Tokyo for up to three years. Training emphasizes language, cultural, and life-style orientation.[22] There are fundamental differences in cultures, but recent studies have found that differences are less important than basic management skills. Good managers share the same supervisory skills worldwide.[23]

The Workforce

Employees change over time. Some significant alterations include the following:

- **An aging workforce.** According to the U.S. Bureau of Labor Statistics, over 70 percent of the workforce is in the 25 to 54 age bracket. In 1975, the average age of the workforce was 28; in 1990 it was 40. The supervisor will be working with older employees; in addition, the supply of cheap entry-level employees is drying up, and increasing numbers of older employees compete for the relatively scarce management jobs.

- **Growing workforce diversity.** The number of women, minorities, and handicapped individuals will continue to increase as the number of white males decreases as a percentage of the workforce. In 1991, 67.2 percent of women with children under 18 were employed.[24] Will the supervisor have trouble relating to this diverse workforce?

- **Changing education levels.** Even though the educational level of our workforce is increasing, illiteracy remains a problem. In the 1990s, over 33 percent of the workforce will be college graduates. Some 15 million college graduates will be competing for the 12 to 13 million jobs that require a degree, and at the same time the functionally illiterate will number 26 million. The U.S. high school graduation rate is 71 percent; the dropout rate in the southeastern states is 33 percent.[25] Will the supervisor have trouble dealing with an over- and undereducated workforce?

- **Changing values and expectations.** Employees are becoming less loyal, more self-centered, and distrustful of management. A survey by two Boston University professors revealed that 78 percent of the respondents don't trust their boss.[26] Workers are also more likely to challenge authority. They expect work to be interesting and to be tailored to their wants, needs, and life-styles. Can supervisors deal effectively with these changing values and expectations?

- **Participative management.** The trend is toward greater employee involvement in traditional management decisions. Keys Curry, executive vice president of Destec Energy, calls employee participation "the most important contributor to the firm's success."

Technology

Experts such as Alvin Toffler (author of *Future Shock*) foresee no end to the rapid pace of technological innovation. Among the most significant applications of technology has been the proliferation of computers. Computers have changed the way we live and do business in the Western world, allowing increasingly sophisticated communications. In fact, author John Naisbitt says we are now in the information age. Scientific and technical information currently increases at a rate of 13 percent per year, which means it doubles every 5.5 years.[27] Many supervisors have desktop computers, and the number is expected to increase. Technical skills will continue to be important to supervisors as they control information.

Challenges to Supervisors

The trends described all affect the supervisor's job. Numerous studies have examined how. One dealt with the question of whether first-level supervision is going to be phased out.[28] The researchers concluded that first-level supervisors are here to stay, but there will be changes. There will be fewer supervisors in the future, and they will perform fewer activities. These supervisors will also need greater technical and human relations skills. Supervisors will need to use more participatory management techniques. There will also be more employee-managed groups. Supervisors will spend more time working with specialized staff and others outside their immediate work unit.

Another study was conducted to determine whether these changes and new systems will require a new and different kind of supervisor.[29] The researchers concluded that good supervisors are good supervisors anywhere. The behavior of successful first-line supervisors won't change from system to system. These supervisors still need technical and human relations skills, as they did in the past. However, being a coach, which was not a prerequisite in the past, probably should be today. The trend toward increasing employee participation in management will continue.

LEARNING
OBJECTIVE
5. Identify the major trends
and challenges facing
supervisors.

Several authors, including Nelsen and Hersey and Blanchard, have concluded that there is no single style of supervision appropriate for all situations. Supervisors must learn to change their leadership styles to fit the situation.[30] Later in this chapter, you will learn how to be such a "situational" supervisor.

CONNECTIONS

6. Give an example of how two of the trends and challenges listed in the text will or do affect you personally as a supervisor.

V. Getting Started as a Supervisor

Up to this point, we've been discussing what a supervisor does and what qualities are needed for successful supervision. In this section, we'll look at how these qualities apply when an employee makes the transition to supervision.

Think and Act Like a Supervisor

As the supervisor you are the boss, but if you are perceived as having an "I'm better than you are" attitude, or you throw your weight around, your employees will resent you. Develop an "I'm a helper" attitude instead.[31]

Set a good example.[32] Be on time for work. Don't take long breaks or lunches. Don't do personal work on the job; don't bring company property home without permission to do so. Keep your promises. When you are wrong, admit it; don't pass the buck. In other words, practice what you preach and you will earn the respect of your employees.

As a supervisor, you are not one of the gang. If you become the supervisor of the department you once worked in, your relationship with your former peers will change. As an employee, you were not responsible for evaluating and changing the behavior of others, but as a supervisor this is part of your job. If you try to be one of the gang, employees may try to take advantage of you. A supervisor-employee relationship should be a close working relationship, but friendship should not stop a supervisor from getting the job done.[33]

Know Your Responsibilities

Make sure you understand the organization's mission and your department's contribution to it. Review your job description—including other duties—with your supervisor. Be familiar with important deadlines and the extent of your authority.[34] Supervisors who do not fully understand their department's functions and responsibilities have less chance of being successful than those who do.

Remember that getting the job done is your first priority; the needs of employees and your own needs and desires must come second and third. Individual needs may take precedence temporarily, but never for long.[35]

Develop Your Relationship with Your Employees, Supervisor, and Others

Employees   Get to know your employees personally and gradually over a period of time. If you try to be too friendly too quickly, employees may believe you are a soft touch and can be taken advantage of. Be available to employees who need help, but don't get hung up on the details of personal problems. Instead, refer employees to the appropriate sources. You are a supervisor, not a counselor.[36]

When you take over a new department, review the personnel files, but don't prejudge employees. Meet with each employee individually to discuss his or her duties, responsibilities, skills, and so forth. During the discussions, assess employee attitudes and morale. Don't get into gripe sessions. Instead, focus on what employees actually do on the job. Don't make any promises without getting all the facts.[37]

Supervisor

Your supervisor will evaluate your performance. Get to know your boss and his or her expectations. Be loyal to your supervisor. If you gossip about your boss, he or she may find out and hold it against you. Don't be afraid to go to your supervisor for help; it's expected, especially when you start the job.[38]

Others

You will have to work with people from other departments. Be cooperative and develop good working relations with these peers. Go on breaks and go to lunch with other supervisors.

You will also work with staff members from personnel, quality control, accounting, and many other departments. Follow their advice and adhere to their policies. Use their services to help you do a better job. If you want to get ahead in the organization, you can use all the friends and support you can get.[39]

In Chapter 6 we discuss developing positive relationships in more detail.

Make Changes Slowly

Part of your job as a supervisor is improving your department. Improvements come through change. However, if you make changes before you have the trust and acceptance of your employees, they may resist your efforts. If employees go outside your department with complaints, your career could be hurt. So make haste slowly.[40] In Chapter 8 we discuss procedures for implementing change.

Delegate

Remember that a supervisor gets the job done through employees. This means that you shouldn't do the work yourself, even if you can do it better or faster. It's your job to train employees to do the work, not to do it for them. Multiply your efforts through delegation.[41] In Chapter 3 you will learn how to delegate work.

Cultivate a Situational Leadership Perspective

LEARNING OBJECTIVE

6. Describe how to make the transition from employee to supervisor.

As a supervisor, you will face many different situations. No single leadership style will be appropriate for all of them. Consequently, you should learn to supervise in a way that meets the demands of the situation.[42] In the next section, you will learn how to be a situational supervisor.

CONNECTIONS

7. Select a few ideas that are most relevant to you in helping you make the transition from employee to supervisor and explain why they are relevant.

VI. Situational Supervision

Determining Your Preferred Supervisory Style

Before reading about situational supervision, you are given the opportunity to determine your preferred supervisory style. Below are 12 situations. Select the one alternative that most closely describes what you would do in each situation. Don't be concerned with trying to pick the right answer; select the alternative you would really use. Circle *a*, *b*, *c*, or *d*. Ignore the C _____ and S _____ , which will be explained later in this chapter and used in class in Skill-Building Exercise 1–1.

C _____   1. Your rookie crew seems to be developing well. Their need for direction and close supervision is diminishing. What do you do?
  a. Stop directing and overseeing performance unless there is a problem. S _____
  b. Spend time getting to know them personally, but make sure they maintain performance levels. S _____
  c. Make sure things keep going well; continue to direct and oversee closely. S _____
  d. Begin to discuss new tasks of interest to them. S _____

C _____   2. You assigned Jill a task, specifying exactly how you wanted it done. Jill deliberately ignored your directions, and did it her way. The job will not meet the customer's standards. This is not the first problem you've had with Jill. What do you decide to do?
  a. Listen to Jill's side, but be sure the job gets done right. S _____
  b. Tell Jill to do it again the right way and closely supervise the job. S _____
  c. Tell her the customer will not accept the job and let Jill handle it her way. S _____
  d. Discuss the problem and solutions to it. S _____

C _____   3. Your employees work well together; the department is a real team. It's the top performer in the organization. Because of traffic problems, the president okayed staggered hours for departments. As a result, you can change your department's hours. Several of your workers have suggested changing. You take what action?
  a. Allow the group to decide the hours. S _____
  b. Decide on new hours, explain why you chose them, and invite questions. S _____
  c. Conduct a meeting to get the group members' ideas. Select new hours together, with your approval. S _____
  d. Send around a memo stating the hours you want. S _____

C _____   4. You hired Bill, a new employee. He is not performing at the level expected after one month's training. Bill is trying, but he seems to be a slow learner. What do you decide to do?
  a. Clearly explain what needs to be done and oversee his work. Discuss why the procedures are important; support and encourage him. S _____
  b. Tell Bill that his training is over and it's time to pull his own weight. S _____
  c. Review task procedures and supervise his work closely. S _____
  d. Inform Bill that his training is over and to feel free to come to you if he has any problems. S _____

C _____   5. Helen has had an excellent performance record for the last five years. Recently you have noticed a drop in the quality and quantity of her work. She has a family problem. What do you do?

    a. Tell her to get back on track and closely supervise her. S _____

    b. Discuss the problem with Helen. Help her realize that her personal problem is affecting her work. Discuss ways to improve the situation. Be supportive and encourage her. S _____

    c. Tell Helen you're aware of her productivity slip and that you're sure she'll work it out soon. S _____

    d. Discuss the problem and solution with Helen and supervise her closely. S _____

C _____   6. Your organization does not allow smoking in certain areas. You just walked by a restricted area and saw Joan smoking. She has been with the organization for 10 years and is a very productive worker. Joan has never been caught smoking before. What action do you take?

    a. Ask her to put it out, and then leave. S _____

    b. Discuss why she is smoking and what she intends to do about it. S _____

    c. Give her a lecture about not smoking, and check up on her in the future. S _____

    d. Tell her to put it out, watch her do it, tell her you will check on her in the future. S _____

C _____   7. Your department usually works well together with little direction. Recently a conflict between Sue and Tom has caused problems. As a result, you take what action?

    a. Call Sue and Tom together and make them realize how this conflict is affecting the department. Discuss how to resolve it and how you will check to make sure the problem is solved. S _____

    b. Let the group resolve the conflict. S _____

    c. Have Sue and Tom sit down and discuss their conflict and how to resolve it. Support their efforts to implement a solution. S _____

    d. Tell Sue and Tom how to resolve their conflict and closely supervise them. S _____

C _____   8. Jim usually does his share of the work with some encouragement and direction. However, he has migraine headaches occasionally and doesn't pull his weight when this happens. The others resent doing Jim's work. What do you decide to do?

    a. Discuss his problem and help him come up with ideas for maintaining his work; be supportive. S _____

    b. Tell Jim to do his share of the work and closely watch his output. S _____

    c. Inform Jim that he is creating a hardship for the others and should resolve the problem by himself. S _____

    d. Be supportive but set minimum performance levels and ensure compliance. S _____

C _____   9. Barbara, your most experienced and productive worker, came to you with a detailed idea that could increase your department's productivity at a very low cost. She can do her present job and this new assignment. You think it's an excellent idea; what do you do?

    a. Set some goals together. Encourage and support her efforts. S _____ *b.* Set up goals for Barbara. Be sure she agrees with them and sees you as being supportive of her efforts. S _____

     c. Tell Barbara to keep you informed and to come to you if she needs any help. S _____

     d. Have Barbara check in with you frequently so that you can direct and supervise her activities. S _____

C _____ 10. Your boss asked you for a special report. Frank, a very capable worker who usually needs no direction or support, has all the necessary skills to do the job. However, Frank is reluctant because he has never done a report. What do you do?

     a. Tell Frank he has to do it. Give him direction and supervise him closely. S _____

     b. Describe the project to Frank and let him do it his own way. S _____

     c. Describe the benefits to Frank. Get his ideas on how to do it and check his progress. S _____

     d. Discuss possible ways of doing the job. Be supportive; encourage Frank. S _____

C _____ 11. Jean is the top producer in your department. However, her monthly reports are constantly late and contain errors. You are puzzled because she does everything else with no direction or support. What do you decide to do?

     a. Go over past reports, explaining exactly what is expected of her. Schedule a meeting so that you can review the next report with her. S _____

     b. Discuss the problem with Jean and ask her what can be done about it; be supportive. S _____

     c. Explain the importance of the report. Ask her what the problem is. Tell her that you expect the next report to be on time and error free. S _____

     d. Remind Jean to get the next report in on time without errors. S _____

C _____ 12. Your workers are very effective and like to participate in decision making. A consultant was hired to develop a new method for your department using the latest technology in the field. What do you do?

     a. Explain the consultant's method and let the group decide how to implement it. S _____

     b. Teach them the new method and closely supervise them. S _____

     c. Explain the new method and the reasons that it is important. Teach them the method and make sure the procedure is followed. Answer questions. S _____

     d. Explain the new method and get the group's input on ways to improve and implement it. S _____

To determine your supervisory style, follow these steps:

1. In the box below, circle the letter you selected for each situation. The column headings (S-A through S-L) represent the supervisory style you selected.

	S-A	S-C	S-P	S-L	
1	c	b	d	a	**S-A Autocratic**
2	b	a	d	c	**S-C Consultative**
3	d	b	c	a	**S-P Participative**
4	c	a	d	b	**S-L Laissez-Faire**
5	a	d	b	c	
6	d	c	b	a	
7	d	a	c	b	
8	b	d	a	c	
9	d	b	a	c	
10	a	c	d	b	
11	a	c	b	d	
12	b	c	d	a	

Total

2. Add up the number of circled items per column. The highest is your preferred supervisory style. Is this the style you tend to use most often?

Your supervisory style flexibility is reflected in the distribution of your answers. The more evenly distributed the numbers are between S-A and S-L, the more flexible your style is. A score of 1 or 0 in any column may indicate a reluctance to use the style.

Note: There is no "right" leadership style. This part of the exercise is designed to enable you to better understand the style you tend to use or prefer to use.

Defining the Situation

Now that you have determined your preferred supervisory style, let's explain the four styles and discuss when to use each.[43] As mentioned, there is no best supervisory style for all situations. Instead, the effective supervisor adapts his or her style to meet the capabilities of the individual or group. Studies have shown that supervisor-employee interactions can be classified into two distinct categories: directive and supportive.

- *Directive behavior.* The supervisor focuses on directing and controlling behavior to ensure that the task gets done. The supervisor tells employees what to do and when, where, and how to do the task and oversees performance.

- *Supportive behavior.* The supervisor focuses on encouraging and motivating behavior. He or she explains things and listens to employee views, helping employees make their own decisions.

In other words, when you, as a supervisor, interact with your employees, you can be focusing on directing (getting the task done), supporting (developing relationships), or both.

These definitions lead us to the question, "What style should I use and why?" The answer is that it depends on the situation. And the situation is determined by the capability of the employees. In turn, there are two distinct aspects of capability:

- *Ability.* Do the employees have the experience, education, skills, and so forth to do the task without direction from you as the supervisor?

- *Motivation.* Do the employees want to do the task? Will they perform the task without your encouragement and support?

Determining Employee Capability: Employee capability may be measured on a continuum from low to outstanding, which you, as a supervisor, will determine. You select the one capability level that best describes the employees' ability and motivation for the specific task. These levels are as follows:

- *Low (C-1).* The employees can't do the task without detailed directions and close supervision. Employees in this category may have the ability to do the task but lack the motivation to perform without close supervision.
- *Moderate (C-2).* The employees have moderate ability and need specific direction and support to get the job done properly. The employees may be highly motivated but still need direction, support, and encouragement.
- *High (C-3).* The employees have high ability but may lack the confidence to do the job. What they need most is support and encouragement to motivate them to get the task done.
- *Outstanding (C-4).* The employees are capable of doing the task without direction or support.

Most people perform a variety of tasks on the job. It is important to realize that their capability may vary depending on the specific task. For example, a bank teller may be a C-4 for routine transactions but a C-1 for opening new or special accounts. Employees tend to start working with a C-1 capability, needing close direction. As their ability to do the job increases, you can begin to be supportive and probably stop supervising closely. As a supervisor, you must gradually develop your employees from C-1 levels to C-3 or C-4 over time.

Using the Appropriate Supervisory Style

As mentioned, the correct supervisory style depends on the situation. And the situation, in turn, is a function of employee capability. Each of the supervisory styles, discussed in greater detail below, also involves various degrees of supportive and directive behavior.

Autocratic style *(S-A) involves high-directive/low-supportive behavior (HD-LS) and is appropriate when interacting with low-capability employees (C-1).* When interacting with employees, you, as the supervisor, give very detailed instructions, describing exactly what the task is and when, where, and how to perform it. You also closely oversee performance. The supportive style is largely absent. You make decisions without input from the employees.

Consultative style *(S-C) involves high-directive/high-supportive behavior (HD-HS) and is appropriate when interacting with moderately capable employees (C-2).* Here, you would give specific instructions as well as overseeing performance at all major stages through completion. At the same time, you would support the employees by explaining why the task should be performed as requested and answering their questions. You should work on relationships as you sell the benefits of completing the task your way. When making decisions, you may consult employees, but you have the final say. Once you make the decision, which can incorporate employees' ideas, you direct and oversee their performance.

Participative style *(S-P) is characterized by low-directive/high-supportive behavior (LD-HS) and is appropriate when interacting with employees with high capability (C-3).* When interacting with employees, you give general directions. You should spend limited time overseeing performance, letting employees do the task their way while you focus on the end result. You should support the employees by encouraging them and building up their self-confidence. If a task needs to be done, don't tell them how to do it; ask them how they will accomplish it. Make decisions together or allow employees to make the decision subject to your limitations and approval.

MODEL 1–1

SITUATIONAL SUPERVISION MODEL

Capability Levels (C)	Supervisory Styles (S)
(C-1) Low The employees are unable or unwilling to do the task without direction.	**(S-A) Autocratic** High directive/low support Tell employees what to do and closely oversee performance. Give little or no support. Make decisions by yourself.
(C-2) Moderate The employees have moderate ability and are motivated.	**(S-C) Consultative** High directive/high support Sell employees on doing the job your way and oversee performance at major stages. You may include their input in your decision. Develop a supportive relationship.
(C-3) High The employees have high ability but may lack self-confidence or motivation.	**(S-P) Participative** Low directive/high support Provide little or general direction. Let employees do the task their way. Spend limited time overseeing performance. Focus on end results. Make decisions together.
(C-4) Outstanding The employees are very capable and highly motivated.	**(S-L) Laissez-Faire** Low directive/low support Provide little or no direction and support. Let employees make their own decisions.

Laissez-faire style *(S-L) entails low-directive/low-supportive behavior (LD-LS) and is appropriate when interacting with outstanding employees (C-4).* When interacting with these employees, you should merely let them know what needs to be done. Answer their questions, but provide little, if any, direction. It is not necessary to oversee performance. These employees are highly motivated and need little, if any, support. Allow these employees to make their own decisions subject to your limitations although your approval will not be necessary.

Model 1–1 summarizes the four supervisory styles.

Applying the Situational Supervision Model

You're already familiar with the following situation from Section IV, where it was part of the exercise for determining your supervisory style. Now we're going to apply the information in Model 1–1 to this situation. (Later, in Skill-Building Exercise 1–1, you'll deal with the remaining 11 situations in class.)

To begin, identify the employee capability level each situation describes. These are listed in the left column of the exhibit. Indicate the capability level (1 through 4) in the line marked "C" to the left of the situation. Now determine the management style that each response (*a, b, c,* or *d*) represents. Indicate that style (A, C, P, or L) on the line marked "S" at the end of each response. Finally, identify the response you think is most appropriate by placing a check mark next to it.

C _____ 1. Your rookie crew seems to be developing well. Their need for close supervision is diminishing. What do you do?

    a. Stop directing and overseeing performance, unless there is a problem. S _____

    b. Spend time getting to know them personally, but make sure they maintain performance levels. S _____

    c. Make sure things keep going well; continue to direct and oversee closely. S _____

    d. Begin to discuss new tasks of interest to them. S _____

Let's see how well you did.

1. Their capability started at C-1, but they have now developed to the C-2 level. If you put the number 2 on the C line, you were correct.

2. Alternative *a* is the laissez-faire style. There is no direction or support.
Alternative *b* is the consultative style. There is both direction and support.
Alternative *c* is the autocratic style. There is direction but no support.
Alternative *d* is the participative style. There is low direction and high support (in discussing employee interests).

3. If you selected *b* as the match, you were correct. However, in the business world there is seldom only one way to handle a problem successfully. Therefore, in this exercise, you are given points based on how successful your behavior would be in each situation. In situation 1, *b* is the most successful alternative because it involves developing the employees gradually; it's a three-point answer. Alternative *c* is the next best alternative, followed by *d.* It is better to keep things the way they are now rather than trying to rush employee development, which would probably cause problems. So *c* is a two-point answer, and *d* a one-point answer. Alternative *a* is the least effective because you are going from one extreme of supervision to the other. This is a zero-point answer because the odds are great that this style will cause problems that will affect your supervisory success.

LEARNING OBJECTIVES

7. State your preferred supervisory style.
8. Explain how to use the situational supervision model and use the model on the job.

The better you are at matching your supervisory style to employees' capabilities, the greater your chances of being a successful supervisor.

During Skill-Building Exercise 1–1, you will apply the model to the remaining situations and be given feedback on your success at applying the model as you develop your situational supervision skills.

CONNECTIONS

8. Identify the supervisory style of your present or past boss. (If you never worked, interview someone who has.) Explain how he or she behaved. Did this supervisor change styles? Which other styles did the person use?

9. Can effective supervisory skills be learned and developed? Explain your answer.

REVIEW

Select one or more methods: (1) fill in the missing key terms from memory; (2) match the key terms from the end of the review with their definitions below; (3) copy the key terms in order from the list at the beginning of the chapter.

Managers are classified as top, middle, or first line. These classifications are called the _____ . _____ are the workers in an organization who do not hold management positions and who report to supervisors. A _____ is a first-line manager responsible for achieving organizational objectives through employees. All supervisors have _____ (physical, financial, and human) to help them get the job done.

Numerous studies have been conducted to determine what it takes to be a successful supervisor. Most of these studies found that technical, human, and conceptual skills are needed. We refer to these skills as _____ .

All managers perform the _____ of planning, organizing, staffing, leading, and controlling. _____ is typically the starting point in the supervisory process and is defined as the process of setting objectives and determining in advance exactly how the objectives will be met. _____ is the process of delegating and coordinating tasks and resources with clear authority, responsibility, and accountability. _____ is the process of selecting, orienting, training, and evaluating employees. _____ is the process of influencing employees to work toward the achievement of objectives. _____ is the process of establishing and implementing mechanisms to ensure that objectives are achieved; it is inseparable from planning.

The supervisor's environment is changing. Some of the external forces affecting the supervisor's job include deregulation, litigation, and shifts toward a service and a global economy. The workforce the supervisor leads is also changing. It is aging, becoming more diverse and better educated, and is changing its values and expectations. Technology will continue to evolve rapidly. The new breed of supervisor needs to be less of a boss and more of a coach, using participative management techniques. The supervisor also needs to adapt leadership styles to fit the situation.

When you make the transition from employee to supervisor, think and act like a supervisor. Know your responsibilities; develop your relationship with employees, supervisor, and others; make changes slowly; delegate; and cultivate a situational leadership style.

The four situational supervision styles are as follows:

_____ high-directive/low-support behavior, which is

appropriate when interacting with low-capability employees;

_____ high-directive/high-support behavior, which is appropriate when interacting with moderately capable employees;

_____ low-directive/high-support behavior, which is appropriate when interacting with highly capable employees;

and _____ low-directive/low-support behavior, which is appropriate when interacting with outstanding employees.

KEY TERMS

autocratic style
consultative style
controlling
employees
laissez-faire style
leading
levels of management
organizing

participative style
planning
staffing
supervisor
supervisory functions
supervisory resources
supervisory skills

REFERENCES

1. Ron Zemke, "Training in the '90s," *Training,* January 1987, p. 49.

2. Richard Gordon, "Six Rules of Getting Started in Management," *Supervisory Management,* December 1984, p. 24.

3. Thomas Peters, "Tom Peters' Formula for Supervisory Excellence," *Supervisory Management,* February 1985, p. 2.

4. Thomas Horton, "The Adolescence of Management: Can Business Survive It?" *Management Review,* December 1984, p. 4.

5. Zemke, "Training in the '90s," p. 49.

6. Claude George, *Supervision in Action* (Reston, VA: Reston Publishing Company, 1982), p. 4.

7. Lester Bittel and Jackson Ramsey, *Summary Report: 1981 National Survey of Supervisory Practices* (Harrisonburg, VA: Center for Supervisory Research, James Madison University, 1982).

8. John Franco, "Supervision: Critical Performance Link," *Industry Week,* April 15, 1985, p. 14.

9. Kent Lineback, "How Management Trainers Miss the Boat," *Training,* March 1984, p. 92.

10. Robert Katz, "Skills of an Effective Administrator," *Harvard Business Review,* September–October 1974, pp. 90–102.

11. Charles MacDonald, *Performance Based Supervisory Development* (Amherst, MA: Human Resources Development Press, 1982), p. 20.

12. Franco, "Supervision: Critical Performance Link," p. 14.

13. "Workers Take Dim View of Bosses," *Chicago Tribune,* July 2, 1984, sec. 2, p. 3.

14. Thomas Peters and Robert Waterman, *In Search of Excellence: Lessons from America's Best-Run Companies* (New York: Harper & Row, 1982).

15. Janice Klein and Pamela Posey, "Good Supervisors Are Good Supervisors—Anywhere," *Harvard Business Review,* November–December 1986, p. 127.

16. *The Wall Street Journal,* November 14, 1980, p. 33.

17. Kenneth Blanchard, "The One-Minute Supervisor," *Supervisory Management,* July 1985, pp. 23–26.

18. Charles Denova, "Requirements of Being a Better Supervisor," *Supervision,* October 1984, p. 5; Clark Caskey, "The Vision in Supervision," *Supervision,* August 1985, pp. 3–4.

19. Most of the information in this section comes from Zemke, "Training in the '90s," pp. 40–53.

20. Alan Murray, "The Service Sector's Productivity Problem," *The Wall Street Journal,* February 9, 1987, p. 1.

21. "Looking Ahead," *The Wall Street Journal,* January 7, 1992, p. 1.

22. Joann Lublin, "Younger Managers Learn Global Skills," *The Wall Street Journal,* March 31, 1992, p. B1.

23. "Good Managers Share Same Skills Worldwide," *The Wall Street Journal,* September 4, 1991, p. B1.

24. "Work & Family," *The Wall Street Journal,* February 12, 1992, p. B1.

25. "Workforce Skills," *The Wall Street Journal,* February 18, 1992, p. 1.

26. *The Wall Street Journal,* February 10, 1987, p. 1.

27. John Naisbitt, *Megatrends* (New York: Warner Books, 1982), p. 24.

28. Kenneth Hill, Steven Kerr, and Laurie Broedling, "The First-Line Supervisor: Phasing Out or Here to Stay?" *Academy of Management Review,* January 1986, pp. 103–17.

29. Klein and Posey, "Good Supervisors," pp. 125–28.

30. Harry Nelsen, "Reality Supervision," *Supervision,* October 1984, pp. 8–10.

31. Alan Farrant, "The New Supervisor," *Supervision,* January 1985, pp. 6–7.

32. Anthony Micolo, "Gaining Acceptance as a New Supervisor," *Supervisory Management,* June 1985, pp. 5–7.

33. Lineback, "How Management Trainers Miss," p. 92.

34. Gordon, "Six Rules of Getting Started," pp. 24–25.

35. Lineback, "How Management Trainers Miss," p. 92.

36. Farrant, "New Supervisor," pp. 6–7.

37. Gordon, "Six Rules of Getting Started," p. 25.

38. Micolo, "Gaining Acceptance," p. 7.

39. Farrant, "New Supervisor," p. 7.

40. Olga Jean Myers, "A New Supervisor: Make Haste Slowly," *Supervision,* February 1986, pp. 14–16.

41. Gordon, "Six Rules of Getting Started," p. 27.

42. Ibid.

43. This discussion is based largely on Paul Hersey and Kenneth Blanchard, *Management of Organizational Behavior: Utilizing Human Resources,* 4th ed. (Englewood Cliffs, NJ: Prentice-Hall, 1982), pp. 149–60.

APPLICATION SITUATIONS

Supervisory Skills

AS 1−1

Below are five statements. Identify each skill as being one of the following:

a. technical   *b.* human   *c.* conceptual

_____ 1. The ability to see things as a whole and as the interrelationship of their parts.

_____ 2. The ability to let employees know how they are doing, what needs to be done, and what is going on within the organization.

_____ 3. The ability to perform departmental tasks.

_____ 4. The ability to determine what's going wrong and correct it.

_____ 5. The ability to relate well to others.

Supervisory Functions

AS 1−2

Below are 10 situations. Identify whether the situation describes one of the five supervisory functions listed or is nonsupervisory (*f*).

a. planning   *c.* leading   *e.* staffing

b. organizing   *d.* controlling   *f.* nonsupervisory

_____ 6. The supervisor is writing out next year's budget.

_____ 7. The supervisor is showing an employee how to set up a machine for production.

_____ 8. The supervisor believes that departmental employees are being a bit lazy; therefore, the supervisor regularly observes the employees as they do their jobs.

_____ 9. The supervisor asks an employee to deliver an envelope to the plant manager.

_____ 10. The supervisor is determining how many units were produced.

_____ 11. An employee has been absent several times. The supervisor is discussing the situation and trying to get the employee to improve attendance.

_____ 12. The supervisor is conducting a job interview to fill the position of a retiring employee.

_____ 13. The supervisor is scheduling employee hours and days for next week.

_____ 14. The supervisor is fixing a broken machine.

_____ 15. The supervisor is conducting a semiannual performance evaluation with an employee who has done poorly.

Differences among Managers

AS 1−3

Below are five descriptions. Identify the level of management each represents as being one of the following:

a. top   *b.* middle   *c.* first-line

_____ 16. Supervises the operating employee.

_____ 17. Has greater need for conceptual than technical skills.

_____ 18. Spends more time leading and controlling.

_____ 19. Reports to an executive.

_____ 20. Are fewest in number.

**John Smith,
Supervisor**

John Smith was asked to describe his job as a supervisor. This is what he said:

"My name is John Smith. I am the distribution foreman for the Crispy Snacks Company. We make our own chips, popcorn, cheese curls, pretzels, and corn chips, which we sell to local businesses. My primary responsibility is to make sure that the snacks are delivered on time. My major accomplishment was the development of a new delivery route schedule that increased delivery speed by 10 percent and cut cost by 15 percent. I developed the new delivery route schedule with the aid of linear programming. I am concerned for my delivery people, so I tried to assign them to the routes they wanted. However, I did tell them that they could not trade or change the routes because company rules do not allow it. This is necessary because we have tight delivery schedules to meet. Our major objective is quick delivery. Supervision is a very challenging and rewarding profession; I highly recommend it to self-starting, motivated individuals."

Select the best alternative for the following questions. Be sure to write a brief explanation to support your answers in the space provided between questions.

_____ 1. John's major responsibility involves
   a. planning   c. leading   e. staffing
   b. organizing   d. controlling

_____ 2. Developing a delivery route schedule is a
   _____ function.
   a. planning   c. leading
   b. organizing   d. controlling

_____ 3. The supervisory function John did not discuss was
   a. planning   c. leading   e. staffing
   b. organizing   d. controlling

_____ 4. John spends more time on
   a. planning and organizing   c. equally on a and b
   b. leading and controlling

_____ 5. Developing a new delivery route schedule illustrates
   the _____ supervisory trait.
   a. integrity   c. ability to get along with people
   b. industriousness

_____ 6. Assigning delivery routes according to employee requests illustrates
   the _____ supervisory trait.
   a. integrity   b. industriousness   c. ability to get along with
                                              people

_____ 7. Assigning delivery routes according to request indicates that John has _____ supervisory skills.
   a. technical   *d.* communication
   b. human   *e.* problem-solving and decision-
   c. conceptual   making

_____ 8. John has a greater need for _____ skills.
   a. technical   *b.* conceptual

_____ 9. John supervises
   a. top managers   *c.* first-line managers
   b. middle managers   *d.* employees

_____ 10. John is a _____ level manager.
   a. top   *b.* middle   *c.* first-line

11. List several other specific supervisory functions that John might perform.

IN-CLASS SKILL-BUILDING EXERCISE

Situational Supervision

SB 1–1

Objectives:

1. To learn to use the situational supervision model.
2. To develop your ability to supervise employees using the appropriate situational supervisory style for their capability level.

Procedure: In groups of two, you will apply Situational Supervision Model 1–1 to situations 2 through 12 in Section VI, "Situational Supervision." After you have finished, your instructor will give you the recommended answers, enabling you to determine your success at selecting the appropriate style.

For each situation, use the left column in Model 1–1 to identify the employee capability level the situation describes. Write the level (1 through 4) in the line marked "C" to the left of each situation. Now identify the supervisory style that each response (*a* through *d*) represents. (These are listed in the right-hand column of the exhibit.) Indicate the style (A, C, P, or L) in the line marked "S" at the end of each response. Finally, choose the management style you think is best for each situation by making a checkmark (✔) next to the appropriate response (*a, b, c,* or *d*).

Step 1
(3–8 minutes)

The instructor reviews the situational supervision model and explains how to use the model for situation 1.

Step 2
(25–45 minutes)

1. Turn to situation 2 in the exercise at the beginning of Section VI and to Model 1–1. (You may tear it out of your book.) Apply the model to the situation and select the best course of action (3 to 4 minutes). The instructor will go over the answers and scoring (3 to 4 minutes).

2. Divide into teams of two; you may have one group of three if there is an odd number in the class. Apply the model as a team to situations 3 through 6. Team members may select different answers if they don't agree (8 to 12 minutes). Do not do situations 7 through 12 until you are told to do so. Your instructor will go over the answers and scoring for situations 3 through 6 (2 to 4 minutes).

3. As a team, select your answers to situations 7 through 12 (11 to 15 minutes). Your instructor will go over the answers and scoring to situations 7 through 12 (2 to 4 minutes).

Integration
(3–5 minutes)

To determine how effective you were at supervising, turn to the next page and do the following:

1. Without consulting the model or the answers you gave in class, repeat the exercise, indicate the responses you would pick on the left side of the following table, labeled "without model." On the right side, circle the letter of the alternative you selected using the model in class.

2. Add the number of circles per column and multiply by 0, 1, 2, or 3 depending on the column. Add the four subtotals to get your total score. The range goes from 0 to 36. The higher the score, the better the match of style and capability levels. Did your score increase when you used the model? Using the model on a daily basis can improve your performance.

Conclusion

The instructor may lead a class discussion and make concluding remarks.

Application
(2–4 minutes)

What did I learn from this experience? How will I use this knowledge in the future?

Sharing

Volunteers give their answers to applications above.

EFFECTIVENESS OF SELECTING RECOMMENDED ACTION

Without Model

	0	1	2	3
1	a	d	c	b
2	c	d	a	b
3	d	b	c	a
4	b	d	a	c
5	a	d	c	b
6	d	c	b	a
7	d	b	a	c
8	c	b	a	d
9	d	b	a	c
10	a	b	c	d
11	d	b	c	a
12	a	d	b	c
Total				

↓   ↓   ↓   ↓

Multiply by:

	0	1	2	3
Subtotals				
Total				

With Model

	0	1	2	3
1	a	d	c	b
2	c	d	a	b
3	d	b	c	a
4	b	d	a	c
5	a	d	c	b
6	d	c	b	a
7	d	b	a	c
8	c	b	a	d
9	d	b	a	c
10	a	b	c	d
11	d	b	c	a
12	a	d	b	c

↓   ↓   ↓   ↓

Multiply by:

	0	1	2	3
Subtotals				
Total				

Caution: There is no proven relationship between how a person performs on a pencil-and-paper test and how he or she actually performs on the job. People have a tendency to choose the answer they think is correct, rather than what they would actually do. The objective of this exercise is to help you better understand your supervisory style and ways in which you can improve it.

Source: Adapted from Paul Hersey and Kenneth Blanchard, *LEAD Directions for Self-Scoring and Analysis* (Center for Leadership Studies, 1973).

IN-CLASS SKILL-BUILDING EXERCISE

Getting to Know You

SB 1–2

Objectives:

1. To get acquainted with some of your classmates.
2. To gain a better understanding of what the course covers.
3. To get to know more about your instructor.

Procedure 1
(8–12 minutes)

Break into groups of five or six, preferably with people you do not know. Each member tells his or her name and two or three significant things about himself or herself. After all the members are finished, they may ask each other questions to get to know each other better.

Procedure 2
(2–4 minutes)

Can anyone in the group call the others by name? If so, he or she should do it. If not, have each member repeat his or her name. Follow with each member calling all members by name. Be sure each person knows everyone's first name.

Procedure 3
(5–10 minutes)

Elect a spokesperson or recorder for your group. Look over the following categories and decide what specific statements or questions you would like your spokesperson to ask the instructor based on these categories. The spokesperson will not identify who asked the questions.

1. *Course expectations.* What do you hope to learn from this course? What topics do you want to learn about? Your instructor will comment on your expectations and tell the class whether the topics are a planned part of the course.

2. *Doubts or concerns.* Is there anything about the course that you don't understand? Express any doubts or concerns that you may have.

3. *Questions about the instructor.* List questions to ask the instructor in order to get to know him or her better.

Procedure 4
(10–20 minutes)

Each spokesperson asks the instructor one question at a time until all questions from procedure 3 have been answered. Spokespeople should skip questions already asked by other groups.

Discussion Question

Was this exercise a worthwhile learning experience or a waste of time? Explain.

Conclusion

The instructor may make concluding remarks.

Application

What did I learn from this experience? How will I use this knowledge in the future?

Sharing

Volunteers may give their answers to the questions above.

2

Planning the Work

Learning Objectives   *After completing this chapter, you should be able to perform the following tasks:*

1. Explain the benefits of planning and some reasons that plans fail.
2. Describe the two distinct phases of the planning process.
3. List the four parts of the writing objectives model and set objectives using the model that meet the six criteria.
4. Describe the three steps of MBO.
5. Explain what policies, procedures, and rules are.
6. Explain what programs, projects, and budgets are.
7. Describe how to use the 11 planning tools.
8. List the five steps of the operational planning model and develop an operational plan.
9. State how much time and detail plans require in a specific situation.

Key Terms   To achieve our objectives in this chapter, it is important that you understand the following 19 key terms. They are presented in the order in which they appear in the chapter. The list of key terms also appears in alphabetical order in the end-of-chapter review.

planning	policies	contingency plans
strategic plans	procedures	Gantt charts
operational plans	rules	PERT
objectives	single-use plans	CPM
management by objectives (MBO)	program	operational planning
standing plans	project	means-end process
	budget	

Sue Forester was a very competent clerical worker. She was promoted to supervisor of the clerical department and now has four employees reporting to her. Sue was excited about her new job, but she is getting frustrated because her job has changed so much. Before, life was so much simpler. Sue's old boss would just give her some of the jobs as they came in. But now Sue has to allocate the jobs among employees. Planning out the schedule has been tough. Some of the work has gone out after the standard three-day time period, but work orders have not increased. Sue is wondering how to get the department back on track. Knowing how to plan is crucial to the success of the supervisor. You will learn this skill in this chapter. Before you begin, complete the Skill-Building Preparation on page 61 at the end of the chapter.

I. Why Planning Is Important

As stated in Chapter 1, supervisors perform five functions: planning, organizing, staffing, leading, and controlling. **Planning** *is the process of setting objectives and determining in advance exactly how the objectives will be met.* Planning is generally believed to be the primary supervisory function because it is the first function in the supervisory process.[1] The supervisor must start by knowing what his or her department has to accomplish and then plan how to accomplish these objectives before he or she can organize, staff, lead, and control employees.

Conceptual skills are needed for successful planning. The supervisor must be able to think things through.[2] In addition, the necessary resources (physical, financial, and human) must be available when needed.[3] The time spent planning pays off despite the uncertainties involved.[4] It is only through planning that you, as a supervisor, can ensure that your department's efforts will lead to better performance in the future.[5] Planning is probably the most critical function in supervision—and the most neglected. In this section, you will learn the benefits of planning; explain some of the reasons that plans fail and that supervisors don't plan; and describe some of the signs of poor planning.

The Benefits of Planning

Planning increases your chances of success. However, plans do not guarantee success.[6] Benefits of planning include the following:

- *Direction and teamwork.* Clear plans enable employees to work together in accomplishing departmental objectives. Each employee can understand his or her role and contribute to the department's common purpose.[7]

- *Preventing problems.* When planning, the supervisor can anticipate possible problems and prevent them from slowing down productivity.[8] Planning to have all the necessary resources available when needed keeps the department on schedule.

- *Better decision making.* Supervisors make daily decisions that affect their departments. If you, the supervisor, keep your department's objectives in mind, you will improve your day-to-day decision making.

- *Efficiency.* Supervisors who plan generally produce more, waste less, and have better quality, lower cost, less duplication of effort, and better coordination than supervisors who do not plan.

- *Control.* Planning enables supervisors to measure their progress and take corrective action to meet objectives. Planning provides a means of determining a supervisor's success.[9] We discuss control in detail in Chapter 4.

The rapid pace of change in the work environment means that the need for planning skills will not only continue but also become more important in future years.[10] The better your planning skills are, the better your chances of success as a supervisor.

Reasons That Plans Fail

Plans fail for a variety of reasons:

- *Poor objectives.* Unclear and unrealistic objectives result in frustrating employees who cannot achieve the desired end results. The essence of good planning is knowing what you are planning for.[11]

- *Inaccurate information.* Plans are only as good as the information they are based on.
- *Uncontrollable circumstances.* If a supervisor needs resources from other departments or organizations that do not deliver, he or she cannot proceed as planned.
- *Lack of communication and follow-through.* Employees need to know what their department's plans are if they are to achieve the desired objectives. Employees may not meet objectives if their supervisor does not measure progress and take corrective action to keep plans on schedule.

Why Supervisors Don't Plan

In the course of conducting training programs for supervisors, the author has found that by far the most common reason for not planning is *lack of time.* "I'm too busy putting out fires to plan" is a typical statement. My response is to ask the supervisor to think of the last few "fires," or crises, in the department. Were they caused by something the supervisor did or did not do? Many crises could have been avoided if the supervisor had planned. Why is it that supervisors find time to do a job over, but can't find the time to plan the job the first time? Successful planners have fewer crises. They are in control of their departments. Nonplanners run out of control from one crisis to the next. Planning is a continuous activity.[12] Plans do not have to be complicated or take a lot of time.[13] Later in this chapter, you will learn about tools supervisors can use to help them plan.

A second reason supervisors don't plan is their *tendency toward action.* When a crisis occurs, many supervisors don't feel comfortable stopping to think and plan how to deal with it. They are more comfortable taking immediate action, but this often leads to further crises. For example, Tom, a supervisor, got a rush order from his manager. Tom immediately stopped all production and began work on the rush order. An hour later Tom's employees told him that although the order is half done, they have run out of the red material needed to finish. Since the customer wants all one color, they have to begin production again in green, of which there is an ample supply. As a result of the rush job, two other orders, which were near completion, were sent out late. Both were for good customers. If Tom had taken the time to plan, all three customers could have been better served, and labor hours and material saved. When you fail to plan, you plan to fail.[14] In addition, planning can be fulfilling if it is approached creatively as an active function.[15]

Indications of Poor Planning

Signs of poor planning include the following:

- *Objectives not met.* Missed deadlines, delivery dates, and schedules, or work not done on time.
- *Crises.* Pushing through rush jobs and using overtime to complete jobs.
- *Idle resources.* Physical, financial, or human resources kept waiting for the supervisor to assign tasks.
- *Lack of resources.* Necessary resources not available when needed.
- *Duplication.* The same task being done more than once.

Exhibit 2–1 summarizes this discussion of the importance of planning.

LEARNING OBJECTIVE

1. Explain the benefits of planning and some reasons that plans fail.

EXHIBIT 2–1

THE IMPORTANCE OF PLANNING

Benefits of Planning

Direction and teamwork

Prevention of problems

Better decision making

Efficiency

Control

Reasons Plans Fail

Poor objectives

Inaccurate information

Uncontrollable circumstances

Lack of communication and follow-through

Why Supervisors Don't Plan

Lack of time

Tendency toward action

Indications of Poor Planning

Objectives not met

Crises

Idle resources

Lack of resources

Duplication

C O N N E C T I O N S

1. Think of a specific supervisory job and identify it. Explain how the supervisor in that job benefits from planning.
2. Think of a plan that has failed and explain why it failed.
3. Describe a situation in which you saw indicators of poor planning. Identify the indicators and describe how proper planning could have prevented the situation.

II. The Planning Process

Ideally, planning begins with top management and works its way down to employees. The planning process has two distinct phases: strategic planning and operational planning.

Strategic Planning

Before top-level managers develop strategic plans, they generally define the organization's purpose and make forecasts about the external environment in which the organization operates. Defining the organization's purpose or mission answers the question "What business are we in?" An organization's primary business is not always evident to customers or employees. For example, what business is McDonald's in? If you answered "fast food," you are only partly correct. McDonald's primary business is real estate. Every new restaurant adds to the company's real estate holdings. An example of a definition of purpose the author has developed is this: "Springfield College Training and Development Services is dedicated to training people and developing their skills in order to maximize performance and productivity on the job and to enhancing individual careers." An organization's statement of purpose or mission can be changed.

The second area to examine before developing strategic plans is the organization's external environment. Top management needs to make forecasts about competitors' future plans, customers' needs, the suppliers' ability to meet the firm's needs, and the effects of government policy, technology, and the economy. Top management also needs a forecast of future sales. With the statement of purpose and forecasts for the external environment and sales in hand, top management is ready to develop strategic plans. The input of lower-level managers will also be sought.

Strategic plans *are long-range plans for the entire organization.* Long-range here usually means more than a year and may be up to 10 years. An organization's strategic plan typically covers a two- to five-year period but is revised every year. A strategic plan may also be called a strategy, master strategy, long-range plan, or corporate strategy.

There are at least four areas that should be covered in a strategic plan.

- *Present and future product and service plans.* What products and services will be offered two to five years from now?

- *Plans for competition.* Where do you stand now and where do you want to be in the future? General Motors used to have a 44 percent market share. However, in 1987 its share fell to 40 percent. GM developed strategic plans to regain its lost market share.

- *Competitive advantage.* What can the organization do that the competition cannot? What can it do better that its competition? Polaroid Corporation stresses its innovation in instant photography.

- *Resource development.* How will the organization use its resources in the future? What new resources will be needed two to five years from now? How will the organization get these resources?

Most major American companies are involved in strategic planning. A *Fortune* magazine survey revealed that the 10 most admired companies are, in order, IBM, Dow Jones, Hewlett-Packard, Merck, Johnson & Johnson, Time, Inc., General Electric, Anheuser-Busch, Coca-Cola, and Boeing.[16] Strategic planning plays a major part in the success of these organizations.

Operational Planning

After the strategic plans have been developed, middle managers must determine how to implement them. In turn, supervisors are responsible for implementation within their specific departments. This is all part of a process called operational planning.

Operational plans *are short-range plans for accomplishing a strategy through functional areas.* They are also called tactical, action, or short-range plans. Short-range plans involve a period of one year or less. As a supervisor, you will be involved in operational planning. Many, and probably most, of the operational plans you develop will be tied indirectly, rather than directly, to accomplishing a strategic plan.

Logically, an organization should have both strategic and operational plans. However, this is not always the case. A survey revealed that only half of the organizations with strategic plans had operational plans, and only 25 percent of

EXHIBIT 2-2

PLANNING DIMENSIONS

Type	Time	Level	Scope
Strategic	Long-range (beyond one year)	Top-level management	The entire organization
Operational	Short-range (one year or less)	Middle managers and supervisors	One unit or department to implement a strategy

LEARNING OBJECTIVE

2. Describe the two distinct phases of the planning process.

those believed that their operating plans were adequate.[17] Coordinating the operational functions of marketing, manufacturing, finance, and personnel to effectively carry out the company's strategic plan poses a major challenge for lower-level managers. Throughout this chapter the focus is on developing and implementing operational plans. Exhibit 2–2 summarizes the differences between strategic and operational planning.

CONNECTIONS

4. Describe your role in the development and implementation of an operational plan.

III. Setting Objectives and MBO

Given the definitions above, you should realize that the first step in planning is to set objectives. Although some management experts differentiate goals and objectives, for our purposes the two are the same. **Objectives** *state what is to be accomplished within a given period of time.* Objectives define the desired end result, but they do not state how the result will be achieved. How to achieve the objective is defined by the plan. In this section you will learn what criteria objectives should meet, how to write objectives, and how to manage using them (management by objectives, or MBO).

Criteria for Objectives

When writing objectives you should try to meet the following criteria.

- *The objectives should be consistent with the organization's purpose.* When setting objectives, a supervisor must bear in mind the organization's purpose and strategic plans, and be sure that the objectives he or she sets will help in accomplishing these larger plans.

- *They should be difficult but achievable.* A number of studies have shown that people perform better when they are assigned difficult objectives, rather than easy ones.[18] To motivate employees to strive for high levels of performance, a supervisor must challenge them with difficult objectives. However, if the employees do not believe the objectives are achievable, they may be frustrated and not try.

- *The results should be observable and measurable.* Studies show that individuals perform better when their performance is measured and evaluated.[19] There-

---

MODEL 2–1

WRITING OBJECTIVES

Infinitive + action verb + singular behavior result + target date

   Example objectives for a student:

To + receive + a B as my final grade in supervision + in December 19 _____ .

To increase my cumulative grade point average to 3.0 by May 19 _____ .

   Examples for supervisors:

To produce 1,000 units per day.

To keep absences to three or fewer per month.

To keep rejects to a 2 percent annual rate.

To decrease accidents by 5 percent during 19 _____ .

To write my budget by June 19 _____ .

---

fore, if employees are to meet objectives, there must be a way to regularly observe and measure their progress.[20]

- *Objectives should be specific and have a target date.* Employees must know exactly what is expected of them and when they are expected to complete these tasks.[21] Supervisors should give and be given deadlines for all tasks.

- *They should be jointly set when possible.* Groups that participate in setting their objectives generally outperform groups with assigned objectives.[22] However, the amount of participation should depend on employee capabilities. The higher the capability, the greater the level of participation should be.

- *The objective must be accepted.* For objectives to be met, they must be accepted by those responsible for their attainment.[23] Even if the five criteria listed above are met, failure may still result if employees do not accept the objectives. Employees may be more likely to accept objectives if they participate in the goal-setting process.[24]

Writing Objectives

Model 2–1 will help you write objectives that meet the six criteria listed above.

   After objectives are set and put in writing, they may also be used as a supervisory tool, as we will see in the section that follows.

CONNECTIONS

5. Using Model 2–1, write down at least three objectives you'd like to achieve. Be sure they meet the six criteria for objectives.

Management by Objectives

Management by objectives (MBO) *is the process by which supervisors and their employees jointly set objectives for the employees, periodically evaluate their performance, and reward them according to the results.* MBO gained recognition in 1954 with the publication of Peter Drucker's book *The Practice of Management.* With MBO as their point of reference, others developed offshoots such as work planning and review, goals management, goals and controls, and management by results. Although MBO is an attractive concept, such a program is difficult to implement. Even among Fortune 500 firms, nearly half of those introducing MBO were unsuccessful.[25] For a planning method to actually be an MBO program, it should be implemented throughout the organization. How MBO programs are structured, what they emphasize, and how they are implemented varies from organization to organization. However, to be successful, writers on the subject suggest that MBO programs include the following elements:

Commitment to and Participation in the MBO Program: For an MBO to be successful, there must be commitment to the program at all levels, from top management to the lowest position in the organization. The first steps involve clearly explaining what MBO is, why the organization is going to implement the program, and how it will affect individual employees. If the members of the organization are not committed (convinced of the benefits to them), the program may be destined to fail. One thing that helps get people committed to MBO is their participation in the program.[26] MBO requires a considerable amount of time and effort on everyone's part.

Organizational Purpose and Objectives: Top management, with the input of lower management, should define its purpose and set objectives for the organization as a whole. All employees should be familiar with the organization's purpose and objectives and should understand how their work contributes to the achievement of those objectives. In operation, an MBO program involves three steps.

- **Step 1:** *Set individual objectives and plans.* The supervisor sets objectives jointly with each of his or her subordinates. These individual objectives must contribute to the accomplishment of the organization's objectives. Participation is the key to motivating employees to accomplish their objectives. Objectives should be written, but paperwork should not be overemphasized. Both the supervisor and the subordinates should agree that the objectives are fair and should be committed to their attainment. The supervisor often must help the subordinate reach his or her objectives. An autocratic supervisor may have trouble using MBO.

  Objectives cannot become a reality without plans and schedules for their completion. How these plans are developed depends on the capability level of the employees.

  The objectives themselves are the heart of the MBO program. If they do not meet the criteria stated earlier in this chapter, the program will not be successful. In some areas (such as sales), it is relatively easy to set objectives, but in other areas (such as the quality of patient care), it is more difficult to set objectives and measure results.

- **Step 2:** *Give feedback and evaluate performance.* Xerox Learning Systems found that giving feedback is the most important supervisory skill.[27] Employees must know how they are progressing toward their objectives. Therefore, communication is the key factor in determining MBO's success or failure.[28] Supervisors and employees must meet frequently to review progress. The length of time between these reviews will vary, depending upon the individual and the job being performed. However, most managers probably don't conduct enough review sessions.[29]

  During the feedback and evaluation sessions, it may be necessary to change objectives. For example, if the economy changes and sales decrease, it is not the fault of the salesperson, and his or her objective should be lowered. The supervisor should also help the employee find ways to meet the objectives during those sessions.

- **Step 3:** *Reward according to performance.* Employees' performance should be measured against their objectives, and they should be rewarded accordingly. Employees who meet their objectives should be rewarded through recognition, praise, pay raises, promotions, and so forth.

The organization you work for may or may not use MBO. If it does not and you like the technique, you can still use it within your own department. However, when production quotas are set by time and motion experts or higher-level managers based on the nature of the job itself, MBO is not appropriate within your department. In this case it is still important to make sure that each employee knows what is expected of him or her. Employees should be given feedback and evaluated, and rewarded according to performance. In other words, as a supervisor it is your responsibility to make sure that employees know and accept their objectives or quotas, understand why they are important to the success of the department and themselves, and realize that they will be rewarded based on their fulfillment of those objectives. This, however, is not MBO because goals are not jointly set.

LEARNING OBJECTIVE

4. Describe the three steps of MBO.

CONNECTIONS

6. Name an organization that uses MBO. Have you ever been involved in MBO? If so, describe the situation.

IV. Standing and Single-Use Plans

As mentioned earlier, objectives state what is to be accomplished, but they do not specify how. The method is a function of plans. Such plans may be either *standing plans,* which are used over and over again, or *single-use* plans, which are nonrepetitive. In the following section, we will also discuss *contingency plans,* which are used on a "what if" basis.

Standing Plans

Operating plans determine how an organization's strategy will be accomplished. This may be done by developing standing plans, which save future planning and decision-making time. **Standing plans** *are policies, procedures, and rules developed for handling recurring, predictable situations.* Their purpose is to guide employees' actions.

Policies *are general guidelines to be followed when making decisions.* Policies exist at all levels within organizations. The board of directors and top management develop policies for the entire organization. It is the supervisor's job to implement these company policies.[30] In doing this, supervisors often establish policies for their own employees. For example, the company policy might state that each employee will be given a paid vacation every year. The length of the vacation may be based on the length of employment. However, a supervisor may develop a departmental vacation policy. He or she may decide that during certain busy periods no one can take a vacation; that only one employee can be on vacation at a time; or that when employees get a vacation will be determined by seniority.

Some policies are dictated by external groups such as the government, labor unions, accrediting associations, and so forth. For example, the government requires organizations to offer equal opportunity to all.

Policy statements may be such things as "The customer is always right"; "We produce high-quality goods and services"; "We promote qualified employees from within"; or "Employees will receive due process in grievances." Notice that policy statements are intentionally general guides that leave employees discretion on how to implement them. As a supervisor, your daily decisions will be guided by policies. It will be your job to interpret, apply, and explain company policies to your employees. In situations where no policy exists, ask your boss to establish one, or issue one yourself, to be used when the situation recurs.

Procedures *are a sequence of actions to be followed in order to achieve an objective.* They are also called standard operating procedures (SOP) and methods. Procedures are more specific than policies, and they entail a series of decisions rather than a single decision and may involve more than one functional area. For example, sales personnel, accounting personnel, production personnel, and shipping personnel may all have to follow a set procedure in order to meet a client's needs in selling the company's product. Procedures ensure that all recurring, routine situations are handled in a consistent, predetermined manner. Many organizations have procedures for purchasing, taking inventory, settling grievances, and so forth. Small firms often do not.

As a supervisor, you should develop procedures for your department in the areas of work operations, work flow, scheduling, personnel assignments, and so on.

Rules *state exactly what an employee should or should not do.* Unlike the other standing plans discussed, employees have no discretion on how to implement rules. Most rules leave little or no room for interpretation. There are to be no exceptions to the rules. Examples include "No smoking or eating in classrooms"; "Everyone must wear a hard hat on the construction site"; and "Stop at a red light." Violating rules usually involves penalties that vary in severity according to the seriousness of the violation and the number of offenses. As a supervisor, you will be responsible for establishing and enforcing rules in a uniform manner.

Policies, procedures, and rules are all standing plans. However, they differ in terms of their definition and purpose. Policies are general guides, procedures delineate a sequence of activities, and rules govern specific actions. The amount of detail varies for each type of standing plan, yet their objective is to guide behavior in recurring situations. It is not always easy to distinguish between a policy, a procedure, and a rule. However, as a supervisor you must, in order to know when you have the flexibility to do it your way and when you do not. The number of rules you establish (usually with the support of your boss) should be consistent with your employees' capability levels. The higher the capability level, the fewer the rules that are needed. The proper use of standing plans can help an organization meet objectives.

LEARNING OBJECTIVE

5. Explain what policies, procedures, and rules are.

C O N N E C T I O N S

7. Give an example of a policy, a procedure, and a rule, preferably from an organization you have worked for.

Single-Use Plans

A strategy may also be implemented by developing single-use plans. **Single-use plans** *are programs, projects, and budgets developed for handling nonrecurring situations.* Single-use plans, unlike standing plans, are developed for a specific purpose and probably will not be used again in the same form. However, a single-use plan may be used as a model for future programs, projects, or budgets.

A **program** *describes a broad set of activities and is designed to accomplish an objective over a relatively long time period.* Programs are not meant to exist over the life of the organization. A program may have its own policies, procedures, budget, and so forth. It may also take several years to complete a given program. Examples include the development of a new product, expansion of facilities, or research and development to find a cure for a disease. Each of these examples involves a variety of plans. Once the program is completed, these plans are no longer used.

A **project** *involves a narrow set of activities and is designed to accomplish an objective within a relatively short time period.* The difference between a program and a project lies in scope, time, and degree of complexity. A project may be a portion or a step in an overall program. For example, an overall program to open a new facility may involve projects such as finding a location, developing a layout, staffing the facility, stocking the facility, and so forth. Each of these is a project.

Programs are usually developed by upper managers, who then assign the various projects in the program to supervisors who plan and complete the projects within a relatively short period of time. As a supervisor, you will develop your own projects as the need arises within your department. Projects at the supervisory level could include designing or changing inventory or quality controls and the selection or installation of new equipment.

When you are developing a project, you may find these guidelines helpful:

- Set project objectives.
- Break the project down into a sequence of steps.
- Assign responsibility for each step.
- Establish starting and ending times for each step.
- Determine the resources needed for each step.[31]

If you use the operational planning sheet shown later in Exhibit 2–7, you will be following these guidelines.

LEARNING OBJECTIVE

6. Explain what programs, projects, and budgets are.

A **budget** *is the funds allocated to operate a department for a fixed period of time.* Many people fear budgets because they have few or no math or accounting skills. In reality, most budgets require planning skills rather than mathematical genius. We will discuss budgeting in more detail in Chapter 4.

CONNECTIONS

8. Give an example of a program and a project, preferably one you were involved in.

Contingency Plans

No matter how effective at planning the supervisor is, there will always be things that go wrong. Often these events are beyond the control of the supervisor; for example, a machine may break down or an employee may call in sick. When the unexpected occurs, the supervisor should be prepared with a backup, or contingency plan. **Contingency plans** *are alternative plans to be implemented if unexpected events occur.* In the case of a key employee calling in sick, a supervisor may have trained another employee to do the job.

To develop a contingency plan for your department, it is helpful to answer three questions:

- What might go wrong in my department?
- How can I prevent it from happening?
- If it does occur, what can I do to minimize its effect?

The answer to question 3 is your contingency plan. When developing single-use plans it is helpful to ask everyone involved what can go wrong and what should be done if it does go wrong. Also ask others within and outside the organization who have implemented similar plans.[32] They may have encountered problems you haven't thought of, and they may have good contingency plans to offer you.

C O N N E C T I O N S

9. Describe a situation in which a contingency plan is appropriate. Explain the plan.

V. Planning Tools

There are a variety of simple and complex tools you can use to plan. In this section we will discuss both simple planning tools, such as the clock, the telephone, meetings, a to-do list, and calendars,[33] as well as complex tools, including mathematics, MBO, Gantt charts, CPM and PERT, the operational planning sheet, and computers.

Simple Planning Tools

- **The clock.** Supervisors look at the clock regularly to determine how much time they have until a meeting, lunch, quitting time, and so forth in order to plan what they can accomplish in the time available.
- **The telephone.** Supervisors call others for information to aid them during planning and planning revisions. They also use the telephone to communicate their plans to others.
- **Meetings.** Supervisors develop, revise, and communicate plans during meetings with one or all of their employees. Employees participate in planning during meetings.
- **To-do list.** Supervisors may write down the things they must accomplish. As they complete each task they cross it off and proceed to the next item. You will learn to use the to-do list in the next chapter.
- **Calendars.** Supervisors write down things they need to do on calendars. Exhibit 2–3 gives an example of how a calendar can be used to plan. You will learn the details of time management in Chapter 17.

Complex Planning Tools

- **Mathematics.** Some of the mathematical techniques available to help supervisors plan include break-even analysis, capital budgeting, linear programming, queuing theory, and probability theory. We will explain these techniques in

---

EXHIBIT 2–3	**CALENDAR PLANNING**	
	Monday 9/2	Interview job applicants. Department meeting.
	Tuesday 9/3	Attend supervising training program. Talk to salesperson.
	Wednesday 9/4	Meet with personnel director.
	Thursday 9/5	Order materials. Meeting with boss.
	Friday 9/6	Develop production schedule. Call payroll to OK overtime pay.

greater detail in Chapter 5. Several are available on computer programs. Teaching you how to calculate these techniques is beyond the scope of this text, but interested readers are advised to take a course in quantitative analysis.

- **MBO.** I discussed MBO earlier in this chapter and its use as a planning tool.

- **Gantt charts.** These charts *graphically illustrate the production schedule and progress over a period of time.* The different activities to be performed are usually shown vertically, with time shown horizontally. A darker color or shading is used to show progress toward completion. Using the chart, a supervisor can see at a glance which projects are on, ahead of, or behind schedule. If a supervisor is aware that a project is behind schedule, he or she can take corrective action to get it back on schedule.

    The technique is not new. Graphic illustrations of production were used when the Great Pyramids of Egypt were built. In modern times Henry Gantt, a management consultant, popularized their use at the turn of this century. Today, these bar diagrams are used extensively.[34] Exhibit 2–4 illustrates a Gantt chart. Assume that today is February 10; which projects are on schedule? Which are ahead of or behind schedule?

- **CPM and PERT.** The Critical Path Method (CPM) and Performance Evaluation and Review Technique (PERT) are popular techniques for planning a variety of activities. Compare Exhibits 2–4, the Gantt chart, and 2–5, which is a CPM/PERT network. In the Gantt chart, each activity is shown separately. In Exhibit 2–5, we see that a variety of tasks must be completed, some simultaneously, to accomplish our objective.

    PERT and CPM are usually used together, but the two techniques are different. **PERT** *is used to identify the various tasks and activities necessary to complete a project.* **CPM** *determines the length of time it will take to complete a project by ascertaining how long each task or activity will take.* The critical path is the most time-consuming series of activities involved in completing the project. It is shown by the double lines in Exhibit 2–5. The Gantt chart is used primarily for routine standing plans, whereas CPM and PERT are used for programs and projects as single-use plans.

To develop a CPM/PERT network, follow these steps:

- **Step 1.** List all the activities that must be completed to reach the specific objective. Assign each a letter. In our example we have 10 activities labeled A through J.

- **Step 2.** Determine the time it will take to complete each activity. In our example, each will take a number of days to complete, as follows: A-2, B-6, C-4, D-10, E-7, F-5, G-7, H-4, I-6, and J-1.

EXHIBIT 2–4 **GANTT CHART**

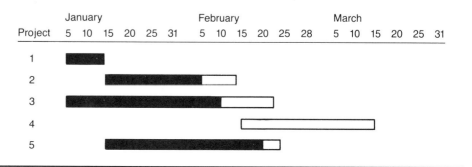

Project	January 5 10 15 20 25 31	February 5 10 15 20 25 28	March 5 10 15 20 25 31
1			
2			
3			
4			
5			

EXHIBIT 2–5   **CPM/PERT NETWORK**

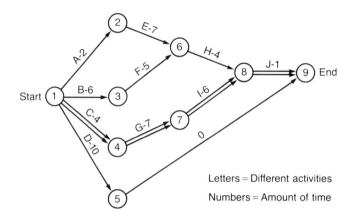

Step 3. Arrange the tasks on the diagram in the sequence in which they must be completed. In Exhibit 2–5, A must be completed before E can begin, E must be completed before H can begin, and H must be completed before J can begin. For example, before you can place a box of cereal on a shelf for sale (J), it must be ordered (A), received (E), and priced (H). Notice that activity D is independent. Each activity is represented by an arrow as well as a letter. The numbered circles signify the completion of an activity leading to the desired outcome. All activities originate and terminate at a circle. In Exhibit 2–5, 1 represents the start of the program or project and 9 its end or completion.

• **Step 4.** Determine the critical path. To do this, you must total the time it takes for each path from start 1 to end 9. Path 1–2–6–8–9 takes 2 + 7 + 4 + 1 days for a total of 14 days. Path 1–3–6–8–9 takes 6 + 5 + 4 + 1 days for a total of 16. Path 1–4–7–8–9 takes 4 + 7 + 6 + 1 days for a total of 18 days. Path 1–5–9 takes 10 + 0 days for a total of 10 days. The critical path, indicated by the double arrow, is 1–4–7–8–9. The program or project should take 18 days to complete.

• **Computers.** Microcomputers have made everything about planning easier, from establishing a schedule to sharing it with others to revising deadlines in the event of a change. There are more than two dozen project-planning software packages on the market.[35] As an example of how they are used, Westhoff Tool and Die employs a computer to track 80 projects. The computer schedules each machine in the plant on a chart, with copies given to six managers who supervise 60 operators.[36]

• **Operational planning sheet.** As an aid to planning, the author has developed an operational planning sheet that he uses personally and in the management training programs he conducts. Exhibit 2–6 is an example. You will learn how to use it in the next section.

Weekly and Daily Planning

L E A R N I N G
O B J E C T I V E
7. Describe how to use
the 11 planning tools

It is recommended that supervisors plan each week and then each day as part of time management. Time management tools are presented in Chapter 17, which you may want to review now.

EXHIBIT 2 – 6   **OPERATIONAL PLAN**

OBJECTIVE: _____

(infinitive + action verb + singular behavior result + target date)

Responsible _____ Starting date _____ Due date _____

Priority _____ Control checkpoints _____

Steps (what, where, how, resources, etc., subobjectives)	When		Who
	Start	End	

VI. Operational Planning

There is an example of an operational planning model in Exhibit 2–6. Feel free to make copies for your own planning. **Operational planning** *involves five steps: (1) setting objectives, (2) determining the type of plan and tools needed, (3) developing and analyzing alternatives, (4) selecting a plan, and (5) implementing the plan and controls.*

**Step 1.
Set Objectives**

Before you can determine how you will do something, you must decide what it is you want to accomplish. So the first step in planning is clearly stating the end result you desire, using the six criteria for setting objectives discussed earlier in the chapter.

**Step 2.
Determine the Type of Plan and Tools Needed**

Type of Plan: Will the situation be recurring so that a standing plan is called for? Or is it a unique situation calling for a single-use plan? Are contingency plans appropriate? Check the appropriate blanks for the type of plan you need:

- Standing plan: policy _____ procedure _____ rule _____ .
- Single-use plan: program _____ project _____ budget _____ .
- Contingency plans: are _____ are not _____ needed.
- Detailed _____ or general _____ .
- The appropriate supervision style:
  autocratic _____ consultative _____ participative _____
  laissez-faire _____ .

Tools Needed: In developing the plan, which tool or tools will be helpful? Check the appropriate blanks:

Clock _____	Computer _____
Telephone _____	Mathematics _____
Meeting _____	MBO _____
To-do list _____	Gantt chart _____
Calendar _____	CPM and PERT _____
	Operational planning sheet _____

**Step 3.
Develop and Analyze Alternatives**

After determining the type of plan and tools needed, you should list the alternative ways you might accomplish your objectives. Analyze the pros and cons of each alternative to determine the best approach. Get the input of others; how much your employees contribute will depend on their capability for this project.

**Step 4.
Select a Plan**

After analyzing the alternatives, select the best method or plan for achieving the objectives. When appropriate, use an operational planning sheet or develop a Gantt chart or CPM/PERT network. Make the plan more specific than you think is necessary and give a copy of the plan to all involved in its implementation.[37]

**Step 5.
Implement the Plan and Controls**

Plans are useless unless someone performs the activities required to complete them. Thus, a plan must be implemented and controls put in place to make sure that the plan is on schedule. The control process involves reviewing the plans

MODEL 2-2

OPERATIONAL PLANNING

Step 1. Set objectives.

Step 2. Determine the type of plan and planning tools needed.

Step 3. Develop and analyze alternatives.

Step 4. Select a plan.

Step 5. Implement and control.

periodically to ensure that all activities are being performed as scheduled. If this is not the case, corrective action may be needed to get the plan back on schedule. Alternatively, the objective, the plan, or both may have to be changed. Good follow-through is needed to make the plan work.[38] I will discuss controlling in detail in Chapter 4.

Model 2-2 summarizes the five steps of operational planning.

Sample Operational Plan

Exhibit 2-7 is an example of an operational plan developed and used by Springfield College Training and Development Services (SCT&DS). As you can see, step 1 (the objective) is clearly stated at the top of the form.

In step 2 the supervisor determined that a detailed standing plan was appropriate and that contingency plans were not needed. He used a consultative supervisory style. The tool used was an operational planning sheet. A Gantt chart or CPM/PERT network could also have been developed if management information systems (MIS) had typed all letters in their entirety on the word processor, rather than using office services to duplicate them, and if the letters had been sent first

EXHIBIT 2-7

MARKETING OPERATIONAL PLAN

OBJECTIVE: To mail a personalized form letter to all target clients by the 15th of each month.

Responsible   _Bob_   Starting date _1st of each month._ Due date _15th of each month._

Priority   _High_   Control checkpoints _6th, 10th, 13th of each month_

Steps (what, where, how, resources needed, etc.)	When		Who
	Start	End	
1. Write the letter and deliver to management information systems (MIS)	1st	3rd	Bob
2. Type the letter on the word processor	3rd	6th	MIS
3. Proofread the letter and deliver to office services (OS)	6th	7th	Bob
4. The original letter is reproduced on the offset machine	7th	10th	OS
5. The letters are delivered to MIS	10th	10th	Mike
6. Envelopes are typed on the word processor	10th	13th	MIS
7. The letters are picked up from MIS, signed by Bob, folded, put into the envelopes, and delivered to the mailroom (MR)	13th	13th	Mike
8. The letters are prepared for bulk mailing and given to the mail carrier at the 4 P.M. pickup	13th	15th	MR

class rather than bulk mail. The reason this alternative was not selected was cost. The U.S. Postal Service informed the supervisor that word-processed letters cannot be mailed bulk rate, and first-class mail cost more than twice as much as bulk mail. In addition, MIS would have charged SCT&DS to type the letters on the word processor. It was decided that the possible benefits did not justify the additional costs. Another alternative would have been to omit from each letter the name and address, personal signature, or all three. All the dates had to be checked to ensure that the time limits could be met by MIS, office services, and the mailroom. As you can see, several more alternatives could have been analyzed.

Step 5, implementing the plan and control, is not so apparent in the exhibit. However, notice the control checkpoints (the 6th, 10th, and 13th are critical times to determine progress to date) that allow for corrective action in meeting the deadline, if necessary.

It took time to develop this plan, but the time spent paid off in two major ways. First, the letters were mailed on time. If the supervisor were to use the "we'll do it when we have time" approach, this would not have happened. Second, Mike, listed in the "who" column of Exhibit 2–7, is the student aide. The turnover rate for student aides is usually one year. This plan saves training time when a new aide comes on board. He or she is given a copy of the plan, which shows the entire process and the aide's role and contribution.

LEARNING OBJECTIVE

8. List the five steps of the operational planning model and develop an operational plan

The Means-End Process

Objectives and plans go together but have different purposes. The relationship between objectives and plans is often referred to as a **means-end process:** *the objective is the end, and the plan is the means to accomplish the end.* Notice in Exhibit 2–7 that the objective does not specify who will mail the letters or when and how the letters will be mailed. The planning section steps state the mailing means.

CONNECTIONS

11. Develop an operational plan following the five steps of Model 2–2. (This may be a plan for one of the objectives you listed in Connections 5.)

VII. Situational Supervisory Planning

In this section we will answer three questions. How much time should a supervisor spend planning? Should plans be detailed and written? How much should employees participate in planning? However, there are no simple answers to these questions that can be applied in all situations, so the situational approach is important.

How Much Time Should a Supervisor Spend Planning?

One study revealed that supervisors plan every day, and that 12 percent of their time is spent planning.[39] Several other studies have concluded that supervisors spend most of their time planning for periods of one week or less. These supervisors develop and implement daily single-use plans while being guided by standing plans. As a supervisor, the time you will spend planning will vary depending upon your situation. As a general guide, you should plan before starting anything new, and you should spend more time developing new plans than revising old plans.[40] Spend as much time planning as is necessary to get the job done right the first time.

How much time a supervisor should spend planning depends on how much time it takes to accomplish the preventive actions versus the corrective actions.

Why is it that so many supervisors can rarely find the time to plan the work, but they can always find the time to redo the work correctly the second or third time? Try to spend your time developing proactive plans that identify and eliminate problems before they occur, rather than reactive plans to solve existing problems. In other words, spend time preventing fires rather than putting them out.

You should probably spend about 30 minutes at the end of each week planning for the coming week. You might also spend about 15 minutes at the end of each day scheduling your activities for the next day or 15 minutes first thing in the morning planning your day. In Chapter 17 you will learn how to manage and plan your time.

Should Plans Be Detailed and Written?

Again, the answer depends upon the situation. There are times, as in Exhibit 2–7, when detailed written plans are appropriate. There are other situations in which detailed plans will not work. For example, before making a telephone call you should plan what you want to talk about, but you cannot write out a detailed script: "I'll say A, the person I'm calling will say B, then I'll say C, and D will be the reply." Instead, you have to listen to what the person is saying before you can respond. As a general guide, major standing plans should be written. Many organizations have handbooks containing appropriate standing plans.

Standing plans vary in terms of the level of detail needed. Policies are general guides, and procedures and rules are more detailed. Among single-use plans, budgets and programs generally should be written in detail. Projects tend to vary. As a general guide, complex projects involving several people should be written in as much detail as possible, and each participant should be given a copy.

Develop detailed written contingency plans when it is critical to meet objectives on time, and when there is a high probability that things will go wrong. This is especially necessary when others will have to carry out complex contingency plans.

Extent of Employee Participation in Planning

The extent of employee participation depends on the time available and their capability. When an employee's capability level is low (C-1), the time available does not matter; develop the plans for the employee without his or her participation, using an autocratic supervisory style. When the employee's capability level is moderate (C-2) and time permits, include the employee's input into the plan using a consultative supervisory style. When the employee's capability level is high (C-3) and time is available, develop the plans together using a participative supervisory style. When the employee has an outstanding capability level (C-4) and can develop the plan in time, let him or her develop the plan while you use a laissez-faire supervisory style.

LEARNING OBJECTIVE

9. State how much time and detail plans require in a specific situation.

For years supervisors have been claiming that they don't have time to allow employee input into planning, and that employees are not capable of planning. You should not make the same excuses. Take the time to develop employee capability, and make the time to include them in planning (if you want to be a successful supervisor, that is).

REVIEW

Select one or more methods: (1) fill in the missing key terms from memory; (2) match the key terms from the end of the review with their definitions below; (3) copy the key terms in order from the list at the beginning of the chapter.

The first or primary supervisory function is _____ . It is defined as the process of setting objectives and determining in advance exactly how the objectives will be met. The benefits of planning include direction and teamwork, prevention of problems, better decision making, efficiency, and control.

The planning process includes two phases or types of plans: _____ , which are long-range plans for the entire organization, and _____ , short-range plans for accomplishing a strategy through functional areas. Supervisors are primarily involved in operational planning.

_____ state what is to be accomplished within a given period of time. They should be consistent with the organization's purpose, difficult but achievable, observable and measurable, specific with a target date, jointly set when possible, and accepted by those who must achieve them. When writing objectives it is helpful to use this model: "infinitive + action verb + singular behavior result + target date." _____ is the process by which supervisors and employees jointly set objectives for the employee, periodically evaluate his or her performance, and reward according to the results.

_____ are policies, procedures, and rules developed for handling recurring, predictable situations. _____ are general guidelines to be followed when making decisions.

_____ are a sequence of actions to be followed in order to achieve an objective. _____ state exactly what an employee should or should not do. _____ are programs, projects, and budgets developed for handling nonrecurring situations. A _____ is a broad set of activities designed to accomplish an objective over a relatively long time period. A _____ is a narrow set of activities designed to accomplish an objective within a relatively short time period. A _____ is the allocated funds to operate a department for a fixed period of time. _____ are alternative plans to be implemented if unexpected events occur.

Some of the planning tools available to the supervisor include the clock, the telephone, meetings, to-do lists, the calendar, mathematics, MBO, and _____ , which graphically illustrate the schedule of production and its progress over a period of time; _____ , a graphic representation of activities and events to be done to complete a program or project; _____ , a technique using a network of activities and events to determine the completion time of a program or project; operational planning sheet; and computers.

Steps in _____ are (1) setting objectives, (2) determining the type of plan and tools needed, (3) developing and analyzing alternatives, (4) selecting a plan, and (5) implementing the plan and controls. Objectives are ends, and plans are means to achieve the ends. This relationship is known as the _____ .

The amount of time situational supervisors spend planning depends on the needs of the situation. These supervisors develop proactive plans and use planning tools appropriate to the situation. The level of detail in their plans also depends on the particular situation. They put their plans in writing when appropriate. And situational supervisors allow employees to participate in planning when capability and time permit.

KEY TERMS

budget	planning
contingency plans	policies
CPM	procedures
Gantt charts	program
MBO	project
means-end process	rules
objectives	single-use plans
operational planning	standing plans
operational plans	strategic plans
PERT	

REFERENCES

1. Richard Sloma, "No-Nonsense Planning for Administrators," *Office Administration and Automation,* April 1985, p. 24.

2. S. Krishnaswami, "A Few Basic Tools for Supervisors," *Supervision,* July 1984, p. 8.

3. Rich Tewell, "Some Simple Action Planning Tools," *Supervisory Management,* August 1985, p. 7.

4. Rick Cook, "Planning for a Better Future," *Computer Decisions,* September 30, 1986, p. 60.

5. Sloma, "No-Nonsense Planning," p. 24.

6. Jewell, Manner, and Jewell, "For the First-Time Planner," *Supervisory Management,* July 1984, p. 28.

7. Bob Powers, "Developing an Operational Plan for Better Performance," *Management Solutions,* September 1986, p. 28.

8. Jewell, Manner, and Jewell, "For the First-Time Planner," p. 40.

9. Powers, "Developing an Operational Plan," p. 29.

10. Hal Mather, "Getting Ready Today for Production Operations of Tomorrow," *Supervisory Management,* May 1986, p. 5.

11. Cook, "Planning for a Better Future," p. 63.

12. Krishnaswami, "A Few Basic Tools," p. 6.

13. Tewell, "Some Simple Action Planning Tools," p. 6.

14. Jewell, Manner, and Jewell, "For the First-Time Planner," p. 40.

15. Alfred Coke, "Mission Planning at the Operational Level," *Supervisory Management,* May 1985, p. 2.

16. Nancy Perry, "America's Most Admired Corporations," *Fortune,* January 9, 1984, p. 51.

17. Roger Schroeder, "Operating Strategy: Missing Link in Corporate Planning?" *Management Review,* August 1984, p. 20.

18. Christina Shalley and Greg Oldham, "Effects of Goal Difficulty and Expected External Evaluation of Intrinsic Motivation," *Academy of Management Journal,* September 1985, p. 628.

19. Ibid.

20. M. R. Hansen, "Better Supervision from A to W," *Supervisory Management,* August 1985, p. 35.

21. Hansen, "Better Supervision from A to W," p. 36.

22. Erez, Zarley, and Hulin, "The Impact of Participation on Goal Acceptance and Performance," *Academy of Management Review,* March 1985, p. 56.

23. Ibid., p. 50.

24. Ibid., p. 51.

25. Joseph Leonard, "Why MBO Fails So Often," *Training and Development Journal,* June 1986, p. 38.

26. Ibid.

27. John Franco, "Supervision: Critical Performance Link," *Industry Week,* April 15, 1985, p. 14.

28. Leonard, "Why MBO Fails So Often," p. 38.

29. Ibid.

30. Franco, "Supervision: Critical Performance Link," p. 14.

31. Adapted from Leonard Aptman, "Project Management: Criteria for Good Planning," *Management Solutions,* September 1986, p. 22.

32. Tewell, "Some Simple Action Planning Tools," p. 8.

33. Ibid., p. 6.

34. Leonard Aptman, "Project Scheduling Tools and Techniques," *Management Solutions,* October 1986, p. 32.

35. Nancy Madlin, "Streamlining the PERT Chart," *Management Review,* September 1986, p. 67.

36. Ibid., p. 68.

37. Jewell, Manner, and Jewell, "For the First-Time Planner," p. 41.

38. Krishnaswami, "A Few Basic Tools," p. 7.

39. Charles MacDonald, *Performance-Based Supervisory Development* (Amherst, MA: Human Resources Development Press, 1982), p. 20.

40. Jewell, Manner, and Jewell, "For the First-Time Planner," p. 40.

APPLICATION SITUATIONS

Identifying Plans

AS 2–1

Below are 10 statements made by different organizations. Identify each in terms of these categories:

Objective	*Standing Plan*	*Single-Use Plan*
a. objective	*b.* policy	*e.* program
	c. procedure	*f.* project
	d. rule	*g.* budget

_____ 1. Quality is job one. (Ford Motor Company)

_____ 2. President John F. Kennedy's plan to land someone on the moon.

_____ 3. To increase our market share by 5 percent next year.

_____ 4. Employees having babies will be given a two-month maternity leave.

_____ 5. How much will it cost to operate your department next month?

_____ 6. Wear safety glasses while touring the factory. (Acme Chain)

_____ 7. Forms for leaves of absence must be approved by the manager and submitted to the personnel office one month in advance of their effective dates.

_____ 8. Maintain the reject rate on watches under 10 percent.

_____ 9. Never take unfair advantage of anyone the firm deals with. (J. C. Penney)

_____ 10. You may spend $1,000 to conduct that seminar.

Developing a Plan

AS 2–2

You have decided to open and manage the Spinning Disc Record Shop on April 1. It is now late December. You plan to move in one month before the store is scheduled to open in order to set up. During March, your assistant will help you set up and you will train him or her. You will start to implement the plan on January 2.

- Develop a plan following the operational planning steps.
- Step 1. Set an objective and write it down.
- Steps 2–4. Determine the type of plan needed and write it down.

Assume that you have decided to use a Gantt Chart and CPM/PERT network. Develop both, in order of your preference, following the text guides for their development, assuming that you have identified the activities and completion times listed below. (The activities may not be given in sequence.)

a. Lease the store fixtures to display your records and tapes; it will take two weeks to receive and arrange them.

b. Order and receive records and tapes. This takes one week.

c. Recruit and select an assistant (three weeks or less).

d. Install the fixtures, paint, decorate, and so on (two weeks).

e. Form a corporation (four weeks).

f. Make arrangements to buy records and tapes on credit (two weeks).

g. Find a store location (six weeks or less).

h. Unpack and display records and tapes (one week).

i. Train the assistant (one week).

j. Select the records and tapes you plan to stock (one week).

k. Determine start-up cost and cash outflow per month through April 31. Your rich uncle will lend you this amount (one week).

When developing the Gantt Chart, use the following format, based on weeks. You may want to change the letter sequence.

(State letter and task for activities a–k)

	January				February				March			
Week	1	2	3	4	1	2	3	4	1	2	3	4
Activity												
Activity												
Activity												
Activity												
Activity												
Activity												
Activity												
Activity												
Activity												
Activity												
Activity												

OBJECTIVE CASE 2

MIS Design

Tom Shawn, president of the RNL Company, decided that the firm's present information system was not adequate considering the growth the company has experienced over the past five years. Tom hired Bob Furry, an expert in computers and management information systems (MIS), to design a new MIS for RNL Company. Bob was given the title of director of MIS and had the present staff of two computer operators reporting to him.

Bob went around to the different functional areas to evaluate the present systems and told the managers what he could do for them with a new MIS.

After several weeks, Bob implemented the new MIS. Six months later, the president decided to see how the new system was working. Tom visited the functional managers and found that very few people were using the information provided. When Tom asked them why they were not using the system, they typically replied, "I have my own system. We don't need an MIS."

Answer the following questions by selecting the best alternative. Use the space between the questions to provide information supporting your answers.

_____ 1. Bob's plan most likely failed for which of the following reasons?
    a. poor objectives   *c.* uncontrollable circumstances
    b. inaccurate information   *d.* lack of communication and
                            follow-through

_____ 2. Assume that Tom had hired you instead of to develop the MIS; what type of plan would you develop?
    a. strategic   *b.* operational   *c.* both

_____ 3. Assume that Tom had hired you to develop the MIS; what type of manager would you be?
    a. top   *b.* middle   *c.* first-line

_____ 4. The plan to design the MIS should be a
    a. standing plan   *b.* single-use plan

_____ 5. A _____ plan is appropriate for the MIS design.
    a. policy   *d.* program
    b. procedure   *e.* project
    c. rule   *f.* budget

_____ 6. Are contingency plans needed?
    a. yes   *b.* no

_____ 7. The appropriate plan would be
    a. detailed   *b.* general

_____ 8. The _____ is an appropriate planning tool for use in the MIS design plan.
   a. Gantt chart   c. operational planning sheet
   b. CPM/PERT   d. all of the above

_____ 9. The appropriate supervisory style to use in developing the MIS plan would be
   a. autocratic   c. participative
   b. consultative   d. laissez-faire

_____ 10. Which functional area or areas should give input into the design and implementation of the MIS?
   a. marketing   d. human resource development/
   b. production   personnel
   c. finance   e. all of the above

11. How would you plan the MIS and overcome the major mistake Bob made?

PREPARATION FOR IN-CLASS SKILL-BUILDING EXERCISE

Course Objectives

SB 2–1

Note: I recommend that you complete part 1 of this preparation before reading Chapter 2. Complete parts 2 and 3 after reading the chapter.

Part 1: Below are 34 statements. Rate yourself on your level of skill in each area using the scale below:

1	2	3	4	5	6	7
Not skilled			Somewhat skilled			Very skilled

_____ 1. Writing effective objectives.

_____ 2. Developing plans to achieve objectives.

_____ 3. Organizing work to get it done.

_____ 4. Assigning work to others.

_____ 5. Establishing methods to ensure work gets done on time.

_____ 6. Following work through to its timely completion.

_____ 7. Solving problems and making decisions.

_____ 8. Knowing when to use a group to make decisions.

_____ 9. Working with people in your department.

_____ 10. Working with people in other departments and organizations.

_____ 11. Communicating with others.

_____ 12. Changing your communication style to meet the situation.

_____ 13. Getting others to change.

_____ 14. Resolving conflicts between yourself and others, and between others as a mediator.

_____ 15. Performing a job analysis and writing a job description.

_____ 16. Conducting a job interview.

_____ 17. Getting people started on a job.

_____ 18. Teaching people how to do things.

_____ 19. Motivating people to do a good job.

_____ 20. Improving productivity.

_____ 21. Evaluating how well people perform.

_____ 22. Conducting a performance appraisal.

_____ 23. Influencing others to meet objectives.

_____ 24. Gaining and using power.

_____ 25. Getting people with problems to do their work.

_____ 26. Disciplining a person for not meeting requirements.

_____ 27. Getting people to work together as a team.

_____ 28. Knowing when to use input from others on the job, and using the input appropriately.

_____ 29. Dealing with union members.

_____ 30. Handling grievances.

_____ 31. Managing your time.

_____ 32. Handling stressful situations.

_____ 33. Planning your career.

_____ 34. Overall ability to manage as a situational supervisor.

Part 2: After reading Chapter 2, record your ratings for the 34 statements on Exhibit SB 2–1. Each statement refers to the skills we will develop during this course. They are grouped by the parts in the book in which they appear. To the right of your answers are the numbers and titles of the chapters in which each topic will be covered. Do not be concerned if some of your skill levels were not high. You should develop them during this course.

Part 3: After completing Exhibit SB 2–1, write down at least five objectives for this course in terms of skills you want to develop. Be sure to use Model 2–1 for writing your objectives. Then review your ratings in Exhibit SB 2–1. The lower the rating, the greater is your need to develop a particular skill. Formulating objectives will help you focus your attention on the skills you most want to develop. You should refer to Exhibit SB 2–1 and to this page when you finish each part of the book to review the past and to think about upcoming material.

Objectives:

IN-CLASS SKILL-BUILDING EXERCISE

Course Objectives

SB 2–1

Objectives:

1. To get an overview of the course content.
2. To determine areas where attention should be given to your supervisory skill building.
3. To develop skills in setting objectives.

Procedure 1
(5–15 minutes)

Break into groups of two to four. You may review each other's profiles (Exhibit SB 2–1). Each member should describe one of his or her objectives to the others. The other group members review each objective to see whether it meets the following criteria:

- Is it difficult but achievable?
- Is it observable and measurable?
- Is it specific with a target date?

If an objective does not meet any of the above criteria, work as a team to help the member make the necessary changes. Remember to keep taking turns until all objectives are stated or until the time is up.

EXHIBIT SB 2 – 1   **PROFILE FORM**

	1	2	3	4	5	6	7	**Part I. The Supervisory Process**
1								Ch. 2. Planning the Work
2								
3								Ch. 3. Organizing and Delegating Work
4								
5								Ch. 4. Controlling Work
6								
								Part II. Supervisory Skills
7								Ch. 5. Problem Solving and Decision Making
8								
9								Ch. 6. Human Relations
10								
11								Ch. 7. Communicating with Others
12								
13								Ch. 8. Managing Change and Conflict
14								
								Part III. Developing Employees
15								Ch. 9. Hiring Employees
16								
17								Ch. 10. Orienting and Training Employees
18								
19								Ch. 11. Improving Productivity
20								
21								Ch. 12. Evaluating and Compensating Employees
22								
								Part IV. Supervising Employees
23								Ch. 13. Leading Employees
24								
25								Ch. 14. Supervising Problem Employees
26								
27								Ch. 15. Supervising Groups
28								

EXHIBIT SB 2-1
(concluded)

	1	2	3	4	5	6	7	**Part IV. Supervising Employees**
29								Ch. 16. Labor Relations
30								
								Part V. Supervising Yourself
31								Ch. 17. Managing Your Time, Stress, and Career
32								
33								
34								Ch. 1–17

Procedure 2
(5–10 minutes)

Select three objectives that are representative of the group. A spokesperson from each group describes the three objectives to the class and writes them on the board. The instructor may make suggestions for improving the objectives and general comments.

Conclusion

The instructor may lead a class discussion and make concluding remarks.

Application
(2–4 minutes)

What did I learn from this experience?
How will I use this knowledge in the future?

Sharing

Volunteers share their answers with the class.

IN-CLASS SKILL-BUILDING EXERCISE

Car Dealer Negotiation

SB 2-2

Objective: To develop your planning ability.

Experience: You will plan for and negotiate the sale or purchase of a car.

Procedure 1
(2–3 minutes)

Break into teams of two and decide who will be the buyer and who will be the seller of the car. At the end of this exercise you will find an appendix called the Car Dealer's Game. Tear it out of the book. The buyer will use the information entitled Confidential Information to the Buyer. The seller uses the seller information. Buyers and sellers should not read the other party's confidential information.

Procedure 2
(4–8 minutes)

Buyers and sellers read their confidential information. They then follow the operational planning steps to develop a plan for the sale or purchase of the car. Do not let the buyer or seller see your plan.

- Step 1. Write an objective.

- Step 2. Determine the type of plan and tools needed.

- Step 3. Develop and analyze alternatives. (What will you do and say?)

- Step 4. Select a plan.

- Step 5. Implement the plan and control.

Procedure 3
(7–10 minutes)

Negotiate the sale of the car. You do not have to buy or sell the car. After you complete the sale or decide not to sell, read the confidential information sheet for your partner in the exercise. Discuss the situation. Do not go on to the next step until your instructor tells you to.

Integration
(2–4 minutes)

Answer the following questions:

_____ 1. Did you set an objective with a specific price limit to pay or accept?
      a. yes   *b.* no

_____ 2. I _____ my objective.
      a. underachieved   *b.* achieved   *c.* overachieved

_____ 3. The type of plan should have been
      a. standing   *b.* single-use

_____ 4. It should have involved a
      a. policy   *c.* rule   *e.* project
      b. procedure   *d.* program   *f.* budget

_____ 5. The plan should have been
      a. detailed   *b.* general

_____ 6. Contingency plans _____ needed.
      a. were   *b.* were not

_____ 7. The _____ supervisory style was used for planning.
      a. autocratic   *c.* consultative
      b. participative   *d.* laissez-faire

_____ 8. Planning tools _____ needed.
      a. were   *b.* were not

9. If you were to do this exercise over, what would you do differently?

Conclusion and Sharing
(3–7 minutes)

The instructor gives the suggested answers to the integration section and students share what they learned from the experience.

Application
(2–4 minutes)

What did I learn from this experience? How will I use this knowledge in the future?

The Car Dealer's Game

Confidential Information to the Buyer

The following information is confidential. No one else has seen this information. However, you may give some or all of the information to other persons during the game.

You are a new and used car dealer in Washington, D.C. One day last week a diplomat from a foreign embassy requested you to locate a 1952 four-door Packard sedan. The diplomat wants the car for a present to his father back home. If this car is found in working order, he will pay $20,000, or $10,000 if in good but not running condition.

After three hours on the phone this morning, you have located a dealer in Columbia, South Carolina, with a 1952 four-door Packard in working order. You talked with the dealer personally. You asked the dealer in Columbia if you could meet tomorrow. You told her that you would stop in Columbia on your way to Florida for a two-week vacation. The dealer in Columbia agreed to meet you tomorrow for lunch.

You have arranged to have a truck ready to bring the 1952 sedan back to Washington. Your travel plans are complete.

You are now thinking about the meeting tomorrow with the car dealer in Columbia.

Confidential Information to the Seller

The following information is confidential. No one else has seen this information. However, you may give some or all of the information to other persons during the game.

You are a new and used car dealer in Columbia, South Carolina. Presently you have an inventory of 250 cars. Half of the cars are late models or new. Your oldest model is a 1952 four-door Packard sedan. You are known locally for offering used cars with a one-week guarantee—"If you can't start it, return it for a full refund in the first week after purchase."

You have decided to junk your older inventory of used cars. All pre-1960 cars will be sold next week to the local iron works at $300 per car. Today you have received a phone call from another dealer in Washington, D.C. This dealer is looking for a 1952 four-door Packard sedan in working order for a customer. The dealer heard that you had such a car. The dealer asked whether he could meet with you tomorrow to purchase the car. He said that he will stop on the way to Florida, where he will be vacationing for two weeks. You agree to meet tomorrow for lunch.

Source: The information for the car dealer negotiation came from Arch G. Woodside, Tulane University. The Car Dealer Game is part of a paper, "Bargaining Behavior in Personal Selling and Buying Exchanges," that was presented at the 1980 Eighth Annual Conference of the Association for Business Simulation and Experiential Learning (ABSEL). It is used with his permission.

3

Organizing and Delegating Work

Learning Objectives *After completing this chapter, you should be able to perform the following tasks:*

1. Explain why organization is important.

2. Describe the 10 organizational principles.

3. Explain the difference between line staff and functional authority and between centralized and decentralized authority.

4. Describe five ways an organization can be departmentalized.

5. Draw an organization chart and explain its structure.

6. State the three questions of the priority determination model and use the model to set priorities.

7. Discuss how to select and train an understudy.

8. List obstacles to delegation and signs of delegating too little, and describe how to overcome these obstacles.

9. State what and what not to delegate.

10. List the five steps in the delegation model and use the model to delegate assignments.

Key Terms To achieve our objectives in this chapter, it is important to understand the following 16 key terms. They are presented in the order in which they appear in the chapter. The list of key terms also appears in alphabetical order in the end-of-chapter review.

organizing	line authority	organizational chart
coordination	staff authority	departmentalization
responsibility	functional authority	priority
authority	centralized authority	understudy
accountability	decentralized authority	delegation steps
delegation		

On February 13, 1992, the front page of *The Wall Street Journal* stated that President Bush had fired Richard Truly, NASA's chief, in a dispute over management style and the direction of policies. The president's primary reason for firing Truly was Truly's unwillingness to delegate authority. Failure to delegate properly is one of the most common mistakes among supervisors. As a supervisor, you get the job done through employees, and the only way to do this is through delegating authority. In this chapter you will learn how to organize and delegate work.

I. Why Organization Is Important

As part of the planning process discussed in Chapter 2, you learned about the need to define the organization's purpose and develop strategic and operational objectives and plans. This entails designing an organizational structure that will allow the firm to achieve its stated objectives. Planning and organizing go hand in hand. When supervisors plan, they are deciding how to organize. **Organizing** *is the process of delegating and coordinating tasks and resources with responsibility, authority, and accountability clearly defined.* Assigning employees tasks and resources is the mechanism for putting plans into action. We tend to take organization for granted. However, without organization there would be havoc and chaos. As a supervisor, the better you organize, the better are your chances of success.

Benefits of Organization

A few of the many benefits of effective organization include the following:

LEARNING OBJECTIVE

1. Explain why organization is important.

- *Defined employee authority and responsibility.* Everyone knows what is expected of him or her.[1]
- *Equitable distribution of work.* Employees have a fair share of the organization's work.
- *Maximum utilization of resources.* Work is not duplicated.
- *Coordination of resources.* Employees work together to achieve objectives.
- *Employee job satisfaction.* Employees prefer a smoothly running organization.
- *Objectives being met.* You cannot meet objectives without organization.

II. Principles of Organization

In the early 1900s Henri Fayol, a French engineer, did pioneering work in administrative theory. Many of the principles of organization that Fayol developed are still used today. In this section, you will learn 10 of these principles: unity of direction; chain of command; span of control; specialization; coordination; balanced accountability, authority, and responsibility; delegation; employment stability; KISS; and flexibility.

Unity of Direction

Unity of direction means that there should be one manager and one plan for all activities directed toward the same objective. Unity of direction in the planning process starts with top-level management's defining the organization's purpose. This statement of purpose, in turn, gives unity of direction in developing a strategic plan. The strategic plan gives unity of direction in developing the operational plans. In terms of management levels, top management develops objectives and plans for the entire organization; middle managers develop objectives and plans for their divisions; and supervisors develop objectives and plans for their departments.

Chain of Command

Chain of command means that authority should be clearly delineated from the top to the bottom of the organization. All members of the firm should know to whom they report and who, if anyone, reports to them. The chain of command forms a hierarchy. In Exhibit 1–2, which demonstrates the three levels of management, you can see that the production manager reports to the president and that supervisors for products A, B, and C report to the production manager. The chain of command is also shown in the organizational chart in Exhibit 3–3.

The chain of command also identifies the normal path for communications. It is generally wise to handle your affairs through this chain of command. You should not go over your boss's head without his or her knowledge. Lisa, a young supervisor, wanted a raise and knew that the plant manager had the authority to grant them. She went directly to the plant manager, going over her boss's head. The plant manager told Lisa that he would have to talk to her boss before making the decision. Lisa's boss not only told the plant manager not to give Lisa the raise, but also lectured Lisa about following the proper channels.

There are times when a supervisor has to go to a higher authority, for example, when his or her boss is unavailable. In most organizations, it is also common for people from different departments to communicate outside the chain of command. It is best to conform to the practice of the organization, but don't betray confidences. If you talk behind a person's back, he or she will usually find out.

Each person should have only one boss. This is known as the *parity principle.* Having more than one boss can be frustrating. Karen once had a job in which she assisted five salespeople. One would give her an assignment, then another would tell her to do something else. The first salesperson would ask for her assignment, and get angry and yell because it wasn't done.

Span of Control

Span of control means that the number of employees reporting to a supervisor should be limited to the number that can be effectively supervised and controlled. The fewer employees supervised, the smaller or narrower the span of control. The more employees supervised, the greater or wider the span of control. There is no best number or best span of control. However, it is generally believed that supervisors can have a wider span of control than higher-level managers. Supervisors don't usually determine their span of control.

The Lockheed Company developed a useful system for determining the optimum span of control. Six variables influence the number of employees that can be supervised: similarity of functions, geographical closeness, complexity of functions, direction and control, coordination, and planning. A suggested span of control is determined by assigning a point value to each variable.

The trend today is toward a wider span of control. Several organizations have cut the number of managers. There will be fewer supervisors in the future, which means that they will have a wider span of control.[2]

Specialization

Specialization means that each person in the organization should have a clear, simple function. Related functions should be grouped together under a single boss. Employees generally have specialized jobs in a functional area such as accounting, production, or sales. Managers usually perform less specialized functions as they move up the management ladder. However, there is a debate in management literature over whether managers should be generalists or specialists. According to some authors, the increasing level of technology means that managers should become more specialized. Others believe that increasing technology requires a generalist who can change with the times. On the supervisory level, some, but not all, authors believe that the trend is toward greater specialization. In the future, supervisors may perform fewer activities.[3]

Coordination

Coordination means that all departments and individuals within the organization should work together to accomplish the strategic and operational objectives and plans. **Coordination** *is the process of integrating organizational or departmental tasks and resources to meet objectives.* Coordination requires conceptual skills. It is important that you coordinate all your department's resources (financial, physical, and human).

Balanced Responsibility, Authority, and Accountability

Balanced responsibility, authority, and accountability means that the responsibilities of each individual in the organization are clearly defined. Each individual is also given the authority needed to meet these responsibilities and is held accountable for meeting them.

Responsibility *is the obligation to achieve objectives by performing required activities.* When strategic and operational objectives are set, the people responsible for achieving them should be identified clearly. Supervisors are responsible for the results of their departments even though they do not actually make the goods or provide the services.

Authority *is the right to make decisions, issue orders, and utilize resources.* A supervisor is given responsibility for achieving departmental objectives. He or she must also have the authority to get the job done. Authority is delegated. The chief executive officer (CEO) is responsible for the results of the entire organization and delegates authority down the chain of command to the supervisors who are responsible for producing the goods or providing the services. We will discuss authority in more detail later in this chapter.

Accountability *is the evaluation of how well individuals meet their responsibility.* All members of the organization should be evaluated periodically and held accountable for achieving their objectives. They must also have the authority to get the job done. The CEO is accountable for the results of the entire organization. Periodically he or she meets with the board of directors to evaluate how well the organization is doing. This procedure goes down the chain of command to the supervisors, who are held accountable for the results of their individual departments. Supervisors, in turn, should hold each employee accountable for the discharge of his or her responsibilities.

Supervisors should delegate responsibility and authority to perform tasks, but they can never delegate their accountability. For example, Karen, a middle manager, delegates responsibility and authority for filling a special customer's order to supervisor Dave. As a supervisor should, Dave delegates the responsibility to employee Chris, who is accountable to Dave. The order was not sent out on time. The organization lost the customer. Karen goes to Dave, who is accountable to her. Dave takes the blame because he is accountable for his employee's performance. Dave, in turn, goes to Chris, who is accountable to him. Hansen states that supervisors should always take the blame for your employees, but give the credit to them.[4]

CONNECTIONS

1. Describe a situation in which you did or did not have balanced responsibility, authority, and accountability.

Delegation

Delegation means that decisions should be made at the lowest level with responsibility and authority assigned as far down the chain of command as possible. In the previous example, Karen delegated the customer's order to Dave. Karen let Dave decide how to fill the order. Dave, in turn, let Chris decide how to fill the order. Unfortunately, Chris was not capable of making the decision. Dave did not do an effective job of delegating. **Delegation** *is the process of assigning responsibility and authority for accomplishing an objective.* Perhaps no skill is more important in the development of a supervisor's career than the ability to delegate.[5] We will discuss delegation in detail later in this chapter.

Employment Stability

Employment stability means that the supervisor's department will be more efficient if employees remain in their jobs for long periods of time. It takes time to become proficient at a job. If there is a high turnover rate, a supervisor must spend a lot of time training new employees.

Employment stability does not mean that supervisors should not train employees to perform each other's jobs as the need arises; they should.

Employment stability also refers to the possibility of layoffs. If production fluctuates so that employees are continually hired and laid off, good employees will tend to find steadier employment elsewhere. Japanese businesses are true believers in employment stability. They generally offer lifetime employment. In the United States, some organizations are stabilizing employment. For example, IBM, despite a few tough years of decreased business and loss of profits, did not lay off employees to cut costs. Instead, the firm offered early retirement, transfers, or retraining to maintain employment stability. Some organizations, such as IBM, believe that the problems caused by layoffs outweigh the benefits of short-term savings.

KISS

KISS (keep it short and simple) means that the supervisor should make things as simple as possible. The more complicated something is, the less chance there is that it will work.[6] Keep things simple but not simplistic. Use 3 words to explain something rather than 10. Don't try to impress your employees; communicate with them. You should use the latest technology available, but explain its use and fully train employees so that the actual use is simple. Too often employees are given jobs or new equipment without sufficient training. A good case in point is the use of computers. Many employees use only a fraction of a computer's capabilities because the computer is too complex for them. Computer applications haven't been simplified through proper training. In writing this text, the author tried to keep the material simple so that it is easy for the student to understand. But he didn't make it simplistic so that students would feel they were being talked down to, or believe that the content would not really be helpful on a supervisor's job.

Flexibility

Flexibility means that there will always be exceptions to the rule. Many principles apply in some situations but not in others. For example, if an organization that is in financial difficulty did not lay employees off, it might go out of business, and everyone would lose.

LEARNING OBJECTIVE

2. Describe the 10 organizational principles.

Supervision is more of an art than a science because its principles cannot always explain and predict with precision. This is one of the major reasons that this book focuses on a situational supervisory approach.

The 10 organizational principles discussed in this section are summarized in Exhibit 3–1.

CONNECTIONS

2. Explain how a specific organization, preferably one you have worked for, does or does not follow any 2 of the 10 organizational principles.

III. Authority

As mentioned earlier, balanced authority is one of the principles of organization. In this section, you will learn the types of organizational authority, including formal and informal authority, line and staff authority, and centralized and decentralized organizational authority.

EXHIBIT 3-1   **ORGANIZATIONAL PRINCIPLES**

1. Unity of direction
2. Chain of command
3. Span of control
4. Specialization
5. Coordination
6. Balanced responsibility, authority, and accountability
7. Delegation
8. Employment stability
9. KISS
10. Flexibility

Types of Authority

Formal Authority: Formal authority starts at the top of the organization and is delegated down the chain of command. The owners (stockholders) of the corporation vote for the board of directors. The board is responsible for overseeing the performance of the entire organization and is given the authority to do so. The board is accountable to the stockholders. The board of directors, in turn, usually has authority to appoint the top managers (CEO and possibly presidents). The CEO is responsible for the day-to-day performance of the entire organization, and the presidents for their divisions. The CEO is accountable to the board of directors and the division presidents are accountable to the CEO. The presidents usually have the authority to appoint the vice presidents, who are responsible for a unit within the division. These vice presidents, in turn, are given the authority to manage their units and are accountable to the presidents. The vice presidents usually have the authority to appoint managers, who are responsible for part of the unit. The managers, in turn, are usually given the authority to appoint supervisors, who are responsible for individual departments. They are given the authority to run their departments and are held accountable by the manager.

The scope of authority narrows as it flows down the organization. The president has more authority than a vice president, who has more authority than a manager, who has more authority than a supervisor. Responsibility and authority flow down the organization, whereas accountability flows up the organization, as indicated in Exhibit 3-2.

Informal Authority: As a supervisor, you will be *given* formal authority, but you will have to *earn* informal authority, unless you have an established reputation coming into the job. The real test of authority is whether employees will accept and perform your orders. Employees will be more willing to follow orders if a supervisor has the following traits:

- *Technical skills.* Full knowledge of the job being done.
- *A performance record.* Has performed successfully in the past.
- *Human relations skills.* The ability to get along with others. How supervisors treat employees influences authority. It's not just the orders; it's how they're issued. Some people don't like to be told what to do. "Tell me what to do and I'll tell you where to go; ask me and I'll do it." We will discuss human relations skills in Chapter 6.
- *Trust.* Openness and honesty in relations.[7]

EXHIBIT 3–2   **SCOPE OF AUTHORITY**

Scope of Authority

Supervisors have the right to make decisions, issue orders, and utilize their departmental resources, all of which constitute their authority. A supervisor's authority should be clearly delineated.[8] A supervisor should also be aware of the scope of his or her authority in different situations.[9] Scope of authority can vary as follows:

1. *Inform authority.* The supervisor informs the boss of possible alternative actions.
2. *Recommend authority.* The supervisor lists alternative actions, analyzes them, and recommends one. However, the supervisor may not implement the recommendation without the boss's okay. The boss may require a different alternative if he or she does not agree with the supervisor's suggestion.
3. *Report authority.* The supervisor is free to select a course of action and carry it out. However, afterward the supervisor must report the action taken to the boss.
4. *Full authority.* The supervisor is free to make decisions and act without the boss's knowledge.

To illustrate, Noel, a supervisor, needs a new machine. If Noel had no authority, it would be up to his boss to get one. With inform authority, Noel would give his boss a list of possible machines to try and a description of their features, prices, and so forth. With recommend authority, Noel would analyze the machines' features and suggest which one to purchase. With report authority, Noel would actually purchase a machine, but would have to tell his boss about it, possibly by sending a copy of the purchase order. With full authority, Noel would purchase the machine without the boss's knowledge.

CONNECTIONS

3. Describe your scope of authority for a position you have held in a specific organization.

Line and Staff Authority

The distinction between line and staff authority is not always clear or universally accepted. **Line authority** *is the right to make decisions and issue orders down the chain of command.* Line managers are primarily responsible for achieving the organization's objectives, and staff people help them. **Staff authority** *is the right to advise and assist line personnel.* Production or operations and sales are usually line departments. In many organizations, financial activities are, too. Personnel and public relations are usually staff departments. An example will make the distinction more clear. Jean, a production (line) supervisor, needs a new employee. The personnel (staff) department will assist by recruiting possible candidates. Personnel may conduct interviews and tests and advise Jean of the results. It may recommend the top candidates for her to interview. It is the supervisor who decides who to hire, with the advice and assistance of staff people.

Staff's primary role is to advise and assist, but there are situations in which they can give orders to line personnel. **Functional authority** *is the right of staff personnel to issue orders to line personnel in established areas of responsibility.* For example, the maintenance department assists production supervisors by keeping the machines operating. But if maintenance determines that a machine is unsafe, the department may issue an order to a line supervisor not to use the machine. Or a payroll manager may order a staff supervisor to get employee time cards in on time.

Staff managers may have both staff and line authority. For example, Ted, a public relations (staff) manager, advises and assists all departments in the organization. However, Ted also issues orders (a line function) to the employees in his department.

There are two major types of staff positions. *General staff* work for only one manager. They are often called "assistant to" and help the manager in any way needed. *Specialist staff* help anyone in the organization who needs it. Personnel, public relations, and maintenance offer specialized advice and assistance.

As reported by Peters and Waterman in their best-seller *In Search of Excellence,* the best-run American companies have "lean" staffs.[10] In fact, during the 1980s many companies cut back on staff personnel. For example, Acme Chesterland's corporate staff was cut from 120 to 50. In other organizations, such as IBM and Bechtel, employees are rotated from line to staff positions.[11]

CONNECTIONS

4. Identify one or more staff positions (general, specialist, or both) in a specific organization. Does the position have any functional authority? What is it?

Centralized and Decentralized Authority

The major difference between centralized and decentralized authority is who makes the important decisions. In **centralized authority,** *important decisions are made by upper-level managers.* In **decentralized authority,** *important decisions are made by lower-level managers.*

The major advantages of decentralization include efficiency and flexibility (decisions are made quickly by people who are familiar with the situation), and development (managers are challenged and motivated to make decisions and solve their own problems).[12] The major advantages of centralization include control (uniform procedures are easier to control, and fewer risks are taken), and reduced duplication of work (few employees perform the same tasks, and specialized staff may be fully utilized).[13] Which type of authority works best? There is no simple answer. Sears, General Electric, and General Motors successfully used decentralized authority, and General Dynamics, McDonald's, and Kmart have successfully used centralized authority.

Authority is a continuum, with decentralized and centralized at each end. With the exception of small companies, which tend to be centralized, most organiza-

LEARNING
OBJECTIVE

3. Explain the difference
between line staff and
functional authority and
between centralized and
decentralized authority.

tions lie somewhere between the two extremes, but can be classified overall. The key to success seems to be having the right balance between the two extremes. This is what Peters and Waterman call "simultaneous loose-tight properties."[14] For example, General Motors is primarily decentralized, but it maintains centralized control over such areas as strategic planning and resource allocation. Production and sales are often decentralized, whereas finances and labor relations are centralized to provide uniformity and control throughout an organization. The rapid pace of change in the external environment means that most organizations need flexibility. As a result, the trend is toward greater decentralization.[15]

CONNECTIONS

5. Describe the type of authority (centralized or decentralized) used by a specific organization, preferably one you have worked for.

IV. Organizing the Entire Firm

In this section you will learn how entire organizations are structured, departmentalized, and coordinated.

Organizational Structure

Organizations are structured in two ways, formal and informal.

Formal Organization: The formal organizational structure defines the working relationships between the organization's members. The formal organization is usually illustrated through an **organizational chart,** *which is a graphic illustration of the organization's departments and their working relationships.* An example is given in Exhibit 3–3, an adaptation of General Motors' organization prior to the firm's restructuring in January 1984.

An organizational chart shows four major aspects of a firm:

- *The division and type of work.* In Exhibit 3–3 work is divided by type of automobile: Buick, Cadillac, Chevrolet, Oldsmobile, and Pontiac. Each vice president within a division is responsible for a function, or type of work, such as sales, production, or finance. The production middle managers are responsible for specific automobile models such as Corvette or Camaro. The supervisors are responsible for specific phases of production—engine, frame, body, paint, and so forth.

- *Chain of command.* As we follow the vertical lines in Exhibit 3–3, we see that the CEO reports to the board of directors, and the division presidents report to the CEO. The managers report to vice presidents, and supervisors report to the managers.

- *The level of management.* In Exhibit 3–3, the CEO and presidents are top-level management, the vice presidents and managers are middle-level management, and the supervisors are first-level management.

- *Departmentalization.* An organizational chart shows how the firm is divided into departments. In Exhibit 3–3, GM is organized by product. An organizational chart does not show the day-to-day activities performed or the structure of the informal organization.

EXHIBIT 3-3   **ORGANIZATIONAL CHART**

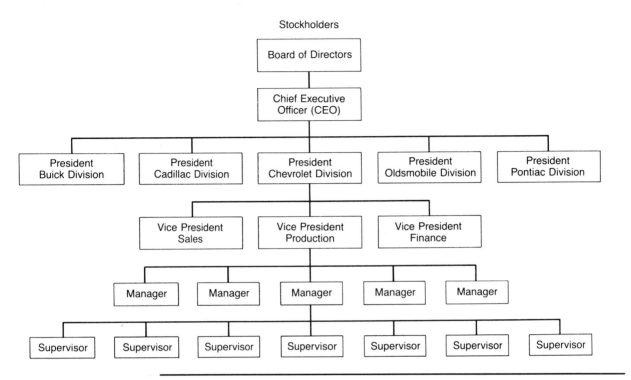

Note: Each vice president of the Chevrolet Division would have middle managers reporting to him or her, and each middle manager would have supervisors reporting. The other four divisions—Buick, Cadillac, Oldsmobile, and Pontiac—would all have their own vice presidents, middle managers, and supervisors, as Chevrolet does (shown here).

- *Succession planning.* For internal use some firms develop organization charts that include succession plans. The name of the person who will eventually replace the present manager is placed in the box under the present manager's name.

Informal Organization: The informal organization is more difficult to see and understand than the formal organization. The informal organization develops from employees' social interactions. Employees may get together during work, such as for lunch or a coffee break, or may see each other after work or on weekends.

Informal organizations or groups may develop to protect and support the members. Informal leaders emerge and are given authority by the group.[16] Although the authority is not given by management, an informal leader can be more powerful than a supervisor. This authority can be positive or negative. For example, the supervisor, Carol, may issue a departmental order to increase productivity. If the informal leader, Ron, tells the employees to go along with it, they probably will increase productivity. On the other hand, if Ron tells employees not to increase productivity, they probably will not.

Supervisors should try to understand the informal structure and gain the support of the informal leader without getting the group to resent either of them. One way to gain the support of the informal leader is through a consultative or participative supervisory style. Make information available to the informal leader and ask for his or her opinion on how the group will react. In the above example, it would be wise for Carol to tell Ron about a possible increase in productivity by *x* percent. If Ron says that he doesn't think the group will do it, Carol would be wise to ask what level increase would be acceptable. If Carol knows the group will be against any increase, it might be wise to back off, rather than fight and lose to the informal group. However, if the increase in productivity comes from a higher level of management, Carol will have to try to enforce the orders.

As a supervisor, the informal organization and leader will affect your ability to get the job done, and possibly even your ability to keep your job. Gain their support.

Departmentalization

Departmentalization *is the grouping of related activities to form internally focused (functional) or externally focused (product, customer, or territory) departments.* Specialized jobs must be grouped together. To determine how many activities should be grouped into one department, the decisions that must be made and the informal flow should be considered. A general rule is to group only specialists who need to interact.

When creating departments, Rosabeth Moss Kanter suggests avoiding "segmentalism." This refers to the way companies go about organizing by setting up walls between units, which cut off communication and damage both productivity and the quality of work life.[17]

Departments may be created around the operations or functions that the employees perform or the resources needed to accomplish the unit's work. This is *functional* departmentalization. *External* or *output* departmentalization is based on activities that focus on departmentalization factors outside the organization.

Functional Departmentalization

Functional departmentalization involves organizing departments around essential input activities, such as production, sales, and finance, that are managerial or technological functions. This functional approach is the most widely used form by small organizations. Its major advantages are the following: (1) it is cost efficient; (2) managing is easier because of the narrow range of skills involved in each department; and (3) because of the specialization, there is little duplication of effort. The major disadvantages are these: (1) little attention is paid to any single product or customer because all must be accommodated; and (2) this approach is not readily adaptable to change; decisions are often slow to get through to top managers. Exhibit 3–4 includes an organizational chart for a firm with an internal or functional focus.

External Departmentalization

Departments are created around products, customers, channels of distribution, or territories. Organizations that are large, have a wide diversity of products or types of customers, or cover a wide territory cannot departmentalize effectively around functions. Instead, they focus on factors that are external to the company. The advantages of external departmentalization include the following: (1) adequate attention can be given to the unique needs of the individual customer; and (2) changes can be made quickly. These are the major disadvantages: (1) duplication of effort; the organization may have, for example, production and sales departments for each product; and (2) managing is more difficult because a wide range of skills (general versus specialty) are needed.

Product departmentalization involves organizing departments around the products or services. Each department becomes, in a sense, a self-contained company, making and selling its own product or service. Departmentalization by product is often called divisionalization. The organizational chart in Exhibit 3–3 gives an example of product divisionalization, as does Exhibit 3–4.

Customer departmentalization involves organizing departments around the needs of different types of customers. The product may be changed and a different

EXHIBIT 3-4   **DEPARTMENTALIZATION**

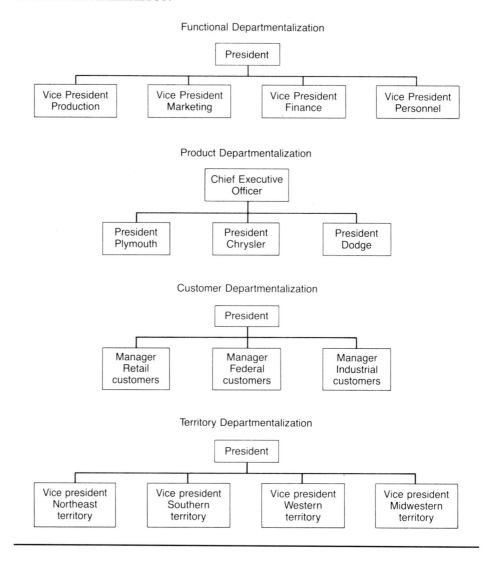

Functional Departmentalization

President

Vice President Production | Vice President Marketing | Vice President Finance | Vice President Personnel

Product Departmentalization

Chief Executive Officer

President Plymouth | President Chrysler | President Dodge

Customer Departmentalization

President

Manager Retail customers | Manager Federal customers | Manager Industrial customers

Territory Departmentalization

President

Vice president Northeast territory | Vice president Southern territory | Vice president Western territory | Vice president Midwestern territory

sales team may serve each group of customers. As with product departmentalization, in a sense, each department becomes a self-contained company. For example, IBM organized by customer because needs varied by industry and size of firm. Organizations that offer a wide diversity of products often use customer departments, as do some nonprofit organizations. For example, a counseling center may offer drug counseling, alcoholism counseling, family counseling, and so on. However, these usually are not self-contained units. Exhibit 3–4 includes an illustration of customer departmentalization.

Territory departmentalization involves organizing departments in each area in which the enterprise does business. The federal government does this. For example, the Federal Reserve System is divided into 12 geographic areas centered in cities such as Boston, New York, and San Francisco. Many large retailers (Sears, for example) are departmentalized by territory. Often the customers in each territory have different needs, for example, for winter clothes in the North and South. Exhibit 3–4 illustrates territory departmentalization.

Multiple Departmentalization: Many organizations, particularly large, complex organizations, use several of the departmental structures described. For example, General Motors Car and Truck Group is departmentalized by product. However,

LEARNING OBJECTIVE

4. Describe five ways an organization can be departmentalized.

each division is functionally departmentalized because each has its own manufacturing, engineering, marketing, and financial departments. GM is also departmentalized by territory, including foreign countries. Any mixture of structures can be used. Some organizations have functional departments with one manufacturing facility, and sales are departmentalized by territory with separate sales managers and salespeople in different areas.

Matrix departmentalization combines the functional and product departmental structures. With matrix departmentalization, the employee works for a functional department and is also assigned to one or more products or projects. The major advantage of matrix departmentalization is supposed to be flexibility. It allows the enterprise to temporarily organize for a project. With this structure, functional departments do not have to be duplicated for each project or product.

The major disadvantage is confusion. A matrix organization dilutes priorities. In addition, each employee has two bosses—a functional boss and a project boss. Role conflict can result when two people give orders. The matrix structure is too complex and confusing; a simple form (internal or external focus) is better. In fact, the popularity of the matrix structure is declining. Of America's best-run companies, only companies organized by project, such as Boeing, say they have a formal matrix structure. But at such companies as Boeing, there is no role conflict.[18]

Dr. W. Edward Deming states that "the employee must work within the system, but it is the manager's job to work on the system." In other words, it is your job as a supervisor to improve the organization—but to do this you must first understand it.[19]

LEARNING OBJECTIVE

5. Draw an organization chart and explain its structure.

CONNECTIONS

6. Draw a simple organization chart for a specific organization. Identify the type of departmentalization and staff positions used.

V. Organizing a Department

In this section you will learn about the ideal departmental organization. You will also learn how to set priorities and develop an understudy.

Developing the Ideal Departmental Organization

As a supervisor, you may be responsible for an existing department, rather than developing a new one. In either case, though, you should conceptualize the "ideal" organizational structure that is most efficient for achieving your department's objectives. This structure should be based on the 10 organizational principles discussed earlier in this chapter. The structure should also focus on how your department will work together with other departments to meet its objectives and the organization's objectives simultaneously.

You should plan improvements to make in the long run, such as the purchase of new equipment, and in the short run, such as redesigning work assignments. Supervisors have the authority to improve their departments, but often don't have the knowledge to make the most effective changes, whereas employees have the knowledge, but no authority.[20] Therefore, the supervisor should ask the employees who do the work how it can be reorganized. Use a consultative or participative supervisory style to develop your department.

Organization Tools

When organizing or reorganizing a department, supervisors have three main tools at their disposal:

Organizational Charts: Drawing an organizational chart for his or her department will help the supervisor visualize the work flow and structure and may give the supervisor ideas for improvement. The chart can also help employees, especially new ones, understand the department's functions and the relationships of their jobs to others.

Manuals: As discussed in Chapter 2, standing plans (policies, procedures, and rules) can be developed and written in a manual. This helps define many of the department's tasks and employee behavior.

Job Descriptions and Job Specifications: The job description states the primary responsibilities, tasks, and functions a job involves. Job specifications state the qualifications needed to perform a job. If employees clearly understand their responsibilities, organization and productivity will improve. If your department does not have job descriptions and specifications, you should consider developing some and putting them in writing. The personnel department should be able to help you. We will discuss job descriptions and specifications in more detail in Chapter 9.

Setting Priorities

One important aspect of organizing a department is setting priorities. At any time there will be several activities to perform. How the supervisor selects the order in which these activities will be completed can affect his or her success. This order involves assigning priorities to the activities. A **priority** *is the preference given to one activity over other activities.* A supervisor's department may not have time to do everything the supervisor wants done, but it does have time to do what's really important—this means having priorities for certain tasks. When scheduling and allocating work, the supervisor should always assign priorities to the tasks and communicate these priorities to employees; alternatively, employees may be involved in selecting priorities. How does a supervisor determine what is important? The major question the supervisor should answer is "Which activity will be the most beneficial in meeting my departmental objectives?" The supervisor's boss is also a source of priorities. When in doubt, check with the boss.

As a first step in assigning priorities, answer the questions in Model 3–1.[21] After the three questions are answered, a high, medium, or low priority can be assigned. The task should be delegated if the answer to question 1 is no. A high priority is assigned if you answer yes to all three questions. It's your responsibility, calling for quick personal action. A medium priority is assigned if you answer yes to question 1 and no to question 2 or 3. You must be personally involved, and it's your primary responsibility, or quick action is needed. A low priority is assigned if you answer yes to question 1 and no to questions 2 and 3. You must be involved, but quick action is not needed. Application Situation 3–3 develops your skill in assigning priorities using this model.

MODEL 3–1   **PRIORITY DETERMINATION QUESTIONS**

1. Do I personally need to be involved because of my unique knowledge or skills? (yes or no)

2. Is the task within my area of responsibility, or will it affect the performance or finances of my department? (yes or no)

3. When is the deadline? _____
   Is quick action needed? (yes or no)

LEARNING OBJECTIVE

6. State the three questions of the priority determination model and use the model to set priorities

Exhibit 3–5 is a to-do list based on the priorities assigned using the model. Feel free to make copies and use it on the job. List each activity on one or more lines and give a priority to each. Remember that priorities may change several times during the day because of unexpected events. You should look at the high (H) priorities and select the most important one to do. When it's done, cross it off and select the next until all high-priority activities are done. Do the same with the medium (M) priorities, and then the low (L) priorities. Be sure to update the priorities. As deadlines come nearer, priorities will change.

Developing an Understudy

Every supervisor occasionally spends time away from the job owing to emergencies, vacations, and so forth. Part of organizing your department is having someone reliable to keep operations going while you are away. The **understudy** *is the supervisor's temporary replacement.* Remember, too, that you cannot be promoted if you don't have an understudy ready to take your place when you leave.[22] Two important steps in developing an understudy are selection and training.

Selecting an Understudy

In some organizations, such as unionized firms, the supervisor cannot select his or her understudy. Assuming you can, look for an employee with the skills necessary for supervision:

1. *Technical skills.* The person should understand the technical aspects of the job but doesn't have to be the most skilled.
2. *Conceptual skills.* The understudy should understand or be capable of understanding how the different parts contribute to the department and to the organization as a whole. The understudy needs good judgment to solve problems and make decisions.
3. *Human relation skills.* Your choice should be respected by the department members and regarded as a leader. The informal leader is a likely candidate. However, once chosen as an understudy, that person may no longer be viewed as the informal leader.

In addition to supervisory skills, the understudy needs outstanding or high capability. He or she must be dependable and willing and able to accept greater responsibilities.[23]

After deciding on one or more possible candidates, talk to each before making a choice. You do not have to announce your choice until you go away. At that time, tell your employees that the understudy will be in charge when you are away. Waiting gives you time to determine whether the understudy will work out.

Training an Understudy

There are no hard and fast rules for developing understudies. However, start by delegating some of your easy activities. As the understudy develops gradually, delegate more complex tasks. If problems arise, include the understudy in solving them. Let the understudy attend supervisory meetings with you, if the company allows it.

Be sure not to overload the understudy or give the person responsibility beyond his or her capability level. Never place an understudy in a sink or swim situation. His or her success is your success.[24] The person you chose has an outstanding or high capability level as an employee, but as an understudy is beginning with low to moderate capability. As a situational supervisor, you must adapt your style to the understudy's capability and gradually change as the understudy's level increases.

LEARNING OBJECTIVE

7. Discuss how to select and train an understudy.

EXHIBIT 3-5   **TO-DO LIST**

	#1 Involvement needed	#2 Responsibility performance/finances	#3 Quick action/deadline	Time needed	Priority

D Delegate — no to #1

H High priority — yes to all three questions (YYY)

M Medium priority — yes to #1 and #2 or #3 (YYN or YNY)

L Low priority — yes to #1, no to #2 and #3 (YNN)

Activity					

VI. Delegation

The definition of supervision states that the first-line manager is responsible for achieving organizational objectives "through employees." As mentioned previously, delegation is the process of assigning responsibility and authority to employees to accomplish an objective. Xerox Learning Systems identified delegation as one of the six skills critical to success at the supervisory level.[25] Cameron and Whetten's research also identified delegation as a critical management skill.[26] If you want to be a successful supervisor, you must delegate effectively.

In this section we will discuss the benefits of delegating, obstacles to delegating, determination of what and what not to delegate and whom to delegate to, and the five steps in delegation.

Benefits of Delegation

Some of the benefits of delegation include the following:[27]

- Delegation increases the supervisor's discretionary time. Delegating frees up time to think and plan.[28] This can allow you to take on more of your boss's duties and become an understudy ready for promotion.
- Delegation helps develop employees' capabilities.
- Delegation demonstrates trust and confidence, which lead to better human relations and job performance.
- Delegation may improve motivation and commitment to the department and organization.[29] However, a recent study cast doubt on the relationship.[30]
- Delegation often improves the quality of decisions. Because it is a means of involving employees, delegation implies moving decision-making authority from one level to a lower level and distributing power.[31] Employees are often more knowledgeable than supervisors about certain problems.
- Delegation allows employees, the supervisor, the department, and the organization to get more work done with fewer resources.
- Delegation enhances the supervisor's personal power within the organization.
- Delegation helps the supervisor to overcome stress.[32] (Stress is discussed in more detail in Chapter 17.)

Obstacles to Delegation

Obstacles to delegation are found in three areas.

1. Obstacles Relating to the Organization: Your boss may affect your ability to delegate. A boss who delegates effectively will train you because supervisors learn from their bosses. However, if your boss is a poor delegator, you don't have to be one too. In any case, know what can and cannot be delegated, according to your boss. You can ask if you are in doubt.

Another obstacle to delegation is the department's work load. If employees are already too busy, time management and productivity improvements may be needed. (These techniques will be discussed later.) If this doesn't relieve the problem, a request for overtime or additional part- or full-time help may be warranted. One researcher believes that situational constraints, rather than personal predispositions, affect delegation in this context.[33]

2. Obstacles Relating to Supervisors: Some supervisors are reluctant to delegate for a variety of reasons:

- *The "I can do it better" attitude.* Being able to do the work better than employees can is not the supervisor's responsibility; getting the work done through employees is. Delegation means letting others become the expert, and hence the best.[34] Don't be a perfectionist; define acceptable standards and be satisfied.

- *The "I can do it faster" attitude.* It can be frustrating to watch others take time doing something you could do twice as fast.[35] Remember, though, part of a supervisor's responsibility is to develop employees' capabilities. Some supervisors don't delegate because they believe that they can do a task in less time than it takes to train an employee to do it. This may be true for a unique task. However, for recurring tasks, taking a few hours' time to train an employee may save the supervisor hundreds of hours in the future.

- *Lack of delegation skills.* Some supervisors lack the confidence to develop delegation skills.[36] Following the guidelines and steps described at the end of this chapter will help you develop these skills. Like any skill, delegation must be developed over time. Supervisors need to practice on simple tasks and gradually move to more complex work.

- *Trust and fear.* Some supervisors don't trust their employees. Supervisors must learn to believe that their employees will learn even if the supervisor can do the work better or faster.[37] Some supervisors fear that employees will make mistakes, or that the job will not get done and he or she will be accountable. In getting the job done through others, risk is part of the supervisory function. The delegation steps at the end of this chapter will decrease the risk. The supervisor must accept the fact that delegation can be an emotionally wrenching process.[38] Supervisors may also fear that employees will outshine them. They must remember that it is their job to delegate.

- *Lack of understanding of their job.* Savary, a management consultant, contends that the major reason supervisors don't delegate is that they don't understand their job.[39] Many supervisors were the best employees. They are often promoted without supervisory training. It is difficult to go from "doer" to "delegator" without an understanding of the change in your position.

3. Obstacles Relating to Employees: Employees may also be reluctant to accept delegated responsibility.

- Some people fear failure or lack confidence. The supervisor must develop employees' confidence through proper training and encouragement on a progressive basis.

- Some people fear criticism from the boss. The supervisor should help employees learn through their mistakes, rather than criticizing them. This topic will be discussed further in later chapters.

- Some employees lack incentive or initiative. They believe that there is no reward for assuming increased responsibility. The supervisor must motivate employees. (Motivation will be discussed in Chapter 11.) Supervisors must also realize that not all employees will want increased responsibility.[40]

Signs of Delegating Too Little

These are some signs indicating that a supervisor does not delegate enough:

- Working longer hours than employees.
- Taking work home.

LEARNING
OBJECTIVE

8. List obstacles to
delegation and signs
of delegating too little,
and describe how to
overcome these obstacles.

- Performing employee tasks.
- Being behind in supervisory work.
- Continual feeling of pressure and stress.
- Rushing to meet deadlines.
- Employees' seeking approval before acting.[41]

CONNECTIONS

8. Describe an obstacle to delegation that you have observed.

What and What Not to Delegate

What to Delegate

The supervisor must decide what and what not to delegate. The following discussion offers some guidelines in making the decision.[42]

As a general guide, the supervisor should delegate anything that he or she does not have to be personally involved with because of his or her unique knowledge or skill. Some possibilities include the following:

- *Paperwork:* reports, memos, letters, and so on.
- *Routine tasks:* checking inventory, ordering, and so on.
- *Technical matters:* have top employees deal with technical questions and problems.
- *Tasks with developmental potential:* give employees the opportunity to learn new things. Prepare them for advancement.
- *Solving employees' problems:* train them to solve their own problems; don't solve problems for them, unless their capability is low.

What Not to Delegate

As a general guide, the supervisor should not delegate anything that he or she needs to be personally involved with because of his or her unique knowledge or skill. Typical examples include these:

- *Personnel matters:* hiring, firing, disciplining, counseling, resolving conflicts, performance appraisals, and so on.
- *Confidential activities:* confidential matters should not be delegated unless the supervisor has permission to do so.
- *Crises:* there is no time to delegate.
- *Activities delegated to supervisors:* for example, if a supervisor is assigned to a committee, he or she shouldn't send someone else without permission.

LEARNING
OBJECTIVE

9. State what and what not
to delegate.

Peter Drucker says: "The purpose of delegation is to enable the supervisor to concentrate on his or her own job, not to delegate it away." He also warns the supervisor against allowing employees to delegate the job back to him or her. Drucker recommends saying something such as, "It's your job. Do it yourself. Just keep me up on what you're doing."[43]

Determining Whom to Delegate To

Once you have decided what to delegate, you must select an employee to do the task. President Reagan once said, "Select the best people you can find and delegate." But don't make his administration's mistake in the Irangate situation by confusing delegation of authority with abdication of responsibility.[44] An obvious choice is the understudy. But don't overload that person. Balance the work load.

When selecting an employee to delegate to, be sure that he or she has the capability to get the job done right. Consider your employees' talents and interests when making a selection.[45] Use employees' full potential.[46] A supervisor may consult with several employees to determine their interest before making the final choice.

Steps in Delegating

There are five steps in delegating that will be discussed in detail in the pages that follow. The **delegation steps** are *(1) explaining the need for delegating and the reasons that the employee was selected; (2) setting objectives that define responsibility, the scope of authority, and the deadline; (3) developing a plan; (4) establishing control checkpoints; and (5) holding employees accountable.*

Following these five steps can increase your chances of successfully delegating.

Step 1. Explain the Need for Delegating and the Reasons That the Employee Was Selected: It is helpful for the employee to understand why the assignment must be completed. In other words, how will the department or organization benefit? Informing employees helps them get the big picture and realize the importance of their job. Telling the employee why he or she was selected should make him or her feel valued. The employee should think that his or her time and talents are being used wisely.[47] Make employees aware of how they will benefit from the assignment. Don't use the "it's a lousy job but someone has to do it" approach. If step 1 is completed successfully, the employee should be motivated or at least willing to do the assignment.

Step 2: Set Objectives That Define Responsibility, the Scope of Authority, and the Deadline: Delegation is planning. As stated in Chapter 2, the first step in planning is setting objectives. The objectives should state the end result the employee is accountable for achieving. They should also define the kind of authority the employee has, as the following choices illustrate:

- Make a list of all supplies on hand and present it to the supervisor each Friday at 2:00 (inform authority).

- Fill out a supply purchase order and present it to the supervisor each Friday at 2:00 (recommend authority).

- Fill out and sign a purchase order for supplies; send it to the purchasing department with a copy put in the supervisor's in-basket each Friday by 2:00 (report authority).

- Fill out and sign a purchase order for supplies and send it to the purchasing department each Friday by 2:00, keeping a copy (full authority).

In each of these options, the objective, responsibility, and authority should be clear to the employee being delegated the task. If the objective is to be put in writing, it might be a good idea to include it on an operational plan sheet such as the one in Exhibit 2–6.

Research indicates that managers change the latitude they give employees when delegating.[48] The scope of authority delegated to an employee should be appropriate for his or her capability level. A low-capability employee (C-1) should probably only have inform authority. An outstanding employee (C-4) can have full authority. Ideally, a supervisor should delegate to an employee with high to outstanding capability. However, such employees are not always available. When an employee proves that he or she is capable, the supervisor should increase the scope of authority delegated to that employee. With time, the employee will hopefully get to full authority.

Step 3. Develop a Plan: Once the objectives are set, a plan is needed to achieve them. The plan may be written on the operational planning sheet. Part of the plan may be to train the employee.

When developing a plan, be sure to identify the resources needed to achieve the objectives, and give the employee the authority necessary to obtain the resources. Inform all parties the employee must work with of his or her authority. For example, if an employee is doing a personnel report, the supervisor should contact the personnel department and tell them the employee must have access to the necessary information.

In developing the plan, the supervisor should use the supervisory style appropriate to the employee's capability level for the delegated assignment, as shown in Model 1–1. When the employee has a low capability level, the supervisor should use an autocratic supervisory style and describe to the employee (verbally, in writing, or both) how to achieve the objective in detail. With moderate capability levels, the supervisor should use the consultative supervisory style and include the employee's input into the plan but oversee performance at major stages. When the employee has a high capability level, the supervisor should use a participative supervisory style, letting the employee develop the plan with appropriate direction and approval, focusing on checking the end result. With outstanding employees, the supervisor should use a laissez-faire style, letting the employee develop the plan without direction and approval. Do not even check end results. The laissez-faire supervisory style is the ideal, but it is generally not used as often as the other styles.

Step 4. Establish Control Checkpoints: The deadline for completion should be stated in the objectives. However, it is often advisable to check progress at predetermined times (control checkpoints). As Drucker puts it, "Build information flow into the delegation system right from the start." The supervisor and employee must agree on the form (phone call, visit, memo, or detailed report) and time frame (daily, weekly, or after specific steps are completed but before going on to the next step) for information regarding the assignment.[49] We will discuss control methods in the next chapter.

When establishing control, the supervisor should consider the employee's capability level. The lower the capability, the more frequent the checks; the higher the capability, the less frequent the checks.

It is helpful to describe the control checkpoints in writing on an operational planning sheet, making copies so that the parties involved and the supervisor have a record to refer to. In addition, all parties involved should record the control checkpoints on their calendars. If the employee to whom the task was delegated does not report as scheduled, follow up to find out why the person did not report, and get the information.

LEARNING OBJECTIVE

10. List the five steps in the delegation model and use the model to delegate assignments.

Step 5. Hold Employees Accountable: Studies show that employees perform better when their performance is measured and evaluated.[50] The supervisor should evaluate performance at each control checkpoint to date and upon completion, and praise or reprimand as appropriate. (We will discuss this further in Chapter 11.)

The five steps of the delegation process are summarized in Model 3–2.

CONNECTIONS

9. Select a manager, preferably one you have worked for, and analyze how well that person implements the five steps of delegation. Which steps does he or she typically follow and not follow?

MODEL 3-2

THE FIVE STEPS OF THE DELEGATION PROCESS

Step 1. Explain the need for delegating and the reasons that the employee was selected.

Step 2. Set objectives that define responsibility, the scope of authority, and the deadline.

Step 3. Develop a plan.

Step 4. Establish control checkpoints.

Step 5. Hold employees accountable.

R E V I E W

Select one or more methods: (1) fill in the missing key terms from memory; (2) match the key terms from the end of the review with their definitions below; (3) copy the key terms in order from the list at the beginning of the chapter.

_____ is the process of delegating, and coordinating tasks and resources with clearly defined responsibility, authority, and accountability.

The 10 principles of organization are unity of direction; chain of command (reporting relationships); span of control (limited number of subordinates); specialization (clear, simple function); _____ (the process of integrating organizational or departmental tasks and resources to meet objectives); balanced _____ (the obligation to achieve objectives by performing the required activities), _____ (the right to make decisions, issue orders, and utilize resources), and _____ (the evaluation of how well individuals meet their responsibilities); _____ (the process of assigning responsibility and authority to accomplish an objective; employment stability (long-term employment); KISS (keep it short and simple); and flexibility (all principles should be implemented to best fit the needs of the organization).

Formal authority is established by top management and is delegated down the chain of command, whereas accountability flows up the chain of command. Informal authority is earned over time rather than delegated. The scope of authority may be informing, recommending, reporting, or full authority.

_____ is the right to make decisions and issue orders down the chain of command, whereas _____ is the right to advise and assist line personnel. _____ is the right of staff personnel to issue orders to line personnel in established situations. There are general and specialist staff positions. With _____ , important decisions are made by upper-level managers, but with _____ , important decisions are made by lower-level managers.

The formal organizational structure is usually shown by an

_____ , which illustrates the organization's departments

and their working relationships. It shows the division and type of work, chain of

command, levels of management, and the type of _____ ,

the grouping of related activities to form internally focused (functional) or

externally focused (product, customer, or territory) departments. The informal

organization is more difficult to see and understand because it develops from

social interactions.

The supervisor should conceptualize the "ideal" departmental structure and

work toward achieving it. A _____ gives preference to one

activity over other activities. When determining priorities, the supervisor should

answer the question "Which activity will be most beneficial in meeting

departmental objectives?" When assigning activities a priority, the supervisor

should answer three questions. (1) Do I personally need to be involved because

of my unique knowledge or skill? (2) Is the task within my area of responsibility,

or will it affect the performance or finances of my department? (3) Is quick

action needed? A no response to question 1 means that the task should be

delegated. Three yes answers mean that the task has a high priority. Two yes

responses mean a medium priority, and two no answers a low priority. The

supervisor should select and develop an _____ as a

temporary replacement.

Delegation is an important skill critical to success as a supervisor. Delegation

has many benefits. When delegating, the supervisor may have to deal with

obstacles relating to the organization, himself or herself, and employees.

Working longer hours than employees and taking work home are two of the

many indications that the supervisor does not delegate enough. It is important

that the supervisor determine what (paperwork, routine tasks, technical matters,

and tasks with developmental potential) and what not (personnel matters,

confidential activities, crises, activities delegated to the supervisor) to delegate.

As a general guide, the supervisor should delegate all activities in which he or

she does not need to be personally involved because of his or her unique

knowledge or skill. When selecting an employee to delegate to, be sure to

consider employee talents, interests, and capability level for the task. The

_____ are as follows: step 1, explain the need for

delegating and why the employee was selected; step 2, set objectives that define

responsibility, the scope of authority, and the deadline; step 3, develop a plan;

step 4, establish control checkpoints; and step 5, hold employees accountable.

KEY TERMS

accountability	functional authority
authority	line authority
centralized authority	organizing
coordination	organizational chart
decentralized authority	priority
delegation	responsibility
delegation steps	staff authority
departmentalization	understudy

REFERENCES

1. Charles Denova, "Requirements of Being a Better Supervisor," *Supervision,* October 1984, p. 5.

2. K. Hall, S. Kerr, and L. Broedling, "The First-Line Supervisor: Phasing Out or Here to Stay," *Academy of Management Review,* January 1986, pp. 103–17.

3. Ibid.

4. M. R. Hansen, "Better Supervision from A to W," *Supervisory Management,* August 1985, p. 3.

5. Charles Pringle, "Seven Reasons Why Managers Don't Delegate," *Management Solutions,* November 1986, p. 26.

6. Hansen, "Better Supervision from A to W," p. 35.

7. Jack Phillips, "Authority: It Doesn't Just Come with the Job," *Management Solutions,* August 1986, pp. 36–37.

8. Richard Gordon, "Six Rules of Getting Started in Management," *Supervisory Management,* December 1984, p. 25.

9. Jack Phillips, "The First Step toward Increasing Supervisory Authority," *Management Solutions,* September 1986, p. 37.

10. Thomas Peters and Robert Waterman, *In Search of Excellence* (New York: Harper & Row, 1982), pp. 3, 6, 18.

11. Ibid., p. 312.

12. Gerald Graham, *Understanding Human Relations* (Chicago: Science Research Associates, 1982), p. 137.

13. Ibid.

14. Peters and Waterman, *In Search of Excellence,* pp. 318–25.

15. P. Levinson, "Why Decentralize," *Management Review,* October 1985, p. 50.

16. Charles Hall, "The Informal Organization Chart," *Supervisory Management,* January 1986, pp. 40–42.

17. Thomas Hortan, "The Adolescence of Management: Can Business Survive It?" *Management Review,* December 1984, p. 3.

18. Peters and Waterman, *In Search of Excellence,* p. 307.

19. Hortan, "The Adolescence of Management," p. 3.

20. S. Baer, "Employee-Managed Work Redesign: New Quality Worklife Development," *Supervision,* March 1986, p. 7.

21. Model adapted from *Training Program Materials* published by Harbridge House, Inc., Boston. For more information on these training programs, contact the publisher directly.

22. Hansen, "Better Supervision from A to W," p. 37.

23. Vermont Royster, "Life with Barney at *The Wall Street Journal,*" *The Wall Street Journal,* March 16, 1987, p. 22.

24. Hansen, "Better Supervision from A to W," p. 37.

25. John Franco, "Supervision: Critical Performance Link," *Industry Week,* April 1985, p. 14.

26. David Whetten and Kim Cameron, *Developing Management Skills* (Glenview, Ill.: Scott Foresman and Company, 1984), p. 5.

27. Ibid., p. 355.

28. Timothy Firnstahl, "Letting Go," *Harvard Business Review,* September–October 1986, p. 16.

29. J.P. Davidson, "Successful Staff Motivation Hinges on Enthusiastic Delegators," *Data Management,* June 1986, p. 17.

30. Carrie Leana, "Predictors and Consequences of Delegation," *Academy of Management Journal,* December 1986, p. 770.

31. Ibid.

32. Firnstahl, "Letting Go," p. 14.

33. Leana, "Predictors and Consequences of Delegation," p. 772.

34. Firnstahl, "Letting Go," p. 14.

35. Ibid.

36. Pringle, "Seven Reasons Why Managers Don't Delegate," p. 27.

37. Kenneth Hall and Lawson Savery, "Tight-Rein, More Stress," *Harvard Business Review,* January–February 1986, p. 162.

38. Firnstahl, "Letting Go," p. 18.

39. M. Savary, "Ineffective Delegation—Symptom or Problem?" *Supervisory Management,* June 1985, p. 29.

40. Hansen, "Better Supervision from A to W," p. 34.

41. "Setting Up to Supervision: Mastering Delegation," *Supervisory Management,* October 1981, pp. 17–18.

42. Trezzie Pressley and Donald Caruth, "Key Factors of Positive Delegation," *Supervisory Management,* July 1984, pp. 6–8.

43. "Drucker on Delegation: Not as Easy as It Seems," *Management Review,* July 1984, p. 4.

44. Peter Drucker, "Management Lessons of Irangate," *The Wall Street Journal,* March 24, 1987, p. 36.

45. Hansen, "Better Supervision from A to W," p. 33.

46. Pressley and Caruth, "Key Factors of Positive Delegation," p. 8.

47. Ibid., p. 6.

48. Leana, "Predictors and Consequences of Delegation," p. 771.

49. "Drucker on Delegation," p. 4.

50. Christina Shalley and Greg Oldham, "Effects of Goal Setting Difficulty and External Evaluation of Intrinsic Motivation," *Academy of Management Journal,* September 1985, p. 628.

APPLICATION SITUATIONS

**Principles of
Organization**

AS 3–1

Identify each statement in terms of the following organizational principles:

a. unity of direction   *f.* balanced responsibility, authority, and accountability

b. chain of command   *g.* delegation

c. span of control   *h.* employment stability

d. specialization   *i.* KISS

e. coordination   *j.* flexibility

_____ 1. Saul told me to pick up the mail. When I got to the post office, I did not have a key, so the postal worker wouldn't give me the mail.

_____ 2. The players on the football team are on the offensive or defensive squad.

_____ 3. "I cannot understand Professor Suffield's lectures; they go right over my head. I need a dictionary to figure out what he's saying."

_____ 4. Middle manager: "I want an employee to deliver this package but I can't order one to do it directly. I have to have one of my supervisors give the order."

_____ 5. "There has been an accident, and the ambulance is on the way. Sue, call Doctor Kildare and have her get to emergency room C in 10 minutes. Bill, get the paperwork ready. Karen, prepare emergency room C."

Departmentalization

AS 3–2

Identify the five organizational charts below as being departmentalized by one of the following methods:

a. function   *d.* territory

b. product/service   *e.* matrix

c. customer

6. G.O.O.D. Consulting Company

7. Production Department

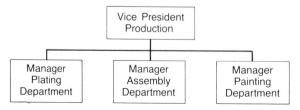

8. Worldwide Marriage Encounter—West County

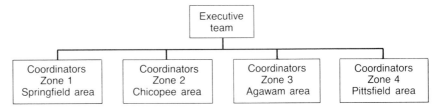

9. Toy Manufacturing Company

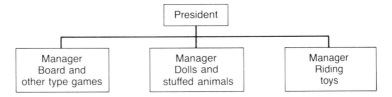

10. Publishing Company

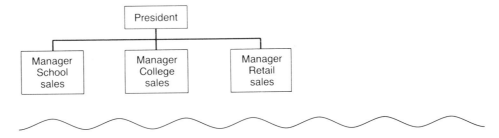

Priority Determination

AS 3-3

You are the first-line supervisor of a production department in a large company. On the following page is your to-do list. It has 10 items on it. Assign priorities to each item as high, medium, low, or delegate.

- *Step 1.* Answer the three priority determination questions by placing a Y for yes or N for no in the columns labeled #1, #2, and #3.
- *Step 2.* Go to the priority determination section and select the appropriate priority.
- *Step 3.* Write the letter H, M, L, or D in the "priority" column. Because you are not the actual supervisor, it is difficult to determine the time needed (column #3). You may leave it blank.

TO-DO LIST	Questions				
Priority Determination	**#1**	**#2**	**#3**		
D Delegate priority — no to #1 H High priority — yes to all three questions (YYY) M Medium priority — yes to #1 and #2 or #3 (YYN or YNY) L Low priority — yes to #1, no to #2 and #3 (YNN) **Activity**	Involvement needed	Responsibility performance/finances	Quick action/deadline	Time needed	Priority
11. John, the sales manager, told you that three customers stopped doing business with the company because your products have decreased in quality.					
12. Your secretary, Rita, told you that there is a salesperson waiting to see you. He does not have an appointment. You don't do any purchasing.					
13. Jan, a vice president, wants to see you to discuss a new product to be introduced in one month.					
14. John, the sales manager, sent you a memo stating that the sales forecast was incorrect. Sales are expected to increase by 20 percent starting next month. Inventories are as scheduled.					
15. Dan, the personnel director, sent you a memo informing you that one of your employees has resigned. Your turnover rate is one of the highest in the company.					
16. Rita told you that a John Smith called while you were out. He asked you to return his call, but wouldn't state why he was calling. You don't know who he is or what he wants.					
17. Sandy, one of your best workers, wants an appointment to tell you about a situation that happened in the shop.					
18. John called and asked you to meet with him and a prospective customer for your product. The customer wants to meet you.					
19. Tom, your boss, called and said that he wants to see you about the decrease in the quality of your product.					
20. In the mail you got a note from Frank, the president of your company, and an article from *The Wall Street Journal*. The note said FYI (for your information).					

Source: Adapted from Harbridge House Training Materials (Boston).

Custom Programmers

About seven years ago, Bill and Bob Smith began Custom Programmers in Springfield, Massachusetts, where they both lived. They went to local businesspeople and told them that they could develop computer programs to meet their unique needs at a low cost. Banks, retail stores, manufacturers, and several other businesses hired them. As the number of clients grew, the Smiths hired additional programmers who were highly skilled and could develop programs for any customer. Within three years, the firm had five professional programmers to whom they simply assigned jobs. Custom Programmers serviced the entire western Massachusetts area. Any programmer could be sent to do a programming job for any organization.

In the fifth year of business, Bob Smith moved to the Boston area and opened a new office servicing eastern Massachusetts. As the number of clients for this office increased, Bob would borrow programmers from the western Massachusetts office, and also hired additional programmers.

Within seven years, the firm offered computer programming services throughout the entire state, with Worcester being the boundary between offices. Each office has five programmers who cover different areas. With one exception, all the programmers are highly skilled and need very little direction and supervision. However, when the work load is uneven, programmers are shifted from one end of the state to the other.

Answer the following questions supporting your answers in writing in the space provided between questions.

_____ 1. Organization is important to Custom Programmers.
      a. true   *b.* false

_____ 2. The span of control would be considered
      a. narrow   *b.* wide

_____ 3. Custom Programmers follows the principle of specialization.
      a. true   *b.* false

_____ 4. Coordination should be a _____ concern.
      a. major   *b.* minor

_____ 5. Custom Programmers follows the flexibility principle of organization.
      a. true   *b.* false

_____ 6. Custom Programmers uses _____ authority.
      a. line   *b.* line and staff   *c.* functional

_____ 7. Custom Programmers' authority should be
      a. centralized   *b.* decentralized

_____ 8. Custom Programmers is departmentalized by
        a. function   *d.* territory
        b. product   *e.* matrix
        c. customer

_____ 9. From the case, one can understand Custom Programmers' informal organization.
        a. true   *b.* false

_____ 10. The most appropriate organizational tool for Custom Programmers to use is
        a. an organizational chart   *b.* a manual   *c.* a job description and specification

11. Would you recommend any organizational changes to Bill and Bob? What would these be?

IN-CLASS SKILL-BUILDING EXERCISE

Delegating Authority

SB 3–1

Objective: To experience and develop skills in delegating authority.

Experience: You will delegate, be delegated to, and observe the delegation of a task, and then evaluate the effectiveness of the delegated task.

Procedure 1

Break into as many groups of three as possible with the remainder in groups of two. Each person in the group picks a number between 1 and 3. Number 1 will be the first to delegate a task, then 2, and then 3. The level of difficulty of the delegation will increase with the number.

Each person then reads his or her delegation situation below (1, 2, or 3) and plans how he or she will delegate the task. If you prefer, you can use an actual delegation from a past or present job. Just be sure to fully explain the situation to the delegation. Be sure to follow the five delegation steps in this chapter. You may use the operational planning sheet in Exhibit 2–6 to help you when you delegate. An observer sheet is included at the end of this exercise for rating each delegation.

Delegation Situation 1: Delegator 1, you are a college student with a paper due in three days for your 10 A.M. class. It must be typed. You don't type well, so you have decided to hire someone to do it for you. The going rate is $1.50 per page. Think of an actual paper you have done in the past or will do in the future. Plan to delegate using the operational planning sheet. Be sure to include the course name, paper title, special typing instructions, and so on. Assume that you are meeting the typist for the first time. He or she doesn't know you and doesn't expect you.

Delegator 2, assume that you do typing and are willing to do the job if the delegation is acceptable to you.

Delegation Situation 2: Delegator 2, you are the manager of a fast-food restaurant. In the past, you have scheduled the workers. Your policy is to keep changing the workers' schedules. You have decided to delegate the scheduling to your assistant manager. This person has never done any scheduling but appears to be very willing and confident about taking on new responsibility (C-2).

Plan your delegation on the operational planning sheet.

Delegator 3, assume that you are interested in doing the scheduling if the manager delegates the task effectively.

Delegation Situation 3: Delegator 3, you own and manage your own business. You have eight employees, one of whom is the organization's secretary. The secretary presently uses an old electric typewriter, which needs to be replaced. You are not sure whether it should be replaced with a newer electric typewriter, a memory typewriter, or a word processor. You can afford to spend up to $2,500. You try to keep costs down and get the most for your money. Because the secretary will use the new machine, you believe that this employee should be involved, or maybe even make the decision. The secretary has never purchased equipment and you believe will be somewhat insecure about the assignment (C-3). Plan your delegation on the operational planning sheet.

Delegator 1, assume that you are able to do the job but are somewhat insecure (C-3). Accept the task if the delegator "participates" effectively.

Procedure 2
(7–14 minutes)

A. *Delegation 1.* Delegator 1 delegates the task (role play) to number 2. Number 3 is the observer. As the delegation takes place, the observer uses the form at the end of this exercise to evaluate the effectiveness of the delegator. Answer the questions on the form.

B. *Integration.* The observer (or number 2) leads a discussion of the effectiveness of the delegation although all team members should participate. Do not continue until you are told to do so.

Procedure 3
(7–14 minutes)

A. *Delegation 2.* Follow procedure 2A, except number 2 is now the delegator, number 3 is the delegatee, and number 1 is the observer.

B. *Integration.* Follow procedure 2B with number 3 as the observer. Do not continue until you are told to do so.

Procedure 4
(7–14 minutes)

A. *Delegator 3.* Follow procedure 2A, except number 3 is now the delegator, number 1 is the delegatee, and number 2 is the observer. If you are in a group of two, be an additional observer for another group.

B. *Integration.* Follow procedure 2B with number 1 as observer.

Conclusion

The instructor may lead a class discussion and make concluding remarks.

Application
(2–4 minutes)

What did I learn from this experience?
How will I use this knowledge in the future?

Sharing

Volunteers give their answers to the application section.

Note: Remember that the process does not end with delegating the task; you must control (check progress at control points and help when needed) to ensure that the task is completed as scheduled.

OBSERVER SHEET

During the delegation process, the observer checks off the items performed by the delegators. Items not checked were not performed. After the delegation, the delegator and delegatee also check off the items. This sheet is used for all three situations. Use the appropriate vertical column for each situation.

		Situation		
Delegation items for all situations		**1**	**2**	**3**
	Did the delegator follow these steps:			
Step 1.	Explain the need for delegating and the reason that the person was selected?			
Step 2.	Set an objective that defines responsibility and scope of authority, and set a deadline?			
Step 3.	Develop a plan? Was it effective?			
Step 4.	Establish control checkpoints?			
Step 5.	Hold the employee accountable? (Can't be done during exercise.)			
Did the delegate				
clearly understand what was expected of him or her and how to follow the plan?				
Improvements:				
How could the delegation be improved if done again? (Explain in the space below.)				

IN-CLASS SKILL-BUILDING EXERCISE

**Organization
Structures—
Communication**

SB 3–2

Procedure 1

Objective: To better understand how organizational structure affects productivity and performance.

Set up three teams of five members each (other class members will observe) seated as shown below.

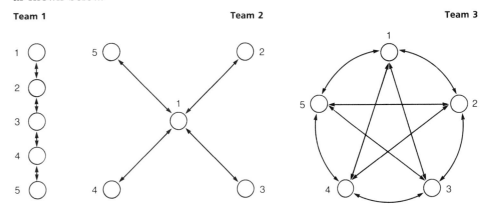

Team 1   Team 2   Team 3

The arrows illustrate communication lines. In team 1, number 1 can talk to 2, 2 can talk to 3, 3 can talk to 4, and 4 can talk to 5. Number 1 cannot talk to 3, 4, or 5; 2 cannot talk to 4 or 5, and so on. In team 2, number 1 can talk to 2, 3, 4, or 5 individually. Members 2, 3, 4, and 5 can only talk to 1. In team 3, anyone can talk to anyone.

Procedure 2

The instructor gives each team member one puzzle piece, and one copy of a 5-inch by 5-inch square in which the puzzle will fit when completed. Each team has up to five minutes to finish the puzzle following the communication lines for its team.

Questions

1. Teams 1, 2, and 3 tell the class how they felt about their organizational structure.
2. Did any team finish? Which team finished first?
3. How did the organizational structure affect the productivity and performance of each team?
4. Which structure was most appropriate for this task?
5. Give examples of when each type of structure is appropriate.

Conclusion

The instructor may make concluding remarks.

Application

What did I learn from this experience?
How will I use this knowledge in the future?

Sharing

Volunteers share their answers to the application section with the class.

4

Controlling Quality Work

Key Terms To achieve our objectives in this chapter, it is important to understand the following 17 key terms. They are presented in the order in which they appear in the chapter. The list of key terms also appears in alphabetical order in the end-of-chapter review.

controlling	key performance areas	budget
characteristics of effective controls	performance report	occasional controls
	input controls	management by walking around
control process	process controls	
standards	output controls	total quality management
strategic control points	constant controls	quality circles
	periodic controls	

In our daily lives we rely on a variety of controls that help us meet objectives. For example, we live in temperature-controlled houses equipped with fire and burglar alarms. Our automobiles are equipped with a variety of gauges that tell us when we need gas, when our lights and brakes are on, when our doors are open, and when we leave our keys in the ignition. As we drive our cars, traffic signals control when we stop and go. Organizations also rely on controls. Controlling *is the process of establishing methods ensuring that the organization's objectives are achieved.*

A supervisor's primary responsibility is to provide a product or service of high quality at a minimum cost on time.[1] In fulfilling that responsibility, the supervisor must make sure that the plans are carried out. And that, as our definition implies, means controlling. The better your skills are at controlling, the greater are your chances of being a successful supervisor. This chapter focuses on how to control the flow of work.

CONNECTIONS

1. Why is control important to the supervisor?

I. Characteristics of Effective Controls

Good controls are generally (1) understandable, (2) timely, (3) economical, (4) indicative, (5) acceptable, and (6) flexible. However, there are some situations in which a control method need not meet all of these criteria to be effective. In this section, we will discuss each characteristic separately.

Understandable

Employees must clearly understand the control methods and their use.[2] This seems self-evident. However, it is not uncommon to find organizations using control systems that give employees information they don't understand, need, or want. As a result, employees don't fully utilize the information. In some situations, frustrated employees totally ignore the formal information system and develop an informal system of their own. To be understandable, controls should be simple, but not simplistic.

Timely

Controls should provide information when it is needed. If plans are not on schedule, the supervisor should know in time to take corrective action before it is too late to meet the objective. For example, a production department's objective is to manufacture 100 desks per day. If a machine breaks down, the supervisor should be told promptly so that it can be fixed as soon as possible. An effective supervisor may send the operator on a break or to lunch while the machine is being fixed. When the employee returns, production resumes and the 100 desks are done at the end of the workday. If the supervisor found out about the machine at the end of the day, production would not have met the objective.

You, the supervisor, must keep the work on schedule. Develop controls that will enable you to take corrective action in time to meet the objective by its target date.

Economical

The benefits of controls must be worth the cost. It is not always easy to determine the cost of controls. But a cost-benefit analysis should be considered. The cost and benefit can change from situation to situation. For example, in a large retail store it may be economical to hire a full-time security guard to keep thefts to a minimum. However, it is not economical to hire a security guard in most small stores because the compensation to the guard can cost more than the merchandise stolen. In a small store, having the employees watch for theft is more economical. It may also be cost-effective to install cameras, mirrors, or both to minimize theft.

With the drop in the price of computers, it is now cost-effective for small businesses to use computers to control accounting, payroll, inventory, and other areas of their business.

A supervisor should do a cost-benefit analysis before establishing control methods.

Indicative

Control methods should also indicate where problems occur. If plans are not on schedule, the supervisor needs to know who or what is causing the problem. For example, in a bank it is helpful to know whether tellers are over or under expected cash balances. However, to correct cash shortages, a supervisor must know *which* tellers are over and under expected cash balances.

As a supervisor, you should set controls that will enable you to determine the exact cause of deviations in plans. In this way, corrective action can be taken to ensure that objectives are met.

Acceptable

Controls should be acceptable to those who must enforce them and to those over whom they are enforced. Employees don't always like controls. In fact, some people resist control. To overcome resistance, it is helpful to get employees to see controls as fair and acceptable. One way to achieve acceptance is to include the employees when developing controls. If participation is not possible or appropriate, employees should clearly understand why the controls are beneficial.

Employees should be aware of the consequences of not complying with controls. Supervisors should not make threats they cannot or will not follow through on. And they should apply controls consistently.[3] When developing and enforcing controls, supervisors should be helpful. They should focus on getting results rather than blaming and punishing employees.[4] When employees see a supervisor as helpful, they are more willing to comply with controls and to report when they are not meeting objectives. Employees who view supervisors as punitive are more apt to resist controls and hide their mistakes. As a result, departmental objectives may not be met.

As a supervisor, be helpful and overcome resistance to controls. Develop controls that are acceptable to employees.

Flexible

A supervisor should realize that times and situations change. Few, if any, departments or organizations enforce all controls all the time. Even the military and prisons make exceptions.[5] Controls should be flexible and should not be followed when inappropriate. There are times when flexibility pays.[6] For example, an organization has a minimum purchase requirement to keep order costs down. However, a salesperson believes that allowing a prospective customer to make a small trial purchase will generate future business. Which is the objective? To make sales? Or to have set minimum purchases? In this case, the control should be violated. Supervisors need to trust their employees, not the control systems. It is the employees who make the control system work, not the other way around.[7]

LEARNING OBJECTIVE

1. List and explain the six characteristics of effective controls.

As a supervisor, develop controls, but be flexible. Trust your employees to know when controls are not appropriate. If the controls you set have the six characteristics discussed, your chances of successfully meeting your objectives are greater than if they do not meet these criteria.

In summary, there are six **characteristics of effective controls:** *such controls are understandable, timely, economical, indicative, acceptable, and flexible.*

CONNECTIONS

2. Give an example of a control (preferably from an organization you have worked for) that has all six characteristics of effective control. Explain how it reflects each characteristic.

II. The Control Process

Now that we have established the characteristics of effective controls, we can look at the steps involved in the control process in greater detail. The **control process** *includes setting objectives; establishing standards, methods, and times for measuring performance; measuring and comparing performance to standards; reinforcing or correcting.*

Step 1. Set Objectives

Planning and controlling are inseparable. The first step in controlling is also a part of planning. As a supervisor, you must set objectives that determine what you want to accomplish within a given period of time. The objective is a statement of the end result desired. Recall that in Chapter 2 we discussed setting objectives and planning in detail.

Step 2. Establish Standards, Methods, and Times for Measuring Performance

Establish Standards

Once objectives are set, you must determine standards used to measure whether you are meeting the objectives. *Complete* **standards** *describe performance levels in the areas of quantity, quality, time, and cost.* Objectives are standards. However, additional standards are also needed if objectives are to be achieved. If your production department has an objective of assembling 200 bicycles per day, you must set additional standards for each employee to achieve this goal. If you have five employees, the standard could be the assembly of 40 bicycles per day. Assembly of 39 bikes is below standard, 40 bikes is at standard, and 41 bikes is above standard. On a per-hour basis, each employee should assemble five bikes ($40 \div 8$) to be at the standard production level.

Some standards may have been established before you got the job. Others may be set by people outside your department. For example, industrial engineers may conduct time and motion studies to determine production standards. Cost accountants may determine how much it should cost to produce your department's product or service. Your boss may also establish standards. But there will also be situations in which you delegate a task and establish the standards yourself.

As a situational supervisor, you will let employees participate in setting standards based on their capability levels. If the capability level is low, you should set the standard yourself. If the employee's capability is moderate, you may ask him or her for input. If the employee's capability level is high, you should establish the standard together. If the employee's capability is outstanding, he or she can establish the standard.

Not all standards cover the four areas described at the beginning of this section. If standards are incomplete, you may not achieve your department's objectives. For standards to be complete they should cover four major areas: quantity, quality, time, and cost.

Quantity: How many units should employees produce to earn their pay? Some examples of quantity standards include the number of words a secretary should type; the number of loans a loan officer must make; and the number of classes an instructor must teach. Quantitative standards are relatively easy to measure and to evaluate to see how well the employee is performing.

Quality: How well must a job be done? How many errors are acceptable? Quality is a relative term. There is a trade-off between cost and benefits. For some products, such as parachutes, defects are unacceptable because the cost of a life is too high traded off against the cost of doing a quality job. For other products, such as clothes, defects are acceptable if the expense of returns does not exceed the savings in quality control. In any situation, you should set quality standards and follow through to make sure employees meet them. If you don't, employees may not produce quality work. Some examples of quality standards include the number of typing errors a secretary may make; the number or percentage of delinquent loans a loan officer may accept; and the acceptable number or percentage of poor student evaluations an instructor may get. Quality standards are often difficult to establish and measure. For example, how does an educational supervisor determine how "good" the teachers are? It's not easy, but quality must be evaluated.

Time: When should the task be completed? Or how fast? When assigning a task, it is important to specify a time period. Have you ever had a boss assign you a task without a deadline? Did you get into trouble as a result? Deadlines are one form of a time-based standard. Performance may also be measured against a specific time period. Examples include how many words per minute a secretary types; how many loans a loan officer makes per month; and how many courses an instructor teaches per semester.

Cost: How much should it cost to do the job? How sophisticated a cost system should an organization have? The answers to these questions depend on the situation. Some production departments use cost-accounting methods to ensure accuracy, whereas other departments have a set budget. Some examples of cost standards include a secretary's typing cost may be reflected in a salary limit; a loan officer's cost may include an expense account to wine and dine customers, as well as the cost of an office, secretarial help, and so on. Or cost could be determined on the basis of delinquent loan losses only. The instructor's cost may include a salary limit and an overhead cost.

In the previous paragraphs we have discussed standards in terms of each of the four areas separately. Now we will set standards for the secretary, loan officer, and instructor that combine all four areas, as effective standards should. The secretary's standard is to type 50 words (quantity) per minute (time) with two errors or less (quality) at a maximum salary of $7.00 per hour (cost). The loan officer's standard is to make $100,000 (quantity) in loans per quarter (time) with delinquency not to exceed $5,000 (quality and cost). The instructor's standard is to teach 24 semester hours (quantity) per year (time), with student evaluations of average or better (quality), at a salary of less than $30,000 (cost). Each of these jobs would have additional standards, as well.

> **CONNECTIONS**
>
> **3.** Give an example of a standard (preferably from an organization you have worked for) that has the four characteristics of a complete standard. Explain how it reflects each characteristic.

Control Methods

While you are setting standards, or once they are in place, you must also establish controls to see that the standards are met. How this is done is the subject of this chapter.

Times to Measure Performance

When and how often should you measure performance? It depends upon the situation. Generally, the more capable the employees are, the less often you need to measure performance. Regardless of capability level, you should identify strategic points that focus on areas most critical to the success of your department. These **strategic control points** *are the critical times to measure key performance areas to ensure that objectives are met.* The **key performance areas,** *in turn, are the parts of the task or department that have to function effectively.*

For a key performance area to be considered a strategic control point, it must meet the following criteria:

1. If a problem occurs in the key performance area, the performance of the entire department is affected.

2. It must be possible to identify deviations from standard in the key performance area before serious damage occurs. Corrective action is taken at a strategic control point to ensure that the objective is met. It is too late if you find out from the customer that the product is defective. Quality control is needed before shipment.

EXHIBIT 4-1   **ESTABLISHING STRATEGIC CONTROL POINTS**

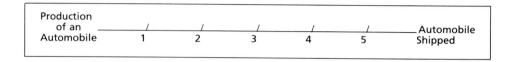

3. Controlling the key performance areas must be affordable. A cost-benefit analysis should be conducted to determine whether the control is economically feasible.

In Exhibit 4–1 the numbers 1 through 5 indicate strategic control points where performance is measured and compared to the standard. If the automobile, in this case, does not meet standards, it is fixed before proceeding to the next strategic control point.

CONNECTIONS

4. Give an example of a strategic control point and key performance area, preferably from an organization or department you have worked for. Explain how it meets the three criteria described in the text.

Step 3. Measure and Compare Performance to Standards

After determining when and how frequently to measure performance, you must follow up by comparing the actual results to the objective or standard. This step is relatively easy if you have performed the first two steps correctly. However, many supervisors do not set dates and times to measure performance, or do not actually perform an evaluation until the deadline. By then, it is too late to take corrective action. The supervisor should check or monitor performance.[8] Fast and frequent feedback is important to enable employees to evaluate their performance.[9]

A performance or variance report such as the one shown in Exhibit 4–2 is commonly used to measure and evaluate. This **performance report** *shows standards, actual performance, and deviations from standards.*

When variances are significant, they should be explained. In Exhibit 4–2, the $300 overtime and $200 material variances would probably be considered significant (a relative term), whereas the $10 under in supplies and $40 in maintenance probably would not. The following is a possible explanation that could accompany the performance report in Exhibit 4–2.

A shipment of faulty materials was received. The materials could have been returned for a refund. However, the employees would have not been able to make the product until a new shipment arrived. Rather than have idle workers, part of the shipment was kept and used. Using the faulty material cost $200 in wasted material that did not meet quality standards. Production was slowed during the period when faulty material was used. There was also idle production time while employees waited for the new shipment of material. In order to meet the budgeted standard production level of 5,000 units, employees had to work 20 hours overtime at a cost of $300.

Step 4. Reinforce or Correct

In Step 3, a comparison is made between the actual performance and the objective or standard. If the plan is on schedule, reinforce employees' achievements through praise. If the plan is not on schedule, take corrective action so that the objective or standard will be met.

In Exhibit 4–2 we realize that it cost $450 more to produce the product than was budgeted. Identifying the deviation and its cause is not enough. Corrective action must be taken to ensure that this material problem does not happen again. There are several ways to prevent the problem from recurring. One would be to keep a larger inventory of good material on hand. With a larger inventory, the faulty materials could have been returned without employee downtime. Another possible solution would be to get a more reliable supplier. Better inspections may also help eliminate the problem in the future.

Sometimes, when unexpected events occur, it is necessary to change the objective or standards rather than the plan. However, when the events are controllable, corrective action should be taken. This was illustrated in Exhibit 4–2. The production supervisor met the production budget of 5,000 units (the standard) at a cost of $450 more than budgeted. The supervisor could have produced less than the 5,000 budgeted units by not taking the corrective action of using overtime. Corrective action may require applying many of the concepts and techniques discussed in this text.

Model 4–1 summarizes the four steps in the control process.

LEARNING OBJECTIVE

2. List and explain the four steps in the control process.

EXHIBIT 4–2

PERFORMANCE REPORT — PRODUCTION DEPARTMENT MONTH OF JUNE 198—

	Standard/ Budget	Actual	Variance (+ over, – under)
Units of Product A	**5,000**	**5,000**	**$ 0**
Labor cost	$10,000	$10,000	$ 0
Overtime	200	500	+300
Materials	1,000	1,200	+200
Supplies	400	390	–10
Maintenance	1,200	1,160	–40
Totals	$12,800	$13,250	$+450

MODEL 4–1   **STEPS IN THE CONTROL PROCESS**

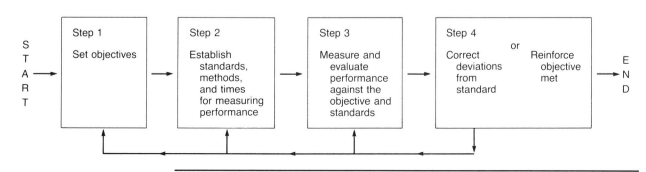

III. Types of Controls

As a supervisor, there are three major types of controls you should use: input, process, and output.

Input Controls

Input controls *are designed to anticipate and prevent possible problems.* A common example is preventive maintenance. Many production departments and trucking companies routinely tune up their machines or trucks to prevent breakdowns that would lower production. Another example is inventory control. Retail stores have designated reorder times so that they will not run out of merchandise, which results in lost sales. One last example of input control is standing plans (discussed in Chapter 2). Policies, procedures, and rules are designed to guide an employee's behavior in recurring situations. Employees do not have to go to the supervisor to be told what to do.

A major difference between the successful and unsuccessful supervisor lies in the ability to be proactive (anticipating and preventing problems), rather than reactive (solving problems after they occur). Supervisors who complain that they have no time to plan because they are too busy putting out fires are in this trap partly because they are reactive. They are controlled by their department rather than being in control. If you plan and establish controls you will be in control of your department. Things should run smoothly most of the time. You will not have to spend all your time putting out fires.

Process Controls

Process controls *measure and evaluate work in progress.* Process controls are used during step 3 of the control process. They allow the supervisor to take corrective action in time to meet objectives.

In the educational setting, tests serve as a process control device that allows students to measure their progress and take corrective action (if needed) to improve performance before receiving a final grade. On the production line, quality control tests identify and remove substandard parts before they become part of the final product. It is often more economical to reject faulty parts than to wait and find out that the finished product does not work properly. Strategic control points illustrated in Exhibit 4–1 are process controls.

A great deal of your time will be spent overseeing the work as it is performed. Using effective process controls will help ensure that your departmental objectives are met.

Output Controls

Output controls *evaluate final results and serve as a guide for future activities.* Output controls do not allow for corrective action, but are designed to guide future performance. In Exhibit 4–2 there were variances in overtime and labor. It was too late to correct the deviations at report time. However, the performance report can be used to help prevent the deviations from recurring. The corrective actions of increasing inventory or getting a more reliable supplier are output controls.

The performance appraisal, which we will discuss more fully in Chapter 12, is an output control that is used in most organizations. During a performance appraisal, the supervisor evaluates an employee's past performance. An employee cannot change past performance. However, the appraisal is used as the basis for improving performance prior to the next performance appraisal. Another output control used by most organizations is the yearly financial report.

As a supervisor, you will use output controls as the basis for improving future performance. Focus on developing plans that prevent problems from recurring rather than on fixing blame, criticizing, and complaining.[10]

In conclusion, you should try to anticipate and prevent problems (input controls). You should measure and evaluate performance as the task is completed (process controls), and take corrective action when needed to meet the objective or standard. You should also evaluate final performance (output controls) and use the evaluation as the basis for improving future performance.

LEARNING OBJECTIVE

3. Describe the three types of controls.

CONNECTIONS

6. Give an example of each of the three types of controls, preferably from an organization you have worked for. Explain why your example is an input, process, or output control.

IV. Control Methods

In this section we will discuss 10 specific methods you can use to control. In turn, these methods fall into one of three categories: constant, periodic, or occasional controls, as follows:

1. *Constant controls.*
   a. Self-control.
   b. Group control.
   c. Standing plans.
2. *Periodic controls.*
   a. Management information systems (MIS).
   b. Audits.
   c. Budgets.
3. *Occasional controls.*
   a. Special reports.
   b. Project controls.
   c. Exception principle.
   d. Personal observation.

Constant Controls

Constant controls *are in continuous use.*

Self-Control: If the supervisor is not watching or somehow monitoring performance, will the employee do the job? Employees with self-control can be left alone while they meet objectives, in contrast to those whom supervisors must control. In any job, there is an element of self-control. A supervisor cannot spend every minute of the day imposing controls. The real issue is the degree of self-control employees are given. Too much or too little imposed control can cause problems.[11] A supervisor must give employees as much autonomy as prudence allows.[12] A supervisor trying to push employees through too much imposed control may meet with resistance, but on the other hand, too little direction and control, especially in ambiguous situations, may lead to frustration.[13] In both cases, objectives may not be met. Allowing employees to use self-control is an intrinsic motivator that can lead to better performance.[14] A supervisor must give up enough control to allow employees to honestly believe that they "own" their jobs and are responsible for them.[15]

How do you, as a supervisor, determine the balance between self-control and imposed control? The answer is not easy, but situational supervision can help guide you. Use more imposed control with low- to moderate-capability employees and more self-control with high-capability and outstanding employees. Different levels of control may be needed for the same employee as he or she performs various tasks.

Group Control: A manager supervises each employee both as an individual and as part of a group. As with individuals, the supervisor must determine the group's capability level and balance group control with imposed control. Chapter 15 will explain group controls further.

Standing Plans: Policies, procedures, and rules (discussed in Chapter 2) are developed to influence employers' behavior in recurring, predictable situations. When standing plans are developed, they are input controls. When they are implemented, they become process controls.

Periodic Controls

Periodic controls *are used at regular intervals.* Unlike constant controls, periodic controls are used on a regular, fixed basis such as once a day, every week, or at the end of the month, quarter, or year.

Management Information Systems (MIS): MIS is a formal system for collecting, processing, and disseminating information that managers need in decision making. The information can be utilized on a daily, weekly, or monthly basis. For example, most banks maintain daily balances on checking and credit card customers to prevent overdrafts. Many organizations maintain weekly inventory balances. A sales manager may get a monthly sales report. Within the same organization, some people and departments will get information daily, whereas others will get it weekly or monthly.

Audits: Part of the accounting function is maintaining records of the organization's assets. Some organizations have an internal auditing department that checks periodically to make sure the assets are reported accurately. Audits are designed to keep theft levels at a minimum. In addition to performing internal audits, many organizations hire outside accountants to verify the organization's financial statements. The auditor states whether the statements reflect the true financial position and were prepared in accordance with generally accepted accounting principles. Companies that sell securities to the public generally must be audited before the securities can be sold and yearly afterward. The auditors usually come in on a yearly basis, but very few people know exactly when they will arrive.

Audits may also be occasional controls when used sporadically; for example, auditors may make unannounced visits at irregular intervals.

Budgets: Budgets are one of the most widely used control tools. Many supervisors fear budgets because they have weak math or accounting skills. In reality, budgeting requires planning skills rather than accounting skills. Budgets and the budgeting process vary from organization to organization. However, supervisors must usually determine in advance how much it will cost to operate their departments while meeting their objectives. The typical budget covers a one-year period and is broken down by month. A sample budget is used in Exhibit 4–2 to evaluate performance. The supervisor may have been told the objective (to produce 5,000 units of product A during the month of June 19—) and asked to determine the cost of labor, overtime, material, supplies, and maintenance. These figures, totaling $12,800, were approved as the budget. As the month of June went by, the supervisor tried to produce 5,000 units at a cost of $12,800. The supervisor produced 5,000 units but overspent the budget by $450. In summary, a **budget** *is the funds allocated to operate a department for a fixed period of time.*

Occasional Controls

Occasional controls *are used on a sporadic basis.* Unlike periodic controls, they do not involve set time intervals. They are used when needed.

Special Reports: When problems are identified, management often requests a special report to be compiled by one employee, a committee within the organization, or outside consultants who specialize in that area. These reports vary in content and nature but are often designed to identify the cause of a problem or an opportunity as well as a solution or a way to take advantage of the situation. For example, a supervisor may have an old piece of equipment. Upper management might ask the supervisor to look into replacing the machine, reporting on the alternatives and their cost, and recommending a purchase.

Project Controls: With nonrecurring or unique projects, strategic control points should be established to monitor progress and allow corrective action. In the machine replacement example, the supervisor should develop a plan (discussed in Chapter 2) with control checkpoints so that he or she can measure progress toward the purchase of the machine. If the supervisor planned to visit three vendors for demonstration during a one-week period but missed some visits, corrective action should be taken to get back on schedule. In this case, the project plan becomes the control method.

Exception Principle: In this instance, control is left up to the employee unless problems occur, in which case he or she goes to the supervisor for help. Corrective action is taken to get the plan back on schedule. For example, Pete, a production worker, may be told to produce 100 units per day. If he produces less than 90 or more than 110 units for any reason, his supervisor, Connie, is to be informed immediately. If the machine breaks down or the necessary materials run out, Pete tells Connie so that she can correct the problem. If Pete produces between 90 and 110 units, Connie checks only on daily or weekly production (output controls). This method can be very effective if used correctly. People are often reluctant to ask for help or to report that they are not performing up to standard until it is too late to take corrective action. Therefore, it is important for the supervisor and employees to agree on what constitutes an exception.[16]

Personal Observation: The supervisor using this control method watches and talks to employees as they perform their jobs. If supervisors want to know what is going on in their departments, they should visit their employees to find out. Tom Peters says that managers who spend more than 25 percent of their time in their offices are probably not doing their jobs.[17] In the best-seller *A Passion for Excellence: The Leadership Difference,* Peters and coauthor Nancy Austin describe what they call **management by walking around (MBWA).**[18] MBWA is not socializing. Instead, it involves three major activities that are usually done at the same time: *listening, teaching,* and *facilitating.*

1. *Listening.* To find out what is going on, the supervisor must do more listening than talking. He or she must accept feedback. Penalizing employees for speaking their minds will stop communications.

2. *Teaching.* Teaching does not mean telling employees what to do. It means helping them to do a better job by solving their own problems. Teach employees how to be more innovative. Use coaching statements such as, "What do *you* think should be done?" Do not encourage employees to blame others. Learn to talk last, not first. When interacting with employees, the values the supervisor wants to instill should be transmitted directly and indirectly. If quality is important, the supervisor should talk and act as though it is.

3. *Facilitating.* Facilitating means taking action to help employees get their job done. When listening, the supervisor should find out what's getting in the way or slowing employees down. This will seldom be big things. Problems are usually caused by petty annoyances that employees believe are too trivial to bother the supervisor with. The supervisor's job is to run interference, to remove the stumbling blocks for the employees. Employees who tell the supervisor what's going on should be told what will be done about a given problem, if anything, and when. Supervisors who listen but don't facilitate through corrective action will find that employees will stop talking.

LEARNING OBJECTIVE

4. List and explain the three categories of control methods and 10 specific control methods.

CONNECTIONS

7. Give an example of a constant, a periodic, and an occasional control method used by a specific organization. Identify each by name (self-control, MIS, special report, and so forth) and explain why it is classified as such.

Exhibit 4–3 summarizes the three types of controls and the 10 control methods. Note that the types and the methods overlap so that neat classifications are not always possible. For example, a budget begins as an input control. During the year, it serves as a process control (as in Exhibit 4–2). At the end of the year, the budget becomes an output control and is used to formulate the upcoming budget. Therefore, when you are developing input, process, or output controls any one or more of the 10 methods may be appropriate.

V. Controlling Quality and Cost

As stated earlier, a supervisor's primary responsibility is to provide, in a timely manner, a high-quality product or service at a minimum cost. A 1977 Harris poll revealed that one of every three consumers surveyed felt short-changed on quality and safety. In the 1970s and into the early 1980s, people believed that the quality of U.S. goods and services had decreased and that the quality of foreign-made goods, particularly from Japan, had increased. As a result, quality and cost control have received a great deal of attention in the 1980s and 1990s. Yet, as mentioned, quality must be balanced against cost. Controlling both is the subject of this section.

Total Quality Management

Quality is the predetermined standard that the product or service should meet. The standards vary. The quality of Ford's Lincoln Town Car is higher than its

EXHIBIT 4-3	**TYPES AND METHODS OF CONTROLS**

Types of Controls

Input

Process

Output

Methods of Control

Constant controls

   Self-control

   Group control

   Standing plans

Periodic controls

   MIS

   Audits

   Budgets

Occasional controls

   Special reports

   Project controls

   Exception principle

   Personal observation

Escort model. But both cars meet their respective quality standards. Quality is a part of the internal environment because the organization has control over it. **Total quality management (TQM)** *requires everyone in the organization to continually improve products and services.* Through TQM, the organization utilizes its resources to provide quality products and services to its customers. The key to achieving TQM is in establishing an agreed-on set of objectives stated as standards to meet for the product or service. Statistical process control (SPC) is used as a feedback method to statistically maintain consistent quality within narrow limits. With TQM the objectives continually change over time as products or services improve. People are the heart of TQM because they are responsible for these continual improvements. TQM uses participative management techniques such as quality circles and work teams to improve quality and productivity. Without effective human relations, TQM will not be effective. According to Taquchi, products need to be designed so that they will not fail in the field. Quality is a virtue of design. If the product is designed effectively, there will be few defects in the factory. Some recommend striving for zero defects as part of the TQM system. However, customer satisfaction is the primary aim of TQM. W. Edwards Deming developed 14 points for creating the TQM environment (see Exhibit 4–4).

LEARNING OBJECTIVE

5. Explain total quality management.

Controlling Quality

How Does Poor Quality Affect the Organization? Poor-quality products often result in dissatisfied customers. In some cases, poor quality may even lead to injuries. Dissatisfaction and injury can cause the loss of customers and sales revenue. Injured people may bring expensive legal suits against the organization. (Liability cases involve some $50 billion a year.[19]) Poor quality has a direct effect on profits.

EXHIBIT 4–4   **DEMING'S 14 POINTS FOR CREATING THE TOTAL QUALITY ENVIRONMENT**

1. Create constancy of purpose toward improvement of product and service, with the aim to become competitive, to stay in business, and to provide jobs.

2. Adopt a new philosophy. We are in a new economic age created by Japan. We can no longer live with commonly accepted styles of American management, nor with commonly accepted levels of delays, mistakes, or defective products.

3. Cease dependence on inspection to achieve quality. Eliminate the need for inspection on a mass basis by building quality into the product in the first place.

4. End the practice of awarding business on the basis of price tag. Instead, minimize total cost.

5. Improve constantly and forever the system of production and service to improve quality and productivity, and thus constantly decrease costs.

6. Institute training on the job.

7. Institute supervision: the aim of supervision should be to help people and machines and gadgets do a better job. Supervision of management is in need of overhaul, as well as supervision of production workers.

8. Drive out fear so that everyone may work effectively for the company.

9. Break down the barriers between departments. People in research, design, sales, and production must work as a team to foresee problems of production and use that may be encountered with the product or service.

10. Eliminate slogans, exhortations, and targets for the workforce that ask for zero defects and new levels of productivity. Such exhortations only create adversarial relationships. The bulk of the causes of low productivity belong to the system, and thus lie beyond the power of the workforce.

11. Eliminate work standards that prescribe numerical quotas for the day. Substitute aids and helpful supervision.

12. Remove the barriers that rob the hourly worker of his right to pride of workmanship. The responsibility of supervisors must be changed from sheer numbers to quality. Remove the barriers that rob people in management and engineering of their right to pride of workmanship. This means abolishment of the annual rating, or merit rating, and management by objective.

13. Institute a vigorous program of education and retraining.

14. Put everybody in the company to work to accomplish the transformation.

What Causes Poor Quality? Supervisors tend to blame poor quality on employees. Many people believe workers don't care about quality and don't take pride in their work. Employees can do a quality job but choose not to. Actually, in most cases poor quality is out of the control of employees and is the result of some combination of the following causes:[20]

- *Resources.* If management furnishes poor-quality tools, equipment, materials, or supplies, employees cannot do a quality job. Remember, in Exhibit 4–2, the cause of the variance was poor-quality material.

- *Supervision.* Poor planning, unclear standards, and poor communication of expectations and instructions often result in poor quality. Supervisors frequently fail to enforce quality standards.

- *Training.* Employees are not always taught how to do a quality job.

- *Production and operations systems.* If the production or operation systems are inefficient, poor quality can result.

What Can Supervisors Do to Ensure High Quality? Following the guidelines below can help your department produce a quality product or service.

- *Use quality resources and systems.* Make sure that your department has the proper quality resources (tools, equipment, material, supplies, and so on) when needed. Periodically check the product or operation system for efficiency. Improve it when possible.

- *Set clear standards.* Every employee should know the exact level of quality expected of him or her. Train employees so that they can produce quality products or services.

- *Talk about and reward quality.*[21] A supervisor should talk about quality regularly. Slogans and signs help communicate the message. Examples include "Quality is job one" (Ford); "Quality, Service, Cleanliness, and Value" (McDonald's); and "We want to give the best customer service of any company in the world" (IBM). Quality should be a part of employees' evaluations. High-quality performers should be rewarded for their results.

- *Enforce standards.* Employees may not produce a quality product or service if supervisors do not check and enforce standards. Each employee's work should be checked by another qualified person. When quality standards are not met, the employee responsible should be informed. Whenever possible, that employee should be required to take corrective action.[22] The employee should redo the job or apologize to the customer. Corrective action should be taken as soon as possible to prevent multiplication of quality problems.

- *Use employee suggestions.* Employees often know their jobs better than their supervisors do and can make valuable suggestions on ways to improve quality.

   You can get suggestions when using MBWA. Another popular, more formal technique is quality circles. They are used by General Motors, Lockheed, American Airlines, Friendly Ice Cream, and the federal government, among others. **Quality circles** *are groups that meet regularly to spot and solve problems in their work area.* There are no universal quality circle procedures. There are different numbers of participants (from 4 to 20 on average). They meet at different intervals (weekly, biweekly, monthly). Some organizations pay participants for their suggestions. (Northrup, for example, pays about 10 percent of any savings from the ideas.) The organization you work for may have a person responsible for employee suggestions. Check with the personnel or human resources department for more information and help in this area.

- *Keep records and plan improvements.* If quality is important, keep a record of your department's performance and communicate it to employees. A bulletin board is a good place to report the results. Compare the current period to previous periods to let employees see their progress, or lack of progress. Make plans to improve quality in the next period.

LEARNING OBJECTIVE

6. Describe six ways to control quality.

CONNECTIONS

8. Explain how a specific organization or department, preferably one you work/worked for, controls quality. How could quality control be improved?

Controlling Cost

Is There a Relationship between Quality and Cost? As stated in the last section, poor quality leads to lost customers and lawsuits. There is also a corrective cost for poor quality, such as the costs of repairing a faulty product; handling and shipping faulty products;

wasted parts, materials, and supplies; and handling customer complaints. Corrective costs may represent anywhere from 2 to 10 percent of an organization's revenue.[23]

Because quality and cost are directly related, the supervisor should focus on controlling both simultaneously.

What Can Supervisors Do to Control Cost? Following these guidelines can help your department control cost:

- *Emphasize profit, not cost.* When purchasing equipment, materials, or supplies don't simply buy the cheapest available. In the long run it may cost less to use higher-quality materials. Delivery is also important. Slower delivery of a lower-cost material may result in idle employees and overtime pay, as we saw in Exhibit 4–2. As a supervisor, evaluate price, quality, and delivery.[24]

  A restaurant that gives only one roll and piece of butter per customer may save a quarter but lose valuable future business worth hundreds of dollars. A sales representative who drives around to find a parking space on the street rather than park in a garage may save a few dollars, but if he or she is late or doesn't have time to properly prepare for a meeting, a sale worth hundreds or even thousands of dollars may be lost.

- *Set clear cost standards.* All employees should know production cost and expectations. Train employees in techniques that will minimize waste.

  The author finds that publishers frequently send him materials via overnight special delivery when he stated that he did not need the materials for several days. Regular first-class mail would save about $5. If this is done for other writers a thousand times a year, publishers incur an unnecessary cost of $5,000.

  To reduce cost, look for drains on financial resources through waste and duplication. Look for cost trends. Change the standards. Be sure to sell the employees on the benefits to them and the organization.

- *Talk about and reward cost consciousness.* Supervisors should focus on cost as well as quality. Discussing cost and quality on a regular basis is essential to cost control. Cost should not be a once-a-year subject when the budget is prepared. Cost control should be part of employee evaluations. Employees should be rewarded for their successful efforts at containing or reducing cost.

- *Enforce standards.* Employees may not be cost conscious if supervisors do not check on and enforce control standards. A supervisor should watch out for theft and intentional damage, which are often two costly areas. We all know what theft is. Employees may also intentionally damage goods if defective merchandise is given to them or sold at minimal cost.

  An individual who worked cleaning up a supermarket at closing time would help herself to cigarettes and candy on her way out. An employee in a shoe factory deliberately damaged shoes in his size. The flaws were in an inconspicuous spot, but the shoes were not salable. This person also took orders for shoes from friends, selling the damaged goods at a profit. This type of activity costs organizations thousands of dollars annually. Supervisors must set the example and enforce controls. It is difficult for supervisors to enforce controls that they don't follow themselves.

CONNECTIONS

9. Explain how a specific organization controls theft. How could this control system be improved economically?

- *Use employee suggestions.* Employees often know or can develop ways to cut cost. You can get employee ideas using MBWA and quality circles.

**LEARNING
OBJECTIVE**

7. Describe six ways to
control cost.

• *Keep records and plan improvements.* If cost control is important, keep a record of your department's performance and communicate it to employees. Performance reports, such as that shown in Exhibit 4–2, can be displayed on bulletin boards. Combine quality and cost into one report. Compare current performance to previous periods. Make plans to improve future performance.

CONNECTIONS

10. Explain how a specific organization or department, preferably one you have worked for, controls cost. How could cost control be improved?

Exhibit 4–5 summarizes what supervisors can do to control quality and cost.

VI. Sample Control Process for a Sales Department

The sales department is a key performance area within an organization, because without sales there is no business. Thus, it is a good place for us to examine how controls work in practice.

Step 1. Set Objectives: To sell $120,000 worth of services during the calendar year 198— (input control).

Step 2. Establish Standards, Methods, and Times for Measuring Performance: The standard is established when the sales manager sits down with each salesperson to set sales goals for the coming year (input control). The yearly sales quota is based on the sales forecast and the individual's actual sales performance for the previous year (output control). The yearly sales quota is broken down by month (process control). Standards would also be set in other areas such as the number of sales calls to make per day, week, or month; an acceptable number of returns; travel budgets; and so forth.

As soon after the end of each month as possible, the accounting department will submit a monthly sales report (periodic control using MIS). The report will state total sales broken down by each salesperson's performance. The sales report will compare actual sales for the month and year-to-date to the quota, with variance amounts stated and identified as positive or negative (output control).

For the sales department, the periodic MIS sales report is the major control method. However, constant controls are always used as well. For example, each

---

EXHIBIT 4–5   **CONTROLLING QUALITY AND COST**

Quality	**Cost**
• Use quality resources and systems.	• Emphasize profit, not cost.
• Set clear quality standards.	• Set clear cost standards.
• Talk about and reward quality.	• Talk about and reward cost consciousness.
• Enforce standards.	• Enforce standards.
• Use employee suggestions.	• Use employee suggestions.
• Keep records and plan improvements.	• Keep records and plan improvements.

salesperson has to use self-control when going out to make sales calls. Will he or she actually spend eight hours per day selling? Some salespeople may need more control than others. Group control is used as a basis of comparison. If one salesperson is selling less than the others, he or she may be inclined to work harder to keep up. However, this information may also slow down the superstars. Standing plans are also needed when making sales calls. The salesperson must know what to do and say in certain situations. Special reports, such as market research, may be required for a prospective new product. Salespeople may be asked to interview their customers and report their findings.

Step 3. Measure and Compare Performance to Standards: Each month, the sales manager reviews the monthly sales report in preparation for step 4.

Step 4. Reinforce or Correct: Each month, the sales manager sits down with each salesperson (periodic process control). If the individual is at or above quota, he or she is praised for a job well done. If the individual is below quota, the salesperson and the manager discuss the reason and work together to correct the situation in the coming months. The individual performing below quota may be given less self-control and more imposed control. Additional training or occasional controls such as managerial observation during a sales call may be added as a corrective measure.

VII. Future Trends in Control

We will experience more changes in the next 15 years than have occurred in the past century. Major changes will come particularly in the area of technology. As a result, Hal Mather recommends engineering and information systems training for future supervisors.[25] In addition, technological controls will take away some of the supervisor's control.[26] Employees will be given more autonomy, both as individuals and as teams. Team control will continue to increase in all sectors of the economy.

The need to control employees as individuals will continue to increase in popularity. To do this effectively, supervisors should understand employee behavior and ways to change their styles to meet an individual employee's needs.[27]

Greenberger and Strasser conducted research revealing that each employee has a desired level of control and a perception of the control he or she possesses.[28] If the employee's desired control is in balance with the actual control, he or she will perform to his or her capability level. However, if the employee is not satisfied with his or her balance of control, he or she will perform below capability level. The imbalance of control desired and actual control will lead to increased stress, depression, absenteeism, sabotage, and a possible change of jobs. This study reinforces the fact that supervisors must work with employees on an individual basis. In other words, situational supervision is a trend of the future.

LEARNING OBJECTIVE

8. Describe the future trends in control.

Situational Supervisory Control

As a situational supervisor, how much time and effort should you devote to controlling? And which type of control should you emphasize? The answers, once again, depend on the situation. The lower the capability level of your employees, the more time and effort you must spend controlling, and process controls should be emphasized. The higher the capability level, the less time and effort are needed for controlling, and output control should be emphasized. Input controls are your responsibility with a low- or moderate-capability employee. They are a shared responsibility with a high-capability employee, and become the responsibility of the outstanding employee.

REVIEW

Select one or more methods: (1) fill in the missing key terms from memory; (2) match the key terms from the end of the review with their definitions below; (3) copy the key terms in order from the key terms at the beginning of the chapter.

_____ is the process of establishing methods ensuring that the organization's objectives are achieved. There are six _____ : understandable, timely, economical, indicative, acceptable, and flexible.

The _____ includes setting objectives; establishing standards, methods, and times for measuring performance; measuring and comparing performance to standards; reinforcing or correcting.

Complete _____ describe performance levels in the areas of quantity, quality, time, and cost. _____ are the critical times to measure key performance areas to ensure that objectives are met. _____ are the parts of the task or department that have to function effectively in order to succeed. A _____ shows standards, actual performance, and deviations from standards.

There are three types of controls. _____ are designed to anticipate and prevent possible problems. _____ involve measuring and evaluating the work in progress. _____ are designed to evaluate final results and serve as a guide for future activities.

There are three categories of control. _____ (including self-control, group control, and standing plans) are controls that are in continuous use. _____ (MIS, audits, and budgets) are controls that are used at regular intervals. _____ (special reports, project controls, exception principle, and personal observations) are controls used on a sporadic basis. A _____ is the funds allocated to operate a department for a fixed period of time. _____ _____ consists of listening, teaching, and facilitating.

_____ requires everyone in the organization to continually improve products or services. Some of the reasons for poor quality include employee errors, poor-quality resources, poor supervision, poor training, and poor production or operations systems. To ensure high quality, a supervisor can make sure that quality resources and systems are available. The supervisor can set clear standards and enforce them. While talking about and rewarding quality, supervisors should listen to and incorporate employee suggestions. One technique for doing so is _____ , groups that meet regularly to spot and solve problems in their work areas. The supervisor should also keep records and plan for improvements.

To control cost, a supervisor should emphasize profit, not cost; set and enforce cost standards; talk about and reward cost consciousness; and use employee suggestions for controlling costs.

In the future, there will be less supervisor-imposed control and more self-control and group control. Situational supervision will be important to present and future supervisors.

KEY TERMS

budget
occasional controls
characteristics of effective control
output controls
constant controls
performance report
control process
periodic controls
controlling
process controls
input controls
quality circles
key performance areas
standards
management by walking around (MBWA)
strategic control points
total quality management

REFERENCES

1. Harian Jessup, "Front Line Control," *Supervisory Management,* October 1985, p. 12.

2. Ibid., p. 14.

3. Lester Bittel, *What Every Supervisor Should Know* (New York: McGraw-Hill, 1985), pp. 130–31.

4. M. R. Hansen, "To-Do List for Managers," *Supervisory Management,* May 1986, p. 38.

5. Fred Lippert, "How Much Leniency?" *Supervision,* August 1986, p. 17.

6. Stephen Finch, "Flexibility Pays," *Supervision,* October 1985, p. 28.

7. M. R. Hansen, "Better Supervision from A to W," *Supervisory Management,* August 1985, p. 35.

8. Robert Chasnoff and Paul Muniz, "How Effective Is Your Follow-through?" *Supervisory Management,* November 1985, p. 20.

9. Hansen, "Better Supervision from A to W," p. 35.

10. Hansen, "To-Do List for Managers," p. 37.

11. "Overmanagement," *Supervision,* February 1986, p. 11.

12. Kenneth Hall and Lawson Savery, "Tight-Rein, More Stress," *Harvard Business Review,* January–February 1986, p. 161.

13. Jack Phillips, "The First Step toward Increasing Supervisory Authority," *Management Solutions,* September 1986, p. 37.

14. Charles Manz, "Self-Leadership: Toward an Expanded Theory of Self-Influence Process in Organizations," *Academy Management Review,* July 1986, p. 595.

15. Tom Peters, "Tom Peters' Formulas for Supervisory Excellence," *Supervisory Management,* February 1985, p. 2.

16. Chansnoff and Muniz, "How Effective Is Your Follow-through?" p. 21.

17. Peters, "Tom Peters' Formulas," p. 4.

18. Tom Peters and Nancy Austin, *A Passion for Excellence* (New York: Random House, 1985), pp. 378–92.

19. Bittel, *What Every Supervisor Should Know,* p. 444.

20. Andrea Nelson, "Who Really Controls Quality?" *Supervisory Management,* October 1985, pp. 8–10.

21. William Gorden, "Gaining Employee Commitment to Quality," *Supervisory Management,* November 1985, pp. 31–33.

22. Hansen, "Better Supervision from A to W," p. 35–36.

23. Bittel, *What Every Supervisor Should Know,* p. 444.

24. Fred Lippert, "Controlling Materials Cost," *Supervision,* October 1985, p. 17.

25. Hal Mather, "Getting Ready Today for the Production Operations of Tomorrow," *Supervisory Management,* May 1986, pp. 3–10.

26. "The Old Foreman Is on the Way Out, and the New One Will Be More Important," *Business Week* 25 (April 1983), pp. 74–75.

27. Thomas Liesz, "Supervisory Toolkit," *Supervision,* October 1986, pp. 14–16; Anthony Alessandra and James Cathcart, "To Supervise Effectively: Know Your Employee Behavior Styles," *Supervisory Management,* September 1985, pp. 37–39.

28. David Greenberger and Stephen Strasser, "Development and Application of a Model of Personal Control in Organizations," *Academy Management Review,* January 1986, pp. 164–75.

APPLICATION SITUATIONS

Identifying Control Characteristics

AS 4–1

Below are five statements about controls. Identify each in terms of one of the six control characteristics listed.

a. understandable *d.* indicative

b. timely *e.* acceptable

c. economical *f.* flexible

_____ 1. Today is the 10th of the month. I just received the agenda for the meeting on the 9th.

_____ 2. When developing controls, a supervisor should let employees participate.

_____ 3. Use your own discretion when completing the project.

_____ 4. Each parachute will be thoroughly inspected to prevent accidents.

_____ 5. When the machine is overheated, it automatically shuts itself off.

Identifying Types of Controls

As 4–2

Following are five types of controls used in different organizations. Identify each as

a. input control

b. process control

c. output control

_____ 6. The production department has scheduled the production of 200 units of product A for next week.

_____ 7. The quality control department will inspect samples of the goods prior to shipment to the customer.

_____ 8. The standing plans for the YMCA as they are implemented by employees on their jobs.

_____ 9. The midterm exam in an accounting course.

_____ 10. The year-end financial statements.

Identifying Control Methods

AS 4–3

Below are 10 situations. Identify each in terms of the control methods listed. Use all answers only once.

Constant	*Periodic*	*Occasional*
a. self-control	*d.* MIS	*g.* special report
b. group control	*e.* audit	*h.* project
c. standing plans	*f.* budget	*i.* exception
		j. observation

_____ 11. No refund will be given without the sales slip.

_____ 12. All purchases over $500 must be approved by the controller.

_____ 13. The president of the company receives his or her monthly financial statement.

_____ 14. The secretary is alone in the office for the day while the manager is out of town. The manager did not give the secretary any special assignments.

_____ 15. At the end of the year, a retail store takes an inventory.

_____ 16. A consulting firm specializes in custom-tailored programs for training and development.

_____ 17. The supervisor's desk faces her employees.

_____ 18. John has finished his training and has been told to see the manager when he needs help.

_____ 19. In a management course, the instructor uses permanent teams of six members who perform exercises and discuss applications and cases. The team members evaluate each other's performance on a regular basis.

_____ 20. Jean has come up with a great way of increasing productivity in the department.

OBJECTIVE CASE 4

MBO at XYZ Wallet Company

Bill Williams of the XYZ Wallet Company wanted to increase productivity in his production department. Each worker makes an average of 32 wallets per eight-hour day. Workers are paid by the hour and not by the number of wallets produced. Different styles produced on different machines take different amounts of time. Bill does not want to change to piece-rate pay to increase production because then he would have to increase the payroll. He wants to increase productivity while keeping the cost the same.

Bill came up with the idea of setting a quota. Employees could leave work early once they met the quota. The average rate was 32 wallets per day, so Bill decided to raise it by around 10 percent to 35 wallets per day. Bill realizes that if the workers push, they can get out of work around a half hour early.

Bill sat down with each employee and set the quota for each worker's machine. For example, he said, "Jean, after you produce 35 wallets in a day you may go home. What do you think of this new MBO idea?" Jean replied, "I don't push too hard; I'd like to get home and spend some extra time with the family. I think it's a good idea." Bill said, "Good, get back to work, and when you meet the quota, punch out and go home."

Things seem to be going well. Production reports show an increase of 7 percent for the first two weeks with the new system. However, one employee, John Farel, is leaving work each day around 2:30, whereas everyone else is leaving work between 4:30 and 5:00 o'clock.

Bill and John have the following conversation:

BILL: John, it's 2:30; where are you going?

JOHN: Home; I produced my 35 wallets.

BILL: Your machine's hourly output average is four wallets. You can't produce 35 wallets in five and a half hours, John.

JOHN: Wrong; the machine used to produce four wallets per hour before I adjusted it and added this little gadget. It took me two hours to fix the machine, but it was worth it. There haven't been any complaints about the quality, have there?

BILL: No, John.

JOHN: Well, I'll see you tomorrow. I'm going to play baseball with my kids.

Select the best alternative to the following questions and use the space between questions to jot down some notes to support your answers.

_____ 1. Is MBO being implemented as an actual MBO program? Why?
   a. yes   *b.* no

_____ 2. Bill's controls were understandable, economical, acceptable, and flexible.
   a. true   *b.* false

_____ 3. Bill set standards in the area or areas of

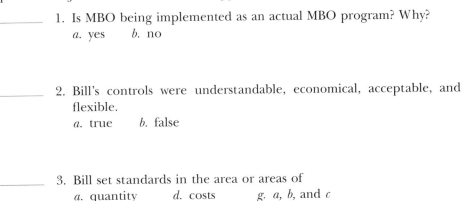

a. quantity	*d.* costs	*g.* *a, b,* and *c*
b. quality	*e.* *a* and *b*	*h.* *a, c,* and *d*
c. timeliness	*f.* *a* and *c*	*i.* *a, b, c,* and *d*

_____ 4. Bill's MBO system has utilized _____ controls.
       a. input   *c.* output   *e.* *a* and *c*
       b. process   *d.* *a* and *b*   *f.* *b* and *c*

_____ 5. Is Bill controlling key performance areas in his department?
       a. yes   *b.* no

_____ 6. In daily production, Bill uses _____ control.
       a. self   *d.* MIS   *g.* project reports
       b. group   *e.* audits   *h.* exception principle
       c. standing   *f.* budgets   *i.* personal observation

_____ 7. Bill's major control method is
       a. self   *d.* MIS   *g.* project reports
       b. group   *e.* audits   *h.* exception principle
       c. standing   *f.* budgets   *i.* personal observation

_____ 8. John is getting out of work early by
       a. resisting controls   *c.* cheating
       b. breaking the rules   *d.* using initiative

_____ 9. Bill's controls focus on
       a. quality   *b.* cost   *c.* profit

_____ 10. Bill did not follow the _____ step in the control process.
       a. first   *d.* fourth
       b. second   *e.* He followed all four steps
       c. third

11. Should Bill continue to let John leave two hours earlier than the other employees? If not, what should he do?

12. Should Bill make any other changes in his controls? If so, what should be changed?

PREPARATION FOR IN-CLASS SKILL-BUILDING EXERCISE*

**Controlling Jones
Employment Agency**

SB 4–1

Paul Jones owns and operates an employment agency. He has no formal control methods because his two recruiters are paid only by commission, so he lets them do their own thing. Paul was pleased with his earnings until he received a report that made him realize his business is not as efficient and profitable as the average employment agency.

Paul has come to you with comparison figures for the year, shown in Exhibit SB 4–1, and has asked you to set up a control system to help his business be as efficient as the average employment agency.

EXHIBIT SB 4–1

INFORMATION FOR LAST YEAR

	Jones	Average
Revenue from placements	$207,000	$225,000
Number of client interviews	621	675
Number of recruiters	3	3
Average salary	$ 24,150	$ 26,250
Refunds	$ 7,000	$ 10,000

Employment agencies in this exercise charge the employer a fee per person hired. The average fee is $1,000. Each agency employee gets 35 percent of the fee charged as a salary. Salary is 100 percent commission. Refunds are made if the person placed does not stay on the job for a set period of time. The number of client interviews per year is an estimate because the Jones Employment Agency keeps no records of this.

Placing yourself in the role of consultant, answer the questions in the space provided in order to implement the control process. The industry forecasts that placements will be the same next year.

Step 1. Set objectives for the Jones Employment Agency.

Step 2(*a*). Establish standards that are viewed as fair; difficult, specific, and descriptive; and complete, observable, and measurable. They should include quantity, quality, timeliness, and cost.

Step 2(*b*). Select control types and methods, and times to measure performance.

Input controls:

Process control and methods:

Source: Adapted from H. J. Bracey and A. Sanford, "Controlling Experience—The Branch Office," in *Basic Management: An Experience-Based Approach* (Plano, TX: Business Publications, Inc., 1977), pp. 177–80.

IN-CLASS SKILL-BUILDING EXERCISE

Controlling Jones Employment Agency,

SB 4–1

Objective: To design a control system.

Experience: You and then your group will design a control system for Jones Employment Agency.

Materials: Preparation for Skill-Building Exercise SB 4–1.

Procedure 1
(10–20 minutes)

Turn to the Preparation for Skill-Building Exercise 4–1 and design the control system.

Procedure 2
(12–18 minutes)

Break into groups of five or six and discuss, analyze, and agree on the best control system for Jones. Have one member write down the group's answers and report them to the class.

Procedure 3
(10–15 minutes)

Each group's spokesperson reports on the control system to the class. Class members may question each spokesperson.

Integration
(4–6 minutes)

Answer the following questions as a group.

1. Our primary control type is
   a. input   *b.* process   *c.* output
   Why?

2. Our control methods are

_____ constant	_____ self	_____ group	_____ standing plans
_____ periodic	_____ MIS	_____ audit	_____ budgets
_____ occasional	_____ special reports		_____ project report
_____ exception principle			_____ personal observation

3. We _____ did _____ did not focus on key performance areas.

4. Our standards are stated in the areas of
   _____ quantity   _____ timeliness
   _____ quality   _____ cost

5. The information system we developed contains
   _____ too little   _____ too much   _____ just enough information to control

6. After listening to descriptions of the other groups' control systems, we could improve ours in the following ways:

Conclusion
(2–5 minutes)

The instructor makes concluding remarks about the exercise.

Application
(3 minutes)

What did I learn from this exercise? How will I use this knowledge in the future?

Sharing

Volunteers may give their answers to the application questions.

IN-CLASS SKILL-BUILDING EXERCISE

**Modern Art
Exhibit**

SB 4–2

Objective: To experience applying the five supervisory functions. To analyze how well your group implemented the five supervisory functions during the exercise.

Experience: In groups, (1) you will develop plans for a modern art exhibit; (2) you will actually build an exact replica of the modern art exhibit displayed; (3) you will determine how well you applied the five supervisory functions.

Material: No preparation is required. The instructor will give you the panels necessary to do the exercise.

*Procedure 1
(2 minutes)*

Read the following rules for this experience.

1. Only one person at a time may leave the group to look at the exhibit. You may not bring anything with you (panels, paper, pens, books, and so on) when you observe the exhibit. The model may not be handled in any way.

2. Until you are ready to start building, you may not exchange your construction panels with those of other team members or put any two pieces together. The panels must stay in front of each person. They can be handled by that person, but not fitted together or lined up in any orderly arrangement.

3. Advise your instructor when you are ready to start building so that your starting order can be ranked.

4. When you are finished building, tell the instructor so that the order in which you finished can be ranked. Once you notify the instructor that you are finished with the planning stage, you may NOT look at the model again.

5. The instructor will determine whether the exhibit has been completed properly. If the instructor finds an error, the team will be advised that the exhibit is not correct, but will not be told what the error is.

6. The team that puts the modern art exhibit together correctly first is the winner. The rank for the team will also be posted. You have up to 20 minutes to complete the modern art exhibit.

*Procedure 2
(2–4 minutes)*

Break into groups of five or six members. Sit in a circle facing each other. The instructor will distribute the 10 panels as evenly as possible. Each member will be given at least one panel.

*Procedures 3–5
(up to 20 minutes)*

Each group proceeds at its own pace. (Read the rest of the procedures now.)

Procedure 3 (up to 15 minutes)—Plan: Use the five supervisory functions in preparing to assemble the modern art exhibit. You may begin to send one member at a time to see the model. When you are ready to begin assembling the modern art exhibit, tell the instructor so that your rank can be listed. Remember, once you begin assembling the panels, you cannot look at the model again. Read procedure 4 now.

Procedure 4—Assemble: You may begin assembling when you are ready. However, you *must* begin no more than 15 minutes after the exercise starts. When your group is finished assembling the exhibit, one member brings it to the instructor so that the group can be ranked and so that the instructor can determine whether the exhibit was assembled correctly. Read procedure 5 now.

Procedure 5—Evaluate: When the group's exhibit is given to the instructor, he or she will tell the group representative either that it is correct, in which case the instructor will then rank the group, or that it is not correct. Your group may continue, without looking at the model, until it is right or until the 20-minute time limit runs out. After all groups assemble the exhibit correctly or the 20 minutes are up, proceed to the integration section.

Integration: Answer the following questions as a group.

From Chapter 1

1. What technical, human, and conceptual skills were needed for completion of the modern art exhibit?
2. How did the group use staffing?
3. How was leadership handled in the group?

From Chapter 2

4. Did your group plan?
5. Were strategic, operational, or both types of plans needed?
6. Did your group have a clear objective?
7. Were standing, single-use, or both types of plans needed?
8. Overall, were policies, procedures, rules, programs, projects, or budgets the most appropriate?
9. Were contingency plans needed?
10. Which, if any, simple planning tools did you use?
11. Did your group follow any of the steps in operational planning (setting objectives; determining the type of plan and tools needed; developing and analyzing alternatives; selecting a plan; implementing the plan and control)?
12. Did your group spend too little or too much time planning?
13. Were detailed or general plans needed?
14. Did your group use participation in developing plans?

From Chapter 3

15. Describe how your group organized. Did it do so in a way that coordinated tasks and resources with clear responsibility, authority, and accountability?
16. Identify any of the 10 principles of organization your group followed (unity of direction; chain of command; span of control; specialization; coordination; balanced responsibility, authority, and accountability; delegation; employment stability; KISS; flexibility).
17. Did your group have line, staff, or line and staff authority?
18. Did your group departmentalize by function, product, customer, or territory?

From Chapter 4

19. How did your group use control? Were the controls understandable, timely, economical, indicative, acceptable, and flexible?
20. Did your group follow the steps in the control process (setting objectives; establishing standards, methods, and times; measuring and comparing performance to standards; reinforcing or correcting)?
21. Classify any controls your group used as input, process, or output controls.
22. Did your group use constant controls (self-control, group control, standing plans), periodic controls (MIS, audits, budgets), or occasional controls (special reports, project controls, exception principle, personal observation)?

Conclusion: The instructor leads a class discussion and makes concluding remarks.

Application
(2–4 minutes)

What did I learn from this experience?
How will I use this knowledge in the future?

Sharing: Volunteers give their answers to the application section.

Supervisory Skills

5

Problem Solving and Decision Making

Key Terms　To achieve our objectives in this chapter, it is important that you understand the following 15 key terms. They are presented in the order in which they appear in the chapter. The list of key terms also appears in alphabetical order in the end-of-chapter review.

problem	unprogrammed	synectics
problem solving	decisions	nominal grouping
decision making	creativity	consensus mapping
problem-solving and	stages in the creative	Delphi technique
decision-making	process	devil's advocate
steps	cost-benefit analysis	approach
programmed	brainstorming	
decisions		

It was late in the day and production was behind schedule. An important customer expected shipment of the product in two days. Louise came to the supervisor and said, "Machine 4 is smoking a bit and I've seen a few sparks fly out the back." The supervisor snapped, "Just finish the job. We're behind schedule now. We don't have time to wait for maintenance to check it out. I'll have them up here during the night when we aren't producing." About a half hour later, there was an explosion and a fire on machine 4. Louise was injured and had to be rushed to the hospital. The entire production process would be halted for a few days until the mess could be cleaned and the machine fixed or replaced.

As a supervisor, you are hired to make sound decisions. Your career success will be based on how well you solve problems and make decisions. Using the information in this chapter will help you develop your problem-solving and decision-making skills.

I. The Importance of Problem Solving and Decision Making

One of the major reasons supervisors are hired is to make decisions and solve problems.[1] Xerox Learning Systems has identified problem solving and decision making as critical skills for success at the supervisory level.[2] Problem solving and decision making are second only to planning in terms of time consumed, requiring 13 percent of a supervisor's time, on average.[3] Some writers state that a supervisor makes about 80 decisions daily, or one every 5 or 6 minutes,[4] and others claim the total is in the hundreds.[5] Making bad decisions can get a supervisor fired.[6] Some decisions can also affect the health, safety, and well-being of consumers, employees, and the community. In fact, ethical decision making is becoming more important.[7]

No one can say for sure how many decisions you will make as a supervisor, but you should realize that problem-solving and decision-making skills will affect your results. As with all the supervisory skills, problem solving and decision making can be developed.

CONNECTIONS

1. Explain why problem-solving and decision-making skills are important to the supervisor.

This section discusses the supervisory functions and problem solving and decision making, decision-making styles, and the problem-solving and decision-making model. But first, let's examine what a problem is and the relationship between objectives and problem solving and decision making.

Objectives and Problem Solving and Decision Making

Problem solving and decision making are based on objectives. As a supervisor, you set objectives. When your objectives are not being met, you have a problem. The better you are at proactive planning the fewer problems you will have to solve. Proactive planning focuses on preventing problems before they occur, and on creating opportunities. Seeking opportunities requires the same consideration as does solving existing problems. The fewer problems you have, the more time you will have to take advantage of opportunities.

A **problem** *exists whenever there is a difference between what is actually happening and what the supervisor wants to happen.* If the supervisor's objective is to produce 500 units per day, but the department produces only 450, there is a problem. Major causes of problems include ineffective materials, tools, methods, or personnel. **Problem solving** *is the process of taking corrective action in order to meet objectives.* Taking corrective action (problem solving) is step 4 in the control process discussed in Chapter 4.

Decision making *is the process of selecting an alternative course of action that will solve a problem.* Decisions must be made when you are faced with a problem. The first is whether to take corrective action. Instead, you can simply choose to change objectives. In the above example, the supervisor can change the objective to 450 units per day.

There is no constant link between problems and decision making. Some problems cannot be solved, and others are not worth the time and effort it would take to solve them. However, your job is to achieve objectives. Therefore, you will have to attempt to solve most problems. Following the suggestions in this chapter can help you develop your problem-solving and decision-making skills.

The Supervisory Functions and Problem Solving and Decision Making

All supervisors perform the same five supervisory functions: planning, organizing, staffing, leading, and controlling. While performing these functions, supervisors must make decisions. In fact, making decisions should precede taking action.[8] For example, when planning, the supervisor must make decisions about objectives and when, where, and how they will be met. When organizing, the supervisor must make decisions about what to delegate and how to coordinate the department's resources. When staffing, the supervisor must decide whom to hire and how to train and evaluate employees. To lead, the supervisor must decide how to influence employees and which control methods are most effective.

Problem solving and decision making are conceptual skills. They are also central to supervisory success.[9]

Decision-Making Styles

Although decision making is important, individuals differ in the way they approach decisions. To determine if your decision-making style is reflexive, reflective, or consistent,[10] answer the 10 questions in Self-Learning Exercise 5–1 by selecting the choice that best describes how you make decisions.

SELF-LEARNING EXERCISE 5–1

Decision-Making Styles

A. Overall, I'm _____ to act.

    1. quick   2. moderate   3. slow

B. I spend _____ amount of time making important decisions as I do making less important decisions.

    1. about the same   2. a greater   3. a much greater

C. When making decisions, I _____ go with my first thought.

    1. usually   2. occasionally   3. rarely

D. When making decisions, I'm _____ concerned about making errors.

    1. rarely   2. occasionally   3. often

E. When making decisions, I _____ recheck my work more than once.

    1. rarely   2. occasionally   3. usually

F. When making decisions, I gather _____ information.

    1. little   2. some   3. lots of

G. When making decisions, I consider _____ alternative actions.

    1. few   2. some   3. lots of

H. When making a decision, I usually make it _____ before the deadline.

    1. way   2. somewhat   3. just

I. After making a decision, I _____ look for other alternatives, wishing I had waited.

   1. rarely   2. occasionally   3. usually

J. I _____ regret having made a decision.

   1. rarely   2. occasionally   3. often

To determine your style, add up the numbers 1 through 3 that represent your answers to the 10 questions. The total will be between 10 and 30. Place an X on the continuum line between 10 and 30 that represents your score number.

Reflexive	Consistent	Reflective
10 _____	16 _____	23 _____ 30

A score of 10–16 indicates a reflexive style; 17–23 indicates a consistent style; and 24–30 indicates a reflective style. You have determined your preferred decision-making style. Groups also have a preferred decision-making style, based on how its members make decisions. You could answer the 10 questions, changing the *I* to *we* and referring to a group rather than to yourself.

Reflexive Style

A reflexive decision maker likes to make quick decisions (shooting from the hip) without taking the time to get all the information that may be needed, and without considering all alternatives. On the positive side, reflexive decision makers are decisive; they do not procrastinate. On the negative side, making quick decisions can lead to waste and duplication when the best possible alternative is overlooked. Employees may see a decision maker as a poor supervisor if he or she consistently makes bad decisions. If you use a reflexive style, you may want to slow down and spend more time gathering information and analyzing alternatives. Following the steps in problem-solving and decision-making Model 5–1 can help you develop these skills.

Reflective Style

A reflective decision maker likes to take plenty of time to make decisions, gathering considerable information and analyzing several alternatives. On the positive side, the reflective type does not make hasty decisions. On the negative side, he or she may procrastinate and waste valuable time and other resources. The reflective decision maker may be viewed as wishy-washy and indecisive. If you use a reflective style, you may want to speed up your decision making. As Andrew Jackson once said, "Take time to deliberate; but when the time for action arrives, stop thinking and go on."

Consistent Style

Consistent decision makers tend to make decisions without rushing or wasting time. They know when they have enough information and alternatives to make a sound decision. Consistent decision makers tend to have the best record for making good decisions. They tend to follow the problem-solving and decision-making steps in Model 5–1.

Problem-Solving and Decision-Making Model

Although management theorists generally agree on the process—how decisions are made—they disagree about the number of steps involved in problem solving and decision making. Nonetheless, five steps can be identified with certainty. The **problem-solving and decision making steps** *include defining the problem; setting* *objectives and criteria; generating alternatives; analyzing alternatives and selecting one; and planning, implementing the decision, and controlling.* These steps are expanded on in Model 5–1. We will also examine them in greater detail in the sections that follow.

Practicing supervisors do not always follow the steps in the model. One reason is that most problems and decisions are recurring; thus, there is no need to proceed through all the steps every time. In addition, some decisions are not suited to the model. However, the model should be followed when making decisions involving people.[11]

Following the steps in the model will not guarantee that you make good decisions; however, it will increase your chances of success in problem solving and decision making.[12] Consult others as you progress through the steps.[13] Consciously use the model in your daily life, and you will improve your ability to solve problems and make decisions.

Model 5–1 summarizes the five steps in problem solving and decision making. Notice that the steps do not simply go from start to the end. At any step you may have to return to a prior step to make changes. For example, if you are in the fifth step and control and implementation are not going as planned, you may have to backtrack to prior steps to take corrective action by generating and selecting a new alternative or changing the objective. If the problem was not defined accurately, you may have to go back to the beginning.

LEARNING OBJECTIVE

1. Describe the five steps in the problem-solving and decision-making model and use the model on the job.

CONNECTIONS

3. Solve the problem listed in Connections 2, following the five steps in the problem-solving and decision-making model. Be sure to clearly label each step and substep.

II. Step 1. Define the Problem

Classify the Problem

Problems may be classified in terms of the decision structure involved[14] or the conditions under which a decision will be made.

Decision Structure

In structured recurring or routine situations, the supervisor should follow established standing plans (discussed in Chapter 2) when making decisions.[15] *Such* **programmed decisions** *are solutions to recurring, routine problems.* Standing plans are designed to save the decision maker time and effort. For example, a specified amount of inventory will be reordered every time stock reaches a specified level. When problems or decisions arise, the supervisor should determine whether existing standing plans apply to the situation.

If the problem or decision is not recurring, standing plans do not apply; the problem is unstructured or unprogrammed. **Unprogrammed decisions** *are solutions to unique, nonroutine problems.* For example, an office is automating and the supervisor must decide which type of personal computer to use in his or her department. However, if it seems as though the situation will recur, the supervisor should develop standing plans for dealing with it. In our example, the unique decisions made in purchasing the PCs can be applied to future purchases. Solving unprogrammed problems should take more time and effort than solving programmed problems. When making programmed decisions, the supervisor usually does not need to follow the problem-solving and decision-making steps; however, the steps should be followed for unprogrammed decisions. As a supervisor, most of the time you spend on problem solving and decision making will involve programmed decisions.

MODEL 5–1   **PROBLEM-SOLVING AND DECISION-MAKING MODEL**

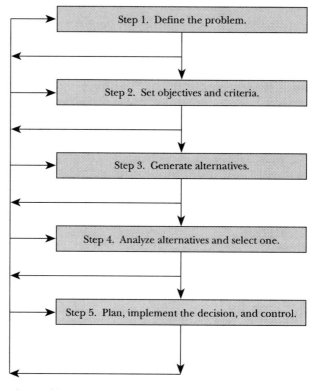

Step 1.   Define the problem.
    a. Classify the problem.
    b. Decide which supervisory style to use.
    c. Determine the causes of the problem.

Step 2.   Set objectives and criteria.
    a. Identify the desired end results.
    b. Select criteria the decision must meet.

Step 3.   Generate alternatives.
    a. Creatively think of several possible ways to solve the problem.

Step 4.   Analyze alternatives and select one.
    a. Compare each alternative to the objective and criteria.
    b. Select the alternative that best solves the problem by meeting criteria.

Step 5.   Plan, implement the decision, and control.
    a. Develop plans for implementing the decision.
    b. Put the decision into action.
    c. Review progress to ensure the problem is solved. If it is, stop. If it is not, repeat the previous steps.

Decision-Making Conditions

Certainty: When making a decision under the conditions of certainty, a supervisor knows the outcome of each alternative in advance. As an example, suppose you were considering making an investment. If you looked at bonds, money market accounts, certificates of deposit, or a regular savings account, you would know the payoff of each of the alternatives and a decision could be made with certainty as to the interest paid. However, you will rarely face decision making under conditions of complete certainty.

Uncertainty: Under conditions of uncertainty, lack of information or knowledge makes the outcome of each alternative unpredictable. Often significant decisions are made under conditions of uncertainty, such as introducing an innovative product or service, for example, the introduction of computers. There were so many variables that it was not possible to predict the likelihood of success with any degree of confidence.

Risk: Complete certainty and complete uncertainty are opposite extremes. Between the two are decisions involving various degrees of risk. When making a decision under conditions of risk, you do not know the outcome of each alternative in advance, but you are aware of the probability of each outcome. Most supervisors make decisions under conditions of risk, but they can predict the likelihood of success based on past history and experience. Usually, risk cannot be avoided.[16] Although risk cannot be eliminated, it can be reduced. For example, June, a sales manager, has a list of potential customers. She does not know for certain who will buy the product. However, based on the information and her experience. June can predict the probability of each customer's buying the product. She can then assign salespeople to call on customers with the highest probability of purchasing. The risk of any decision varies based on the reliability and complexity of the information and knowledge involved. The more reliable and less complex the information is, the more certain the results.

LEARNING OBJECTIVE

2. Explain the difference between programmed and unprogrammed decisions and between conditions of certainty, uncertainty, and risk.

CONNECTIONS

4. Give an example of a programmed and an unprogrammed decision.

Decide Which Supervisory Style to Use

When a problem exists, the supervisor must decide who should participate in solving it.[17] As a rule of thumb, only the key people involved should participate.[18] However, the current trend in management is toward increased employee participation. Thus, the major question is not whether a supervisor should allow employees to participate in problem solving and decision making, but when and how this should be done. When solving problems and making decisions, you should use the supervisory style (autocratic, consultative, participative, or laissez-faire, discussed in Chapter 1) appropriate to the situation. We will address this issue in more detail in a later section of this chapter.

Determine the Causes of the Problem

Owing to time pressures in crisis situations, supervisors are often in a hurry to solve problems. In their haste, they may neglect the first step in problem solving, defining the problem.[19] To define the problem, a supervisor must determine its cause. In determining the causes of the problem, the supervisor needs time to think, preferably in a quiet, reflective, and focused manner.[20] Determining the causes of a problem involves looking back to understand the past and then forward to predict the future.[21] The supervisor must also get the necessary information and facts.[22]

Distinguish Symptoms from the Cause of the Problem

To do this, list the observable and describable occurrences (symptoms) that indicate a problem exists. Once this is done, you must determine the cause of the problem. If the cause is eliminated, the symptoms should disappear.

For example, Wayne, an employee with five years on the job, has been an excellent producer. However, in the last month, Wayne has been out sick or late more times than he was in the past two years. What is the problem? If you say "absenteeism" or "lateness," you are confusing symptoms and causes. They are symptoms of the problem. If the supervisor simply disciplines him, Wayne may be late or absent less often, but the problem will not be solved. It would be wiser for his supervisor to talk to Wayne and discover the reason for the problem (the cause).[23] The cause may be a personal problem at home or on the job.[23] The key is that the decision maker must define the problem correctly in order to solve it.

III. Step 2. Set Objectives and Criteria

In defining the problem, the supervisor has determined what type of decision must be made, who should be involved, and what the problem is. The supervisor is now ready to set an objective and develop criteria. The supervisor should have an objective.[24] Research indicates that supervisors with specific objectives formulate better operational plans and make better decisions.[25] Unfortunately, this is not as simple as it sounds. The objective must state exactly what is to be accomplished[26] (see Chapter 2.)

You should also specify the criteria for achieving the objective. It is helpful to distinguish "must" and "want" criteria. Must criteria have to be met whereas want criteria are desirable but not necessary.

An example of an objective and criteria for hiring a manager might be as follows: objective—to hire a store manager by June 30, 19—. The must criteria are a college degree and a minimum of five years' experience as a store manager. The want criterion is that the person should be a minority group member. The supervisor wants to hire a minority but will not hire one who does not meet the must criteria. We will discuss criteria again later in this chapter.

IV. Step 3. Generate Alternatives

After the problem is defined and objectives and criteria are set, the decision maker is ready to generate possible alternatives for solving the problem. There are usually many possible ways to solve a problem; in fact, if you don't have two or more alternatives, you don't have to make a decision. Supervisors should also consider the time, energy, and cost of gathering information. Supervisors can neither expect nor afford complete information.[27]

In programmed decision making, the alternatives are fairly straightforward. However, in unprogrammed decision making, new and creative solutions are needed.

Creativity

Creativity *is the ability to develop unique alternatives for solving problems.* Several U.S. industries have not been as creative as their foreign counterparts and have lost sales to them. The automotive and steel industries are examples. On the other hand, Adelphi University provides an example of a creative solution to a problem. The university wanted to expand its graduate business program. However, many potential students felt that they did not have the time to further their education. The alternative that Adelphi developed was the "classroom on wheels," which offers classes four days a week on commuter trains into and out of New York City. Needless to say, imaginative and creative thinking are scarce resources.[28] Nonetheless, creativity can be developed by supervisors and their employees.[29]

The Creative Process: There are four **stages in the creative process:** *preparation, possible solutions, incubation, and evaluation.*[30]

Following these guidelines, summarized in Exhibit 5–1, can help you improve your creativity.

EXHIBIT 5-1 | **STAGES IN THE CREATIVE PROCESS**

Stage 1. Preparation

Stage 2. Possible solutions

Stage 3. Incubation

Stage 4. Evaluation

LEARNING OBJECTIVE

3. List and explain the four stages in the creative process.

1. *Preparation.* The supervisor must become familiar with the problem. Get others' opinions, feelings, and ideas, as well as the facts.[31] When solving a problem, look for new angles, use imagination and invention, and don't limit boundaries.[32]

2. *Possible solutions.* Generate as many possible solutions as you can think of without making a judgment.

3. *Incubation.* After generating alternatives, take a break; sleep on the problem. Take some time before working on the problem again. During the incubation stage, you may gain an insight into the solution. Have you ever worked hard on something and become discouraged but found that when you gave up or took a break, the solution came to you?

4. *Evaluation.* Before implementing a solution, you should evaluate the alternative to make sure the idea is practical. Evaluation often leads to more creativity.

CONNECTIONS

5. Give an example of how you solved a problem using the stages in the creative process, or solve an existing problem using it.

V. Step 4. Analyze Alternatives and Select One

A supervisor may not always select the best alternative. In many cases, the factors involved will dictate a compromise.[33] In evaluating alternatives, a supervisor should think forward and try to predict the possible outcome of each.[34] Several popular analysis techniques are briefly presented in this section.

Cost-Benefit Analysis

Cost-benefit analysis *is a technique for comparing the cost and benefit of each alternative course of action.* Each alternative has positive and negative aspects, or pros and cons, including cost and benefits. However, these are not always easy to determine. The supervisor needs to use intuition and judgment when performing a cost-benefit analysis. Bear in mind that the cost of some alternatives will be greater than the benefits they provide. These alternatives must not be selected.

The Kepner-Tregoe Method

The Kepner-Tregoe Method is a technique for comparing alternatives using the criteria selected as step 2 in the problem-solving and decision-making model. An example of its use is shown in Exhibit 5–2. You should refer to the exhibit to clarify the discussion.

EXHIBIT 5-2   **KEPNER-TREGOE ALTERNATIVE ANALYSIS**

Must criteria	Car A	Car B	Car C	Car D
Cost under $5,000	Yes	Yes	Yes	Yes
Available within two weeks	Yes	Yes	Yes	No

Want criteria				Meets Criteria					
	Importance	A	WS*	B	WS*	C	WS*	D	WS*
Gas mileage	7 ×	5 =	35	6	42	8	56		
Sporty	8 ×	5 =	40	7	56	4	32		
Blue	3 ×	10 =	30	0	0	0	0		
AM/FM stereo	5 ×	7 =	35	8	40	3	15		
Cruise control	3 ×	0 =	0	0	0	0	0		
Good condition	10 ×	5 =	50	6	60	8	80		
Low mileage	6 ×	6 =	36	4	24	5	30		
Total weighted score			226		222		213		

*Weighted score

Step 1: Compare each alternative to the must criteria. Any alternative that does not meet the must criteria is eliminated. To illustrate, let's state that our objective is to buy a car within two weeks. This is an unprogrammed decision, and you will decide by yourself. The must and want criteria for each alternative are listed in the exhibit. (These correspond to steps 2 and 3 in Model 5–1.) As you can see, alternative D does not meet all the must criteria and is eliminated.

Step 2: Rank each want criterion on a scale of 1 to 10 (10 being most important). These ranks are listed in the "importance" column in Exhibit 5–2.

Step 3: Assign a value of 1 to 10 (10 being the highest) to how well each alternative meets the want criteria. These values are shown in the vertical columns labeled A–D.

Step 4: Calculate the weighted score for each alternative by multiplying (horizontally) the importance value by the meets criteria value. Next add the total weight for each want criteria.

Step 5: Select the alternative with the highest total weighted score as the solution to the problem. Car A should be selected because it has the highest weighted score.

Quantitative Techniques

Quantitative techniques use math to aid in analyzing alternative solutions. We will discuss some of these techniques below. The intent is to make you aware of the techniques, not to make you a mathematician. If you are interested in the actual calculations, you might want to take a course in quantitative analysis.

Supervisors are generally not expected to calculate the math, or even use these techniques. However, if you know when to use these techniques you can seek help from specialists within or outside the organization. Going to your boss and suggesting using any of these techniques appropriately will show initiative on your part.

Break-Even Analysis

This technique allows calculation of the volume of sales that will result in a profit. It involves forecasting the volume of sales and the cost of production. The break-even point is the level at which there is no profit or loss. Combinations of costs versus sales above this point yield a profit; those below it, a loss. Break-even analysis is often shown in chart form with the revenue or cost on the vertical axis and the units produced or sold on the horizontal axis.

Capital Budgeting

These techniques are used to analyze alternative investments. One is the *payback* approach, which allows calculation of the number of years it will take to recover the initial cash invested. The alternative having the quickest payback is preferred. Another technique is used to calculate the *average rate of return*. It is appropriate when the yearly returns are not equal. A more sophisticated technique is the *discounted cash flow* method, which takes into account the time value of money. The assumption is that a dollar today is worth more than a dollar in the future. Organizations including AMF, Kellogg, Procter & Gamble, and 3M use discounted cash flow.

Linear Programming

Optimum allocation of resources is determined using linear programming (LP). The resources a supervisor typically allocates include time, money, space, material, equipment, and employees. It is primarily used for programmed decisions under conditions of certainty. LP is widely applied to product-mix decisions. Lear Siegler, Inc. uses LP when determining work flow, to optimize the use of its equipment and production. Bendix Corporation uses LP to minimize transportation (shipping) costs for its truck fleet.

Queuing Theory

An organization can have any number of employees providing service to customers. These employees cost the company money in salaries. If there are too few employees, the company can lose customers, and this costs money in lost revenue. Queuing theory helps the company balance these two costs. Queuing theory is used by retail stores to determine the optimum number of checkout clerks; by airports to determine the optimum number of takeoffs and landings on runways; and by production departments to schedule preventive maintenance on equipment.

Probability Theory

LEARNING
OBJECTIVE

4. Understand how to use seven techniques for analyzing alternatives.

This method enables the user to make decisions under the condition of risk. A probability of success or failure is assigned to each alternative. The expected value, which is the payoff or profit from each combination of alternatives and outcomes, is then calculated. The calculations are usually done on a payoff matrix or decision tree by multiplying the probability of the outcome by the benefit or cost. Probability theory is used to determine whether to expand facilities, and to what size; to select the most profitable investment portfolio; to determine the amount of inventory to stock; and to choose a job.

CONNECTIONS

6. Give an example in which it would be appropriate for a supervisor to use the Kepner-Tregoe alternative analysis.

7. Give examples of situations in which it would be appropriate for the supervisor to seek mathematical assistance in order to use break-even analysis, capital budgeting, linear programming, queuing theory, and probability theory.

VI. Step 5. Plan, Implement the Decision, and Control

The final step in problem solving and decision making involves three phases.

Plan

After making a decision, a supervisor must develop a plan of action with a schedule for implementation.[35] Refer to Chapter 2 for a detailed description of how to develop plans.

Implement the Decision

After a decision has been made and plans developed, the plans must be implemented. Communicating the plan to all employees is critical to successful implementation. (We will discuss communications further in Chapter 7.) Delegation may be necessary (refer to Chapter 3 for details on how to delegate).

Control

Controlling was dealt with in Chapter 4. As mentioned, controls should be developed while planning. Checkpoints should be established to determine whether the alterative chosen is solving the problem. If it is not, corrective action may be needed. A supervisor should not be locked into a decision and wind up throwing good money after bad.[36] When a supervisor makes a poor decision, he or she should admit the mistake and try to rectify it by going back over the steps in the problem-solving and decision-making model.

VII. Participation in Problem Solving and Decision Making

In this section you will learn the advantages and disadvantages of using groups in decision making and a method for selecting the appropriate supervisory style to meet the needs of the situation. First, let's examine ways in which groups can be used to generate solutions.

Using Groups to Generate Alternatives

There are a variety of methods available when using group participation to generate alternative solutions to a problem. Following are some of the more popular techniques.

Brainstorming

Brainstorming *is the process of suggesting as many alternatives as possible without evaluation.* The group is presented with a problem and asked to develop as many solutions as possible. When brainstorming, employees should be encouraged to make wild, extreme suggestions. They should also build on suggestions made by others. Status differences should be ignored. Everyone should have an equal voice.[37] None of the alternatives should be evaluated until all possibilities are exhausted. Brainstorming can be used for problems requiring creative ideas such as naming a new product or service. This technique is not appropriate for decisions made under conditions of uncertainty such as whether to introduce a new product or service.

Synectics

Synectics *is the process of generating novel alternatives through role playing and fantasizing.* Synectics focuses on generating novel ideas rather than a quantity of ideas. At first, the leader does not even state the exact nature of the problem so that group members avoid preconceptions. For example, when Nolan Bushnell wanted to develop a new concept in family dining, he began by discussing leisure activities generally. Bushnell then moved to leisure activities having to do with eating out. The idea that came out of this synectic process was a restaurant–electronic game complex where families could entertain themselves while eating pizza and hamburgers. The complex is called Showbiz/Pizza Time Inc. and its mascot is Chuck E. Cheese.

Nominal Grouping

Nominal grouping *is the process of generating and evaluating alternatives using a structured voting method.* This process usually involves six steps. (1) Each employee generates ideas in writing. (2) The supervisor lists all ideas where everyone can see them. (3) Alternatives are clarified through a guided discussion, and any additional ideas are listed. (4) Each employee rates the ideas and votes; the voting eliminates alternatives. (5) An initial discussion of the voting is conducted for clarification, not persuasion. During this time, employees should explain their choices and their reasons for making them.[38] (6) A final vote is taken to select the alternative that will be presented to the supervisor. The supervisor may or may not implement the decision. (This is an example of the participative supervisory style.)

Consensus Mapping

Consensus mapping *is the process of developing a group consensus to solving a problem.*[39] It represents a cooperative attempt to develop a solution acceptable to all employees rather than a competitive battle in which a solution is forced on some members of the group.[40] Consensus mapping is an extension of nominal grouping. The principal difference is that in consensus mapping the group categorizes or clusters ideas rather than choosing a single solution. A major benefit of consensus mapping is that because the solution is the group's, members generally are more committed to implementing it.

The Delphi Technique

The **Delphi technique** *involves using a series of anonymous questionnaires to refine a solution.* Responses on the first questionnaire are analyzed and resubmitted to participants on a second questionnaire. This process may continue for five or more rounds before a consensus emerges. The Delphi technique is primarily used for technological forecasting such as projecting the next computer breakthrough and its effect on the banking industry.

Synectics and Delphi techniques are more commonly used by upper-level managers rather than supervisors. If you use brainstorming, nominal grouping, or consensus mapping, be on guard against responses that kill creativity. Some of these statements are listed in Exhibit 5–3. If your employees make such statements, make everyone realize that this demonstrates a negative attitude and is unproductive.

LEARNING OBJECTIVE

5. Describe the five methods of generating group alternatives.

CONNECTIONS

8. Give examples of situations in which it would be appropriate for the supervisor to use brainstorming, nominal grouping, and consensus mapping.

EXHIBIT 5 – 3   **RESPONSES THAT KILL CREATIVITY**

- It isn't in the budget.
- Don't be ridiculous.
- We've never done it before.
- Has anyone else ever tried it?
- It won't work in our company (industry).
- That's not our problem.
- We tried that before.
- It can't be done.
- It costs too much.
- That's beyond our responsibility.
- It's too radical a change.
- We did all right without it.
- We're doing the best we can.
- We don't have the time.
- That will make other equipment obsolete.
- We're too small (big) for it.
- Let's get back to reality.
- Why change it? It's still working okay.
- We're not ready for that.
- You're years ahead of your time.
- You can't teach an old dog new tricks.
- Let's form a committee.

Advantages of Group Problem Solving and Decision Making

Better Decisions: Participative management is beneficial. Groups usually do a better job in solving complex problems.[41] Using groups to solve problems and make decisions is appropriate for unprogrammed decisions made under conditions of risk or uncertainty.

More Alternatives: A diverse group offers different points of view and a variety of alternative solutions.[42] A group may be more creative than an individual. Members can build on each others' ideas to improve the quality of alternatives.

One approach to improving the quality of decisions is called the **devil's advocate approach,** *which involves an individual explaining and defending his or her position before the group.* The group asks the presenter questions and tries to shoot holes in the idea. This way, any possible problems in implementation are identified. This approach requires focus and maturity. While in graduate school, I used this technique with a study group to analyze cases. One member would present his or her solution to the case while the other members came up with reasons why the solution would not work. After a period of time, the solution was refined.

Acceptance: The chances of successfully implementing a decision can be greatly increased if those affected are involved in the decision-making process.[43] How the decision is made is often more important than the decision itself. Consensus builds ownership, enthusiasm, and a commitment to action.[44]

Morale: Participation in problem solving and decision making is tangibly reward-ing and personally satisfying to all parties involved. With participation comes better understanding of why decisions are made and improved communications within the department.

Disadvantages of Group Problem Solving and Decision Making

Time: It takes longer for a group to make a decision. Employees involved in problem solving and decision making are not on the job producing. Thus, group involvement costs the organization time and money.

Domination: One group member or subgroup may dominate and nullify the group decision. Subgroups may develop and destructive conflict may result. Conflicting secondary goals may also develop. An individual or subgroup may try to win an argument rather than find the best solution, or may put personal needs before the group's needs.

Conformity: Group members may feel pressured to go along with the group's solution without questioning it out of fear of not being accepted. This nullifies the advantage of diversity. This conformity has been labeled "groupthink."

Responsibility: The supervisor is responsible for the decision regardless of how it is made. A supervisor may delegate authority to the group but he or she remains responsible. As a result, a supervisor must be able to effectively utilize the group when solving problems and making decisions.[45]

LEARNING OBJECTIVE

6. List and explain the advantages and disadvantages of group problem solving and decision making.

Selecting the Appropriate Supervisory Style

Supervisors adopt different styles depending on the type of decisions they must make.[46] In addition to capability level, discussed in Chapter 1, a supervisor must also consider time, information, and acceptance. There are two steps in selecting the appropriate situational supervisory style for problem solving and decision making: diagnosing the situation and selecting the appropriate style.

**Step 1.
Diagnose
the Situation**

The first step involves diagnosing the situational variables, including time, infor-mation, acceptance, and employee capability.

Time: The supervisor must determine whether there is enough time to include employees in decision making. If there is not, the supervisor should use the autocratic style, regardless of preference. When there is no time to include employees in problem solving and decision making, the supervisor should ignore the other three variables; they are irrelevant if there is no time. A short time frame may permit use of the consultative style, but not the participative or laissez-faire styles. Time is a relative term. In one situation, a few minutes may be considered a short time period, but in another a month may be a short period of time.

Information: Does the supervisor have enough information to make a quality decision alone? If the supervisor has all the necessary information, there is no need for employee participation, and the autocratic style is appropriate. When the supervisor has some information but needs more, the consultative style may be appropriate. If the supervisor has little information, the appropriate style may be participative or laissez-faire.

Acceptance: The supervisor must decide whether employee acceptance of the decision is critical to implementation. If the supervisor makes the decision alone, will the employee or group implement it? If the employee or group will be accepting, the appropriate style is probably autocratic. If the employee or group will be reluctant, the appropriate style may be consultative or participative. If the employee or group will probably reject the decision, the participative or laissez-faire style may be appropriate.

Capability: The supervisor must decide whether the employee or group has the ability and willingness to be involved in problem solving and decision making. Does the employee or group have the experience and information needed to be involved? Will the employee or group put the organization's or department's goals ahead of personal goals? Does the employee or group want to be involved in problem solving and decision making? Employees are more willing to participate when the decisions personally affect them.

If the employee's or group's capability level is low (C-1), an autocratic style may be appropriate. When an employee's or group's capability is moderate (C-2), a consultative style may be appropriate. If the employee's or group's capability level is high (C-3), a participative style might be adopted. If the employee's or group's level of capability is outstanding (C-4), choose the laissez-faire style. Remember that an employee's or group's capability level can change from situation to situation.

Step 2. Select the Appropriate Supervisory Style

After considering the four variables, a supervisor must select the appropriate style. In some situations, all variables will indicate that the same style is appropriate, whereas in other cases, the appropriate style is not so clear. For example, a supervisor may have time to use any style, may have all the information necessary (autocratic), employees may be reluctant (consultative or participative), and their capability may be moderate (consultative). In situations where different styles are indicated for different variables, the supervisor must determine which variable should be given more weight. In the above example, assume that acceptance was critical for successful implementation of the decision. Acceptance takes precedence over information. Because the employees involved have moderate capability, the consultative style would be appropriate. Model 5–2 summarizes use of the four situational supervisory styles in decision making.

Applying the Situational Problem-Solving and Decision-Making Model

We will apply the model to the following situation; more situations are presented in Skill-Building Exercise SB 5–1.

Ben, a supervisor, can give one of his employees a merit pay raise. He has a week to make the decision. Ben knows how well each employee performed over the past year. The employees really have no option but to accept getting or not getting the pay raise, but they can complain to upper management about the selection. The employees' capability levels vary, but as a group they have a high capability level under normal circumstances.

_____ time _____ information _____ acceptance _____ capability

Step 1. Diagnose the Situation: Ben has plenty of time to use any level of participation. He has all the information needed to make the decision (autocratic). Employees have no choice but to accept the decision (autocratic). And the group's capability level is normally high (participative).

Step 2. Select the Appropriate Style for the Situation: There are conflicting styles to choose from (autocratic and participative):

  yes time   S-A information   S-A acceptance   S-P capability

The variable that should be given precedence is information. The employees are normally capable, but in a situation like this they may not put the department's goals ahead of their own. In other words, even if employees know who deserves the

| MODEL 5-2 | **SITUATIONAL PROBLEM-SOLVING AND DECISION-MAKING MODEL** |

Step 1. Diagnose the situation.

Variable	Use of Supervisory Style
Time	No: S-A Yes: S-C, S-P, or S-L
Information	All: S-A Some: S-C Little: S-P or S-L
Acceptance	Acceptance: S-A Reluctance: S-C Rejection: S-P or S-L
Capability	Low: S-A Moderate: S-C High: S-P Outstanding: S-L

Step 2. Select the appropriate style for the situation.

Autocratic (S-A)
The supervisor makes the decision alone and announces it after the fact. An explanation of the rationale for the decision may be given.

Consultative (S-C)
The supervisor consults the group for information and then makes the decision. Before implementing the decision, the supervisor explains the rationale for the decision and sells the benefits to the employees. The supervisor may invite questions and have a discussion.

Participative (S-P)
The supervisor may present a tentative decision to the group and ask for its input. The supervisor may change the decision if the input warrants a change. Or the supervisor presents the problem to the group for suggestions. Based on employee participation, the supervisor makes the decision and explains its rationale.

Laissez-faire (S-L)
The supervisor presents the situation to the group and describes limitations to the decision. The group makes the decision. The supervisor may be a group member.

raise, they may fight for it anyway. Such a conflict could cause future problems. Some possible ways to make the decision include the following:

- Autocratic (S-A). The supervisor would select the person to be given the raise without discussing it with any employees. Ben would simply announce the decision after submitting it to the payroll department.

- Consultative (S-C). The supervisor would get information from the employees concerning who should get the raise. Ben would then decide who would get the raise. He would announce the decision and explain the rationale for it. He may invite questions and discussion.

- Participative (S-P). The supervisor could tentatively select the employee who gets the raise, but be open to change if a group member convinces him that someone else should. Or Ben could explain the situation to the group and lead a discussion concerning who should get the raise. After considering their input, Ben would make the decision and explain the rationale for it. Notice

LEARNING
OBJECTIVE

7. Explain how to use
the problem-solving
and decision-making model
and use it on the job.

that the consultative style does not allow for discussion as the participative style does.

- Laissez-faire (S-L). The supervisor would explain the situation and allow the group to decide who gets the raise. Ben may be a group member. Notice that this is the only style that allows the group to make the decision.

The autocratic style is appropriate for this situation. Skill-Building Exercise SB 5-1 will help develop your ability to select the appropriate situational problem-solving and decision-making supervisory style.

CONNECTIONS

9. Identify the primary situational supervisory problem-solving and decision-making styles used by your present or past boss. Give an example of when the boss used this style.

10. Give examples of situations in which the autocratic, consultative, participative, and laissez-faire supervisory styles would be appropriate.

VIII. Guidelines for Problem Solving and Decision Making

The following guidelines should help you improve your skill in problem solving and decision making.

- Don't avoid problems or procrastinate; be proactive; try to anticipate and prevent problems.
- Follow the five steps in the problem-solving and decision-making model, step by step.
- When defining a problem, don't jump to conclusions. Focus only on the information directly related to the problem or decision.[47]
- Involve the necessary people when solving problems, and use the appropriate situational supervisory style.
- Do not generate and evaluate alternatives at the same time.
- Use the appropriate technique for analyzing alternatives.
- Always give an answer, whether yes or no, once you have sufficient information. Do not vacillate or give a pocket veto.[48]
- Remember that most decisions can be changed if they do not solve the problem or if better alternatives appear.
- Do not bring a problem to your boss without a solution. You were hired to solve problems, not create them.[49]
- Do not dwell on the past, but learn from it.[50]
- Make decisions during your prime time, when you are at your best (morning, afternoon, or night). Also try to see your boss during his or her prime time.[51]
- Give people credit for helping; you need all the friends you can get when taking risks to solve problems.

Decision Responsibility   You should use the appropriate style for the given situation. Whichever decision style you use, be sure that you realize that, as a supervisor, you have ultimate decision responsibility. Whether you make the decision alone or give the group the authority to make the decision, you are held responsible and accountable by higher-level management.

REVIEW

Select one or more methods: (1) fill in the missing key terms from memory; (2) match the key terms from the end of the review with their definitions below; (3) copy the key terms in order from the key terms at the beginning of the chapter.

A _____ exists whenever there is a difference between what is actually happening and what the supervisor wants to happen. _____ is the process of taking corrective action to meet objectives. _____ is the process of selecting an alternative that will solve a problem. The supervisor cannot perform the supervisory functions without making decisions. There are three decision-making styles; reflexive, consistent, and reflective. The _____ include defining the problem; setting objectives and criteria; generating alternatives; analyzing alternatives and selecting one; and planning, implementing the decision, and controlling.

Defining the problem involves three stages: The first is classifying the decision in terms of structure and condition. The decisions can be _____ , solutions to recurring routine problems; or _____ , solutions to unique, nonroutine problems. Decisions may be made under conditions of certainty, risk, or uncertainty. A supervisor must also decide which supervisory style to use when making the decision. And he or she must distinguish symptoms from the cause in defining the problem.

Once the problem has been defined, the supervisor should know what type of decision must be made and who should be involved. The supervisor is now ready to proceed to step 2 in the problem-solving and decision-making model: setting objectives and criteria that will solve the problem.

The third step in problem solving and decision making is to generate alternative solutions. When doing this, the supervisor should use _____ , the ability to develop unique alternatives for solving problems. The _____ steps are (1) preparation, (2) generation of possible solutions, (3) incubation, and (4) evaluation.

The fourth step in problem solving and decision making is analyzing the alternatives and selecting one. When analyzing alternatives, the supervisor should perform a _____ , a technique for comparing the cost and benefit of each alternative. The supervisor may also use the Kepner-Tregoe method to analyze alternatives. Or he or she may employ quantitative techniques such as break-even analysis, capital budgeting, linear programming, queuing theory, or probability theory.

The fifth and last step in problem solving and decision making is to develop a plan, implement the plan, and control to ensure that the problem is solved.

There are advantages (better decisions, more alternatives, acceptance, and morale) and disadvantages (time, domination, conformity, and responsibility) to using a group when solving problems or making decisions. Techniques for group problem solving include _____ , suggesting as many alternatives as possible; _____ , generating novel alternatives through role playing and fantasizing; _____ , generating and evaluating alternatives using a structured voting method; _____ , developing a group consensus on the solution to a problem; and the _____ , which refines a solution using a series of anonymous questionnaires. The _____ , in which an individual explains and defends his or her position before the group, can improve the quality of decisions. When selecting an appropriate situational supervisory style, the supervisor must consider four variables: time, information, acceptance, and capability.

KEY TERMS

brainstorming
consensus mapping
cost-benefit analysis
creativity
decision making
Delphi technique
devil's advocate approach
nominal grouping

problem
problem solving
problem-solving and decision-making steps
programmed decisions
stages in the creative process
synectics
unprogrammed decisions

REFERENCES

1. M. R. Hansen, "Better Supervision from A to W," *Supervisory Management,* August 1985, p. 36.

2. John Franco, "Supervision: Critical Performance Link," *Industry Week,* April 15, 1985, p. 14.

3. Charles MacDonald, *Performance-Based Supervisory Development* (Amherst, MA: Human Resources Press, 1982), p. 20.

4. Lester Bittel, *What Every Supervisor Should Know* (New York: McGraw-Hill, 1985), p. 137.

5. Hillel Einhorn and Robin Hogarth, "Decision Making: Going Forward in Reverse," *Harvard Business Review,* January–February 1987, p. 66.

6. W. H. Weiss, "Cutting Down the Risk in Decision Making," *Supervisory Management,* May 1985, p. 14.

7. Linda Trevino, "Ethical Decision Making in Organizations: A Person-Situationist Model," *Academy of Management Review,* July 1986, pp. 601, 615.

8. Walter Kiechel, "Getting Organized," *Fortune,* March 3, 1986, p. 24.

9. Daniel Isenberg, "Thinking and Managing: A Verbal Protocol Analysis of Managerial Problem Solving," *Academy of Management Review,* December 1986, p. 775.

10. Paul Preston and Thomas Zimmerer, *Management for Supervisors* (Englewood Cliffs, NJ: Prentice-Hall, 1983), pp. 80–82.

11. Peter Drucker, "How to Make People Decisions," *Harvard Business Review,* July 1985, p. 22.

12. Boris Blai, "Eight Steps to Successful Problem Solving," *Supervisory Management,* January 1986, p. 9.

13. "Building the Power Base to Sway a Decision Your Way," *Supervisory Management,* May 1986, p. 19.

14. Thomas Horton, "Deciding about Decisions," *Management Review,* November 1985, p. 3.

15. Hansen, "Better Supervision from A to W," p. 35.

16. Weiss, "Cutting Down the Risk," p. 15.

17. Michael Bowen, "The Escalation Phenomenon Reconsidered: Decision Dilemmas or Decision Errors?" *Academy of Management Review,* January 1987, p. 52.

18. Blai, "Eight Steps to Successful Problem Solving," p. 7.

19. Charles White, "Problem Solving: The Neglected First Step," *Management Review,* January 1983, p. 52.

20. Timothy Firnstahl, "Letting Go," *Harvard Business Review,* September–October 1986, p. 16.

21. Einhorn and Hogarth, "Decision Making: Going Forward in Reverse," p. 66.

22. Blai, "Eight Steps to Successful Problem Solving," p. 7.

23. White, "Problem Solving: The Neglected First Step," p. 52.

24. Weiss, "Cutting Down the Risk," p. 15.

25. Isenberg, "Thinking and Managing," p. 775.

26. "Building the Power Base to Sway a Decision," p. 17.

27. Isenberg, "Thinking and Managing," p. 785.

28. Jerry Conrath, "The Imagination Harvest: Training People to Solve Problems Creatively," *Supervisory Management,* September 1985, p. 6.

29. Ibid.

30. Horton, "Deciding about Decisions," p. 3.

31. M. Hensey, "Consulting Patterns of Successful Managers," *Supervisory Management,* May 1986, p. 32.

32. Conrath, "The Imagination Harvest," p. 7.

33. Horton, "Deciding about Decisions," p. 3.

34. Einhorn and Hogarth, "Decision Making: Going Forward in Reverse," p. 69.

35. Blai, "Eight Steps to Successful Problem Solving," p. 8.

36. Bowen, "The Escalation Phenomenon Reconsidered," p. 52.

37. Andrew Grove, "How High-Output Managers Reach Agreement in a Know-How Business," *Management Review,* December 1983, p. 9.

38. John Rohrbaugh, "Social Judgment Analysis," *Pryor Report,* March 1986, p. 3.

39. S. Hart, M. Boroush, G. Enk, and W. Hornick, "Managing Complexity through Consensus Mapping: Technology for the Structuring of Group Decisions," *Academy of Management Review,* July 1985, pp. 587–600.

40. Jane Allen, "How to Solve the Right Problem," *Training,* February 1987, p. 45.

41. Ichak Adizes and Efrain Turban, "An Innovative Approach to Group Decision Making," *Personnel,* April 1985, p. 49.

42. John Wanous and Margaret Youtz, "Solution Diversity and the Quality of Group Decisions," *Academy of Management Journal,* March 1986, p. 42.

43. Adizes and Turban, "An Innovative Approach," p. 45.

44. Colleen Cooper and Mary Ploor, "The Challenges That Make or Break a Group," *Training and Development Journal,* April 1986, p. 32.

45. Norman Maier, "Assets and Liabilities in Group Problem Solving: The Need for an Integrative Function," in Hackman, Lawler, and Porter, eds., *Perspectives on Business Organization,* 2nd ed. (New York: McGraw-Hill, 1983), pp. 385–93.

46. August Smith, "Choosing the Best Decision-Making Styles for Your Job," *Supervisory Management,* May 1985, p. 30.

47. Isenberg, "Thinking and Managing," p. 776.

48. Hansen, "Supervision form A to W," p. 34.

49. Ibid., p. 36.

50. Frank Vander Wert, "Guidelines for Decision Making," *Supervision,* December 1984, p. 7.

51. Weiss, "Cutting Down the Risk," p. 16.

APPLICATION SITUATIONS

Steps in Problem Solving and Decision Making

AS 5–1

Identify the step in the problem-solving and decision-making model that each statement represents.

a. Step 1   *c.* Step 3   *e.* Step 5

b. Step 2   *d.* Step 4

_____ 1. Today we will be using the brainstorming technique.

_____ 2. Chuck, is the machine still jumping out of sequence?

_____ 3. We should state what it is we are trying to accomplish.

_____ 4. What symptoms have you observed?

_____ 5. I suggest that we use linear programming to help us in this situation.

Classify the Problem

AS 5–2

Classify the five problems according to the structure and condition under which the decision is being made.

a. programmed, certainty   *c.* programmed, risk   *e.* unprogrammed, uncertainty

b. programmed, uncertainty   *d.* unprogrammed, certainty

f. unprogrammed, risk

_____ 6. A recent college graduate has decided to buy an existing business rather than to get a job working for someone else.

_____ 7. The owner-supervisor of a small business has had a turnaround in business. She wants to keep the excess cash liquid so that she can get it quickly when it is needed.

_____ 8. A purchasing agent must select new cars for the business. This is the sixth time in six years he has made this decision.

_____ 9. In the early 1970s investors had to decide whether to start the World Football League.

_____ 10. A supervisor in a department with high turnover must hire a new employee.

Selecting Quantitative Methods

AS 5–3

Select the appropriate quantitative method to use in the following five situations.

a. break-even analysis   *c.* linear programming   *e.* probability theory

b. capital budgeting   *d.* queuing theory

_____ 11. The manager of a small store wants to determine the quantity of items to place on the shelves for sale.

_____ 12. The supervisor must decide whether to repair his or her favorite old machine or to replace it.

_____ 13. A supervisor wants to invest money to make a profit.

_____ 14. The manager of a fast-food restaurant wants to even the work load in the store. At times employees sit idle, and other times they work for hours without stopping.

_____ 15. The accountant is preparing the budget for next year and has been given the sales forecast.

**Using Groups to
Generate Alternatives**

AS 5–4

In the five situations below, identify the most appropriate group technique to use in generating alternatives.

a. brainstorming   *c.* nominal grouping   *e.* Delphi

b. synectics   *d.* consensus mapping

_____ 16. The supervisor wants to develop some new toys. He is consulting employees and children together.

_____ 17. The department is suffering from morale problems.

_____ 18. The supervisor must choose new furniture for the office.

_____ 19. The supervisor wants to reduce waste in the department.

_____ 20. The supervisor wants to project future trends in the business.

Supervisor Sam

Sam started working for the organization five years ago. Everyone likes Sam; he's a nice guy. Sam was the top producer in his department. When the supervisor's job was open, he got it. He is responsible for maintaining the department's productivity. Sam supervises 10 employees. He received a raise for his increased responsibility. Sam was enthusiastic; he believed he could do an excellent job without any training. The organization has no training program for supervisors, and his boss, Betty, does not spend much time with him.

At first, Betty was pleased with Sam's performance. However, recently Sam has started being late. He never used to be out sick, but Sam has been absent twice in the past two weeks.

Betty decided to have a talk with Sam. She found out that Sam is rude to his employees and that they are no longer his friends. However, the department's performance is up to standard. Only Sam's work is below standard. During the discussion, Sam assured Betty that he did not have any problems and that he would do a better job in the future.

Two weeks passed. Sam has not been late or absent, but has been taking longer breaks. And his performance has not improved.

Answer the following questions. Use the space between questions to explain your answers. (The questions follow the five steps in the problem-solving and decision-making model.)

_____ 1. Betty has a problem.
   a. true   *b.* false

Step 1. Define the problem.

_____ 2. The problem Betty has can be classified as
   a. programmed, certainty   *d.* unprogrammed, certainty
   b. programmed, uncertainty   *e.* unprogrammed, uncertainty
   c. programmed, risk   *f.* unprogrammed, risk

_____ 3. Which situational supervisory problem-solving and decision-making style is appropriate for Betty to use in this situation?
   _____ time _____ information _____ acceptance _____ capability
   a. autocratic   *c.* participative
   b. consultative   *d.* laissez-faire

_____ 4. _____ . This is the most likely cause of the problem. The other alternatives are symptoms of the problem.
   a. Sam is often absent and late.   *d.* Sam was promoted without supervisory training.
   b. Sam cannot get along with people.   *e.* Sam is not capable of being a good supervisor.
   c. Sam has personal problems.

Step 2. Set objectives and criteria

———— 5. _____ is the most appropriate objective for Betty at this point.
   a. Firing Sam
   b. Getting Sam to stop taking long breaks
   c. Talking to Sam to determine whether he want to continue as a supervisor
   d. Developing Sam into an effective supervisor

Step 3. Generate alternatives

———— 6. _____ is an appropriate technique to use in developing alternative solutions to this problem.
   a. Brainstorming
   b. Synectics
   c. Nominal grouping
   d. Consensus mapping
   e. Delphi
   f. None of the above

Step 4. Analyze alternatives and select one

———— 7. _____ is the most appropriate method to use when analyzing the alternative solutions to this problem.
   a. Cost-benefit analysis
   b. Break-even analysis
   c. Capital budgeting
   d. Linear programming
   e. Queuing theory
   f. Probability theory

Step 5. Plan, implement the plan, and control

———— 8. A plan should be developed to solve this problem.
   a. true   *b.* false

———— 9. Implementing a plan to improve Sam's supervisory skills should be _____ responsibility.
   a. Betty's   *b.* Sam's   *c.* shared

———— 10. Betty should set _____ control points.
   a. frequent   *b.* infrequent

11. Assume that you replaced Betty as Sam's supervisor; what would you do?

PREPARATION FOR IN-CLASS SKILL-BUILDING EXERCISE

Deciding Which Situational Supervisory Problem-Solving and Decision-Making Style to Use

SB 5–1

Below are 10 situations calling for a decision. Select the appropriate problem-solving and decision-making style. Be sure to use Model 5–2 when determining the style to use.

S-A autocratic   S-P participative

S-C consultative   S-L laissez-faire

_____ 1. You have developed a new work procedure that will increase productivity. Your boss likes the idea and wants you to try it in a few weeks. You view your employees as fairly capable, and believe that they will be receptive to the change.
_____ time _____ information _____ acceptance _____ capability

_____ 2. There is new competition in your industry. Your organization's revenues have been dropping. You have been told to lay off 3 of your 10 employees in two weeks. You have been supervisor for over one year. Normally, your employees are very capable.
_____ time _____ information _____ acceptance _____ capability

_____ 3. Your department has been facing a problem for several months. Many solutions have been tried and failed. You've finally thought of a solution, but you're not sure of the possible consequences of the change required or of acceptance by your highly capable employees.
_____ time _____ information _____ acceptance _____ capability

_____ 4. Flex-time has become popular in your organization. Some departments let each employee start and end work when they choose. However, because of the cooperation required of your employees, they must all work the same eight hours. You're not sure of the level of interest in changing the hours. Your employees are a very capable group and like to make decisions.
_____ time _____ information _____ acceptance _____ capability

_____ 5. The technology in your industry is changing too fast for the members of your organization to keep up. Top management hired a consultant who has made recommendations. You have two weeks to decide what to do about the recommendations. Your employees are usually capable; they enjoy participating in the decision-making process.
_____ time _____ information _____ acceptance _____ capability

_____ 6. A change has been handed down by top management. How you implement it is your decision. The change takes effect in one month. It will affect everyone in your department. Their acceptance is critical to the success of the change. Your employees are usually not interested in making decisions.
_____ time _____ information _____ acceptance _____ capability

_____ 7. Your boss called to tell you that someone requested an order for your department's product; the delivery date is very short. She asked you to call her back with a decision about taking the order in 15 minutes. Looking over the work schedule, you realize that it will be very difficult to deliver the order on time. Your employees will have to push hard to make it. They are cooperative, capable, and enjoy being involved in decision making.
_____ time _____ information _____ acceptance _____ capability

_____ 8. Top management has decided to make a change that will affect all of your employees. You know that they will be upset because it will cause them hardship. One or two may even quit. The change goes into effect in 30 days. Your employees are very capable.
_____ time _____ information _____ acceptance _____ capability

_____ 9. You believe that productivity in your department could be increased. You have thought of some ways to do it, but you're not sure of them. Your employees are very experienced; almost all of them have been in the department longer than you have.

_____ time _____ information _____ acceptance _____ capability

_____ 10. A customer offered you a contract for your product with a quick delivery date. The offer is open for two days. To meet the contract deadline, employees would have to work nights and weekends for six weeks. You cannot require them to work overtime. Filling this profitable contract could help get you the raise you want and feel you deserve. However, if you take the contract and don't deliver on time, it will hurt your chances of getting a big raise. Your employees are very capable.

_____ time _____ information _____ acceptance _____ capability

IN-CLASS SKILL-BUILDING EXERCISE

Deciding Which Situational Supervisory Problem-Solving and Decision-Making Style to Use

SB 5–1

Objective: To develop your situational supervisory problem-solving and decision-making skills.

Experience: You will try to select the appropriate problem-solving and decision-making style for each of 10 situations described.

Materials: The completed Preparation for Exercise 5–1.

Procedure 1 (5–12 minutes)

The instructor reviews Model 5–2 and explains how to use it to select the appropriate supervisory style for the first situation.

Procedure 2 (12–20 minutes)

Break into teams of two or three. Apply the model to situations 2 through 5 as a team. You may decide to change your original answers. (It might be helpful to tear Model 5–2 out of the book so you don't have to keep flipping pages.) The instructor goes over the recommended answers and scoring for situations 2 through 5. Do not continue on to situation 6 until the instructor goes over the answers to situations 2 through 5.

Procedure 3 (12–20 minutes)

In the same teams, select problem-solving and decision-making styles for situations 6 through 10. The instructor will go over the recommended answers and scoring.

Conclusion: The instructor may lead a class discussion and make concluding remarks.

Application (2–4 minutes): What did I learn from this experience? How will I use this knowledge in the future?

Sharing: Volunteers give their answers to the application section.

IN-CLASS SKILL-BUILDING EXERCISE

Individual versus Group Decision Making

SB 5–2

Objective: To compare individual and group decision making to better understand when to use a group to make decisions.

Experience: As preparation you should have answered Application Situations 5–1 and 5–2. During class you will work in a group that will make the same decisions and then analyze the results.

Materials: Application Situations 5–1 and 5–2.

Procedure 1
(1–2 minutes)

Place your answers to the application situations in the "individual answer" column in the table.

Application Situation	Individual Answer (a–f)	Group Answer (a–f)	Recommended Answer (a–f)	Score	
				Individual	Group
1.					
2.					
3.					
4.					
5.					
6.					
7.					
8.					
9.					
10.					
Total score					

Procedure 2
(18–22 minutes)

Break into teams of five, with smaller or larger groups as necessary. As a group, come to an agreement on the answers to the application situations. Place the group answers in the "group answer" column. Try to use the consensus mapping rather than the nominal grouping technique in arriving at the answers.

Procedure 3
(4–6 minutes)

Scoring: The instructor will give the recommended answers. Determine how many you got right as an individual and as a group. Total your individual and the group's score.

Calculate the average individual score by adding all the individual scores and dividing by the number of group members. Average _____ .

Now calculate the difference between the average individual score and the group score. If the group's score is higher than the average individual score, you have a gain of _____ points; if the group score is lower, you have a loss of _____ points.

Determine the highest individual score _____ .

Determine the number of individuals who scored higher than the group's score _____ .

Procedure 4 (4–8 minutes) — Integration: As a group, discuss the advantages or disadvantages of being in a group while making the decisions in this exercise.

Advantages

- *Better decisions.* Did your group make better decisions? Was the group's score higher than the highest individual score? If not, why not? Were knowledgeable members nonassertive? Were they listened to?

- *More alternatives.* Did the group get members to think about alternatives they did not consider as individuals? Did your group use the devil's advocate approach?

- *Acceptance.* Did group members accept the answers?

- *Morale.* Were members more satisfied making the decisions in a group?

Disadvantages

- *Time.* Did it take longer to answer as a group? Was the time spent worth the benefits?

- *Domination.* Did any one person or subgroup dominate? Did everyone participate?

- *Conformity.* Were members nonassertive when presenting their answers in order to be accepted? Did group pressure force them to agree with the majority?

- *Responsibility.* Because no one person was held responsible for the group's answers, did members have an "I don't care" attitude?

Improvements: Overall, were the advantages of using a group greater than the disadvantages? If your group continues to work together, how could it improve its problem-solving and decision-making ability? Write your answer below.

Conclusion: The instructor leads a class discussion and makes concluding remarks.

Application (2–4 minutes): What did I learn from this experience? How will I use this knowledge in the future?

Sharing: Volunteers give their answers to the application section.

6

Human Relations: Power, Politics, and Ethics

Learning Objectives

1. Explain the goal of human relations.
2. List and explain the five forces influencing behavior at work.
3. Describe the two sources and seven bases of power and ways to increase your power.
4. Discuss the nature of organizational politics.
5. Describe how you will develop political skills.
6. Explain the difference between ethical and unethical politics.
7. Describe how to develop good relations with your boss.
8. Describe how to develop good relations with your subordinates.
9. Describe how to develop good relations with your peers.
10. Describe how to develop good relations with other departments.
11. Describe how to develop good relations with customers.

Key Terms

To achieve our objectives in this chapter, it is important that you understand the following 17 key terms. They are presented in the order in which they appear in the chapter. The list of key terms also appears in alphabetical order in the end-of-chapter review.

human relations	**connection power**	**reciprocity**
goal of human relations	**reward power**	**ethics**
self-fulfilling prophecy	**legitimate power**	**ethical politics**
power	**referent power**	**unethical politics**
coercive power	**information power**	**open-door policy**
	expert power	
	politics	

Bob and Sally are at the water fountain talking.

BOB: "I'm sorry the Peterson account was not assigned to you. You deserved it. Roger's claim of being more qualified to handle the job is not true. I'm really surprised that our boss, Ted, believed Roger's claim."

SALLY: "I agree. Nobody likes Roger because he always has to get his own way. I can't stand the way Roger puts down co-workers and members of other departments to force them to give him his own way. Roger has pulled the old emergency routine so many times now that purchasing and maintenance ignore his request. This hurts our department."

BOB: "You're right. Roger thinks only of himself; he never considers what other people want or what's best for the company. I've overheard Ted telling him he has to be a team player if he wants to get ahead."

SALLY: "The way he tries to beat everyone out all the time is sickening. He'll do anything to get ahead. But the way he behaves, he will never climb the corporate ladder."

Besides good work, what does it take to get ahead in an organization? To climb the corporate ladder, you will have to gain power and utilize ethical political skills with your superiors, subordinates, and peers, and with members of other departments.

I. Human Relations Skills

As stated in Chapter 1, supervisors need three types of skills to be successful: conceptual, technical, and human. Human relations skills are at least as important as technical skills. Because supervisors work with people they should put as much effort into studying human nature as into technical expertise.[1] Supervisors work with three organizational resources: physical, financial, and human. Of the three, people are the most important. We are living in a service economy where relationships are becoming more important than physical products.[2] The most common cause of supervisory failure is faulty human relations skills.[3]

Obviously, then, human relations are and will continue to be a major part of any supervisor's job. As we know, all supervisors perform five functions: planning, organizing, staffing, leading, and controlling. In each of these, human relations play a role. When planning, the supervisor often works with employees in development and implementation. In organizing, the supervisor must decide what to delegate and to whom while coordinating the department's resources. The staffing functions of hiring, orienting, training, and evaluating employees require good human relations skills. The supervisor cannot lead effectively without these skills, nor can he or she control employees' behavior. **Human relations** *are interactions among people.* Personal conflicts, cooperative effort, and group interaction are all examples of human relations. It is generally agreed that from 50 to 90 percent of a supervisor's time is spent interacting with people.

Goal of Human Relations

The **goal of human relations** *is to create a win-win situation by satisfying employee needs while achieving organizational objectives.* A win-win situation occurs when the organization and employees get what they want. When an employee asks "What's in it for me?" that employee is expressing his or her needs. When a supervisor expects high levels of performance from his or her employees, that supervisor is identifying organizational objectives. Many employees and union representatives have argued that company owners don't share their profits or that management exploits employees, creating an organization wins–employees lose situation. When employees feel as though management is taking advantage of them, they often hold back performance to create an employees win–management loses situation. Actually, unmet employee needs often result in a lose-lose situation. For example, Carla has a college degree in education. However, because she cannot find a teaching job, she took a job as a computer data-entry typist, which she finds boring. Carla makes many careless errors and her performance level is low. She has been caught using the company telephone during work hours to call several schools about jobs. Because Carla's needs for job satisfaction are not being met, she is not helping the organization meet its objectives. In her current job, Carla is not working to her full capability. However, as a teacher, Carla's performance level would probably be higher and she could help the school meet its objectives. Have you ever had a job in which your needs were not being satisfied? Was your performance level low or high in this situation?

Conflicts usually arise because a win-win situation is absent. In Chapter 8 you will learn to create win-win situations when facing conflicts.

The concept of human relations is not a gimmick to give you power to manipulate people. Nor does it offer simple solutions to the employee problems you will face as a supervisor. Having good human relations skills does not mean you will be popular. No positive correlation exists between popularity and the speed at which people are promoted to the top of the management ladder.[4]

LEARNING OBJECTIVE

1. Explain the goal of human relations.

Forces Influencing Behavior at Work

A key in human relations is understanding why people behave as they do, particularly in the workplace, which is your principal concern as a supervisor. There are five major forces that influence every employee, regardless of the size of the organization: organizational culture, supervisory influence, work group influence, job influence, and personal characteristics of the worker.[5]

Organizational Culture: Organizational culture is the shared values and expectations of organizational members. Examples include IBM's code of customer service, respect for the individual, and superior performance and McDonald's Q.S.C.V. policy—quality, service, cleanliness, and value. Peters and Waterman in their best-seller *In Search of Excellence* reinforced the idea that strong organizational cultures lead to success.

Supervisory Influence: Supervisors hold the key to both employee outlook and performance. They are the organization's spokespersons. An employee's image of the organization and its concern for his or her welfare is influenced by the supervisor's human relations abilities. If you have a positive attitude and expect employees to be highly productive, they will be highly productive. This is what J. Sterling Livingston called the self-fulfilling prophecy.[6] According to the **self-fulfilling prophecy,** *a supervisor's attitude and expectations and his or her treatment of employees largely determine performance.* In a popular study of the self-fulfilling prophecy, teachers were told that certain groups of students were "intellectual bloomers" who should perform well. Actually, the students were selected at random. Groups were similar. The only difference was teacher expectations for the groups. Nonetheless, the so-called intellectual bloomers did significantly outperform the other groups. The teacher's expectations became the students' self-fulfilling prophecy. This carries over to the workplace. More often than not, employees do what they are expected to do.[7] Expect and get the best in your supervisory role.

Work Group Influence: An employee's peers will affect his or her job performance. The work group helps the employee meet social needs. Some people really enjoy the people they work with and allow them to be a major influence in their work. The work group also provides emotional support. When an employee is having a tough time, peers can help get him or her through it. The work group can help the employee meet other needs as well.

Job Influence: The job itself can help employees meet their needs. Some employees really enjoy their work and look forward to the challenge it presents. However, not everyone likes his or her job. People like Carla would rather be somewhere else. In either case, the job influences the employee's behavior.

Personal Characteristics: Every employee is different. Each brings a unique combination of abilities, interests, needs, aptitudes, values, and expectations to the job. These personal characteristics have a major influence on employee behavior.

LEARNING OBJECTIVE

2. List and explain the five forces influencing behavior at work.

These five forces, summarized in Exhibit 6–1, have a complex influence on employee behavior. You can understand why employee-oriented problems are so common in organizations, given this complexity.

EXHIBIT 6-1   **FORCES INFLUENCING BEHAVIOR AT WORK**

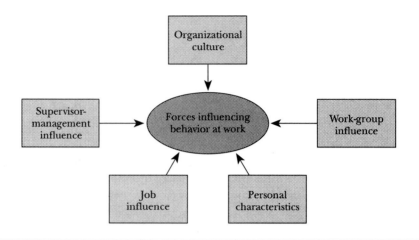

CONNECTIONS

2. Give an example, personal if possible, of how one of the five forces
influenced your behavior and performance at work.

II. Power

To be effective in an organization, you must understand how power is used. You
will learn the importance of power in organizations, bases of power, and ways to
increase your power. Begin by completing Self-Learning Exercise 6–1 to determine your preferred use of power.

SELF-LEARNING
EXERCISE 6-1

Power Base

When you want to get something and need others' consent or help, which approach do you
use more often? Think of recent specific situations in which you tried to get something. If
you cannot develop your own example, assume that you and a co-worker both want the same
job assignment for the day. How would you get it? Rank all seven approaches below from 1,
the first approach you would most commonly use, to 7, the last approach you would most
commonly use. Be honest.

_____ I did/would somehow use a form of *coercive power*—pressure, blackmail, force,
threat, retaliation, and so forth, to get what I want.

_____ I did/would use the influential *connection power* I have. I'd refer to my friend, or
actually have the person tell the person with authority to do it (like your boss).

_____ I did/would use *reward power* by offering the co-worker something of value to him
or her as part of the process, or in return for compliance.

_____ I did/would convince the co-worker to give me what I want by making a *legitimate*
request (like referring to your seniority over the co-worker).

_____ I did/would convince the coworker using *referent power*—relying on our
relationship. Others comply because they like me or are my friends.

_____ I did/would convince my co-worker to give me what I want with *information power.*
The facts support the reason why he or she should do what I want. I have
information my co-worker needs.

_____ I did/would convince my co-worker to give me what I wanted by making him or her realize that I have the skill and knowledge. I'm the *expert,* so it should be done my way.

Your selection rank (1–7) prioritizes your preferred use of power. Each power base is a key term and will be explained in this chapter.

Organizational Power

Some people view power as the ability to make people do what they want them to do, or the ability to do something to people or for people. These definitions may be true, but they tend to give power a manipulative, negative connotation, as does the adage "Power corrupts and absolute power corrupts absolutely." Within an organization, power should be viewed in a positive sense. Without power, managers could not achieve organizational objectives. Employees are not influenced without a reason, and the reason is often related to the power a supervisor wields over them. People do not actually have to use power to influence others. Often it is the perception of power, rather than the actual power, that influences employees.[8] It has been said that power in all its varieties drives performance forward. Power is the ability to lead and inspire. Leadership and power go hand in hand. For our purposes, **power** *is a person's ability to influence another person's behavior.*

Power generally begins at the top of an organization and works its way down the hierarchy. The president has more power than a vice president, who has more power than a general manager, who has more power than a production supervisor, who has more power than a worker. Over the past 10 years, CEOs have been delegating more power to lower levels.[9] The buzzword for giving more power to employees is *empowerment.* Power and empowerment are popular business topics today.

Bases of Power and Ways to Increase Your Power

Amital Etzioni differentiated two sources of power—positional power and personal power.

Positional Power: Positional power is derived from top-level management and is delegated down the chain of command.

Personal Power: Personal power is derived from the follower, rather than delegated by management. Everyone has personal power to various degrees. Personal power is largely due to one's personality. Leaders with personal power get it from followers because they meet followers' needs. In other words, President Kennedy is said to have had charisma; yet, even though he didn't satisfy the needs of all Americans, most liked him and were struck by him. Personal power can be gained or lost. For example, President Reagan had a lot of personal power, but he lost much of it through the Iran-Contra affair. President Bush lost power as the economy stagnated.

Etzioni postulates that it is best to have both positional power and personal power. There is no universal acceptance of which source of power is more important. However, more people pick personal power as being the more important of the two.

Etzioni's two sources of power have been expanded by many authors. Entirely new systems of classification have been developed. The most popular framework was devised by John French and Bertram Raven.[10] They proposed five bases of power—coercive, legitimate, expert, reward, and referent. Later, French and Kruglanski identified a sixth power base—information power. In 1979 Hersey and Goldsmith proposed adding a seventh power base—connection power. In the following sections you will learn the definitions of seven bases of power and ways to increase each. You do not have to take power away from others to increase your power base. Generally, power is given to those who get results. Performance is the key to gaining power. High-level performers are given increased power as they take on more responsibility. Ask not what the company can do for you, *ask what* you can do for the company. If you want more resources, pay raises, and promotions, you must perform to gain the power to achieve these things.[11]

Coercive Power

The use of **coercive power** *involves threats, punishment, or both to influence compliance.* Out of fear that noncompliance will lead to reprimands, probation, suspension, or dismissal, employees often do as the supervisor requests. Other examples of coercive power include verbal abuse, humiliation, and ostracism. In the opening case, when Roger puts co-workers and members of other departments down to force them to give him his own way, he is using coercive power.

Coercive power is appropriate to use in maintaining discipline when enforcing rules. When an employee is not willing to do as the manager requests, he or she may use coercive power to gain compliance. However, it is advisable to keep the use of coercive power to a minimum because it hurts human relations and often productivity as well.[12]

Increasing Coercive Power: To have true coercive positional power, you need to have a management job that enables you to gain and maintain the ability to hire, discipline, and fire your employees. However, some people can pressure others to do what they want without positional authority.

Connection Power

One way is to use **connection power,** *which is based on the user's relationship with influential people.* It relies on the use of contacts or friends who can influence the person you are dealing with. The right connections can give you the perception of having power, and they can actually give you power. If people know that you are friendly with people in power, they are more apt to do as you request. For example, if the boss's son has no positional power but wants something done, he can gain compliance by making a comment about speaking to his father or mother. The case at the end of the chapter illustrates how people use networking connection power to get ahead.

Increasing Connection Power: To increase your connection power, expand your network of contacts with important managers who have power. Join the "in-crowd," and the "right" clubs. Sports such as golf may help you meet influential people. The golfvine may be stronger than the grapevine.[13] When you want something, identify the people who can help you attain it, make alliances, and win them over to your side.[14] Get people to know your name. Get all the publicity you can. Have your accomplishments known by the people in power; send them notices.

Reward Power

Another alternative to position authority is **reward power,** *which is based on the user's ability to influence others with something of value to them.* In a management position, use positive reinforcement with incentives such as praise, recognition, pay raises, and promotions to ensure compliance. With peers you can exchange favors as a reward, or give something of value to the other party.

When appropriate, let people know what's in it for them. If you have something attractive to others, use it. For example, when Professor Smith is recruiting a student aide, he tells candidates that if they are selected and do a good job, he will recommend them for an MBA fellowship at Suffolk University, where he has connection power. As a result he gets good, qualified help for minimum wages while helping both his student aide and his alma mater. Professor Smith meets the goal of human relations by creating a win-win situation for himself, the student, and the university.

Increasing Reward Power: Get a management position and gain and maintain control over evaluating your employees' performance and determining their raises and promotions. Find out what others value, and try to reward them in that way. Using praise can help increase your power. Employees who feel they are appreciated rather than simply used will give the manager more power.

Legitimate Power

Another type of power, **legitimate power,** *is based on the user's positional power,* which is given by the organization. Employees tend to feel that they ought to do what the supervisor says within the scope of the job. For example, the supervisor may ask an employee to take out the trash. The employee does not want to do it but thinks, "The boss made a legitimate request and I ought to do it," and takes it out. If the employee was hesitant to take out the trash, the supervisor could refer to his or her positional power as well.

The use of legitimate power is appropriate when asking people to do something that is within the scope of their job. Most day-to-day interactions are based on legitimate power.

Increasing Legitimate Power: Let people know the power you possess, and work at gaining people's perception that you do have power. Remember—people's perception that you have power gives you power.

Referent Power

You may use **referent power,** *which is based on the user's personal power.* The supervisor relies on personality and his or her relationship with employees to gain compliance. For example, say "Will you please do it for me?" not "This is an order." Identification stems primarily from the employee's attractiveness to the person using power, and is manifested in personal feelings of "liking." Because Roger is not well liked in the organization, he has weak referent power.

The use of referent power is particularly appropriate for people with weak, or no, positional power. Roger has no positional power, so he should increase his referent power.

Increasing Referent Power: To gain referent power, develop your relationship with others; stand up for them.[15] Using the nine guidelines for effective human relations can help you win referent power. Remember that your boss's success depends upon you. Gain his or her confidence in order to get more power; work at your relationship with the boss.[16]

Information Power

Another type of power you can use is **information power,** *which is based on the user's information desired by others.* Managers rely on the other person's need for the information they possess. The information is usually related to the job, but not always. Some secretaries have more information than the managers they work for. For example, Professor Wilkins asked his department chairperson a question. The chairperson did not know the answer, so she told the professor to call and ask the manager's secretary. He was specifically told to ask the secretary because she had more information than the manager.

Increasing Information Power: Have information flow through you. Know what is going on in the organization. Provide service and information to other departments. Serve on committees; it gives you both information and a chance to increase connection power.

EXHIBIT 6-2   **SOURCES AND BASES OF POWER**

Personal power ————————————————————————— Position power

Expert   Referent   Reward   Coercive

Information   Legitimate   Connection

Expert Power

You may also use **expert power,** *which is based on the user's skill and knowledge.* Supervisors rely on their unique ability to do or explain something to others. Being an expert makes other people dependent upon you. The fewer the people who possess the skill or knowledge, the more power you have. People often respect an expert. For example, because there are so few people possessing the ability to become top athletes, they command multimillion-dollar contracts.

Expert power is essential to people who have to work with people from other departments and organizations. They have no direct positional power to use, so being seen as an expert gives credibility and power. Roger, rather than Sally, got the Peterson account because he convinced Ted of his expertise.

Increasing Expert Power: To become an expert, take all the training and educational programs your organization provides. Stay away from routine tasks in favor of more complex, hard-to-evaluate tasks. Project a positive image.

Remember to use the appropriate type of power in a given situation. Exhibit 6-2 matches the two sources of power with the seven bases of power.

LEARNING OBJECTIVE

3. Describe the two sources and seven bases of power and ways to increase your power.

CONNECTIONS

3. Of the many suggestions for increasing your power bases, which two are your highest priority for using on the job? Explain.

4. Give two examples, preferably from an organization you have worked for, of individuals' use of power. Identify the power base and describe the behavior and its effect on human relations and performance.

III. Organizational Politics

You will learn the nature of politics and ways to develop political skills. Begin by determining your use of political behavior by completing Self-Learning Exercise 6–2.

SELF-LEARNING EXERCISE 6–2

Political Behavior

Select the response that best describes your actual or planned use of the following behavior on the job. Place the number 1–5 on the line before each statement.

(5) usually (4) frequently (3) occasionally (2) seldom (1) rarely

_____ 1. I get along with everyone, even those recognized as difficult. I avoid or delay giving my opinion on controversial issues.

_____ 2. I try to make people feel important and compliment them.

_____ 3. I compromise when working with others and avoid telling people they are wrong; instead, I suggest alternatives that may be more effective.

_____ 4. I try to get to know the managers and functions of as many other departments as possible.

_____ 5. I take on the same interests as those in power (watch or play sports, join the same clubs, and so forth).

_____ 6. I purposely seek contacts and network with higher-level managers so that they will know who I am by name and face.

_____ 7. I seek recognition and visibility for my accomplishments.

_____ 8. I form alliances with others to increase my ability to get what I want.

_____ 9. I do favors for others and use their favors in return.

_____ 10. I say I will do things when I am not sure I can deliver; if I cannot meet the obligation I explain why it was out of my control.

To determine your political behavior add the 10 numbers you selected as your answers. The number will range from 10 to 50. The higher your score, the more political behavior you use. Place your score on the continuum below.

Nonpolitical   10   20   30   40   50   Political

The Nature of Organizational Politics

You cannot keep out of politics and be successful. Politics is a fact of organizational life. In our economy, money is the medium of exchange; in an organization, politics is the medium of exchange. Managers are, and must be, political beings in order to meet their objectives. Politics is the network of interactions by which power is acquired, transferred, and exercised upon others.[17] **Politics** _is the process of gaining and using power._ As you can see from the definition, power and politics go hand in hand.

Managers cannot meet their objectives without the help of other people and departments over which they have no authority or positional power. For example, Tony, a production department supervisor, needs materials and supplies to make the product, but he must rely on the purchasing department to acquire them. If Tony does not have a good working relationship with purchasing, he may not get the materials when he needs them.

Using **reciprocity** _involves creating obligations and debts, developing alliances, and using them to accomplish objectives._ When people do something for you, you incur an obligation that they may expect to be repaid. When you do something for people, you create a debt that you may be able to collect on at a later date when you need a favor. Over a period of time, when the trade-off results in both parties getting something they want, an alliance usually develops to gain group power in attaining mutually desirable benefits. You should work at developing a network of alliances that you can call on for help in meeting your objectives. When the trade-off of help with alliances creates a win-win situation for all members of the alliances and the organization, the goal of human relations is met.

Like power, politics often has a negative connotation resulting from people's abuse of political power. Ethical politics helps the organization by meeting the goal of human relations without negative consequences. No amount of power can eliminate political dimensions in organizations.[18] The amount and importance of politics varies from organization to organization. However, larger organizations tend to be more political; and the higher the level of management, the more important politics becomes.[19] In fact, one consultant has said that long-term career success in large, highly competitive organizations depends 10 percent on

LEARNING
OBJECTIVE

4. Discuss the nature
of organizational politics.

performance, 30 percent on image, and 60 percent on exposure, which requires successful political behavior.[20]

As you can see, organizational politics is an integral part of everyday corporate life. You should develop your political behavior to take advantage of political realities that can help you and the organization and to avoid being hurt by politics. Developing political skills is the next topic.

CONNECTIONS

5. Give an example of reciprocity, preferably from an organization you have worked for. Explain the trade-off.

Developing Political Skills

If you want to climb the corporate ladder, you should develop your political skills. Human relations skills are critical to political success in organizations.[21] In June 1988 *The Wall Street Journal* reported that few women know how to play the "corporate game." Following the human relations guidelines can help you develop political skills. More specifically, review the 10 statements in Self-Learning Exercise 6–2 and consciously increase your use of these behaviors, especially any that had a low frequency of use. However, use number 10 (saying you will do something when you are not sure you can) sparingly, and don't use the word "promise." You don't want to be viewed as a person who doesn't keep his or her word.

Use reciprocity. When you want something, determine who else will benefit and create alliance power to help you, the other party or parties, and the organization. Ongoing alliances are also known as political coalitions. The average manager belongs to two or three coalitions.[22]

LEARNING
OBJECTIVE

5. Describe how you will
develop political skills.

Successfully implementing these behaviors results in increased political skills. However, if you don't agree with one of the political behaviors, don't use it. You may not need to use all of the political behaviors to be successful. Learn what it takes in the organization where you work.

CONNECTIONS

6. Of the 10 political behaviors listed in Self-Learning Exercise 6–2, which two require the most effort on your part? The least? Explain your four answers.

IV. Business Ethics and Politics

Are all power and political behaviors ethical? What is the relationship between ethics and politics? You will learn about ethical and unethical politics, and a simple guide to ethical decisions. But first, complete Self-Learning Exercise 6–3.

SELF-LEARNING
EXERCISE 6–3

Ethical Behavior

Below are 15 statements. Identify the frequency of which you do, have done, or would do these things in the future when employed full time. Place the letter R, O, S, or N on the line before each statement.

R—regularly   O—occasionally   S—seldom   N—never

_____ 1. I come to work late and get paid for it.

_____ 2. I leave work early and get paid for it.

_____ 3. I take long breaks or lunches and get paid for it.

_____ 4. I call in sick to get a day off, when I'm not sick.

_____ 5. I use the company phone to make personal long distance calls.

_____ 6. I do personal work while on company time.

_____ 7. I use the company copier for personal use.

_____ 8. I mail personal things through the company mail.

_____ 9. I take home company supplies or merchandise.

_____ 10. I give company supplies or merchandise to friends, or allow them to take them without saying anything.

_____ 11. I put in for reimbursement for meals and travel or other expenses that I did not actually eat or make.

_____ 12. I use the company car for personal business.

_____ 13. I take my spouse or friend out to eat and charge it to the company expense account.

_____ 14. I take my spouse or friend on business trips and charge the expense to the company.

_____ 15. I accept gifts from customers or suppliers in exchange for giving them business.

Give yourself 1 point for each N answer, 2 points for each S answer, 3 points for each O answer, and 4 points for each R answer. Total your score. It will be between 15 and 60. Place it on the continuum below.

Ethical   15   20   25   30   35   40   45   50   55   60   Unethical

All of these items are considered unethical behavior by most organizations. However, many of these actions happen regularly in organizations. If many employees do them, does that make it all right for you to do them too?

Some experts distinguish between moral behavior and ethical behavior. Morals refers to absolute worldwide standards of right and wrong behavior, such as "Thou shalt not commit murder." Ethical behavior, on the other hand, reflects established customs and mores that may vary throughout the world and that are subject to change from time to time. For our purpose we combine the two: **ethics** *is the moral standard of right and wrong behavior.*

Right behavior is considered ethical behavior, and wrong behavior is considered unethical behavior. In the business world, the difference between right and wrong behavior is not always clear. Many unethical behaviors are illegal, but not all. People have different values, which leads to behaviors that some people view as ethical but that others do not. Ethics is also considered to be relative. In one situation people may believe that a certain behavior is ethical but that the same behavior in a different situation is unethical. For example, giving someone a gift is legal, but giving a gift as a condition of attaining business (a bribe) is illegal. A gift versus a bribe is not always clear.

In your daily life, you face decisions in which you can make ethical or unethical choices. You make your choices based on your past learning from parents, teachers, friends, co-workers, and so forth. Our combined past makes up what many refer to as our conscience, which helps us to choose right from wrong.

Ethical and Unethical Politics

Politics can be helpful or harmful to an organization depending upon the behavior. We will classify political behavior into two categories: ethical and unethical. **Ethical politics** *includes behavior that benefits both the individual and the organization.* Ethical politics creates a win-win situation, meeting the goal of human relations. On the other hand, **unethical politics** *includes behavior that benefits the individual and hurts the organization.* Unethical politics creates a win-lose situation; it does not meet the needs of both the organization and the individual. Unethical politics also includes management behavior that helps the organization but hurts the individual. At this point, we are focusing on individual behavior. In Chapter 14 we will look at organizational ethics. Behavior that helps the individual but does not hurt the organization is also considered ethical. The term *organization* includes people because if employees are hurt, so is the organization.

The 10 political behavior statements in Self-Learning Exercise 6–2 are generally considered ethical. Another example of ethical political behavior includes Tom, the computer manager, who wants a new computer. He talks to several of the powerful managers and sells them on the benefits of getting one. They form an alliance and attain the funds to purchase the computer. Tom benefits because he now manages a new and more powerful computer. He also looks good in the eyes of the other managers, who will also benefit through the use of the new computer. Overall, the organization's performance increases.

Examples of unethical behavior that hurt the organization include the following: (1) Kate, a production manager, wants to be promoted to the general manager's position. To increase her chances, she spreads untrue gossip about her main competitor. (2) There is a vacant office, which is large and well furnished. Sam, a sales manager who spends most of his time on the road, sees the office as prestigious, so he requests it, even though he knows that Cindy, a public relations manager, wants it and will get better use from it. Sam speaks to his friends in high-level management positions and gets the office.

Does unethical political behavior pay? According to Dr. Klein, at first one may be richly rewarded for knifing people in the back, but retaliation follows, trust is lost, and productivity declines.[23] This is illustrated in the opening case. Roger uses unethical politics in hopes of getting ahead. But according to his peers, he will not climb the corporate ladder. It is difficult to get ahead when people don't like you and you make a lot of enemies. Unethical behavior and stress appear to be linked. Highly ethical managers are less likely to feel hostility, anxiety, and fear.[24]

LEARNING OBJECTIVE

6. Explain the difference between ethical and unethical politics.

CONNECTIONS

7. Give an example of ethical and unethical politics, preferably from an organization you have worked for. Describe the behavior and consequences for all parties involved.

A Human Relations Guide to Ethical Decisions

When making decisions, try to meet the goal of human relations by creating a win-win situation for all parties. Some of the relevant parties include peers, your boss, subordinates, other department members, the organization, and people and organizations outside the organization you work for. The relevant parties will often change from situation to situation. The higher up in the organization, the more relevant parties there are to deal with. For example, if you are not a manager, you will not have any subordinates to deal with. If, after making a decision, you are proud to tell all these relevant parties your decision, the decision is probably ethical. If you are embarrassed to tell others your decision, or if you keep rationalizing the decision, it may not be ethical. Throughout the rest of this chapter, you will learn how to use ethical politics with your boss, subordinates, peers, members of other departments, and customers. The human relations guide to ethical decisions is also presented in Exhibit 6–3 at the end of the chapter.

V. Vertical Politics

Vertical politics are your relations with superiors and subordinates. Your superiors are people in the organization who are on a higher level than you. The most important person to develop effective relations with is your boss. Your subordinates are people who are on a lower level than you. The employees you supervise and who report to you are the most important people with whom to develop effective relations. You will learn how to develop effective vertical politics.

Relations with Your Boss

Your relationship with your boss will affect your job satisfaction and can mean the difference between success or failure on the job. Not getting along with your boss can make life miserable for you.[25] Needless to say, you should work at developing a good working relationship with your boss.

Analyze your boss's style and, if necessary, change your style to match it.[26] For example, if your boss is very businesslike and you are very informal and talkative, be businesslike when you are with your boss. Remember, people generally like people who behave like themselves.

Knowing your boss can lead to better human relations between the two of you. It is helpful to know what your boss's primary responsibility is, what your boss regards as good performance, how your performance will be evaluated, and what your boss expects of you.

Common Expectations of Bosses

Your boss will most likely expect loyalty, cooperation, initiative, information, and openness to criticism. Let's discuss each separately.

Loyalty: Your boss will expect your respect and support. You will be expected to carry out the organization's standing plans and any special orders with the proper attitude. You should not talk negatively about your boss behind his or her back, even if others are doing so. You should defend your boss as honestly as you can, even if you are not in total agreement. At least state his or her reasons for the actions. Regardless of how careful you are, or how trustworthy the other person is, gossip always seems to get back to the boss. When it does it can seriously hurt your relationship. Your boss may never forget it or forgive you for doing it. The benefits, if any, don't outweigh the cost of disloyalty. In fact, you should never talk negatively about anyone; it can only get you into trouble. The adage "If you can't say anything good about someone, don't say anything at all" is a good one to follow. Continuing to listen to, and especially agreeing with, negative statements only encourages others to continue this behavior. The discussion between Bob and Sally is an example of negative talk about others. If people are talking negatively about others, encourage them to stop in a nice way, change the subject, or leave them. For example, try saying, "Complaining about Roger really doesn't change anything. Why don't we talk about the things we can change like . . ." or "Did you/anyone see the movie/game on TV last night?"

Cooperation: Your boss expects you to cooperate with him or her and with everyone you must work with. If you cannot get along with others, you can be an embarrassment to your boss. And bosses don't like to be embarrassed. Roger is not cooperative; his boss Ted has told him that if he wants to get ahead he will have to be a team player.

Initiative: Your boss will expect you to know your responsibility and authority and to act without having to be told to do so. If there is a problem, the boss may expect you to solve it rather than to bring it to him or her. If it is appropriate to include the boss in solving a problem, at least analyze the situation and have a solution to recommend.

Information: Your boss expects you to keep him or her informed about what your objectives are and how you are progressing. If there are problems, your boss expects you to tell him or her about them. You should not cover up your mistakes, your employees' mistakes, or your boss's mistakes. You can cause your boss the embarrassment of looking stupid by finding out from others what's going on in his or her department. Bosses don't like to be surprised.

Openness to Criticism: We all make mistakes; part of your boss's job is to help you avoid repeating them. When your boss criticizes you, try not to become defensive and argumentative. Remember that criticism is a means of improving your skills; be open to it even though it may hurt. Don't take it personally.

LEARNING OBJECTIVE

7. Describe how to develop good relations with your boss.

If you get to know your boss, find out your boss's problem and work on it, and meet his or her expectations, you should develop a good relationship. If you meet your boss's expectations, he or she will most likely be willing to help you meet your needs. Meeting your boss's expectations can help you meet the goal of human relations by creating a win-win situation for both of you.

CONNECTIONS

> **8.** Of the common expectations of bosses, which is your strongest area? Which is your weakest? Explain your answers.

Relations with Subordinates

If the goal of human relations is to satisfy employee needs while achieving organizational objectives, why are poor human relations so common? One reason is the fact that the supervisor must consider the work to be accomplished as ultimately more important than the needs and desires of those doing the work, including the supervisor's own needs.[27] Supervisors get so busy getting the job done that they forget about the needs of the employees doing the work. Employees tend to start a job enthusiastically, but the supervisor often does not take the time to develop the human relations necessary to maintain that enthusiasm.[28] As a supervisor, you must take the time to develop effective human relations.

Developing Supervisor-Employee Relations

Human relations skills are important today and will be even more important in the future with the changing work environment.[29] In developing supervisor-employee relations, one should follow the guidelines to human relations discussed in this chapter. Perfect human relations probably don't exist. The supervisor should strive for harmonious relations where differences of opinion are encouraged and settled in a peaceful manner. He or she should keep morale at high levels but should not try to please all of the people all of the time. As a supervisor, you may face resentment from an employee who resents you for *what* you are (the supervisor), rather than for *who* you are.[30] Others may not like you for any number of reasons. A supervisor can have good human relations without being well liked personally or being popular.

Friendship

The relationship between supervisor and employee is not, and cannot be, one of real friendship. The nature of supervision excludes true friendship because the supervisor must evaluate the employee's performance; true friends don't evaluate or judge each other in any formal way. The supervisor must also give employees directions; friends don't order each other around. In addition, the supervisor might have to get the employee to change; friends usually don't seriously try to change each other.[31]

Trying to be friends can cause problems for you, the employee, and the department. Will your friend try to take advantage of your friendship to get special favors? Will you be able to treat your friend like the other members of the department? The other employees may say that you play favorites. They may resent your friend and ostracize him or her. Your friendship could adversely affect department morale.

Because supervisors cannot be true friends to employees does not mean that they should not be friendly. If the supervisor takes an "I'm the boss" attitude, employees may resent him or her and morale problems could result.[32]

Developing the proper supervisor-employee relationship can be stressful. Yet the relationship can help supervisors deal more effectively with job stress through the social support system. Your friends at work should be your peers. Go to breaks and lunch with your peers.[33] As in most cases, there are exceptions to the rule. Some supervisors are friends with employees and are still very effective supervisors.

CONNECTIONS

9. Assume that you get hired or promoted for a supervisory position. Will you develop a relationship with your employees based on friendship? Describe the relationship you plan to develop.

The Open-Door Policy

The **open-door policy** *is the supervisory practice of being available to employees.* Your supervisory ability is directly proportional to the amount of time your door is open, both literally and figuratively.[34] For effective human relations, the supervisor must be available to employees to give them the help they need when they need it. If employees view the supervisor as too busy or unwilling to help them, poor human relations and low morale can result. An open-door policy does not mean that supervisors must stop everything whenever an employee wants to see them. For nonemergencies the employee should make an appointment to see the supervisor. The supervisor should prioritize spending time with an employee along with other responsibilities.

Following these guidelines should help you develop effective human relations with your subordinates. Use your power wisely to meet the goal of human relations. Remember, your success as a manager depends on your subordinates. If you want employees to meet your expectations, create a win-win situation. Help your subordinates meet their needs while attaining the high performance that will make you a success. When you ask subordinates to do something, answer their unasked question, "What's in it for me?" The Professor Smith–student aide example under reward power is a superior example of a subordinate win-win situation.

LEARNING OBJECTIVE

8. Describe how to develop good relations with your subordinates.

VI. Horizontal Politics

Horizontal politics are your relations with your peers and members of other departments. Your peers are the people who are on the same level in the organizational hierarchy as you. Your direct peers also report to your boss. You will learn how to develop effective horizontal politics.

Relations with Peers

To be successful you must cooperate, compete with, and sometimes even criticize your peers. We will discuss how to do each in the following sections.

Cooperating with Peers

Your success as an employee is linked to other employees in the organization, such as your peers. If you are cooperative and help them, they should have a positive attitude toward you and be willing to help you meet your objectives. If you don't cooperate with your peers, your boss will know it.

Competing with Peers

Even though you cooperate with your peers, you still compete with them. Your boss will compare you to them when evaluating your performance, giving raises, and granting promotions. Like a great athlete, you must learn to be a team player and help your peers to be successful, but at the same time you have to look good as well.

Criticizing Peers

Do not go looking for faults in your peers. But if your peers do something they shouldn't, you owe it to them to try to correct the situation or prevent it from recurring in the future. Tactfully and sincerely telling a peer of a shortcoming is often appreciated. Sometimes peers are not aware of the situation. Chapter 8 contains the details on how to approach peers, and others, to resolve conflicts.

Do not go to the boss unless it is a serious offense, such as disregarding safety rules that endanger the welfare of employees. Unless your own safety is in danger, tell the boss only after discussing it with the peer and warning him or her of the consequences of continuing the behavior. Do not cover for a peer in trouble—you will only make things worse for everyone involved. And don't expect or ask others to cover for you.

LEARNING OBJECTIVE

9. Describe how to develop good relations with your peers.

Roger violates peer relations. He always has to get his own way. Roger is uncooperative, too competitive, and critical of co-workers and members of other departments to force them to give him his own way.

Relations with Other Department Members

You will most likely need the help of other departments. You will need personnel to hire new employees, accounting to approve budgets, purchasing to get materials and supplies, maintenance to keep the department's equipment running efficiently, quality control to help maintain the quality of the product, payroll to okay overtime pay, and so forth.

Some of these departments have procedures you should follow. Develop good human relations by being cooperative and following the guidelines set by the organization.

Roger's "pulling the old emergency routine" so many times has resulted in purchasing's and maintenance's ignoring him. This is an embarrassment for Ted and the department, and it is hurting performance.

Following the guidelines in the text should help you develop effective human relations with others. Make your peers and members of other departments your friends and allies. Use your power wisely to meet the goal of human relations. Your success may depend on others. When you want something, remember to use effective horizontal politics to create a win-win situation for all involved. Answer people's unasked question, "What's in it for me?" Tom, the computer manager in the example under ethical politics, used horizontal politics to get the new computer.

LEARNING OBJECTIVE

10. Describe how to develop good relations with other departments.

Customer Relations

Not all supervisors are responsible for customer relations, but the quality of relations with customers affects everyone in the organization. Total quality management requires everyone in the organization to focus on the customer to improve products and services.

Is Customer Service Important? Many Americans are critical of the quality of service they receive, and they want something done about it. As a result, U.S. business has made customer service a focal point.[35] For example, organizations like Southern California Gas Company have developed extensive training programs to improve the quality of customer service.[36] A Strategic Planning Institute study revealed that organizations that emphasized service increased their market share by 6 percent per year; their return on sales was 12 percent. Organizations that deemphasized service had a 2 percent loss in market share and a return on sales of 1 percent. There is no question that customer service has an economic impact.[37]

How Do Customer Complaints Affect the Organization? Customers complain because products or services are poor. Complaints can result in lost customers, sales, and profits.

According to Technical Assistance Research Programs (TARP), the average business never hears from 96 percent of its unhappy customers. For every complaint received, the average company, in fact, has 26 customers with problems, 6 of which are serious. Complainers are more likely than noncomplainers to do business again with the company even if the problem is not satisfactorily resolved. Of the customers who register a complaint, between 54 and 70 percent will do business again if their complaint is resolved. That figure goes up to a staggering 95 percent if the customer feels that the complaint was resolved quickly. The average customer who has had a problem with an organization tells 9 to 10 people about it. Thirteen percent of the people who have a problem recount the incident to more than 20 people, but only 5 percent of complainers who had their complaint resolved satisfactorily tell only five people about it.[38] Clearly, supervisors must give a very high priority to customer service and satisfactorily resolving complaints if they want to be successful.

Developing Good Customer Relations

Supervisors can control the quality of customer service. In addition to the control techniques discussed in Chapter 4, a supervisor can take the following steps to develop good customer relations:

- Select employees with good interpersonal skills. Hire people who are outgoing and enjoy meeting and talking to people. Generally, introverts do not make good customer service representatives.[39]

- Set a good example. Employees will only show customers the same respect, courtesy, and attention that they receive from their supervisor. The supervisor sets the tone for customer service.[40]

- Train customer service representatives. Employees should be polite and project a positive image of the organization. Customers do not like to be ignored. Customers should be greeted with a polite statement such as, "May I help you?"[41]

- Evaluate and reward performance. Employees must realize the importance of customer service. The supervisor should evaluate employee performance often.[42] Employees who give customers good service should be rewarded with praise, recognition, and pay raises. Employees who do not give good customer service should be reprimanded, disciplined, or even fired if they do not produce to standard.

- Keep the shelves stocked with basics. It is irritating to go to the store for a basic item like sugar only to find out that the supermarket is out.[43] You can't put a rain check in your coffee.

LEARNING OBJECTIVE

11. Describe how to develop good relations with customers.

VII. How Politics and Ethics Affect Performance

Generally, people who use ethical politics are more productive in the long run than people who use unethical politics. Unethical behavior can affect the performance of the individual and one or more of the following groups: superiors, subordinates, peers, other department members, and people and organizations outside the organization you work for.

People who use unethical politics may get short-run performance results, but in the long run, performance will be lower. Roger's use of emergencies may have worked for a while, but the purchasing and maintenance departments now ignore his emergency requests. As a result of Roger's behavior, his performance, his peers' performance, his boss's performance, other departments' performance, and the performance of the organization as a whole are affected negatively.

Unethical behavior can get you fired, which will stop your performance within an organization completely, and can also result in your going to prison.

See Exhibit 6–3 for an illustration that puts the concepts of power, politics, and ethics together.

As has been clearly illustrated in this chapter, human relations skills are critical to your success as a supervisor. Begin to develop these skills today.

EXHIBIT 6-3 **HUMAN RELATIONS GUIDE TO ETHICAL DECISION MAKING**

If you are proud to tell all relevant parties your decision, it is probably ethical.

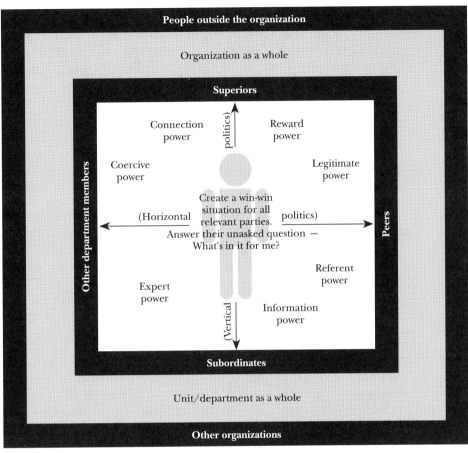

If you are embarrassed to tell all the relevant parties your decision or keep rationalizing, it is probably unethical.

REVIEW

Select one or more methods: (1) fill in the missing key terms from memory; (2) match the key terms from the end of the review with their definitions below; (3) copy the key terms in order from the key terms at the beginning of the chapter.

_____ are interactions among people.

The _____ _____ is to create a win-win situation by satisfying employee needs while achieving organizational objectives. Human relations skills are one of the three skills necessary for success as a supervisor. They are important to the implementation of the five supervisory functions. The forces influencing behavior at work include organizational culture, supervisory influence, work group influence, job influence, and personal characteristics of the worker. According to the

_____ , a supervisor's attitude and expectations and his or her treatment of employees largely determine performance.

_____ is a person's ability to influence another person's behavior. Generally, the higher the management level, the more power one has.

The two sources of power are positional power and personal power, and the seven bases of power include _____ , based on threats, punishment, or both to influence compliance; _____ , based on the user's relationship with influential people;

_____ , based on the user's ability to influence others with something of value to them; _____ , based on the user's positional power; _____ , based on the user's personal power; _____ , based on the user's information desired by others; and _____ , based on the user's skill and knowledge. The use of power affects behavior, human relations, and performance. The power used should be appropriate for the situation.

_____ , the process of gaining and using power, is an important part of meeting organizational objectives. _____ involves creating obligations and debts, developing alliances, and using them to accomplish objectives.

_____ are the moral standards of right and wrong behavior. _____ includes behavior that benefits both the individual and the organization, while _____ includes behavior that benefits the individual and hurts the organization. The human relations guide to ethical decisions seeks to meet the goal of human relations by creating a win-win situation for all parties including superiors, subordinates, peers, members of other departments, and people and other organizations outside the organization. If you are proud to tell all relevant parties your decision, that decision is probably ethical; if you are embarrassed to tell or if you rationalize, it is probably unethical behavior.

Relations with your superiors and subordinates, known as vertical politics, are important to career success. Get to know your boss and his or her expectations. Common expectations of bosses include loyalty, cooperation, initiative, information, and openness to criticism. With your employees develop a professional relationship rather than friendship, and use the

_____ , the supervisory practice of being available to employees.

Relations with peers and other departments, known as horizontal politics, are also important to career success. Learn to cooperate and compete with your peers and criticize them when necessary. Be cooperative and follow company guidelines in working with other departments and customers.

In general, ethical politics have a positive effect on behavior, human relations, and performance in the long run. In the short run, unethical behavior may increase performance, but in the long run, it tends to have a negative effect on behavior, human relations, and performance.

KEY TERMS

coercive power

connection power

ethical politics

ethics

expert power

goal of human relations

human relations

information power

legitimate power

open-door policy

politics

power

reciprocity

referent power

reward power

self-fulfilling prophecy

unethical politics

REFERENCES

1. M. R. Hansen, "Better Supervision for A to W," *Supervisory Management,* August 1985, p. 35.

2. Barry Reece and Rhonda Brandt, *Effective Human Relations in Organizations* (Boston: Houghton Mifflin Company, 1987), p. 5.

3. W. Richard Plunket, *Supervision: The Direction of People at Work* (Dubuque, IA: Wm. C. Brown, 1983), p. 161.

4. Srully Blotnick, "Enemies," *Forbes,* June 30, 1986, p. 152.

5. Reece and Brandt, *Effective Human Relations,* pp. 10–14.

6. J. Sterling Livingston, "Pygmalion in Management," in *Harvard Business Review on Human Relations* (New York: Harper & Row, 1979), p. 181.

7. Ibid.

8. Steven Skinner, James Donnelly, and John Ivancevich, "Effects of Transactional Form on Environmental Linkages and Power-Dependence Relations," *Academy of Management Journal,* September 1987, p. 585.

9. John Byrne and Laurie Baum, "The Limits of Power," *Business Week,* October 23, 1987, p. 34.

10. John French and Bertram Raven, "A Comparative Analysis of Power and Preference," in J. T. Tedeschi, ed., *Prospectives on Social Power* (Hawthorne, NY: Adline Publishing, 1974).

11. A. J. Patrellis, "Your Power as an Employee," *Supervisory Management,* April 1985, p. 40.

12. Fernando Bartolome and Andre Laurent, "The Manager: Master and Servant of Power," *Harvard Business Review,* November–December 1986, p. 81.

13. Jolee Edmondson, "Foreplay, Some of the Best Business Deals Begin on the Golf Course," *Success,* April 1985, pp. 28–31.

14. "Building the Power Base to Sway a Decision Your Way," *Supervisory Management,* May 1986, p. 17.

15. Bartolome and Laurent, "The Manager: Master and Servant of Power," p. 79.

16. Patrellis, "Your Power as an Employee," p. 41.

17. Wayne Mondy and Shane Premeaux, "Power, Politics, and the First-Line Supervisor," *Supervisory Management,* January 1986, pp. 36–39.

18. Stanley Young, "Politicking: The Unsung Managerial Skill," *Personnel,* June 1987, p. 62.

19. John Miner, *Organizational Behavior: Performance and Productivity* (New York: Random House, 1988), p. 498.

20. Walter Kiechell, "The Importance of Being Visible," *Fortune,* June 24, 1985, p. 141.

21. Young, "Politicking," p. 68.

22. Ian MacMilan and William Guth, "Strategy Implementation and Middle Management Coalitions," *Advances in Strategic Management* 3, 1985, pp. 233–54.

23. "The '90s May Tame the Savage M.B.A.," *The Wall Street Journal,* June 14, 1990, p. B1.

24. "Unethical Behavior, Stress Appear Linked," *The Wall Street Journal,* April 11, 1991, p. B1.

25. Donald Sanzotta and Lois Drapin, "Getting Along with the Boss," *Supervisory Management,* July 1984, p. 40.

26. Ibid., p. 41.

27. Kent Lineback, "How Management Trainers Miss the Boat," *Training,* March 1984, p. 92.

28. Kenneth Blanchard, "The One-Minute Supervisor," *Supervisory Management,* July 1985, pp. 23–26.

29. Kenneth H. Hill, Steven K. Kerr, and Laurie B. Broedling, "The First-Line Supervisor: Phasing Out or Here to Stay?" *Academy of Management Review,* January 1986, p. 105.

30. Keith Denton, "If You Want Your Ideas Approved," *Management Solutions,* September 1986, p. 11.

31. Lineback, "How Management Trainers Miss the Boat," p. 93.

32. Alan Farrant, "The New Supervisor," *Supervision,* January 1985, p. 6.

33. Ibid., p. 7.

34. Hansen, "Better Supervision from A to W," p. 36.

35. Karl Albrecht and Ron Zemke, *Service America!* (Homewood, IL: Dow Jones-Irwin, 1985), p. v.

36. Chris Lee, "Training the Front Line to Train the Front Line," *Training,* March 1987, pp. 77–81.

37. "What Goes Around Comes Around," *News from Cally Curtis* 8, issue 1, p. 3.

38. Ibid., pp. 3–4.

39. C. Hobson, R. Hobson, and J. Hobson, "People Skills: A Key to Success in the Service Sector," *Supervisory Management,* October 1984, p. 9.

40. "Key Management Skills to Improve Customer Service," *Key Management Strategies* (Western Massachusetts Chapter: American Society of Training and Development, April 30, 1985).

41. Hobson et al., "People Skills," p. 4.

42. Ibid., p. 9.

43. Ralph Shaffer, "Keep the Shelves Stocked with Basics," *The Wall Street Journal,* April 13, 1987, p. 22.

APPLICATION SITUATIONS

Forces Influencing Behavior at Work

AS 6–1

Identify each statement in terms of one of the work-behavior influences listed below:

a. organizational culture   *c.* work group   *e.* personal characteristics

b. supervisory   *d.* job

_____ 1. "I can't stand the manager's style of telling everyone what to do all the time."

_____ 2. "I really enjoy the feeling I get when I see a car roll off the assembly line."

_____ 3. "We have a great bunch of guys; we kid each other all the time."

_____ 4. "I do try; maybe I don't have much aptitude for the task."

_____ 5. "At Springfield College we have the humanics philosophy." (We educate the spirit, mind, and body.)

Using Power

AS 6–2

Identify the appropriate power to use in each situation.

a. coercive   *c.* reward or legitimate   *e.* information or expert

b. connection   *d.* referent

_____ 6. Carl is one of the best workers you supervise. He needs little direction, but he has slowed down his production level. You know he has a personal problem, but the work needs to get done.

_____ 7. You want a new personal computer to help you do a better job.

_____ 8. José, one of your best workers, wants a promotion. He has asked you to help prepare him for when the opportunity comes.

_____ 9. Your worst employee has ignored one of your directives again.

_____ 10. Wonder, who needs some direction and encouragement to maintain production, is not working to standard today. Wonder claims to be ill, as she does occasionally.

Ethical and Unethical Politics

AS 6–3

Identify each statement as

a. ethical politics   *b.* unethical politics

_____ 11. Pete goes around telling everyone about any little mistake his peer Sue makes.

_____ 12. Tony is taking tennis lessons so that he can challenge his boss.

_____ 13. Carol delivers her daily figures at 10:00 A.M. each day because she knows that she will run into Ms. Big Power on the way.

_____ 14. Carlos goes around asking about what is happening in other departments during his work time.

_____ 15. Frank sent a copy of his department's performance record to three high-level managers to whom he does not report.

Relations with Others

AS 6—4

Identify the party mentioned in each statement:

a. employees   *d.* other departments

b. boss   *e.* customers

c. peers

_____ 16. "As a supervisor, I report to a middle manager named Kim."

_____ 17. "The guys in sales are always trying to rush us to ship the product."

_____ 18. "Willy is reluctant to accept the tasks I delegate to him."

_____ 19. "I'm sorry it doesn't work; here's your money back."

_____ 20. "The supervisors are getting together for lunch; will you join us?"

OBJECTIVE CASE 6

Politicking

Karen Whitmore is going to be promoted in two months. She will be replaced by one of her subordinates—Jim Green or Lisa Fesco. Both Jim and Lisa know that they are competing for the promotion. Their years of experience and quality and quantity of work are about the same. Following is a description of some of the political behavior each used to help them get the promotion.

Lisa has been going to night classes and company training programs in supervision to prepare herself for the promotion. Lisa is very upbeat; she goes out of her way to be nice to people and compliment them. She gets along well with everyone. Knowing that Karen was an officer in a local businesswomen's networking organization, Lisa joined the club six months ago and now serves on a committee. At work Lisa talks regularly to Karen about the women's organization. Lisa makes an effort to know what is going on in the organization. One thing Karen doesn't like about Lisa is the fact that when she points out Lisa's errors, she always has an answer for everything.

Jim is good at sports and has been playing golf and tennis with upper-level managers for over a year now. In the department, especially with Karen, Jim refers to conversations with managers all the time. When Jim does something for someone, they can expect to do a favor in return. Jim really wants this promotion, but he fears that with more women being promoted to management positions, Lisa will get the job just because she is a woman. To increase his chances of getting the job, Jim stayed late and made a few changes—errors—in the report Lisa was working on. Jim sees nothing wrong with making the changes to get ahead. When Lisa handed in the report without checking prior work, Karen found the errors. The one thing Karen doesn't like about Jim is the fact that, on occasion, she has to tell him what to do before he acts.

Answer the following questions. Then in the space between the questions, state why you selected that answer. (*Note:* Meetings between Lisa and Jim, Karen and Jim, or all three may be role-played in class.)

_____ 1. We know that Karen has _____ power.
        a. positional   *b.* personal

_____ 2. To be promoted, Lisa is stressing _____ power. Refer to the opening statement about Lisa.
        a. coercive   *c.* reward   *e.* referent   *g.* expert
        b. connection   *d.* legitimate   *f.* information

_____ 3. To be promoted, Jim is stressing _____ power. Refer to the opening statement about Jim.
        a. coercive   *c.* reward   *e.* referent   *g.* expert
        b. connection   *d.* legitimate   *f.* information

_____ 4. _____ appears to use reciprocity the most.
        a. Lisa   *b.* Jim

_____ 5. Lisa _____ conducted unethical political behavior.
        a. has   *b.* has not

_____ 6. Jim _____ conducted unethical political behavior.
   a. has   *b.* has not

_____ 7. Jim and Karen are primarily playing _____ politics to get promotions.
   a. horizontal   *b.* vertical

_____ 8. Who was *not* affected by Jim's changing the report?
   a. supervisors   *c.* peers   *e.* other departments
   b. subordinates   *d.* Karen's department   *f.* the organization

_____ 9. Lisa does not meet Karen's expectation of
   a. loyalty   *c.* initiative   *e.* openness to criticism
   b. cooperation   *d.* information

_____ 10. Jim does not meet Karen's expectation of
   a. loyalty   *c.* initiative   *e.* openness to criticism
   b. cooperation   *d.* information

11. Lisa suspects that Jim made the changes in the report, but she has no proof. What would you do?

12. Karen suspects that Jim made the changes in the report, but she has no proof. What would you do?

IN-CLASS SKILL-BUILDING EXERCISE

Bases of Power

SB 6–1

Procedure 1
(10–20 minutes)

Objectives: To better understand the seven bases of power and when to use each.

Preparation: You should understand the seven bases of power.

The instructor shows the video or has two students read the scripts. As you view each of the seven scenes, identify the power base being used by the manager.

Scene 1. _____   *a.* coercive power
Scene 2. _____   *b.* connection power
Scene 3. _____   *c.* reward power
Scene 4. _____   *d.* legitimate power
Scene 5. _____   *e.* referent power
Scene 6. _____   *f.* information power
Scene 7. _____   *g.* expert power

    After viewing each of the seven scenes, identify the power base used by the manager by placing the letter of the power base on the scene line.

Option A: View all seven scenes and identify the power base used by the manager. After viewing all seven scenes, discuss and have the instructor give the correct answers.

Option B: After each scene the class discusses the power base used by the manager. The instructor states the correct answer after each of the seven scenes.

Procedure 2
(2–5 minutes)

Select the one power base you would use to get the employee to take the letter to the mail room. Which other power bases are also appropriate? Which power bases would you not use (are not appropriate) for this situation? Next to each power base listed above, write the letter A for appropriate or N for not appropriate.

Discussion:

Option A: In groups of four to six, answer the questions below.

Option B: As a class answer the questions below.

1. Which power bases are not appropriate to use in this situation?

2. Which power bases are appropriate to use in this situation?

3. Is there one base of power most appropriate in this situation?

Conclusion: The instructor may make concluding remarks.

Application (2–4 minutes): What did I learn from this exercise? How will I use this knowledge in the future?

Sharing: Volunteers give their answers to the application section.

PREPARATION FOR IN-CLASS SKILL-BUILDING EXERCISE

Ethics

SB 6–2

For each of the following statements, place an O on the line if you observed someone doing this behavior. Also place an R on the line if you reported this behavior within the organization.

O—observed   R—reported

_____ 1. Coming to work late and getting paid for it.

_____ 2. Leaving work early and getting paid for it.

_____ 3. Taking long breaks or lunches and getting paid for it.

_____ 4. Calling in sick to get a day off when not sick.

_____ 5. Using the company phone to make personal long-distance calls.

_____ 6. Doing personal work while on company time.

_____ 7. Using the company copier for personal use.

_____ 8. Mailing personal things through the company mail.

_____ 9. Taking home company supplies or merchandise.

_____ 10. Giving company supplies or merchandise to friends or allowing them to take them without saying anything.

_____ 11. Putting in for reimbursement for meals and travel or other expenses that wasn't actually eaten or taken.

_____ 12. Using the company car for personal business.

_____ 13. Taking spouse or friends out to eat and charging it to the company expense account.

_____ 14. Taking spouse or friends on business trips and charging the expense to the company.

_____ 15. Accepting gifts from customers or suppliers in exchange for giving them business.

_____ 16. A student cheating on homework assignments.

_____ 17. A student passing off another's term paper as his or her own work.

_____ 18. A student cheating on an exam.

19. For items 1 through 15, select the three which you consider to be the most severe unethical behavior. Who is harmed and who benefits by these unethical behaviors?

20. For items 16 through 18, who is harmed and who benefits from these unethical behaviors?

21. If you observed unethical behavior but didn't report it, why didn't you report the behavior? If you did report the behavior, why did you report it? What was the result?

22. As a supervisor, what can you do to minimize these unethical behaviors?

IN-CLASS SKILL-BUILDING EXERCISE

Ethics

SB 6–2

Objectives: To better understand ethics and whistleblowing.

Preparation: You should have answered the questions in the preparation.

Experience: You will share your answers to the preparation questions.

Procedure 1 (5–30 minutes):

Option A: Break into groups of five or six and share your answers to the preparation questions.

Option B: The instructor leads a discussion in which students share their answers to the preparation questions. (The instructor may begin by going over the 18 statements and having students who have observed the behavior raise their hand.) Then the instructor will have them raise their hand if they reported the behavior.

Conclusion: The instructor may lead a class discussion and make concluding remarks.

Application (2–4 minutes): What did I learn from this exercise? How will I use this knowledge in the future?

Sharing: Volunteers give their answers to the application section.

7

Communicating with Others

Key Terms   To achieve our objectives in this chapter, it is important that you understand the following 15 key terms. They are presented in the order in which they appear in the chapter. The list of key terms also appears in alphabetical order in the end-of-chapter review.

communication
goals of
   communication
encoding
message
decoding
media
nonverbal
   communication

message-sending process
empathic listening
feedback
paraphrasing
autocratic
   communication style
consultative
   communication style

participative
   communication style
laissez-faire
   communication style

Sara, a manager at Sears, needs a report typed. She has decided to assign the task to David following the five steps in the message-sending process. Here's how Sara and David communicated for each step.

- *Step 1.* **Develop rapport.**

SARA: David, how are you doing today?

DAVID: Okay. How about you?

SARA: Fine, thanks. Is the work on schedule?

DAVID: Yes, things are running smoothly.

- *Step 2.* **State the communication objective.**

SARA: David, I have a report that I'd like you to type for me.

DAVID: Let's see it.

• *Step 3.* **Transmit the message.**

SARA: Here are five handwritten pages. Please type the first page on my letterhead and the others on regular bond. Place the exhibit on a separate page; it will probably be on page 3. Then run the rest.

DAVID: It sounds easy enough.

SARA: I need it for a presentation to Paul at two o'clock today, and I'd like some time to review it before then. How soon will you have it ready?

DAVID: Well, it's 10 now, and I go to lunch from 12 to 1. I've got to finish what I'm working on now, but I should have it by noon.

SARA: Good. That will allow me to look it over at noon and get it back to you at one o'clock if it needs changes.

• *Step 4.* **Check understanding.**

SARA: I want to make sure I clearly explained what I need so that it will not need to be redone. Will you please tell me how you are going to do the job?

DAVID: Sure. I'm going to type it on regular bond. I'll run it until I get to the exhibit; the exhibit will be on its own page; then I will run the rest of it.

SARA: Did I mention that I wanted the first page to be on my letterhead?

DAVID: I don't remember, but I'll put page one on your letterhead.

SARA: Good!

• *Step 5.* **Get a commitment and follow up.**

SARA: So you agree to type it as directed and deliver it to my office by noon today.

DAVID: Yes, I'll get it to you before noon.

SARA: *(thinking to herself as she walks back to her office):* I'm confident he'll do it. But I'll follow up. If David doesn't show up by 11:55, I will be back, and he'll do it during his lunchtime.

How would you have communicated the typing job? The five steps in the message-sending process above are part of the communication process that you will learn in this chapter.

I. Why Communication Skills Are Important

Some of the reasons communication skills are important include the following:

• Talking and listening account for 75 percent of each workday. Yet 75 percent of what we hear, we hear imprecisely. We forget 75 percent of what we hear accurately within three weeks. Communications, the skill we need the most at work, is the skill we most lack.[1]

• Supervisors spend 70 percent of their time communicating in some way, broken down as follows: reading, 9 percent; writing, 16 percent; talking, 30 percent; and listening, 45 percent.[2]

• Communication is the most difficult and important task of the supervisor.[3]

• Your success as a supervisor depends largely on your ability to get messages across convincingly and effectively.[4]

• Various research studies have revealed that as much as 70 percent of all business communications fail to achieve the intended purpose.

The Supervisory Functions and Communication Skills

Without communication, a supervisor cannot get the job done. Plans cannot be implemented without communications. A supervisor cannot organize and delegate a task without communicating with an employee. The staffing and leadership processes require communication with employees. When controlling, the supervisor relies on information to determine progress toward objectives. When corrective action is needed, it must be communicated. In other words, you cannot supervise without communicating. Your success as a supervisor is directly affected by your ability to communicate.

Defining Communication

LEARNING OBJECTIVE

1. Define communication and state why it is important.

There is no universally accepted definition of communication. In fact, one study found over 95 definitions. For our purposes, **communication** *is the process of transmitting a mutually understood message from a sender to a receiver.* The important element is mutual understanding. If the two or more parties involved do not agree on the meaning of the message, communication has not taken place. We often send messages and assume that the receiver understands them without checking. As a supervisor, don't assume. The tendency to assume is probably the major reason that as much as 70 percent of all business communication fails to achieve its intended purpose. There are at least three major **goals of communication:** *to influence, to inform, or to express feelings.* When communicating, a person may do all three simultaneously rather than only one.

II. The Communication Process

Communication requires a sender to encode a message and transmit it to a receiver, who decodes it. Let's examine these three components separately.

The Sender

The sender of the message is the source or person who initiates the communication. Once people have a need, desire, or reason (to influence, inform, or to express feelings) to communicate, they encode the message. **Encoding** *is the sender's process of putting the message into a form that the receiver will understand.* The sender should consider who the receiver of the message is and determine the best way to encode it for mutual understanding to take place. For example, supervisors who are highly knowledgeable in their field must remember that, when encoding a message to a new, inexperienced employee, they must explain technical terms in a way that the receiver can relate to and understand.

Message Transmission

The **message** *is the physical form of the encoded information.* The message can be transmitted in three major ways—orally, in writing, or nonverbally. The sender should determine the most appropriate media or channel of transmission to meet the needs of the situation. In the next section of this chapter, you will learn recommended transmission media for different messages.

The Receiver

The person receiving the message decodes it. **Decoding** *is the receiver's process of translating the message into a meaningful form.* The receiver interprets what the sender is communicating. An example of the stages of communication process would be a professor preparing for a class; he or she encodes by preparing a lecture. The message (lecture) is transmitted orally during class. The students (receivers) decode the lecture (message) by listening and taking notes in a way that is meaningful to them. Students generally select from the lecture what to write down in notes. The notes are usually decoded rather than taken verbatim.

Steps in the Communication Process

The four steps in the communication process are selecting transmission media, sending the message, receiving the message, and responding to the message. Not all messages require a response. During a conversation the sender and receiver can reverse roles several times. Exhibit 7–1 illustrates the communication process. Each step will be fully explained under separate sections of this chapter.

In the opening case, Sara is the sender of an oral message, with a handwritten report to be typed. Although you could not see it in the case, Sara also used nonverbal communications. David was the receiver of the message, who responded to the message by agreeing to finish the report by noon. Now you will learn the details of each step in the communication process.

LEARNING OBJECTIVE

2. List and explain the four steps in the communication process.

EXHIBIT 7–1   **THE COMMUNICATION PROCESS**

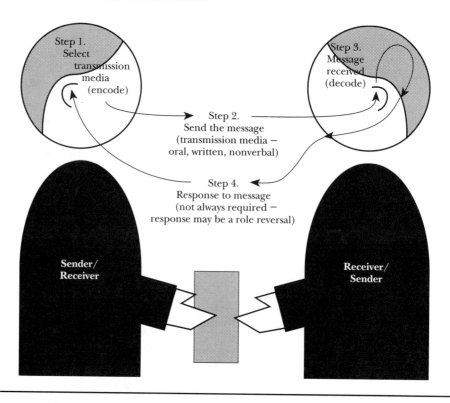

III. Message Transmission Media

When encoding the message, the sender should give careful consideration to selecting media. **Media** *are the forms of the transmitted message.* In this section you will learn the three major media you can use when transmitting messages: oral, written, and nonverbal.

Oral Communications

Oral communication is by far most managers' preferred medium for sending messages.[5] Four common types of oral communication include face to face, telephone, meetings, and presentations.

Face to Face

Face-to-face communication is the appropriate medium for delegating tasks, coaching, disciplining, instructing, sharing information, answering questions, checking progress toward objectives, and developing and maintaining human relations. Managers also spend one-on-one, face-to-face time communicating with their bosses, colleagues, and peers.

Telephone

The amount of time spent on the telephone varies greatly with the job. The telephone is the appropriate medium for quick exchanges of information and checking up on things. It is especially useful for saving travel time. However, it is inappropriate for personal matters such as discipline.

Meetings

The supervisor's most common meeting is the brief, informal get-together with two or more employees. It is appropriate for coordinating employee activities, delegating a task to a group, and resolving employee conflicts. (Conflict resolution is covered in Chapter 8.) In Chapter 15 you will learn how to conduct meetings.

Presentations

On occasion, a manager may be required to make a formal presentation. Prepare your presentations and be sure they have the following three parts:

1. *A beginning.* The presentation should begin with a purpose statement and an overview of the main points to be covered.
2. *A middle.* The presentation supports its purpose through a discussion of the main points in the detail necessary to get the message across.
3. *An end.* The presentation should summarize the purpose, main points, and any action required of the audience.

Written Communications

Written communications are appropriate for sending general information; for messages requiring future action; for sending formal, official, or long-term messages; and for messages that affect several people in a related way.

Some of the written forms commonly used in organizations include the following:

Memos: Memos are commonly used for interorganizational use. Many organizations have a standard form that usually has *to, from, subject, date,* and *copy* lines. Memos are appropriate for informal inquiries and replies; for keeping others informed of progress toward objectives; and for extensive messages, especially ones containing facts and figures.

Letters: Letters are commonly used for communicating to people outside the organization. They represent you and the organization to customers, suppliers, and so forth. You and the organization will be judged on the letters you send. Most organizations that use letters regularly have organizational stationery. Letters may also be used within the organization for long communications and for more personal and formal communication.

Reports: Reports are used to convey information. They usually involve an evaluation, analysis, and recommendations to management or colleagues. You may be required to write reports on your progress toward departmental objectives.

Bulletin Board Notices: Bulletin boards are appropriate for making formal announcements. They usually are a supplement to another form of communication. Bulletin boards should be updated regularly.

Posters: Posters are appropriate reminders of important information such as safety, quality, and good housekeeping. Ford has posters to remind employees that "Quality Is Job One."

Computers: Many people use computers to send messages. With the increased use of personal computers in organizations, you may use a computer to send and receive messages. With the increased amount of information made available through computers, managers are often dazzled; they don't know what to do with it all.

Fax Machines: The facsimile machine has fostered speed, clarity, and impatience. The fax is subtly changing how people communicate and do business because it allows delivery of documents almost instantaneously.

Nonverbal Communications

Every time we use oral face-to-face communications, we also use nonverbal communications. **Nonverbal communications** *are the facial expressions, vocal qualities, gestures, and posture used while transmitting messages.* Nonverbal communication can be anything that sends a message. The adage, "Actions speak louder than words," is true. Or, as Emerson put it, "What you do thunders so loudly in my ears, I cannot hear what you say." For example, if Amy, a supervisor, tells employees to do a quality job but does not do a quality job herself and does not reward quality performance, employees will most likely ignore the quality message.

Communicating is much more complex than selecting the right words. In fact, Dr. Albert Mehrabian, a specialist in nonverbal communications, conducted research identifying three dimensions of face-to-face communication:[6] verbal—the spoken word; vocal—the pitch, tone, and timbre of the voice; facial expression—mouth and eye movement. Mehrabian also showed the weight each one carries, as follows: verbal, 7 percent; vocal, 38 percent; and facial expression, 55 percent. In other words, the saying, "It's not what you say, but how you say it that counts," is true. For example, if Ward, a supervisor, tells Wally, an employee, he did a good job (verbal) in a sarcastic tone (vocal) with a look of disgust (facial expression), Wally will most likely disregard the verbal message.

Nonverbal communications are used together and may send different messages. For example, a person may be smiling (a sign of openness to communications) while having his or her arms and legs crossed (a sign of being closed to communications).

It is important for you to be aware of your nonverbal communications and to make sure they are consistent with your oral and written communications. You can use nonverbal communications, such as a nod of the head, to facilitate face-to-face communications. Be aware of other people's nonverbal communications. They tell you their feelings and attitudes toward the communications and you as a person and supervisor.[7]

CONNECTIONS

1. Give a specific example of a nonverbal communication that did not support the verbal message.

Combining Media

As stated previously, nonverbal communications are always combined with face-to-face communications. The supervisor can also combine oral and written communication. Repetition is often needed to ensure that the message has been conveyed with mutual understanding.[8] It is common for a manager to give an oral message followed by a written message to reinforce it. For example, the supervisor could conduct a safety program orally with the support of a written manual. Posters could also be placed in the work area to remind employees to follow the safety rules.

Oral communication followed by written communication is appropriate for developing objectives and plans; communicating new or changed standing plans; delegating complex tasks; communicating safety, quality, and good housekeeping; and reporting progress toward departmental objectives.

Before you send a message, be sure to select the best medium or media. Exhibit 7–2 lists the major media sources from which to select.

LEARNING OBJECTIVE

3. Discuss the three major transmission media.

EXHIBIT 7–2   **MESSAGE TRANSMISSION MEDIA SELECTION**

Oral communication media

1. Face to face
2. Telephone
3. Meetings
4. Presentations

Written communication media

1. Memos
2. Letters
3. Reports
4. Bulletin boards
5. Posters
6. Computers
7. Fax

Nonverbal communication media

1. Facial expressions
2. Vocal quality
3. Gestures
4. Posture

2. Which message transmission media are you strongest and weakest in? How will you improve your ability to communicate using your weakest medium?

IV. Sending Messages

Have you ever heard a manager say, "This isn't what I asked for"? When this happens, it is usually the manager's fault. Managers often make incorrect assumptions and do not take 100 percent of the responsibility for ensuring the message is transmitted with mutual understanding. To transmit messages effectively, managers must state exactly what they want, how they want it done, and when they need it done.[9]

Sending the message is the second step in the communication process. Before you send a message, you should carefully select your medium and plan how you will send the message.

Planning the Message

Before sending a message the sender should plan the following message elements:

- *What.* What is the goal of the message? Is it to influence, inform, or to express feeling? What do you want as the end result of the communication? Set an objective. When appropriate, consult others for information and participation in defining the objective.
- *Who.* Determine who should receive the message.
- *How.* With the receiver in mind, plan how you will encode the message so that it will be understood. Select the appropriate medium for the audience and situation. What will be said, done, written, and so forth?
- *When.* When will the message be transmitted? Timing is important. For example, if it is going to take 15 minutes to transmit a message, don't approach an employee five minutes before quitting time. Wait until the next day. Make an appointment when appropriate.
- *Where.* Decide where the message will be transmitted—your office, another's office, and so on. And remember to keep distractions to a minimum.

Sending the Message One on One

When sending a one-on-one message, it is helpful to follow the steps in the **message-sending process:** *developing rapport, stating the communication objective, transmitting the message, checking understanding, and getting a commitment and following up.*

In the opening case, Sara followed the five steps in the message-sending process. Following is a discussion of the five steps. After reading them, return to the opening case and review the process.

Step 1. Develop Rapport. Put the receiver at ease. It is usually appropriate to begin communications with small talk correlated to the message. It helps prepare the employee to receive the message. Developing rapport is perfected through practice and trust.

Step 2. State the Communication Objective. In business communications with the goal of influencing, it is helpful for the receiver to know the end result of the communication before getting to all the details.

MODEL 7–1

THE MESSAGE-SENDING PROCESS

Step 1. Develop rapport.

Step 2. State the communication objective.

Step 3. Transmit the message.

Step 4. Check understanding.

Step 5. Get a commitment and follow up.

Step 3. Transmit the Message. If the communication goal is to influence, tell the people what you want them to do, give instructions, and so forth. And be sure to set deadlines for completing tasks. If the goal is to inform, tell the people the information. If the goal is to express feelings, do so.

Step 4. Check Understanding. About the only time you may not want to check understanding is when the goal is to express feelings. When influencing and giving information, one should ask direct questions and use paraphrasing. To simply ask "Do you have any questions?" does not check understanding.

Step 5. Get a Commitment and Follow Up. When the goal of communication is to inform or express feelings, a commitment is not needed. However, when the goal of communication is to influence, it is important to get a commitment to the action. Managers must make sure that employees can do the task and have it done by a certain time or date. In situations in which the employee does not intend to get the task done, it is better to know when sending the message, rather than to wait until the deadline to find out. When employees are reluctant to commit to the necessary action, managers can use persuasive power within their authority. When communicating to influence, follow up to ensure that the necessary action has been taken.

Model 7–1 lists the five steps in the message-sending process.

LEARNING OBJECTIVE

4. List and explain the five steps in the message-sending process and use the model.

Criticizing Others

Most people do not enjoy criticizing others. However, part of the job of a supervisor, teacher, or parent is to criticize subordinates to improve their performance. How criticism is given makes a difference in how it is accepted. The goal of criticism should be to change undesirable behavior while maintaining human relations, not to get even or to show superiority. When criticizing others, follow these guidelines:

Give More Praise than Criticism: As a manager, try to praise 80 percent of the time and give criticism 20 percent. Research has shown that employees who receive above-average numbers of negative criticisms generally decrease, rather than increase, performance. Praise produces better results. For example, a manager should praise an employee for setting up a display nicely rather than giving criticism to the employee for being too slow. The praise resulted in increased performance. Criticism probably would not have worked.

Criticize Immediately: Criticism should be given as soon after the performance as is feasible. Criticism loses its effect with time. Give feedback immediately, unless people are emotional. When people are emotional, as when they are angry, following the other criticism guidelines is difficult.

Give Performance-Oriented Criticism: Focus on the task, not the person. Distinguish between the employee and his or her performance. For example, do not say things like "You are lazy," which is an attack on the person. It would be more useful to the employee to hear "Your rate of production is 10 percent slower than the standard," or "You are letting our group down by only doing five, while we all do seven."

EXHIBIT 7–3   **GUIDELINES FOR GIVING EFFECTIVE CRITICISM**

- Give more praise than criticism.
- Criticize immediately.
- Give performance-oriented criticism.
- Give specific and accurate criticism.
- Open on a positive note and close by repeating what action is needed.

Give Specific and Accurate Criticism: Generalities are of little use to employees. The more descriptive the feedback the more useful it is to the receiver. For example, do not say things like "You always make mistakes." It would be more useful to the employee to hear "Your work has three errors; they are. . . ." Giving inaccurate information can cause problems and embarrassment.

Open on a Positive Note and Close by Repeating What Action Is Needed: People remember longest what was said first and last. The opening statement sets the stage for criticism, and the conclusion the reinforcement of it. Try to let the employee realize that you like and value him or her as a person, and that it is some small aspect of his or her behavior that needs to be changed. For example, a customer who had just had her car fixed complained to the manager, Ruth, that the car rug has grease on it. Ruth tells the customer that the technician will clean it right away. Ruth approaches the auto mechanic and says, "Bill, overall you're a good technician; you did a good tune-up on that last car, but the owner complained about grease on the rug. You know you have to put a mat down on the floor to keep it from getting dirty. By putting the mat on the floor, you will do a better job by having fewer customer complaints; and you will save yourself the time it takes to clean the rug. From now on you must put a mat down in each and every car. Do you agree to using the mats?" Bill says, "Okay." Ruth says, "Good. Clean the woman's rug; then bring in the next car with a mat."

Generally, employees are open to criticism. Employees prefer to be told when they are not performing to standards, rather than to receive no criticism at all. They cannot improve performance without the necessary praise or criticism. However, employees do not like to be criticized in a negative way. Chastising, sarcasm, and joking should not take place when giving criticism. This type of behavior generally makes things worse. Exhibit 7–3 lists the guidelines for giving effective criticism.

LEARNING OBJECTIVE

5. List and explain the five guidelines for giving effective criticism.

C O N N E C T I O N S

3. Give a specific example (do not simply say poor performance) of a situation in which a supervisor should give an employee criticism.

4. Give an example of a situation in which a supervisor gave you criticism. List all five guidelines from the text, stating whether or not each was followed. If you have no example, interview and report another person's example.

V. Receiving Messages

Complete Self-Learning Exercise 7–1 to determine how good a listener you are.

SELF-LEARNING
EXERCISE 7–1

Listening Skills

Select the response that best describes the frequency of your actual behavior. Place the letter A, U, F, O, or S on the line before each of the 15 statements.

A — almost always   U — usually   F — frequently   O — occasionally   S — seldom

_____ 1. I like to listen to people talk. I encourage them to talk by showing interest, smiling, nodding, and so forth.

_____ 2. I pay closer attention to speakers who are more interesting or similar to me.

_____ 3. I evaluate the speaker's words and nonverbal communication ability as he or she talks.

_____ 4. I avoid distractions; if it's noisy, I suggest moving to a quiet spot.

_____ 5. When people interrupt me to talk, I put what I was doing out of sight and mind and give them my complete attention.

_____ 6. When people are talking, I allow them time to finish. I do not interrupt, anticipate what they are going to say, or jump to conclusions.

_____ 7. I tune people out who do not agree with my views.

_____ 8. While the other person is talking or the professor is lecturing, my mind wanders to personal topics.

_____ 9. While the other person is talking, I pay close attention to the nonverbal communications to help me fully understand what the sender is trying to get across.

_____ 10. I tune out and pretend I understand when the topic is difficult.

_____ 11. When the other person is talking, I think about what I am going to say in reply.

_____ 12. When I think there is something missing or contradictory, I ask direct questions to get the person to explain the idea more fully.

_____ 13. When I don't understand something, I let the sender know.

_____ 14. When listening to other people, I try to put myself in their position and see things from their perspective.

_____ 15. During conversations I repeat back to the sender what has been said in my own words (paraphrase) to be sure I understand correctly what has been said.

If you were to have people to whom you talk regularly answer these questions about you, would they have the same responses that you selected? Have friends fill out the questions for you and compare answers.

To determine your score, give yourself 5 points for each A, 4 for each U, 3 for each F, 2 for each O, and 1 for each S for statements 1, 4, 5, 6, 9, 12, 13, 14, and 15. Place the numbers on the line next to your response letter. For items 2, 3, 7, 8, 10, and 11 the score reverses: 5 points for each S, 4 for each O, 3 for each F, 2 for each U, and 1 for each A. Place these score numbers on the lines next to the response letters. Now add your total number of points. Your score should be between 15 and 75. Place your score on the continuum below. Generally, the higher your score, the better your listening skills.

Poor listener 15   25   35   45   55   65   75 Good listener

Active Listening

Step 3 of the communication process is receipt of the message. Communication does not take place unless the message is received with mutual understanding. The message cannot be received accurately unless the receiver listens. Poor listening is caused in part by the fact that people speak at an average rate of 120 words per minute, whereas they are capable of listening at a rate of over 500 words per minute. The ability to comprehend words more than four times faster than the speaker can talk often results in minds wandering.

To help overcome the discrepancy in the speed between your ability to listen and people's rate of speaking, use the speed of your brain positively. Listen actively by organizing, summarizing, reviewing, interpreting, and critiquing often. These activities will help you to actively listen.

To become an active listener, take 100 percent of the responsibility for ensuring mutual understanding. Work to change your behavior to become a better active listener. Review the 15 statements in Self-Learning Exercise 7–1. Examine items 1, 4, 5, 6, 9, 12, 13, 14, and 15. Do not look at items 2, 3, 7, 8, 10, and 11. True active listening requires responding to the message to ensure that mutual understanding takes place.

LEARNING OBJECTIVE

6. List and explain the characteristics of active listening.

CONNECTIONS

5. What is your weakest listening skill? How will you improve your listening ability?

Dealing with Emotional Employees

As a supervisor, you will most likely have an employee come to talk to you in an emotional state. As a supervisor and an employee, you should understand emotions and how to deal with them.

Understanding Feelings

We should all realize that feelings are subjective; they tell us people's attitudes and needs. Feelings are usually disguised as factual statements. For example, when people are hot, they tend to say, "It's hot in here," rather than, "I feel hot." Most important, feelings are neither right nor wrong.[10]

We cannot choose our feelings or control them. However, we can control how we express them. For example, if Vern, an employee, says "You *!!" (pick a swear word that would make you angry) to Bonnie, his supervisor, she will feel its effect. However, Bonnie can express her feelings in a calm manner, or she can yell, hit, give Vern a dirty look, and so on. Supervisors should encourage employees to express their feelings in a positive way. But they shouldn't allow employees to go around yelling, swearing, or hitting others. And they should not get caught up in others' emotions.

Calming the Emotional Employee

When an emotional employee comes to you, NEVER make statements such as, "You shouldn't be angry"; "Don't be upset"; "Be a man/woman, not a baby"; "Just sit down and be quiet"; or "I know how you feel." (No one knows how anyone else feels. Even people who experience the same thing at the same time don't feel the same.) These types of statements only make the feelings stronger. True, you may get the employee to shut up. But communication will not take place. The problem will still exist and your human relations with the employee will suffer because of it, as will your relations with others who see or hear about what you said and did. When the employee complains to peers, he or she will tend to feel you were too hard or easy on him or her. You lose either way.

Empathic Listening

To calm emotional employees, don't argue with them. Encourage them to express their feelings in a positive way. Show them that you understand how they feel; we all want to be understood. Do not agree or disagree with the feelings; simply identify them verbally. Paraphrase the feeling to the employee. Use statements such as, "You were *hurt* when you didn't get the assignment," "You *resent* Bill for not doing his share of the work; is that what you mean?" or "You are *doubtful* that the job will be done on time; is that what you're saying?"

After you deal with emotions, you can go on to work on content (solving problems). It may be wise to wait until a later time. You will find that understanding the employee's feelings is often the solution. The receiver's attempt to stand in the sender's shoes is also called empathic listening. To listen with empathy does not mean you have to agree with the person. **Empathic listening** *is the ability to understand and relate to another's situation and feelings.* Most messages have two components—feelings and content. Try to relate to both.

LEARNING OBJECTIVE

7. Explain how to deal with an emotional employee.

CONNECTIONS

6. Give an example of a situation in which a supervisor dealt with an emotional employee. Did the supervisor calm the employee using empathic listening? Explain.

VI. Responding to Messages

The fourth and last step to the communication process is responding to the message. Not all messages require a response. For example, if top management sends around a memo to all employees telling them that the company will close at noon on Christmas Eve, rather than the usual 5:00 P.M., top management does not expect employees to respond to the message. However, when you are sending a message face to face, the best way to ensure mutual understanding is to get feedback from the receiver.

Feedback

Feedback *is the process of verifying messages.* Questioning, paraphrasing, and allowing comments and suggestions are all forms of feedback. Feedback when giving and receiving messages facilitates job performance.

For motivation to take place, employees need to know how they are doing. However, many employees do not know how they are doing. It is not unusual for employees to go to a formal performance appraisal thinking that they are doing a good job, only to find out that the boss does not agree. In fact, the higher you move up the corporate ladder, the less likely you are to receive feedback on your performance.[11]

The benefits of feedback have been clearly illustrated in a study conducted among clerical employees.[12] The workers were asked about the frequency and usefulness of different types of feedback. The most frequent and most useful information came from the employee himself or herself. Peers were the second most frequent source of feedback, but they were ranked fourth for the usefulness of their information. Supervisors were ranked third for their frequency of feedback, but second (the first-rated external source of feedback) in usefulness of the feedback given. Watching others was the fourth most frequent source of feedback, but watching was ranked third in usefulness.

Getting Feedback

Mutual understanding must exist for communication to take place. The best way to make sure communication has taken place is to get feedback from the receiver of the message through questioning and paraphrasing.

The Common Approach to Getting Feedback and Why It Doesn't Work[13]

The most common approach to getting feedback is to send the entire message, followed by asking "Do you have any questions?" Feedback usually does not follow because people have a tendency not to ask questions. There are three good reasons why people do not ask questions:

- They feel ignorant. To ask a question, especially if no one else does, is considered an admission of not paying attention or not being bright enough to understand the issue.
- They are ignorant. Sometimes people do not know enough about the message to know whether it is incomplete, incorrect, or subject to interpretation. There are no questions because what was said sounds right. The receiver does not understand the message, or does not know what to ask.
- Receivers are reluctant to point out the sender's ignorance. This is very common when the sender is a supervisor and the receiver is an employee. The employee fears that asking a question suggests that the supervisor has done a poor job of preparing and sending the message. Or it suggests that the supervisor is wrong. Regardless of the reason, the end result is the same: employees don't ask questions; generally, students don't either.

After supervisors send their messages and ask for questions, they then proceed to make another common error. They assume that a lack of questions means communication is complete, that the message is mutually understood. In reality, the message is often misunderstood. When "This isn't what I asked for" happens, the task has to be done all over again. The end result is often wasted time, materials, and effort.

The most common cause of communication error is the sender's lack of the feedback that ensures mutual understanding. The proper use of questioning and paraphrasing can help you ensure that your messages are communicated.

How to Get Feedback on Messages

Following are four guidelines managers should use when getting feedback on messages. They are also appropriate for nonmanagers.

Be Open to Feedback: First of all, you must be open to feedback. The open-door policy encourages feedback. When an employee asks a question, the supervisor needs to be responsive and patiently answer questions and explain things. There are no stupid questions, only stupid answers. Make the employee feel comfortable emotionally and physically.

Be Aware of Nonverbal Communication: You must also be aware of your nonverbal communications and make sure that they encourage feedback. For example, if supervisors say that they encourage questions, but act impatient or look at employees as though they are stupid when employees ask questions, employees will learn not to ask questions. The supervisor must also be aware of employees' nonverbal communications. For example, if the supervisor is explaining a task to Larry, the employee, and Larry has a puzzled look on his face, he is probably confused but may not be willing to say so. In such a case, the supervisor should stop and clarify things before going on.

Ask Questions: When you send messages, it is better to know whether or not the messages are understood before action is taken so that the action will not have to be changed or repeated. Because communicating is entirely the responsibility of message senders, they should ask questions to check understanding, rather than simply asking, "Do you have any questions?" Direct questions dealing with the specific information you have given will indicate whether the receiver has been listening and whether he or she understands enough to give a direct reply. If the response is not accurate, repeating, giving more examples, or further elaborating on the message is needed. The supervisor can also ask indirect questions to attain feedback. The supervisor could ask "How do you feel?" questions about the message. The supervisor could also ask "If you were me" questions, such as, "If you were me, how would you explain how to do it?" Or the supervisor can ask third-party questions, such as, "How will employees feel about this?" The response to indirect questions will tell the supervisor the employee's attitude and can convey misunderstandings.

Paraphrasing: The most accurate indicator of understanding is **paraphrasing**—*the process of having the receiver restate the message in his or her own words.* How the supervisor asks the employee to paraphrase will affect his or her attitude. For example, the supervisor's saying, "John, tell me what I just said so that I can be sure you will not make a mistake as usual," would probably result in defensive behavior on John's part. John would probably make a mistake in fulfillment of the supervisor's self-fulfilling prophecy (as discussed in Chapter 6). Following are two examples of proper requests for paraphrasing:

- "Now tell me what you are going to do so we will be sure that we are in agreement."
- "Would you tell me what you are going to do so that I can be sure that I explained myself clearly?"

LEARNING OBJECTIVE

8. Discuss the four guidelines for getting feedback on messages.

Notice that the second statement takes the pressure off the employee. The supervisor is asking for a check on his or her ability, not that of the employee. These types of requests for paraphrasing should result in a positive attitude toward the message and the supervisor. They show concern for the employee and for effective communication.

CONNECTIONS

7. Describe how your present or past boss used feedback. How could his or her feedback skills be improved?

Response Styles

As the sender transmits a message, how you as the receiver respond to the message directly affects the communications. There is no one best response style. The response should be appropriate for the situation. You will learn six response styles: evaluating, confronting, diverting, probing, reassuring, and reflecting.[14] For each alternative you will be given an example of a response to the employee message, "You supervise me so closely that you disrupt my ability to do my job."

Evaluating and Advising

People tend to feel obligated to make a judgment about a message they receive. An evaluative response accepts or rejects, passes judgment, or offers advice. Such a response tends to close, limit, or direct the flow of communication.

Evaluative responses used during the early stages of receiving the message may cause the sender to become defensive. People often feel the need to justify the message.

Appropriate Use of Evaluative Responses: The evaluative response is particularly appropriate when the situation calls for an autocratic or consultative supervisory style. Situations in which you are asked for advice, direction, or your opinion call for an evaluative response.

An example of a supervisor's evaluative response to the employee's message is, "You need my supervision; you lack experience."

Confronting

Confronting responses tend to challenge the sender to clarify the message, usually by pointing out inconsistencies in the message. They tend to reject the message and close, limit, or direct the flow of communication.

Confronting responses used during the early stages of receiving a message may cause the sender to become defensive. They are generally more useful after trust and acceptance have occurred.

Appropriate Use of Confronting Responses: Confrontation is most appropriate when the sender is not aware of the mistake or omission in the message, or when clarity is needed. A supervisor should view employees' confronting responses as requests for clarification rather than as threatening or questioning of your authority.

An example of a supervisor's confronting response to the employee's message is, "I disagree. You need my direction to do a good job."

Diverting

Diverting responses switch the focus of the communication to a message of the receiver. The receiver becomes the sender of a different message. It is often called changing the subject. Diverting responses tend to redirect, close or limit the flow of communication.

Diverting responses used during the early stages of receiving the message may cause the sender to feel that his or her message is not worth discussing, or that the other party's message is more important.

Appropriate Use of Diverting Responses: The diverting response is appropriate when using the autocratic or consultative supervisory style. When you want the job done your way, you must convey that message. Diverting responses may be helpful when they are used to share personal experiences of feelings that are similar to that of the sender.

An example of a supervisor's diverting response to the employee's message is, "You've reminded me of a supervisor I once had who. . . ."

Probing

A probing response asks the sender to give more information about some aspect of the message. It is useful to get a better understanding of the situation. When probing, "what" questions are preferred to "why" questions.

Appropriate Use of Probing Responses: Probing is appropriate during the early stages of the message to ensure understanding. It is used with the consultative and participative supervisory styles.

An example of a supervisor's probing response to the employee's message is, "What do I do to cause you to say this?" not, "Why do you feel this way?"

Reassuring

A reassuring response is given to reduce the intensity of the emotions associated with the message. Essentially you're saying, "Don't worry; everything will be okay." You are pacifying the sender.

Appropriate Use of Reassuring Responses: Reassuring is appropriate to use when the other person lacks confidence. Encouraging responses can help employees develop.

An example of a supervisor's reassuring response to the employee's message is, "I will not do it for much longer."

Reflecting

The reflective response is used by the empathic listener. Most messages have two components—feelings and content. A reflective response paraphrases the message back to the sender to show him or her that the receiver understands, values, accepts him or her. The sender can then feel free to explore the topic in more depth. Empathizing has been found to significantly affect employees' attitudes and behavior in positive ways.

The empathic responder deals with content, feelings, and the underlying meaning being expressed in the message (generally in that order). Carl Rogers, a noted psychological expert, believes that reflective responses should be used in the beginning stages of most communications. Reflective responses lead to mutual understanding and develop human relations. They should be used with the consultative and participative supervisory styles.

The example statements used to calm an emotional employee are reflective responses. An example of a supervisor's reflective response to the employee's message is, "My checking up on you annoys you!"

The opening case illustrated the four steps in the communication process. Sara was the sender of an oral message, with a handwritten report to be typed. Although you could not see it in the case, Sara also used nonverbal communications. David was the receiver of the message and he did respond to the message by agreeing to finish the report by noon. David "reassured" Sara that he would have the report done on time.

Sara also followed the five steps in the message-sending process. She developed a rapport with David and stated the objective of the communication as typing a report. She transmitted the message, stating the directions, and they agreed on a noontime completion of the report. Sara checked understanding with David by getting feedback; she asked him to paraphrase how he was going to do the report. Getting the feedback allowed Sara to clarify that the first page was to be on letterhead. David had missed this point. David did agree to the noon delivery time and Sara had a follow-up plan.

LEARNING OBJECTIVE

9. List and explain the six response styles.

CONNECTIONS

8. Give situations in which any two of the six response styles would be appropriate. Give the sender's message and your response. Identify its style.

VII. Communication Barriers

Communication is important, yet there are many barriers to effective communication. In this section, you will learn some of the major barriers and how to overcome them. The 10 barriers include perception, semantics, noise, emotions, filtering, trust and credibility, information overload, not listening, time and place, and medium selection.

Perception

As a message is transmitted, the receiver decodes it. In the process of decoding, the person's background, experience, interest, values, and so forth all affect how the message is interpreted. We usually see the message from our point of view, rather than from the sender's. For example, if a supervisor changes a work procedure in order to increase productivity, he or she views the change as positive. However, an employee may perceive it negatively, as a means of making him or her do more work.

Semantics

Semantics also causes perception problems. The same word often means different things to different people. For example, a supervisor gives a secretary a letter to type, saying, "Do it as soon as you can." The supervisor returns 30 minutes later to find that the letter is not typed. The secretary perceived the instructions to mean "when you get around to it."

To overcome such problems, we need to consider how the other person will most likely perceive the message, and try to encode and transmit it appropriately.

Noise

Noise can disturb or confuse communications. For example, there may be a machine making a noise that is distracting; the sender may not speak loudly enough for the receiver to hear well; or a radio or TV may distract the receiver, causing him or her to miss the message.

To overcome noise we need to consider the physical surroundings before transmitting the message. Try to keep noise to a minimum.

Emotions

Emotions such as anger, hurt, fear, sorrow, or happiness make it difficult to be objective and listen. For example, a supervisor is trying to get an employee to increase productivity. The supervisor makes a comment such as, "You're a lazy bum." Chances are good that the employee will get angry and defensive (emotional). The employee and supervisor may end up arguing. Generally, mutual understanding is impossible in this situation.

To avoid emotional problems when communicating, we should try not to become emotional ourselves. And we should follow the four guidelines for effective feedback so that we don't make others emotional. If anyone does become emotional, it is usually more productive to postpone communications until everyone calms down.

Filtering

People often filter—alter, color, or distort—information to project a more favorable image. For example, if a supervisor is asked to report progress in meeting objectives, he or she may stress the positive and deemphasize or even leave out the negative side of the situation. Employees often filter information as a means of hiding problems from an overly critical boss.

To help eliminate filtering, the supervisor should treat errors as a learning experience, rather than as an opportunity to blame and criticize employees. Using the open-door policy can create and support two-way communications.[15]

Trust and Credibility

A receiver may accept or reject a message depending on how much he or she trusts the sender. The sender's credibility also affects acceptance of a message. A person perceived as an expert has a good chance of having his or her message accepted. When people hear two different versions of the same message, they tend to believe the more credible source. For example, if a classmate told you your next class was canceled, but a professor (not the instructor) said it was not, you would probably go to the classroom.

To increase the trust people have in you, be open and honest with others. If you are caught in a lie, people may never trust you again. To gain and maintain credibility, it is important to get the facts straight before you communicate. Send clear, correct messages.

Information Overload

We all have a limit to the amount of information we can decode and understand at any given time. For example, you would find it difficult to read and comprehend several chapters the night before an exam if you had never looked at them before.

To minimize information overload, don't send more messages than the receiver can decode and understand. When communicating, check to be sure the receiver is decoding the message as you intended; use paraphrasing. If you talk for too long, the receiver can become bored or lose the thread of the message. For example, if you are explaining a procedure, don't go through it completely and then ask whether there are any questions. The receiver may be lost and not know what to ask. Instead, break the procedure down into parts. Explain one part at a time, allowing employees to ask questions. When you have explained one part, have the employee paraphrase. Do this for each part of the procedure. Then summarize by repeating the steps for the total procedure.

Not Listening

People usually hear what the sender is saying, but they often do not *listen to* or *understand* the message. Not listening can sometimes be the result of not paying attention. The receiver's mind may wander. Or the receiver may be formulating a reply rather than listening.

To help ensure that people are listening to your message, ask questions and have them paraphrase your message. If they can, they have listened to you. If they cannot, keep trying until they can.

When listening, if you find your mind wandering, bring it back on track as quickly as you can.[16] Don't listen for long without giving feedback to the sender. When you cannot understand the message, say so, and encourage others to do the same for you. Regard old messages as new; don't assume that you know what the other party is saying or going to say; listen.[17]

Time and Place

When and where you send a message affects communication. Selecting a poor time or place to send the message often results in missed communications. For example, the professor is about to start class and a student comes to the front of the room to discuss a personal matter. The professor's mind is on starting class and he or she will tend to rush the student. It is better to wait until after class or, better still, go to the professor's office during office hours. In the business setting, it is usually not a good idea to start giving employees long, detailed information when it is minutes from quitting time. Wait until the next morning.

Medium Selection

LEARNING OBJECTIVE

10. Describe the 10 barriers to communication and ways to overcome them.

The medium used to send the message is also important. It is also interrelated with time and place. Use of an inappropriate medium can result in missed communication. For example, if a supervisor catches an employee in the act of breaking a rule, the best medium selection is one-on-one, face-to-face communication. Before sending a message, give careful thought to which medium is the most effective. See Exhibit 7–4 for a list of the 10 barriers to communication.

CONNECTIONS

9. Give examples of 3 of the 10 barriers to communication you have encountered. Explain the situation.

VIII. Situational Communications

When you work with people outside your department, you have no authority to give them direct orders. You must use other means to achieve your goal. Situational communication is a model for conducting communications with people outside

EXHIBIT 7–4　　**HOW BARRIERS AFFECT THE COMMUNICATION PROCESS**

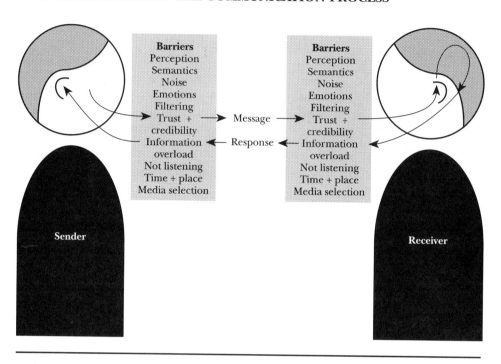

your department or organization or with people who are peers and managers in higher levels of management than you. The situational communications model will teach you how to analyze a given situation and select the most appropriate style of communications.

This section focuses on the interactive process system, situational communication styles, situational variables, and selection of the most appropriate communication style in a given situation. Begin by determining your preferred communication style.

Determining Your Preferred Communication Style

To determine your preferred communication style, select the *one* alternative that most closely describes what you would do in each of the 12 situations below. Do not be concerned with trying to pick the correct answer; select the alternative that best describes what you would actually do. Place the letter *a, b, c,* or *d* in the blank next to each question. Ignore the time, information, acceptance, capability, style, and S lines. They will be explained later in this chapter, and will be used with Model 7–2 during In-Class Skill-Building Exercise 7–1 at the end of the chapter.

_____ 1. Wendy, a knowledgeable person from another department, comes to you, the engineering supervisor, and requests that you design a special product to her specifications. You would _____ time _____ information _____ acceptance _____ capability _____ style

 a. Control the conversation and tell Wendy what you will do for her. S _____

 b. Ask Wendy to describe the product. Once you understand it, you would present your ideas. Let her realize that you are concerned and want to help with your ideas. S _____

   c. Respond to Wendy's request by conveying understanding and
      support. Help clarify what she wants you to do. Offer ideas, but do
      it her way. S _____

   d. Find out what you need to know. Let Wendy know you will do it
      her way. S _____

_____ 2. Your department has designed a product that is to be fabricated by
         Saul's department. Saul has been with the company longer than you
         have; he knows his department. Saul comes to you to change the
         product design. You decide to _____ time _____ information
         _____ acceptance _____ capability _____ style

   a. Listen to the change and the reasons that it would be beneficial. If
      you believe Saul's way is better, change it; if not, explain why the
      original design is superior. If necessary, insist that it be done your
      way. S _____

   b. Tell Saul to fabricate it any way he wants to. S _____

   c. You are busy; tell Saul to do it your way. You don't have time to
      listen and to argue with him. S _____

   d. Be supportive; make changes together as a team. S _____

_____ 3. Upper management has a decision to make. They call you to a
         meeting and tell you they need some information to solve a problem
         they describe to you. What do you do? _____ time _____ infor-
         mation _____ acceptance _____ capability _____ style

   a. Respond in a manner that conveys personal support and offer
      alternative ways to solve the problem. S _____

   b. Respond to their questions. S _____

   c. Explain how to solve the problem. S _____

   d. Show your concern by explaining how to solve the problem and
      why it is an effective solution. S _____

_____ 4. You have a routine work order. The work order is to be placed
         verbally and completed in three days. Sue, the receiver, is very
         experienced and willing to be of service to you. You decide to
         _____ time _____ information _____ acceptance
         _____ capability _____ style

   a. Explain your needs, but let Sue make the order decision.
      S _____

   b. Tell Sue what you want and why you need it. S _____

   c. Decide together what to order. S _____

   d. Simply give Sue the order. S _____

_____ 5. Work orders from the staff department normally take three days;
         however, you have an emergency and need the job today. Your
         colleague Jim, the department supervisor, is knowledgeable and
         somewhat cooperative. You decide to _____ time _____ infor-
         mation _____ acceptance _____ capability _____ style

   a. Tell Jim that you need it by 3 P.M. and will return at that time to
      pick it up. S _____

   b. Explain the situation and benefits to the organization. Volunteer
      to help expedite the order in any way you can. S _____

   c. Explain the situation and ask Jim when the order will be ready.
      S _____

   d. Explain the situation and together come to a solution to your
      problem. S _____

_____ 6. Danielle, a peer with a record of high performance, has recently had
         a drop in productivity. Her problem is affecting your performance.
         You know that Danielle has a family problem. What do you do?

_____ time _____ information _____ acceptance
_____ capability _____ style

a. Discuss the problem; help Danielle realize the problem is affecting her work and yours. Supportively discuss ways to improve the situation. S _____

b. Tell the boss about it and let him decide what to do about it. S _____

c. Tell Danielle to get back on the job. S _____

d. Discuss the problem and tell Danielle how to solve the work situation; be supportive. S _____

_____ 7. You are a knowledgeable supervisor. You buy supplies from Peter regularly. He is an excellent salesperson and very knowledgeable about your situation. You are placing your weekly order. You decide to _____ time _____ information _____ acceptance _____ capability _____ style

a. Explain what you want and why. Develop a supportive relationship. S _____

b. Explain what you want and ask Peter to recommend products. S _____

c. Give Peter the order. S _____

d. Explain your situation and allow Peter to make the order. S _____

_____ 8. Jean, a knowledgeable person from another department, has asked you to perform a routine staff function to her specifications. You decide to _____ time _____ information _____ acceptance _____ capability _____ style

a. Perform the task to her specifications without questioning her. S _____

b. Tell her that you will do it the usual way. S _____

c. Explain what you will do and why. S _____

d. Show your willingness to help; offer alternative ways to do it. S _____

_____ 9. Tom, a salesperson, has requested an order for your department's services with a short delivery date. As usual, Tom claims it is a take-it-or-leave-it offer. He wants your decision now, or within a few minutes, because he is in the customer's office. Your action is to _____ time _____ information _____ acceptance _____ capability _____ style

a. Convince Tom to work together to come up with a later date. S _____

b. Give Tom a yes or no answer. S _____

c. Explain your situation and let Tom decide whether you should take the order. S _____

d. Offer an alternative delivery date. Work on your relationship; show your support. S _____

_____ 10. As a time and motion expert, you have been called in regard to a complaint about the standard time it takes to perform a job. As you analyze the entire job, you realize that the one element of complaint should take longer, but that other elements should take less time. The end result is a shorter total standard time for the job. You decide to _____ time _____ information _____ acceptance _____ capability _____ style

a. Tell the operator and foreman that the total time must be decreased and why. S _____

    b. Agree with the operator and increase the standard time.
    S _____

    c. Explain your findings. Deal with the operator's and foreman's concerns, but ensure compliance with your new standard.
    S _____

    d. Together with the operator, develop a standard time. S _____

_____ 11. You approve budget allocations for projects. Marie, who is very competent in developing budgets, has come to you. What do you do? _____ time _____ information _____ acceptance _____ capability _____ style

    a. Review the budget, make revisions, and explain them in a supportive way. Deal with concerns, but insist on your changes.
    S _____

    b. Review the proposal and suggest areas where changes may be needed. Make changes together, if needed. S _____

    c. Review the proposed budget, make revisions, and explain them.
    S _____

    d. Answer any questions or concerns Marie has and approve the budget as is. S _____

_____ 12. You are a sales manager. A customer has offered you a contract for your product with a short delivery date. The offer is open for two days. The contract would be profitable for you and the organization. The cooperation of the production department is essential to meet the deadline. Tim, the production manager, and you do not get along very well because of your repeated request for quick delivery. Your action is to _____ time _____ information _____ acceptance _____ capability _____ style

    a. Contact Tim and try to work together to complete the contract.
    S _____

    b. Accept the contract and convince Tim in a supportive way to meet the obligation. S _____

    c. Contact Tim and explain the situation. Ask him whether you and he should accept the contract, but let him decide. S _____

    d. Accept the contract. Contact Tim and tell him to meet the obligation. If he resists, tell him you will go to his boss.
    S _____

To determine your preferred communication style, below, circle the letter you selected in situations 1 through 12. The column headings indicate the style you selected.

	Autocratic (S-A)	Consultative (S-C)	Participative (S-P)	Laissez-Faire (S-L)
1.	*a*	*b*	*c*	*d*
2.	*c*	*a*	*d*	*b*
3.	*c*	*d*	*a*	*b*
4.	*d*	*b*	*c*	*a*
5.	*a*	*b*	*d*	*c*
6.	*c*	*d*	*a*	*b*
7.	*c*	*a*	*b*	*d*
8.	*b*	*c*	*d*	*a*

9.	*b*	*d*	*a*	*c*
10.	*a*	*c*	*d*	*b*
11.	*c*	*a*	*b*	*d*
12.	*d*	*b*	*a*	*c*
Total				

Add up the number of circled items per column. The total across the bottom row should equal 12. The column with the highest number represents your preferred communication style. There is no one best style in all situations. The more evenly distributed the numbers are between the four styles, the more flexible are your communications. A total of 0 or 1 in any column may indicate a reluctance to use that style.

The Interactive Process System

According to Anderson and Erlandson, communication has the following five dimensions, all of which can be described on a continuum:[18]

Initiation ——————————————————————— **Response**

Initiation: The sender starts, or initiates, the communication. The sender may or may not expect a response to the initiated message.

Response: The receiver's reply or action to the sender's message. In responding, the receiver can become an initiator. As two-way communication takes place, the role of initiator (sender) and responder (receiver) may change.

Presentation ————————————————————— **Elicitation**

Presentation: The sender's message is structured, directive, or informative. A response may not be needed, although action may be called for. ("We are meeting to develop next year's budget." "Please open the door.")

Elicitation: The sender invites a response to the message. Action may or may not be needed. ("How large a budget do we need?" "Do you think we should leave the door open?")

Closed ——————————————————————————— **Open**

Closed: The sender expects the receiver to follow the message. ("This is a new form to fill out and return with each order.")

Open: The sender is eliciting a response as a means of considering the receiver's input. ("Should we use this new form with each order?")

Rejection —————————————————————— **Acceptance**

Rejection: The receiver does not accept the sender's message. ("I will not fill out this new form for each order!")

Acceptance: Agreement with the sender's message. ("I will fill out the new form for each order.")

Strong ——————————————————————————— **Mild**

Strong: The sender will use force or power to have the message acted upon as directed. ("Fill in the form or you're fired.")

Mild: The sender will not use force or power to have the message acted upon as directed. ("Please fill in the form when you can.")

Situational Communication Styles

The interactive process can be used with situational supervision. For example, use of the autocratic style requires a closed, strong presentation, whereas the laissez-faire style calls for an open, mild elicitation. The mild to strong component can be used with any of the styles, but the strong messages tend to be used more often with the autocratic and consultative styles. Acceptance or rejection can come from any of the styles because, to a large extent, it is beyond the sender's control.

Following is the interactive process, as it is used with each of the four situational supervisory styles.

One style, the **autocratic communication style** *(S-A), demonstrates high-task/low-relationship behavior (HT-LR), initiating a closed presentation.* The other party has little, if any, information and has low capability.

- Initiation/response. You initiate and control the communication with minimal, if any response.
- Presentation/elicitation. You make a presentation letting the other parties know they are expected to comply with your message; there is little, if any, elicitation.
- Closed/open. You use a closed presentation; you will not consider the receiver's input.

The **consultative communication style** *(S-C) demonstrates high-task/high-relationship behavior (HT-HR), using a closed presentation for the task with an open elicitation for the relationship.* The other party has moderate information and capability.

- Initiation/response. You initiate the communication by letting the other party know that you want him or her to buy into your influence. You desire some response.
- Presentation/elicitation. Both are used. Use elicitation to determine the goal of the communication. For example, you may ask questions to determine the situation and follow up with a presentation. When the communication goal is known, little task elicitation is needed. Relationship communication is elicited in order to determine the interest of the other party and acceptance of the message. The open elicitation should show your concern for the other party's point of view and motivate him or her to follow your influence.
- Closed/open. You are closed to having the message accepted (task), but open to the person's feelings (relationship). Be empathetic.

The **participative communication style** *(S-P) demonstrates low-task/high-relationship behavior (LT-HR), responding with open elicitation, some initiation, and little presentation.* The other party has much information and high capability.

- Initiation/response. You respond with some initiation. You want to help the other party solve a problem or get him or her to help you solve one. You are helpful and convey personal support.
- Presentation/elicitation. Elicitation can occur with little presentation. Your role is to elicit the other party's ideas on how to reach objectives.
- Closed/open. Open communication is used. If you participate well, the other party will come to a solution you can accept. If not, you may have to reject the other party's message.

The fourth style, the **laissez-faire communication style** *(S-L), demonstrates low-task/low-relationship behavior (LT-LR), responding with the necessary open presentation.* The other party has a great deal of information and very high capability.

- Initiation/response. You respond to the other party with little, if any, initiation.
- Presentation/elicitation. You present the other party with information, structure, and so forth, that the sender wants.

• Closed/open. Using open communication, you convey that the other party is in charge; you will accept the message.

Situational Variables

When selecting the appropriate communication style, you should consider four variables: time, information, acceptance, and capability. Answering the questions in the following sections can help you select the appropriate style for the situation.

Time

Do I have enough time to use two-way communication? When there is no time, the other three variables are not considered; the autocratic style is appropriate. When time is available, any of the other styles may be appropriate, depending on the other variables. Time is a relative term; in one situation a few minutes may be considered a short time period, whereas in another a month may be a short period of time.

Information

Do I have the necessary information to communicate my message, make a decision, or take action? When you have all the information you need, the autocratic style may be appropriate. When you have some of the information, the consultative style may be appropriate. When you have little information, the participative or laissez-faire style may be appropriate.

Acceptance

Will the other party accept my message without any input? If the receiver will accept the message, the autocratic style may be appropriate. If the receiver will be reluctant to accept it, the consultative style may be appropriate. If the receiver will reject the message, the participative or laissez-faire style may be appropriate to gain acceptance. There are situations where acceptance is critical to success, such as in the area of implementing changes.

Capability

Capability has two parts:

Ability: Does the other party have the experience or knowledge to participate in two-way communications? Will the receiver put the organization's goals ahead of personal goals?

Motivation: Does the other party want to participate? Choose your supervisory style according to the other party's capability.

Capability levels can change from one task to another. For example, a professor may have outstanding capability in classroom teaching, but low capability for advising students.

Selecting Communication Styles

Successful supervisors rely on different communication styles according to the situation.[19] There are three steps to follow when selecting the appropriate communication style in a given situation.

Step 1. Diagnose the Situation: Answer the questions for each of the four situational variables. At the beginning of this section, you were asked to select an alternative to 12 situations. You were told to ignore the section with time, information, acceptance, capability, style, and S lines. Now you will complete this part in In-Class Skill-Building Exercise 7–1 by placing the style letters (S-A, S-C, S-P, S-L) on the lines provided for each of the 12 situations.

Step 2. Select the Appropriate Style for the Situation: After analyzing the four variables, you will select the appropriate style for the situation. In some situations, where variables may have conflicting styles, you should select the style of the most important variable for the situation. For example, an employee may have outstanding capability (C-4), but you have all the information you need (S-A). If the information is more important, use the autocratic style even though the capability is outstanding. When doing Skill-Building Exercise 7–1, place the letters S-A, S-C, S-P, or S-L for the appropriate styles on the style lines.

Step 3. Implement the Appropriate Communication Style: During Skill-Building Exercise 7–1, you will identify one of the four communication styles for each alternative action; place the S-A, S-C, S-P, or S-L on the S lines. Select the alternative *a, b, c,* or *d* that represents the appropriate communication for each of the 12 situations.

Model 7–2 summarizes the material in this section. Use it to determine the appropriate communication style in situation 1 and during Skill-Building Exercise 7–1.

Determining the Appropriate Communication Style for Situation 1

Step 1. Diagnose the Situation: Answer the four variable questions from the model, and place the letters on the four variable lines below.

1. Wendy, a knowledgeable person from another department, comes to you, the engineering supervisor, and requests that you design a special product to her specifications. What would you do?

   _____ time   _____ information   _____ acceptance
   _____ capability   _____ style

   a. Control the conversation and tell Wendy what you will do for her. S _____
   b. Ask Wendy to describe the product. Once you understand, you would present your ideas. Let her realize that you are concerned and want to help with your ideas. S _____
   c. Respond to Wendy's request by conveying understanding and support. Help clarify what you are to do. Offer ideas, but do it her way. S _____
   d. Find out what you need to know. Let Wendy know you will do it her way. S _____

Step 2. Select the Appropriate Style for the Situation: Review the four variables. If they are all consistent, select one style. If they conflict, select the most important variable as the style to use. Place its letters (S-A, S-C, S-P, or S-L) on the style line.

Step 3. Select the Appropriate Action: Review the four alternative actions. Identify the communication style for each, placing its letters on the S line, and then check the appropriate match alternative.

Let's see how you did.

1. Time is available; it can be S-C, S-P, or S-L. You have little **information,** so you need to use a participative or laissez-faire style to find out what Wendy wants done: S-P or S-L. If you try to do the project your way rather than Wendy's way, she will probably not **accept** your solution. You need to use a participative or laissez-faire style: S-P or S-L. Wendy is knowledgeable and has a high level of **capability:** S-P.

2. Reviewing the four variables, you see that there is a mixture of S-P and S-L. Because you are an engineer, it is appropriate to participate with Wendy to give her what she needs. Therefore, the choice is S-P.

3. Alternative *a* is S-A; this is the autocratic style, high task/low relationship. Alternative *b* is S-C; this is the consultative style, high task/high relationship. Alternative *c* is S-P; this is the participative style, low task/high relationship. Alternative *d* is S-L; this is laissez-faire, low task/low relationship behavior.

If you selected *c* as your action, you chose the most appropriate action for the situation. This was a three-point answer. If you selected *d* as your answer, this is also a good alternative; it scores two points. If you selected *b,* you get one point for overdirecting. If you selected *a,* you get zero points; this is too much directing and will most likely hurt communications.

MODEL 7–2

SITUATIONAL COMMUNICATIONS MODEL

Step 1. Diagnose the situation.

Resource	Use of Resource Style
Time	No: S-A Yes: S-C, S-P, or S-L
Information	All: S-A Some: S-C Little: S-P or S-L
Acceptance	Acceptance: S-A Reluctance: S-C Rejection: S-P or S-L
Capability	Low: S-A Moderate: S-C High: S-P Outstanding: S-L

Step 2. Select the appropriate style for the situation.

Autocratic (S-A)
High task/low relationship
Initiate a closed presentation.

Consultative (S-C)
High task/high relationship
Initiate a closed presentation for the task. Use open elicitation for feelings and relationship.

Participative (S-P)
Low task/high relationship
Respond with open elicitation, some initiation, and little presentation.

Laissez-faire (S-L)
Low task/low relationship
Respond with the necessary open presentation.

Step 3. Implement the appropriate communication style.

During Skill-Building Exercise 7–1, you will identify each communication style and select the alternative *a, b, c,* or *d* that represents the appropriate style.

LEARNING OBJECTIVE

11. Explain how to use the situational communications model.

The better you match your communication style to the situation, the more effective you will be at communicating. In Skill-Building Exercise 7–1, we will apply the model to the other 11 situations in Self-Learning Exercise 7–2 to develop your situational communication skills.

Now that you have read this chapter, you should better understand organizational communications, barriers to communications and ways to overcome them, and ways to become a situational communicator.

CONNECTIONS

10. Which of the four situational communication styles has your boss used most often? Explain his or her behavior.

11. Has your boss changed communication styles? If so, which other styles has he or she used?

REVIEW

Select one or more methods: (1) fill in the missing key terms from memory;
(2) match the key terms from the end of the review with their definitions below;
(3) copy the key terms in order from the key terms at the beginning of the chapter.

Communication skills are important because they are required for performance
of the five functions of supervision. _____ is the process of
transmitting a mutually understood message by a sender to a receiver.
The _____ are to influence,
inform, or express feelings.

   The sender initiates the communication, beginning by
_____ , which is the sender's process of putting the
message into a form that the receiver will understand. The sender then
transmits the _____ , the physical form of the encoded
information, to the receiver, who in turn goes through
_____ , the receiver's process of translating the message
into a meaningful form. If the sender and receiver don't mutually agree on the
meaning of the message, communication has not taken place. The four steps in
the communication process are selecting transmission media, sending the
message, receiving the message, and responding to the message. Not all
messages require a response. During a conversation the sender and receiver can
reverse roles several times.

   _____ are the forms of the transmitted message. The
major media include oral (face to face, telephone, meetings, and presentations);
written (memos, letters, reports, bulletin board notices, posters, fax machines,
and computers); and _____ , the facial expressions, vocal
qualities, gestures, and posture used while transmitting messages.

   The sender should plan the message by predetermining what the message is,
who should receive it, and when and where the message will be transmitted.
The _____ steps include developing rapport, stating the
communication objective, transmitting the message, checking understanding,
and getting a commitment and following up. When criticizing others, follow
these guidelines: give more praise than criticism, criticize immediately, make the
criticism performance-oriented, give specific and accurate criticism, open on a
positive note, and close by repeating what action is needed.

   _____ is the ability to understand and relate to
another's situation and feelings. Use empathy when dealing with emotional
employees. Be an active listener.

_____ is the process of verifying messages. After sending a message, verify mutual understanding by asking questions and having the other person paraphrase the message. _____ is the process of having the receiver restate the message in his or her own words.

When responding to a message, the receiver has six styles to choose from: evaluating, confronting, diverting, probing, reassuring, and reflecting.

Ten common barriers to organizational communication include perception, semantics, noise, emotions, filtering, trust and credibility, information overload, not listening, time and place, and medium selection.

The interactive process system has five dimensions, which are on a continuum. They are initiation—response, presentation—elicitation, closed—open, rejection—acceptance, and strong—mild. The four situational communication styles are _____ , high-task/low-relationship behavior (HT-LR), initiating a closed presentation; _____ , high-task/high-relationship behavior (HT-HR), using a closed presentation for the task with an open elicitation for the relationship; _____ , low-task/high-relationship behavior (LT-HR), responding with open elicitation, some initiation, and little presentation; and _____ , low-task/low-relationship behavior (LT-LR), responding with the necessary open presentation. To determine the appropriate communication style to use in a situation, the supervisor should diagnose the situation by considering the variables of time, information, acceptance, and capability.

KEY TERMS

autocratic communication style
communication
consultative communication style
decoding
empathic listening
encoding
feedback
goals of communication

laissez-faire communication style
media
message
message-sending process
nonverbal communications
paraphrasing
participative communication style

REFERENCES

1. Robert Maidment, "Listening—The Overlooked and Underdeveloped Other Half of Talking," *Supervisory Management,* August 1985, p. 10.

2. Clark Caskey, "The Vision in Supervision," *Supervision,* August 1985, p. 3.

3. Keith Denton, "A Manager's Toughest Job: One-on-One Communication," *Supervisory Management,* May 1985, p. 37.

4. Andrew Sherwood, "Galvanizing Your Communications," *Training and Development Journal,* May 1985, p. 14.

5. Walter Kiechel, "Memo Punctilio," *Fortune,* September 15, 1986, p. 185; Dru Scott, "The Art of Taking Telephone Messages," *News from Cally Curtis* 8, no. 1, p. 8.

6. Thomas Sheppard, "Silent Signals," *Supervisory Management,* March 1986, pp. 31–33.

7. Ibid.

8. Alan Farrant, "Talking to Subordinates," *Supervision,* November 1986, p. 9.

9. Roni Abrams, "Do You Get What You Ask For?" *Supervisory Management,* August 1986, p. 34.

10. Kent Baker and Philip Morgan, "Building a Professional Image: Using Feeling-Level Communication," *Supervisory Management,* January 1986, pp. 20–25.

11. "How Am I Doing? Few Executives Know," *The Wall Street Journal,* February 1, 1988, p. 29.

12. Philip Quaglieri, "Feedback on Feedback," *Supervisory Management,* January 1980, p. 37.

13. Paul Preston, "Feedback," *Credit Union Management,* March 1982, pp. 24–27.

14. David Whetten and Kim Cameron, *Developing Management Skills* (Glenview, Ill.: Scott, Foresman, 1984), pp. 224–30.

15. Charles Beck and Elizabeth Beck, "The Manager's Open Door and the Communication Climate," *Business Horizons,* January–February 1986, pp. 15–19.

16. "Mind Wandering," *News from Cally Curtis* 8, no. 1, p. 13.

17. Maidment, "Listening," p. 10.

18. Eugene Anderson, "Communication Patterns: A Tool for Memorable Leadership Training," *Training,* January 1984, pp. 55–57.

19. August Smith, "Choosing the Best Decision-Making Styles for Your Job," *Supervisory Management,* May 1985, p. 30.

APPLICATION SITUATIONS

Media Selection

AS 7−1

Select the most appropriate medium for each message.

a. one on one   *c.* meeting   *e.* memo   *g.* report

b. telephone   *d.* presentation   *f.* letter   *h.* poster

_____ 1. The supervisor has to assign a new customer order to Karen and Ralph.

_____ 2. The supervisor is expecting needed material for production this afternoon. She wants to know whether it will arrive on time.

_____ 3. Employees have been leaving the lights on when no one is in the stockroom. The supervisor wants this practice to stop.

_____ 4. The boss has asked for the production figures for the month.

_____ 5. An employee has broken a rule and needs to be discouraged from doing it again.

Identifying Response Styles

AS 7−2

Identify the style represented by each response to the situations described.

a. evaluating   *c.* diverting   *e.* reassuring

b. confronting   *d.* probing   *f.* reflecting

MS. WALKER: Mr. Tomson, do you have a minute to talk?

MR. TOMSON: Sure, what's up?

MS. WALKER: Can you do something about all the swearing the men do around the plant? It carries through these thin walls into my work area. It's disgusting. I'm surprised you haven't done anything.

MR. TOMSON:

_____ 6. I didn't know anyone was swearing. I'll look into it.

_____ 7. You don't have to listen to it. Just ignore it.

_____ 8. What kind of swear words are they using?

_____ 9. You find this swearing offensive?

JIM: Mary, I have a complaint.

MARY: Sit down and tell me about it.

JIM: Since you're the athletic director, you know that I use the weight room after the football team uses it. Well, my track team has to return the plates to the racks, put the dumbbells back, and so forth. I don't get paid to pick up after the football team. After all, they have the use of the room longer than we do.

I've complained to Ted, the football coach, but all he says is that's the way he finds it, or that he'll try to get the team to do a better job. But nothing happens.

MARY:

_____ 10. Before I forget, congratulations on beating Harvard.

_____ 11. Don't you think you're being a bit picky about this?

_____ 12. You feel it's unfair to pick up after them?

_____ 13. Are you sure you're not jealous because they get to use the weight room longer than you do?

In the two situations, which response is the most appropriate?

Communication Barriers

AS 7–3

Identify the communication barriers as being one of the following:

a. perception   *e.* filtering   *h.* not listening

b. semantics   *f.* trust and credibility   *i.* time and place

c. noise   *g.* information overload   *j.* media selection

d. emotions

_____ 14. You shouldn't be upset. Listen to me.

_____ 15. Buddy, last week you took a long break. Don't do it again.

_____ 16. That's a lot to remember; I'm not sure I got it all.

_____ 17. Why did you say the job was going well, when you know it's not? You haven't even finished the . . . or the. . . .

_____ 18. I can't hear you. Shut that thing off! Now, what did you say?

_____ 19. I said I'd do it in a little while. It's only been 10 minutes. Why do you expect it done now?

_____ 20. Why should I listen to you? You don't know what you're talking about.

OBJECTIVE CASE 7

Communication?

In the following dialog, Chris is the supervisor and Sandy is an employee.

CHRIS: I need you to get a metal plate ready for the Stern job.

SANDY: Okay.

CHRIS: I need a ¾-inch plate. I want a ½-inch hole a little off center. No, you'd better make it ⅝. In the left corner, I need about a ⅜ hole. And on the right top portion, about ⅞ of an inch from the left side, drill a ¼-inch hole. You got it?

SANDY: I think so.

CHRIS: Good, I'll be back later.
    (*Later*)

CHRIS: Do you have the plate ready?

SANDY: It's right here.

CHRIS: This isn't what I asked for. I said a ½-inch hole a little off center; this is too much off center. Do it again so that it will fit.

SANDY: You're the boss; I'll do it again.

Answer the following questions, using the space between questions to explain your answers.

_____   1. Chris and Sandy communicated.
        a. true   *b.* false

_____   2. Chris's primary goal of communication was to
        a. influence   *b.* inform   *c.* express feelings

_____   3. Chris was the
        a. sender/decoder   *c.* sender/encoder
        b. receiver/decoder   *d.* receiver/encoder

_____   4. Chris followed which guidelines to getting feedback on messages?
        a. open to feedback   *c.* ask questions
        b. awareness of nonverbal *d.* paraphrasing
            common   *e.* none of these

_____   5. The message transmission medium was
        a. oral   *c.* nonverbal
        b. written   *d.* combined

_____   6. _____ was (were) the primary barrier to communication.
        a. Perception   *e.* Trust and credibility
        b. Noise   *f.* Information overload
        c. Emotions   *g.* Not listening
        d. Filtering

_____ 7. Which step or steps did Chris follow in the message-sending process?
(You may select more than one answer.)
a. step 1   *d.* step 4
b. step 2   *e.* step 5
c. step 3

_____ 8. Sandy was an active listener.
a. true   *b.* false

_____ 9. Sandy's response style was primarily
a. evaluating   *d.* probing
b. confronting   *e.* reassuring
c. diverting   *f.* reflecting

_____ 10. Chris used the _____ situational communication style.
a. autocratic   *c.* participative
b. consultative   *d.* laissez-faire

11. In Chris's situation, how would you have given Sandy the instructions?

IN-CLASS SKILL-BUILDING EXERCISE

Situational
Communications

SB 7–1

Objectives: To develop your ability to communicate using the appropriate style for the situation.

Experience: You will try to select the appropriate style for the 12 situations described Self-Learning Exercise 7–2.

Material: You will need your responses to the 12 situations.

Procedure 1
(3–8 minutes)

The instructor reviews Model 7–2 and explains how to apply it to determine the appropriate style for situation 1.

Procedure 2
(6–8 minutes)

Turn to situation 2. Using Model 7–2, select the appropriate style. If you have time, identify each alternative style (3–4 minutes). The instructor will then go over the recommended answer (3–4 minutes).

Procedure 3
(20–50 minutes)

1. Break into groups of two or three. As a team, apply Model 7–2 to situations 3 through 7 (15–20 minutes). The instructor will go over the appropriate answers when all teams are done or the time is up (4–6 minutes).

2. Break into new groups of two or three, and examine situations 8 through 12 (15–20 minutes). The instructor will go over the appropriate answers (4–6 minutes).

Conclusion: The instructor leads a class discussion and makes concluding remarks.

Application (2–4 minutes): What did I learn from this experience? How will I use this knowledge in the future?

Sharing: Volunteers give their answers to the application section.

IN-CLASS SKILL-BUILDING EXERCISE

Giving Instructions

SB 7–2

Objective: To develop your ability to give and receive messages (your communication skills).

Experience: You will plan, give, and receive instructions for drawing three objects.

Materials: No preparation is necessary. The instructor will provide the original drawings, which will be copied.

Procedure 1
(3–7 minutes)

Read all of procedure 1 twice. The supervisor is supposed to give an employee instructions for drawing three objects. They must be drawn to scale and look like a photocopy of the original. You will have 15 minutes to complete the task.

The exercise has four separate steps.

1. The supervisor plans.
2. The supervisor gives the instructions.
3. The employee does the drawing.
4. The results are evaluated.

Rules: The rules are numbered to correspond with the four steps above.

1. Planning. While planning, the supervisor may write out instructions for the employee but may not do any drawing of any kind.

2. Instructions. While giving the instructions, the supervisor may not show the original drawing to the employee. (The instructor will give the original to the

student.) The instructions may be given orally, in writing, or both, but no hand gestures are allowed. The employee may take notes while the instructions are being given but cannot do any drawing. The supervisor must give instructions for all three objects before the employee begins drawing.

3. Drawing. Once the employee begins drawing, the supervisor may no longer communicate in any way, although he or she may watch.

4. When the employee is finished or the time is up, the supervisor shows the employee the original drawing. Discuss how you did. Turn to the integration section and answer the questions. The supervisor should write down the answers.

Procedure 2
(2–5 minutes)

Half of the class members will be supervisors and give instructions. Supervisors should spread out and move their seats to the walls. They should be facing the center of the room; backs should be close to the wall.

Employees sit in the middle of the room until called for by a supervisor. When called, bring your chair and sit facing the supervisor so that you cannot see the drawing.

Procedure 3
(15–20 minutes)

The instructor gives each supervisor a copy of the drawing. Be careful not to let any employees see it. The supervisor plans the instructions. When supervisors are ready, they call an employee and give the instructions. It may be helpful to use the message-sending process. Be sure to follow the rules. The employee should do the drawing on the page entitled Employee Drawing at the end of this exercise. He or she has 15 minutes to complete the drawings. When the employee finishes the drawings, the employee and supervisor should answer the questions in the integration section.

Procedure 4
(15–20 minutes)

The employees now become the supervisors. Repeat procedure 3. The instructor will give the supervisors different drawings. Do not work with the same person as before.

Evaluation Questions:
You may select more than one answer.

_____ 1. The goal of communication was to
    a. influence   *b.* inform   *c.* express feelings

_____ 2. Feedback was
    a. immediate   *c.* performance oriented
    b. specific and accurate   *d.* positive

_____ 3. _____ communication was used
    a. vertical   *b.* horizontal

_____ 4. How did the supervisor transmit the message?
    a. orally   *c.* nonverbally
    b. in writing   *d.* all of the above

_____ 5. We encountered _____ barriers to communications. Describe how you dealt with them and how they influenced your results.
    a. perception   *d.* trust and credibility
    b. noise   *e.* information overload
    c. filtering   *f.* not listening

_____ 6. The supervisor spent _____ time planning (what, who, when, where, how).
    a. too much   *b.* too little   *c.* the right amount of

Questions 7–11 relate to the message-sending process.

_____ 7. The supervisor developed rapport (step 1).
　　　　a. true   *b.* false

_____ 8. The supervisor stated the communication objective (step 2).
　　　　a. true   *b.* false

_____ 9. The supervisor transmitted the message (step 3).
　　　　a. effectively   *b.* ineffectively

_____ 10*a.* The supervisor checked understanding by using (step 4).
　　　　a. direct questions   *c.* both
　　　　b. paraphrasing   *d.* neither

_____ 10*b.* Checking was:
　　　　a. too frequent   *b.* too infrequent   *c.* about right

_____ 11. The supervisor got a commitment and followed up (step 5).
　　　　a. true   *b.* false

_____ 12. The supervisor, employee, or both got emotional.
　　　　a. true   *b.* false

_____ 13. The primary response style the supervisor used was

_____ 14. The primary response style the employee used was
　　　　a. evaluating   *d.* probing
　　　　b. confronting   *e.* reassuring
　　　　c. diverting   *f.* reflecting

_____ 15. The supervisor used the _____ style. The appropriate style
　　　　was _____ .
　　　　a. autocratic   *c.* participative
　　　　b. consultative   *d.* laissez-faire

16. Were the objects drawn to approximate scale? If not, why not?

17. Did you follow the rules? If not, why not?

18. If you could do this exercise over again, what would you do differently?

Conclusion: The instructor leads a class discussion and makes concluding remarks.

Application (2–4 minutes): What did I learn from this experience? How will I use this knowledge in the future?

Sharing: Volunteers give their answers to the application section.

Employee Drawing

PREPARATION FOR IN-CLASS SKILL-BUILDING EXERCISE

Giving Criticism

SB 7–3

In class you will be given the opportunity to role-play giving criticism. Think of a job situation in which you or another employee should have been criticized to improve performance. If you prefer, you can act as criticizer in a nonjob situation in which criticism is warranted. Below, briefly state the situation; then write some notes on what you would say when giving the criticism. Be sure to follow the five guidelines in Exhibit 7–3 for giving effective criticism. Remember to maintain human relations while criticizing.

You will get more from the exercise if you think of your own situation. However, if you cannot think of your own situation after making a serious effort, you may use this situation. The employee is a waiter or waitress in an ice cream shop. He or she knows that the tables should be cleaned up quickly after customers leave so that the new customers do not have to sit at a dirty table. It is a busy night. You the supervisor notice customers seated at two dirty tables. The employee responsible for clearing the tables is socializing with some friends at one of the tables. Employees are supposed to be friendly. When criticized, the employee may use this fact as an excuse for the dirty tables.

IN-CLASS SKILL-BUILDING EXERCISE

Giving Criticism

SB 7–3

Objective: To develop your skill at improving performance through giving criticism while maintaining human relations.

Preparation: You should have developed criticism to role-play in class.

Experience: You will give criticism, be criticized, and observe criticism following the guidelines for giving effective criticism.

Procedure 1
(2–4 minutes)

Break into groups of three. Make one or two groups of two if necessary. It is recommended that only one person per group use the example given in the preparation. The other two should have their own situation.

Each member selects a number from one to three to determine the order of giving, receiving, and observing criticism.

Procedure 2
(5–8 minutes)

Number 1 will give the criticism to number 2, and number 3 will be the observer. Number 1 explains the situation to numbers 2 and 3. If the person criticized would most likely make some comment in response, tell number 2 what it is so that he or she can make it. When number 2 and 3 understand the situation, number 1 role-plays giving the criticism while number 3 observes and takes notes on the observer sheet. When the role play is finished, the observer leads a discussion on how well number 1 criticized number 2 using the observer sheet.

Do not go on to the next criticism until told to do so. If you finish early, wait for the others to finish.

Observer Sheet

For each question, think of what was done well and how the criticizer could improve. Telling others how to improve is criticism. The person criticized and the observer now criticize the criticizer.

1. Was criticism given immediately (if appropriate)?

2. Was the criticism performance oriented?

3. Was the criticism specific and accurate?

4. Did the criticizer open on a positive note?

5. Did the criticizer close by repeating what action is needed (if appropriate)?

6. Do you think the person criticized will change the behavior? Why or why not?

7. Was criticism given in a way that will maintain human relations? Explain your answer.

Procedure 3
(5–8 minutes)

Number 2 will give the criticism to number 3, and number 1 will be the observer. Number 2 explains the situation to numbers 1 and 3. If the person criticized would most likely make some comment, tell number 3 what it is so that he or she can make it. When number 1 and 3 understand the situation, number 2 role-plays giving the criticism while number 1 observes and takes notes on the observer sheet. When the role play is finished, the observer leads a discussion on how well number 2 criticized number 3 using the observer sheet.

Do not go on to the next criticism until told to do so. If you finish early, wait for the others to finish.

Procedure 4
(5–8 minutes)

Each person plays the role not yet played, following the same procedures as described.

Conclusion: The instructor leads a class discussion and makes concluding remarks.

Application (2–4 minutes): What did I learn from this experience? How will I use this knowledge in the future to give effective criticism while maintaining human relations?

Sharing: Volunteers give their answers to the application section.

8

Managing Change and Conflict

Learning Objectives

1. List and explain the four types of change.
2. Explain why people are resistant to change and how to overcome this resistance.
3. Discuss the use of the five OD techniques.
4. List the steps in the change model and use the model.
5. Explain the types and sources of conflict.
6. Explain the five conflict management styles and the appropriate use of each style.
7. List and explain the steps in the initiating, responding, and mediating conflict resolution models and use the models.

Key Terms

To achieve our objectives in this chapter, it is important that you understand the following 18 key terms. They are presented in the order in which they appear in the chapter. The list of key terms also appears in alphabetical order in the end-of-chapter review.

automation	team building	collaborating conflict
management	conflict	style
information	forcing conflict style	initiating conflict
systems	avoiding conflict	resolution steps
resistance to change	style	XYZ model
organizational	accommodating	responding conflict
development	conflict style	resolution steps
force field analysis	compromising	mediating conflict
survey feedback	conflict style	resolution steps
Grid OD		

Judy Monetti has been supervisor of the typing pool at Ace Stationery Company for seven years. At long last, she has received the go-ahead from her superiors to change the typing pool to a word-processing department. "This change shouldn't be too tough," she reasons to herself. "After all, we're at least a decade late getting computerized. Besides, several of my employees have been bugging me about word processors for years."

Imagine Judy's surprise when she discovers that out of her staff of 16, only 7 are really behind her in making this change. Two have a "don't know yet" attitude, and the other seven are downright hostile about such a change. To make matters worse, her announcement about the change seems to have created two warring factions, one for and one against.

Judy is facing two classic problems of the supervisor—change and conflict. She needs to do something fast. Where should she start?

I. Why Managing Change Is Important

Following are a few of the many reasons why managing change is important:

- Plato said, "Change takes place no matter what deters it."
- John F. Kennedy described change as "the law of life."
- There is no progress without change.[1]
- Corporate histories reveal that organizations that fail have often continued to operate in the same old way, even after successful competitors demonstrated how to do things better.[2]
- Books like Alvin Toffler's *Future Shock* have helped make managers realize that one of their most important functions is managing change.
- A survey of 506 executives revealed that "innovation is a major determinant of the growth and success of enterprises."[3]
- One of the supervisor's key tasks is getting employees to change. Every supervisor spends considerable time helping employees change their behavior, increase or adapt their skills, change points of view, or increase their understanding.[4]
- Each day the supervisor is faced with numerous decisions that involve change.[5]

Forces Producing Change

Every organization interacts with its external environment. In the course of this interaction, certain forces, including competition, consumer tastes, technology, government regulations, economic conditions, and technological advances, may cause change in the organization.

Aspects of the organization's internal environment, such as redefined purpose and strategies, financial position, reorganization, and mergers, may also lead to change.

In terms of your position as a supervisor, the five functions discussed in earlier chapters will engender change. Most plans that the supervisor develops require changes. When the supervisor organizes and delegates tasks, employees are often required to make some changes in their routine. When the supervisor hires, orients, trains, and evaluates performance (staffing), change is involved. Leadership calls for influencing employees, often to change in some way. And control may require new methods or techniques. Supervisors are often reluctant to get involved with change and conflict because they are not aware of what constitutes their job description, and what limitations are imposed on their position by the organization.

CONNECTIONS

1. Give reasons other than those listed in the text why change and conflict management skills are important to a supervisor.

II. Types of Change

In the early 1960s, Harold J. Leavitt developed a model that identifies four interaction variables in every organization. These variables—task, structure, technology, and people—listed in Exhibit 8–1, are also key areas of change.

Task

The organization's task is reflected in its statement of purpose, objectives, and strategic plans (discussed in Chapter 2). And this task should change with changes in the environment. For example, as customers' tastes change, the product or

EXHIBIT 8–1   **TYPES OF CHANGES**

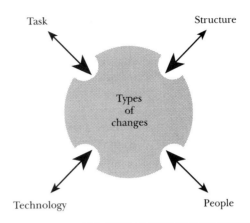

service should also change to continue to meet their needs. If it does not, the organization will lose customers. Changing the product will involve redefining objectives and strategic plans.

As Leavitt points out, a change in task will affect the other variables as well. If the organization changes its product or service, changes in structure, technology, and people may also be required. Thus, any change involves a *systems approach.* Thus, a supervisor should consider the repercussions of change in one variable on the other variables and plan accordingly.

Structure

Structure involves departmentalization, chain of command, span of control, coordination methods, and type of authority, as discussed in Chapter 3. Of Leavitt's four variables, change in structure is the one that people most often resist.[6] Yet structural or administrative reorganization is quite common. For example, each time a new president takes office, there are substantial administrative changes in the federal government, which, in turn, cause change in task, technology, and people.

Technology

Technological innovations such as the computer have dramatically increased the rate of change. In fact, change is so rapid that machinery often becomes obsolete even though it is still in usable condition. Changes in technology are often introduced to increase productivity. This may involve automation.

Automation *is the simplification or reduction of the human effort needed to do a job.* Computers and other machines may even replace people in some jobs. For example, robots inspect, clean, guard, and assemble parts. One writer predicted that 100,000 robots would be in use by 1990.[7] Some people fear that automation will reduce the number of employees. This fear is only partly justified. Although some people have lost their jobs to automation, other jobs have been created. As changes in technology increase, there will be a growing need for skilled workers, and the demand for unskilled labor will decline.

Technology may also affect the way a job is done. This is called *process change.* Process change may result because of a task change, or a process can be changed while the task remains the same. Jobs are often redesigned. A significant area of change here is in the way organizations process information, particularly with the use of a computer. For example, **management information systems (MIS)** *are formal structures for collecting, processing, and disseminating necessary information.* The MIS is an attempt to centralize and integrate all or most of the relevant information in an organization, involving areas such as finance, production, inventory, and sales. As a result, different departments can coordinate their efforts. The first part of creating an MIS involves collecting the information (input) needed to make decisions. Once the information has been collected, it must be organized, stored, and processed or transformed into a form that managers can use. The third part of MIS is disseminating the information (output) in a usable form so that managers can make better decisions.

People

When changing task, structure, or technology, never forget the effect of the changes on people. In addition, attempts to change any of these other variables will not be effective without the cooperation of people.

As stated above, people's skills must change with the level of technology. In some cases, new people with the necessary skills must be hired. Recruiting, selecting, orienting, and training employees has become more important in the recent past.

Although some believe that people resist technological changes, there is no agreement on the subject. According to Lawrence, "People do not resist technological changes as such and most resistance which does occur is unnecessary. What people resist is the social change brought about by technological changes."[8] To guard against such technological resistance, you need the input and participation of those who will be most affected.[9]

LEARNING OBJECTIVE

1. List and explain the four types of change.

In the early 1950s, Kurt Lewin developed a technique for changing people's behavior, skills, and attitudes. This technique is still used today. Three steps are involved. In step 1, unfreezing, the person becomes aware of why the present behavior should be changed. In step 2, change, he or she learns new behavior. In step 3, refreezing, the person is reinforced and supported for the new behavior in order to solidify the change.

CONNECTIONS

2. Give one or more examples of a type of change you have experienced in an organization.

3. Describe the MIS in an organization, preferably one you have been associated with.

4. Describe a change in automation in an organization, preferably one you have been associated with.

III. Resistance to Change

As mentioned, without people there can be no change in the other three variables. In this section, you will learn why people resist change and how to overcome that resistance.

Resisting Change

Some people believe that managers are for change and that employees are against it. This simply is not true.[10] Supervisors and managers are often more resistant to change than employees.[11] For example, engineers in a communications training program complained that they were hired to make changes, but that management was often reluctant to allow the changes. In fact, most of us resist change, except for the occasions on which it offers guaranteed immediate benefits.[12]

Resistance to change by itself is neither good nor bad.[13] *Three variables—intensity, source, and focus—cause* **resistance to change.**[14]

Intensity

People have different attitudes toward change. Some thrive on it, some are upset by it, and many resist it at first but gradually accept it.[15] As a supervisor, you must anticipate employee resistance to change. Will it be strong, weak, or somewhere in between? You should also evaluate your own resistance to change. Avoid the counterproductive "we-they" syndrome—"*We* have to because *they* say so."

Source

There are three major sources of resistance:

1. *Facts.* Because change represents a threat to our security and because it is natural to fear the unknown, the facts concerning a change are often misrepresented.[16] They are often circulated inaccurately through the grapevine or used selectively to prove a point. Stating the facts accurately helps to overcome fear of the unknown.

2. *Beliefs.* Beliefs are subjective. Our beliefs lead us to think and feel that a change will be good or bad. These perceptions can cause resistance to change.[17] We use our experience to predict what the new change will be like. If employees have had a bad experience with similar changes, they may believe the new change will also be for the worse.

3. *Values.* Values reflect what people believe is worth pursuing or doing. What we value is important to us. Because change often requires learning new ways of doing things, employees may see it as an inconvenience and place a low value on it.[18] If the facts are presented in such a way that employees believe the change will be of value to them, they will offer less resistance.

Focus

There are three major focuses of resistance:

1. *Self.* It's natural to ask, "What's in it for me? What will I gain or lose?" If a change will have a negative effect on an employee's economic well-being, such as lower pay or longer hours without additional pay, he or she will resist the change.[19] Employees also resist changes that result in a loss of status or esteem.[20]

2. *Others.* After considering what's in it for them, or when they're not affected by the change, people tend to consider how the change will affect their friends, peers, and colleagues. If an employee believes the change will affect others negatively, he or she may still resist.

3. *Work environment.* The work environment includes the physical setting and the climate. People like to be in control of their environment and resist changes that take away that control.[21] If employees believe the changed environment is not of value, they will resist. For example, if a salesperson has a Ford Thunderbird as a company car that the firm wants to replace with a Ford Escort, the salesperson will probably resist. A change from the Escort to the Thunderbird would probably not be resisted. Changes in the work environment may also cause changes in social interactions or relationships. And, as we stated earlier, people resist changes in social relationships.

As shown in Exhibit 8–2, there is a relationship between the source (facts, beliefs, or values) and the focus (self, others, or the work environment) of resistance to change. However, resistance may come from more than one focus or source. Use the matrix to identify the source and focus of resistance. Once you have done this, you can work at overcoming it. Overcoming resistance to change is our next topic.

EXHIBIT 8-2   **RESISTANCE MATRIX**

	Self	
1. Facts about self I never did it before. I failed the last time I tried. All my friends are here.	**4. Beliefs about self** I'm too busy to do it. I'll do it, but I'll mess up. I don't think I can accept the change.	**7. Values pertaining to self** I like the job I have now better. I don't want to change; I'm happy. I like working alone.
	Others	
2. Facts about others He's on probation. She has two children. Other people told me it's hard to do.	**5. Beliefs about others** She pretends to be busy to avoid extra work. He's better at it than I am; let him do it. She never understands our side.	**8. Values pertaining to others** Let someone else train her. I'm not interested. What you think really doesn't matter to me. I don't give a . . . about him.
	Work Environment	
3. Facts about the work environment Why should I do it? I'm not getting paid extra. I haven't been trained to do it. I make less than anyone else in the department.	**6. Beliefs about the work environment** This is a lousy place to work. The pay here is terrible. It's who you know, not what you know that counts around here.	**9. Values pertaining to the work environment** Who cares what the goals are? I just do my job. The salary is more important than the benefits. This job gives me the chance to work outside.

Focus: Facts / Beliefs / Values

Source: Adapted from Ken Hultman, *The Path of Least Resistance* (Austin, TX: Learning Concepts, 1979).

Overcoming Resistance to Change[22]

Develop a Positive Climate for Change: Develop and maintain good relations with employees. Make employees realize that you have their best interest in mind. Because trust and an affirmative attitude toward change are so closely intertwined, the supervisor's first concern should be to develop a trusting relationship with employees.[23] There should be cooperation and interdependence within the department. Cooperation carries over when change is implemented.

Encourage an Interest in Improvement: Encourage employees to do their best. Continually give them opportunities to develop new skills and abilities. Help employees to be creative. Constantly look for better ways to do things. Get employees to view change in a positive way.[24] Effective leaders find excitement in making change a way of life and allowing others to be change agents.[25] Encourage employees to suggest changes; listen to and implement their ideas.[26]

EXHIBIT 8-3   **OVERCOMING RESISTANCE TO CHANGE**

Old .... **New**

1. Develop a positive climate
2. Encourage an interest in improvement
3. Plan
4. Give facts
5. Avoid getting people emotional
6. Avoid direct confrontation
7. Involve employees
8. Provide support

Plan: It takes planning to implement changes successfully. Identify possible areas of resistance to change and plan how to overcome them. Put yourself in the employee's position instead of considering how you would react. A supervisor perceives things differently. What seems very simple and logical to you may appear complex to an employee. Set clear objectives so that employees know exactly what the change is and how it affects them.[27] Use a systems approach. As mentioned earlier, a change in one variable, such as technology, will also have effects on social relations and other factors.

Give Facts: Get all the facts and plan how you will present them to the employees. Remember to relate the change to employees' values. Sell employees on the benefits to themselves. Giving the facts as far in advance as possible helps to overcome the fear of the unknown. If the grapevine starts to spread inaccurate facts, correct the rumors as quickly as possible.

Avoid Getting People Emotional: Recall that emotional people tend to be defensive. In addition, emotional people may hear, but often don't listen well. Emotion makes people more resistant to change. If the supervisor gets emotional, employees will probably get emotional, too. Try not to do or say things that will make people emotional. Avoid statements such as, "You're wrong," "You don't know what you're talking about," or "It's not hard; it's easy." Maintain people's self-respect.

Avoid Direct Confrontation: Confrontation tends to make people emotional and more resistant to change. A subtle approach is preferable. Trying to persuade people that their facts, beliefs, and values are wrong leads to resistance. Such confrontational debate is risky. What if the supervisor loses the debate?

Involve Employees: A commitment to change is usually critical to successful implementation. Employees who participate in developing changes are more committed to them than are employees who are told about the changes after the fact. Participative groups outperform the others.[28] (Remember to use the appropriate level of participation for the situation.) Upper management can overcome major resistance by involving both supervisors and employees in the change process from the very start.

Provide Support: Allow employees to express their feelings in a positive way. Training is very important in making a change successful.[29] Give as much advance notice and training as possible before the change takes place. Thorough training helps reduce frustration. Employees will realize that they have successfully adapted to the change. Remember that mistakes are both inevitable and even necessary when a change is made. Mistakes should be learning experiences.[30] Exhibit 8–3 summarizes the eight ways to overcome resistance to change.

Responding to Resistance

You have learned why employees resist change and how you can create a climate conducive to change. But suppose, despite your best efforts, an employee still resists. Below is a list developed by H. P. Karp to classify resistant employees.[31] You are also given some ideas about how to handle the different types.

- *The blocker.* "I don't want to do it that way." Supervisor: "What are your objections to the change? How would you prefer to do it?"
- *The roller.* "What do you want me to do?" Supervisor: "I want you to. . . ." (Be specific and describe the change in detail; use communication skills.)
- *The staller.* "I'll do it when I can." Supervisor: "What's more important?"
- *The reverser.* "That's a good idea." (But never does it.) Supervisor: "What is it that you like about the change?"
- *The sidestepper.* "Why don't you have XYZ do it?" Supervisor: "I asked you to do it because. . . ."
- *The threatener.* "I'll do it, but the guys upstairs won't like it." Supervisor: "Let me worry about that. What are *your* objections?"
- *The politician.* "You owe me one; let me slide." Supervisor: "I do owe you one, but I need to make the change. I'll pay you back later."
- *The traditionalist.* "That's not the way we do things around here." Supervisor: "This is a unique situation; it needs to be done."
- *The assaulter.* "You're a . . . [pick a word]." Supervisor: "I will not tolerate that type of behavior." Or "This is really upsetting you, isn't it?"

LEARNING OBJECTIVE

2. Explain why people are resistant to change and how to overcome this resistance.

These types of responses will be helpful in most situations, but not all. If employees continue to resist the change, they may be considered problem employees and handled accordingly. You will learn about problem employees in Chapter 14. As a supervisor, try not to use these responses with your boss.

CONNECTIONS

5. Describe a situation in which you were resistant to change. Identify the intensity, source, and focus, and identify it in terms of the box number and statement in Exhibit 8–2.

IV. Organizational Development

Up to this point, we have mainly dealt with change on the supervisory level. Now we will turn to organizationwide implementation of change. **Organizational development (OD)** *is the ongoing planned process of change to improve the organization's effectiveness in solving problems and achieving objectives.* There are several OD techniques including force field analysis, survey feedback, Grid OD, change masters, and team building.

The first step in organizational development is diagnosis of the problem. Indicators that problems exist, such as conflict, decreasing productivity or profits, excessive absenteeism or turnover, and so forth, may lead management to call in a change agent to study the problem. This change agent is responsible for the OD program. He or she can use a variety of methods to diagnose the problem.

Force Field Analysis   **Force field analysis** *is used to diagram the current level of performance as well as the hindering and driving forces.* An example is given in Exhibit 8–4. The analysis begins by appraising the current level of performance. This is shown in the middle of the diagram. The hindering forces holding back performance are listed on the top part of the diagram. The driving forces keeping performance at the present level

EXHIBIT 8–4   **FORCE FIELD ANALYSIS**

Hindering Forces:	H-1	H-2	H-3	H-4	H-5	H-6
	high production cost	longevity of product	slow delivery	high sales-people turn-over	poor performance of three sales-people	inadequate sales training

Present Performance—1,000 Units Sold Per Month

	good reputation of organization	high quality product	quality advertising	good service	seven excellent salespeople	skilled sales supervisor
Driving Forces:	D-1	D-2	D-3	D-4	D-5	D-6

are listed on the bottom of the diagram. Once the forces are identified, strategies are developed for maintaining or increasing the driving forces while simultaneously decreasing hindering forces. For example, in Exhibit 8–4, the solution could be to have the salespeople go through a training program. The supervisor could spend more time working with the poor salespeople. Delivery time could be decreased. If all of the driving forces are maintained, higher sales volume could result.

Force field analysis is particularly useful for group problem solving. Once the diagram is developed, the solution often becomes clear to the group.

Survey Feedback

Survey feedback is one of the oldest and most popular OD techniques. **Survey feedback** *uses a questionnaire to gather data that are used as the basis for change.* Different change agents will use slightly different approaches; however, a survey feedback program would commonly include six steps:

1. Management and the change agent do some preliminary planning to develop an appropriate questionnaire.
2. The questionnaire is administered to all members of the organization or unit.
3. The survey data are analyzed to uncover problem areas.
4. The change agent feeds the results back to management.
5. Managers evaluate the feedback and discuss the results with their subordinates.
6. Plans for corrective action are developed and implemented.

The author was called in as a consultant to a large manufacturer. The industrial and manufacturing engineering managers informed him that a survey had been conducted (steps 1 through 3) and that the feedback showed low performance among engineers (step 4). The three managers had met with their engineers and discussed the reasons for the low rating and ways to change (step 5). They decided to have the engineers go through a human relations and communications training program to improve their ability to interact with the organizational members whom they served. The author developed and conducted a training program that helped change and correct the situation (step 6).

Grid OD®

Robert Blake and Jane Mouton developed a "packaged" approach to OD with a standardized format and procedures and fixed goals. **Grid OD** *is a six-phase program designed to improve management and organizational effectiveness.* The phases include the following:

- *Phase 1: training.* Teams of five to nine managers, ideally from different functional areas, are formed. During a week-long seminar, each team member assesses his or her leadership style and develops skills in the areas of team building, communication, and problem solving.
- *Phase 2: team development.* Managers return to their jobs and try to use their new skills.
- *Phase 3: intergroup development.* Work groups improve their ability to cooperate and coordinate their efforts. This fosters joint problem solving.
- *Phase 4: organizational goal setting.* Management develops a model for the organization.
- *Phase 5: goal attainment.* Changes necessary to become the model organization are identified and implemented.
- *Phase 6: stabilization.* The first five phases are evaluated to identify and stabilize positive changes, and to identify areas that need improvement or alteration.[32]

Change Masters

Dr. Rosabeth Moss Kanter, considered by many to be the foremost authority on innovation and change, is the author of the best-selling book *Change Masters: Innovation for Productivity in the American Corporation.* She also developed a video-cassette training program outlining the change process and how to apply it.[33] Kanter has identified and explained the seven key characteristics of a change master, the person who facilitates change:

- Tuning into the environment.
- Kaleidoscope thinking.
- Communicating a clear vision.
- Building coalitions.
- Working through teams.
- Persisting and persevering.
- Making everyone a hero.

Change masters encourage people to embrace change in three ways: (1) through broad job assignments that focus on results rather than procedures; (2) by organizing people into teams with complete responsibility for every function and for the end product; and (3) by creating a "culture of pride" that emphasizes the value of the people involved.

Team Building

Team building is probably the most widely used OD technique. It recognizes that within an organization, small groups of individuals work closely and interdependently in teams. The effectiveness of each team and of all the teams working together directly affects the results of the entire organization. **Team building** *is designed to help work groups operate more effectively.*

Team building can be used as a comprehensive OD technique. Top executives first go through the program and then repeat it with their middle managers. In turn, middle managers go through it with their supervisors, who then go through it with their employees. The agenda tends to change to meet the needs of each group. However, team building is most widely used to help new or existing groups improve effectiveness. For example, Dr. Miriam Hirsch and the author were called in as consultants by a medical center that had restructured administrative responsibility. The center had changed to three-member team management. Doctors were no longer sole managers; they had to work with a nurse and an administrative manager. Because these managers were not used to teamwork, we were asked to propose a team-building program to help develop these skills.

The goals of team-building programs will vary considerably depending on group needs and the change agent's skills. Some typical goals are as follows:

- To clarify the objectives of the team and the responsibilities of each team member.
- To identify problems preventing the team from accomplishing its objectives.
- To develop team problem-solving, decision-making, objective-setting, and planning skills.
- To determine a preferred style of teamwork, and to change to that style, if necessary.
- To fully utilize the resources of each individual member.
- To develop open, honest working relationships based on trust and an understanding of group members.

The Change Agent's Responsibilities: In team building the change agent usually first meets with the supervisor to discuss the reasons for conducting the program. They discuss the goals of the program. The change agent assesses the supervisor's willingness to get feedback from the team about the supervisor's style and practices. The supervisor's receptiveness to the program will directly affect the potential results.

The change agent and supervisor meet with the team. An atmosphere of openness and trust is developed as the change agent describes the goals, agenda, and procedures of the team-building program. The change agent describes his or her agreement with the supervisor.

The change agent may interview each team member privately and confidentially to identify group problems. A survey feedback questionnaire, such as the one in the Preparation for Skill-Building Exercise 8–1, may be used instead of or in addition to the interviews. The team-building program may take one or more days, depending upon the number of problems and the size of the team.

Team-Building Program: The actual team-building program varies with team needs and the change agent's skills. Typical topics include the following:

1. *Climate building.* The program begins by trying to develop a climate of trust, support, and openness. The program's purpose and objectives are discussed. Team members learn more about each other and share what they would like to accomplish in the session.
2. *Evaluation.* The team evaluates the strengths and weakness of how members work together and communicate, rather than how well they perform technical job functions. The team explores and selects ideal standards of behavior that members abide by.
3. *Problem identification.* The team identifies its strengths and then its weaknesses or areas where improvement is possible. The problems may be identified in the change agent's interviews, the feedback survey, or both. The team lists several areas where improvement is possible and assigns priorities to help itself improve performance.
4. *Problem solving.* The team takes the top-priority item and develops a solution. It then moves to the second, third, and fourth item, and so on.
5. *Training.* Team building often includes some form of training that addresses the problems facing the group.
6. *Closure.* The program ends by summarizing what has been accomplished. Follow-up responsibility is assigned. Team members commit to improving performance.[34]

Although the techniques discussed are appealing, there is much controversy over the results of OD programs. Some organizations believe that they are very effective. For example, Butler Manufacturing of Iowa claims that productivity is up by 20 percent and profitability by 35 percent owing to team building.

However, critics point out that few studies provide evidence of specific results. OD is used selectively within departments, rather than comprehensively throughout the organization.

As a supervisor you may be involved in any of these OD techniques. However, you would not conduct Grid OD with your employees because it is a management program. You could use survey feedback, although it is commonly used by upper-level managers. You can follow the guidelines for being a change master. Supervisors do conduct force field analyses and team building, but they usually are given training by the organization first.

LEARNING OBJECTIVE

3. Discuss the use of the five OD techniques.

CONNECTIONS

6. Identify an OD technique and explain how it is used by a specific organization, preferably one you have worked for.

V. A Change Model

To summarize what we've discussed up to this point, Model 8–1 lists the steps involved in implementing change. As you'll see in the following discussion, many of the techniques we've discussed are applicable as the steps are followed.

Step 1. Define the Change

Clearly state what the change is. Is it a task, structural, technological, or people change? What are the systemic effects on the other variables? Set objectives following the guidelines in Chapter 2.

Step 2. Identify Possible Resistance

Determine the intensity, source, and focus of possible resistance to the change. Use the resistance matrix in Exhibit 8–2.

Step 3. Plan the Change

Plan the change following the guidelines in Chapter 2. Use the appropriate supervisory style for the situation. You may use force field analysis to help you overcome resistance to change by reducing hindering forces while maintaining or increasing the driving forces for change.

MODEL 8–1   **A CHANGE MODEL**

Step 1. Define the change.

Step 2. Identify possible resistance to the change.

Step 3. Plan the change.

Step 4. Implement the change.

  Give the facts.

  Involve employees.

  Provide support.

Step 5. Control the change.

Step 4. Implement the Change

Give the Facts: Give the facts and explain why the change is necessary; do this as far in advance of the change as possible. Explain how the change will affect the employees. Relate the change to their values.

Involve Employees: Involve employees as much as you can, but use the appropriate supervisory style for the situation. Follow the guidelines in Chapters 1, 5, and 7.

Provide Support: Allow employees to express their thoughts and feelings in a positive way. Answer their questions openly and honestly. Make sure that they receive the training necessary to implement the change.

Step 5. Control the Change

LEARNING OBJECTIVE

4. List the steps in the change model and use the model.

Follow up to ensure that the change is implemented and maintained. Make sure the objective is met. If it is not, take corrective action. (Follow the guidelines in Chapter 4.) For major changes, be sure to change employee job descriptions and performance appraisals to reflect the new job accurately.[35]

CONNECTIONS

> **7.** Give a specific example of a situation in which the change model would be helpful to a supervisor.

VI. Why Conflict Management Skills Are Important

Conflict *exists whenever two or more parties disagree.* As we have seen, change may result in conflict. So may many other aspects of organizational life. Consider the following points:

- Complex organizations are marked with chronic episodes of conflict.[36]
- You cannot avoid conflict. Coping with it successfully is one of the most important skills you can acquire.[37]
- Inability to handle conflict effectively may well be the single greatest barrier to satisfaction and success as a supervisor.[38]
- Unresolved conflicts can decrease the productivity of a department or organization for years.[39]
- Conflict is familiar to every supervisor. One survey revealed that managers spend about 20 percent of their time resolving conflicts, and that managing conflict is becoming more important.[40]
- Understanding how to confront and resolve conflict can lead to both organizational productivity and improved interpersonal relationships.[41]

People often think of conflict as fighting and view it as disruptive, but conflict can be creative and beneficial.[42] The devil's advocate approach to group problem solving is one example. The question is not whether conflict is good or bad but rather how it should be managed to benefit the organization. Too little or too much conflict is a bad sign, usually indicating management's unwillingness or lack of ability to adapt to a changing environment. A challenge to present methods or an innovative change can cause conflict but can also lead to improved productivity. While performing any of the supervisory functions (planning, organizing, staffing, leading, or controlling), a supervisor may encounter conflict.

VII. Types and Sources of Conflict

In this section we will examine conflict in terms of two classifications as well as the reasons conflict exists.

Types of Conflict

There are at least two ways to classify conflict. One is to determine whether the conflict is constructive or destructive. *Constructive* (also called *functional*) *conflict* helps the department achieve its objectives; *destructive* (also called *dysfunctional*) *conflict* hinders the department's efforts in achieving its objectives. The supervisor's job is to either eliminate destructive conflict or change it into constructive conflict.

A second method of classifying conflict is in terms of the people involved.

1. Conflict *within the individual* is common when a person is faced with contradictory priorities. If you are asked to work overtime and have another commitment, what do you do?

2. *Interpersonal conflict* occurs when two people disagree. When people interact over any period of time, there is bound to be conflict.

3. Conflict *between an individual and a group* occurs when a group member breaks the group's norms.

4. *Intergroup conflict* is a conflict between two different groups or departments. Conflict is common when groups or departments have different objectives and are dependent on each other to meet their objectives.

5. *Conflict between organizations* often results from competing in a free-enterprise system.

Reasons for Conflict

There are at least four major reasons for conflict.

Personal Differences: People have different needs, beliefs, and values. Our perceptions and expectations can also differ. Differences in values often produce conflicts that are difficult to resolve. Personal differences are often incorrectly called personality clashes. As a supervisor, don't generalize. Determine whether the conflict is due to different needs, beliefs, values, perceptions, or expectations, and resolve it.

Information: People tend to use different sources of information. At times, the sources will not agree, or the same information will be interpreted differently. Conflicts caused by information can usually be resolved through the clarification of the information and with a minimum of resentment. The more effective you are at communicating, the fewer information conflicts you will have to resolve.

Different Objectives: Individuals and groups sometimes have different or incompatible objectives. For example, the salesperson's objective is to sell as much as possible, whereas the credit person's objective is to give credit only to people who are good risks. These two groups are known to have conflicts. Conflict also can arise when priorities are not clear. Employees can be in conflict over what should be done and when.

Environmental Factors: There is often conflict over forecasts of changes in the environment, which are used in planning. Employees or departments often have to compete for scarce organizational resources. Here, conflict is common, for example, when budgets are set. People are also territorial; conflict can occur if someone tries to infringe on another's turf. Clearly defining employees' authority and responsibility helps prevent such territorial disputes.[43]

LEARNING OBJECTIVE

5. Explain the types and sources of conflict.

8. Describe a conflict you observed in an organization, preferably one you have worked for. Identify the type of conflict in terms of the people involved and the source of the conflict.

VIII. Conflict Management Styles

We have examined the causes of conflict in an organization. Now you will learn how to manage conflict. But first turn to Self-Learning Exercise 8–1 to determine your preferred style of conflict management.

SELF-LEARNING EXERCISE 8–1

Determining Your Preferred Conflict Management Style

Following are four situations. Rank all five alternative actions from 1, the first approach you would use (most desirable), to 5, the last approach you would use (least desirable). Don't try to pick a best answer. Select the alternative that best describes what you would actually do in the situation based on your past experiences.

1. You are the general manager of a manufacturing plant. The purchasing department has found a source of material at a lower cost than the one being used. However, the production manager says the current material is superior, and he doesn't want to change. The quality control manager says that both will pass inspection with similar results. You would

_____ *a.* Do nothing; let the purchasing and production managers work it out between themselves.

_____ *b.* Suggest having the purchasing manager find an alternative material that is cheaper but acceptable to the production manager.

_____ *c.* Have the purchasing and production managers compromise.

_____ *d.* Decide who is right and make the other comply.

_____ *e.* Get the purchasing and production managers together and work out an agreement acceptable to both parties.

2. You are a college professor. You have started a consulting organization and have the title of director of consulting services, which the dean has approved. You run it through the business department, using other faculty and yourself to consult. It has been going well. Randy, the director of continuing education, says that your consulting services should come under his department and not be a separate department. You would

_____ *a.* Suggest that some services be under continuing education, but that others, such as your consulting, remain with you in the business department.

_____ *b.* Do what you can to stop the move; you go to the dean and request that the consulting services stay under your direction in the business department, as the dean okayed originally.

_____ *c.* Do nothing. The dean will surely see through this "power grab" and turn Randy down.

_____ *d.* Talk to Randy. Try to come up with an agreement you are both satisfied with.

_____ *e.* Go along with Randy's request. It's not worth fighting about; you can still consult.

3. You are a branch manager for a bank. One of your colleagues cut you off twice during a managers' meeting that just ended. You would

_____ *a.* Do nothing; it's no big deal.

_____ *b.* Discuss it in a friendly manner, but try to get the colleague to stop this behavior.

_____ *c.* Don't do or say anything because it might hurt your relations, even if you're a little upset about it.

_____ *d.* Forcefully tell the colleague that you put up with being cut off, but will not tolerate it in the future.

_____ *e.* Tell the colleague that you will listen without interrupting if he or she does the same for you.

4. You are the human resources and personnel manager. You have decided to have visitors sign in and wear guest passes. However, only about half of the employees sign their guests in before taking them to their offices to do business. You would

_____ *a.* Talk to the general manager about why employees are not signing in visitors.

_____ *b.* Try to find a method that will please most employees.

_____ *c.* Go to the general manager and request that he require employees to follow your procedures. If the general manager says to do it, employees will.

_____ *d.* Do not require visitors to sign in; only require them to wear guest passes.

_____ *e.* Let employees do things the way they want to.

To determine your preferred conflict management style, place your ranking numbers 1 through 5 on the lines below.

Situation 1

_____ *a.* forcing
_____ *b.* avoiding
_____ *c.* accommodating
_____ *d.* compromising
_____ *e.* collaborating

Situation 3

_____ *a.* avoiding
_____ *b.* collaborating
_____ *c.* accommodating
_____ *d.* forcing
_____ *e.* compromising

Situation 2

_____ *a.* compromising
_____ *b.* forcing
_____ *c.* avoiding
_____ *d.* collaborating
_____ *e.* accommodating

Situation 4

_____ *a.* collaborating
_____ *b.* accommodating
_____ *c.* forcing
_____ *d.* compromising
_____ *e.* avoiding

Now place your ranking numbers 1 through 5 that correspond to the styles from the four situations in order; then add the four numbers.

Situation 1	Situation 2	Situation 3	Situation 4		
_____ *a.*	_____ *b.*	_____ *d.*	_____ *c.*	= _____	total, forcing style
_____ *b.*	_____ *c.*	_____ *a.*	_____ *e.*	= _____	total, avoiding style
_____ *c.*	_____ *e.*	_____ *c.*	_____ *b.*	= _____	total, accommodating style
_____ *d.*	_____ *a.*	_____ *e.*	_____ *d.*	= _____	total, compromising style
_____ *e.*	_____ *d.*	_____ *b.*	_____ *a.*	= _____	total, collaborating style

The total with the lowest score is your preferred conflict management style. There is no one best conflict style in all situations. Like situational supervision and communications, the best style depends upon the situation. The more even the totals are, the more flexible you are at changing conflict management styles. Very high and very low totals indicate less flexibility.

The five conflict management styles—forcing, avoiding, accommodating, compromising, and collaborating—will be presented next.[44] See Exhibit 8–5 for an overview of the five styles.

Forcing Conflict Style   *A person using the* **forcing conflict style** *attempts to resolve the conflict by getting his or her own way.* The forcing approach is an assertive, uncooperative, autocratic attempt to satisfy your own needs at the expense of others, if necessary. A win-lose situation is created. Forcers use authority, threats, and intimidation and call for majority rule

EXHIBIT 8–5   **CONFLICT MANAGEMENT STYLES**

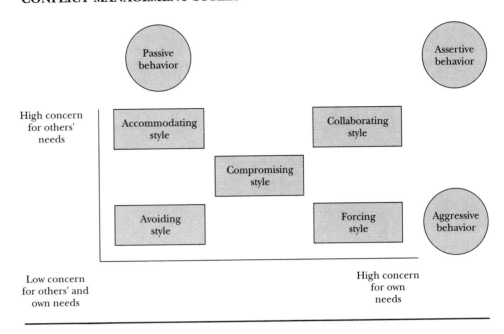

when they know they will win. This is believed to be the style most commonly used by managers.

The advantage of the forcing style is that better organizational decisions will be made (assuming the forcer is correct) because compromise decisions are often less effective. The disadvantage is that overuse of this style leads to feelings of hostility and resentment toward the forcer.

The forcing style is appropriate when the conflict is over personal differences (particularly values, which are hard to change); when maintaining close, supportive relationships is not critical; or when conflict resolution is urgent.

Avoiding Conflict Style

Someone using the **avoiding conflict style** *attempts to ignore the conflict rather than resolve it.* The avoiding approach is unassertive and uncooperative, and represents an attempt to satisfy your needs by avoiding or postponing confrontation. A lose-lose situation is created because the conflict is not resolved. People avoid conflict by refusing to take a stance, physically leaving, or escaping mentally (tuning out).

The advantage of the avoiding style is that it may maintain relationships that would be hurt by resolving the conflict. The disadvantage is that conflicts are not resolved. An overuse of this style leads to conflict within the individual. People tend to walk all over the avoider. Supervisors use this style when they allow employees to break rules and do not confront them. Avoiding problems does not make them go away; instead, they usually get worse.

The avoiding style is appropriate when your stake in the issue is not high, when confrontation will damage a critical working relationship, or when a time constraint necessitates avoidance. Some people use the avoiding style out of fear that they will handle the confrontation poorly, making the situation worse rather than better.[45] After studying this chapter and following its guidelines, you should be able to handle confrontations effectively.

Accommodating Conflict Style

Those using the **accommodating conflict style** *attempt to resolve a conflict by giving in to the other party.* The accommodating approach is unassertive and cooperative. It is an attempt to satisfy the other party while neglecting your own needs. A win-lose situation is created, with the other party being the winner.

The advantage of the accommodating style is that relationships are maintained. The disadvantage is that giving in to the other party may be counterproductive in that the accommodator may have a better solution. People may take advantage of someone who overuses this style. When using this style, the relationship the accommodator is trying to maintain is often lost nonetheless.

The accommodating style is appropriate when maintaining the relationship outweighs all other considerations; when the changes agreed to are not important to the accommodator, but are to the other party; or when time to resolve the conflict is limited. This is often the only style you can use with an autocratic boss.

Compromising Conflict Style

A user of the **compromising conflict style** *attempts to resolve conflict through give and take and by making concessions.* The compromising approach involves both assertiveness and cooperation. It is an attempt to meet a person's need for harmonious relationships. A win-lose or lose-lose situation may be created through compromise.

The advantages of the compromising style are that conflict is resolved quickly and relationships are maintained. The disadvantage is that compromise may have counterproductive results in that suboptimum decisions are made. Overuse of this style leads to playing games. For example, someone may ask for twice as much as he or she needs in order to get what he or she really wants. This style is commonly used in collective bargaining.

The compromise style is appropriate when the issues are complex and critical and there is no simple and clear solution, when all parties have a strong interest in different solutions, or when time is short.

Collaborating Conflict Style

Someone using the **collaborating conflict style** *attempts to jointly resolve conflict with the best solution that is agreeable to all parties.* This is also called the *problem-solving style.* The collaborating approach is assertive and cooperative. The collaborator attempts to fully address the concerns of all. The focus is on finding the best solution to a problem that is satisfactory to all parties. Unlike the forcer, the collaborator is willing to change if a better solution is presented. This is the only style that creates a win-win situation.

The advantage to the collaborating style is that it tends to lead to the best solution. The disadvantage is the time and effort it takes to resolve a conflict.

The collaborating style is appropriate when maintaining relationships is important, when time is available, or when it is a peer conflict.

As a supervisor, you would be wise to work at preventing conflict. It generally takes less time and effort than resolving conflicts. Allowing employees to work together, defining their own responsibility, authority, and accountability, is a good way to prevent conflict.[46] However, you will never eliminate conflict completely. When a conflict does arise, you must determine the appropriate style to use. A person's preferred style tends to reflect his or her needs. Some people enjoy forcing, others prefer to avoid conflict, and so forth. However, as with other aspects of situational supervision, success lies in your ability to use the style appropriate to the situation. Of the five styles, the most difficult to implement successfully (and probably the most underutilized) is the collaborative style. You learn this style in the next section of this chapter.

LEARNING OBJECTIVE
6. Explain the five conflict management styles and the appropriate use of each style.

CONNECTIONS

9. Give an example of a conflict and identify and explain the appropriate conflict management style to use in resolving it.

IX. Using the Collaborating Conflict Management Style

Collaboration is not always appropriate in supervisor-employee conflicts. However, it is generally the appropriate style for conflict between colleagues and peers.

The objective of this section is to develop your ability to confront (or be confronted by) people you are in conflict with, in a manner that resolves the conflict without damaging interpersonal relationships. This may involve initiating, responding, or mediating in conflict resolution.[47]

Initiating Conflict Resolution

To initiate conflict resolution, you must confront the other person or people. Your attitude will have a major effect on the outcome of the confrontation. We tend to get what we are looking for. If you go into a confrontation expecting to argue and fight, you probably will. If you expect a successful resolution, you probably will get it.[48]

The three **initiating conflict resolution steps** *are planning to maintain ownership of the problem using the XYZ model, implementing your plan persistently, and making an agreement for change.*

Step 1. Plan to Maintain Ownership of the Problem Using the XYZ Model

Part of the reason confronters are not successful at resolving is that they wait too long before approaching the other party, and they do it in an emotional state without planning. They end up saying things they didn't mean because they don't give thought to what it is they want to say and accomplish through confrontation. They ignore the fact that it is *their* problem, not the other person's. For example, you don't smoke and a smoker comes into your office all lit up. The smoke, but not the smoker, bothers you. It's your problem. Open the confrontation by asking the smoker to help you solve your problem. This approach reduces defensiveness and establishes an atmosphere conducive to problem solving.

Approach a conflict knowing what you want to accomplish and say ahead of time. Be descriptive, not evaluative. Avoid trying to determine who is to blame. Both parties are usually partly to blame. Fixing blame only gets people defensive, which is counterproductive to conflict resolution. Keep your opening statement short. The longer the statement, the longer it will take to resolve the conflict. People get defensive when they must wait for their turn to talk. Use the XYZ model. The **XYZ model** *describes a conflict in terms of behavior, consequences, and feelings.* When you do X (behavior), Y (consequences) happens, and I feel Z (feelings). For example, when you smoke in my office (behavior), I have trouble breathing and become nauseated (consequences), and I am uncomfortable and irritated (feelings). When you approach the other party, vary the sequence, starting with a feeling or consequence as the situation dictates.[49]

Timing is also important. Don't confront people when they are involved in something else. For example, don't confront a professor when he or she is about to start class. Instead wait until after class, or better still, see the professor during office hours (when possible). If the other party is busy, make an appointment to discuss the conflict. In addition, don't confront a person concerning several unrelated issues at once.

Step 2. Implement Your Plan Persistently

After making your short, planned XYZ statement, let the other party respond. If the confronted party acknowledges the problem and says he or she will change, you may have succeeded. Often, people do not realize that there is a conflict, and when approached properly, are willing to change. However, if the other party does not understand or avoids acknowledging the problem, persist. You cannot resolve a conflict if the other party will not even acknowledge its existence. Repeat your planned statement several times, explain it in different terms, or both, until you get an acknowledgement, or realize it's hopeless. But don't give up too easily.

If the other party acknowledges the problem, but is not responsive to resolving it, appeal to common goals. Make the other party aware of the benefits to the organization as well as to him or her.

Step 3. Make an Agreement for Change

Try to come to an agreement about specific action you will both take to resolve the conflict. Remember that you are collaborating, not forcing. If possible, get a statement describing the change.

Below is an example of conflict resolution following these guidelines:

PAM: Hi, Bill! Got a few minutes to talk?

BILL: Sure, what's up?

PAM: Something's been bothering me lately, and I wanted you to know about it. When you come to class without doing your homework [*behavior*] I get irritated [*feeling*], and our group has to wait for you to read the material, or make a decision without your input [*consequences*].

BILL: Hey, I'm busy!

PAM: Do you think the rest of the group isn't?

BILL: No.

PAM: Are grades important to you?

BILL: Yeah, if I don't get good grades, I can't play on the football team.

PAM: You get a grade for doing your homework, and we all get the same group grade. Your input helps us all to get a better grade.

BILL: You're right; sometimes I forget about that. Well sometimes I don't do it because I don't understand the assignment.

PAM: I'll tell you what; when you don't understand it call me or come over, and I'll explain it. You know my phone number and address.

BILL: I'd appreciate that.

PAM: So you agree to do your homework before class, and I agree to help you when you need it.

BILL: Okay, I'll do it from now on.

Responding to Conflict Resolution

The person responding is the supposed source of the conflict. If you are the responder, an initiator has confronted you. Most initiators do not follow the initiating steps described. Therefore the person responding should take responsibility for successful conflict resolution by using the **responding conflict resolution steps:** *listening to and paraphrasing the problem using the XYZ model; agreeing with some aspect of the complaint; asking for, and giving, alternative solutions; and making an agreement for change.*

Step 1. Listen to and Paraphrase the Problem Using the XYZ Model

When discussing a conflict, listen. Do not get defensive and justify your actions as your first response. Even when you disagree, listen to the other party's side. Avoid trying to place blame.

Let people blow off some steam as long as they don't verbally attack you. If they do, calmly tell them you are willing to discuss a genuine problem, but you will not tolerate personal attacks or scapegoating. When a person is too emotional, it may be better to postpone the discussion until everyone is calm. Deal with emotions following the guidelines in Chapter 7. If someone confronts you when you don't have time to talk, explain your situation and make an appointment to discuss the problem.

Using the XYZ Model: The untrained initiator often makes general statements and simply blames the responder. To resolve the conflict, you must transform the general and personal accusations into specific descriptions of behavior. To do this, use the XYZ model, which breaks down the conflict in terms of behavior (X), consequences (Y), and feelings (Z).

1. Ask for a specific example. "When do I do X? Can you give me a specific example of what I do that causes the conflict or problem?" Keep at it until you clearly understand the specific behavior.

2. Have the initiator describe the consequences of the behavior (Y happens). "When I do X what are the results?" Keep at it until you understand the consequences of your behavior.

3. Ask the person how he or she feels, if feelings were not expressed. "And you feel Z?" Use the model to paraphrase the conflict for the initiator: "When I get back from break late (X), you have to wait on my customer (Y), and you get upset (Z). Is that your complaint?" If the initiator agrees that this is the problem, go to the second step. If it is not, keep paraphrasing until you get it. Paraphrasing does not mean you agree with the initiator's complaint. It simply shows your true understanding of the conflict.

Step 2. Agree with Some Aspect of the Complaint

This is important but difficult, especially when you do not agree with the complaint. It is tempting to change from the collaborative style to the avoiding, forcing, accommodating, or compromising styles. But don't. State your position in an assertive and cooperative way. Find a point you can agree on. There is generally a grain of truth in even the most outlandish complaints. If there is nothing else you agree with, at least agree about the person's perception. For example, "I agree that my behavior is upsetting you."

Again, you are not agreeing with the total complaint, nor are you conceding your position. Being agreeable will lead to problem solving. Generally, people who complain have a long list of arguments to support their position. They will keep them coming until you agree with something. The longer it takes to agree on something, the broader the base of the argument/conflict will be. And the longer it will take to resolve.

Step 3. Ask for and Give Alternative Solutions

By asking for solutions, you show your regard for the initiator and shift the focus away from the negative past to the positive future. Together, you will try to find a solution that is satisfactory to all parties (a win-win situation). You do not have to compromise or accommodate, and you should not force or avoid.

Step 4. Make an Agreement for Change

Come to an agreement on a solution, and develop a plan stating each party's responsibility. If possible, have each person paraphrase what he or she agrees to do in the future.

Mediating Conflict Resolution

Frequently employees in conflict cannot resolve their dispute. In such cases, the supervisor should mediate to help them resolve their differences. With corporate downsizing, the amount of time supervisors spend resolving conflict is growing.[50]

The mediating supervisor should first decide whether to start with joint or individual meetings. If an employee has a complaint but has not confronted the other person or people involved, or there is serious discrepancy in employee perceptions, the supervisor should meet with each party individually before bringing them together. On the other hand, when both parties have similar awareness of the problem and motivation to solve it, the supervisor can begin with a joint meeting, assuming all parties are calm. The supervisor should be a mediator, not a judge. Get the employees to resolve the conflict, if possible. Remain impartial, unless one party is violating company policies. Don't belittle the parties in conflict. Don't make comments like "I'm disappointed in you two; you're acting like babies."

When bringing conflicting parties together, follow the **mediating conflict resolution steps:** *have each party state his or her complaint using the XYZ model; agree on the problem; develop alternative solutions; and make an agreement for change and follow up.*

Step 1. Have Each Party State Its Complaint Using the XYZ Model

Teach the employees to use the XYZ model (behavior, consequences, and feelings), and have them state their complaint using it. It is helpful to have them write out their complaints first.

Step 2. Agree on the Problem

Do not try to place the blame on any one party. If either party blames the other, make a statement such as, "We are here to resolve the conflict; placing blame is not productive." Focus on how the conflict is affecting their work. Discuss the issues, not personalities. The discussion should make the parties aware of the consequences of their behavior. The supervisor may ask questions or make statements to clarify what is being said. He or she should develop one statement of the problem that is agreeable to all parties, if possible. If not, each party's statement should be taken separately.

Step 3. Develop Alternative Solutions

Have both parties suggest possible solutions to the problem. Focus on the changes in behavior needed to eliminate the negative consequences and feelings. "If I do X, then Y and Z will no longer result in conflict." Combining ideas is often helpful. The supervisor may suggest alternatives but should try not to force acceptance. Develop alternatives that create a win-win situation.

Step 4. Make an Agreement for Change and Follow Up

Come to a solution satisfactory to all parties. Have all parties state what they will or will not do in the future. The supervisor should paraphrase these statements to ensure all are in agreement and to get a commitment to the changed behavior. "To summarize, Kit, you are going to do X, and Wayne, you are going to do X. Do you both agree to this action?" Set a follow-up meeting to determine whether the conflict has been resolved. The steps involved in initiating, responding to, and mediating conflict resolution are summarized in Model 8–2.

LEARNING OBJECTIVE

7. List and explain the steps in the initiating, responding to, and mediating conflict resolution models and use the models.

CONNECTIONS

10. Describe a situation in which the initiating, responding, or mediating conflict resolution model would be appropriate.

MODEL 8–2

CONFLICT RESOLUTION

Initiating Conflict Resolution

Step 1. Plan to maintain ownership of the problem using the XYZ model.

Step 2. Implement your plan persistently.

Step 3. Make an agreement for change.

Responding to Conflict Resolution

Step 1. Listen to and paraphrase the problem using the XYZ model.

Step 2. Agree with some aspect of the complaint.

Step 3. Ask for, and give, alternative solutions.

Step 4. Make an agreement for change.

Mediating Conflict Resolution

Step 1. Have each party state its complaint using the XYZ model.

Step 2. Agree on the problem.

Step 3. Develop alternative solutions.

Step 4. Make an agreement for change and follow up.

REVIEW

Select one or more methods: (1) fill in the missing key terms from memory; (2) match the key terms from the end of the review with their definitions below; (3) copy the key terms in order from the key terms at the beginning of the chapter.

Managing change is important for the supervisor when performing the five functions of supervision.

There are four major types of change: task, structure, technology, and people. A change in one variable affects one or more of the other variables. _____ is the simplification or reduction of the human effort needed to do a job. _____ are formal structures for collecting, processing, and disseminating the necessary information that aids supervisors in decision making.

Three variables—intensity, source, and focus—cause _____ . Intensity refers to the level of resistance people have toward the change. There are three sources of resistance: facts, beliefs, and values. The three focuses of resistance to change are self, others, and the work environment. To overcome resistance to change, the supervisor can encourage an interest in improvement, plan, give the facts, avoid getting people emotional, avoid direct confrontation, involve employees, and provide support. An understanding of various types of employee resistance can help the supervisor respond to that resistance.

_____ is the ongoing planned process of change to improve the organization's effectiveness in solving problems and achieving objectives. _____ is used to diagram the currentlevel of performance as well as the hindering and driving forces. _____ uses a questionnaire to gather data that is used as the basis for change. _____ is a six-phase program to improve management and organizational effectiveness. _____ is designed to help work groups operate more effectively.

The steps in the change model are defining the change, identifying possible resistance to the change, planning the change, implementing the change (give facts, involve employees, and provide support), and controlling the change.

_____ exists whenever two or more parties disagree. Conflict management skills are important when performing the five functions of supervision.

There are two methods of classifying conflict: as constructive versus destructive; and in terms of the people involved, as conflict within the individual, interpersonal conflict, conflict between an individual and a group, intergroup conflict, or conflict between organizations. The reasons for conflict include personal differences, information, different objectives, and environmental factors.

There are four conflict management styles. A person using the _____ attempts to resolve the conflict by getting his or her own way. Someone using the _____ attempts to ignore the conflict rather than resolve it. Those using the _____ attempt to resolve a conflict by giving in to the other party. A user of the _____ attempts to resolve the conflict through give and take and making concessions. Someone using the _____ attempts to jointly resolve conflict with the best solution agreeable to all parties. Each style has its advantages and disadvantages, and each is appropriate in certain situations.

The _____ are planning to maintain ownership of the problem using the XYZ model, implementing your plan persistently, and making an agreement for change. The _____ describes a conflict in terms of behavior, consequences, and feelings. The _____ are listening to and paraphrasing the problem using the XYZ model; agreeing with some aspect of the complaint; asking for and giving alternative solutions;

and making an agreement for change. The _____ are as follows: have each party state his or her complaint using the XYZ model; agree on the problem; develop alternative solutions; and make an agreement for change and follow up.

KEY TERMS

accommodating conflict style

automation

avoiding conflict style

collaborating conflict style

compromising conflict style

conflict

force field analysis

forcing conflict style

Grid OD

initiating conflict resolution steps

management information systems (MIS)

mediating conflict resolution steps

organizational development (OD)

resistance to change

responding conflict resolution steps

survey feedback

team building

XYZ model

REFERENCES

1. M. R. Hansen, "Better Supervision from A to W," *Supervisory Management,* August 1985, p. 34.

2. Thomas Horton, "Building through Change," *Management Review,* October 1983, p. 3.

3. Perry Pascarella, "Making Change a Way of Life," *Industry Week,* October 13, 1986, p. 59.

4. Kent Lineback, "How Management Trainers Miss the Boat," *Training,* March 1984, p. 92.

5. Dorothy Schaeffer, "Change Has Its Headaches," *Supervision,* June 1985, p. 5.

6. David Oromaner, "Winning Employee Cooperation for Change," *Supervisory Management,* December 1985, p. 18.

7. Jeremy Main, "Work Won't Be the Same Again," *Fortune,* June 28, 1982, pp. 58–65.

8. P. Lawrence, "How to Deal with Resistance to Change," *Harvard Business Review,* March–April 1986, p. 178.

9. Horton, "Building through Change," p. 3.

10. Lawrence, "How to Deal with Resistance," p. 178.

11. Oromaner, "Winning Employee Cooperation for Change," p. 21.

12. Perry Pascarella, "Creating Change," *Industry Week,* April 14, 1986, p. 7.

13. Lawrence, "How to Deal with Resistance," p. 178.

14. Ken Hultman, *The Path of Least Resistance* (Austin, TX: Learning Concepts, 1979).

15. Horton, "Building through Change," p. 2.

16. Ibid.

17. Kent Baker and Stevan Holmberg, "Stepping Up to Supervision: Coping with Change," *Supervisory Management,* March 1982, p. 23.

18. Schaeffer, "Change Has Its Headaches," p. 6.

19. Waldron Berry, "Overcoming Resistance to Change," *Supervisory Management,* February 1983, p. 27.

20. Oromaner, "Winning Employee Cooperation for Change," p. 19.

21. Ibid.

22. Hultman, *Path of Least Resistance.*

23. Horton, "Building through Change," p. 3.

24. Pascarella, "Making Change a Way of Life," p. 64.

25. Pascarella, "Creating Change," p. 7.

26. Oromaner, "Winning Employee Cooperation for Change," p. 21.

27. Berry, "Overcoming Resistance to Change," p. 27.

28. Miriam Erez, P. Christopher Earley, and Charles L. Hulin, "The Impact of Participation on Goal Acceptance and Performance," *Academy of Management Journal,* March 1985, pp. 50–66.

29. Schaeffer, "Change Has Its Headaches," p. 7.

30. Dennis Gillen, "Harnessing the Energy from Change Anxiety," *Supervisory Management,* March 1986, p. 43.

31. H. P. Karp, "Resistance," *Supervision,* March 1985, pp. 32–35.

32. Robert Blake and Jane Mouton, *The New Managerial Grid* (New York: Gulf Publishing, 1978).

33. Rosabeth Moss Kanter, *The Change Masters* (Lake Orion, MI: Britannica Videos Training and Development Program, 1987).

34. D. D. Warrick, *Managing Organizational Change and Development* (Chicago: Science Research Associates, 1984), pp. 32–33.

35. "Byproducts of Change," *Personnel Administrator,* March 1986, p. 19.

36. Deborah Kolb and Priscilla Glidden, "Getting to Know Your Conflict Options," *Personnel Administrator,* June 1986, p. 77.

37. Kent Baker and Phillip Morgan, "Building a Professional Image: Handling Conflict," *Supervisory Management,* February 1986, p. 24.

38. J. Wilcox, E. Wilcox, and K. Cowan, "Communicating Creatively in Conflict Situations," *Management Solutions,* October 1986, p. 18.

39. Peter Muniz and Robert Chasnoff, "Assessing the Cause of Conflict and Confronting the Real Issues," *Supervisory Management,* March 1986, p. 34.

40. Wilcox et al., "Communicating Creatively," p. 18.

41. Steven Schoonover and Murry Dalziel, "Developing Leaders for Change," *Management Review,* July 1986, p. 59.

42. Karen Watkins, "When Co-Workers Clash," *Training and Development Journal,* April 1986, p. 26.

43. Mary Jean Parson, "The Peer Conflict," *Supervisory Management,* May 1986, p. 25.

44. A. C. Filley, *Interpersonal Conflict Resolution* (Glenview, IL: Scott, Foresman, 1975).

45. David Whetten and Kim Cameron, *Developing Management Skills* (Glenview, IL: Scott, Foresman, 1984), pp. 407–16.

46. Robert Chasnoff and Peter Muniz, "Training to Manage Conflict," *Training and Development Journal,* January 1985, p. 49.

47. Whetten and Cameron, *Developing Management Skills,* pp. 416–33.

48. Wilcox et al., "Communicating Creatively," p. 19.

49. T. Gordon, *Parent Effectiveness Training* (New York: Wyden, 1970).

50. *The Wall Street Journal,* January 14, 1992, p. 1.

APPLICATION SITUATIONS

Identifying Resistance to Change

AS 8−1

Following are five statements made by employees asked to make a change on the job. Identify the source, focus, and intensity of their resistance using Exhibit 8−2. Place the number of the box (1 through 9) that best describes the resistance.

_____ 1. The police sergeant asked Sue to take a rookie cop as her partner. Sue said, "Do I have to? I broke in the last rookie."

_____ 2. The tennis coach asked Bill, the star player, to have Jim as his doubles partner. Bill said, "Come on; Jim is a lousy player. Peter is better; don't break us up." The coach disagreed and forced Bill to concede.

_____ 3. The supervisor realized that Sharon always used the accommodating conflict style. The supervisor told her to stop giving in to everyone's wishes. Sharon said, "But I like people, and I want them to like me, too."

_____ 4. An employee went to Sim, her supervisor, and asked whether she could change the work order form. Sim said, "That would be a waste of time; the current form is fine."

_____ 5. Ann, an employee, is busy at work. Her supervisor tells her to stop what she is doing and begin a new project. Ann says, "The job I'm working on now is more important."

OD Techniques

AS 8−2

Following are five situations in which OD would be beneficial. Identify the most appropriate technique for each.

_a._ force field analysis   _d._ change masters

_b._ survey feedback   _e._ team building

_c._ Grid OD

_____ 6. "We need to make the jobs broader in scope with more teamwork. Employees need to be more involved and valued."

_____ 7. "We are a progressive company; we believe in developing our people. We'd like to make a good organization even better."

_____ 8. "To improve productivity, we should identify the things that are holding us back and the things that are helping us to be productive, too."

_____ 9. "We want an OD program that will enable us to better utilize the input of each manager."

_____ 10. "Morale and motivation are low in our organization. We'd like to know why and change it."

Selecting Conflict Management Styles

AS 8–3

Identify the most appropriate conflict management style for each of the following 10 situations.

a. forcing   *d.* accommodating

b. avoiding   *e.* collaborating

c. compromising

_____ 11. You are in a supervision class where small groups work together for the entire semester. Under normal conditions, the most appropriate style is _____ .

_____ 12. You have joined a committee in order to meet people. Your interest in the committee's actual function is low. While serving on the committee, you make a recommendation that was opposed by another member. You realize that you have the better idea. The other party is using a forcing style.

_____ 13. You are the supervisor of a production department. An important order is behind schedule. Two of your employees are in conflict, as usual, over how to meet the deadline.

_____ 14. You are on a committee that has to select a new computer. The four alternatives available will all do the job. It's the brand, price, and service that people disagree on.

_____ 15. You are a sales manager. One of your competent salespeople is trying to close a big sale. The two of you are discussing the next call the person will make. You disagree on strategy.

_____ 16. You are on your way to an important meeting and you're late. As you leave your office, you see one of your employees goofing off instead of working.

_____ 17. You have a crisis in your department. Your boss calls you up and tells you, in a stern voice, to get up to her office right away.

_____ 18. You are in a special one-hour budget meeting with your boss and fellow supervisors. You have to finalize the total budget for each department.

_____ 19. You and a fellow supervisor are working on a report. You disagree on the format to use.

_____ 20. You're over budget for labor this month. It's slow today, so you asked a part-time employee to go home early. (You control the hours.) The employee needs the money and doesn't want to leave.

OBJECTIVE CASE 8

Supervisor Carl's Change

Carl was an employee at Benson's Corporation. He applied for a supervisor's job at Hedges Inc., and got it. Carl wanted to do a good job. He observed the employees at work to determine ways to improve productivity. Within a week, Carl thought of a way.

On Friday afternoon, he called the employees together. Carl told them that starting on Monday he wanted them to change the steps they follow when assembling the product. He demonstrated the new steps a few times and asked whether everyone understood them. There were no questions. So Carl said, "Great, start it on Monday first thing."

On Monday, Carl was in his office for about an hour doing the week's scheduling. When he came out to the shop floor he realized that no one was following the new procedure he had described on Friday.

Carl called the crew together and asked why no one was using the procedure.

Debbie said: "On Friday at the tavern we were talking about it, and we agreed that it's not a good method."

Answer the following questions. Use the space between questions to explain your answers.

_____ 1. The type of change Carl introduced was
      a. task   *c.* technology
      b. structure   *d.* people

_____ 2. Using Exhibit 8–2, identify the box that describes the employees' resistance to the change.
      a. 1   *f.* 6
      b. 2   *g.* 7
      c. 3   *h.* 8
      d. 4   *i.* 9
      e. 5

_____ 3. Which major means of overcoming resistance to change should Carl have used when implementing his new procedure?
      a. Develop a positive   *d.* Give facts.
          climate.   *e.* Avoid emotions.
      b. Encourage interest in *f.* Avoid direct confrontation.
          improvement.   *g.* Involve employees.
      c. Plan.   *h.* Provide support.

_____ 4. Debbie's comment was a _____ resistance statement.
      a. blocker   *f.* threatener
      b. roller   *g.* politician
      c. staller   *h.* traditionalist
      d. reverser   *i.* assaulter
      e. sidestepper

_____ 5. The best OD technique for Carl to have used for this change was
  a. force field analysis   *d.* change masters
  b. survey feedback   *e.* team building
  c. Grid OD

_____ 6. Carl followed the steps in the change model.
  a. true   *b.* false

_____ 7. At the end of the case, this was a _____ .
  a. conflict within Carl   *d.* intergroup conflict
  b. interpersonal conflict   *e.* organizational conflict
  c. conflict between an individual
    and a group

_____ 8. The primary source of the conflict is
  a. personal differences   *c.* different objectives
  b. information   *d.* environmental factors

_____ 9. The conflict management style Carl should use in this situation is
  a. forcing   *d.* accommodating
  b. avoiding   *e.* collaborating
  c. compromising

_____ 10. When Carl called the crew together and asked why no one was
  following the new procedure, he was _____
  conflict resolution.
  a. initiating   *b.* responding to   *c.* mediating

11. Assume that you have Carl's job. How would you have made the change?

Team Building

SB 8–1

Below is a survey feedback questionnaire. There are no right or wrong answers. Indicate how each question applies to your class group by checking the appropriate line.

	Strongly Agree	Agree Somewhat	Neutral	Disagree Somewhat	Strongly Disagree

Conflict or Fight

1. Our group's atmosphere is friendly.

2. Our group has a relaxed (rather than tense) atmosphere.

3. Our group is very cooperative (rather than competitive).

4. Members feel free to say what they like.

5. There is much disagreement in our group.

6. Our group has problem people (silent, talker, bored, wanderer, arguer).

Apathy

7. Our group is committed to its tasks. (All members actively participate.)

8. Our group has good attendance.

9. Group members come to class prepared. (All assignments are complete.)

10. All members do their share of the work.

11. Our group should consider firing a member for not attending and/or doing his/her share of the work.

Decision Making

12. Our group's decision-making ability is good.

13. All members participate in making decisions.

14. One or two members influence most decisions.

15. Our group follows the five steps in the decision-making model (Chapter 5).

Step 1. Define the problem.

Step 2. Set objectives and criteria.

	Strongly Agree	Agree Somewhat	Neutral	Disagree Somewhat	Strongly Disagree
Step 3. Generate alternatives.	———	———	———	———	———
Step 4. Analyze alternatives (rather than quickly agreeing on one).	———	———	———	———	———
Step 5. Plan, implement the decision, and control.	———	———	———	———	———

16. Our group uses the following ideas:
    a. Members sit in a close circle.

——— ——— ——— ——— ———

    b. We determine the approach to the task before starting.

——— ——— ——— ——— ———

    c. Only one member speaks at a time, and everyone discusses the same question.

——— ——— ——— ——— ———

    d. Each person persents answers with specific reasons.

——— ——— ——— ——— ———

    e. We rotate order for presenting answers.

——— ——— ——— ——— ———

    f. We listen to others rather than rehearsing our own answers.

——— ——— ——— ——— ———

    g. We eliminate choices not selected by group members.

——— ——— ——— ——— ———

    h. All members defend their answers (when they believe they are correct) rather than change to avoid discussion, conflict, or to get the task over with.

——— ——— ——— ——— ———

    i. We identify the answers remaining and reach a consensus on one (no voting).

——— ——— ——— ——— ———

    j. We come back to controversial questions.

——— ——— ——— ——— ———

17. List other relevant questions.

18. Our group uses the_____conflict-management style.
    a. forcing   *c.* avoiding   *e.* collaborating
    b. accommodating   *d.* compromising

19. Our group resolves its conflicts in a way that is satisfactory to all.
    a. true   *b.* false

Team Building

SB 8–1

This exercise is designed for groups that have worked together for some time.

Objectives: To experience a team-building session. To improve your group's effectiveness.

Experience: This exercise is discussion oriented.

Material: Preparation for Skill-Building Exercise 8–1.

Procedure 1a
Climate Building
(5–30 minutes)

To develop a climate of trust, support, and openness, group members will learn more about each other through a discussion based on asking questions.

Rules: When asking the questions listed below, you must observe these rules:

1. Take turns asking questions.
2. You may refuse to answer a question as long as you did not ask it (or plan to).
3. You do not have to ask the questions in the order they are listed.
4. You may ask your own questions. (Add them.)

Review the questions below and in the appropriate blank place the name of one or more group members of whom you want to ask the questions. If you prefer to ask the entire group, put "group" next to the question. When everyone is ready, begin asking the questions.

1. How do you feel about this course? _____
2. How do you feel about this group? _____
3. How do you feel about me? _____
4. How do you think I feel about you? _____
5. Describe your first impressions of me. _____
6. What do you like to do? _____
7. How committed to the group are you? _____
8. What do you like most about this course? _____
9. What do you plan to do after you graduate? _____
10. What do you want out of this course? _____
11. How do you react to deadlines? _____
12. Who in the group are you the closest to? _____
13. Who in the group do you know the least? _____

Other: _____

Source: Adapted from John E. Jones, "Twenty-Five Questions: A Team-Building Exercise," in *A Handbook of Structured Experiences for Human Relations Training* (La Jolla, CA: University Associates, 1973), no. 118, pp. 88–91.

Procedure 1b
(2–4 minutes)

Participants determine what they would like to accomplish during the team-building session. Below are six major goals of team building; you may add to them. Rank them according to your preference.

_____ To clarify the teams objectives.
_____ To identify areas for improving group performance.
_____ To develop team skills.
_____ To determine and utilize a preferred team style.
_____ To fully utilize the resources of each group member.
_____ To develop working relationships based on trust, honesty, and understanding.
_____ Your own goals (list them).

Procedure 1c
(3–6 minutes)

Participants share their answers to Procedure 1*b*. The group can come to a consensus on its goals if it wants to.

Procedure 2
Process and Structure
(3–8 minutes)

As a team, discuss strengths and weaknesses in how the group works together and communicates. Below, list norms (do's and don'ts) for the group to abide by.

Procedure 3a
Problem Identification
(10–15 minutes)

As a team, answer the survey feedback questionnaire (Preparation for Exercise 8–1). Place a G on the line to signify the team's answer. Don't rush; fully discuss what the issues are and how and why they affect the group.

Procedure 3b
(3–7 minutes)

Based on the above information, list 8 to 10 ways in which the team could improve its performance.

Procedure 3c
(3–6 minutes)

Assign priorities to the above list (1 = most important).

Procedure 4
Problem Solving
(6–10 minutes)

Take the top priority item and do the following:

1. Define the problem.
2. Set objectives.
3. Generate alternatives.
4. Analyze alternatives and select one.
5. Develop an action plan for its implementation.

Procedure 5
Training (1 minute)

Team building often includes training to address the problems facing the group. Because training takes place during most exercises, we will not do any now. Remember that the agendas for team building vary and usually last for one or more full days, rather than one hour.

Application: Do I intend to implement the team's solutions? Why? What did I learn from this experience? How can I apply this knowledge in my daily life? How can I apply this knowledge as a manager?

Procedure 6
(1–3 minutes)

Group members summarize what has been accomplished and state what they will do (commit) to improve the group.

Sharing (4–7 minutes): A spokesperson from each team describes the group's top three areas for improvement. The instructor records them on the board.

PREPARATION FOR IN-CLASS SKILL-BUILDING EXERCISE

**Initiating Conflict
Resolution**

SB 8–2

During the in-class exercise you will be given the opportunity to reenact a conflict you now face or have faced in the past in order to develop your conflict resolution skills. Fill in the information requested in the spaces below and also record your answers on a separate sheet of paper.

Name (real or fictitious) of other party or parties _____

You _____

Define the situation:

1. Pertinent information about the other party or parties. (Relationship with you, knowledge of situation, years of service, background, age, beliefs, values, and so forth.)

2. State what you want to accomplish:

3. Identify the other party's or parties' possible reaction to your confrontation, resistance to change (intensity, source, focus), and so forth.

4. Plan how you will initiate a resolution to the conflict. On a separate sheet of paper, outline your approach to the three steps in initiating a conflict resolution.

IN-CLASS SKILL-BUILDING EXERCISE

**Initiating Conflict
Resolution**

SB 8–2

Objective: To experience and develop skills in resolving a conflict.

Experience: You will initiate, respond to, and observe a conflict, and then evaluate the effectiveness of its resolution.

Material: The questionnaire in the Preparation for Exercise 8–2.

*Procedure 1
(2–3 minutes)*

Break into as many groups of three as possible. You do not have to be with members of your permanent team, if you have one. Make one or two groups of two, if necessary. Each member selects the number 1, 2, or 3. Number 1 will be the first to initiate a conflict resolution, then 2, followed by 3.

*Procedure 2
(8–15 minutes)*

Initiator number 1 gives the information in the preparation for this exercise to number 2 (the responder) to read. Number 3 will be the observer and will fill out the feedback form at the end of the exercise. Once number 2 understands the conflict, the initiator and responder enact the resolution. When the role playing is over, the observer leads a discussion on the effectiveness of the conflict resolution. This should be discussion, not a lecture. Do not go on to procedure 3 until you are told to do so.

*Procedure 3
(8–15 minutes)*

Same as procedure 2, only number 2 is now the initiator, number 3 the responder, and number 1 the observer.

*Procedure 4
(8–15 minutes)*

Same as procedure 2, only number 3 is the initiator, number 1 is the responder, and number 2 is the observer.

Conclusion: The instructor leads a class discussion and makes concluding remarks.

Application (2–4 minutes): What did I learn from this experience? How will I use this information in the future?

Sharing: Volunteers give their answers to the application section.

Feedback Sheet

For each of the steps below, indicate where the initiator did well, and where he or she could improve.

Step 1. Did the initiator maintain ownership of the problem?
(positive)   (improvement)

Step 2. Did the initiator have and implement a well-thought-out XYZ *plan?*
(positive)   (improvement)

Did the initiator *persist* until the responder acknowledged the problem?
(positive)   (improvement)

Step 3. Did the initiator get the responder to *agree* to a change or solution?
(positive)   (improvement)

PART

III

Developing
Employees

9

Hiring Employees

Key Terms   To achieve our objectives in this chapter, it is important that you understand the following 15 key terms. They are presented in the order in which they appear in the chapter. The list of key terms also appears in alphabetical order in the end-of-chapter review.

human resource planning	structured interview	open-ended question
job analysis	unstructured interview	probing question
job description	semistructured interview	hypothetical question
job specifications	closed-ended question	interview preparation steps
recruiting		interviewing steps
selection		

Kristy Hammer just found out something that scares her. She is going to be responsible for hiring two new hosts for the restaurant where she is supervisor of the serving staff. No one told her that staffing was going to be a part of her job. Luckily, she has a sympathetic manager to whom she can turn for advice. "Neena, this has really got my mind going in a lot of different directions. I mean, don't I have to be really careful how I word interview questions, with the EEO laws and all? I don't know anything about those laws! And what questions should I ask, anyway? How can I be sure I'm being fair, but—more important—how can I be sure that the people I hire won't turn out to be rotten employees?"

Could you answer all of Kristy's questions? They are all both typical and quite important. What was wrong with the planning here? Should something like this take a supervisor completely by surprise?

I. Human Resource Staffing

Staffing is one of the five functions of supervision. In Chapter 1 we defined staffing as the process of selecting, orienting, training, and evaluating employees. Now, we will look at each step in staffing in depth. In this chapter we will discuss selecting employees. In Chapter 10 we will discuss orienting and training, and in Chapter 12 we will discuss evaluating employees.

We will begin by examining reasons that employee selection is important, human resource planning, and working with the human resource or personnel department.

Why Employee Selection Is Important

Employee selection involves choosing the right person for the job. As we will see, it is vital to organizational success.

- Nobody wants a company staffed with mediocre people. Organizational success depends on attracting and retaining competent people.[1]

- According to a Princeton University study, 80 percent of all Americans are in the wrong job. In addition, in this century we are facing the largest decrease ever in the growth of the labor force, while the number of jobs continues to increase.[2]

- According to the Bureau of National Affairs, the attrition rate for new hires is 52 percent.[3] One of every two new employees does not stay on the job for one year. This is a national average; you may have a higher or lower turnover rate in your department. In some industries, such as fast foods, the rate greatly exceeds 52 percent.

- It is not unusual for a manufacturer to spend over $4,000 hiring an assembly worker, and over $10,000 for a technician, engineer, or programmer.[4]

- Discrimination lawsuits over hiring policies have cost companies millions of dollars.

A supervisor's success depends on his or her employees. Hiring the right person for the right job directly affects the department's and organization's productivity.

Human Resource Planning

Human resource planning *is the process of ensuring that the organization or department has the necessary people to attain its objectives.* The term *necessary people* refers to the correct number of employees who have the right skills when they are needed. Supervisors should have input in human resource planning, but they often do not. Human resource planning is a sequential process involving three major inputs:

Inputs

1. The organization's purpose and strategic objectives and plans. If the strategy calls for growth, new employees will be needed. If it calls for retrenchment, layoffs may be necessary. Or some departments may grow while others are shrinking, requiring both hiring and layoffs.

2. The environment. Competition, customers, technology, government, suppliers, the economy, and other environmental factors affect the supply of labor and the organization's ability to attract and retain workers.

3. The organization's sales forecast. Sales directly affect the number of employees needed. Some organizations tend to hire during boom periods and lay off during slack times.

Analysis of Current Human Resources

When planning human resources, an analysis of the present work force is conducted to determine ability, training needs, and possible candidates for future positions. Employees must be evaluated to determine who might be promoted. Often a replacement chart is used that lists years of experience, level of performance, and promotability. The chart is used to identify replacements for retirees and in cases of unexpected employee turnover or planned expansion.

Forecasting Future Human Resource Needs

Given the organization's strategy, environmental and sales forecasts, and current human resource analyses, the number and types of employees needed for the long and short run can be forecast. Budgets must be developed for selecting and training the necessary employees.[5]

Supervisors may have to forecast their departmental human resource needs. This can be done by following the four steps listed.

1. Determine your department's production requirements. The sales forecast is usually the basis for production levels. Assume your department has to produce 10,000 units per month over the next three months.

2. Calculate the number of hours it takes to produce 10,000 units. Staff experts such as time and motion analysts or cost accountants may develop a standard rate of employee hours needed to produce certain quantities in your department. If such a study is not available, use past records to estimate the number of hours. Industry averages may also be available to help you determine how long it should take to produce the units. Assume the standard is 15 minutes per unit or four units per hour; it will take 2,500 hours to produce 10,000 units a month ($10,000 \div 4$).

3. Calculate the number of employees needed to produce 10,000 units. Divide the number of production hours (2,500) by the number of work hours per month. Assume a 40-hour work week. If you have a high rate of employee absence or downtime, or other factors that take away work hours, deduct them from the average work week. Assume that you lose two hours per week per employee so that each employee works 38 hours per week times 4½ weeks per month, which equals 171 hours per month. It will take 14.6 employees (2,500 production hours $\div$ 171 work hours = 14.619) to produce 10,000 units per month.

4. Determine the amount of support your employees will need. You may need other departments (setup, maintenance, secretarial, and so on) to assist your employees in producing the 10,000 units per month for the next three months. Other departments may have a waiting list, so get your request in as early as possible.[6]

Once you know the number of employees needed (14.6 in the previous example), you can compare it to the current number of employees. Assume you have 14 employees; you could have employees work overtime. Assume you currently have 13 employees; you may want to request additional help.

As a supervisor, you may not be involved in selecting employees. The human resource department, your boss, or both may select your employees for you. However, in this chapter we will assume that you will be involved and have the final say as to who is offered the positions in your department.

You may need to replace employees who are promoted, who transfer, who retire, who get fired, or who leave for any number of reasons. Or your department may expand and you'll need new employees.

Working with the Human Resource Department

The *human resource department* is a current term for the *personnel department*, although both titles are still used. The human resource services offered vary from organization to organization and often depend on the size of the firm. Human

LEARNING
OBJECTIVE
1. Describe the human
resource planning process.

resources is a staff department intended to help line managers do their jobs. Get to know what services are offered and use them. In many cases, you will be required to work with the human resource department in selecting employees, perhaps filling out a written requisition before human resources will begin to recruit employees.

CONNECTIONS

1. Give several reasons, other than those stated in the text, why staffing skills are important to supervisors.

2. Explain how human resource planning is done by a specific supervisor, perhaps one you have worked for.

II. Job Analysis

Before employee recruiting begins, you must determine the nature of the position you're offering and the skills needed to do the job. This will involve job analysis, job descriptions, and job specifications, all of which are discussed in this section.

Human resource planning helps determine the number of people needed, but it does not specify how the job will be done. **Job analysis** *determines what the job entails and what qualifications are needed to perform the job.* In other words, a job analysis results in separate parts: job description and job specifications. A job analysis is used in four ways.

1. The job analysis determines employee compensation. How much the person will be paid must be decided before an employee is hired.

2. The job analysis is the prerequisite for recruiting and selecting employees. It states what the job applicant will actually do and what qualifications are needed to do the job.

3. The job analysis is the prerequisite for determining training needs. Often people with the specific skills needed cannot be hired, so company training will be necessary. Even when experienced workers are hired, they often need to be trained to work in the specific department or organizational environment.

4. The job analysis is also the prerequisite for evaluating employee performance. The job description states the expected level of performance. A supervisor must determine whether employees are meeting or exceeding these standards. This performance appraisal, in turn, is the basis for raises, promotions, transfers, training, and development. The performance appraisal form used by the supervisor should be based on the job analysis. Employees should have input into the job analysis and performance appraisal form for motivational reasons.

The job analysis can be performed by an expert in this field, by the supervisor of the job, by employees who hold the job, or by a combination of these people. Job analysis should be high on the supervisor's list of responsibilities, but often it is not.

The job analyst can observe an employee performing the job, interview the employee about the job, have the employee fill out a job questionnaire, or have the employee keep a log of what he or she actually does and when. A combination of these methods may also be used.

The Position Analysis Questionnaire (PAQ) is popular for job analysis. The PAQ contains 194 questions that require specific answers. The answers serve as the basis for the job description and job specifications, which will be discussed shortly.

The Dictionary of Occupational Titles (DOT), published by the federal government, may also be used. It contains information on over 20,000 jobs. Each job is coded to enable an analyst to describe its "functions." The functions determine the degree of complexity in terms of working with people, data, and things. The DOT information is often adjusted for the specific job and presented in a format appropriate for the organization.

Job Descriptions

The first part of the job analysis results in a job description, which tells an employee what the job entails. A **job description** *states the basic tasks and responsibilities of a position.* Job descriptions generally include:

- The job title. (Clerk, bookkeeper, technician, etc.)
- Supervision. (Who you report to; who, if anyone, reports to you.)
- Location. (Where the job is performed—shop, office, etc.)
- Tasks, duties, activities, etc. (What the person actually does on the job.)
- Performance standards. (The level of acceptable performance, e.g., the sale of $100,000 worth of merchandise per year.)
- Working conditions. (It specifies any hazards, heat, noise, etc.)
- Tools, equipment, materials, etc. (Typewriters, computers, forklifts, etc.)

As a supervisor, you may be involved in developing job descriptions for your employees.

Job Specifications

The second part of job analysis results in developing job specifications. **Job specifications** *identify the qualifications needed to perform a job satisfactorily.* The specifications answer the question, "What type of people are needed?" There are two methods commonly used to determine job specifications. The most popular method is the educated guess. Supervisors and/or human-resource specialists decide what they think it takes to do a job. They may use sources like the DOT or job specifications from other organizations. The second method is statistical analysis. It involves testing workers to determine which traits distinguish successful from unsuccessful performers. The traits identified become part of the job specification. Job specifications may include:

- Skills and ability. (Type 60 words per minute.)
- Credentials. (College degree, teacher certification.)
- Training. (Trained to operate XYZ machine.)
- Experience. (Having held the same or a similar job for a certain period of time, usually stated in years of experience.)
- Personal qualities. (Good judgment, initiative, personality, ambition.)
- Physical effort. (Able to lift 50-pound bags.)
- Sensory demands. (Specific level of sight, hearing, smell.)

When determining job specifications, it may be helpful to use Kepner-Tregoe analysis, identifying must and want criteria (as discussed in Chapter 5). For example, a high school diploma is required (must) and a college degree is preferred (want).

One thing not listed on the job specifications is the personal traits needed to "fit in" with the department. Not getting along with peers—not fitting in—is the most common reason employees are unhappy on the job.[7] The author recalls one job interview that was so informal it seemed more like a social encounter. He

EXHIBIT 9-1

JOB DESCRIPTION

DEPARTMENT: Plant Engineering

JOB TITLE: Lead Sheet Metal Specialist

JOB DESCRIPTION:

Responsible for the detailed direction, instruction, and leading of sheet metal department personnel in the construction and repair of a wide variety of sheet metal equipment. Also must perform similar related or more complex phases of the work most of the time. Receives verbal or written instructions from foreman as to sequence and type of jobs or special methods to be used. Allocates work to members of the group. Directs the layout, fabrication, assembly, and removal of sheet metal units according to drawings or sketches and generally accepted trade procedures. Obtains material or supplies needed for specific jobs according to standard procedures. Trains new employees, as directed, regarding metalworking procedures and safe working practices. Checks all work performed by the group. Usually makes necessary contacts for the group with supervision or engineering personnel. May report irregularities to higher supervision but has no authority to hire, fire, or discipline other employees. Must be thoroughly experienced and skilled in the performance of all types of sheet metal work performed by the group.

LEARNING OBJECTIVE

2. Explain the content and use of the job description and job specifications.

later realized that the potential boss knew he was qualified; but the boss really wanted to know whether the author would fit in with the department members and whether the students would feel comfortable with him. When selecting employees be sure to consider their personal traits, appearance, and so on to be sure they will fit in with your department.[8] Exhibit 9-1 is a sample job description.

C O N N E C T I O N S

3. Complete a job analysis for a job you hold or have held; write a job description and job specifications. If you have never worked, get an example from someone who has.

III. Recruiting

After hiring needs have been determined, usually the human resource department, not the supervisor, recruits people to fill the positions. **Recruiting** *is the process of attracting qualified candidates to apply for job openings.* To fill an opening, possible candidates must first be made aware that the organization is seeking employees. They must then be persuaded to apply for the jobs. When matching jobs and people, it helps to have an adequate number of applicants to choose from. However, the recruiter should give a realistic job preview in order to get qualified people who will be satisfied and stay on the job.[9]

Most organizations divide recruitment into *general recruiting* for lower-level positions and *specific recruiting* for technical, professional, and managerial positions. Jobs in the general category tend to open frequently. Recruiting for them is usually an ongoing process. Specific recruiting is usually more time-consuming and difficult. In either case, an organization may look within its own ranks to fill a position or use external recruiting sources.

Internal Recruiting

Internal recruiting involves filling job openings with current employees. Some of the advantages of internal recruiting include the following: it costs less in many situations; it fosters performance among those who aspire to be promoted; and it helps reduce turnover. In addition, the organization knows the strengths and weaknesses of the employee and the employee is familiar with the organization.

One disadvantage of internal recruiting is the "ripple effect." The person promoted must also be replaced. Depending on the level and nature of the job, this may involve substantial shifts in personnel. One organization experienced 545 job movements to fill 195 initial openings.[10] Another disadvantage to internal recruiting is that employees who are not promoted may be dissatisfied, particularly when their new boss is an old peer. In addition, this "inbreeding" can mean that fewer new ideas are generated. Training costs tend to increase as well.

Promotions from Within: Many organizations post job openings on bulletin boards, in company newspapers, and so on. Current employees may apply or bid for the open positions. It has been estimated that as many as 90 percent of all managers are promoted from within. Promotion from within is used extensively for both general and specific recruiting.

Employee Referrals: When job openings are posted internally, employees may be encouraged to refer friends and relatives for the positions. Some organizations pay employees a finder's fee if a referral is hired. Generally, employees will only refer good candidates. Studies have shown that referral employees tend to stay on the job for a significant length of time. However, the government has stated that the referral method is not acceptable when current employees are predominantly white or male since it tends to perpetuate the present composition of the work force, resulting in discrimination.

Skills Inventory: A skills inventory is similar to a replacement chart, but is used for nonmanagement positions. The inventory contains detailed descriptions of the skills, experience, and abilities of current employees. Inventories are checked to identify qualified employees who are encouraged to apply for open positions.

External Recruiting

Some of the major advantages of external recruiting include: more potential candidates; hiring experienced workers reduces training costs; new ideas and insights are brought in; and changes are accomplished more easily.

Some of the major disadvantages of external recruiting include: the high cost; the possibility of lowered morale of present employees; the time it takes a new person to adjust to the organization; and the risk of not knowing the candidate's true ability, including potential to fit in.

External Recruiting Sources

Walk-Ins: Without actually being recruited, good candidates may come to the organization "cold" and ask for a job. According to some estimates, one in three people gets a job by walking in and asking. When no job openings exist, walk-in applications are placed on file and candidates are called when an opening occurs. Walk-ins are rare for specific recruiting. Professionals tend to send a résumé and cover letter asking for an interview.

Educational Institutions: Recruiting also takes place at high schools, vocational/technical schools, and colleges. Several schools offer career planning and placement services to aid the students and potential employers.

Advertising: It has been estimated that some 90 percent of organizations that recruit use advertising. It is important to use the appropriate source to reach

EXHIBIT 9-2   **RECRUITING SOURCES**

Internal Sources

Promotion from within
Employee referrals
Skills inventory

External Sources

Walk-ins
Educational institutions
Advertising
Agencies
Executive recruiters

qualified candidates. A newspaper is good for most positions, but professional and trade magazines may be more suitable for specific recruiting.

Agencies: There are three major types of agencies: (1) Temporary agencies, like Kelly Services, provide part- or full-time help for limited periods. They are useful for replacing employees who will be out for a short period of time or for supplementing the regular work force during busy periods. (2) Public agencies; there are state employment services nationwide. They generally provide job candidates to employers at no direct cost. (3) Private employment agencies. They are privately owned and charge a fee for their service, which is paid either by the employer or the candidate. Agencies are good for general recruiting and for some specific recruiting.

Executive Recruiters: They are often referred to as "headhunters." They specialize in recruiting managers and/or those with specific technical skills, like engineers and computer experts. They tend to charge the employer, rather than the employee, for their services. They are often used as a last resort when employers cannot find a qualified applicant on their own.

Exhibit 9–2 lists the internal and external sources of recruiting.

LEARNING OBJECTIVE

3. List and explain several internal and external recruiting sources.

CONNECTIONS

4. Identify the recruiting source used to hire you for one or more jobs. If you have never worked, get an example from someone who has.

IV. The Selection Process

Once candidates are recruited, one must be selected to fill the position. **Selection** *is the process of choosing the most qualified applicant recruited for a job.* No set sequence is universally followed. Organizations may even use different selection methods for different jobs. In this section, we will discuss some common selection methods: the application form, screening interviews, testing, background and reference checks, interviewing, and the physical examination. Bear in mind that these are not mutually exclusive. Several will be used in combinations dictated by the job in question.

Application Form

As part of the selection process, the recruited applicants will be asked to complete an application. Organizations may use different application forms for different jobs. In specific recruiting, candidates may be asked to send in a résumé, which may replace the application. The application form typically includes the following information:

- Personal data: name, address, telephone number, social security number, medical data, and so forth.
- Education: schools attended with dates, majors, and certificates or degrees earned.
- Experience: previous employers, job titles, duties, dates employed, salary, supervisor, reason for leaving, and so on.
- Skills: machines operated, certifications, and so forth.
- References: the names of (usually) three people who can vouch for the applicant in some way, with their addresses, telephone numbers, occupations, and relationship to the candidate.

The selection process can be thought of as a series of obstacles that the applicant must overcome to be offered the job. The first obstacle is typically the application. The data on it are compared to the job specifications. If they match, the applicant may progress to the next obstacle; if they do not, that person is out of the running.

Screening Interview

Specialists in the human resource department often conduct screening interviews to select the top candidates who will continue on in the selection process. This is especially helpful in saving the supervisor time when there are large numbers of candidates.

Testing

Tests can be used to predict job success. Tests must meet Equal Employment Opportunity (EEO) guidelines for validity and reliability. Illegal tests can result in lawsuits.

    Tests should not be the sole criterion for selection. Some people do not test well. Tests also do not measure motivation, and employees will not perform well unless they are motivated to do a good job.[11] If tests are used they should only be used to assess against the specific job criteria. The major types of tests include the following:

Achievement Tests

An achievement test measures actual performance. What is measured are skills that can be learned. Examples of achievement tests include a typing test, a programming test, a driver's test, or a final exam in college. People who do well on this type of test should do well on the job.

Aptitude Tests

Rather than measuring actual performance, the aptitude test measures potential to do the job. Intelligence quotient (IQ) tests are aptitude tests. They are used by the Dallas Cowboys and other National Football League teams as predictors of a player's ability to learn the plays and to be successful in the league.

Personality Tests

Personality tests measure or describe personality dimensions such as emotional maturity, self-confidence, objectivity, and subjectivity. Examples include the Rorschach inkblot tests and the Edwards Personal Preference test.

Interest Tests

These tests measure interest in various kinds of activities. It is assumed that people perform best at what interests them. Examples include the Strong-Campbell Interest Inventory and the Kuder Preference Record.

Additional Tests

The primary purpose of testing is to predict how well an applicant might perform in a given job. Some organizations test potential employees for other reasons.

Drug Tests: Drug testing is becoming more common. In a survey conducted by Taiani and Bolz of Indiana University of Pennsylvania, nearly half of the major companies responding required urine tests of all job applicants and current employees.[12] The government also administers drug tests to candidates for certain jobs. This is controversial; some claim drug tests are a violation of privacy.

AIDS Tests: Some states, such as California, Wisconsin, and Florida, prohibit AIDS testing of job candidates. Even when it is permissible, AIDS testing is questionable because it does not reveal whether a person has the disease. It only shows whether the person was exposed to the AIDS virus. In addition, an organization using AIDS testing may be charged with discriminating against the handicapped. The risk of AIDS in the workplace is a controversial issue. However, it has been definitively determined that AIDS is *not* contracted through casual contact such as that (generally) occurring in the workplace.

Some organizations use assessment centers for testing. We will discuss this in the next chapter.

Background and Reference Checks

A background check verifies the information on a candidate's application form or résumé. It has been estimated that up to one-half of all applications contain false or erroneous material. References are used on the assumption that past performance is a good predictor of future success. Unfortunately, due to privacy legislation, many organizations will only verify employment and give the job title, dates of employment, and last salary, but will make no statements concerning the candidate's performance. People are more apt to give more accurate references orally, rather than in writing. Calling for a reference might get you the information you want.

Interviewing

The interview is costly and inefficient, and is usually an invalid predictor of job performance. Different interviewers often evaluate the same candidate differently. Yet it is the most heavily weighted selection criterion.[13] A human resource manager for Xerox told the author that the interview was given about 60 percent of the weight in the selection process. The interview is usually the final hurdle in the selection process. The other methods are usually considered supplemental to the interview.

The interview allows two-way communication between the candidate and the supervisor or organization. It gives both the applicant and the employer a chance to determine whether there is a match that should end in employment. The interview gives the candidate a chance to learn about the job and organization. Therefore, it is important for the interviewer to give the candidate a realistic job preview (RJP).[14] The RJP helps ensure the appropriate match between people and jobs. (The RJP will be explained later in this chapter.) The interview also gives a supervisor a chance to learn things about candidates that can't be obtained from an application, test, or references, such as the candidate's ability to communicate, personality, appearance, and motivation. We will discuss aspects of an interview in greater detail in the next two sections.

Physical Examination

The job offer is often contingent on the candidate's ability to pass a physical examination. Several organizations make arrangements for candidates to be examined by a designated company doctor. The physical exam is used to determine whether the candidate can perform the job, to protect other employees from contagious disease, to establish a health record, and to protect the organization from unjustified worker's compensation claims.

Selection

After obtaining information using the selection methods discussed, compare the candidates without bias, and decide who is best for the job, next best, and so on. Kepner-Tregoe analysis (discussed in Chapter 5) can help you make an objective comparison.

   Contact the most qualified candidate and offer him or her the job. If the person asks for time to think about it, set a deadline for the answer. If the candidate does not accept the job, or accepts but leaves after a short period of time, contact the next best candidate. If a qualified candidate is not available, you should try to determine why. Is the salary too low? Are your expectations too high? You may need to begin recruiting again or obtain the services of an agency or executive recruiter.

LEARNING OBJECTIVE

4. Describe the selection process components.

C O N N E C T I O N S

> **5.** Identify the selection methods used for a job you were offered. List each method from the selection process, and state whether it was used or not. If a test was used, be sure to specify the type of test it was. If you have never worked, get an example from someone who has.

V. Legal Considerations in Staffing

In this section, we will discuss laws affecting staffing and the issue of discrimination.

Laws Affecting Staffing

You are aware that an organization cannot discriminate against a minority. Who is legally considered a minority? Just about anyone who is not a white male of European heritage with an adequate education is considered a minority. The Equal Employment Opportunity Commission (EEOC) guidelines list Hispanics, Asians, blacks, native Americans, and Alaskan natives as minorities. Women are also protected by law from discrimination in employment, but they are not considered a minority. Disadvantaged young people, handicapped workers, and persons over 40 and up to 70 years of age are also protected.

The EEOC specifically protects minorities. It has 47 field offices across the nation. The commission offers seminars for employees who feel they aren't getting a fair shake, as well as an around-the-clock hotline (1-800-USA-EEOC) to provide information on employee rights.[15]

As this information suggests, organizations are not always completely free to hire whomever they want. The human resources department is usually responsible for seeing that the organization complies with the law.

The two pieces of legislation that have the greatest effect on staffing are the Equal Employment Opportunity (EEO) and Affirmative Action (AA) amendments. EEO, a 1972 amendment to the Civil Rights Act of 1964, prohibits employment discrimination on the basis of race, sex, religion, color, or national origin, and applies to virtually all private and public organizations that employ 15 or more persons. AA, a 1977 amendment to Executive Orders of 1965 and 1968, requires firms doing business with the federal government to make special efforts to recruit, hire, and promote women and members of minority groups. Companies with over $50,000 in federal contracts and more than 50 employees must have a written Affirmative Action Program (AAP).

Some of the other laws affecting staffing include the Equal Pay Act of 1963, Age Discrimination in Employment Act of 1967, Vocational Rehabilitation Act of 1973 (applies to the handicapped), Vietnam Era Veterans' Readjustment Act of 1974, Title VII Sex Harassment and Pregnancy Discrimination, and the Americans with Disability Act of 1991.

Violation of any of these laws can lead to investigation by the EEOC or to legal action. Courts find discrimination when selection criteria are vague, elusive, unstructured, undefined, or poorly conceived.[16] As a supervisor, you should be familiar with your organization's EEO and AAP guidelines.[17]

Discrimination

On the application and during interviews, discriminatory questions are illegal. There are two rules of thumb in deciding whether a question is discriminatory. (1) Every question should be job related. You should have a reason relating to the selection process for asking each question. (2) Any general question should be asked of all candidates. We will discuss in greater detail what you can and cannot ask during a job interview in order to disqualify applicants.

Name

Can Ask: Current legal name and whether the candidate has ever worked under a different name.

Cannot Ask: Maiden name or whether the person has changed his or her name.

Address

Can Ask: Current residence and length of residence.

Cannot Ask: Whether the candidate owns or rents his or her home unless it is a bona fide occupation qualification (BFOQ) for the job.

Age

Can Ask: If the candidate is between 21 and 70, to meet job specifications. For example, an employee must be 21 to serve alcoholic beverages.

Cannot Ask: You cannot inquire about a candidate's exact age, nor can you ask to see a birth certificate. Do not ask an older person how much longer he or she plans to work before retiring.

Gender	*Can Ask:* Only if gender is a BFOQ. *Cannot Ask:* If it is not a BFOQ. To be sure you are not violating sexual harassment laws, do not ask questions or make comments remotely considered flirtatious.
Marital and Family Status	*Can Ask:* Whether the candidate can comply with the work schedule and whether the candidate's activities, responsibilities, or commitments may affect attendance requirements. The same questions should be asked of candidates of both sexes. *Cannot Ask:* To indicate marital status, or any questions regarding children or other family matters.
National Origin, Citizenship, Race, or Color	*Can Ask:* Whether the candidate is legally eligible to work in the United States, and whether he or she can prove this if hired. *Cannot Ask:* To identify national origin, citizenship, race, or color (or that of parents and other relatives).
Language	*Can Ask:* To list languages the candidate speaks or writes fluently (or both). The candidate may be asked whether he or she speaks or writes a specific language if it is a BFOQ. *Cannot Ask:* The language spoken off the job, or how the applicant learned the language.
Convictions	*Can Ask:* Whether the candidate has been convicted of a felony, and other information if the felony is job related. *Cannot Ask:* Whether the candidate has ever been arrested. (An arrest does not prove guilt.) For information regarding a conviction that is not job related.
Height and Weight	*Can Ask:* Whether the candidate meets BFOQ height or weight requirements or both, and whether this can be proved if the person is hired. *Cannot Ask:* The candidate's height or weight if it isn't a BFOQ.
Religion	*Can Ask:* Whether the candidate is a member of a specific religious group when it is a BFOQ. Whether the candidate can comply with the work schedules, or anticipated absences caused by religious observance. *Cannot Ask:* Religious preference, affiliations, or denominations.
Credit Ratings or Garnishments	*Can Ask:* If it is a BFOQ. *Cannot Ask:* If it is not a BFOQ.
Education and Work Experience	*Can Ask:* For information that is job related. *Cannot Ask:* For information that is not job related.
References	*Can Ask:* For the names of people willing to provide references or for the names of people who suggested that the candidate apply for the job. *Cannot Ask:* For a reference from a religious leader.

Military

Can Ask: For information on education and experience gained that relates to the job.

Cannot Ask: Dates and conditions of discharge. About eligibility for military service. National Guard or National Reserve Units of candidates. About experience in foreign armed services.

Organizations

Can Ask: To list membership in job-related organizations such as unions or professional or trade associations.

Cannot Ask: To identify membership in any non-job-related organization that would indicate race, religion, and so on.

Handicaps

Can Ask: Whether the candidate has any disabilities that would prevent him or her from performing the specific job.

Cannot Ask: For information that is not job related. Under the Americans with Disabilities Act, employers cannot ask applicants about any disabilities. Focus on abilities. Don't ask about medical history, work absenteeism, and past treatment for alcoholism or mental illness before you offer a position. In states where people with AIDS are protected under discrimination laws, you should not ask whether the candidate has AIDS. (A survey revealed that 88 percent of corporate department heads and 91 percent of equal employment officers at 921 companies rated handicapped employees as "good" or "excellent" workers.)[18]

LEARNING OBJECTIVE

5. Give examples of questions that you can and cannot ask before offering a candidate a job.

CONNECTIONS

6. Were you, or anyone you know of, asked illegal discriminatory questions during an interview or on an application blank? If so, specify the area or areas (age, gender, race, and so on).

VI. Interviewing

Most supervisors dislike conducting job interviews. A major reason is that they have not been trained to interview. Employees responsible for interviewing should be trained to do so within the organization. Supervisors usually don't interview frequently enough to develop the skill on their own.[19] After completing this chapter, you should be more confident about your ability and more skillful in conducting job interviews.

In this section, we will discuss the details of interviewing, including problems to avoid, types of interviews, types of questions, preparing for the interview, conducting the interview, and selecting the candidate.

Problems to Avoid

Interruptions: When you are conducting a job interview, it is important not to be interrupted. Interruptions are very distracting to you and to the candidate. Before beginning the interview, tell others not to disturb you unless it is an emergency.

Rushing: Try not to be pressured into hiring any candidate. Find the best person available.

Stereotyping: Don't prejudge or leap to conclusions. Do a thorough review of the job description and job specifications. Match the candidate to the job based on reason.

"Like Me" Syndrome: Don't look for a candidate who is your clone. People who are not like you may do an excellent job.

Halo Effect: Do not judge a candidate on the basis of one or two favorable characteristics. Look at the candidate's total qualifications.

Horn Effect: Do not judge a candidate based on one or two unfavorable characteristics. Most candidates will have both favorable and unfavorable characteristics. Make the selection on the basis of the total qualifications of all candidates.

Premature Selection: Don't make your selection based on the application or after interviewing a candidate who impressed you. Do not compare candidates after each interview. The order in which applicants are interviewed can influence you. Be open-minded during all interviews and make a choice only after all interviews are finished. Compare each candidate on each job specification.

Types of Interviews

There are three basic types of interviews. The structured and the unstructured interviews are extremes with the semistructured interview somewhere in between.

Structured Interview

In the **structured interview,** *the interviewer has a list of questions that all candidates are asked.* The structured interview is also called the *directive* or *patterned* interview. The questions are usually put on a form with space for the interviewer to record the candidate's answers. The structured form helps the interviewer control the interview. And the interviewer does not forget any points, because they are all written down.

Unstructured Interview

In the **unstructured interview,** *the interviewer has no preplanned questions or sequence of topics.* The unstructured interview is also called the *nondirective* interview. The interviewer asks open-ended questions and allows the candidate to direct the interview. Each question is often based on the candidate's last answer.

Semistructured Interview

In the **semistructured interview,** *the interviewer has a list of questions to ask, but also asks unplanned questions.* The semistructured interview is generally preferred because, although it helps ensure against discrimination in that all candidates are asked the same set of questions, it also allows the interviewer to ask each candidate questions relating to his or her own situation. The interviewer may depart from the structure, if appropriate. At the same time, using a standard set of questions makes it easier to compare candidates. And the structured questions are considered more legally valid for selection purposes.

How much structure should the supervisor use? It depends on his or her experience. The less experienced you are, the more structure you need. As you develop your interviewing skills, you can be less structured.

Other Interview Types

Group interviews are also used in which several candidates are interviewed at the same time. *Panel interviews* involve one candidate being interviewed by two or more interviewers. The group interview allows the interviewer to compare candidates head-on, and the panel interview allows a group to work together in selecting a candidate. A less popular type is the *stress interview,* in which the candidate is intentionally intimidated or put on the spot so that the interviewer can observe him or her under stress. All of these interview types may be structured, unstructured, or somewhere in between.

Types of Questions

The questions you ask give you control over the interview; they allow you to get the information you need to make your decision. Questions should not just involve restating what is on the application form; use them to verify and expand upon the information. Keep questions short.[20] Remember that all questions should have a purpose and be job related, and ask all candidates the same set of questions.

There are five types of questions you might use during an interview.

The Closed-Ended Question: The **closed-ended question** *requires a limited response and is appropriate for dealing with fixed aspects of the job.* Closed-ended questions often require a yes or no answer. Examples include the following:

- "Is there anything that will interfere with your working from 3:00 to 11:00?"
- "Are you over 21 years of age?"
- "Do you have a class one license and can you produce it if hired?"
- "Have you ever been convicted of a felony?"
- "How long have you been a grocery bagger?"
- "Do you prefer the day or night shift?"

Overusing closed-ended questions may frustrate candidates who would like a chance to explain their situations.

The Open-Ended Question: The **open-ended question** *requires an unlimited response and is appropriate for determining abilities and motivation.* An open-ended question allows a candidate to respond as he or she chooses. Avoid asking too many "why" questions; they tend to put candidates on the defensive. Ask "what" and "how" questions as well, to break the interview sequence up. Examples of open-ended questions might include these:

- "What do you know about our company?"
- "What prompted you to take the commercial course in high school?"
- "Why do you want to be a computer programmer?"
- "What is it about the job that interests you?"
- "What was your major achievement?"
- "What do you see as a major strength you can bring to our company? What is your major weakness?"
- "Explain what you did on your last job."
- "What was the reason for leaving your last job?"

The Probing Question: The **probing question** *requires a clarification response and is appropriate for improving understanding.* Probing is used in semistructured and unstructured interviews. The probing question is not planned. It is used to clarify the candidate's response to an open-ended question. Does the candidate understand the terms he or she is using? When in doubt, ask a probing question to verify the candidate's job knowledge.[21] Examples might include the following:

- "What do you mean by 'it was tough'?"
- "What was the dollar increase in sales you achieved?"
- "Can you give me an example of how you cut costs?"

- "How often did this happen?"
- "How many times were you late for work?"
- "Can you describe how it works?"

The Hypothetical Question: The **hypothetical question** *requires the candidate to describe what he or she would do and say in a given situation; it is appropriate in assessing capabilities.* Develop case situations that are critical for job success, and assess the candidate's capability for handling these situations.[22] Ask hypothetical questions that also assess the candidate's technical ability. Examples include these:

- "What would you do and say if a customer swore at you?"
- "What job would you do first: A, B, or C?" (Describe each task to determine the candidate's ability to assign priorities.)
- "What would you do if the machine broke?"
- "What would the problem be if the machine made an XYZ sound?"
- "What model would you recommend to a family of four?"
- "What temperature setting would you use for an XYZ?"

The Leading Question: The final type is the *leading question.* A leading question suggests a response. The interviewer should use a limited number of leading questions, if any. Don't lead candidates or they will tell you what you want to hear rather than give their own answers. Examples of leading questions include the following:

- "You do know how to operate the machine, don't you?"
- "You will be on time for work, won't you?"

CONNECTIONS

8. Identify the types of questions you were asked during a job interview. Write down some of the questions, identifying their types. If you have never worked, get examples from someone who has.

Preparing for the Interview

Supervisors are often ineffective at interviewing because they do not plan, or they plan poorly. Following the preparation guidelines will help you improve your interviewing skills. The **interview preparation steps** *are as follows: review the job description and specifications; plan a realistic job preview; develop questions to ask all candidates; develop a format; and develop specific questions for each candidate.*

Step 1. Review the Job Description and Specifications: You cannot effectively match the candidate to the job if you do not thoroughly understand the job. Read and become familiar with the job description and job specifications. If they are outdated, or do not exist, conduct a job analysis.

Step 2. Plan a Realistic Job Preview: Candidates should understand what the job is and what they are expected to do. They should know the good and bad points of the job. Candidates given a realistic job preview (RJP) are more likely to turn down a job offer. However, if they do accept, they are also better able to cope with the demands of the job and more likely to be satisfied with the job, and will probably remain on the job longer than candidates who are not given an RJP. The RJP helps to lower inflated job expectations.[23] Candidates will be less likely to complain that "this job isn't what I thought it would be." Plan how you will present the RJP using the job description.

MODEL 9-1   **INTERVIEW PREPARATION STEPS**

Step 1. Review the job description and specifications.

Step 2. Plan a realistic job preview.

Step 3. Develop questions to ask all candidates.

Step 4. Develop a format.

Step 5. Develop specific questions for each candidate.

Step 3. Develop Questions to Ask All Candidates: Recall that your questions should be job related, nondiscriminatory, and asked of all candidates. Use the job description and specifications to develop a few questions that relate to each requirement.[24] Use a mixture of closed-ended, open-ended, and hypothetical questions. Don't be concerned about the order of questions; just write them out at this point. As an extension of hypothetical questioning, you can have the candidate role-play a situation to see what he or she would do and say. If you want to use role playing, prepare in advance. Also, if you feel it is appropriate, you can use the devil's advocate approach to challenge or pressure a candidate to see how he or she responds.[25]

Step 4. Develop a Format: Once you have completed your list of questions, determine the sequence. Start with the easy questions.[26] One approach is to start with closed-ended questions, moving on to open-ended questions, and then to hypothetical questions; use probing questions as needed. Another approach is to structure the interview around the job description and specifications; explain each, and then ask questions relating to each responsibility.

Write out the questions in sequence, leaving space for checking off closed-ended responses, and room to make notes on the responses to open-ended and hypothetical questions. Information gained from probing questions is added where appropriate. You are guided through the interview as you record the candidate's responses on the form. Make a copy of the form for each candidate, and a few extras for future use when filling the same job, or as a reference when developing forms for other jobs.

Step 5. Develop Specific Questions for Each Candidate: Review each candidate's application. You will most likely want to verify or clarify some of the information given during the interview. Examples include the following. "I noticed that you did not list any employment during 1985; were you unemployed?" "On the application you state you had computer training; what computer were you trained to operate?" Be sure the individual questions are not discriminatory; for example, do not ask only women whether they can lift 50 pounds; this is a question for all candidates.

You can either add the individual questions to the standard form, writing them in where appropriate, or you can add a list at the end of the form. Model 9-1 lists the interview preparation steps.

Conducting the Interview

The interview should take place in a private, quiet place, without interruptions. It may be appropriate to begin the interview in an office and then tour the facilities while asking questions. Plan when the tour will take place, and what questions will be asked. Take your form if you intend to ask several questions.

Following the four guidelines listed can help you do a better job of interviewing candidates. The **interviewing steps** *include opening the interview, giving a realistic job preview, asking your questions, and closing the interview.*

MODEL 9-2

INTERVIEWING STEPS

Step 1. Open the interview.   Step 3. Ask your questions.

Step 2. Give a realistic job preview.   Step 4. Close the interview.

Step 1. Open the Interview: Develop a rapport. Put the candidate at ease by talking about some topic not related to the job. You may add a little humor when appropriate. According to Adia Personnel Services, 63 percent of the personnel executives surveyed said that humor is appropriate during job interviews.[27] But be sure the humor is not sexist, racial, offensive, or discriminatory in any way. Maintain eye contact in a way that is comfortable for you and the candidate. Use the communication skills discussed in Chapter 7.

Step 2. Give a Realistic Job Preview: Be sure the candidate understands the job requirements. Answer any questions the candidate has about the job and the organization. If the job is not what the candidate expected, or wants to do, allow the candidate to disqualify himself or herself.[28] Close the interview at that point.

Step 3. Ask Your Questions: Steps 2 and 3 can be combined if you like. Tell the candidate that you have prepared a list of questions you will be asking. Also tell him or her you plan to take notes and why.

During the interview, you should not talk more than 20 percent of the time.[29] Ask a question, and then seal your lips. Give the candidate a chance to think and respond.[30] If the candidate did not give you all the information you want or need, ask an unplanned probing question. However, if it is obvious that the candidate does not want to answer the question, don't force it. Go on to the next question or close the interview. End with a closing question such as, "I'm finished with my questions. Is there anything else you want to tell me about, or ask me?"

Step 4. Close the Interview: Do not lead candidates on. Be honest without making a decision during the interview. Thank candidates for their time, and tell them what the next step in the interview process is, if any. Tell candidates when you will contact them. For example, say, "Thank you for coming in for this interview. I will be interviewing over the next two days and will call you with my decision by Friday of this week." After the interview, be sure to jot down general impressions that were not covered by specific questions. Model 9-2 lists the interview steps.

Selecting the Candidate

LEARNING OBJECTIVE

6. List and explain the steps in interview preparation and interviewing and use these models when interviewing.

After all interviews are completed, compare each candidate's qualifications to the job specifications to determine who would be best for the job. You may use the Kepner-Tregoe analysis, as described earlier.

Contact the candidate you select. If he or she accepts the job, contact the other candidates and tell them that they were not selected. If the other candidates ask why, be sure not to give any discriminatory reasons. If you have made an objective, nondiscriminatory decision, you should be able to state the reason without fear of a discrimination charge being brought against the organization.

> ### CONNECTIONS
>
> **9.** Using Model 9-2, identify the steps used or not used when you were interviewed for a job. How could the process have been improved? If you have never worked, get an example from someone who has.

VII. Future Trends in Employment

There is a dwindling supply of labor, particularly workers under 25. The Bureau of Labor Statistics forecasts that by 1990 there will be 11 percent fewer workers aged 16 through 24 than there were in 1984. In the period from 1981 through 1995, there will have been a 20 percent drop in this age group. During the next decade, the service and retail sales sectors of the economy alone will add 9 million jobs, but the labor shortage will continue.[31]

To combat this shortage, companies like Dunkin' Donuts are redesigning their shops in an attempt to provide the same level of service with fewer people. Another trend in organizations such as Burger King is focusing on retention of the people they do hire.[32]

In spite of shortages in some areas, one survey shows that three-quarters of the nation's employers may be planning managerial and administrative cuts on top of their recent wrenching cutbacks.

Another trend is increasing use of outside contractors who work for an organization without receiving all the company benefits.[33] Temporary and part-time employees make up nearly one-quarter of the work force, with projections that this segment will continue to grow by 10 percent to 15 percent a year. Companies now want an as-needed work force.[34]

Employee leasing firms are also growing. They put employees of small businesses on their payroll and then lease them back as a way to provide better benefit packages.[35]

For the reasons discussed, the job market is changing.[36] With a growing number of job openings and a declining number of candidates to fill them, it will be increasingly difficult for the supervisor to recruit, hire, and retain good employees.

LEARNING OBJECTIVE

7. Identify some of the employment trends of the future.

CONNECTIONS

10. Give the name of an organization that uses temporary or contract help or employee leasing.

REVIEW

Select one or more methods: (1) fill in the missing key terms from memory; (2) match the key terms from the end of the review with their definitions below; (3) copy the key terms in order from the key terms at the beginning of the chapter.

_____ is the process of ensuring that the organization or department has the necessary people to attain its objectives. It is a sequential process that includes inputs, analysis of current human resources, and forecasting future human resource needs. The supervisor works with the human resource department in staffing.

_____ determines what the job entails and the qualifications needed to perform the job. It results in a _____ , which states the basic tasks and responsibilities of a position, and

_____ , which identify the qualifications needed to perform a job satisfactorily.

_____ is the process of attracting qualified candidates to apply for job openings. Recruiting may be general or specific. Internal recruiting sources include promotion from within, employee referrals, and skills inventories. External recruiting sources include walk-ins, educational institutions, advertising, agencies, and executive recruiters.

_____ is the process of choosing the most qualified applicant recruited for the job. Common selection methods include the application form, the screening interview, testing (achievement, aptitude, assessment center testing, personality, interest, and drug and AIDS testing), background and reference checks, the interview, and the physical examination.

There are several legal factors to consider when staffing. Although a supervisor may ask for information such as name, address, age, sex, marital and family status, national origin, citizenship, race or color, language, convictions, height and weight, religion, credit rating or salary garnishment, education and work experience, military service, membership in organizations, and handicaps/AIDS, these questions should be job related and nondiscriminatory.

Interview problems to avoid include interruptions, rushing, stereotyping, the "like me" syndrome, the halo and horn effects, and making a selection before interviewing all candidates. There are three major types of interviews. In the _____ , the interviewer has a list of questions that all candidates are asked. In the _____ , the interviewer has no preplanned questions or sequence of topics. And in the _____ , the interviewer has a list of questions to ask, but also asks unplanned questions. There are also group, panel, and stress interviews. Five major types of questions include the _____ , which requires a limited response and is appropriate for dealing with fixed aspects of the job; the _____ , which requires an unlimited response and is appropriate for determining abilities and motivation; the _____ , requiring a clarification response and being appropriate for improving understanding; the _____ , which requires the candidate to describe what he or she would do and say in a given situation, appropriate in assessing capabilities; and the leading question, which suggests a response. The   are as follows: review the job description and specifications; plan a realistic job preview; develop a list of questions to ask all candidates; develop a format; and develop specific questions for each candidate. The _____ are opening the interview, giving a realistic job preview, asking your questions, and closing the interview.

The job market is changing. The supply of labor is dwindling, with no sign of a letup. Companies are using more part-time, temporary, and contract employees. Employee leasing is also growing.

KEY TERMS

closed-ended question

human resource planning

hypothetical question

interview preparation steps

interviewing steps

job analysis

job description

job specifications

open-ended question

probing question

recruiting

selection

semistructured interview

structured interview

unstructured interview

REFERENCES

1. "In Quest of the Ideal Employee," *Nation's Business,* November 1986, p. 38.

2. M. Rutigliano, "Naisbitt and Aburdene on Reinventing the Workplace," *Management Review,* October 1985, p. 35.

3. Elizabeth Dickerson, "The Hiring Decision: Assessing Fit into the Workplace," *Management Review,* January 1987, p. 24.

4. Lester Bittel, *What Every Supervisor Should Know* (New York: McGraw-Hill, 1985), p. 187.

5. R.W. Beatty and C.E. Schneier, *Personnel Administration: An Experiential Skill Building Approach* (Reading, MA: Addison-Wesley, 1981).

6. Adapted from Bittel, *What Every Supervisor Should Know,* pp. 188–89.

7. "Fitting in Determines Job Success," *Training and Development Journal,* August 1986, p. 11.

8. Dickerson, "Hiring Decision," pp. 26–27.

9. Mary Suszko and James Breaugh, "The Effects of Realistic Job Previews on Applicant's Self-Selection and Employee Turnover, Satisfaction, and Coping Ability," *Journal of Management,* Winter 1986, p. 513.

10. E.H. Burack and N.J. Mathys, *Human Resource Planning: A Pragmatic Approach to Manpower Staffing and Development* (Lake Forest, IL: Brace-Park Press, 1980).

11. Dickerson, "Hiring Decision," p. 24.

12. "Drug Tests Spread," *The Wall Street Journal,* April 7, 1987, p. 1.

13. Stephen Cohen and Frank Gump, "Using Simulations to Improve Selection Decisions," *Training and Development Journal,* December 1984, p. 85.

14. Suszko and Breaugh, "Effects of Realistic Job Previews," p. 513.

15. Kirkland Ropp, "How the Courts Affect Management Policy," *Personnel Administration,* January 1987, pp. 45, 47.

16. Victoria Corcoran, "Surviving the Preemployment Legal Minefield," *Management Review,* October 1986, p. 37.

17. Ibid.

18. "The Handicapped Worker," *The Wall Street Journal,* May 19, 1987, p. 1.

19. Darrel Brown, "Shaping Your Job Interview Techniques," *Supervisory Management,* August 1985, p. 29.

20. Milt Grassell, "The Power of Questions," *Nation's Business,* November 1986, p. 58.

21. Brown, "Shaping Your Job Interview Techniques," p. 31.

22. Dickerson, "Hiring Decision," p. 28.

23. Suszko and Breaugh, "Effects of Realistic Job Previews," pp. 513–23.

24. Brown, "Shaping Your Job Interview Techniques," p. 30.

25. Dickerson, "Hiring Decision," p. 28.

26. Grassell, "Power of Questions," p. 58.

27. "Going for Laughs," *The Wall Street Journal,* July 16, 1987, p. 31.

28. Brown, "Shaping Your Job Interview Techniques," p. 32.

29. Ibid., p. 30.

30. Grassell, "Power of Questions," p. 58.

31. Dale Feuer, "Coping with the Labor Shortage," *Training,* March 1987, pp. 64–65.

32. Ibid., p. 65.

33. Amanda Bennett, "Growing Small," *The Wall Street Journal,* May 4, 1987, p. 1.

34. Ibid.

35. "Employee Leasing Firms Regroup after Tax Law Changes," *The Wall Street Journal,* February 24, 1987, p. 1.

36. Bennett, "Growing Small," p. 1.

APPLICATION SITUATIONS

Job Description or Job Specifications

AS 9–1

Below are five statements. Identify each as either of the following:

a. job description   *b.* job specification

_____ 1. The employee must produce at least 50 units per day.

_____ 2. The employee will work in the generator room.

_____ 3. The employee must be a high school graduate.

_____ 4. The employee will operate an IBM personal computer.

_____ 5. The employee should have two years of retail sales experience.

Recruiting Sources

AS 9–2

Select the major recruiting source that should be used for each of the five job openings described below.

Internal Sources

a. promotion from within

b. employee referrals

c. skills inventory

d. walk-in

External Sources

e. educational institutions

f. advertising

g. agencies

h. executive recruiters

_____ 6. One of your workers was hurt on the job and will be out for one month. The person must be replaced.

_____ 7. One of the first-line supervisors is retiring in two months.

_____ 8. You need an engineer who has very specific qualifications. There are very few people who can do the job.

_____ 9. Your sales manager likes to hire young people without experience in order to train them to sell using a unique approach.

_____ 10. Your maintenance department needs a person to perform routine cleaning services.

Legal Questions

AS 9–3

Identify the five questions below as:

a. legal (can be asked)   *b.* illegal (cannot be asked)

_____ 11. What is your mother tongue, or the principal language you speak?

_____ 12. Are you married or single?

_____ 13. Are you a member of the Teamsters Union?

_____ 14. Have you been arrested for stealing on the job?

_____ 15. Can you prove you are legally eligible to work?

Types of Questions

AS 9–4

Identify the five questions below as being one of the following:

a. closed-ended   *c.* probing

b. open-ended   *d.* hypothetical

_____ 16. When was the last time you did this type of task?

_____ 17. Would you prefer to be a cashier or a bagger?

_____ 18. How did you find out about the job opening?

_____ 19. Why should I hire you for the job?

_____ 20. If you were playing second, with two outs, and there were runners on first and second bases when the ball was hit to you, what would you do?

Selecting a Payroll Manager

Carla Smith, the controller in a large organization, sent a request to the human resources department for a payroll manager. She asked that they recruit and select the top three candidates, send her copies of their applications and any other pertinent information, and set up the three interviews for her.

The assignment was given to Jack and Sue, who had the following conversation:

JACK: John Goldberg is retiring in three months.

SUE: His payroll department handles a large volume of work.

JACK: We've staffed more positions in his department than any other department in the company.

SUE: It's not our fault people leave. We've recruited some excellent people for John.

JACK: Let's develop the job description and specifications for the payroll manager position.

SUE: OK, the candidate should have a B.S. degree in accounting.

JACK: The person gets to work in a nicely heated and air-conditioned office.

SUE: The candidate should have excellent accounting skills.

JACK: The candidate will have to maintain all the payroll records and pay all the organization's people on time.

SUE: You just reminded me of the many times that the payroll department had to work overtime to get the checks ready on time. And the few times we got paid late. Everyone was so mad!

JACK: Give me another idea we can use.

SUE: The person must be computer literate.

JACK: The person will report to the controller and supervise 10 employees.

SUE: The payroll department is at corporate headquarters.

JACK: Sound decision-making skills are needed.

SUE: Well, I guess that does it.

JACK: Yes, let's decide on a recruiting method and go through the selection process.

Sue and Jack recruited and selected the following finalists for Carla to interview:

- Mark Brown, B.S. in accounting, grade-point average "A –." Mark has two years' experience in auditing as a staff accountant for a large certified public accounting (CPA) firm. His supervisor said, "Mark is a very intelligent young man; he catches on quickly. He works hard and pushes others to do the same. Mark has done an excellent job for our firm, and I'm sure he'll do the same for yours."

- Sara Soucy, B.S. in accounting, grade-point average "C +." She has three years of experience working as the assistant tax collector for a nearby city. Most of her time is spent handling complaints and supervising five clerical workers. Sara's supervisor said, "Sara is successful because she enjoys working with people. She has excellent supervisory skills. Sara keeps everything running smoothly. I hate to lose her. I'm confident she will be successful at the job of her choice."

- Mike Jones, B.S. in accounting, grade-point average "B +." He has four years of accounting experience, two in budgeting and two in cost accounting. Mike's supervisor said, "Mike has a good analytical mind. He has developed more accurate accounting methods in several areas of operations. I highly recommend him."

Answer the following questions using the space between the questions to explain your answers.

———— 1. Jack and Sue performed a job analysis.
   a. true   *b.* false

———— 2. Jack's statements were primarily job
   a. analysis   *b.* descriptions   *c.* specifications

———— 3. Sue's statements were primarily job
   a. analysis   *b.* descriptions   *c.* specifications

———— 4. Which external recruiting source should they have used? (Assume no internal candidates are available.)
   a. walk-ins   *d.* agencies
   b. educational institutions   *e.* executive recruiters
   c. advertising

———— 5. A screening interview should be used in the selection process.
   a. true   *b.* false

———— 6. Testing should be used in the selection process.
   a. true   *b.* false

———— 7. It would be ————————————— to ask candidates whether they belong to any community groups or clubs.
   a. legal   *b.* illegal

———— 8. Jack and Sue's primary mistake (or mistakes) was (were):
   a. interruptions   *c.* stereotyping   *e.* halo effect
   b. rushing   *d.* like-me syndrome *f.* horn effect

———— 9. Based on the case information, the payroll manager faces the following problem or problems:
   a. poorly trained employees   *f.* *a* and *b*
   b. fatigued employees   *g.* *b* and *c*
   c. deadlines not met   *h.* *c* and *e*
   d. poor work standards   *i.* *a*, *b*, and *c*
   e. high turnover   *j.* *b*, *c*, and *d*

_____ 10. As you know, you should not select a candidate before the interviews are over. However, assume you cannot interview the candidates in this case. Select the most qualified candidate for the payroll manager position.

    a. Mark   *b.* Sara   *c.* Mike

11. Explain your selection in question 10.

12. Did Jack and Sue do an effective staffing job? Explain your answer.

PREPARATION FOR IN-CLASS SKILL-BUILDING EXERCISE

Interview Questions

SB 9–1

Part 1. Open-Ended Questions: Below are five closed-ended questions. Use the space provided to rephrase each, making it an open-ended question.

1. Do you work well under pressure?

2. Do you think you will like the job?

3. Do you require a lot of supervision?

4. Do you get along well with people?

5. Do you want to tell me anything else about yourself?

Part 2. Probing Questions: Even though you ask an open-ended question, you may get a closed-ended answer. Assume you asked your five open-ended questions in part 1 and got the closed-ended responses below. Use the space provided to write probing questions that will get the candidate to elaborate on his or her answers.

1. Pressure doesn't bother me.

2. I just like working.

3. I don't need anyone telling me what to do.

4. Everyone likes me.

5. No.

IN-CLASS SKILL-BUILDING EXERCISE

Interview Questions

SB 9–1

Objective: To develop your ability to ask open-ended and probing questions during a job interview.

Experience: You will share and discuss your questions with class members.

Materials: The completed questions in the Preparation for Skill-Building Exercise 9–1.

Procedure 1
(10–40 minutes)

- *Option A.* Volunteers read their questions to the class for comments or questions. The instructor or a student may write several of the questions on the board.

- *Option B.* Break into groups of five or six members and share and discuss your questions.
- *Option C–1.* Same as option B, with one group member presenting the group's best question for each alternative to the entire class.
- *Option C–2.* Each spokesperson writes the group's 10 questions on the board.

Conclusion: The instructor may lead a class discussion and make concluding remarks.

Application (2–4 minutes): What did I learn from this experience? How will I use this knowledge in the future?

Sharing: Volunteers give their answers to the application section.

PREPARATION FOR IN-CLASS SKILL-BUILDING EXERCISE

Selecting a Tennis Coach

SB 9–2

You are in your first year as athletic director of a local high school. While planning your human resource needs, you realize the position of tennis coach will be open. You must staff the position.

The compensation for the job is set in the budget. It is to be paid in one lump sum at the end of the season. It is competitive with the pay of other tennis coaches in the area.

Recruiting

Because you have no recruiting budget, you do some internal recruiting and contact some athletic directors in your area to spread the word about the opening. You recruit three candidates for the coaching position. Below is a brief listing of their qualifications.

Candidate A. Has been a history teacher at your school for 10 years. This person was the tennis coach for two years. It's been five years since the teacher coached the team. You don't know why the candidate stopped coaching or how good a job was done. Candidate A never played competitive tennis. However someone told you the candidate plays regularly and is pretty good. You guess the teacher is about 35 years old.

Candidate B. Works as a supervisor on the 11 P.M. to 7 A.M. shift for a local business. This candidate has never coached before. However, the person was a star player in high school and college. Candidate B still plays in local tournaments and you see the name in the paper now and then. You guess this candidate is about 25 years old.

Candidate C. Has been a basketball coach and physical education teacher at a nearby high school for the past five years. The person has a master's degree in physical education. You figure it will take the person 20 minutes to get to your school. Candidate C has never coached tennis, but did play on the high school team. The candidate plays tennis about once a week. You guess the person is about 45 years old.

Preparing for the Interviews

Follow the five interview preparation steps in Model 9–1. For step 1, there are no job descriptions and specifications. Write them out, as well as what you intend to do for the other steps. Because there are only three candidates, you have decided to interview them all, even if they do not meet your job specifications.

Conducting the Interviews

During the in-class part of this exercise you will conduct a job interview. Be sure to bring your preparation material for class use.

IN-CLASS SKILL-BUILDING EXERCISE

Selecting a Tennis Coach

SB 9-2

Objectives: To perform a job analysis. To develop skills in selecting employees.

Experience: You will discuss your preparation. You will also conduct a job interview, be an interviewee, and observe an interview.

Material: The completed Preparation for Skill-Building Exercise 9–2.

Procedure 1
(5–10 minutes)

Break into groups of five or six, pass your preparation materials around to the other members, and discuss them. You may make changes to improve your preparation. For example, you may want to add some good questions you did not think of.

Procedure 2
(3–5 minutes)

Break into groups of three with class members other than the group in procedure 1. Make one or two groups of two, if necessary. Each person selects one of the three candidates (A, B, or C) he or she will play during the interview. Use your own name, but assume you have the person's qualifications; ad lib realistically.

Procedure 3
(25–75 minutes)

1–1. *Interview 1 takes place.* The person who chose A is the interviewer; B is the interviewee; and C is the observer. A conducts the interview using his or her interview materials, while B answers the questions. C observes quietly, and fills in the answers to the integration section at the end of this exercise. (If there are only two in your group, B is also the observer.) You may not be able to ask all your questions in the allotted time (5 to 20 minutes). Keep the opening short and be sure to close when you are ready to or the time is up.

1–2. *Integration (3–5 minutes).* C gives his or her observation of the interview. All three group members discuss the interview and how it could be improved. Do not go on to the next interview until you are told to do so.

2–1. *Interview 2 takes place.* B is the interviewer; C is the interviewee; and A is the observer. Follow the guidelines for 1–1.

2–2. *Integration.* Follow the guidelines for 1–2.

3–1. *Interview 3 takes place.* C is the interviewer; A is the interviewee; and B is the observer. Groups of two join other triads as observers. Follow the guidelines for 1–1.

3–2. *Integration.* Follow the guidelines for 1–2.

Procedure 4
(2–4 minutes)

Individually select the candidate you would offer the job to. Students vote to select a candidate.

Conclusion: The instructor may lead a class discussion and make concluding remarks.

Application (2–4) minutes): What did I learn from this experience? How will I use this knowledge in the future?

Sharing: Volunteers give their answers to the application section.

Integration Sheet

Interview Problems to Avoid.

Did the interviewer avoid:

— Interruptions?

— Rushing?

— Stereotyping?

— The like-me syndrome?

— The halo effect?

— The horn effect?

— A premature selection?

Types of Interviews.

The interviewer used the _____ interview.

— Structured   — Unstructured   — Semistructured

Types of Interview Questions.

The interviewer used _____ questions.

— Closed-ended   — Open-ended   — Probing   — Hypothetical   — Leading

Preparation for the Interview.

The interviewer:

— Step 1. Developed a job description and specifications

— Step 2. Planned a realistic job preview

— Step 3. Developed a list of questions for all candidates

— Step 4. Developed a format

— Step 5. Developed questions for each candidate

Conducting the Interview.

The interviewer:

— Step 1. Opened the interview. Developed a rapport, putting the candidate at ease by discussing a topic unrelated to the job.

— Step 2. Gave a realistic job preview. The candidate understood what the duties and responsiblities were.

— Step 3. Asked questions. Asked legal questions, talked less than 20 percent of the time, and ended with a closing question.

— Step 4. Closed the interview. Specifically informed the candidate of when the selection would be made.

Recommendations.

Give specific ideas on how the interviewer can improve future performance.

10

Orienting and Training Employees

1. List and explain five areas of orientation programs.
2. List and explain the five steps in the training cycle.
3. List and explain the four job instructional training steps and use the model when training.
4. Describe the use of the 14 training methods.
5. Discuss the supervisor's role in company safety programs.
6. Identify six common causes of accidents and explain how to prevent them.

Key Terms   To achieve our objectives in this chapter, it is important that you understand the following 12 key terms. They are presented in the order in which they appear in the chapter. The list of key terms also appears in alphabetical order in the end-of-chapter review.

orientation	development	job instructional training
psychological contract	vestibule training	safety
orientation program	training cycle	accident
training	assessment center	disabling injuries

Joe Jacobs was excited about being hired as a part of the weatherization program at his local Community Action Council. After his supervisor had introduced him to the other members of the crew, he took Joe into a small office, handed him a rather thick, dog-eared book, and said, "This is our policies and procedures manual; read it as fast as you can and let me know when you're done. I've got lots more stuff you need to know about this place, and I'm going to be gone tomorrow."

Reading as rapidly as he could, Joe had finished the first 20 pages of the 220-page document when the supervisor came back in. "Hey, if you're not done with that yet, just read it when you can; I've got a bunch of stuff that can't wait." The "bunch of stuff" turned out to be two weatherization jobs that took the rest of the day to complete. The supervisor left each job after half an hour. Joe felt incompetent and useless. Except for one fellow employee who was also quite new, no one would tell him what he should be doing. By the end of the day, Joe was wondering whether or not he should quit. A week later, he still hadn't gotten a chance to read the policies and procedures manual.

Joe's experience is not unusual. Many supervisors place far too little emphasis on orienting and training new employees. In fact, on October 22, 1991 the front page of *The Wall Street Journal* **stated that 89 percent of American workers never receive any formal training from their employers. How would you have treated Joe?**

I. Orientation

After you hire new employees, you must orient them to the organization and the job. Orientation is one of the supervisor's most important responsibilities. Experiences the first day on the job will affect employees' morale and productivity throughout their employment.[1] However, probably no supervisory skill is more poorly handled than orientation.[2]

Orientation *is the process of getting a new employee to function comfortably and effectively on the job.* The time it takes for orientation varies greatly with the complexity of the job. Simple jobs may take a week, and complex jobs may take months. Orientation is learning the ropes or the rules of the game.

In this section you will learn the benefits of orientation and one aspect of orientation, helping new employees fit in.

The Benefits of Orientation

One survey revealed that about 85 percent of businesses provide some kind of formal orientation program, but approaches to orientation vary widely. Regardless of how employees are oriented, there are several benefits.

Reduced Start-Up Costs: New employees need time to reach standard rates of performance. Research has revealed that properly oriented employees reach these levels faster.[3] In addition, the employee's supervisor and co-workers spend less time answering questions, showing the new employee how to do the work, and so forth.

Accurate Expectations: The orientation program tells the new employee what is expected of him or her from the start. Organizational standing plans should be covered. In this way, the employee learns what the job duties and responsibilities are. It is important for the new employee to understand what quality and quantity standards are expected, and when he or she should perform at standard rates.[4] As stated in Chapter 6, high expectations lead to higher levels of performance as part of the self-fulfilling prophecy.

Reduced Turnover: After an organization spends thousands of dollars selecting employees, it is important to retain them.[5] But if you don't manage new employees properly from the start, you can kiss them good-bye.[6] Because employees are most likely to quit during the breaking-in period, it is important to help new employees fit in and be successful on the job right from the start.[7]

Reduced Anxiety: Whenever people face new and unknown situations they tend to be fearful. They are anxious about how they will perform, whether they will be appreciated, whether they will fit in, and so forth. Orientation should help eliminate this fear of the unknown. In addition, anxiety over human relations tends to be more significant than anxiety over the technical aspects of a job.[8]

Positive Attitude and Performance: Performance is often directly related to attitude.[9] Employees usually begin with a positive attitude. The supervisor should work to develop and maintain that positive attitude, which affects morale, job satisfaction, motivation, and performance. Here, orientation is important because an employee's first impressions are often lasting impressions.

CONNECTIONS

1. Identify benefits of orientation for a specific supervisor's department, preferably one you have worked in.

Helping New Employees Fit In

Not fitting in is the most common reason for job dissatisfaction.[10] It is your responsibility as a supervisor to help the new employee fit in with the rest of the department. Some of the things a supervisor can do to help the new employee include the following:

Overcoming "Newness" Behavior: The employee at first will behave like someone new to the job. He or she will think of co-workers in terms of "them" versus "me." A new employee needs a "we" attitude and must become part of the group. The new employee also needs to stop talking about the past and comparing the present workplace and methods to those of previous employers.

Newness behavior is common. However, if it continues for too long, it can keep the new employee from fitting in. The supervisor should be aware of newness behavior, and if it is a problem, he or she should talk to the new employee about it.[11]

Use the Buddy System: With the buddy system, the new employee is assigned to an experienced co-worker who acts as a mentor. The mentor must be willing to help and be capable of helping the new employee. The mentor should be available to answer the new employee's questions and teach him or her necessary skills. The mentor should also take the new employee to breaks and lunch or see to it that others do, until the new employee is fully oriented to the job and has made friends.[12]

Prepare for the First Day at Work: Prepare for the new employee's first day on the job.[13] Have his or her work area ready with a nameplate on it. Pass out a brief written statement about the new employee to department members.[14] Keep your calendar as open as possible on the first day. Meet the new employee when he or she arrives. Begin the orientation by going to your office and developing a rapport. Start getting to know the new employee and discuss topics unrelated to the job. Tell the new employee how you want to be addressed, and ask how he or she prefers to be addressed. Explain the orientation process and the day's schedule. Begin your planned orientation. Try to take the new employee to lunch. If you cannot, have the mentor do it. Meet with the new employee about 30 minutes before quitting time to discuss the day, answer any questions, and continue the orientation.

Develop a Psychological Contract: Edgar Schein coined this term; the **psychological contract** *comprises the unwritten but understood expectations of the supervisor and employee.* The employer is saying what is expected no matter who is hired, and the employee is saying what he or she expects no matter what the job is.

Through the orientation process, the supervisor and employee learn what they expect from each other. It is important that the psychological contract be realistic; if either party believes it has been violated, there will be conflict and possible problems. Be sure to be open and honest. Make sure the new employee clearly knows your expectations, and follow through on what you say you will do.

II. Orientation Programs

Orientation programs vary in formality and content. Some organizations have formal orientation sessions conducted by the human resources department before the new employee reports to the job. Others simply allow the new employee to learn the ropes from the old timers during work, breaks, and lunch. As a supervisor, you should be familiar with your human resources department's orientation program and coordinate yours with theirs.[15]

Customize your orientation program to meet your new employee's and the department's needs. To avoid information overload, it may be best to spread the orientation over several days. Experiment and find out what works best. An **orientation program** *might include descriptions of organization and department functions, job duties and responsibilities, and standing plans, as well as tours and introductions to co-workers.*[16] We will discuss each area. It is recommended that you select and add items that relate to your job situation. Some of the items may be covered by the human resources department and may only need a quick review at most. Develop a checklist for use during the orientation to ensure that you cover each item as planned. The list will also show you what still needs to be covered.

Organization and Department Functions

Start with the organization and then discuss your specific department. Talk about the organization's history, culture, and products or services. Develop pride in working for the organization.

- Explain the organization's structure. Show the new employee the organizational chart.[17]
- Explain the functions and relationship of the departments.
- Inform the employee of the organization's benefits.
- Explain your department's purpose and objectives.
- Give the employee any handbooks or other relevant materials.
- Help the employee fill out all the necessary paperwork.
- Explain the department's structure and the job's relation to the department.

Job Duties and Responsibilities

Be sure the new employee's workstation is clean and well supplied before his or her arrival.[18]

- Explain why the employee's job is important and how it affects other jobs in and outside of the department.
- Give the employee a copy of the job description. Review the duties and responsibilities together. Describe any training that will be given and when it will take place.[19]
- Explain what the employee's authority is, what assistance is available, and how the employee can get help.
- Clearly explain job standards; tell the employee how long it should take to reach standard levels of performance.
- Explain the probation period and evaluation procedures.
- Show the employee a copy of the performance appraisal you will use. Explain the rating system.
- Discuss what common problems are and how to handle them.
- Go over the work hours, pay rates, and payment system.
- Explain any overtime needs and extra duty assignments.
- Explain any records or reports the employee is responsible for.
- Explain where and how to get any needed supplies, materials, tools, and so on.
- Give the employee a company telephone directory and explain how to use the phone system.

Standing Plans

Explain the policies, procedures, and rules of the organization and your department. Some areas to cover include the following:

- Break and lunch times.
- Safety requirements. (We will discuss this topic later in this chapter.)
- Eating, drinking, smoking, chewing gum, and so on.
- Removal of company property (theft).
- Making and receiving personal telephone calls.
- Job bidding and requesting assignments.
- The use of time clocks or timesheets.
- Policies on absence and lateness.

Tours

The new employee should be given a tour of the organization and the department. Areas you should consider touring include the following:

- Workstations of co-workers.
- Rest rooms and locker rooms.
- Water fountain.
- Lounges and cafeterias.
- Departments the employee will work with.
- Locations of supplies, tools, equipment, files, and so forth.
- Safety equipment location (such as the fire alarm, fire extinguisher, and first aid).

Introduction to Co-Workers

Co-workers should be introduced when the new employee tours their workstations. Be enthusiastic when introducing the new employee; make him or her feel important and wanted. Say something like, "This is Steve Wagner; he is highly qualified and we're glad to have him as a member of our team." It is difficult to remember several people's names all at once. Reintroduce new employees on several occasions until they know everyone by name.

During the introduction, do not give your opinions of current workers to the new employee. Let the new employee develop his or her own opinions without your prejudice, either pro or con.[20] Exhibit 10–1 summarizes the five major elements in orientation.

LEARNING OBJECTIVE

1. List and explain five areas of orientation programs.

CONNECTIONS

2. Recall an orientation you experienced. Which parts of an orientation program did it include? How would you improve that orientation? Describe the entire orientation.

EXHIBIT 10–1   **ORIENTATION PROGRAM**

1. Organization and department functions
2. Job duties and responsibilities
3. Standing plans
4. Tour
5. Introduction to co-workers

III. Training and the Supervisor

Most people will have to be trained to do a new job, regardless of whether they were just hired or have been working for the organization in another capacity. Orientation and training may and often do take place simultaneously. **Training** *involves acquiring the skills necessary to perform a job.* Training typically develops the technical skills of nonmanagers. The terms *training* and *development* are often used together.

Development *involves the ability to perform both present and future jobs.* Development, as opposed to training, is less technical and aimed at managerial and professional employees.

Existing employees need training and development as changes occur in the department and organization. In this section we will discuss the importance of training and the supervisor's role in training.

The Importance of Training

Training is important for many reasons, including the following:

- Training and development is a billion-dollar-a-year industry. Large companies, high-tech companies, firms in highly or newly competitive industries, and companies in service or service-intensive industries spend heavily on training. Companies believe that if they train more, and more effectively, they will have happier, more loyal employees and less turnover.[21]

- The best and brightest people gravitate to organizations that foster personal growth.[22]

- Training is the most vital and necessary function within an organization. Teaching and training are among the supervisor's most important skills.[23]

- Employees and supervisors are the determining factor in quality and quantity of production.[24] The better they are trained, the more productive employees will be.

- A study revealed that most supervisors spend 10 percent of their time training and developing employees. It is a daily task.[25]

- Trained employees enable supervisors to take on more responsibility and enhance their own promotability.

- Training employees produces a safer work environment.

The Supervisor's Role in Training

Training should have an organizationwide commitment; it is not just one person's job. Training is not a one-time event. It should be ongoing from orientation through retirement. The supervisor's role in training varies with the size of the organization. In large organizations with training departments, the supervisor may get help in training employees. In small organizations, the supervisor may have sole responsibility for training employees. Regardless, training will take place in one of two contexts, and more than likely your employer will not teach you how to conduct training.

Off-the-Job Training: As the name implies, this training is done away from the work site. It is often conducted in some sort of classroom setting. A common method is vestibule training. **Vestibule training** *develops technical skills in a simulated setting.* It is used when teaching job skills at the work site is impractical. For example, many large retail stores have training rooms where new employees learn how to run the cash registers and other equipment. Once they achieve the desired level of performance, they work with the same type of equipment in the store. The training is usually conducted by a training specialist. Employees may undergo training before they start on the job or leave the job for training and return when it is over. Off-the-job training does not mean that the supervisor is not involved. The supervisor should work with the training department to ensure that the employees are being effectively taught the skills they need. The supervisor is the technical expert, and the trainer is the instructional expert. The two should work together. Supervisors should talk to their employees about the training and follow up to ensure that the skills taught are used on the job.

On-the-Job Training (OJT): This training is done at the work site. It is usually conducted by the supervisor or an employee selected by the supervisor. In either case, it is the supervisor's responsibility to see that the employees are taught the skills needed to do their jobs effectively. We will discuss how to conduct OJT in the next section.

Even when employees receive off-the-job training, it is often necessary to do some on-the-job training. In other words, the supervisor cannot avoid having input into and responsibility for training.

IV. The Training Cycle

Following the steps in the training cycle will help ensure that training is done in a systematic way. The **training cycle** *involves needs assessment, setting objectives, preparing for training, conducting the training, and measuring and evaluating training results.*

Step 1. Needs Assessment

Before you begin training, you must determine your employees' training needs. These needs will differ depending on whether you are training new or existing employees.

Needs Assessment for New Employees

To train inexperienced workers, you must review the job description and specifications and identify the specific skills a new employee will need. Then proceed to the next step in the training cycle.

Needs Assessment for Existing Employees

Symptoms indicating that training is needed include excessive scrap, missed deadlines, accidents, poor morale, and so forth. Whenever employees do not produce at standard levels of performance, you have a problem. The first step in problem solving is to determine the cause. A needs assessment determines whether poor skills are the problem, and whether training is the solution. If the organization has a training department, the supervisor may contact a specialist for help in conducting the needs assessment. The needs assessment consists of three steps:

1. Determine acceptable performance standards. If standards exist, evaluate them; if they don't exist, set them.

2. Compare actual departmental or employee performance to the standard and measure discrepancies.

3. Determine the cause of the discrepancies. Is the problem lack of skill? Or is it caused by job design, equipment, materials, or motivation? If lack of skill is the problem, continue to the second step in the training cycle; if it is not, training isn't needed.

Assessment Centers

An assessment center may be used to determine training needs. An **assessment center** *is a facility where people undergo several days of concentrated tests and interviews, the results of which are used for selection and training.* People who do well on the assessment tests are commonly promoted to management positions at all levels. The analysis of strengths and weaknesses resulting from the tests is used to develop specific training programs for the individual. The tests assess management skills and other traits such as potential, flexibility, energy, initiative, self-direction, resistance to stress, and originality. Assessment simulations such as in-basket exercises, leaderless group discussions on a variety of management issues, management games, and presentations of solutions to problems are used. We will discuss these simulations later.

Step 2. Set Objectives

The key to any training program is having well-defined, performance-based objectives.[26] As with all plans, you should begin by determining the end result you want to achieve. The criteria for objectives discussed in Chapter 2 apply to training objectives:

- The objectives should be difficult but achievable, challenging the trainee.
- They should be observable and measurable; you must be able to determine the success of the training program.[27]
- Objectives should be specific, and they should have a target date; at the beginning of the training program, the trainees should know specifically what they will be able to do and by when.
- They should be jointly set, when possible. Participation is usually not possible with inexperienced employees. However, you may be able to use employee input when training experienced workers. Determining what skills they have and the skills they need requires participation.
- Objectives must be accepted; employees must be willing to work toward developing the skills.

Sample Training Objectives

Examples of training objectives that meet the criteria would include the following:

- Participants will type a minimum of 40 words per minute by the end of the one-week training period.
- Assemblers will be able to assemble 10 sets per hour by the end of the one-day training period.
- Customer service representatives will serve an average of 20 customers per hour by the end of the one-month training period.

Step 3. Prepare for Training

A supervisor should plan whenever he or she does anything for the first time. Before conducting a training session, the supervisor should have written plans and all the necessary materials ready. If you ever had an instructor come to class obviously unprepared, you know why I recommend preparation before training.

In preparing a training session, it is important to break the task down into steps. What we do as part of our routine seems simple to us. But to the new employee it may seem very complicated. Write out each step and go through the steps to make sure they work.[28]

An often neglected step in training is preparing the learner. If trainees are to learn, they must be motivated and prepared for the experience.[29] We will discuss preparing the learner later in this section.

As with all plans, training plans should answer the who, what, when, where, and how questions.

- *Who.* During the needs assessment, you should have identified the employees who will be trained.
- *What.* Your objectives should state what the trainees should learn.
- *When.* Dates and times for training should be specified.
- *Where.* Places for training should be specified. If reservations are needed, they should be made as far in advance as possible.
- *How.* The methods used are very important to the success of the training program. There are a variety of training methods available.

We will discuss several training methods in the next section of this chapter. For now, we will focus on the on-the-job training method most often used by supervisors, job instructional training (JIT). **Job instructional training** *involves preparation of the learner, presentation of the operation, performance tryout, and follow-up.* These steps are discussed in greater detail in Model 10–1. Use the model when developing your own training programs.

Step 4. Conduct the Training

Regardless of the training method used, follow your plans. Be sure to have your written plan with you, as well as any other materials needed.

Step 5. Measure and Evaluate Training Results

During training and at the end of the program, you should measure and evaluate the results to determine whether or not the objectives were achieved. If they were, the training is over; if they were not, you may have to continue the training until objectives are met. Or take employees off the job if they cannot meet the standards. Revise and improve your written plans. The training cycle is summarized in Exhibit 10–2.

C O N N E C T I O N S

3. Identify which steps of job instructional training your supervisor used to train you for a present or past job.

EXHIBIT 10–2   **THE TRAINING CYCLE**

MODEL 10-1   **JOB INSTRUCTIONAL TRAINING**

Step 1. Preparation of the learner

1. Put the learner at ease — relieve the tension.

2. Explain why he is being taught.

3. Create interest, encourage questions, and find out what the learner already knows about her job or other jobs.

4. Explain the why of the whole job, and relate it to some job the worker already knows.

5. Place the learner as close to his normal working position as possible.

6. Familiarize her with the equipment, materials, tools, and trade terms.

Step 2. Presentation of the operation

1. Explain quantity and quality requirements.

2. Go through the job at the normal work pace.

3. Go through the job at a slow pace several times, explaining each step. Between operations, explain the difficult parts, or those in which errors are likely to be made.

4. Go through the job at a slow pace several times, explaining the key points.

5. Have the learner explain the steps as you go through the job at a slow pace.

6. Have the learner explain the key points as you go through the job at a slow pace.

Step 3. Performance tryout

1. Have the learner go through the job several times, slowly, explaining to you each step. Correct his mistakes, and, if necessary, do some of the complicated steps for him or her the first few times.

2. You, the trainer, run the job at the normal pace.

3. Have the learner do the job, gradually building up skill and speed.

4. As soon as she demonstrates that she can do the job, put her on her own, but don't abandon her.

Step 4. Follow-up

1. Designate to whom the learner should go for help if he needs it, or if he needs to ask questions.

2. Gradually decrease supervision, checking her work from time to time against quality and quantity standards.

3. Correct faulty work patterns that begin to creep into his work, and do it before they become a habit. Show him why the learned method is superior.

4. Compliment good work; encourage her and keep her encouraged until she is able to meet the quality and quantity standards.

Source: William Berliner and William McLarnery, *Management Practice and Training* (Homewood, IL: Richard D. Irwin, 1974), pp. 442–43. Reproduced by permission of the publisher.

V. Training Methods and Tips

In this section you will look at some of the other training methods available. Also listed are several tips to help improve your ability in training.

Training Methods

When selecting a training method, keep in mind the following statistics:[30]

- People learn 10 percent of what they read.
- They learn 20 percent of what they hear.
- They learn 30 percent of what they see.
- People learn 50 percent of what they see and hear.
- They learn 70 percent of what they talk over with others.
- People learn 80 percent of what they use and do in real life.
- They learn 95 percent of what they teach someone else.

Given these facts, there are several ways the supervisor can present the material to trainees.

Written Material

The trainer may write his or her own material or use existing sources such as the company handbook, which employees are expected to read. There is no limit to the number of people who can be trained using written material. It is appropriate for teaching the technical aspects of a job. In terms of cost, using written materials is somewhere in the middle of the spectrum of training methods. Using written material requires no special skill on the part of the trainer.

Lecture

The trainer presents the information verbally. The lecture can be used with any number of trainees. However, the greater the number of trainees, the greater the need for presentation skills on the part of the lecturer. A lecture is appropriate for technical training. It is inexpensive unless you bring in professional lecturers, who can greatly increase the cost.

Video

The major advantage of video is that it can be used repeatedly. Like the lecture, video can be used with any number of trainees for technical training. If the video is made by the organization, it is relatively expensive, and it takes a high level of training skills to lecture effectively in front of a camera. Videos may also be rented or purchased. In such cases, no training skills are needed.

Question and Answer

The trainer lectures and then either asks the trainees questions or allows them to ask questions. The maximum number of people who can be trained with this format is about 20, and it is effective for technical training. It is relatively low cost and requires moderate training ability. However, it takes technical ability to answer the questions.

Discussion

The trainer allows the trainees to express their ideas about and opinions of the information. It is appropriate for teaching technical skills and even better for developing human relations and problem-solving and decision-making (conceptual) skills. It is a low-cost method but moderate to high training skills are needed to lead an effective discussion. It is best used with 5 to 15 participants. This group size is large enough to generate different views but not so large as to discourage participation.

Programmed Learning and Computer-Assisted Instruction (CAI)

Programmed learning and CAI are the same basic training method, but programmed learning materials generally are in book form, whereas CAI is done via a computer terminal. They both involve three steps. (1) The trainee is presented with a question or problem. (2) The trainee selects a response to the question or problem. (3) The trainee receives feedback on the accuracy of the response. Study guides are a form of programmed learning. Some also come in CAI versions. These methods are appropriate for training in technical, human relations, and conceptual skills. With these methods, people are taught individually. Both programmed learning and CAI are relatively expensive to develop. Prepackaged programs are available at moderate cost. The methods are economical if a large number of trainees will use the material, such as in large organizations with many employees to train or those that experience high turnover. It takes no training skills to use them.

Demonstration

The demonstration shows the trainee how to perform the task. (This is step 2, presentation of the operation, in JIT.) The demonstration can be used with any number of trainees. It is appropriate for teaching technical and human relations skills. It is a low-cost method, but a great deal of training skill is needed to demonstrate properly.

Job Rotation

With this method, a trainee moves from job to job. Management trainees often do job rotations before being assigned to one area. Job rotation, or cross-training, is important to ensure that when one employee is not on the job, someone else can get the work done. It is common for employees to know how to perform two or three jobs. Job rotation usually involves one employee, or two or three at most. It is appropriate for technical training. Job rotation also develops conceptual ability because employees get to understand the relationships between different departments and jobs. It is a low-cost method but requires moderate to high training skills.

Projects

To develop employees' skills, the supervisor can delegate certain responsibilities, such as reports, studies, serving on committees, and so forth. A supervisor should take these opportunities to develop employees' technical, human relations, and conceptual skills. One employee or a small group (up to five employees) can work on a given project. Projects are a low-cost training method requiring a moderate to high level of training skill to motivate and teach the employees to do the extra tasks.

Role Playing

In role playing, employees act out a situation in order to develop skills needed in handling similar situations on the job. The number of trainees can range from 2 to about 20. Role playing is appropriate for development of human relations skills. It is a low-cost training method calling for moderate to high training skills.

Behavior Modeling

Behavior modeling involves four steps. (1) The trainees observe how to perform the task correctly. This may be done via a live demonstration or a videotape. (2) Trainees role-play a situation using the observed skills. (3) Trainees receive feedback on how well they performed. (4) Trainees develop plans for using the new skills on the job. This method is appropriate for from 2 to 20 trainees. Regardless of whether an organization develops, rents, or buys the demonstration materials, it is relatively expensive. Behavior modeling is appropriate for developing human relations skills and requires a highly skilled trainer to give effective feedback. Notice that role playing is a part of behavior modeling, although the latter is superior.

Management Games

In management games, the trainees manage a simulated company. They make decisions in teams and get the results back on a quarterly basis, over a period of several game "years." Teams usually have from three to five members and are in an "industry" with several competitors. A total of 10 to 25 trainees in different teams is optimum with this method. Management games are appropriate for developing conceptual skills in areas such as planning, problem solving, and decision making. Although usually not the focus, human relations skills are often developed through working in the teams. Many colleges now offer business courses that use computer-simulated management games. Games are a relatively expensive training method, especially when computers are used. A moderately skilled trainer is needed.

In-Basket Exercise

The in-basket exercise presents the trainee with actual or simulated letters, memos, reports, telephone messages, and so forth that would typically be found in the in-basket of a person holding the job for which training is given. Trainees are asked what, if any, action they would take for each item, and to assign priorities to the material. In-basket exercises are appropriate for developing conceptual skills. Participants usually work alone, possibly followed by group discussion. The optimum size when group discussion is used is 5 to 20. It is moderately costly to develop or buy the in-basket materials. It takes a moderately to highly skilled trainer to lead the group discussion and review the possible answers.

Cases

With the case approach, the trainee is presented with a situation and asked to diagnose and solve the problems involved. The trainee is usually asked to answer questions. Trainees often work alone, and then discuss their analysis in a group. The optimum group size is 5 to 35 participants. Cases are appropriate for developing conceptual skills. They are relatively low cost and require a moderately to highly skilled trainer to lead the discussion.

Exhibit 10–3 is designed to help you select training methods. The first column lists the training method. The second column lists the optimum number of people who can be trained with the method. The third column indicates the type of skill the exercise is designed to develop. The fourth column lists the relative cost of the method. The fifth column shows the level of skill needed by the trainer.

Supervisor Use of Training Methods

Reading, lecture, video, question and answer, discussion, programmed learning and CAI, demonstration, job rotation, and projects are commonly used by supervisors to train employees how to perform their jobs.

Role playing and behavior modeling are not commonly used by supervisors. However, they are appropriate for supervisors who need to train employees how to handle human relations such as customer complaints. The supervisor can teach employees by example.

Management games, in-basket exercises, and cases are commonly used to train managers, not employees. Therefore, supervisors may be trained with these methods, but will probably not use these training methods with their employees.

Training Tips

Following are some tips you can use to improve your training ability.[31]

- Direct questions back to the trainees; get them to think.
- Share your experience with the trainees.

EXHIBIT 10-3   **SELECTING TRAINING METHODS**

Method	Number of Trainees	Use*	Cost†	Trainer Skill†
Reading	unlimited	T	M	L
Lecture	unlimited	T	L	M, H
Video	unlimited	T	H	L, H
Questions and answers	1-20	T	L	M
Discussion	5-15	T, H, C	L	M, H
Programmed learning/CAI	1	T, H, C	M, H	L
Demonstration	unlimited	T, H	L	H
Job rotation	1-3	T, C	L	M, H
Projects	1-5	T, H, C	L	M, H
Role playing	2-20	H	L	M, H
Behavior modeling	2-20	H	H	H
Management games	10-25	C	H	M
In-basket exercise	1-20	C	M	M, H
Cases	5-35	C	L	M, H

*T = technical; H = human; C = conceptual.
†L = low; M = moderate; H = high.

- Admit it if you don't know the answer.
- Show that you enjoy training.
- Spend the time necessary to train employees properly.
- Adopt the trainees' point of view; meet their needs, not yours.
- Be positive. Never say things such as "This is hard to do." Develop the trainee's confidence.
- Ask the trainee easy questions to develop confidence.
- Put the trainee at ease.
- Follow up to be sure the trainee is using the new skills.
- Develop your relations with the trainees and help them develop their human relations, as well as technical, skills.[32]
- Praise the trainees' attempts and accomplishments. Never put down the trainee.[33] Don't make comments like, "Are you stupid?" "What's wrong with you? Don't you understand it?" or "What's your problem? It's easy."

LEARNING OBJECTIVE

4. Describe the use of the 14 training methods.

CONNECTIONS

4. Explain the type of training you received for a job. Which training methods were used? Describe how you would improve your training.

VI. Safety and the Supervisor

Among the areas in which training is important, safety is number one.

- The Bureau of Labor Statistics reports that approximately 6 million work-related injuries or illnesses occur in the United States each year.
- An estimated 28 million workdays are lost each year because of job-related injuries or illnesses.
- An injury occurs on the job to 1 in every 10 workers.
- Injuries cost an annual $2 billion in lost production and $1.5 billion in lost wages.
- A company with 1,000 employees could expect to have 27 lost workdays due to injuries. With a 4.5 percent profit margin, the company would need $11.3 million in sales to offset the cost.[34] Safety is a wise investment.

Safety *is the effort aimed at preventing accidents and illnesses.*

The Supervisor's Role in Safety

Among the supervisor's main concerns are reducing time lost from injuries and controlling the cost of insurance while improving the general quality of the work environment.[35] The supervisor's major role is to eliminate unsafe conditions and actions in their departments and throughout the entire organization.[36] Management (this includes the supervisor) is legally responsible for ensuring that new and existing employees are taught safety procedures on an ongoing basis. Safety should be a part of the orientation and training program.

A supervisor may be responsible for developing and maintaining a safety program, implementing safety changes, keeping safety records, or investigating and reporting accidents. The time spent preventing accidents can be far less than the time it takes to investigate an accident, fill out the necessary forms, attend meetings concerning it, and recommend future action. Productivity suffers when accidents occur.

The supervisor's attitude toward and enforcement of safety regulations will affect employee compliance. If the supervisor has a negative attitude and does not enforce the safety rules, employees will ignore them, too.

Occupational Safety and Health Administration

Part of any ongoing safety program will be compliance with federal regulations. In 1970 Congress passed the Occupational Safety and Health Act (OSHA) with the purpose of ensuring safe and healthy working conditions. The Occupational Safety and Health Administration, under the aegis of the U.S. Department of Labor, was created to enforce the act. OSHA covers virtually every business with one or more employees. The Occupational Safety and Health Administration is authorized to take the following actions:

- Encourage employers and employees to reduce workplace hazards and to implement new or improved safety and health programs.
- Establish "separate but dependent responsibilities and rights" for employers and employees for the achievement of better safety and health conditions.
- Maintain a reporting and record-keeping system to monitor job-related injuries and illnesses.
- Develop mandatory job safety and health standards and enforce them effectively.
- Provide for the development, analysis, evaluation, and approval of state occupational safety and health programs.[37]

Injuries and illnesses resulting in death, lost workdays, loss of consciousness, restriction of work or motion, transfer to another job, or medical treatment (other than first aid) must be reported to OSHA within six working days from the time the employer learns about the accident or illness.

OSHA conducts more than 100,000 on-site inspections yearly. A supervisor is frequently asked to accompany OSHA officials as they inspect the organization's physical facilities. Therefore, the supervisor should be familiar with OSHA regulations affecting his or her department. Exhibit 10–4 summarizes these regulations. Cooperating with OSHA officials is recommended.

OSHA's original focus was the manufacturing sector. However, the agency is following a court order to explore ways of expanding the standards to protect workers in other sectors of the economy.

LEARNING OBJECTIVE
5. Discuss the supervisor's role in company safety programs.

CONNECTIONS

5. Describe the supervisor's role in safety for a job you have held.
6. Describe the safety procedures, rules, and program for a job you have held.

VII. Creating and Maintaining Safety in the Workplace

The saying "Safety is no accident" has a double meaning. It means that safety doesn't happen by chance, and it means that a company should be free of accidents. The supervisor can't prevent all accidents, but he or she can greatly reduce the number that take place.

In this section you will learn about accidents, prevention of accidents, and safety measurement.

Accidents

An **accident** *is an unforeseen incident that may or may not result in injury or property damage.* A person who slips but does not fall or drops something that does not break has still had an accident.

Causes of Accidents

Human Error: Human error accounts for 80 percent of all accidents.[38] Among the causes of these human-error accidents are inadequate training, bad examples, boredom, goofing off, operating without authority, unsafe speeds, making safety devices inoperative, using unsafe equipment, failure to use safety equipment, unsafe loading, poor positioning and posture, and distractions.

Examination of safety records shows that the majority of accidents happen to a minority of employees. The employees who are injured frequently are called *accident prone*. These accident-prone employees tend to be relatively young (between 20 and 24), single, emotionally insecure, low in motivation, aggressive, and hostile toward themselves. Identifying accident-prone employees and closely supervising them can help them to have fewer accidents.

Environmental Conditions: The other major cause of accidents is environmental conditions. Unsafe tools, machines, or equipment; unsafe chemicals; poor design or construction; damaged protective equipment; inadequate lighting; and poor housekeeping are among the environmental factors that can lead to accidents.

EXHIBIT 10–4 **OSHA GUIDELINES**

JOB SAFETY & HEALTH PROTECTION

The Occupational Safety and Health Act of 1970 provides job safety and health protection for workers by promoting safe and healthful working conditions throughout the Nation. Requirements of the Act include the following:

Employers

All employers must furnish to employees employment and a place of employment free from recognized hazards that are causing or are likely to cause death or serious harm to employees. Employers must comply with occupational safety and health standards issued under the Act.

Employees

Employees must comply with all occupational safety and health standards, rules, regulations and orders issued under the Act that apply to their own actions and conduct on the job.

The Occupational Safety and Health Administration (OSHA) of the U.S. Department of Labor has the primary responsibility for administering the Act. OSHA issues occupational safety and health standards, and its Compliance Safety and Health Officers conduct jobsite inspections to help ensure compliance with the Act.

Inspection

The Act requires that a representative of the employer and a representative authorized by the employees be given an opportunity to accompany the OSHA inspector for the purpose of aiding the inspection.

Where there is no authorized employee representative, the OSHA Compliance Officer must consult with a reasonable number of employees concerning safety and health conditions in the workplace.

Complaint

Employees or their representatives have the right to file a complaint with the nearest OSHA office requesting an inspection if they believe unsafe or unhealthful conditions exist in their workplace. OSHA will withhold, on request, names of employees complaining.

The Act provides that employees may not be discharged or discriminated against in any way for filing safety and health complaints or for otherwise exercising their rights under the Act.

Employees who believe they have been discriminated against may file a complaint with their nearest OSHA office within 30 days of the alleged discrimination.

Citation

If upon inspection OSHA believes an employer has violated the Act, a citation alleging such violations will be issued to the employer. Each citation will specify a time period within which the alleged violation must be corrected.

The OSHA citation must be prominently displayed at or near the place of alleged violation for three days, or until it is corrected, whichever is later, to warn employees of dangers that may exist there.

Proposed Penalty

The Act provides for mandatory penalties against employers of up to $1,000 for each serious violation and for optional penalties of up to $1,000 for each nonserious violation. Penalties of up to $1,000 per day may be proposed for failure to correct violations within the proposed time period. Also, any employer who willfully or repeatedly violates the Act may be assessed penalties of up to $10,000 for each such violation.

Criminal penalties are also provided for in the Act. Any willful violation resulting in death of an employee, upon conviction, is punishable by a fine of not more than $10,000, or by imprisonment for not more than six months, or by both. Conviction of an employer after a first conviction doubles these maximum penalties.

Voluntary Activity

While providing penalties for violations, the Act also encourages efforts by labor and management, before an OSHA inspection, to reduce workplace hazards voluntarily and to develop and improve safety and health programs in all workplaces and industries. OSHA's Voluntary Protection Programs recognize outstanding efforts of this nature.

Such voluntary action should initially focus on the identification and elimination of hazards that could cause death, injury, or illness to employees and supervisors. There are many public and private organizations that can provide information and assistance in this effort, if requested. Also, your local OSHA office can provide considerable help and advice on solving safety and health problems or can refer you to other sources for help such as training.

Consultation

Free consultative assistance, without citation or penalty, is available to employers, on request, through OSHA supported programs in most State departments of labor or health.

More Information

Additional information and copies of the Act, specific OSHA safety and health standards, and other applicable regulations may be obtained from your employer or from the nearest OSHA Regional Office in the following locations:

Atlanta, Georgia
Boston, Massachusetts
Chicago, Illinois
Dallas, Texas
Denver, Colorado
Kansas City, Missouri
New York, New York
Philadelphia, Pennsylvania
San Francisco, California
Seattle, Washington

Telephone numbers for these offices, and additional area office locations, are listed in the telephone directory under the United States Department of Labor in the United States Government listing.

Washington, D.C.
1985
OSHA 2203

William E. Brock, Secretary of Labor

U.S. Department of Labor
Occupational Safety and Health Administration

Under provisions of Title 29, Code of Federal Regulations, Part 1903.2(a)(1) employers must post this notice (or a facsimile) in a conspicuous place where notices to employees are customarily posted.

Preventing Accidents

There are six common causes of accidents in the workplace, summarized in Exhibit 10–5. In the following sections we will examine each in terms of prevention of that type of accident.

Posture and Positioning

About one-half of the human-error accidents are caused by unsafe posture and positioning. For example, lifting heavy objects with the back rather than bending and using the legs results in strains and dislocations. Poor positioning of ladders often results in falls.[39]

To help prevent posture and positioning accidents, the supervisor must properly train employees and follow up. The supervisor should (1) stop the employee, (2) explain proper procedures and why they are important, (3) observe the employee do it correctly, and (4) follow up to ensure proper methods are used in the future.

Not Using or Wearing Safety Equipment

Safety equipment should be provided by the organization. Nonetheless, employees may not use or wear seat belts, safety goggles, hard hats, and so forth.

To help ensure that employees use and wear safety equipment the supervisor should: (1) Train employees to use or wear the safety equipment. (2) Explain how the equipment protects them. (3) Make sure that everyone, especially the supervisor him- or herself, uses/wears it all the time. (4) Allow employees to participate in selecting the safety equipment and offer them a variety to choose from; this may encourage employees to use/wear it.

Machines

There are a lot of accidents on cutting edges, exposed gears, belts, chains, and so forth. Accidents caused by machinery produce the most severe injuries.

To help prevent machinery accidents, the supervisor should make sure that employees are familiar with proper operations. It is especially important that employees be able to shut off a machine quickly in case of emergencies. Employees should be aware of possible hazards and how to prevent them.

Falls

Falls on slippery surfaces are sometimes due to improper footwear. Employees may also trip over objects that were left where they shouldn't be. When climbing stairs, ladders, and scaffolds, falls are likely. Employees often fall when grabbing for objects that are out of reach.

To help prevent falls, surfaces should be kept free of all types of debris. Proper footwear should always be required. And employees should be instructed in proper climbing techniques. Stairs, ladders, and scaffolds should be regularly checked for safety.

Hand Tools

Injuries may be caused by using the wrong tool or a tool in poor condition.

To help prevent accidents involving hand tools, be sure to properly train employees to use the correct tool for the job, and to replace worn tools. Hand tools should be checked and replaced periodically.

Electric Shocks

Though it is surprising to many people, a shock from ordinary household current (110 volts) can result in death. Live wires, live parts, short circuits, accidental grounds, overloads on the systems, and broken connections are among the causes of electric shock.

EXHIBIT 10–5	**CAUSES OF ACCIDENTS**
	1. Posture and positioning
	2. Not using/wearing safety equipment
	3. Machines
	4. Falls
	5. Hand tools
	6. Electric shocks

To help prevent electric shocks, be sure all machinery, equipment, tools, and so forth are properly grounded before they are connected to an electrical outlet. Have employees report hot wires, abnormal sparks, frayed insulation, loose connections, and any other electrical fault. Have the faults checked by an electrician right away. And have the electrical system checked by electricians regularly.

Other Safety Precautions

It is important to make safety everyone's responsibility. One technique that helps is the *buddy system,* which means that all employees look out for each other. When they see a co-worker violate safety rules, they don't run to the boss or ignore the violation. They inform or remind their friend of the possible dangers of accidents, and encourage compliance with the safety rules. This reflects the same philosophy as the slogan "Friends don't let friends drive drunk."[40] Employees should also be trained to handle possible emergencies. Proper training can save lives.[41]

The *safety checklist* is used to identify areas where accidents are highly possible. (When developing your list, refer to Exhibit 10–5.) The areas identified are periodically inspected by the supervisor.[42] During the safety check, try to be positive, praising employees who are using proper safety procedures.[43] But also correct those who are not. Safety can be discussed during MBWA (Chapter 4).

Measuring Safety

LEARNING OBJECTIVE

6. Identify six common causes of accidents and explain how to prevent them.

The two most widely accepted methods of measuring safety are the frequency rate and the severity rate. Both calculate only **disabling injuries,** *which require the employee to miss one or more days of work.* The *frequency rate* indicates how often disabling injuries occur. The *severity rate* indicates how serious the accidents were and the length of time the injured employees were out of work. The calculations for frequency and severity are compared to those for similar organizations to determine the firm's safety record.

CONNECTIONS

7. Describe an accident you had on the job. If you have never had one, describe one you saw. Classify the condition and cause of the accident. How could the supervisor have helped prevent this accident?

8. Exhibit 10–5 lists the six major causes of accidents. Which types have you had or witnessed?

9. Develop a safety checklist for a department you have worked in. How often would you check safety in this department?

REVIEW

Select one or more methods: (1) fill in the missing key terms from memory; (2) match the key terms from the end of the review with their definitions below; (3) copy the key terms in order from the key terms at the beginning of the chapter.

_____ is the process of getting a new employee to function comfortably and effectively on the job. The benefits of orientation include reduced start-up cost, accurate expectations, reduced turnover, reduced anxiety, and positive attitude and performance. To help the new employee fit in, the supervisor can help him or her overcome newness behavior, use the buddy system, make the employee's first day successful, and develop a realistic _____ , the unwritten but understood expectations of the supervisor and employee.

An _____ might include descriptions of organization and department functions, job duties and responsibilities, and standing plans, as well as tours and introductions to co-workers.

_____ involves acquiring the skills necessary to perform a job. _____ involves the ability to perform both present and future jobs. The terms *training* and *development* are often used together. Training may take place off or on the job. _____ develops technical skills in a simulated setting.

The _____ involves needs assessment, setting objectives, preparing for training, conducting the training, and measuring and evaluating training results. The _____ is a facility where people undergo several days of concentrated tests and interviews, the results of which are used for selection and training. _____ involves preparation of the learner, presentation of the operation, performance tryout, and follow-up.

Employees may be trained using written materials, lectures, videos, question and answer sessions, discussion, programmed learning and CAI, demonstration, job rotation, projects, role playing, behavior modeling, management games, in-basket exercises, and cases.

_____ comprises efforts aimed at preventing accidents and illness. Management—including the supervisor—is legally responsible for ensuring that employees are taught safety procedures on an ongoing basis. The supervisor may also be responsible for developing and maintaining a safety program, implementing safety changes, keeping safety records, and investigating or reporting accidents. The supervisor must be familiar with the Occupational Safety and Health Act (OSHA) and comply with its standards.

An _____ is an unforeseen incident that may or may not result in injury or property damage. Human error and environmental conditions cause accidents, with the former accounting for 80 percent of accidents. The supervisor should identify accident-prone employees and closely supervise them to help prevent accidents. The six major causes of accidents are: posture and positioning, not using safety equipment, machines, falls, hand tools, and electric shocks. Using the buddy system makes safety everyone's responsibility. The supervisor should have emergency plans and train employees to handle emergencies. Developing a checklist and periodically checking on safety can help prevent accidents. Safety is measured by frequency rate and severity rate. _____ cause the employee to miss one or more days of work because of an accident.

KEY TERMS

accident
assessment center
development
disabling injuries
job instructional training (JIT)
orientation

orientation program
psychological contract
safety
training
training cycle
vestibule training

REFERENCES

1. Lana Chandler, "Welcoming the New Employee," *Supervision,* October 1985, p. 14.

2. Claude George, *Supervision in Action: The Art of Managing Others* (Reston, VA: Reston Publishing, 1982), p. 305.

3. William Glueck, *Personnel: A Diagnostic Approach* (Plano, TX: Business Publications, 1982), Chapter 11.

4. A. G. Bedeian and W. F. Glueck, *Management* (Chicago: CBS College Publishing, 1983), p. 440.

5. "In Quest of the Ideal Employee," *Nation's Business,* November 1986, p. 38.

6. Dale Feuer, "Coping with the Labor Shortage," *Training,* March 1987, p. 75.

7. Bedeian and Glueck, *Management,* p. 440.

8. Ibid.

9. H. Lon Addams, "Up to Speed in 90 Days: An Orientation Plan," *Personnel Journal,* December 1985, p. 35.

10. "Fitting in Determines Job Success," *Training and Development Journal,* August 1986, p. 11.

11. Linda Segall, "Integrating Your New Employee into the Organization," *Supervisory Management,* February 1986, pp. 12–14.

12. Addams, "Up to Speed in 90 Days," p. 36.

13. Diane Arthur, "The First Day at Work," *Management Solutions,* October 1986, pp. 37–42.

14. Chandler, "Welcoming the New Employee," p. 14.

15. Addams, "Up to Speed in 90 Days," p. 36.

16. Walter St. John, "The Complete Employee Orientation Program," *Personnel Journal,* May 1980, p. 47.

17. Chandler, "Welcoming the New Employee," p. 16.

18. Arthur, "First Day at Work," p. 40.

19. Chandler, "Welcoming the New Employee," p. 16.

20. Arthur, "First Day at Work," p. 39.

21. Lawrence Olson, "Training Trends: The Corporate View," *Training and Development Journal,* September 1986, pp. 33–34.

22. M. Rutigliano, "Naisbitt and Aburdene on Reinventing the Workplace," *Management Review,* October 1985, p. 33.

23. Melvin Smith, "Training—Supervisory Responsibility or Not?" *Supervision,* May 1986, p. 3.

24. Michael Cohen, "Training Employees for On-the-Job Survival," *Personnel Administration,* November 1985, p. 28.

25. Charles MacDonald, *Performance-Based Supervisory Development* (Amherst, MA: Human Resources Press, 1982), p. 20.

26. Robert Sullivan and Donald Miklas, "On-the-Job Training That Works," *Training and Development Journal,* May 1985, p. 118.

27. Feuer, "Coping with the Labor Shortage," p. 75.

28. Fred Lippert, "Analyze before You Train," *Supervision,* December 1985, pp. 17–18.

29. Raymond Noe, "Trainees' Attributes and Attitudes: Neglected Influences on Training Effectiveness," *Academy of Management Review,* October 1986, pp. 743–46.

30. Clayton Lafferty, *Supervisory Skills Manual* (Plymouth, MI: Human Synergistics, 1982), p. 44.

31. Eugene Fetteroll, "16 Tips to Increase Your Effectiveness," *Training and Development Journal,* June 1985, pp. 68–70.

32. Cohen, "Training Employees for On-the-Job Success," p. 28.

33. Fred Lippert, "Tear Down or Build Up?" *Supervision,* June 1985, pp. 17–18.

34. "A Disabling Injury," *The Wall Street Journal,* April 14, 1987, p. 1.

35. Charles Goodroe, "Nontraditional Advantages of a Safety Program," *Supervision,* September 1985, p. 5.

36. Fred Lippert, "Why Correct Unsafe Acts?" *Supervision,* November 1986, p. 19.

37. *All About OSHA,* rev. ed. (Washington, DC: U.S. Department of Labor, 1982).

38. Lippert, "Why Correct Unsafe Acts?" p. 19.

39. Fred Lippert, "Cure or Prevention," *Supervision,* May 1986, pp. 18–19.

40. Fred Lippert, "Keeping Up with OSHA," *Supervision,* November 1985, p. 17.

41. S. Nelton, "Planning That Saves Lives," *Nation's Business,* May 1986, pp. 41–42.

42. Bernard Thompson, "Managing for Safeness," *Management Solutions,* March 1987, p. 42.

43. Goodroe, "Nontraditional Advantages of a Safety Program," p. 6.

APPLICATION SITUATIONS

Orientation Contents

AS 10—1

Identify the five statements below as being one of the following:

a. organization and department functions

b. job duties and responsibilities

c. standing plans

d. a tour

e. introduction to co-workers

_____ 1. "Joe, I'd like you to meet Carol, our new receptionist."

_____ 2. "Make sure the floors are kept clean and free of debris."

_____ 3. "This is our cafeteria. On the right is the hot meal line, and on the left is the sandwich line."

_____ 4. "When you enter the shop area, you must put on a safety hat."

_____ 5. "We make the highest-quality tools in the industry."

The Training Cycle

AS 10—2

Identify each of the five statements below as one of the following steps in the training cycle:

a. needs assessment

b. set objectives

c. prepare for training

d. conduct the training

e. measure and evaluate results

_____ 6. "I will now demonstrate the proper technique."

_____ 7. "At the end of this training session, you will be able to operate the machine."

_____ 8. "In reviewing your performance, I've decided that you need more training to increase your speed."

_____ 9. "You passed the test with a perfect score; you're certified."

_____ 10. "Where did I put that JIT sheet? I need to revise it."

Training Methods

AS 10—3

In the situations below, select the most appropriate training method.

a. written material	*h.* job rotation
b. lecture	*i.* projects
c. video	*j.* role play
d. questions and answers	*k.* behavior modeling
e. discussion	*l.* management games
f. programmed learning/CAI	*m.* in-basket exercise
g. demonstration	*n.* cases

_____ 11. You have a large department with a high turnover rate. Employees must learn several rules and regulations in order to perform their jobs.

_____ 12. You occasionally have new employees whom you must teach to handle the typical daily problems they will face on the job.

_____ 13. Your boss has requested a special report.

_____ 14. You want to be sure that employees can cover for each other when they are out.

_____ 15. You need to teach employees how to handle customer complaints.

Accidents

AS 10—4

Identify the condition and cause (select two answers) of the accidents described below.

Condition: *a.* human error   *b.* environmental

Cause: *a.* posture and positioning   *b.* not using safety equipment

   c. machines   *d.* falls   *e.* hand tools   *f.* electric shocks

_____ 16. "I swung the sledgehammer back and the head came off and hit John in the back."

_____ 17. "I tripped on this Coke bottle on the floor."

_____ 18. "I got a chip of wood in my eye while using the saw."

_____ 19. "I don't know what happened; it was grounded. I just plugged it in and jumped in pain."

_____ 20. "I bent over and grabbed the box. But it took me a while to straighten my back again."

Welcome to the Machine

Sharon Waters is the supervisor of the machine department. She recently hired Pete Coleson. Below is a description of Pete's first few hours on the job. The conversation begins in Sharon's office.

SHARON: Welcome to the machine, Pete; we think pink around here.

PETE: Thanks, it's nice to be here. I'm a Pink Floyd fan.

SHARON: We are behind on our production schedule, so I want to get through your orientation quickly and get you right to work.

PETE: Okay.

SHARON: As I told you during the job interview, you are a machinist. You are expected to produce 10 products per hour, 40 per day. You have two weeks to get up to this level. The sooner you can, the better off we will be. The department is behind schedule now. Do you have any questions?

PETE: No, it's pretty straightforward.

SHARON: Good. I also want you to take this booklet and read it when you get a chance. It explains all the rules and things you need to know.

PETE: Sure thing.

SHARON: Now that the orientation is over, let's go to your machine and I'll teach you to operate it. It's not hard to do.

(On the work floor) SHARON: This is it. Let me tell you a little story about these machines. . . .

PETE *(laughing):* That's a funny story.

SHARON: I'll begin by naming the various parts. If you have any questions at all, just ask as we go. This is the _____ . Can you name the parts, Pete?

PETE: Sure, this is the _____ .

SHARON: Great; you're catching on fast. As you know, you will be expected to produce 10 products per hour. Now I'll go through the steps of producing the products a few times. This is step 1, 2, 3, 4, 5 . . . 10. Now you name the steps as I perform them again. Good, now you know all 10 steps. You do it while I watch.

PETE: No problem. Step, 1, 2, 3.

SHARON: Hold it, that's not quite right. Move it to the left a bit. OK.

PETE: Step 4 . . . 10.

SHARON: That's it. Let me see you do it again, naming each step as you go.

PETE: Step 1 . . . 10.

SHARON: That's it. Now in this drawer is a list of the 10 steps in case you forget any. If you have any questions, come see me. If you don't have any questions, you're on your own.

PETE: No questions; you explained everything clearly.

SHARON: It's only been an hour since you got here. You're a fast learner. Welcome to the machine.

About a half hour later, Becky, one of the machinists, ran into Sharon's office and said, "That new guy Pete cut his finger." Sharon went out and looked at Pete's finger.

SHARON: It's only a scratch. Let's go over to the first aid kit and I'll take care of it. *(While taking care of the cut)* How did this happen?

PETE: The machine jammed, so I reached in and pulled the piece out.

SHARON: You're not supposed to do that.

PETE: I didn't know I wasn't supposed to.

SHARON: It's in the booklet I gave you. Why didn't you come and get me?

PETE: You said we were behind schedule. Going to get you would have wasted time.

SHARON: Not really; I don't want you to get hurt. If it jams again I want you to. . . . Do you understand how to unjam it correctly? And are you okay to go back to work?

PETE: Yes to both questions.

SHARON: Okay, get back to work, and come see me if you have any other problems you're not sure of.

Answer the following questions. Use the space between questions to explain your answers.

_F_ 1. The orientation was sufficient for Pete to function comfortably and effectively on the job.
   a. true   *b.* false

_F_ 2. Sharon used the buddy system.
   a. true   *b.* false

_F_ 3. Sharon made Pete's first day on the job like the one suggested in the text.
   a. true   *b.* false

_F_ 4. During Pete's first few hours on the job, a psychological contract developed.
   a. true   *b.* false

_____ 5. Pete's orientation included what elements. (You may select more than one answer.)
   a. organization and department functions
   b. job duties and responsibilities
   c. standing plans
   d. tours
   e. introduction to co-workers

_T_ 6. Sharon followed the JIT steps.
   a. true   *b.* false

_____ 7. The primary training method Sharon used to teach Pete how to operate the machine was
   a. written material
   b. lecture
   c. video
   d. questions and answers
   e. discussion
   f. programmed learning/CAI
   g. demonstration
   h. job rotation
   i. projects
   j. role play
   k. behavior modeling
   l. management games
   m. in-basket exercise
   n. cases

_A_   8. The condition causing the accident was
     a. human error   *b.* environment

_____   9. The accident was caused by
     a. posture and positioning   *d.* falls
     b. not using/wearing safety   *e.* hand tools
        equipment
     c. machines   *f.* electric shocks

_F_   10. The accident was a disabling injury.
     a. true   *b.* false

11. Could this accident have been avoided? If so, how?

Human error. Pete did not
have time to read Booklet on
~~Woodchia~~ Machine operations.
Pete should have gone to Sharon.

12. If you were in Sharon's supervisory position, how would you have oriented and
    trained Pete?

There should not have been
a rush to pressure Pete to be
productive so quickly. Safety training
should have been more intense for
Pete. Hazards should have been
explained, like jamming, and how to
avoid them.

PREPARATION FOR IN-CLASS SKILL-BUILDING EXERCISE

Developing Orientation, Training, and Safety Programs

SB 10–1

For this exercise think of a supervisory job you would like to have in the future (or have now). Assume you will be responsible for orienting and training the employees you supervise, and that you must develop a safety program for your department. (You may contact a supervisor who holds this position for help with this exercise.)

Write Out a Description of Your Orientation Program: What will you do and say? (Cover each of the five areas in an orientation program.) How will you help the new employee fit in? Describe the new employee's first day at work.

Write Out a Description of Your Training Program: Will off-the-job training, on-the-job training, or both be used? Which training methods will you use? If you are not doing Skill-Building Exercise 10–2, explain what you will do for each step in the training cycle.

Write Out a Description of Your Safety Program: How will you prevent accidents? Develop a safety checklist.

IN-CLASS SKILL-BUILDING EXERCISE

Developing Orientation, Training, and Safety Programs

SB 10–1

Procedure 1 (10–50 minutes)

Objectives: To experience developing orientation, training, and safety programs.

Experience: You will share and discuss the orientation, training, and safety programs you developed in the preparation section.

Materials: You will need your completed preparation for this exercise.

Option A. Students describe their programs to the class. The instructor then asks questions, leads a class discussion, and makes comments. To allow more participation, each student should describe only one program, not two or three.

Option B. Break into groups of five or six and discuss your programs. Try to help each other improve your programs.

Option C. Same as option B, but the group selects a member to present his or her example to the entire class.

Conclusion: The instructor may lead a class discussion and make concluding remarks.

Application (2–4 minutes): What have I learned from this experience? How will I use this knowledge in the future?

Sharing: Volunteers give their answers to the application section.

PREPARATION FOR IN-CLASS SKILL-BUILDING EXERCISE

The Training Cycle

SB 10–2

For this exercise, you will develop a JIT following the five steps in the training cycle.

Step 1. Needs Assessment: Select a task you are familiar with and can teach someone else to do in 10 minutes (knitting, a job function, an athletic technique, how to play a game, and so on).

Step 2. Set Objectives: Write down your objectives for the training session, following the text criteria.

Step 3. Prepare for Training: Write out a description of your plan, following the four steps in the JIT model. Be sure to develop steps for the presentation of the operation. The "who" will be determined in class. The "when" and "where" will be in class.

Step 4. Conduct the Training: The training will be done in class. Be sure to bring all the materials you will need.

Step 5. Measure and Evaluate Results: This will be done in class. But make sure that your plan includes how you will measure and evaluate your training results.

IN-CLASS SKILL-BUILDING EXERCISE

The Training Cycle

SB 10–2

Objective: To develop skills in designing and implementing training using the training cycle and JIT.

Experience: You will give, receive, and observe JIT.

Materials: You will need your completed preparation.

Procedure 1
(2–3 minutes)

Break into groups of three, preferably with people who are not familiar with the task you will be teaching. Make some groups of two, if necessary. Decide who will be the trainer, trainee, and observer for the first training session. During the training session, the trainer teaches the trainee to perform the task while the observer makes notes on the integration sheet at the end of this exercise.

Procedure 2
(10–15 minutes)

a. Training session 1 takes place.
b. When the training is over, or the time is up, the observer leads a group discussion on which steps the trainer did and did not follow in the training cycle and JIT. Focus on how the trainer can improve his or her skills. Do not go on to the next training session until you are told to do so.

Procedure 3
(10–15 minutes)

a. Training session 2 takes place. The previous trainer is now the trainee; the previous observer becomes the trainer; and the trainee becomes the observer.
b. Same as procedure 2b.

Procedure 4
(10–15 minutes)

a. Training session 3 takes place. Each person plays the role he or she hasn't played yet.
b. Same as procedure 2b.

Conclusion: The instructor may lead a class discussion and make concluding remarks.

Application (2–4 minutes): What did I learn from this experience? How will I use this knowledge in the future?

Sharing: Volunteers give their answers to the application section.

Integration Sheet

The observer gives feedback to the trainer by specifying which steps the trainer did and did not follow before and during the training session. Check off steps performed well.

Step 1. Needs Assessment: The trainer identified a training need.

Step 2. Set Objectives: The trainer stated an objective that was difficult but achievable; observable and measurable; specific, with a target date; and accepted.

Step 3. Prepare for the Training: The trainer was well prepared to conduct the training. Could the trainer have been better prepared? How?

Step 4. Conduct the Training: Did the trainer perform the JIT steps listed in Model 10–1? How could the trainer improve?

Step 5. Measure and Evaluate Training Results: Did the trainee achieve the objective?

Overall: How could the trainer improve?

11

Improving Productivity

Learning Objectives

1. Explain the three factors of the performance formula and the ways in which each affects performance.
2. Describe the process of measuring productivity and three ways to increase productivity.
3. Explain the four methods of increasing employee ability.
4. List the five steps in the increasing productivity model and use the model.
5. Describe and contrast four content motivation theories.
6. Describe and contrast the two process motivation theories.
7. State how the four types of reinforcement are used.
8. List the four steps in the giving praise model and use the model.
9. List possible limitations of using motivation theories outside North America.
10. Describe ways to increase productivity through capital, job enrichment, job design, and job simplification.

Key Terms

To achieve our objectives in this chapter, it is important that you understand the following 17 key terms. They are presented in the order in which they appear in the chapter. The list of key terms also appears in alphabetical order in the end-of-chapter review.

performance	needs hierarchy	reinforcement
performance	two-factor theory	theory
formula	manifest needs	giving praise
productivity	theory	job enrichment
increasing-	process motivation	job design
productivity model	theories	job simplification
motivation	expectancy theory	
content motivation	equity theory	
theories		

Latoia Henderson was recently promoted to a management position at State Potato Chip Co. She is enthusiastic about her work. Generally things are going well, but Latoia is having a problem with Hank. Hank is often late for work, and even though he can do a good job, he does not regularly perform to expectations. Latoia had a talk with Hank to find out what the problem was. Hank said that the money and benefits were okay, and that the people in the department were nice, but that the job was boring. He complained that he didn't have any say about how to do his job and that Latoia was always checking up on him. Hank believes he is treated fairly because of the union, which gives him job protection. But because everyone is paid the same, working hard is a waste of time. If you were in Latoia's position, how would you motivate Hank? In this chapter you will learn specific motivation theories and techniques that can be used to motivate Hank and employees in all organizations.

349

I. Performance and Productivity

Organizational success comes through employees. The supervisor is closest to the employees, and his or her behavior affects their attitude and performance.[1] **Performance** *is the ability to use organizational resources effectively and efficiently.* Performance is not an absolute; it is a continuum. As our definition indicates, there are three components of performance: resources, effectiveness, and efficiency.

Peter Drucker distinguished effectiveness and efficiency as follows: effectiveness is "doing the right thing" and efficiency is "doing it right." To perform at high levels, the supervisor must use organizational resources (human, physical, and financial) effectively. A supervisor is effective if he or she sets objectives that coordinate with the organization's objectives and assigns priorities to and accomplishes the objectives. There is usually more than one way to meet objectives. Selecting the right way results in higher levels of performance.

A supervisor can be efficient without being effective. Some supervisors are very efficient at doing things that should not be done at all, or that have low priority. You must determine the right thing to do before doing it right.

The Performance Formula

Generally, an employee who is motivated will try harder to do a good job than one who is not motivated. However, performance is not simply based on motivation. The level of performance attained is determined by three interdependent factors: ability, motivation, and resources. Stated as a **performance formula,** *performance = ability × motivation × resources.*

For performance levels to be high, all three factors must be high. If any one is low or missing, the performance level will be adversely affected. For example, Roland, a student, wants to get an A on an exam (high performance). He has the books, notes, and so on (resources), and studies long and hard (motivation). However, Roland is low in academic ability and does not get the A. Mary Lou, a very intelligent student, has the books, but because she does not care about an A, she does not study (low motivation) and does not get an A either. Poindexter, an intelligent, motivated student, has an outdated edition of the book with material missing. Because several questions on the exam are from the new material he gets a B. Veronica has all three factors and gets the A.

As an employee and manager, if you want to attain high levels of performance, you must be sure that you and your employees have the ability, motivation, and resources to meet objectives. When performance is not at the standard level or above, you must determine which performance factor needs to be improved, and improve it. In the opening case, Hank has the ability and resources, but he lacks motivation.

When employee needs are not met through the organization, employees are dissatisfied and are generally lower performers. This is the case with Hank; he finds the job boring and is not performing to expectations. To increase Hank's performance, Latoia must meet the goal of human relations. She must create a win-win situation so that Hank's needs are met to motivate him to perform to her expectations. As each motivation theory and technique is presented, you will learn how Latoia can apply it to motivate Hank or others.

There is no single universally accepted theory of how to motivate people. In this chapter you will learn seven major motivation theories and ways you can use them to motivate yourself and others. After studying all the theories, you can select one theory to use, take from several to make your own theory, or apply the theory that best fits the specific situation.

LEARNING OBJECTIVE

1. Explain the three factors of the performance formula and the ways in which each affects performance.

Defining Productivity

Productivity has been the premiere issue in business for more than a decade. Productivity has increased at a much faster rate in other industrial nations than it has in the United States. Among the 11 major industrial countries, the United States was 10th in productivity gains. The leaders included Norway (6.4 percent gain), Japan (5.8 percent), and the United Kingdom (5.1 percent) compared to the 2 percent gain of the United States.[2] Yet, according to Wickham Skinner, the harder companies pursue productivity, the more elusive it becomes.[3] U.S. manufacturing does seem to be catching up, but the service sector is still languishing.[4] Joji Arai, director of the Washington, D.C., office of the Japan Productivity Center, has stated that productivity is a state of mind.[5] Supervisors and employees have to be constantly thinking of ways to increase productivity.

Productivity *is a performance measure relating inputs to outputs.* The inputs include employee's time, materials, equipment, and so forth. The outputs are the products or services produced. Productivity tells supervisors how efficient they are in utilizing their department's resources. Some organizations have increased productivity by working better and faster with fewer employees. For example, Xerox halved both the number of employees and the amount of time needed to design a product. Harley-Davidson reduced total plant employment by 25 percent while cutting the time it takes to make a motorcycle by more than half.[6]

Measuring Productivity

Productivity can be measured by dividing the outputs by the inputs. For example, a trucking company wants to measure productivity on a delivery. The truck traveled 500 miles and used 50 gallons of gas. Its productivity was 10 miles to the gallon:

$$\frac{\text{output: 500 miles traveled}}{\text{inputs: 50 gallons of gas}} = \text{productivity of 10 mpg}$$

Another fairly simple example involves measuring the productivity of an accounts payable department. (1) Select a base period of time, such as an hour, day, week, month, quarter, or year. We'll use a week. (2) Determine how many bills were sent out during that period of time (outputs): 600. (We checked the records.) (3) Determine the cost of sending out the bills (inputs). Determining cost can become complicated if you use overhead, depreciation, and so forth. We'll calculate cost based on direct labor charges. We have three employees. Each is paid $5 per hour. They all worked 40 hours during the week, or a total of 120 hours. The total cost is $5 per hour times 120 hours, or $600. (4) Divide the number of bills by the costs:

$$\frac{\text{output: 600 bills sent}}{\text{input: \$600 cost}} = 1$$

The performance of 1 can be stated differently. It is usually stated as a ratio (in this case, 1:1), or as a percentage (100 percent). It can also be stated as a cost per unit. To determine the cost per unit, you reverse the process and divide the input by the output. In this case, it cost $1 to send out each bill. Productivity measures are more meaningful when they are compared to other productivity rates. For example, you can compare your department's productivity to that of other departments. You can also compare your productivity during one period to your productivity in other periods. This comparison will enable you to identify increases or decreases in productivity. As indicated at the beginning of this discussion, increasing productivity is desirable.

Increasing Productivity

There are three ways to increase productivity:

1. Increase the value of the outputs while maintaining the value of the inputs ($\uparrow O \leftrightarrow I$).

2. Maintain the value of the outputs while decreasing the value of the inputs ($\leftrightarrow O \downarrow I$).

3. Increase the value of the outputs while decreasing the value of the inputs ($\uparrow O \downarrow I$).

To illustrate, we will use the accounts payable department example above.

1. The supervisor conducted a training program for the employees (ability). As a result of the training, they sent out 650 bills the following week (outputs increased), without getting a raise in pay (inputs maintained). The productivity is figured as follows:

$$\frac{650}{600} = 1.08\text{: 1 ratio}$$

or 108 percent (move the decimal right two places). The ratio has gone up by .08. Calculate the percentage change by dividing the change in the ratio by the base ratio figure. (Change in ratio: 1.08 − 1.00 = .08 increase.) Percentage change = .08 ÷ 1.00 = .08; productivity increased by 8 percent. The cost per bill has decreased by 8 cents, to 92 cents (600/650 = .923 subtracted from the previous $1).

2. One employee quit work on Thursday. The supervisor helped out a little on Friday, and convinced the other two employees to push hard to maintain the 600 billing level (motivation). Productivity level is calculated thus:

$$\frac{600}{560} = 1.0714\text{: 1 ratio}$$

or 107 percent, a productivity increase of 7 percent.

3. The supervisor bought a new computer (resources). The three employees were given jobs in another department. An experienced computer operator was hired at $8 per hour for a 40-hour workweek ($320 per week). During the week, 800 bills were sent out. The productivity level is calculated as follows:

$$\frac{800}{320} = 2.5\text{:1 ratio}$$

or 250 percent, a productivity increase of 150 percent.

In determining productivity, several costs must be considered. When new resources must be purchased, it is important to consider the cost of these resources. Direct labor costs, as mentioned, are relevant in determining produc-

EXHIBIT 11–1	**INCREASING PRODUCTIVITY**
	Step 1. Define productivity.
	Step 2. Measure productivity.
	Step 3. Improve productivity.
	Step 4. Follow through.

Source: Joan Harmann, "Getting More Output from Your Department," *Management Solutions,* August 1986, p. 6.

tivity. In a production department where materials costs are significant, these costs should also be added to the direct labor cost. Here, simply decreasing waste will increase your department's productivity. For a more accurate measure, include depreciation of the resource, overhead, and so forth. The accounting department can help you measure productivity. If you don't know and can't find out the cost of running your department, you can measure productivity based on hours of labor rather than on cost.

It is important to calculate productivity rather than just production because you can increase production while decreasing your productivity.[7] For example, the accounts payable department sends out 650 bills (production). However, it took 10 hours of overtime, which cost time-and-a-half at $7.50 per hour, or $75. Productivity has decreased to .9629:1 or 96 percent (650/675 = [600 + 75 overtime]) from 1:1 or 100 percent.

Increasing productivity can help gain pay raises for your employees. It can also help you get a raise and promotion. It is advisable to document productivity. To increase productivity, follow the four steps in Exhibit 11–1. We will examine specific ways of improving productivity (step 3) in the sections that follow.

LEARNING OBJECTIVE

2. Describe the process of measuring productivity and three ways to increase productivity.

II. Increasing Productivity through Employee Ability

Ability is the first factor in the performance formula. In this section, we will discuss how improving employee ability can increase productivity. This can be done through training or participation. We will also discuss a model for increasing productivity.

Some question whether productivity can be increased through people. They suggest putting the time, effort, and money into resources such as robots. The author agrees that productivity can and should be increased through resources, but he also believes that it is the supervisor's job to maintain and increase productivity through employees (ability and motivation). In support of his belief, he would like to point out that the 1981 congressional hearing on the human factor in technological innovation and productivity improvement revealed that collaborative employee-management relationships had equal to or greater potential for increasing productivity than did hard technologies. In addition, the National Science Foundation reported that the Japanese automakers are more productive than their American counterparts because of management-employee collaboration, not technology.[8]

Training

One way to increase productivity is through training. Organizations spend billions of dollars each year on training because they realize that it increases productivity. We discussed training in detail in Chapter 10, so we will spend no more time on this topic.

Participation

Participation affects employee satisfaction and productivity.[9] Today's employees want to know what is going on in the organization. They want to be involved in work decisions.[10] When you include employees in decision making you are utilizing their abilities. Employees tend to know their jobs better than the so-called experts who design them. Let employees do the job the way they want to, as long as productivity levels are maintained or increased. What difference does it make how they do the job? What seems awkward to the supervisor may be very comfortable to an employee. Focus on the end result, not the process. There doesn't have to be one right or best way to do every job, and the method suggested by a supervisor or other expert may not be the best way. Using the participative supervisory style, when appropriate, can increase productivity. Develop employees' creativity and awareness of productivity. Encourage and allow employees to experiment and make changes without getting permission.[11]

We have already discussed some participation techniques, such as quality circles. Another that may be useful in improving productivity is the suggestion system.

The Suggestion System   Successful organizations such as IBM, Frito-Lay, and 3M use suggestion systems to increase productivity. If the suggestion system is managed properly, the department or organization can get lots of good ideas that work. At a Canon plant, the system averages 50 suggestions per employee per year. At Fuji Electric, the average is 300 annual suggestions from each worker. Supervisors in this environment manage ideas, not people. Although most organizations tailor their suggestion systems to their unique situation, there are some guidelines for developing and using suggestion systems:

- Make participation voluntary.
- Stress all improvements, not just major ideas worth thousands of dollars in savings.
- Evaluate all suggestions and evaluate fairly.
- Give employees quick feedback on their suggestions.
- Clearly explain to employees the reason for not implementing their ideas.
- Have the person doing the job implement suggested changes.
- Reward employees whose suggestions are used. Rewards do not have to be monetary, but it helps if they are.[12]

Suggestion systems do not have to be companywide or complicated. One supervisor developed a successful system in which employees post their suggestions on a special bulletin board during the week. Every Friday, a half hour before quitting time, a committee meets to review the week's suggestions. The committee determines which ideas will be adopted and follows up to see that earlier suggestions have been implemented. This system may not work for every department. As a supervisor, you should develop one that will work for your department.

The Increasing Productivity Model

The increasing productivity model is designed to improve ability to deal with motivation problems. The **increasing productivity model** *involves referring to past feedback, describing current performance, describing desired performance, getting a commitment to the change, and following up.* To illustrate each step, I have included an example. In the example, Fran is the supervisor of the vending machine repair department, and Dale is a relatively new repair technician.

**Step 1.
Refer to Past Feedback**

This assumes that the employee was told or trained to do something in the past and never did, or no longer does it properly. If the employee has never received feedback, begin by explaining the situation.

FRAN: Hi, Dale. I called you into my office because I wanted to discuss your repair record.

DALE: What about it?

FRAN: We haven't discussed your performance since you started, but I've noticed a problem and wanted to correct it quickly.

**Step 2.
Describe Current
Performance**

In detail, using specific examples, describe the current performance that needs to be changed.

FRAN: In reviewing the repair reports, I realized that you repaired vending machines at the Big Y Supermarket, the United Cooperative Bank, and the Springfield YMCA. You had to return to all three places to repair the same machine again within a month.

DALE: That's right. But if you look at my report, you'll see that the repeat trips were for different problems. I fixed the machines right the first time.

FRAN: I realize that. That's not the problem. The problem is that the average time before returning for any repair on a machine is three months. Did you realize that?

DALE: Now that you mentioned it, I did hear it in the training class.

FRAN: I want to find out why you have to return to the same machine more often than the average. My guess is that it's because when you repair a machine, you only fix the problem; you don't go through the entire machine to perform routine maintenance.

DALE: My job is to fix the machines.

**Step 3.
Describe Desired
Performance**

Tell the employee, in detail, exactly what the desired performance is. If a skill is needed, teach it using job instrumental training (JIT). Explain why it is important to change performance.

FRAN: During the training program, did they tell you to go through the entire machine for routine maintenance or just to fix it?

DALE: I don't remember.

FRAN: Do you know why it is important to do maintenance rather than just fix the machines?

DALE: I guess it's so I don't have to go back within a month and repair the same machine.

FRAN: That's right. You'd be more productive. From now on I want you to go through the machines and perform maintenance instead of just fixing them.

**Step 4.
Get a Commitment
to the Change**

If possible, get the employee to commit to changing his or her performance. This is important because if the employee is not willing to make a commitment, he or she will not make the change. It's better to know now that the employee is not going to change, than it is to wait and find out when it may be too late. The employee can commit and not make the change. But at least you have done your job, and can refer to past commitments when you discipline the employee. We'll discuss discipline in Chapter 14.

FRAN: From now on will you do maintenance, rather than just repairs?

DALE: I didn't do it in the past because I didn't realize I was supposed to. But in the future, I will.

**Step 5.
Follow Up**

The follow-up meeting is important to make sure that the employee knows you are serious about the change. When employees know their performance will be evaluated, they are more likely to make a suggested change. A meeting is not always necessary, but the employee should be told how the supervisor will follow up.

FRAN: In the future, I will review the records for frequent repairs of the same machine. I don't think it will continue, but if it does, I'll call you in again.

DALE: That won't be necessary.

FRAN: Great. I appreciate your cooperation, Dale. This was my only concern about your work. Other than this one area, you're doing a good job. I'll see you later.

DALE: Have a good one.

During the discussion with the employee, preferably near the end, it is important to be positive while correcting performance. This helps motivate the employee to make the necessary change. For an example, refer to Fran's last statement. Model 11–1 summarizes the five steps in increasing productivity.

**LEARNING
OBJECTIVES**

3. Explain the four methods of increasing employee ability.
4. List the five steps in the increasing productivity model and use the model.

CONNECTIONS

3. Describe a specific situation in which it would be appropriate to use the steps for increasing productivity listed in Model 11–1.

III. Increasing Productivity through Content Motivation

Increasing productivity through the organization's human resources (employees) may involve motivation as well as ability. Motivation is the second factor in the performance formula. In this section you will learn about motivation and why it is important; four content motivation theories will be explained.

What Is Motivation and Why Is It Important?

The term **motivation** *means the willingness to achieve the organization's objectives.* Have you ever wondered why people do the things they do? The primary reason people do what they do is to meet their needs or wants. The process people go through to meet their needs is as follows:

need → motive → behavior → satisfaction or dissatisfaction

For example, you are thirsty (need) and would like (motive) to get a drink. You get a drink (behavior) that quenches (satisfaction) your thirst. However, if you could

---

MODEL 11–1   **INCREASING PRODUCTIVITY**

Step 1. Refer to past feedback.

Step 2. Describe current performance.

Step 3. Describe desired performance.

Step 4. Get a commitment to the change.

Step 5. Follow up.

not get a drink, or a drink of what you really wanted, you would be dissatisfied. Satisfaction is usually short-lived. Getting that drink satisfied you, but soon you will need another drink.

Managers often view motivation as an employee's willingness to put forth effort to achieve organizational objectives. Latoia is concerned because Hank is not motivated to work hard.

Why Knowing How to Motivate Employees Is Important

There are many reasons for which employee motivation is important:

- Motivation is the number one problem facing business today.[13] Today's employees have less interest in extra hours, job dedication, attendance, and punctuality.[14] Knowing how to motivate will help you eliminate or reduce these performance problems.

- $160 billion a year is lost through wasted time on the job. This figure does not include the cost of absenteeism, alcoholism and drug abuse, or personal problems. Many employees just do enough to get by without being fired. They operate at about 60 percent efficiency. With proper motivation, their efficiency could be raised to 80 percent or higher.[15]

- The old belief was that if you paid people adequately they would be motivated. However, today we realize that people don't work just for money. Money is not the prime motivator; job satisfaction is.[16]

- Motivation is a major part of a supervisor's job. Charles Shipley, a vice president of SL Industries, says that managers have to learn more about motivating our workers and guiding them.[17] Motivational skills with subordinates is critical for advancement.[18]

A satisfied employee is more productive.[19] Job satisfaction is the primary motivator.[20] If an organization wants to increase performance, it must meet employees' needs. Each year hundreds of millions of dollars are spent on employee need satisfaction programs to increase productivity. To increase performance, managers must know their own needs and their employees' needs, and they must satisfy them.[21] This is the goal of human relations.

The **content motivation theories** *focus on identifying people's needs in order to understand what motivates them.* You will learn four content motivation theories: needs hierarchy, ERG theory, two-factor theory, and manifest needs theory; and how organizations use them to motivate employees.

Needs Hierarchy

The **needs hierarchy** *is based on five categories of needs.* In the 1940s Abraham Maslow developed one of the most popular and widely known motivation theories.[22] His theory is based on three major assumptions:

- People's needs are arranged in order of importance (hierarchy), going from basic needs (physiological) to more complex needs (self-actualization).

- People will not be motivated to satisfy a higher-level need unless the lower-level needs have been at least minimally satisfied.

- Maslow assumed that people have five classifications of needs. Following is a list of these five needs in order of importance to the individual.

Physiological Needs: These are people's primary or basic needs. They include air, food, shelter, sex, and relief or avoidance of pain. In an organizational setting, these needs include adequate salary, breaks, and working conditions.

Safety Needs: Once the physiological needs are met, the individual is concerned with safety and security. In the organizational setting, these needs include safe

EXHIBIT 11-2   **NEEDS HIERARCHY AND ERG THEORY**

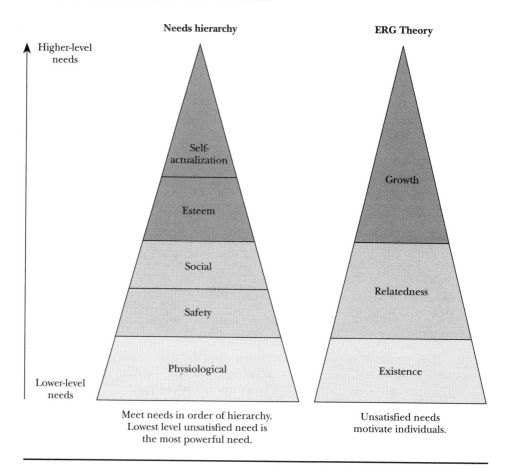

Needs hierarchy

Higher-level needs

- Self-actualization
- Esteem
- Social
- Safety
- Physiological

Lower-level needs

Meet needs in order of hierarchy.
Lowest level unsatisfied need is
the most powerful need.

ERG Theory

- Growth
- Relatedness
- Existence

Unsatisfied needs
motivate individuals.

working conditions, salary increases to meet inflation, job security, and fringe benefits that protect the physiological needs.

Social Needs: After establishing safety, people look for love, friendship, acceptance, and affection. In the organizational setting, these needs include the opportunity to interact with others, to be accepted, and to have friends.

Esteem Needs: After the social needs are met, the individual focuses on ego, status, self-respect, recognition for accomplishments, and a feeling of self-confidence and prestige. In the organizational setting, these needs include titles, the satisfaction of completing the job itself, merit pay raises, recognition, challenging tasks, participation in decision making, and the chance for advancement.

Self-Actualization: The highest level of need is to develop one's full potential. To do so, one seeks growth, achievement, and advancement. In the organizational setting, these needs include the development of one's skills, the chance to be creative, achievement and promotions, and the ability to have complete control over one's job.

Many research studies do not support Maslow's hierarchy theory. However, it has a sound foundation and is still used today. In fact, Maslow's work served as a basis for several other theories.

Maslow himself saw limits to the five steps. He also spoke of other needs that motivate people. Maslow called them "cognitive" and left them outside of the hierarchy. One of Maslow's cognitive needs is a thirst for knowledge; he referred to people motivated by that need as "unsung Galileos."

See Exhibit 11-2 for an illustration of Maslow's five needs.

ERG Theory

The classification of needs has been debated. Some say there are only two needs, and others claim there are seven. Several researchers have combined categories to simplify the theory. ERG is a well-known simplification. As Exhibit 11–2 illustrates, Clayton Alderfer reorganized Maslow's needs hierarchy into three levels of needs: existence (physiological and safety needs), relatedness (social), and growth (esteem and self-actualization). Alderfer maintained the higher- and lower-order needs. He agreed with Maslow that unsatisfied needs motivate individuals. In the opening case, Hank's performance was poor, but he can be motivated to meet Latoia's expectations if his performance results in satisfying his needs.

Motivating with Needs Hierarchy and ERG Theory

Based on Maslow's work, we can conclude that managers should concentrate mainly on meeting employees' lower-level needs so that they will not dominate the employees' motivational process. Managers should get to know and understand people's needs and meet them as a means of increasing performance.

To use ERG theory, answer six questions:

1. What need does the individual have?

2. What needs have been satisfied?

3. Which unsatisfied need is the lowest in the hierarchy?

4. Have some higher-order needs been frustrated? If so, how?

5. Has the person refocused on a lower-level need?

6. How can be unsatisfied needs be satisfied?

Latoia observed Hank and took the time to talk to him to determine his needs. Hank's need for existence and relatedness have been met. However, his need for growth has been frustrated. To motivate Hank, Latoia must meet his need for growth. Later in this chapter you will learn ways to satisfy growth needs.

Two-Factor Theory

The **two-factor theory** *classifies needs as hygienes or motivators.* Before learning Herzberg's theory, complete Self-Learning Exercise 11–1 to learn what motivates you.

SELF-LEARNING EXERCISE 11–1

Motivators or Hygienes

Most workers want job satisfaction.[23] Below are 12 job factors that contribute to job satisfaction. Rate each according to its importance to you. Place the number 1 through 5 on the line before each factor.

Very important		Somewhat important		Not important
5	4	3	2	1

_____ 1. An interesting job

_____ 2. A good boss

_____ 3. Recognition and appreciation for the work I do

_____ 4. The opportunity for advancement

_____ 5. A satisfying personal life

_____ 6. A prestigious or status job

_____ 7. Job responsibility

_____ 8. Good working conditions (nice office)

_____ 9. Sensible company rules, regulations, procedures, and policies

_____ 10. The opportunity to grow through learning new things

_____ 11. A job I can do well and succeed at

_____ 12. Job security

To determine if hygienes or motivators are important to you, copy your answers in the appropriate blanks below.

Hygiene factors score	Motivational factors score
2. _____	1. _____
5. _____	3. _____
6. _____	4. _____
8. _____	7. _____
9. _____	10. _____
12. _____	11. _____
Totals _____	_____

Add each column vertically. Did you select hygienes or motivators as being more important to you? Now we'll find out what the difference is.

In the 1950s Frederick Herzberg and associates interviewed 200 accountants and engineers.[24] They were asked to describe situations in which they were satisfied or motivated and dissatisfied or unmotivated. Their findings disagreed with the traditional view that satisfaction and dissatisfaction were at opposite ends of a continuum.

Maslow classified five needs, Alderfer classified three needs, and Herzberg classified two needs that he calls factors. Herzberg combines lower-level needs

EXHIBIT 11–3   **TWO-FACTOR THEORY**

Hygiene Factors (Needs)
(physiological, safety, and social/existence and relatedness needs)

	Extrinsic Motivation	
Dissatisfaction	(Environment)	No Dissatisfaction

* Pay

* Status

* Job security

* Working conditions

* Fringe benefits

* Policies and administrative practices

* Human relations

(physiological, safety, and social or existence and relatedness) into one classification he called hygienes; and higher-level needs (esteem and self-actualization or growth) into one classification he called motivators. Hygienes are also called extrinsic motivators because motivation comes from outside the job itself, such as pay, job security, and title; working conditions; fringe benefits; and relationships. Motivators are called intrinsic motivators because motivation comes from the job itself, such as achievement, recognition, challenge, and advancement. See Exhibit 11–3 for an illustration of Herzberg's theory.

Herzberg contends that providing maintenance factors will keep people from being dissatisfied, but that it will not motivate people. For example, if people are dissatisfied with their pay and they get a raise, they will no longer be dissatisfied. They may even be satisfied for a short period of time. However, before long they get accustomed to the new standard of living and will no longer be satisfied. They will need another raise to be satisfied again. The vicious cycle goes on. If you got a pay raise, would you be motivated and be more productive? How many people do you know who increased their level of productivity and maintained it until the next pay raise?

To motivate, Herzberg says that you must first ensure that hygiene factors are adequate. Once employees are satisfied with their environment, they can be motivated through their jobs. However, Herzberg's theory has been argued, as well as supported, in scholarly articles.

One thing is clear, however. There *is* a difference between the job itself and the work environment. Therefore, simply because a person enjoys great maintenance factors such as high pay and benefits does not mean that he or she will be a high producer. It does mean that he or she will not be unhappy with the workplace. On the other hand, if a person dislikes the job, he or she will have little or no motivation to do well. What all this means is that you cannot make an employee do well by insisting, "We pay you well. You must be happy," if the employee doesn't like the job he or she is doing.

Understanding this theory is helpful when you are dealing with people who have boring jobs. In such cases you can at least make sure the "environment" is clean—that there is good pay, and so forth. Then you will be able to maintain an adequate level of productivity. However, if you are dealing with employees who have boring, meaningless jobs *and* low pay, you get little productivity at all.

Motivator Factors (Needs)
(esteem and self-actualization/growth needs)

Intrinsic Motivation

No Job Satisfaction	(The Job Itself)	Job Satisfaction

* Meaningful and challenging work

* Recognition for accomplishments

* Feeling of achievement

* Increased responsibility

* Opportunity for growth

* Opportunity for advancement

Review Self-Learning Exercise 11–1. According to Herzberg, if you seek and attain these job factors, you may not be dissatisfied, but you will not be satisfied. To be satisfied you must seek and attain motivators.

Using Two-Factor Theory to Motivate Employees

In the opening case, Hank said that he was not dissatisfied with hygiene factors. He lacked job satisfaction. If Latoia is going to motivate him, she will have to focus on intrinsic motivation, not hygiene. Hank says the job is boring, but will a pay raise or better working conditions make the job more interesting and challenging? Motivation comes from doing what you like and enjoy doing. According to Herzberg, the best way to motivate employees is to build challenge and opportunity for achievement into the job itself. Herzberg developed a method for increasing motivation, which he called job enrichment. Under the Motivation Techniques section of this chapter, you will learn about job enrichment and how Latoia could use it to motivate Hank.

Manifest Needs Theory

Like Maslow, Alderfer, and Herzberg, manifest needs theorists believe people are motivated by their needs. However, they classify needs differently. **Manifest needs theory** *classifies needs as achievement, power, and affiliation.* McClelland does not have a classification for lower-level needs. His affiliation needs is the same as social and relatedness, and power and achievement are related to esteem and self-actualization and growth. See Exhibit 11–4 for a comparison of the classification of needs by four theories of motivation.

Manifest needs theory was originally developed by Henry Murry, and then adapted by John Atkins and David McClelland.[25] Unlike Maslow, they believe that needs are based on personality and are developed as people interact with the environment. All people possess the need for achievement, power, and affiliation, but to various degrees. One of the three needs tends to be dominant in each of us and motivates our behavior. Before getting into the details of each need, complete Self-Learning Exercise 11–2 and determine your dominant or primary need.

E X H I B I T   1 1 – 4   **CLASSIFICATION OF NEEDS BY FOUR THEORIES OF MOTIVATION**

Maslow Needs Hierarchy Theory	Alderfer ERG Theory	Herzberg Two-Factor Theory	McClelland Manifest Needs Theory
Self-actualization	Growth	Motivators	Power
Esteem			Achievement
Social	Relatedness	Hygiene	Affiliation
Safety	Existence		
Physiological			

Manifest Needs

Identify each of the 15 statements according to how accurately it describes you. Place the number 1 through 5 on the line before each statement.

Like me		Somewhat like me		Not like me
5	4	3	2	1

_____ 1. I enjoy working hard.

_____ 2. I enjoy competition and winning.

_____ 3. I want or have lots of friends.

_____ 4. I enjoy a difficult challenge.

_____ 5. I enjoy leading and being in charge.

_____ 6. I want to be liked by others.

_____ 7. I want to know how I am progressing as I complete tasks.

_____ 8. I confront people who do things I disagree with.

_____ 9. I enjoy frequent parties.

_____ 10. I enjoy setting and achieving realistic goals.

_____ 11. I enjoy influencing other people to get my way.

_____ 12. I enjoy belonging to lots of groups and organizations.

_____ 13. I enjoy the satisfaction of completing a difficult task.

_____ 14. In a leaderless situation I tend to take charge.

_____ 15. I enjoy working with others more than working alone.

To determine your primary need, copy your answers in the appropriate blanks below. Each statement/column represents a specific need.

Achievement	Power	Affiliation
1. _____	2. _____	3. _____
4. _____	5. _____	6. _____
7. _____	8. _____	9. _____
10. _____	11. _____	12. _____
13. _____	14. _____	15. _____
Totals _____	_____	_____

Add up the total of each column. Each column total should be between 5 and 25 points. The column with the highest score is your dominant or primary need.

Now that you have a better understanding of your needs, you will learn more about all three needs.

The Need for Achievement (_n_Ach)

People with a high _n_Ach tend to have the following characteristics:

- They want to take personal responsibility for solving problems.
- They are goal oriented; they set moderate, realistic, attainable goals.
- They seek a challenge, excellence, and individuality.
- They take calculated, moderate risks.

- They desire concrete feedback on their performance.
- They are willing to work hard.

People with a high *n*Ach think about ways to do a better job, accomplish something unusual or important, and generally make progress in their careers. They perform well in nonroutine, challenging, and competitive situations, whereas people low in *n*Ach do not perform well in these situations.

McClelland's research shows that only about 10 percent of the U.S. population has a dominant need for achievement. There is evidence of a positive correlation between high achievement need and high performance. People with a high *n*Ach tend to enjoy sales and entrepreneurial-type positions. Managers tend to have a high, but not dominant, *n*Ach.

Motivating Employees with a High n*Ach:* Give them nonroutine, challenging tasks in which there are clear, attainable objectives. Give them fast and frequent feedback on their performance. Continually give them increased responsibility for doing new things.

The Need for Power (*n*Pow)

People with a high need for power tend to have the following characteristics:

- They want to control the situation.
- They want influence or control over others.
- They enjoy competition in which they can win; they do not like to lose.
- They are willing to confront others.

People with high *n*Pow think about controlling a situation, and the people in it, while seeking positions of authority and status. People with high *n*Pow tend to have a low need for affiliation. Managers tend to have a dominant need for power. Power is essential for successful supervision.

Motivating Employees with a High n*Pow:* Let them plan and control their jobs as much as possible. Try to include them in decision making, especially when they are affected by the decision. They tend to perform best alone rather than as team members. Try to assign them to a whole task rather than just a part of a task.

People are motivated to gain power because having it meets their needs. In the opening case, Hank's primary need seems to be power. Hank wants more say on how to do his job, and wants Latoia to do less checking up on him. If Latoia empowers Hank by giving him more job-related responsibility, it may satisfy Hank's needs and create a win-win situation, resulting in higher performance.

The Need for Affiliation (*n*Aff)

People with a high *n*Aff tend to have the following characteristics:

- They seek close relationships with others.
- They want to be liked by others.
- They enjoy lots of social activities.
- They seek to belong; they join groups and organizations.

People with a high *n*Aff think about friends and relationships. They tend to enjoy developing, helping, and teaching others. They tend to have a low *n*Pow. People with high *n*Aff seek jobs as teachers, in personnel, and in other helping professions. They tend to avoid supervision because they like to be one of the group rather than its leader.

LEARNING OBJECTIVE

5. Describe and contrast four content motivation theories.

Motivating High n*Aff Employees:* Be sure to let them work as part of a team. They derive satisfaction from the people they work with rather than the task itself. Give them lots of praise and recognition. Delegate responsibility for orienting and training new employees to them. They make great buddies and mentors.

EXHIBIT 11-5   **HOW ORGANIZATIONS MEET EMPLOYEE NEEDS**

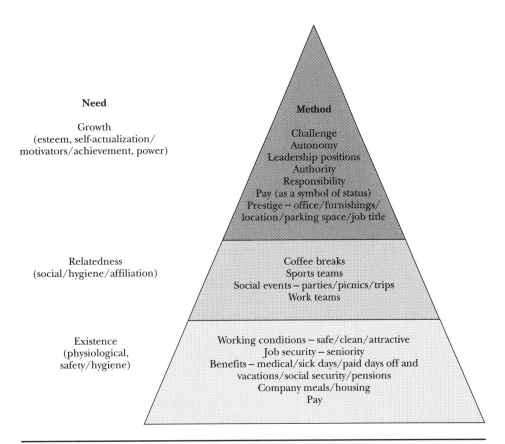

How Organizations Meet Employee Needs

See Exhibit 11–5 for a list of methods that organizations use to meet employee needs. Note that pay can meet both higher- and lower-level needs.

CONNECTIONS

4. Explain how your personal *n*Ach, *n*Pow, and *n*Aff affect your motivation. How can you use manifest needs theory to motivate employees?

IV. Increasing Productivity through Process Motivation

Content motivation theory attempts to understand what motivates people, whereas **process motivation theories** *attempt to understand how and why people are motivated.* Why do people select certain goals to work toward? Why do people select particular behavior to meet their needs? How do people evaluate need satisfaction? Expectancy and equity theories attempt to answer these questions.

Expectancy Theory

The **expectancy theory** *states that motivation = expectancy × valence.* Under Victor Vroom's theory, motivation depends on how much people want something, and how likely they are to get it.[26] The theory is based on the following assumptions:

- Both internal (needs) and external (environment) factors affect behavior.
- Behavior is the individual's decision.
- People have different needs, desires, and goals.
- People make behavior decisions based on their perception of the outcome.

Two important variables in Vroom's formula must be met for motivation to take place.

Expectancy: Expectancy refers to the person's perception of his or her ability (probability) to accomplish an objective. Generally, the higher one's expectancy, the better the chance for motivation. When employees do not believe that they can accomplish objectives, they will not be motivated to try.

Also important is the perception of the relationship between performance and the outcome or reward. Generally, the higher one's expectancy of the outcome or reward, the better the chance for motivation. If employees are certain to get the reward, they probably will be motivated. When unsure, employees may not be motivated. For example, Dan believes he would be a good supervisor and wants to get promoted. However, Dan has an external locus of control and believes that working hard will not result in a promotion anyway. Therefore, he will not be motivated to work for the promotion.

Valence: Valence refers to the value a person places on the outcome or reward. Generally, the higher the value (importance) of the outcome or reward, the better the chance of motivation. For example, the supervisor, Jean, wants an employee, Sim, to work harder. Jean talks to Sim and tells him that working hard will result in a promotion. If Sim wants a promotion, he will probably be motivated. However, if a promotion is not important to Sim, it will not motivate him.

Motivating with Expectancy Theory

Expectancy theory can accurately predict a person's work effort, satisfaction level, and performance, but only if the correct values are plugged into the formula.[27] Therefore, this theory works in certain contexts but not in others. The following conditions should be met to make the theory result in motivation:

1. Clearly define objectives and the necessary performance needed to achieve them.
2. Tie performance to rewards. High performance should be rewarded. When one employee works harder to produce more than other employees and is not rewarded, he or she may slow down productivity.
3. Be sure rewards are of value to the employee. The supervisor should get to know his or her employees as individuals. Develop good human relations.
4. Make sure your employees believe you will do as you promise. For example, they must believe you will promote them if they do work hard. And you must do as you promise so that employees will believe you.

Expectancy theory also works best with employees who have an internal locus of control because if they believe they control their destiny, their efforts will result in success. Expectancy theory does not work well with employees who have an external locus of control because they do not believe their efforts result in success. Believing that success is due to fate, or chance, why should they be motivated to work hard?

In the opening case, Hank says that because of the union everyone is paid the same, so working hard is a waste of time. In the expectancy formula, because expectancy is low, there is no motivation. Paying more for higher performance motivates many employees. However, in a union organization, Latoia has no control over giving Hank a raise if he does a better job. However, the chance for advancement to a higher-level job that pays more may motivate him to work harder. Organizations generally do not promote people to a higher-level job unless they are good performers at the present job. Assuming Hank is interested in advancement, Latoia can explain to Hank that, provided he does a good job, she will recommend him for a promotion when an advancement comes up. If a promotion is not important to Hank, Latoia may find some other need to help him meet. If Latoia can find a need with expectancy and valence, Hank will be motivated to perform to expectations, creating a win-win situation for all parties.

CONNECTIONS

5. Give an example of how expectancy theory has affected your motivation. How can you use expectancy theory to motivate employees?

Equity Theory

The **equity theory** *is based on the comparison of perceived inputs to outputs.* J. Stacy Adams popularized equity theory with his contention that people are motivated to seek social equity in the rewards they receive (output) for their performance (input). Based on the knowledge of equity, one can predict behavior.[28]

According to equity theory, people compare their inputs (effort, experience, seniority, status, intelligence, and so forth) and outputs (praise, recognition, pay promotions, increased status, supervisor's approval, and so on) to that of relevant others. A relevant other could be a co-worker or group of employees from the same or different organizations, or even from a hypothetical situation. Notice that our definition says *perceived* and not *actual* inputs to outputs. Equity may actually exist. However, if employees believe there is inequity, they will change their behavior to create equity. Employees must perceive that they are being treated fairly, relative to others.

Most employees tend to inflate their own efforts or performance when comparing themselves to others. They also overestimate what others earn. Employees may be very satisfied and motivated until they find out that a relevant other is earning more for the same job or earning the same for doing less work. When inequity is perceived, employees attempt to reduce it by reducing input or increasing output.

A comparison with relevant others leads to one of three conclusions: the employee is equitably rewarded, underrewarded, or overrewarded.

Equitably Rewarded: Inputs and outputs are perceived as being equal; motivation exists. Employees may believe that relevant others should have greater outputs when they have more experience, education, and so on.

Underrewarded: When employees perceive that they are underrewarded, they may reduce the inequity by trying to increase outputs (get a raise); reducing inputs (do less work, being absent, or taking long breaks); rationalizing (finding a logical explanation for inequity); changing others' inputs or outputs (get them to do more, or get less); leaving the situation (get transferred, or leave for a better job); or changing the object of comparison (they get less than I do).

Overrewarded: Being overrewarded is not too disturbing to most employees. However, research suggests that employees may reduce perceived inequity by increasing inputs (work harder or longer); reducing output (take a pay cut); rationalizing (I'm worth it); or trying to increase others' output (give them the same as me).

Motivating with Equity Theory

Research supporting equity theory is mixed. Using equity theory in practice can be difficult because you don't know who the employee's reference group is, and what his or her view of inputs and outcomes is. However, it does offer some useful general recommendations:

- The supervisor should be aware that equity is based on perception, which may not be correct. It is possible for the supervisor to create equity or inequity. Some managers have favorite subordinates who get special treatment; others don't.
- Rewards should be equitable. When employees perceive that they are not treated fairly, morale and performance problems occur.
- High performance should be rewarded, but employees must understand the inputs needed to attain certain outputs.

In the opening case, Hank said that he was equitably treated because of the union. Therefore, Latoia does not need to be concerned about equity theory with Hank. However, it could be an issue with another employee.

LEARNING OBJECTIVE

6. Describe and contrast the two process motivation theories.

CONNECTIONS

6. Give an example of equity theory's effect on your motivation. How can you use equity theory to motivate employees?

V. Increasing Productivity through Reinforcement

Average employees can easily double or triple output without even exerting themselves.[29] Several organizations, including 3M, Frito-Lay, and B. F. Goodrich, have used reinforcement to increase productivity. Michigan Bell had a 50 percent improvement in attendance and above-standard productivity and efficiency level. Emery Air Freight went from 30 percent of employees meeting standard to 90 percent after using reinforcement. Emery estimates that its reinforcement program has resulted in a $650,000 yearly savings.

As you have seen, content motivation theories focus on what motivates people and process motivation theories focus on how and why people are motivated; reinforcement theory focuses on getting people to do what you want them to do. **Reinforcement theory** *contends that behavior can be controlled through the use of rewards.* It is also called *behavior modification* and *operant conditioning.*

B. F. Skinner contends that people's behavior is learned through experiences of positive and negative consequences. He believes that rewarded behavior tends to be repeated, and that unrewarded behavior tends not to be repeated. The three components of Skinner's framework are as follows:[30]

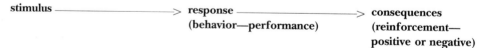

stimulus ——————————> response ——————————> consequences
                                        (behavior—performance)   (reinforcement—
                                                                                   positive or negative)

An employee learns what is, and is not, desired behavior as a result of the consequences for specific behavior.

Reinforcement theory is concerned with maintaining desired behavior (motivation) over time. In other words, people behave in ways that are rewarding. For example, if Beth, a student, wants to get an A on an exam, she will study for the outcome. If Beth gets the A (reward), she will probably study in the same way for the next exam. However, if Beth does not get the A, she will probably change her method of study for the next exam. We tend to learn to get what we want through trial and error.

Skinner states that supervisors can control and shape employees' behavior while making them feel free. The two important concepts used to control behavior are the types of reinforcement and the schedule of reinforcement.

Types of Reinforcement

The four types of reinforcement are as follows:

Positive Reinforcement: One method of encouraging continued behavior is to offer attractive consequences (rewards) for desirable performance. For example, an employee is on time for a meeting and is rewarded by the supervisor thanking him or her. The praise is used to reinforce punctuality. Other reinforcers are pay, promotions, time off, increased status, and so forth. Positive reinforcement is the best motivator for increasing productivity.

Avoidance Reinforcement: Avoidance is also called *negative reinforcement.* As with positive reinforcement, you are encouraging continued desirable behavior. The employee avoids the negative consequence. For example, an employee is punctual for a meeting to avoid negative reinforcement, such as a reprimand. Standing plans, especially rules, are designed to get employees to avoid certain behavior.

Extinction: Rather than encourage desirable behavior, extinction (and punishment) attempts to reduce or eliminate undesirable behavior by withholding reinforcement when the behavior occurs. For example, an employee who is late for the meeting is not rewarded with praise. Or a pay raise may be withheld until the employee performs to set standards. Supervisors who do not reward good performance can cause its extinction.

Punishment: Punishment is used to provide an undesirable consequence for undesirable behavior. For example, an employee who is late for a meeting is reprimanded. Notice that with avoidance there is no actual punishment; it's the threat of the punishment that controls behavior. Other methods of punishment include harassing, taking away privileges, probation, fining, demoting, and so forth. Using punishment may reduce the undesirable behavior, but it may cause other undesirable behavior, such as poor morale, lower productivity, and acts of theft or sabotage. Punishment is the most controversial method and the least effective at motivating employees.

LEARNING OBJECTIVE

7. State how the four types of reinforcement are used.

Schedule of Reinforcement

The second reinforcement consideration in controlling behavior is when to reinforce performance. The two major classifications are continuous and intermittent:

Continuous Reinforcement: With a continuous method, each and every desired behavior is reinforced. Examples of this method would be a machine with an automatic counter that lets the employee know, at any given moment, exactly how many units have been produced, a piece rate of $1 for each unit produced, or a supervisor who comments on every customer report.

Intermittent Reinforcement: With intermittent reinforcement the reward is given based on the passage of time or output. When the reward is based on the passage of time, it is called an *interval schedule.* When it is based on output, it is called a *ratio schedule.* When electing to use intermittent reinforcement, you have four alternatives:

1. Fixed interval schedule (giving a salary pay check every week, breaks and meals at the same time every day).
2. Variable interval schedule (giving praise only now and then, a surprise inspection, a pop quiz).
3. Fixed ratio schedule (giving a piece rate or bonus after producing a standard rate).
4. Variable ratio schedule (giving praise for excellent work, a lottery for employees who have not been absent for a set time).

Ratios are generally better motivators than intervals. The variable ratio tends to be the most powerful schedule for sustaining behavior.

Motivating with Reinforcement

Generally, positive reinforcement is the best motivator. Continuous reinforcement is better at sustaining desired behavior; however, it is not always possible or practical. Some general guidelines include these:

- Make sure employees know exactly what is expected of them. Set clear objectives.
- Select appropriate rewards. A reward to one person could be considered a punishment by another. Know your employees' needs.
- Select the appropriate reinforcement schedule.
- Do not reward mediocre or poor performance.
- Look for the positive and give praise, rather than focus on the negative and criticize. Make people feel good about themselves (Pygmalion effect).
- Never go a day without giving praise.
- Do things for your employees, instead of to them, and you will see productivity increases off the scales.[31]

In the opening case, Hank has been coming to work late and performing below expectations. If Latoia offers Hank the possible promotion (expectancy theory), she has used a positive reinforcement with a variable interval schedule. There is no set time before an opening comes up, and Hank doesn't get it after completing a specific amount of work. If the recommendation for a promotion does not change Hank's behavior, Latoia should try some other positive reinforcement such as job enrichment. If positive reinforcement doesn't change Hank's behavior, Latoia can use avoidance reinforcement. Based on her authority, she could tell Hank that the next time he is late or performs below a specific level, he will receive a specific punishment, such as withholding part of his pay. If Hank does not avoid this behavior, Latoia must follow up and give the punishment. As a manager try the positive first. Positive reinforcement is a true motivator because it creates a win-win situation by meeting the employee's needs and the manager's or organization's. From the employee's perspective, avoidance and punishment create a lose-win situation. The organization or manager wins by forcing them to do something they really don't want to do.

Organizational Reinforcement for Getting Employees to Come to Work and to Be on Time

The traditional attempt to get employees to come to work and to be on time has been avoidance and punishment. If employees miss a specific number of days, they don't get paid. If an employee is late, the time card indicates this, and the employee receives punishment.

Many organizations today are using positive reinforcement by offering employees rewards for coming to work and being on time. For example, ADV Marketing Group, a Stamford, Connecticut, company, uses continuous reinforcement by offering prizes simply for showing up and being on time: a $100 dinner certificate after 13 on-time weeks and an $800 vacation plus two days off after a year of on-time performance. Mediatech, a Chicago company, uses variable ratio schedule by holding a lottery. Each week Mediatech puts up $250. On Friday they spin a wheel to determine if a drawing will be held that week. If not, the money goes into the pot for the next week. When a drawing is held, only the employees who have attended on time up to the drawing are included.

A popular technique used by many organizations, which virtually eliminates the problem of being late for work, is flextime. Flextime allows employees to determine when they start and end work, provided they work their full number of hours, with certain restrictions on working hours. A typical schedule permits employees to begin work between 6:00 A.M. and 9:00 A.M. and complete their workday between 3:00 P.M. and 6:00 P.M. Flextime helps meet the goal of human relations because it allows employees to schedule their time to accommodate meeting their personal needs and job requirements.

CONNECTIONS

7. What type(s) and schedule(s) of reinforcement does or did your supervisor, coach, or teacher use to motivate you? Explain each. How can you use reinforcement to motivate employees?

Giving Praise

In the 1940s, Lawrence Lindahl conducted a survey revealing that what employees want most from a job is full appreciation for work done. Similar studies have been performed over the years with little change in results. One survey showed that managers want personal recognition more than salary by four to one.[32] Another survey revealed that 27 percent of workers would quit to move to a company known for giving praise and recognitions; 38 percent of workers said they rarely or never get praise from the boss.[33] When was the last time your boss gave you a thank-you or some praise for a job well done? When was the last time your boss complained about your work? If you are a manager, when was the last time you praised or criticized your employees? What is the ratio of praise to criticism?

Giving praise develops a positive self-concept in employees and leads to better performance—the Pygmalion effect. Praise is a motivator (not a hygiene) because it meets employees' needs for esteem and self-actualization, growth, and achievement. Giving praise creates a win-win situation. It is probably the most powerful and simplest, yet most underused, motivational technique there is.

Ken Blanchard and Spencer Johnson have recently popularized giving praise through their best-selling book *The One-Minute Manager*.[34] They developed a technique that involves giving one-minute feedback of praise. Model 11–2 is an adaptation. The steps in **giving praise** are as follows: *tell the person exactly what was done correctly; tell the person why the behavior is important; stop for a moment of silence; encourage repeat performance.* Blanchard calls it one-minute praise because it should not take more than one minute to give the praise. It is not necessary for the employee to say anything. The four steps are illustrated below.

Step 1. Tell the Person Exactly What Was Done Correctly: When giving praise, look the person in the eye. Eye contact shows sincerity and concern. It is important to be very specific and descriptive. General statements such as "You're a good worker" are not as effective. But, on the other hand, don't talk for too long, or the praise again loses its effectiveness.

SUPERVISOR: John, I just overheard you deal with that customer's complaint. You did an excellent job of keeping your cool; you were polite. That person came in angry and left happy.

Step 2. Tell the Person Why the Behavior Is Important: Briefly state how the organization, the person, or both benefit from the action. It is also helpful to tell the employee how you feel about the behavior. Be specific and descriptive.

MODEL 11–2   **GIVING PRAISE**

Step 1. Tell the person exactly what was done correctly.

Step 2. Tell the person why the behavior is important.

Step 3. Stop for a moment of silence.

Step 4. Encourage repeat performance.

SUPERVISOR: Without customers we don't have a business. One customer bad-mouthing us can cause hundreds of dollars in lost sales. It really made me proud to see you handle that tough situation the way you did.

Step 3. Stop for a Moment of Silence: This is a tough one. Most supervisors I train have trouble being silent. The rationale for the silence is to give the employee the chance to "feel" the impact of the praise. It's the pause that refreshes.

SUPERVISOR: (*Silently counts to five.*)

Step 4. Encourage Repeat Performance: This is the reinforcement that motivates the employee to keep up performance. Blanchard recommends touching the employee. Touching has a powerful effect. However, he recommends it only if both parties feel comfortable. Others say not to touch employees; it could lead to a sexual harassment charge.

SUPERVISOR: Thanks, John; keep up the good work (*while touching John on the shoulder, or shaking hands*).

As you can see, giving praise is easy, and it doesn't cost a penny. Several supervisors I have trained to give praise say it works wonders. It's a much better motivator than giving a raise or other monetary reward. One supervisor stated that an employee was taking his time stacking cans on a display. He gave the employee praise for stacking the cans so straight. The employee was so pleased with the praise that the display went up with about a 100 percent increase in productivity. Notice that the supervisor looked for the positive and used positive reinforcement, rather than punishment. The supervisor could have made a comment such as, "Quit goofing off and get the display up faster." That statement would not have motivated the employee to increase productivity. All it would have done was hurt human relations, and could have ended in an argument. Notice that in the above supervisor's example the cans were straight. The employee was not praised for the slow work pace. However, if the praise had not worked, the supervisor should have used another reinforcement method.

LEARNING OBJECTIVE

8. List the four steps in the giving praise model and use the model.

In the opening case, if Hank is interested in changing behavior to get a promotion, Latoia should give him praise for coming in on time and increasing his performance to encourage him to continue this behavior. Praise is a reinforcement that is very effective when used with a variable ratio schedule.

Motivation Review

For a review of the major motivation theories, see Exhibit 11–6. For a review of the four steps in the motivation process, see Exhibit 11–7.

VI. Do Motivation Theories Apply Globally?

The motivation theories you have learned were developed in North America. As firms become global, they must be aware of the cultural limitations to theory generalizations. For example, a U.S. firm in Mexico gave workers a raise to motivate

EXHIBIT 11–6   **MOTION THEORIES**

MOTIVATION THEORIES

CONTENT MOTIVATION THEORIES

Focus on identifying people's
needs in order to understand
what motivates them.

1. Needs Hierarchy

Maslow's theory of motivation
that is based on five needs.

2. ERG Theory

Alderfer's classification of
needs as existence, relatedness,
and growth.

3. Two-Factor Theory

Herzberg's classification
of needs as hygienes
and motivators.

4. Manifest Needs Theory

McClelland's classification of
needs as achievement, power,
and affiliation.

Major Theories
of Motivation

PROCESS MOTIVATION THEORIES

Attempt to understand how
and why people are motivated.

5. Expectancy Theory

Vroom's formula, which states
that Motivation = Expectancy ×
Valence.

6. Equity Theory

Adam's motivation theory,
which is based on the comparison of perceived inputs to
outputs.

7. REINFORCEMENT THEORY

Skinner's motivation theory,
which contends that behavior
can be controlled through the
use of rewards.

them to work more hours. The raise actually motivated the employees to work fewer
hours. Because the employees could now make enough money to live and enjoy life
(one of their primary values) in less time, why should they work more hours?

One major cultural difference is in the focus on individualistic versus a group
approach to business. Individualistic societies (United States, Canada, Great
Britain, Australia) tend to value self-accomplishment. Collective societies (Japan,
Mexico, Singapore, Pakistan) tend to value group accomplishment and loyalty.[35,36]
Cultural differences suggest that there might not be a hierarchical superiority to
self-actualization as a motivator in collective societies. Cultures also differ in the
extent to which they value need for achievement. The need for achievement tends
to be more group oriented in Japan, and more individualistic in North America.
Intrinsic motivation of higher-level needs might be more relevant to wealthy
societies than to third-world countries.

Equity theory calls for higher producers to be paid more. This tends to be more
of a motivator in individualistic countries than it is in collective countries, where
people tend to prefer equality and arrangements in which all are paid the same
regardless of output.

Expectancy theory holds up fairly well cross-culturally because it is flexible. It
allows for the possibility that expectations and valences may be different across
cultures. For example, societal acceptance may be of higher value than individual
recognition in collective societies.[37]

**LEARNING
OBJECTIVE**

9. List possible limitations
of using motivation theories
outside North America.

Deming's View of North American Motivation Methods

As stated in Chapter 1, the United States has fallen behind in productivity gains.
Dr. W. Edwards Deming, often credited with making Japan a world business leader,
said in an interview with *The Wall Street Journal,*[38]

EXHIBIT 11–7   **THE MOTIVATION PROCESS**

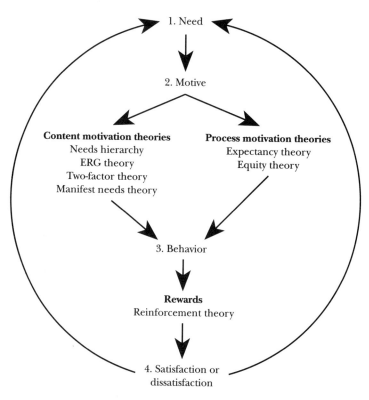

Notice that the motivation process is circular, or ongoing, because meeting our needs is a never-ending process.

We are all born with intrinsic motivation, self-esteem, dignity, an eagerness to learn. Our present system of management crushes that all out. Instead of working for the company, people compete with each other. The Japanese are more successful than the U.S. because they live by cooperation, not competition. American firms will have to learn to support each other, rather than continue with the everybody for himself approach. That's how business should be.

Deming is saying that North America must change from an individualistic society to a collective society if it is to survive in the global economy. He is pessimistic that U.S. business will make the changes he thinks necessary to compete.

Following the suggestions from this chapter can help you motivate yourself and employees. What is your motivation theory?

CONNECTIONS

8. Do you agree with Deming's statement—to survive in the global economy the United States must change to the group approach to doing business? Explain your answer.

9. Which motivation theory do you like best? Explain.

10. What are the major methods and techniques you plan to use to increase performance, motivation, and productivity?

VII. Increasing Productivity through Resources

We have already discussed improving productivity through ability and motivation. In this section you will learn about the last factor in the performance formula: resources. Improving capital utilization, job enrichment, and job design and simplification will be dealt with.

Capital

Management specialist Peter Drucker says that organizations should focus on increasing productivity through capital, rather than labor.[39] *Capital* is the financial and physical resources of the organization. There are five areas in which productivity can be increased through capital.

1. Capital Equipment: A major way of increasing productivity is through capital equipment. New equipment can often save time. Organizations should invest in the latest technology such as computer-assisted design and manufacturing (CAD/CAM), robots, and flexible machine centers.[40] Capital equipment purchases are often postponed because organizations cannot be sure of the results until the equipment is up and running.[41] In addition, when equipment is introduced, productivity usually declines in the first year. However, organizations need to focus on the long run. Despite short-run results, new equipment ultimately tends to increase productivity for a 10-year period.[42]

2. Reduce Waste: Avoiding waste of your capital resources can also increase productivity. Most supervisors can find waste in their departments and reduce it. This is often the major focus of cost cutting. However, be careful. Too many organizations carry waste reduction to the point where efficiency and productivity also decrease.[43]

3. Inventories: It is expensive to have excess inventories of raw materials, work in process (WIP), and finished goods. To keep inventories to a minimum, many organizations are using just-in-time inventory. As a supervisor, finish WIP as fast as possible.[44]

4. Budgets: When developing and spending the budget, the supervisor should get the best value for the department and organization.

5. Space: Use the department's space as productively as possible.

Job Enrichment

Job enrichment *is the process of building motivators into the job itself by making it more interesting and challenging.* It differs from job rotation, in which employees learn to perform other employees' jobs, and job enlargement, in which the employee is assigned more tasks of a similar nature.

Organizations including IBM, AT&T, Polaroid, Monsanto, General Motors, Motorola, Maytag, and The Traveler's Insurance Company have used job enrichment successfully.

Before implementing job enrichment, the manager should be sure that the job is of low motivation potential and that the employees want their jobs enriched. Many people with an external locus of control are happy with the jobs the way they are. Hygienes must also be adequate before job enrichment is used.

Some simple ways managers can enrich jobs include delegating more variety and responsibility, forming natural work groups, making employees responsible for their own identifiable work, and giving employees more autonomy.

1. Delegate More Variety and Responsibility: Give employees challenging assignments that help them to grow and to develop new skills. New tasks require the challenge of new learning. The variety of tasks relieves monotony that develops from repetition. Variety gives employees a greater sense of accomplishment because they can perform more tasks. Managers can delegate some of the responsibility and tasks they perform themselves.

2. Form Natural Work Groups: Allow the team of employees to work together. For example, at AT&T, service order representatives who prepared service orders to be typed were in separate areas of the office. To enrich the jobs, the service order representatives were moved to one geographical location and assigned their own typist to work together as a team. As a result, orders typed on time increased from 27 to over 90 percent, with improved accuracy. The work group can also perform its own identifiable work with increased responsibility.

3. Make Employees Responsible for Their Own Identifiable Work: Let employees make the entire product rather than one part of it. For example, at Motorola, assemblers who worked on one or two components had their jobs enriched. The enriched jobs enabled the assemblers to work on eight different components, and their names were put on the units they assembled. Units not meeting quality control were returned to the proper employee for repair, rather than to a random assembler.

4. Give Employees More Autonomy: Allow employees to plan, schedule, organize, and control their own jobs. For example, at Banker's Trust Company of New York, typists had their jobs enriched by being allowed to schedule their own work and correct their own errors on computer output tape, rather than having a specialist make the change. Making typists responsible for checking their own work eliminated the need for checkers. Job enrichment resulted in an annual savings of $360,000, improved attitudes, and greater job satisfaction.

Job Design

Poorly designed jobs cause more performance problems than supervisors realize.[45] **Job design** *involves employee transformation of inputs into outputs.* The more effective and efficient the method, the more productive the employee. Job design focuses on increasing performance through job design improvements. Do it better by doing it differently.[46] Jobs can be designed by one of three major groups: (1) time and motion experts, who analyze the job to determine the one best method and the amount of time it should take to do the task; (2) managers, who supervise the jobs; and (3) employees, who are the most knowledgeable about their jobs and can make the most effective changes.[47] Allowing employees to design their own jobs, or at least change the jobs to their specifications, can motivate employees to perform at higher levels.

A common approach to job design is work simplification. The idea behind work simplification is to work smarter, not harder. **Job simplification** *involves a combination of eliminating, combining, and changing the work sequence to increase productivity.* To motivate employees, have them break the job down into steps and see whether they can do the following:

- *Eliminate.* Does the task have to be done at all? If not, don't waste time doing it. At Intel they decided it was not necessary to fill out a voucher for expenses amounting to less than $100. Work volume went down by 14 percent in 30 days.

- *Combine.* Doing more than one thing at a time often saves time. Make one trip to the mail room at the end of the day instead of several throughout the day.

- *Change sequence.* Often a change in the order of doing things results in a lower total time.

When used appropriately, work simplification can be effective at motivating employees. However, the danger lies in making a job too simple and boring rather than making it more interesting and challenging, as suggested under job enrichment.

Job enrichment and job design can be motivators (not hygienes) because they can meet employees' need for esteem and self-actualization, growth, and power and achievement. They empower employees to increase responsibility with an opportunity for creating meaningful, challenging work to help them grow and accomplish what they and the manager want to accomplish, creating a win-win situation.

In a union situation such as the opening case, job enrichment or job redesign may not be possible without union consent and input. Assuming Latoia can use these techniques, she and Hank could work together following the foregoing guidelines to transform Hank's present boring job into a challenging and interesting one. This is the most appropriate motivation technique to use with Hank because it directly addresses the boring job. Hopes of a promotion in the unknown future will not change the present situation; however, if job enrichment is not possible, it may at least make the job tolerable until the promotion comes. If Hank finds his job interesting, he will most likely come to work on time and perform to expectation, creating a win-win situation.

LEARNING OBJECTIVE

10. Describe ways to increase productivity through capital, job enrichment, job design, and job simplification.

CONNECTIONS

11. Describe how an organization you have worked for can increase productivity through better utilization of capital.

12. Describe how a present or past job could be enriched.

13. Describe how a present or past job could be simplified. Specify whether elimination, combination, or a change in sequence would simplify the job.

REVIEW

Select one or more methods: (1) fill in the missing key terms from memory; (2) match the key terms from the end of the review with their definitions below; (3) copy the key terms in order from the key terms at the beginning of the chapter.

_____ is the ability to use organizational resources effectively and efficiently. The _____ is as follows: performance = ability × motivation × resources. All three factors are necessary for performance to be high. _____ is a performance measure relating inputs to outputs. The three ways to increase productivity are increasing the value of the outputs while maintaining the value of the inputs, maintaining the value of the outputs while decreasing the value of the inputs, and increasing the value of the outputs while decreasing the value of the inputs. The steps to follow when increasing productivity are defining productivity, measuring productivity, improving productivity, and following up.

The supervisor can increase productivity by improving employees' ability to do the job through training, participation, and the suggestion system. The _____ involves referring to past feedback, describing current performance, describing desired performance, getting a commitment to the change, and following up.

_____ is the willingness to achieve the organization's objectives. _____ focus on identifying people's needs in order to understand what motivates them. _____ is based on five categories of needs. ERG theory is Alderfer's reorganization of Maslow's needs hierarchy into three levels: existence, relatedness, and growth.

_____ classifies needs as hygienes or motivators.

_____ classifies needs as achievement, power, and affiliation.

_____ attempt to understand how and why people are motivated. _____ states that motivation = expectancy × valence. _____ is based on the comparison of perceived inputs to outputs.

_____ contends that behavior can be controlled through the use of rewards. The types of reinforcement include positive, avoidance, extinction, and punishment. The schedule of reinforcement includes continuous and intermittent (fixed interval, variable interval, fixed ratio, and variable ratio). The steps in _____ are as follows: tell the person exactly what was done correctly; tell the person why the behavior is important; stop for a moment of silence; and encourage repeat performance.

As firms become global, they must be aware of the cultural limitation to theory generalizations. One major cultural difference is in the focus on the individualistic (U.S.) versus the group approach to business (Japan). Dr. Deming says that to survive in the global economy, the United States must change to the group approach toward business.

Capital may be used to increase productivity through capital equipment, reducing waste, inventories, budgets, and space. _____ is the process of building motivators into the job itself by making it more interesting and challenging. _____ involves how inputs are transformed into outputs. _____ involves eliminating, combining, and changing the work sequence to increase productivity.

KEY TERMS

content motivation theories	increasing-productivity model
equity theory	job design
expectancy theory	job enrichment
giving praise	job simplification
manifest needs theory	process motivation theories
motivation	productivity
needs hierarchy	reinforcement theory
performance	two-factor theory
performance formula	

REFERENCES

1. Thomas Peters, "The Tom Peters Formula for Supervisory Excellence," *Supervisory Management*, February 1985, p. 2.

2. *The Wall Street Journal*, August 21, 1990, p. 1.

3. Wickham Skinner, "The Productivity Paradox," *Harvard Business Review*, July–August 1986, p. 55.

4. "Pursuing Efficiency," *Fortune*, June 9, 1986, p. 31.

5. Jeff Hallett, "Productivity: A State of Mind," *Personnel Administrator*, May 1985, p. 18.

6. Thomas Hout and George Stalk, "Working Better and Faster with Fewer People," *The Wall Street Journal*, May 15, 1987, p. 14.

7. Fred Lippert, "Production versus Productivity," *Supervision*, April 1985, pp. 17–18.

8. Ken Macher, "The Politics of People," *Personnel Journal*, January 1986, p. 50.

9. Katherine Miller and Peter Monge, "Participation, Satisfaction, and Productivity: A Meta-Analytic Review," *Academy of Management Journal*, December 1986, p. 748.

10. Oliver Niehouse, "Job Satisfaction: How to Motivate Today's Workers," *Supervisory Management*, February 1986, p. 9.

11. Bruce Nixon and Richard Allen, "Creating a Climate for DIY Development," *Personnel Management*, August 1986, p. 34.

12. Norman Bodek, "The Unifying Theory of Productivity (UTOP): How to Manage Human Resources," *Supervisory Management*, May 1985, pp. 17–26.

13. Adam Radizik, "What Managers Want to Know," *Nation's Business*, August 1985, p. 37.

14. "Employee Attitudes," *The Wall Street Journal*, April 28, 1987, p. 1.

15. Richard Baran, "Interpersonal Relationships Skills, or How to Get Along for Productivity and Profit," *Personnel Administrator*, April 1986, p. 12.

16. Oliver Niehouse, "Job Satisfaction: How to Motivate Today's Workers," p. 9.

17. Selwyn Feinstein, "Pointing Workers to a Common Goal," *The Wall Street Journal*, February 16, 1988, p. 1.

18. Roger Ailes, "Secrets of Successful Leaders," *Reader's Digest*, May 1988, p. 134.

19. Vincent Kafka, "A New Look at Motivation-Productivity Improvements," *Supervisory Management*, April 1986, p. 24.

20. Niehouse, "Job Satisfaction: How to Motivate Today's Workers," p. 8.

21. Kafka, "A New Look at Motivation-Productivity Improvements," p. 24.

22. Abraham Maslow, "A Theory of Human Motivation," *Psychological Review* 50 (1943), pp. 370–96; *Motivation and Personality* (New York: Harper & Row, 1954).

23. Selwyn Feinstein, "Pointing Workers to a Common Goal," p. 1.

24. Frederick Herzberg, "One More Time: How Do You Motivate Employees?" *Harvard Business Review,* January–February 1968, pp. 53–62.

25. Henry Murry, *Explorations in Personality* (New York: Oxford Press, 1938); John Atkinson, *An Introduction to Motivation* (New York: Van Nostrand Reinhold, 1964); David McClelland, *The Achieving Society* (New York: Van Nostrand Reinhold, 1961); McClelland and D. H. Burnham, "Power Is the Great Motivator," *Harvard Business Review,* March–April 1978, p. 103.

26. Victor Vroom, *Work and Motivation* (New York: John Wiley & Sons, 1964).

27. Daniel Ilgen, Delbert Nebeker, and Robert Pritchard, "Expectancy Theory Measures: An Empirical Comparison in an Experimental Simulation," *Organizational Behavior and Human Performance* 28 (1981), pp. 189–223.

28. J. Stacy Adams, "Toward an Understanding of Inequity," *Journal of Abnormal and Social Psychology* 67 (1963), pp. 422–36.

29. Jack Falvey, "To Raise Productivity, Try Saying Thank You," *The Wall Street Journal,* December 6, 1982, p. 16.

30. B. F. Skinner, *Beyond Freedom and Dignity* (New York: Alfred A. Knopf, 1971).

31. Falvey, "To Raise Productivity," p. 16.

32. "A Pat on the Back," *The Wall Street Journal,* January 3, 1989, p. 1.

33. "Odds and Ends," *The Wall Street Journal,* April 18, 1989, p. B1.

34. Kenneth Blanchard and Spencer Johnson, *The One-Minute Manager* (New York: Wm. Morrow & Co., 1982).

35. C. Kagitcibasi and J. W. Berry, "Cross-Culture Psychology: Current Research and Trends," *Annual Review of Psychology* 40 (1989), pp. 493–531.

36. G. Hofstede, *Culture's Consequence: International Differences in Work-Related Values* (Beverly Hills, CA: Sage, 1980).

37. N. J. Alder, *International Dimensions of Organizational Behavior* (Boston: Kent, 1986).

38. "Deming's Demons," *The Wall Street Journal,* June 4, 1990, pp. R39, 41.

39. Amanda Bennett, "Management Guru: Peter Drucker Wins Impressive Following," *The Wall Street Journal,* July 28, 1987, p. 12.

40. W. Skinner, "The Productivity Paradox," p. 57.

41. Joan Harmann, "Getting More Output from Your Department," *Management Solutions,* August 1986, p. 5.

42. Robert Hayes and Kim Clark, "Why Some Factories Are More Productive than Others," *Harvard Business Review,* September–October 1986, p. 67.

43. W. Skinner, "The Productivity Paradox," p. 56.

44. W. T. Buchanan, "Managing to Motivate," *SAM Advanced Management Journal,* Spring 1987, p. 18.

45. Michael Campion and Paul Thayer, "Job Design: Approaches, Outcomes, and Trade-Offs," *Organizational Dynamics,* Winter 1987, p. 66.

46. "Systems to Raise Output," *Personnel Administrator,* October 1985, p. 16.

47. L. Baer, "Employee-Managed Work Redesign—New Quality of Work Life Development," *Supervision,* March 1986, p. 7.

APPLICATION SITUATIONS

The Performance Formula

AS 11−1

Identify the factor contributing to poor performance in the five situations below.

a. ability   *b.* motivation   *c.* resources

_C_ 1. In the recent past, the U.S. steel industry was not as productive as the foreign competition.

_B_ 2. "I don't think you produce as much as the other department members because you're lazy."

_A_ 3. "I practice longer and harder than Heather and Linda, who are also on the track team. I don't understand why they beat me in the races."

_B_ 4. "I could get all A's in school, if I wanted to. But I'd rather relax and have a good time in college."

_C_ 5. The government would be more efficient if it cut down on waste.

Measuring Productivity

AS 11−2

The standard monthly rate of productivity in the department is as follows:

$$\frac{\text{output 10,000 units}}{\text{inputs } \$5,000 \text{ costs}} = 2.00{:}1 \text{ ratio or } 200\%$$

Calculate the ratio, percentage, and percentage increase or decrease for the next five months.

_____ 6. Month 6: output was 9,500, input cost $5,000.

_____ 7. Month 7: output was 10,300, input cost $5,000.

_____ 8. Month 8: output was 10,000, input cost $5,200.

_____ 9. Month 9: output was 10,000, input cost $4,900.

_____ 10. Month 10: output was 10,200, input cost $4,800.

⑥ 1.9:1, 190%, 5% decrease 9,500/5,000 = 1.9 or 190%
200 − 1.90 = .10/2.00 = .05 or 5%

Motivation Theories

AS 11–3

Identify the 10 statements below in terms of one of the following motivation theories:

a. expectancy   *d.* manifest needs

b. equity   *e.* two-factor

c. needs hierarchy   *f.* reinforcement

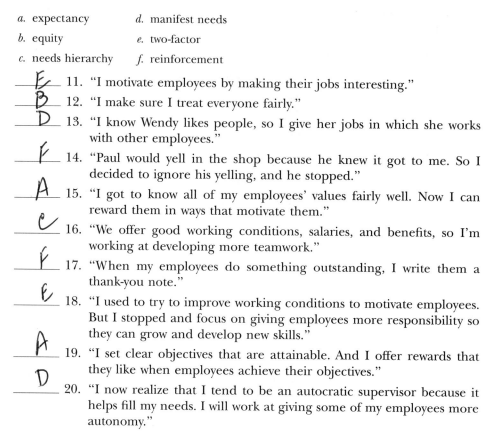

___E___ 11. "I motivate employees by making their jobs interesting."

___B___ 12. "I make sure I treat everyone fairly."

___D___ 13. "I know Wendy likes people, so I give her jobs in which she works with other employees."

___F___ 14. "Paul would yell in the shop because he knew it got to me. So I decided to ignore his yelling, and he stopped."

___A___ 15. "I got to know all of my employees' values fairly well. Now I can reward them in ways that motivate them."

___C___ 16. "We offer good working conditions, salaries, and benefits, so I'm working at developing more teamwork."

___F___ 17. "When my employees do something outstanding, I write them a thank-you note."

___E___ 18. "I used to try to improve working conditions to motivate employees. But I stopped and focus on giving employees more responsibility so they can grow and develop new skills."

___A___ 19. "I set clear objectives that are attainable. And I offer rewards that they like when employees achieve their objectives."

___D___ 20. "I now realize that I tend to be an autocratic supervisor because it helps fill my needs. I will work at giving some of my employees more autonomy."

Friedman's Business Technique

The following conversation takes place between Art Friedman and the author. In 1970, Art Friedman introduced the business technique described at Friedman's Appliances. At that time, the Oakland, California, organization employed 15 workers. Friedman's is an actual business that uses the technique you will read about.

BOB: What is the reason for your success in business?

ART: My business technique.

BOB: What is it? How did you implement it?

ART: I called my 15 employees together and told them, "From now on, I want you to feel as though the company is ours, not mine. We are all bosses. From now on, you decide what you're worth and tell the accountant to put it in your pay envelope. You decide which days and hours you work and when to take time off. We will have an open petty cash system that will allow anyone to go into the box and borrow money when they need it."

BOB: You're kidding, right?

ART: No, it's true. I really did do these things.

BOB: Did anyone ask for a raise?

ART: Yes, several people did. Charlie asked for and received a $100-a-week raise.

BOB: Did he and the others increase their productivity to earn their raises?

ART: Yes, they all did.

BOB: How could you run an appliance store with employees coming and going as they pleased?

ART: The employees made up schedules that were satisfactory to everyone. We had no problems with under- or overstaffing.

BOB: Did anyone steal from the petty cash box?

ART: No.

BOB: Would this technique work in any business?

ART: It did work, it still works, and it will always work [for me]!

In 1976, Art Friedman changed his strategy. Art's present business is Friedman's Microwave Ovens. It is a franchise operation that utilizes his technique of making everyone a boss. In its first three years, Art's business grew from one store in Oakland to 20 stores that sold over 15,000 microwaves. In 1988 Art had over 100 stores nationwide. Friedman's now sells around 125,000 microwaves per year.

Answer the following questions. Use the space between questions to explain your answers.

_____T_____ 1. Art's business technique improved performance and productivity.
　　　　　　　　a. true   *b.* false

_____B_____ 2. Art focused on the _____ factor in the performance formula.
　　　　　　　　a. ability   *b.* motivation   *c.* resources

_____A_____ 3. Art used participation.
　　　　　　　　a. true   *b.* false

_A_ 4. Victor Vroom would say that Art uses expectancy motivation theory.
   a. true   *b.* false

_A_ 5. Art
   a. offers equitable rewards   *b.* underrewards   *c.* overrewards

_E_ 6. Art's employees seem to be on the _____ needs level.
   a. physiological   *c.* social   *e.* self-actualization
   b. safety   *d.* esteem

_C_ 7. Art's technique has little emphasis on meeting _____ needs.
   a. achievement   *b.* power   *c.* affiliation

_B_ 8. Herzberg would say Art is using
   a. hygienes   *b.* motivators

_A_ 9. Art uses _____ reinforcement.
   a. positive   *b.* avoidance   *c.* extinction   *d.* punishment

_C_ 10. Art used
   a. job rotation   *c.* job enrichment
   b. job enlargement   *d.* job design

11. Do you know of any organizations that use any of Art's techniques or other unusual techniques? If you do, what is the organization's name? What techniques does it use?

   students may or may not have examples

12. Could Art's techniques work in all organizations?

   discuss

13. In a position of authority, would you use Art's techniques?

   personal choice

IN-CLASS SKILL-BUILDING EXERCISE

What Do You Want from a Job?

SB 11–1

Objectives: To help you better understand how job factors affect motivation. To help you realize that people are motivated by different factors. What motivates you may turn someone else off.

Preparation: You should have completed Self-Learning Exercise 11–1.

Experience: You will discuss the importance of job factors.

Procedure 1
(8–20 minutes)

Break into groups of five or six, and discuss job factors selected by group members in Self-Learning Exercise 11–1. Come to a consensus on the three factors that are most important to the group. They can be either motivators or hygienes. If the group mentions other job factors not listed, such as pay, you may add them.

Procedure 2
(3–6 minutes)

A representative from each group goes to the board and writes his or her group's three most important job factors.

Conclusion: The instructor leads a class discussion and makes concluding remarks.

Application
(2–4 minutes)

What did I learn from this experience? How will I use this knowledge in the future?

Sharing: Volunteers give their answers to the application section.

PREPARATION FOR IN-CLASS SKILL-BUILDING EXERCISE

Giving Praise

SB 11–2

Think of a job situation in which you did something well, deserving praise and recognition. For example, you may have saved the company money, turned a dissatisfied customer into a happy one, and so forth. If you have never worked, interview someone who has. Put yourself in a supervisory position and write out what you would say to an employee who deserved praise for doing what you did, using the steps described.

Briefly describe the situation:

Step 1. Tell the employee exactly what was done correctly.

Step 2. Tell the employee why the behavior is important.

Step 3. Stop for a moment of silence. (Count to 5 silently.)

Step 4. Encourage repeat performance.

IN-CLASS SKILL-BUILDING EXERCISE

Giving Praise

SB 11–2

Objective: To develop your skill at giving praise.

Experience: You will give and receive praise.

Material: You will need the preparation for Exercise 11–2.

Procedure
(12–17 minutes)

Break into groups of five or six. One at a time, you will praise another group member using the statements in the preparation.

1. Explain the situation.

2. Select a group member to praise.

3. Praise the person. (Talk. Don't just read the statement off the paper.) Try to select the position you would use (both standing, both sitting, and so on) if you were actually giving praise on the job.

4. Integration. The group gives feedback on how the praise was given.

   • *Step 1.* Was the praise very specific and descriptive? Did the giver look the employee in the eye?

   • *Step 2.* Was the importance of the behavior clearly stated?

   • *Step 3.* Did the giver stop for a moment of silence?

   • *Step 4.* Did the giver encourage repeat performance? Did the giver of praise touch the receiver [optional]?

   • Did the praise take less than one minute? Was the praise sincere?

Conclusion: The instructor leads a class discussion and makes concluding remarks.

Application (2–4 minutes): What did I learn from this experience? How will I use this knowledge in the future?

Sharing: Volunteers give their answers to the application section.

12

Evaluating and Compensating Employees

Learning Objectives

1. List and explain the five steps in performance appraisal.
2. Describe six performance appraisal measurement methods.
3. List and explain the five steps for improving performance and use the model.
4. Explain 11 problems to avoid when conducting a performance appraisal.
5. List the steps in preparing for the evaluation and developmental performance appraisal.
6. List the steps in the evaluation and developmental interview and use these models.
7. Describe the supervisor's role in compensation.

Key Terms To achieve our objectives in this chapter, it is important that you understand the following 13 key terms. They are presented in the order in which they appear in the chapter. The list of key terms also appears in alphabetical order in the end-of-chapter review.

performance appraisal	ranking	job evaluation
critical incident file	coaching	point system
rating scales	evaluation interview	compensation
behaviorally anchored rating scales	developmental interview reward systems	comparable worth

Each year in November, all personnel at Ilco Insurance Corporation are given a performance appraisal. Jill Allen was no exception. She said to a friend in her department, "My supervisor hasn't said one negative thing to me all year. I'm pretty confident about the whole thing. I think I'll ask for that raise I've been wanting for months." "I don't know," her friend countered. "Last year I walked out of my appraisal about as depressed as I've ever been."

When the day of the interview came, Jill was shocked to hear her supervisor bring up an extended list of negative things, most of which seemed rather trivial to Jill. Jill's question was, "Why didn't you mention these things before today?" The supervisor just shrugged and muttered something about being busy and not being one to nitpick all the time. "Nitpick?" Jill nearly screamed, "What do you say about this interview?" The supervisor had no answer, and ended the job appraisal at that point, without any discussion of salary.

What did the supervisor do wrong? What would you have done differently?

I. The Performance Appraisal Process

In this section you will learn why performance appraisals are important, why performance is appraised, why supervisors and employees both dislike performance appraisals, legal aspects of performance appraisals, and the steps in a performance appraisal.

Why Performance Appraisal Is Important

Performance appraisal *is the ongoing process of evaluating employee effectiveness and efficiency.* Performance appraisal is also called *performance evaluation, performance review, merit rating,* and *performance audit.* Regardless of the name, performance appraisal is one of the supervisor's most important—yet most difficult—functions.[1] Supervisors spend about 10 percent of their time providing performance feedback. It is a daily function.[2] Handled properly, performance appraisal can increase productivity and morale and decrease absenteeism and turnover.[3] But handled poorly, it can decrease performance.

Why Performance Is Appraised

Performance is appraised for purposes of development as well as evaluation. In other words, an appraisal should affect future performance as well as assess past performance. It is used to make *administrative decisions,* such as pay raises and promotions, as well as *developmental decisions* involving areas where the employee could or should improve.

Development

To improve future performance, an appraisal should do the following:

- Ensure that employees know what their responsibilities are and the standards of performance they are expected to achieve.
- Give employees feedback of how well they are doing their jobs.
- Recognize and praise good performance.
- Diagnose individual and organizational problems.
- Develop objectives and plans for improved performance.
- Help employees develop new skills.
- Increase motivation, morale, and positive attitudes.
- Strengthen supervisor-employee relations.

Evaluation

An appraisal is meant to tell an employee how well he or she has done the job. To do this, it should fulfill the following functions:

- Give employees feedback on how well they performed over the period since the last appraisal.
- Make compensation decisions, that is, wage and salary increases, bonus pay, and so forth.
- Make transfer and promotion decisions.
- Make demotion and termination decisions.

Because the performance appraisal has two separate objectives, the actual appraisal interview should also separate the two topics.[4]

The evaluative focus is on the past, whereas the developmental focus is on the future ("Where do we go from here?"). Separate meetings make the objectives clear. When conducted together, the development is often less effective, especially when the employee disagrees with the evaluation.

Why Supervisors and Employees Dislike Performance Appraisals

Neither supervisors nor employees look forward to performance appraisals.[5] Reasons supervisors give for disliking this important function include the following:

- They take too much time.
- It's not easy giving bad news.
- I have other, more important, things to do.
- I'm not good at it.[6]

Employees dislike the appraisal interview for the following reasons:

- It's too tense.
- I don't know what to expect.
- I don't get to say much.
- The boss is defensive if I disagree.
- I'm afraid to disagree with my boss; the boss will hold it against me.
- I'm criticized a lot more than praised.
- My boss is not prepared.[7]
- The appraisal is not based on objective data; it does not adequately reflect my ability or performance.[8]

In reviewing this list, you can see that all of the reasons performance appraisals are unpopular can be controlled by the supervisor, with the support of middle and top management. Supervisors should be trained to conduct effective performance appraisals. After studying this chapter, you should understand how to conduct effective performance appraisals.

CONNECTIONS

1. Do you look forward to performance appraisals? Explain your answer from the supervisor's and the employee's perspectives.

Legal Aspects of Performance Appraisal

Supervisors are held accountable for what they say during performance appraisals. Employees who believe that supervisors are not giving them a fair shake are going to court, and, more times than not, they are winning.[9] Supervisors who make promises they do not keep may face litigation. For example, the supervisor who says "work hard and you will get a promotion" could end up in court. Supervisors should not make statements they cannot, or will not, follow through on.

Administrative decisions, such as raises, promotions, demotions, or discharges, must meet the EEOC Uniform Guidelines on Employee Selection Procedures. As was true in the selection of new employees, such administrative decisions should not be discriminatory. As in the selection process, management is not completely free to promote or discharge anyone it pleases. These decisions should be based on objective job criteria.

An organization cannot develop a perfect system because performance appraisals are based on human judgment, which is subject to error. However, following these guidelines can help the organization prevent and defend its decisions:

- A job analysis should determine the skills needed to perform the job successfully.

- The job analysis should be incorporated into the performance appraisal. Only objective, measurable, job-related characteristics should be used in an appraisal. If criteria must be used, keep them to a minimum and back them up with objective measures.

- Performance standards must be clearly communicated to employees. They should know the difference between outstanding, superior, good, average, and below-average performance. Employees who perform below standard must be told of the consequences. Employees should not be discharged for poor performance without being given a warning. It is also advisable to have the employee sign a written statement as proof that the warning was given.

- Supervisors should be trained to conduct performance appraisals. One reason many supervisors dislike performance appraisals is that they have not been trained to conduct them.

- Evaluations should be documented. When an employee is given a poor appraisal that results in discharge, you should have documented the reason. It is also advisable to have the employee sign the documents as proof that he or she has seen them. If an employee gets acceptable performance ratings and is discharged, the courts may conclude that the reason for the discharge was discrimination. We will discuss how to document performance in the next section of this chapter.

- The system should be monitored. As jobs change with time, the evaluation system should also change.[10]

Steps in a Performance Appraisal

Following is a brief discussion of the five steps in a performance appraisal. In later sections, you will be given a more detailed explanation of each step.

Step 1. Job Responsibilities: Based on the organization's strategic and operational objectives and plans (Chapter 2), the work and responsibilities are assigned to employees. Job responsibilities are determined through the job analysis (Chapter 9). Job responsibilities should be ranked in order of importance. Because we have already discussed job analysis, we will not deal with this subject in detail again.

Step 2. Develop Standards and Measurement Methods: After determining what it takes to do the job, standards and methods for measuring performance can be developed. In the next section of this chapter, we will discuss setting standards and describe several common performance appraisal methods.

Step 3. Informal Performance Appraisals—"Coaching": Performance appraisals should not merely be once-a-year, one-hour sessions.[11] Employees need regular feedback on their performance. The employee performing below standard may need daily or weekly coaching. The supervisor's new role is that of a coach, rather than the dictator of the past.[12] In the third section of this chapter, we will discuss coaching.

Step 4. Preparing for the Formal Performance Appraisal: Failure to plan for the performance appraisal is planning to fail. In the fourth section of this chapter, we will discuss how to prepare for the interview. That section also lists problems to avoid when conducting the interview.

EXHIBIT 12-1   **STEPS IN A PERFORMANCE APPRAISAL**

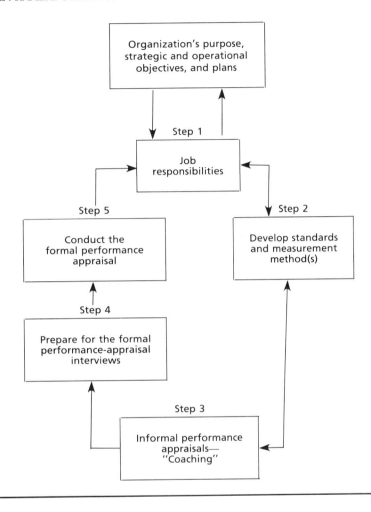

Step 5. Conducting a Formal Performance Appraisal: In the fifth section of this chapter, we will discuss the steps to follow when conducting the actual performance appraisal.

Exhibit 12-1 lists the steps in a performance appraisal. Notice that the arrows in steps 1 through 3 go forward to the next step and back. This is because developments at one step may require the supervisor to backtrack and make changes. For example, during an informal appraisal, the supervisor may realize that environmental changes require a change in the employee's job, performance standards, or both. Note also that performance appraisal is an ongoing process; step 5 brings the supervisor back to step 1.

LEARNING OBJECTIVE

1. List and explain the five steps in performance appraisal.

II. Developing Performance Standards and Measurement Methods

Step 2 in a performance appraisal is developing standards and measurement methods. This is the topic of this section. We will also discuss responsibility for performance appraisals.

Standards

Standards are the backbone of a performance appraisal.[13] (See Chapter 4 for details on how to set standards in the areas of quantity, quality, time, and cost.) Clear objectives and standards can make the experience much easier.[14] Standards for performance appraisals should encompass a range. For example, the standard range for typing could be as follows: 70 words per minute (WPM)—excellent; 60 WPM—good; 50 WPM—average; 40 WPM—satisfactory; 30 WPM—unsatisfactory.

Vagueness of the performance form, poorly defined criteria, inappropriate measures, and meaningless assessment items are all signs that standards are poorly developed.[15] Failure to communicate standards is another major problem with performance appraisals. Research by William Weitzel indicates that over 50 percent of the time, supervisors actually do not tell employees what is expected of them.[16]

As a supervisor, make sure that your employees know what the standards are. If an employee gets an average rather than a good rating, you should be able to clearly explain why. The employee should understand what needs to be done during the next performance period to get the higher rating. With clear standards, there shouldn't be any surprises during the formal performance appraisal. Courts do not look favorably upon surprises.[17]

CONNECTIONS

2. Describe the performance standards for a job you have held. Describe how you would improve them.

Measurement Methods

Use of a standard rating method throughout an organization is becoming less common. In the litigious environment most organizations face, it is preferable to develop job-specific methods. The measurement method is often selected by the human resources department. Thus, as a supervisor, you may have no choice in the performance appraisal process and form used. If you do not like the procedures or forms, offer suggestions on how to improve them, rather than complaining and criticizing.[18]

In the following sections we will discuss some common measurement methods, including critical incident files, rating scales, behaviorally anchored rating scales, ranking, management by objectives, and narrative.

Critical Incident File   The **critical incident file** *is a record of an employee's positive and negative performance.* Because the review period is usually long, it is very difficult to remember an employee's performance from appraisal to appraisal. The critical incident file provides a record of what an employee did three, six, or even nine months ago. The critical incident file also provides documentation, which is needed in this litigious environment.

There are no hard and fast rules as to what a critical incident file should contain. Basic guidelines include these:

- Keep a record of uncommonly good or poor performance. Most supervisors focus on the negative only; don't.

- Record the facts soon after the incidents. Be sure to include the date.

- Some supervisors use a notebook. Others use folders. The author uses 8½ × 11 file folders. He makes notes on the inside of the folder itself and stores performance forms inside the folder.

- Some supervisors make weekly summaries of performance.
- Be specific and descriptive so that others, such as a jury, can understand what you wrote.[19] For example, see the following list:

1/10/94: 10 minutes late for work.

2/11/94: Voluntarily stayed a half hour late to finish a job.

3/12/94: Took an extra 15 minutes for lunch.

4/13/94: Pushed to meet a contract deadline; produced 10 extra units.

5/14/94: Produced five units below standard.

A critical incident file helps the supervisor to evaluate the entire review period, not just the recent past. Documentation of poor performance is especially critical when discharging the employee is being considered.

Critical incident files are appropriate for developmental decisions. They are not appropriate for administrative decisions such as pay raises and promotions. Referring to critical incidents can help change an employee's performance. For example, if you want to improve an employee's lateness record, don't say, "You're always late." (This is too general.) The employee will probably say, "No, I'm not." Say, "On January 5, 11, and 17 you were late." (This is specific.) It is difficult to argue with accurate facts.

Rating Scales

The **rating scale** *is a form on which the supervisor simply checks off the employee's level of performance.* Some of the possible areas evaluated include quantity of work, quality of work, dependability, judgment, attitude, cooperativeness, initiative, and so forth.

Rating scales are probably the most common measurement method, probably because they are relatively easy to develop and use. When checking off rating scales, the supervisor should refer to the critical incident file to refresh his or her memory of past performance. Employee performance should be compared to the scales, not to the performance of other employees. A rating scale is used in preparation for Skill-Building Exercise 12–2.

Rating scales geared to the specific job are appropriate for both developmental and administrative decisions. The scale indicates strengths and areas where improvement is needed. It can be used to develop objectives and plans for improved performance. It can also be used as the basis for pay raises, promotions, and other administrative decisions. Rating scales for all employees can be compared to identify superior performers.

Behaviorally Anchored Rating Scales (BARS)

Behaviorally anchored rating scales *combine rating scales and critical incident files.* This appraisal method is growing in popularity because it is more objective and accurate than either method used separately. In courts, BARS tend to be viewed more favorably than rating scales. Rather than just a rating of excellent, good, average, and so on, the form includes a statement that describes the employee's performance. Standards are clear when good BARS are developed.

The major drawback to BARS is the time it takes to develop the instrument. The BARS are usually several pages long (often with one page per responsibility) rather than one or two pages like the rating scales. BARS are also very specific and cannot be used for a variety of different jobs as the rating scales can. Like the rating scales, BARS can be used to make both developmental and administrative decisions.

Ranking

Ranking *is used to compare employee performance.* It is used to compare employees to each other rather than comparing them to a standard measurement. Employees are often rated too high during appraisals. To offset this, some organizations require a ranking in addition to the rating scales because all employees may perform the job well, but only one can be the best. An offshoot of ranking is the forced distribution method, which is similar to grading on a curve. A predetermined percentage of employees are placed in each performance category, for example, excellent 5 percent, above average 15 percent, average 60 percent, below average 15 percent, and poor 5 percent.

Ranking methods are appropriate for administrative decisions such as merit pay raises and promotions. They are more accurate when the ranking is based on a standard such as rating scales or BARS. Ranking is not appropriate for development decisions. Let all employees be winners; don't rank them and make them compete. Compare them to the standard.

Management by Objectives (MBO)

MBO dictates that supervisors and their employees jointly set objectives for the employee, periodically evaluate their performance, and reward the employees based on the results. (See Chapter 2 for details.)

MBO is appropriate for developmental decisions. It is often difficult to make administrative decisions based on MBO alone.

Narrative

With the narrative method, the supervisor writes a description of the employee's performance. How this is done can vary. Supervisors may be allowed to write whatever they like, or they may be required to write answers to specific questions about the employee's performance. The free-form narrative often becomes subjective. In addition, many supervisors lack the writing skills for this method to be effective. Answering a series of questions makes the method more objective and uniform.

Some prefer the written statement of performance to the rating scales or BARS.[20] However, the written statement is not popular, possibly because it is more subjective and difficult to use. The narrative is often combined with another method.

The narrative is appropriate for developmental decisions because the objectives and plans can be written down. It can be difficult to use the narrative method for administrative decisions involving employees who have different supervisors because there is no uniform measurement.

Which Performance Appraisal Method Is Best?

The answer to the question of choosing an appraisal method depends on the objectives of the system. A combination of methods is usually superior to using any single method. For developmental objectives, the critical incident file and MBO work well. For administrative decisions, a ranking method based on rating scales or BARS works well.

The real success of performance appraisal does not lie in the method or form used. It depends on the supervisor. The effective supervisor will have success with any format because he or she will communicate standards clearly. The ineffective supervisor can have the best format in the world and do a poor job.

Responsibility for Performance Appraisal

Up to this point, we have been assuming that the supervisor evaluates employees. However, appraisals may also be conducted by a group, a committee, or peers. Self-evaluation is also done. Another approach is the employee evaluation of the supervisor.

Supervisor: Most often, the immediate supervisor evaluates the employee. The supervisor is usually in the best position to evaluate performance. The other three methods are usually used in addition to, rather than in place of, the supervisor's appraisal. A combination of methods often results in a more objective performance appraisal.

Group or Committee: A group or committee is able to offer a variety of insights. This type of evaluation is often used for decisions involving administrative promotions. It is common in matrix structures (see Chapter 3) when employees report to more than one superior.

Peer Evaluations: Peer evaluation is helpful when making administrative decisions. Co-worker evaluation has proven to be an effective predictor of future supervisory success. Peer ranking can also help the supervisor distribute merit raises.[21] Skill-Building Exercise 12–2 is a peer evaluation.

Self-Evaluation: Even if it is not part of the appraisal system, employees tend to evaluate themselves and their job performance. It is advisable to incorporate this and have employees evaluate their own performance before and during informal and formal appraisals. We will discuss this in more detail later. (Skill-Building Exercise 12–2 requires a self-evaluation of your performance in this course.)

Subordinate Evaluation of Superiors: This method is commonly used in colleges to assess professors' teaching ability. The results are often considered in making tenure and promotion decisions. Employees also evaluate supervisors in some organizations to assess supervisory training needs. The evaluation should be anonymous for obvious reasons.

LEARNING OBJECTIVE

2. Describe six performance appraisal measurement methods.

CONNECTIONS

3. Identify the measurement methods used to evaluate performance in a job you have held.

4. Identify who appraised your performance for a job you have held.

III. Coaching

Coaching is the third step in the performance appraisal process. As our definition states, performance appraisal is an ongoing process. This is largely achieved through coaching. **Coaching** *is the process of giving feedback to maintain and improve performance.* Coaching is needed to ensure maximum performance; it should begin on the employee's first day of orientation.[22] A supervisor should set aside time to coach employees and develop an atmosphere of understanding in which the employees feel free to come to him or her for help.[23]

When some people hear the word "coaching," they think of athletes. Like the athletic coach, the supervisor should be looking for steady performance and constant improvement. When the New England Patriots went to the Super Bowl in 1986, everyone was asking "How did they do it?" A major factor was their coach, who asked his team for play-calling suggestions. The next time you watch a sporting event, keep an eye on the coaches and learn some ways to coach employees.[24]

Coaching's objectives are to maintain and improve performance. Your efforts to maintain performance can result in improved performance.

Maintaining and Improving Performance

To maintain or improve performance, employees need feedback on how they are doing. Effective feedback should provide an employee with a feeling of accomplishment so that he or she will work harder, take on more difficult assignments, and take more risks.[25] Following are some guidelines for giving feedback.

Separate Positive and Negative Feedback: Give employees either positive or negative feedback. When you give both at the same time, often called the *sandwich technique,* employees tend to get confused. "The supervisor told me I'm doing a good job, and I'm not doing a good job, and then I'm doing a good job again. Which is it?" Because the sandwich technique starts out with positive feedback, employees tend to think to themselves, "When is the bad news coming?" They focus on the negative feedback and discard the positive.[26] In addition, when giving sandwich feedback, supervisors often talk about more than one topic. It's better to give feedback on one topic at a time. Feedback on several topics can result in information overload.

Give More Positive than Negative Feedback: At least give equal amounts of both. One simple technique to determine the ratio of positive to negative feedback is to keep a 3″ × 5″ card in your pocket. Every time you give positive feedback put a plus (+) on one side of the card. Every time you give negative feedback put a minus (−) on the other side of the card. After a few days or a week, add up the number of plus and minus signs. The typical supervisor will have more minus signs.[27] If this is true in your case, you should work at giving more positive feedback. Stress the positive. If you want to maintain good performance, you must reinforce it through positive feedback. Focusing on the positive builds employees up. They feel like winners and are more willing to try to maintain and improve performance.

Jack Falvey takes the positive versus negative feedback ratio to the point of recommending only positive feedback.

> *Criticism is to be avoided at all costs (there is no such thing as constructive criticism; all criticism is destructive). If you must correct someone, never do it after the fact. Bite your tongue and hold off until he is about to do the same thing again and then challenge him to make a more positive contribution.*[28]

Giving praise following the model in Chapter 11 is an excellent method of giving positive feedback.

Improving Performance

Performance appraisal's primary objective is to facilitate performance improvement and personal development.[29] Like an athletic coach, a supervisor is fine-tuning performance to ensure constant improvement. In the last chapter, the steps in Model 11–1 were followed to increase productivity. In the example that follows, we will see how the model can be used to improve performance. In the example, a diagnosis of the problem and training are not necessary. Rita is the branch manager of a bank and Tony is a customer service representative who handles mail passbook transactions. Tony has just returned from his 10:00 A.M. break and finds Rita waiting.

Step 1. Refer to Past Feedback: Let the employee know what the feedback refers to.

RITA: Tony, you know you're not supposed to leave passbooks unattended, don't you?

TONY: Yes, I do.

Step 2. Describe Current Performance: In detail and using specific examples, describe the current behavior that needs to be changed.

RITA: During your 10:00 break, I walked past your desk and found this passbook sitting on it.

Step 3. Describe Desired Performance: Tell the employee exactly what the desired performance is in detail. Have the employee state why the performance is important.

MODEL 12–1

IMPROVING PERFORMANCE

Step 1. Refer to past feedback.

Step 2. Describe current performance.

Step 3. Describe desired performance.

Step 4. Get a commitment to the change.

Step 5. Follow up.

TONY: I left in such a hurry that I must have forgotten to lock it in my desk. You know how you stress taking breaks at the proper times.

RITA: Why does the bank insist on not leaving passbooks unattended?

TONY: For security and confidentiality.

RITA: That's right. Would you like to have your passbook left unattended where someone could take it, or look at the amount in it?

TONY: Not really!

Step 4. Get a Commitment to the Change: This is important because, if the employee is not willing to commit to the change, he or she will not make the change.

RITA: Is there something we can do to prevent this from happening again in the future?

TONY: Yes, I can be more conscientious and lock the passbooks in my drawer whenever I leave my desk.

RITA: So you agree to stop leaving passbooks unattended?

TONY (*Sarcastically*): I'll try not to do it again, okay?

RITA: Will you make a sincere effort not to do it again?

TONY: Yes.

Step 5. Follow Up: Remember, employees do what a supervisor inspects, not what he or she expects.[30] The supervisor should always follow up to ensure that the employee is behaving as desired. An actual meeting is not always necessary, but the employee should realize how the supervisor will follow up.

RITA: I'm glad to hear you say that. In the future, I don't expect to find any passbooks on your desk when you're not there.

Model 12–1 lists the five steps for improving performance.

LEARNING OBJECTIVE

3. List and explain the five steps for improving performance and use the model.

CONNECTIONS

5. Recall a past or present supervisor. How would you rate his or her coaching ability? Explain your answer using critical incidents.

6. Describe a specific situation in which the increasing productivity model would be appropriate for improving performance.

IV. Preparing for a Performance Appraisal

You have learned what you should cover in a performance appraisal. Now you will examine how to use this information in preparing for and actually conducting an appraisal. In this section, you will learn problems to avoid when conducting a performance appraisal and when preparing for an evaluation and a developmental interview.

Problems to Avoid When Conducting a Performance Appraisal

There are 11 significant problem areas to avoid when conducting a performance appraisal: interruptions, rushing, recency trap, activity trap, bias, halo effect, horn effect, central tendency, leniency, strictness, and memory.

Interruptions: It is important to avoid interruptions during a performance appraisal. It is very distracting to both the supervisor and employee. Before beginning the interview, tell others not to disturb you unless an emergency arises.

Rushing: Supervisors often underestimate the time the appraisal will take. When pressed for time, they rush through the end of the appraisal. Be sure to leave plenty of time. Do not plan anything for some time after you think the appraisal will end so that you can carry on until a natural ending. Do not schedule the appraisal too late in the work day.

Recency Trap: Do not give more weight to recent performance during the evaluation. Keeping a good critical incidents file will help you remember past performance.

Activity Trap: Do not evaluate employees based on how active or busy they appear to be. Evaluate results. The employee who appears to be the busiest may actually be the least productive.

Bias: Evaluate actual performance, not personality, race, religion, and so forth. Supervisors develop feelings for employees based on work-related interactions. Be aware of your feelings toward each employee. Separate objective judgment from subjective feelings when evaluating performance. Feelings can be positive, neutral, or negative. Feelings also affect other problem areas in the appraisal.[31]

Halo Effect: The halo effect means that the supervisor rates the employee favorably on all criteria based on performance in a few. When a supervisor has positive feelings about a specific employee, the halo effect may take hold.[32] When evaluating performance, the supervisor should deal with each criterion separately. An employee may be outstanding in some areas and poor in others.

Horn Effect: The horn effect is the opposite of the halo effect. A supervisor rates the employee low on all criteria based on unfavorable performance in a few. This may be especially true when a supervisor has negative feelings about the employee.[33] Evaluate each performance criterion separately.

Central Tendency: The central tendency means that a supervisor rates all employees as average or that all ratings in a single evaluation are within a narrow range. There should be a distribution of ratings because employees do not perform at the same level all the time or on every task. When a supervisor has neutral feelings about employees, the central tendency may be observed.[34]

Leniency: Supervisors with the leniency problem rate employees higher than actual performance warrants. In one study, 62 percent of the 267 corporations responding cited inflated ratings as the most severe problem in performance appraisal.[35] Supervisors with positive feelings about employees tend to be lenient.

Strictness: The opposite of leniency is strictness. The supervisor rates employees lower than actual performance warrants. This may reflect a supervisor's negative feelings about employees.[36]

Memory: It is difficult to remember what happened six months to a year ago. Using the critical incident file can help minimize memory problems.

Exhibit 12–2 summarizes the 11 problems to avoid when appraising performance.

LEARNING OBJECTIVE

4. Explain 11 problems to avoid when conducting a performance appraisal.

EXHIBIT 12-2   **PROBLEMS TO AVOID WHEN APPRAISING PERFORMANCE**

1. Interruptions
2. Rushing
3. Recency trap
4. Activity trap
5. Bias
6. Halo effect
7. Horn effect
8. Central tendency
9. Leniency
10. Strictness
11. Memory

CONNECTIONS

7. Recall an appraisal of your performance. Did the supervisor avoid all 11 problem areas? If not, which problems did the supervisor have?

Preparing for an Evaluation

As stated earlier, a performance appraisal has two objectives: to evaluate past performance and to help an employee improve or develop. Therefore, a formal performance appraisal should involve two separate interviews. The first should evaluate past performance. When preparing for this interview, the supervisor should make an appointment, have the employee do a self-appraisal, assess performance, and identify strengths and areas for improvement. The supervisor should also predict how the employee will react and plan how to handle it.

Make an Appointment: About one week before the supervisor plans to conduct the performance appraisal interview, he or she should make an appointment with the employee. Agree on a date, time, and place. Let the employee select the place—the supervisor's office, the employee's work area, or a neutral area such as a conference room (reserve it). Don't break the appointment; this sends a signal that the employee is not important.

Have the Employee Perform a Self-Appraisal: When you make the appointment, give the employee a copy of the evaluation form. Ask him or her to fill it out (explain how, if necessary) and bring it to the interview.[37] Also ask the employee to identify his or her strengths and areas where improvement is needed.

Assess Performance: Gather the data you need to make the assessment: employee records, critical incidents file, and so on. Fill out the evaluation form, but not in final form. You may change your evaluation during the interview. Review the 11 problem areas in Exhibit 12-2 and be sure you avoid them all.

Identify Strengths and Areas for Improvement: Notice that I did not say *weaknesses*. That term has a negative connotation. An employee may say, "I have no weaknesses," but there are always areas where improvement is possible.

Predict Employee Reactions and Plan How to Handle Them: Supervisors who know their employees should have a good idea of how the employee will react to the evaluation. Having a list of specific critical incidents to back up the evaluation will help the supervisor overcome disagreement.

Preparing for a Developmental Interview

After the evaluation is completed, the supervisor should prepare for the developmental interview. To do this, a supervisor should make an appointment, have the

EXHIBIT 12–3   **PREPARING FOR PERFORMANCE APPRAISAL INTERVIEWS**

Evaluation interview	Developmental interview
1. Make an appointment.	1. Make an appointment.
2. Have the employee perform a self-appraisal.	2. Have the employee develop objectives and plans for improving performance.
3. Assess performance.	3. Develop objectives and plans for improving employee performance.
4. Identify strengths and areas for improvement.	
5. Predict employee reactions and plan how to handle them.	

employee develop objectives and plans for improving performance, and develop his or her own objectives and plans for improving employee performance.

Make an Appointment: Set a date, time, and place for the developmental interview. This date can be set at the end of the evaluation interview or later. Scheduling the development interview about a week after the evaluation is fine.

Have the Employee Develop Objectives and Plans for Improving Performance: During the evaluation interview, the supervisor and employee should have agreed on strengths and areas for improvement. The areas for improvement serve as the basis for developmental objectives and plans.

Develop Objectives and Plans for Improving Employee Performance: The degree of detail in the objectives and plans the supervisor develops should depend on the employee's capability level. Use the supervisory style (discussed in Chapter 1) appropriate to the situation. If the employee is low in capability (C-1), the supervisor should use an autocratic style and have detailed written objectives and plans ready. Use the operational planning sheet in Exhibit 2–6 for this purpose. When the employee has medium capability (C-2), the supervisor should use a consultative style and have written objectives and plans, but be open to changing them. For employees with a high capability level (C-3), the supervisor should use a participative style and think of objectives and plans but should not write them down. With the outstanding employee (C-4), the supervisor should use the laissez-faire style and does not need to develop objectives and plans.

Exhibit 12–3 lists the steps in preparing for performance appraisal interviews.

LEARNING OBJECTIVE

5. List the steps in preparing for the evaluation and developmental performance appraisal.

CONNECTIONS

8. Before an evaluation performance appraisal, would you prefer to do a self-appraisal? Why? Have you ever done one?

V. Conducting a Performance Appraisal

When actually conducting a performance appraisal, the supervisor should compare the employee's performance to the established standards; avoid comparing the employee to other employees. Encourage the employee to talk. The appraisal should be a give-and-take interview with both parties contributing on a 50-50 basis. In fact, the supervisor usually does 85 to 90 percent of the talking.[38] How the actual appraisal is conducted will depend on whether it is an evaluation or a developmental interview.

Conducting an Evaluation Interview

The steps in an **evaluation interview** *are as follows: open; go over the form; agree on strengths and areas for improvement; and close.*

Step 1. Open the Interview: Put the employee at ease. Develop a rapport by discussing some topic of interest to the employee, such as sports, hobbies, and so forth. You may tell a joke if it's inoffensive. In one study, 58 percent of the personnel executives surveyed stated that humor is appropriate for performance reviews.[39] Once a rapport is established, state the purpose of the interview to actually begin.

Step 2. Go Over the Form: Start with the first item and go over the items on the form in order. You can begin with the employee's self-evaluation for each item, and his or her reason for the rating. Follow with the rating you gave on the item and your reasons for it. Use critical incidents to support the rating. The supervisor can also begin with his or her rating on the item and reasons it was selected, using critical incidents. The supervisor then asks for the employee's rating and reason for it.

With either method, the supervisor should praise good performance and express appreciation of it. In most interviews, there will be at least one area of disagreement on the rating the employee should receive. When this occurs, do the following:

- Listen to the employee's side without becoming hostile, defensive, or argumentative.
- Be willing to change the rating if the employee is correct.
- Stand firm if you are correct. Do not let the employee bluff you into changing ratings if you disagree.[40]
- If the employee continues to disagree, tell him or her to submit a written statement. The statement can be written directly on the form—several include space for this purpose—or it can be attached to the form.

Step 3. Agree on Strengths and Areas for Improvement: After going over each item on the form, ask the employee to describe his or her strengths. You should also describe what you believe are the employee's strengths, and then come to an agreement. Follow the same procedure to identify areas for improvement. Keep the latter to two or three items, at most. Unless the employee has low capability, this is a good time to tell the employee to develop objectives and plans for improvements in these areas. You can also set up the appointment for the developmental interview.

If the supervisor has the authority to give pay raises, the amount of the raise can be discussed at this point.

Step 4. Close the Interview: Summarize the meeting with an overall rating of the employee's performance. End on a positive note such as, "I'm glad we had a chance to discuss your performance," "You're doing a great job," "I'm sure that if we work together, you can improve the evaluation next time," and so on.[41]

Model 12–2 lists the steps in an evaluation interview.

MODEL 12–2   **CONDUCTING AN EVALUATION INTERVIEW**

Step 1. Open the interview.

Step 2. Go over the performance appraisal form.

Step 3. Agree on strengths and areas for improvement.

Step 4. Close the interview.

Conducting a Developmental Performance Appraisal

A **developmental interview** *involves opening the interview, agreeing on objectives, developing plans for meeting objectives, making a follow-up appointment, and closing.*

Step 1. Open the Interview: Open the interview in the same way as you did with the evaluation interview.

Step 2. Agree on Objectives: Keep the number of objectives to two or three, at most. This discussion depends upon the employee's capability level. If the employee has low capability (C-1), he or she may not have been asked to develop objectives and plans. Instead, you will go over objectives you developed with the employee. Ask employees who have medium (C-2) or high (C-3) capability to describe the objectives they developed. With the medium-capability employee, "sell" the employee on your written objectives unless you agree with the objectives the employee developed. With the high-capability employee, use the employee's objectives with modifications, if necessary. The outstanding employee should present acceptable objectives.

In any case, write each objective on an operational planning sheet (Exhibit 2–6) following the criteria for good objectives.

Step 3. Develop Plans for Meeting Objectives: To meet each objective, a plan must be developed. How much guidance the supervisor gives depends upon the employee's capability level. The lower the level, the more guidance is needed; the higher the level, the less guidance is needed.

In any case, each objective and the plans should be written on an operational planning sheet. Be sure to set control checkpoints to review progress in meeting the objectives.

Step 4. Make a Follow-Up Appointment: Be sure to schedule a meeting to review progress at the first control checkpoint.

LEARNING OBJECTIVE

6. List the steps in the evaluation and developmental interview and use these models.

Step 5. Close the Interview: The supervisor and employee should each have copies of the operational plans or make arrangements to get copies. The supervisor may review action items. Close with a positive statement such as, "I'm confident that you will achieve the objectives."

Model 12–3 lists the steps in conducting a developmental performance appraisal interview.

CONNECTIONS

9. Identify the steps that a present or past supervisor followed when conducting an evaluation or developmental interview. List each step described in the appropriate model and indicate whether it was followed.

MODEL 12–3

CONDUCTING A DEVELOPMENTAL PERFORMANCE APPRAISAL INTERVIEW

Step 1. Open the interview.

Step 2. Agree on objectives.

Step 3. Develop plans for meeting objectives.

Step 4. Make a follow-up appointment.

Step 5. Close the interview.

VI. Compensating Employees

Once performance is evaluated, good or superior performance must be recognized in some way. **Reward systems** *are the mechanisms for defining, evaluating, and recognizing performance.* Organizations attempt to motivate employees through reward systems. Rewards can be *financial* (such as pay, commission, bonus, profit sharing, pensions, employee stock options, or fringe benefits) or *nonfinancial* (for example, praise, promotions, status, additional assignments, special awards, or commendations).

In this section, you will learn about financial rewards: pay systems, wage and salary determination, total compensation, increasing compensation, trends in compensation, and the supervisor's role in compensation.

Pay Systems

An employee may receive an hourly wage, a straight salary, or be compensated according to some sort of incentive system. An organization may use one or more of these methods in its compensation system.

Hourly Wages: Pay is based on the number of hours worked. If an employee receives $7 per hour and works 40 hours, his or her gross pay for the week is $280. Hourly wages are common for blue-collar workers.

Straight Salary: Pay is based on a set rate for a week, month, or year. The salary is usually paid regardless of the number of hours worked. Straight salary is common for white-collar workers and managers.

Incentive Systems: Incentive systems are based on results. For example, some salespeople receive a commission only on the sales they make. If Ben, a salesperson, is paid a 25 percent commission and sells $4,000 worth of goods for the week, he is paid $1,000. Most organizations combine incentive pay with wages or salaries. For example, production workers are often paid a wage plus a bonus for all units over the standard rate. Assume that a $1 bonus is paid for each unit above the standard of 50 per week; Coleen earns $6 per hour and produced 75 units in 40 hours. Her gross pay is $265 [hourly wage ($6 × 40 hours = $240) + bonus (75 – 50 = 25 × $1 = $25) $240 + $25 = 265]. Incentive pay is common for production and sales employees.

Wage and Salary Determination

Organizations must determine how much they will pay their employees. Usually the human resources department is responsible for wage and salary administration. External or internal criteria may be used to determine compensation. The same organization may use both.

External Criteria   Organizations using external criteria base compensation on how much other organizations pay their employees for doing the same or similar jobs. Several professional and trade associations publish average pay figures for various jobs. Most organizations pay within a narrow range of the average; 52 percent pay within 7 percent of average, and 71 percent pay within 9 percent of the average. However, there is often a lack of consistency within an organization; pay may be below average for some jobs and above average for others.[42]

Internal Criteria   Most large companies and state and federal agencies use internal criteria to compensate employees; small businesses usually do not. Job evaluation is used to determine compensation. **Job evaluation** *is the process of determining the worth of each job relative to the other jobs within the organization.* The objective is to pay equally for jobs of equal worth or value. Pay must be nondiscriminatory and meet EEO guidelines. A job analysis must be done before the job evaluation because the analysis serves as the basis of comparison for the different jobs. There are four major ways to evaluate jobs: ranking, classification, factor comparison, and the point system.

Ranking: Jobs are ranked in order of their importance to the organization. This becomes very complex in organizations with hundreds of different jobs. This is the simplest and most subjective job evaluation method.

Classification: This method involves determining a certain number of job classifications, often called grades. Each job is categorized by classification or grade. This method is used by the federal civil service, which assigns GS ratings. Generally, the higher the grade level, the higher the pay.

Factor Comparison: A series of factors that are important to the organization are identified. They may include mental ability, skills, education, working conditions, responsibility, and so forth. After the factors are identified, they are weighted according to their importance, and an amount of pay is assigned to each factor. The pay for each factor is added up to determine total wage or salary for each job.

Point System: Over 95 percent of major U.S. corporations using job evaluation have a point system.[43] The **point system** *assigns a value to each job factor.* As with factor comparison, a series of factors are identified; however, each factor is assigned a point value rather than a dollar value. The points are totaled to determine job grades or classes. Jobs at each grade receive a specified pay range. The higher the points, the higher the pay. Exhibit 12–4 illustrates a job evaluation using the point system. The total number of points determines the job level.

Total Compensation

So far we have talked about pay, which is money given directly to employees. However, employees receive more than direct pay. Organizations also give employees a great deal of indirect pay, usually in the form of *benefits.* **Compensation** *is the direct and indirect pay that employees receive.*

Some benefits are required by law; these include social security, unemployment compensation, and workers' compensation. Other benefits commonly offered, but not required by law, include health, dental, and life insurance; sick pay; paid vacations; pension plans; profit sharing; stock options; tuition payments; and child care. The cost of these benefits to the organization varies. However, most estimate that benefits average around 35 percent of employees' direct pay. For example, if an employee's direct pay is $10,000 per year, benefits received cost $3,500 ($10,000 × 35 percent). In other words, compensation, or the total cost to the organization, is $13,500.

To so-called *cafeteria plan* is becoming increasingly popular. It allows the employee to select the benefits that meet his or her needs. Most organizations provide some basic coverage and then allow the employee to select additional benefits.

Increasing Compensation

After a period of time, often once a year following the performance appraisal, employees are eligible for an increase in compensation. The increase can be in direct pay, benefits, or a combination of both. An increase in direct pay can be a flat rate or a percentage increase, or it can be based on merit.

EXHIBIT 12-4

JOB EVALUATION—POINT SYSTEM

Job Name __Material-Handling Operator__   Class _____ Job Level __13__ Code __676__
Dept. __Resimenes__

Factor	Basis for Degree of Difficulty	Deg.	Pts.
Education	Two years of high school or equivalent required to keep records of transfers, inventories, shipments. Need to understand simple ratios and percentages.	4	40
Experience	One to two years required to become familiar with products, storage areas, job routine, etc.	5	100
Initiative	Requires frequent making of simple decisions, but only where precedents are available. Occasionally decision or action required where only general procedures are available.	4	60
Physical Effort	Moderately heavy physical activity. Medium-weight objects handled generally, with occasional heavy lifting, pushing, or pulling (not to exceed 20 percent of job cycle).	4	40
Concentration	Fairly diversified job requiring planning and organization in addition to alertness.	4	60
Responsibility for Materials and Equipment	Damage to equipment causing moderate production delay, resulting in moderate expenditures for material replacements or equipment repair.	5	50
Responsibility for Reports and Records	Keeps record of samples, shipments, materials, inspections, status of work. May require 25–50 percent of time spent on records.	5	25
Working Conditions	Continuous exposure to some very disagreeable conditions, dust, and outside weather conditions.	5	50
Unavoidable Hazards	If injured, employee is likely to receive such injuries as severe cuts, bruises, fractures. Some exposure to minor health hazards.	4	20
		Total	445

Flat Rate: All employees receive a fixed dollar amount, regardless of present pay. For example, all employees get a $500 raise for the year.

Percentage Increase. This is more popular than the flat rate. All employees get a set percentage increase in their present pay. For example, the increase is 5 percent. An employee now getting $10,000 a year will receive $10,500 after the raise. An employee getting $20,000 annually will receive $21,000. Employees are concerned about getting a percentage increase that exceeds the increase in the cost of living for that year to ensure that their standard of living will improve. For example, if the cost of living rises by 5 percent and you get a 3 percent raise, your standard of living is going down. Some organizations give cost-of-living adjustments.

Merit: Under the merit system, the amount of the increase is based on performance. The intent of merit raises is to tie performance to rewards. However, the system is often flawed. Unfortunately, many merit compensation systems simply reward longevity, all but ignoring performance and creativity.[44] Merit raises can also be based on politics rather than on performance. Many supervisors give all employees virtually the same percentage increases regardless of performance. Or they give merit raises to all employees on a rotating basis.

A Research Institute survey revealed that only 20 percent of U.S. workers believe that performance and pay are related.[45] To be considered equitable to employees, a merit raise should amount to 10 to 20 percent of current salary.[46] To motivate employees to increase productivity, the merit raises given must be distinct. It should be obvious that superior performance is rewarded. One way to distribute merit raises is as follows: establish five categories called outstanding (only 5 percent of employees should be given this rating), superior (15 percent of employees), good (60 percent of employees), adequate (15 percent of employees), and unacceptable (5 percent of employees).[47]

Merit increases should be determined as follows:

Employee Category	Merit Raise (percentage of current salary)
Outstanding	12–14%
Superior	11–9
Good	8–6
Adequate	5–3
Unacceptable	0

Peer ranking is helpful in placing employees in the categories.[48] Many organizations use a combination of flat rate, percentage, and merit increases. For example, all employees receive a cost-of-living percentage increase and a merit raise based on performance.

Trends in Compensation

Each year, a smaller number of employees say that traditional pay practices are fair.[49] Perhaps some of the current trends in employee compensation will redress this balance. For example, in the 1990s compensation will be more directly tied to individual performance and contributions to corporate goals.[50]

Organizations will also view compensation as having a fixed and a variable element.[51] The fixed portion (wage and salary, benefits, and so on) will decrease, and the variable portion (profit sharing, bonuses, and so forth) will increase.[52] In 1986, bonuses were granted in lieu of salary increases by 1 of every 15 companies in one survey.[53]

The All-Salaried Work Force: Organizations including Dow Chemical, IBM, and Gillette are giving blue-collar workers a salary rather than an hourly wage.

Skills-Based Compensation: Employees are paid based on the number of jobs they can do rather than for one specific job they may be doing at the present time.

Organizations using skills-based compensation described the following benefits: 90 percent reported having a more flexible work force; 80 percent reported reduced defects; 75 percent reported increased quality of output; 70 percent reported reduced absenteeism, turnover, and production costs; and 45 percent reported reduced labor cost. They all reported that the system is at least moderately successful.[54]

Comparable Worth: **Comparable worth** *means that jobs that are distinctly different but require similar levels of ability should have the same pay scale.* Today, on average, women are paid less than men. Advocates of comparable worth want the pay for jobs traditionally held by women, such as secretarial positions to be comparable to that for jobs traditionally held by men, such as electrician work, when they require the same ability. People opposing it claim that supply and demand for labor sets the pay rates, not discrimination against women.

Comparable worth has received much attention from certain women's groups, with mixed support from government agencies and the courts. In 1984, the issue was tabled by the Civil Rights Commission as unenforceable. However, it could become a major issue in the future with the more liberal federal administration elected in 1992. Comparable worth could very well become the hottest employment issue of the rest of the century.

The Supervisor's Role in Compensation

The supervisor often gives input into the job analysis and job evaluations. The supervisor can also be helpful in identifying job factors and assigning values to them. The supervisor often determines or gives input deciding the amount of increased compensation employees receive. When the supervisor does not directly recommend a specific raise, his or her performance appraisal is often used as the basis for someone else's decision. The supervisor may be responsible for awarding the increases, although the amount may be determined elsewhere in the organization. For example, the supervisor may be allowed to give employees a percentage increase of between 3 and 7 percent, or may be given a set amount to distribute as merit raises.

LEARNING OBJECTIVE

7. Describe the supervisor's role in compensation.

CONNECTIONS

10. Identify the methods of payment you receive or have received.

11. Identify how compensation is increased at an organization you have worked for. If merit is used, how would you improve the method? If merit is not used, how would you use merit?

12. Identify any current compensation trends in an organization you have worked for.

REVIEW

Select one or more methods: (1) fill in the missing key terms from memory; (2) match the key terms from the end of the review with their definitions below; (3) copy the key terms in order from the key terms at the beginning of the chapter.

_____ is the ongoing process of evaluating employee effectiveness and efficiency. Performance is appraised for developmental and evaluative reasons. Neither supervisors nor employees look forward to performance interviews. Performance appraisal interviews must meet EEO guidelines. The performance appraisal steps are as follows: determine job responsibilities, develop standards and measurement methods, give informal performance appraisals (coaching), prepare for the formal performance appraisal, and conduct a formal performance appraisal.

Standards of performance should be clearly established and communicated to employees and should cover a range of performance. Measurement methods include the _____ , a record of an employee's positive and negative performance; the _____ , a form on which the supervisor simply checks off the employee's level of performance; _____ , combining rating scales and critical incident files; _____ , used to compare employee performance; management by objectives; and the narrative. Performance can be evaluated by the immediate supervisor, a group or committee, peers, and by the employee himself or herself. Sometimes employees evaluate supervisors.

_____ is the process of giving feedback to maintain and improve performance. To maintain performance, the supervisor should separate positive and negative feedback, give more positive than negative feedback, and give praise every day. To improve performance, the supervisor should follow the five steps in the increasing productivity model.

When preparing for a performance appraisal, the supervisor should avoid interruptions, rushing, the recency trap, the activity trap, bias, the halo effect, the horn effect, the central tendency, leniency, strictness, and the memory problem. When preparing for an evaluation the supervisor should make an appointment, have the employee perform a self-appraisal, assess performance, identify strengths and areas for improvement, and predict employee reactions and plan how to handle them. When preparing for a developmental interview, the supervisor should make an appointment, have the employee develop objectives and plans for improving performance, and develop his or her own objectives and plans for improving employee performance.

Steps in an _____ are open, Step 2. go over the form, agree on strengths and areas for improvement, and close. A _____ involves opening, agreeing on objectives, developing plans for meeting objectives, making a follow-up appointment, and closing.

_____ are the mechanisms for defining, evaluating, and recognizing employee performance. Employees are paid an hourly wage or a straight salary or are paid through an incentive system. Wages and salaries are determined using external or internal criteria. The _____

is the process of determining the worth of each job relative to the other jobs

within the organization. The four methods used to evaluate jobs are ranking,

classification, factor comparison, and the _____ , which

assigns a value to each job factor. _____ is the direct and

indirect pay that employees receive. A compensation increase can be a flat rate

or a percentage increase or can be based on merit. The supervisor often gives

input into the job analysis and job evaluation. The supervisor may also be

involved in determining an employee's increase in compensation.

_____ means that jobs that are distinctly different but

require similar levels of ability should have the same pay scale.

KEY TERMS

behaviorally anchored rating scales (BARS)

coaching

comparable worth

compensation

critical incident file

developmental interview

evaluation interview

job evaluation

performance appraisal

point system

ranking

rating scales

reward systems

REFERENCES

1. Ted Pollock, "Are You Ready to Conduct that Appraisal?" *Supervision*, January 1986, p. 24.

2. Charles MacDonald, *Performance Based Supervisory Development* (Amherst, MA: Human Resources Development, 1982), p. 20.

3. Lawrence Bonifant, "The 423-Minute Manager," *Personnel Administrator*, July 1986, p. 25.

4. William Weitzel, "How to Conduct Effective Performance Appraisals," *BNA Communicator*, Spring 1987, p. 11.

5. Phillip Grant, "A Better Approach to Performance Reviews," *Management Solutions*, March 1987, p. 11.

6. Bonifant, "The 423-Minute Manager," p. 22.

7. Donald Kirkpatrick, "Performance Appraisal: Your Questions Answered," *Training and Development Journal*, May 1986, p. 70.

8. "The Trouble with Performance Appraisal," *Training*, April 1984, p. 91.

9. "Will Your Next Performance Appraisal Land You in Court?" *Management Solutions*, July 1986, p. 5.

10. Shelley Burchett and Kenneth De Meuse, "Performance Appraisal and the Law," *Personnel*, July 1985, pp. 29–37.

11. Stephen Harper, "Adding Purpose to Performance Reviews," *Training and Development Journal*, September 1986, p. 53.

12. Rutigliano, "Naisbitt and Aburdene on: Reinventing the Workplace," *Management Review*, October 1985, p. 33.

13. Kenneth Phillips, "Red Flags in Performance Appraisal," *Training and Development Journal*, March 1987, p. 80.

14. D. Keith Denton, "How to Conduct Effective Appraisal Interviews," *Administrative Management*, February 1987, p. 15.

15. Mark Mallinger and Tom Cummings, "Improving the Value of Performance Appraisals," *SAM Advanced Management Journal*, Spring 1986, p. 19.

16. Weitzel, "How to Conduct Effective Performance Appraisals," p. 11.

17. "Will Your Next Performance Appraisal Land You in Court?" p. 9.

18. Kirkpatrick, "Performance Appraisal," p. 70.

19. Michael Smith, "Putting Their Performance in Writing," *Management Solutions*, March 1987, pp. 5–10.

20. Gary Kreutz, "Is the Appraisal System Going the Way of the Dinosaur?" *Personnel Administrator*, August 1986, p. 10.

21. John Bache, "Merit Increase Programs—Do We Really Pay for Performance?" *Supervision*, May 1986, p. 17.

22. Richard Concilio, "Will Coaching Pay Off?" *Management Solutions*, September 1986, p. 18.

23. Bonifant, "The 423-Minute Manager," p. 25.

24. Rosabeth Moss Kanter and Joseph Zolner, "What New Coaches Can Teach Managers," *Management Review*, November 1986, pp. 10–11.

25. Weitzel, "How to Conduct Effective Performance Appraisals," p. 11.

26. Michael Smith, "Feedback as a Performance Management Technique," *Management Solutions*, April 1987, p. 29.

27. Ibid.

28. Jack Falvey, "To Raise Productivity, Try Saying Thank You," *The Wall Street Journal*, December 6, 1982.

29. Roy Serpa, "Why Many Organizations—Despite Good Intentions—Often Fail to Give Employees Fair and Useful Performance Reviews," *Management Review*, July 1984, p. 41.

30. Weitzel, "How to Conduct Effective Performance Appraisals," p. 11.

31. Anne Tsui and Bruce Barry, "Interpersonal Affect and Rating Errors," *Academy of Management Journal*, September 1986, p. 595.

32. Ibid.

33. Ibid.

34. Ibid.

35. "Performance Appraisals—Reappraised," *Management Review*, November 1983, p. 5.

36. Tsui and Barry, "Interpersonal Affect and Rating Errors," p. 595.

37. Kirkpatrick, "Performance Appraisal," p. 70.

38. Ibid., p. 71.

39. "Going for Laughs," *The Wall Street Journal*, p. 26.

40. Denton, "How to Conduct Effective Appraisal Interviews," p. 16.

41. Kirkpatrick, "Performance Appraisal," p. 71.

42. Kenneth Foster, "An Anatomy of Company Pay Practices," *Personnel*, September 1985, pp. 67, 69.

43. Edward Lawler, "What's Wrong with the Point-Factor Job Evaluation," *Management Review*, November 1986, p. 44.

44. R. Meehan, "Many Merit Compensation Systems Simply Reward Longevity, All but Ignoring Performance and Creativity," *Office Administration and Automation*, September 1985, p. 84.

45. Bache, "Merit Increase Programs," p. 14.

46. Ibid., p. 15.

47. Charles Tharp, "Linking Annual Incentives and Individual Performance," *Personnel Administrator*, January 1986, p. 85.

48. Bache, "Merit Increase Programs," p. 17.

49. Rosabeth Moss Kanter, "The Attack on Pay," *Harvard Business Review*, March–April 1987, p. 61.

50. "Compensation Changes Coming," *Personnel Administrator*, January 1987, p. 20.

51. Ibid.

52. Kanter, "Attack on Pay," p. 67.

53. "Bonus Pay Gains Favor as More Companies Tie Salaries to Performance," *The Wall Street Journal*, March 31, 1987, p. 1.

54. William Curington, Nina Gupta, and Douglas Jenkins, "Labor Issues and Skill-Based Compensation Systems," *Labor Law Journal*, August 1986, p. 581.

APPLICATION SITUATIONS

Performance Appraisal Steps

AS 12–1

Identify which step in the performance appraisal process (Exhibit 12–1) is represented by the statements below.

a. Step 1   *d.* Step 4
b. Step 2   *e.* Step 5
c. Step 3

_____ 1. "You really did a great job of fixing that machine."

_____ 2. "Review this job description, and then we will go over it together."

_____ 3. "Have a seat. As you know, we are going to evaluate your performance over the past year."

_____ 4. "We use the rating scale to evaluate employee performance."

_____ 5. "I'd like you to do a self-appraisal of your performance using this form."

Performance Appraisal Methods

AS 12–2

Select the performance appraisal method that should be used in each situation.

a. critical incident file   *d.* ranking
b. rating scales   *e.* MBO
c. BARS   *f.* narrative

_____ 6. You work for a small organization that does not have a formal performance appraisal system. You are overworked, but you want to develop an evaluative tool or form.

_____ 7. You have been promoted from a supervisory position to a middle management position. You have been asked to select your replacement.

_____ 8. Wally is not performing up to standard. You have decided to talk to him in order to improve his performance.

_____ 9. You want to develop a system for developing employees.

_____ 10. You have a master's degree in human resources development (HRD) and work in the HRD department. You have been assigned to develop an objective performance appraisal system, meeting EEO guidelines, for the entire organization.

Performance Appraisal Problems

AS 12–3

Below are 10 employee statements about their performance appraisal. Identify the problem or mistake made by the supervisor.

a. interruptions	*f.* halo effect
b. rushing	*g.* horn effect
c. recency trap	*h.* central tendency
d. activity trap	*i.* leniency
e. bias	*j.* strictness
	k. memory

_____ 11. "I have five major responsibilities. Because I do the more important one so well, the super rates me high on all items."

_____ 12. "I went five months without making a mistake. This month I made one and got a good rating instead of very good."

_____ 13. "I took the supervision course from Professor Luke because I heard she gives all A's and B's for grades."

_____ 14. "I wanted to explain my feeling about the interview at its conclusion, but the super said there wasn't time; he had to go to lunch."

_____ 15. "I'm not concerned about how I perform because I always get the same rating. Almost everyone gets an average rating."

_____ 16. "I don't type well. I only type about 10 percent of the time anyway. But because of typing, the super rates me low on other items."

_____ 17. "I take my time and pace myself. I do as much work as anyone in the department. But because I don't look like I'm pushing it, like some others do, I don't get high evaluations."

_____ 18. "During my interview, the super got three phone calls."

_____ 19. "I did not take accounting with Professor Vader because he gives the most D and F grades in the department."

_____ 20. "Although the super did not say it, she gave me a low rating because of the way I dress. She's always on my case about it."

Shawn's Performance Appraisal of Joan

The following conversation takes place between Shawn, the supervisor, and Joan, the employee.

SHAWN: Joan, I called you into my office because it's time for your first yearly performance appraisal.

JOAN: It's been a year already? I didn't realize it had been that long.

SHAWN: The check marks on this two-page form show how I rated you. I wanted you to look at the form and sign it.

JOAN: (*Several minutes later*) You only gave me an average overall rating! Why? I'm as good a worker as anyone else in the department.

SHAWN: That's right. But there are no superstars in this department. You're all about the same, average.

JOAN: I'll sign it, but I think you underrated me.

SHAWN: Don't worry about it. You presently make $200 a week. I'm authorized to give you a raise of between 2 and 6 percent, and I'm recommending you for a 5 percent increase. I never give the max.

JOAN: That's only $10 a week.

SHAWN: It's the best I can do. Don't forget about our child-care center.

JOAN: Yes, it does help save me money. Day-care centers are expensive.

SHAWN: Overall, you're doing a good job, and you're getting a 5 percent raise. Thank you for coming in for this meeting. I'm glad to have you in my department.

JOAN: I'll see you later.

Answer the following questions, supporting your answers in the space between questions.

_____ 1. The objective of this performance appraisal was
   a. evaluation   *b.* developmental

_____ 2. Shawn is in step _____ of the performance appraisal process.
   a. 1   *d.* 4
   b. 2   *e.* 5
   c. 3

_____ 3. Performance standards are clear.
   a. true   *b.* false

_____ 4. The performance method used by Shawn is
   a. critical incident file   *d.* ranking
   b. rating scales   *e.* MBO
   c. BARS   *f.* narrative

_____ 5. Shawn's primary performance appraisal problem is
      a. interruptions   *f.* halo effect
      b. rushing   *g.* horn effect
      c. recency trap   *h.* central tendency
      d. activity trap   *i.* leniency
      e. bias   *j.* strictness

_____ 6. It appears that Shawn _____ prepare for the interview as suggested in the text.
      a. did   *b.* did not

_____ 7. Which step did Shawn follow as recommended in the text?
      a. 1. open   *c.* 3. agree on strengths and areas for improvement
      b. 2. go over the form   *d.* 4. close

_____ 8. Joan is paid _____ .
      a. wages   *c.* through incentives
      b. a salary

_____ 9. Joan received a _____ pay raise.
      a. flat rate   *c.* merit
      b. percentage

_____ 10. Shawn's statement about child care relates to _____ pay.
      a. direct   *b.* indirect

11. If you were in Shawn's position, how would you have conducted the performance appraisal?

IN-CLASS SKILL-BUILDING EXERCISE

Improving Performance—Coaching

SB 12-1

Objective: To develop your skill at improving performance through coaching.

Experience: You will coach, be coached, and be observed coaching using the improving performance model.

Material: There is no preparation; all materials follow.

Procedure 1
(2–4 minutes)

Break into groups of three. Make some groups of two, if necessary. Each member selects one of the three situations below in which to be the supervisor, and a different one in which to be the employee. You will take turns coaching and being coached.

1. Employee 1 is a clerical worker. The person uses files, as do the other 10 employees in the department. The employees all know that they are supposed to return the files when they are finished so that others can find the files when they need them. Employees should only have one file out at a time. The supervisor notices that employee 1 has five files on the desk, and another employee is looking for one of them. The supervisor thinks that employee 1 will complain about the heavy work load as an excuse for having more than one file out at a time.

2. Employee 2 is a server in an ice cream shop. The person knows that the tables should be cleaned up quickly after customers leave so that new customers do not have to sit at dirty tables. It's a busy night. The supervisor finds dirty dishes on two of this employee's occupied tables. Employee 2 is socializing with some friends at one of the tables. Employees are supposed to be friendly; employee 2 will probably use this as an excuse for the dirty tables.

3. Employee 3 is an auto technician. All employees at the garage where this person works know that they are supposed to put a paper mat on the floor of each car so that the carpets don't get dirty. When the service supervisor got into a car employee 3 repaired, the car did not have a mat and there was grease on the carpet. Employee 3 does excellent work and will probably make reference to this fact when coached.

Procedure 2
(3–7 minutes)

Prepare for coaching to improve performance. Below, each group member writes an outline of what he or she will say when coaching employee 1, 2, or 3, following the steps below:
  Step 1. Refer to past feedback.
  Step 2. Describe current performance.
  Step 3. Describe the desired behavior. (Don't forget to have the employee state why it is important.)
  Step 4. Get a commitment to the change.
  Step 5. Follow up.

Procedure 3
(5–8 minutes)

a. Role playing. The supervisor of employee 1, the clerical worker, coaches him or her as planned. (Use the actual name of the group member playing employee 1.) Talk—do not read your written plan. Employee 1, put yourself in the worker's position. You work hard; there is a lot of pressure to work fast. It's easier when you have more than one file. Refer to the work load while being coached. Both the supervisor and the employee will have to ad-lib.

The person not playing a role is the observer. He or she notes on the observer form at the end of this exercise on what the supervisor did well and how the supervisor could improve.

b. Feedback. The observer leads a discussion of how well the supervisor coached the employee. (This should be a discussion, *not* a lecture.) Focus on what the supervisor did well and how the supervisor could improve. The employee should also give feedback on how he or she felt and what might have been more effective in getting him or her to change.

Do not go on to the next interview until you are told to do so. If you finish early, wait for the others to finish.

Procedure 4
(5–8 minutes)

Same as procedure 3, but change roles so that employee 2, the server, is coached. Employee 2 should make a comment about the importance of talking to customers to make them feel welcome. The job is not much fun if you can't talk to your friends.

Procedure 5
(5–8 minutes)

Same as procedure 3, but change roles so that employee 3, the auto technician, is coached. Employee 3 should comment on the excellent work he or she does.

Conclusion: The instructor leads a class discussion and makes concluding remarks.

Application (2–4 minutes): What did I learn from this experience? How will I use this knowledge in the future?

Sharing: Volunteers give their answers to the application section.

OBSERVER FORM

Try to make positive comments and point out areas for improvement. Give the supervisor alternative suggestions for what he or she could have said to improve the coaching session.

Step 1. How well did the supervisor refer to past feedback?

Step 2. How well did the supervisor describe current behavior?

Step 3. How well did the supervisor describe desired behavior? Did the employee state why the behavior is important?

Step 4. How successful was the supervisor at getting a commitment to the change? Do you think the employee would change?

Step 5. How well did the supervisor describe how he or she was going to follow up to ensure that the employee performed the desired behavior?

PREPARATION FOR IN-CLASS SKILL-BUILDING EXERCISE

Performance-Appraisal Interviews

SB 12–2

Note: This exercise is designed for groups that have been working together over a period of time. During this exercise, you will do a self-appraisal. Your performance will also be evaluated by each member in your group, and you will evaluate the performance of each member of your group. During class, you will conduct evaluative and developmental interviews.

Preparing for an Evaluation Interview:

Step 1. Make an appointment. The interviews will take place during class.

Step 2. Have the student perform a self-appraisal. All group members will do this as part of the preparation. At the end of the preparation there is an evaluation appraisal form and a developmental objective and plan sheet. The copy in the book is for your use. You will have to make copies of it for your appraisal of the other group members. After making the copies, do a self-appraisal on your form following the directions below.

Step 3. Assess performance. Put your name on the lines labeled "evaluator" and "student." Also put your name on the "evaluator" line on each of your copies and indicate one group member as the student on each copy. Follow the directions for each evaluation, including your own self-appraisal.

a. Attendance. Determine the student's attendance record and check the appropriate box. To do this, take the number of times the group worked together. (The instructor may tell you, or make an estimate.) Determine the number of times the student attended (total minus the number of absences). Calculate a percentage by dividing the number of classes attended by the total number of classes. For example, 15 classes, 10 attended (5 absences) = 10/15 = .6666 or 67 percent. Check the 69 to 60 percent column.

b. Preparation. Determine the student's level of preparation. Follow the procedure above but use the number of times the student was prepared for class. This percentage may be lower than the attendance percentage because students don't always do their preparation or homework. If the student missed class, you cannot assume that he or she was prepared unless he or she handed in the work.

c. Knowledge. A rating of 100-95 percent could be considered excellent (a grade of A); 94-90 percent outstanding (A–); 89-80 percent good (B+/B); 79-70 percent average (C+/C); 69-60 poor (D+/D); 59-50 percent failure (F); and 49-40 percent low failure (F).

d. Involvement. Use the rating scale described.

Step 4. Identify strengths and areas of improvement. On the bottom of the form, list one or two strengths and areas for improvement.

Step 5. Predict student reactions and plan to handle them. Think of critical incidents to back up your evaluations.

Preparing for a Developmental Interview:

Step 1. Make an appointment. This has been done for you.

Step 2. Have the student develop objectives and plans for improving performance. Use the developmental objective and plan form at the end of this preparation to write out a developmental objective for the area in which you need the most improvement; develop a plan for the objective. This need not be a detailed, step-by-step plan.

Step 3. Develop objectives and plans for improving performance. Identify one major area that needs improvement for each group member.

EVALUATION PERFORMANCE APPRAISAL FORM

Student _____ Evaluator _____

I. Attendance

What percentage of group meetings did the student attend?

100-95	94-90	89-80	79-70	69-60	59-50	49-0

II. Preparation

What percentage of the time did the student come prepared?

100-95	94-90	89-80	79-70	69-60	59-50	49-0

III. Knowledge

What percentage of the time did the student:

	100-95	94-90	89-80	79-70	69-60	59-50	49-0
Understand text terms							
Apply text concepts to the assignment							
Back up answers with text references							
Give correct answers							

IV. Involvement

What percentage of the time did the student contribute to group morale, motivation, and performance by:

	100-95	94-90	89-80	79-70	69-60	59-50	49-0
Showing interest in the subject							
Expressing ideas							
Fully discussing the assignment without rushing							
Getting along with members							

DEVELOPMENTAL
PERFORMANCE-
APPRAISAL FORM

Operational Plan

Objective: _____

(infinitive + action verb + singular behavior result + target date)

Responsible _____   Starting date _____   Due date _____

Control Checkpoints _____

Steps (What, where, how, resources, etc., subobjectives)	When	
	Start	End

IN-CLASS SKILL-BUILDING EXERCISE

Performance Appraisal Interviews

SB 12–2

Note: This exercise is designed for groups that have been working together over a period of time.

Objectives: To develop plans to improve your performance in class. To develop skills in conducting performance appraisals.

Experience: You will be both the evaluator and the employee in this exercise.

Material: You will need the performance appraisal forms filled out in the preparation for this exercise. Be sure to follow the guidelines in Models 12–2 and 12–3 when doing this exercise.

Procedure 1
(2–3 minutes)

Break into your usual groups and, beginning with A, have each member select a letter of the alphabet.

Procedure 2
(8–20 minutes)

Pair off as follows: A and B, C and D, E and F, and so on. If there is an odd number in the group, each member will sit out one round. A, C, and E (and so forth) conduct the evaluation performance appraisal, directly followed by the developmental interview for B, D, and F. Be an evaluator or employee; do not act as peers having a discussion. The instructor will tell you when the time for this round is half over. When the interview is over or the time is up, reverse roles. (B, D, and F become the evaluators.)

Do not go on to procedure 3 until you are told to do so. If you finish early, wait for the others to finish.

Procedure 3
(8–20 minutes)

Form new groups of two. Decide who will be the evaluator first. Follow the directions for procedure 2.

Procedures 4–6

Continue to change groups of two and conduct the interviews until every group member has appraised and been appraised by every other group member.

Integration (2–5 minutes): Evaluate how well you conducted the evaluation and developmental performance appraisals.

- Did you prepare properly for the interviews?
- Did you avoid the 11 interview problems? (Review Exhibit 12–2, which lists them.)
- How well did you follow the guidelines when conducting the evaluation interview? (Review Model 12–2, which lists the steps.)
- How well did you follow the guidelines for a developmental performance appraisal? (The five steps are listed in Model 12–3.)

Conclusion: The instructor leads a class discussion and makes concluding remarks.

Application (2–4 minutes): What did I learn from this experience? How will I use this knowledge in the future?

Sharing: Volunteers give their answers to the application section.

Supervising Employees

13

Leading Employees

Key Terms   To achieve our objectives in this chapter, it is important that you understand the following 14 key terms. They are presented in the order in which they appear in the chapter. The list of key terms also appears in alphabetical order in the end-of-chapter review.

leadership	contingency leadership theories	normative leadership theory
leadership trait theory		situational leadership
behavioral leadership theories	contingency leadership theory	autocratic style
	leadership continuum	consultative style
Managerial Grid®		participative style
System 4		laissez-faire style

Mike Templeton is a branch manager at the Westfall Bank. Mike has authority over subordinates to make decisions regarding hiring and firing, raises, and promotions. Mike gets along well with his subordinates. The branch atmosphere is friendly. His boss has asked for a special report about the loans the branch has made so far this year. Mike could have done the report himself, but he thought it would be better to delegate the task to one of the three loan officers. After thinking about the qualifications of the three loan officers, Mike selected Jean. He called her into his office to talk about the assignment.

MIKE: Hi, Jean, I've called you in here to tell you that I've selected you to do a year-to-date loan report for the branch. It's not mandatory; I can assign the report to someone else. Are you interested?

JEAN: I don't know; I've never done a report before.

MIKE: I realize that, but I'm sure you can handle it. I selected you because of my faith in your ability.

JEAN: Will you help me?

MIKE: Sure. There is more than one way to do the report. I can give you the details on what must be included in the report, but you can use any format you want, as long as I approve it. We can discuss the report now; then, as you work on it, you can come to me for input. I'm confident you'll do a great job. Do you want the assignment?

JEAN: Okay, I'll do it.

Mike and Jean discuss how she will do the report together.

What leadership style would you use to get the report done? In this chapter you will learn 11 leadership theories. Each theory will be applied to the loan report.

Leadership

Leadership is one of the most talked about, researched, and written about management topics. Peter Drucker, a top management consultant, professor, and author, recently wrote, "Leadership is all the rage just now."[1] **Leadership** *is the process of influencing employees to work toward the achievement of objectives.* Our definition applies to the workplace.

In this section you will learn why leadership skills are important; what the difference is between leadership and management; and how leadership affects behavior, human relations, and performance.

Why Leadership Skills Are Important

Following are some reasons why leadership skills are important to managers:

- The most fundamental task of any manager is that of being an effective leader.[2]

- Failure to lead properly results in missed deadlines, poor quality, and lower productivity.[3]

- Survey results have revealed that academicians and practitioners alike agree that leadership is the most important topic of all within the realm of organizational behavior.[4]

- Ralph Stogdill's well-known *Handbook of Leadership* contains over 3,000 references on the topic, and Bass's revision of it contains well over 5,000 references. Between 1972 and 1983, there was an annual average rate of 250 scholarly studies and articles written on the subject.[5] In the 1990s leadership is just as popular.

- Employees learn by watching. They constantly observe the supervisor's behavior as a guide for their own behavior.[6]

- The unique exchange that develops between the leader and members of the group influences employee behavior.[7]

- Managers are responsible for getting the job done through employees. Without the ability to influence them to achieve objectives, managers cannot be successful.

Leadership and Management Are Not the Same

People tend to use the terms *manager* and *leader* interchangeably. However, this is not correct. Managers and leaders are different.[8] Leadership is one of the five supervisory functions. The five functions include planning, organizing, staffing, leading, and controlling. A manager can have this position without being a true leader. There are managers—you may know of some—who are not leaders because they do not have the ability to influence others. They tell employees to do something, but the employees don't do it. There are also good leaders who are not managers. The informal leader, an employee group member, is a case in point. You may have worked in a situation where one of your peers had more influence in the department than the manager. To summarize, management is broader in scope than leadership; leading is only one of the five supervisory functions. There are successful managers who are not considered leaders.

In this chapter we will focus on managers who have the positional power to lead employees. We will discuss leadership theories that can help you become a better leader. Two other important components of leadership are motivation, discussed in Chapter 11, and communications, discussed in Chapter 7.

Leadership and the Supervisory Functions

As you know, the five supervisory functions are planning, organizing, staffing, leading, and controlling. The ability to lead affects the other four functions. The supervisor who is a great planner but who cannot get employees to implement the plans will not be successful. When organizing through delegating, the supervisor needs leadership skills to get the employee to complete the task. The various aspects of staffing discussed in Chapters 9 through 12 all require leadership ability. The supervisor cannot control without leadership skills. The skills discussed in Chapters 5 through 8 (problem solving and decision making, human relations, communications, and managing change and conflict) are all part of leadership.

How Leadership Affects Behavior, Human Relations, and Performance

There are different styles of leadership. The leader's style affects the leader's behavior. In other words, the leader's behavior actually makes the leader's style. An autocratic leader displays different behavior than a democratic leader does. The human relations between leader and follower will differ according to the leadership style. This will be explained in more detail throughout the chapter.

Leadership, although mediated by a host of intervening variables, does have a causal effect on performance.[9] It is difficult to prove the direct relationship between performance and leadership because of the number of variables. For example, is IBM successful because of its present CEO, John Akers, and past CEOs, or because the company entered the computer business when there was little competition? Or are there other possible reasons? Leadership has been stated as a major reason for IBM's success. IBM is known for developing good leaders. When a survey asked top executives to name a company that develops good leaders, 64 percent named IBM.[10]

Research indicates that leadership can make a difference in performance, although it does not always do so.[11] The leader's behavior can have a positive or negative effect on others' performance. Truly outstanding leaders tend to elicit highly effective performance from others. However, the number of such leaders is small. One study estimated the percentage of leaders who really make a difference in this manner to be about 15 percent in any given organization.[12] These outstanding leaders are called *transformational leaders*; we will discuss them later in this chapter.

For years researchers have been trying to answer the questions of what it takes to be an effective leader and what the most effective leadership style is. There is no universal agreement to the answers to these questions or even to the definition of

LEARNING
OBJECTIVE
1. Define leadership and
state how it affects behavior,
human relations, and
performance.

leadership. Relatively little is known about the process of leadership. We will now turn to a primarily chronological review of researchers' attempts to answer these questions. After studying the major leadership theories, you can select the one you like best, or develop your own.

CONNECTIONS

1. Why are leadership skills important to a specific supervisor?

II. Leadership Trait Theory

In the early 1900s, an organized approach to studying leadership began. The early studies were based on the assumption that leaders are born, not made. This was later called the "great man" theory of leadership. Researchers wanted to identify a set of characteristics or traits that distinguished leaders from followers or effective from ineffective leaders. **Leadership trait theory** *assumes that there are distinctive physical and psychological characteristics accounting for leadership effectiveness.* Researchers analyzed traits, or qualities, such as appearance, aggressiveness, self-reliance, persuasiveness, and dominance in an effort to identify a set of traits that all successful leaders possessed. The list of traits was to be used as a prerequisite for promotion of candidates to leadership positions. Only candidates possessing all the identified traits were to be given leadership positions.

Inconclusive Findings: In 70 years, over 300 trait studies were conducted.[13] However, no one has come up with a universal list of traits that all successful leaders possess. In all cases, there were exceptions. For example, several lists identified successful leaders as being tall. However, Napoleon was short. On the other hand, some organizations came up with a list of traits and found people who possessed them all, only to find that these people were not successful leaders. In addition, some people were successful in one leadership position but not in another.

People also questioned whether traits such as assertiveness and self-confidence were developed before or after one became a leader. In fact, one 1978 study concluded that it is practically impossible to uncover a universal set of traits. Peter Drucker says that there is no such thing as "leadership qualities or a leadership personality."[14]

Indeed, if leaders were simply born and not made (or in other words, if leadership skills could not be developed), there would be no need for courses in management and supervision.

The Ghiselli Study

Probably the most widely publicized trait theory study was conducted by Edwin Ghiselli. Professor Ghiselli studied over 300 managers from 90 different businesses in the United States and published his results in 1971.[15] His study concluded that there are traits important to effective leadership, although not all are necessary for success. Ghiselli identified the following six traits, in order of importance, as being significant traits for effective leadership:

1. *Supervisory ability.* Getting the job done through others. Basically, the ability to perform the five functions of supervision, which you are developing through this course.

2. *Need for occupational achievement.* Seeking responsibility. The motivation to work hard to succeed.

3. *Intelligence.* The ability to use good judgment, reasoning, and thinking capacity.

4. *Decisiveness.* The ability to solve problems and make decisions competently.

5. *Self-assurance.* Viewing oneself as capable of coping with problems. Behaving in a manner that shows others that you have self-confidence.

6. *Initiative.* Self-starting in getting the job done with a minimum of supervision from one's boss.

In the opening case, Mike appears to have supervisory ability. He is getting the job done through Jean, using the supervisory process. Based on the case, one cannot determine if Mike has traits two through six.

Current Studies

Even though it is generally agreed that there is no universal set of leadership traits or qualities, people continue to study and write about leadership traits. For example, in a *Wall Street Journal* Gallup survey, 782 top executives in 282 large corporations were asked, "What are the most important traits for success as a supervisor?"[16] In Self-Learning Exercise 1–1 you were asked to determine if you have the qualities necessary to be a successful supervisor—integrity, industriousness, and the ability to get along with people.

Other traits listed were business knowledge, intelligence, leadership ability, education, sound judgment, ability to communicate, flexibility, and ability to plan and set objectives. The survey also identified traits that lead to failure as a supervisor: a limited viewpoint, inability to understand others, inability to work with others, indecision, lack of initiative, failure to assume responsibility, lack of integrity, inability to change, reluctance to think independently, inability to solve problems, and a desire to be popular.

One article, "The Qualities of Leadership,"[17] identified desire to achieve, mental energy, persistence, decisiveness, integrity, confidence, persuasiveness, and the ability to handle people as the traits needed for successful leadership.

Another study also revealed that CEOs scored much higher than the general population in such traits as achievement drive, integrity, leadership, willingness to accept norms of society, and self-confidence.[18]

It is clear that certain traits can help you to be a successful supervisor, professional, or worker. You should try to develop these traits. Do you possess all the traits listed above? If you do, it will help you to be a successful leader. During this course you should develop your abilities through the skill-building approach the text takes.

CONNECTIONS

2. What are your views on trait leadership theory? Recall a supervisor you have had. Which of Ghiselli's six traits does he or she have? Which traits does the supervisor lack?

III. Behavioral Leadership Theories

By the late 1940s, most of the leadership research had changed from the trait theory and had focused on what the leader did. In the continuing quest to find the one best leadership style in all situations, studies attempted to identify the differences in the behavior of the effective leaders versus the ineffective leaders.

Behavioral leadership theories *assume that there are distinctive styles that effective leaders use consistently.*

Douglas McGregor developed Theory X and Theory Y. Theory X supervisors assume people don't like to work and must be closely supervised; Theory Y is the opposite. He advocated that managers of the time (late 1950s and early 1960s) were primarily Theory X oriented and should change to a Theory Y approach to leadership. McGregor did not give specific details on how to lead; he suggested a reorientation in management thinking. Theory X and Theory Y influenced other behavioral writers.

In this section you will learn five leadership theories: basic leadership styles, two-dimensional leadership styles, the Managerial Grid, System 4, and transformational leadership.

Basic Leadership Styles

In the 1930s, before behavioral theory became popular, Kurt Lewin, Ronald Lippitt, and Ralph White conducted studies at the University of Iowa that concentrated on the manner or style (behavior) of the leader. Their studies identified three basic leadership styles:

Autocratic: The leader makes the decisions and closely supervises employees. This can be related to Theory X assumptions.

Democratic: The leader allows participation in decisions and does not closely supervise employees. This can be related to Theory Y assumptions.

Laissez-Faire: The leader takes a "leave the employees alone" approach. This is neither Theory X nor Theory Y. It is sometimes called free rein.

The studies concluded that the democratic style was the most desirable and productive. However, later research revealed cases in which the democratic style was not more productive. The contingency theorists contend that the appropriate style will change with the situation. Contingency theory is explained later.

The Iowa studies contributed further to the human relations movement and ushered in an era of behavioral rather than trait research.

In the opening case, Mike is using the democratic style because he is allowing Jean to participate in the format of the report.

Two-Dimensional Leadership Styles

Structuring and Consideration Styles

In 1945, the Personnel Research Board of Ohio State University, under the principal direction of Ralph Stogdill, began a study to determine effective leadership styles. In the attempt to measure leadership styles, they developed an instrument known as the Leader Behavior Description Questionnaire (LBDQ). Respondents to the questionnaire perceived their leader's behavior toward them on two distinct dimensions:

- *Initiating structure.* The extent to which the leader takes charge to plan, organize, direct, and control as the employee performs the task.
- *Consideration.* The extent to which the leader communicates to develop trust, friendship, support, and respect.

Job-Centered and Employee-Centered Styles

At approximately the same time the Ohio State studies began, the University of Michigan's Survey Research Center began leadership studies under the principal direction of Rensis Likert. Their research also identified the same two dimensions or styles of leadership behavior. However, they called the two styles:

- *Job-centered.* This is the same as initiating structure. The Managerial Grid (to be discussed next) refers to this dimension as concern for production.

- *Employee-centered.* This is the same as consideration. The Managerial Grid refers to this dimension as concern for people.

Using Leadership Styles

When interacting with employees, the supervisor can engage in directive (initiating structure, job-centered, concern for production) and/or supportive (consideration, employee-centered, concern for people) behavior. In an attempt to determine how these two variables affect employee satisfaction and performance, various studies were conducted. The studies concluded that, generally, high support leads to high employee satisfaction. However, the performance results were inconclusive. Some managers with low support (concern for employees) had high performance levels.

Different combinations of the two dimensions of leadership result in four leadership styles, illustrated in Exhibit 13–1, The Ohio State (University of Michigan) Leadership Model.

In the opening case, Mike is using the high consideration (employee-centered) and low structure (job-centered) style, box three, because he is telling Jean what needs to be in the report, but how she does the report is up to her. Mike also offers supportive statements.

The Managerial Grid®

As stated above, the Managerial Grid is based on the two leadership dimensions called concern for production and concern for people. The **Managerial Grid** *identifies the ideal leadership style as having a high concern for both production and people.* The grid has 81 possible combinations of concern for production and people. However, they identify five major styles:[19]

(1,1) *The impoverished manager.* This leader has low concern for both production and people. The leader does the minimum required to remain employed in the position.

EXHIBIT 13–1   **THE OHIO STATE (UNIVERSITY OF MICHIGAN) LEADERSHIP MODEL**

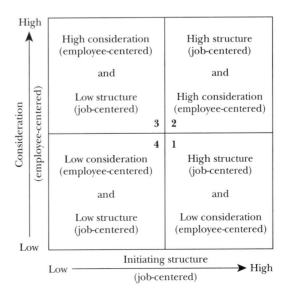

(9,1) *The sweatshop manager.* This leader has a high concern for production and a low concern for people. The leader uses position power to coerce employees to do the work. People are treated like machines.

(1,9) *The country club manager.* This leader has a high concern for people and a low concern for production. The leader strives to maintain relations and a friendly atmosphere.

(5,5) *The organized man manager.* This leader has balanced, medium concern for both production and people. The leader strives to maintain satisfactory middle-of-the-road performance and morale.

(9,9) *The team manager.* This leader has a high concern for both production and people. This leader strives for maximum performance and employee satisfaction. Participation, commitment, and conflict resolution are emphasized.

The horizontal axis of the grid (see Exhibit 13–2) represents concern for production, and the vertical axis represents concern for people. Each axis is on a 1 to 9 point scale. A 1 indicates low concern, and a 9 indicates high concern.

Through grid training, which is still being used today, managers fill in an instrument that indicates what they would do in certain situations. The results are scored to indicate where they are on the Managerial Grid, one of the 81 combinations of concern for production and people. They go through training designed to help them become ideal 9,9 managers, having a high concern for both production and people.

There is no research focusing directly on the superiority of 9,9 leadership, as measured by managerial grid scales and by organizational indexes of performance effectiveness. However, groups of experienced managers from various organizations have judged the 9,9 style as the style they favor.[20]

In the opening case, Mike has a high concern for getting the report done, and a high concern for Jean. If you had to select one of the five major styles, you would probably choose the 9,9 team leader. However, Mike is giving more support to Jean than direction for doing the report. Mike is actually using closer to a 9,7 leadership style.

EXHIBIT 13–2   **THE MANAGERIAL GRID**

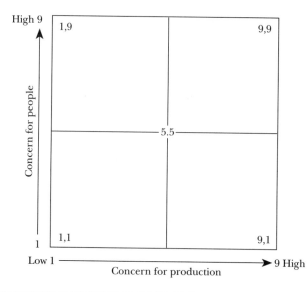

System 4

Rensis Likert and his associates attempted to differentiate the leadership attitudes of supervisors of high-producing and low-producing sectors of a wide variety of industries. The differentiations they discovered were based on a long agenda of research and developing theory.[21] Rensis's study concluded by stating that the supervisors with the best production records focus on the human aspects of their subordinates' problems and were described as employee centered. They did not maintain close supervision and were helpful and supportive in solving problems caused by mistakes. They tended to use group methods and develop effective teams with high performance standards. Supervisors with low-producing units were not viewed as people oriented. They tended to use close supervision and use punishment in solving problems caused by mistakes. They tended to use one-on-one rather than group supervision.[22]

Likert developed four systems of leadership:[23]

1. Exploitative/authoritative.
2. Benevolent/authoritative.
3. Consultative.
4. Participative group.

Comparisons can be made on how "operating characteristics"—such as decision making, goal setting, leadership, motivation, and communications—are conducted in each of the four systems. In a sense, System 1 is Theory X, and System 4 is a Theory Y approach to leadership using a 9,9 style. Likert suggested that the supervisor move from the traditional System 1 to the more contemporary System 4. In **System 4** *the ideal leadership style is called participative group.*

The attitudes and techniques found in the more effective organizations are the three basic concepts of System 4 leadership:[24]

- *The principle of supportive relationships.* Employees view management as supportive and maintain a sense of personal worth and importance.

- *Group decision making and group methods of supervision.* Employees participate in management. However, final accountability for decisions, their execution, and the results remain with managers.

- *High performance goals.* High goals and expectations of performance are a part of the manager's approach to organizational or departmental effectiveness.

In the opening case, Mike is using the participative group system of leadership. Mike and Jean are a group of two.

Transformational Leadership

Transformational leadership, a contemporary view of leadership, is a behavioral theory because it focuses on the behavior of successful leaders. Studies conducted looked at successful leaders to determine the behavior they use to make their organizations successful. The focus of transformational leadership is on top-level managers, primarily chief executive officers of large organizations.

Transformational leadership is about change, innovation, and entrepreneurship. According to research by Tichy and Devanna, the transformational leaders perform, or take the organization through, three acts, on an ongoing basis:[25]

Act 1. Recognizing the need for revitalization. The transformational leader recognizes the need to change the organization in order to keep up with the rapid changes in the environment and to keep ahead of the global competition, which is becoming more competitive all the time.

Act 2. Creating a new vision. The transformational leader visualizes the changed organization and motivates people to make it become a reality.

Act 3. Institutionalizing change. The transformational leader guides people as they make the vision become a reality.

A good example of an effective transformational leader is Lee Iacocca, CEO of Chrysler Corporation. During a survey, when top executives were asked to name a corporate leader they admired, nearly half named Iacocca.[26] Other transformational leaders include Mary Ann Lawlor, CEO, Drake Business Schools; Michael Blumenthal, CEO, Burroughs Corporation; Jeffery Campbell, president, Burger King; James Sparks, CEO, Whirlpool Corporation; Jack Welch, chairperson, General Electric; and James Renier, vice chairperson, Honeywell.

Some of the characteristics or traits of transformational leaders include the following:

- They see themselves as change agents.
- They are courageous individuals who take risks.
- They believe in people and motivate them.
- They are value driven.
- They are life-long learners.
- They have the ability to deal with complexity, ambiguity, and uncertainty.
- They are visionaries.

In the opening case, Mike is not a true transformational leader. A branch manager is not a top-level manager capable of changing the entire bank. However, he could transform his own branch.

LEARNING OBJECTIVE

2. Define and contrast the five behavioral leadership theories.

Behavioral leadership theories attempt to create a win-win situation. In general, behavioral theories suggest a high concern for employees, allowing them to participate in decision making that meets their higher-level needs. Participation is a motivator (not a hygiene) because it meets employees' needs for esteem and self-actualization, growth, and power and achievement.

IV. Contingency Leadership Theories

Both the trait and behavioral leadership theories were attempts to find the one best leadership style in all situations. In the late 1960s, it became apparent that there is no best leadership style in all situations. Both the Ohio State and University of Michigan studies revealed that no set of leader behaviors is effective in all situations. **Contingency leadership theories** *assume that the appropriate leadership style varies from situation to situation.*

In this section you will learn the four most popular contingency leadership theories, including contingency leadership theory, the leadership continuum, normative leadership theory, and situational leadership.

Contingency Leadership Theory

In 1951, Fred E. Fiedler began to develop the first situational leadership theory. He called it the "contingency theory of leader effectiveness."[27] Fiedler believed that one's leadership style is a reflection of one's personality (trait theory oriented) and is basically constant. Leaders do not change styles. **Contingency leadership theory** *uses a model to determine whether one's leadership style is task or relationship oriented, and whether one's situation matches one's style.* If there is no match, Fielder recommends changing the situation, rather than their leadership styles, and trains people to do so.

Leadership Style: The first major factor is to determine one's leadership style as being task or relationship oriented. To do so, the leader fills in the least preferred co-worker (LPC) scales. This is followed by determining the favorableness of the leader's situation.

Situational Favorableness: Situational favorableness refers to the degree a situation enables the leader to exert influence over the followers. The three variables, in order of importance, are as follows:

1. *Leader-member relations.* Is the relationship good or poor? Do the followers trust, respect, accept, and have confidence in the leader? Is it a friendly, tension-free situation? Leaders with good relations have more influence. The better the relations, the more favorable the situation.

2. *Task structure.* Is the task structured or unstructured? Do employees perform routine, unambiguous, standard tasks that are easily understood? Leaders in a structured situation have more influence. The more structured the jobs are, the more favorable the situation.

3. *Positional power.* Is positional power strong or weak? Does the leader have the power to assign work, reward and punish, hire and fire, give raises and promotions? The leader with positional power has more influence. The more power, the more favorable the situation.

Determining the Appropriate Leadership Style: To determine whether task or relationship leadership is appropriate, the user answers the three questions pertaining to situational favorableness, using the Fiedler contingency theory model. See Exhibit 13–3 for an adapted model. The user starts with question 1 and follows the decision tree to good or poor depending upon the relations. The user then answers question 2 and follows the decision tree to structured or unstructured. When answering question 3, the user ends up in one of eight possible situations. Situations 1, 2, 3, and 8 are very favorable or unfavorable and call for task-oriented leadership. Situations 4, 5, and 6 are moderate in favorableness and call for relationship-oriented leadership. In Situation 7, either style is appropriate.

Even though Fielder's theory is based on 80 studies conducted over more than a decade in a variety of situations, the theory has many critics. One of the major criticisms is the view that the leader should change his or her style rather than the situation. The other contingency writers in this chapter take this position. Fiedler has thus helped contribute to the other contingency theories. More recently, Fielder has written about the leader's knowing when to lead and when to stand back.[28]

In the opening case, Mike has good relations with Jean, the task is unstructured, and Mike's positional power is strong. This is Situation 3, in which the appropriate leadership style is task. However, Mike is using a relationship style. Fiedler would suggest that Mike change the situation to meet his preferred relationship style.

EXHIBIT 13–3   **FIELDER'S CONTINGENCY THEORY MODEL**

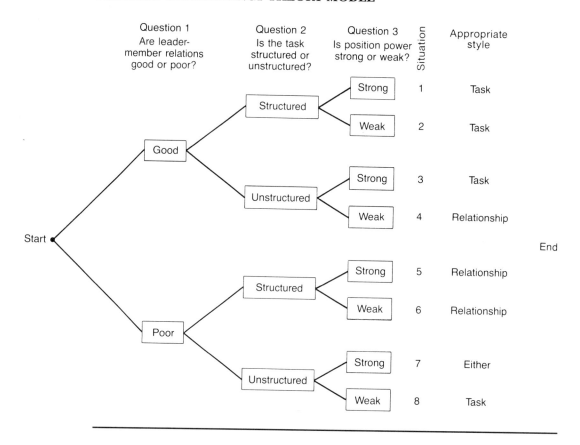

C O N N E C T I O N S

5. What are your views on contingency leadership theory? Do you agree with Fiedler's recommendation to change the situation rather than the leader's style?

Leadership Continuum

Robert Tannenbaum and Warren Schmidt stated that leadership behavior is on a continuum from boss-centered to employee-centered leadership. Their model focuses on who makes the decisions. They identify seven major styles the leader can choose from. Exhibit 13–4 is an adaptation of their model, which lists the seven styles.[29] The **leadership continuum** *identifies seven leadership styles based on one's use of boss-centered versus employee-centered leadership.*

Before selecting one of the seven leadership styles, the user must consider the following three factors or variables:

- *The manager.* What is the leader's preferred style, based on experience, expectation, values, background, knowledge, feeling of security, and confidence in the subordinates?

- *The subordinates.* What is the subordinate's preferred style for the leader, based on experience, expectation, and so on as above? Generally, the more willing

EXHIBIT 13-4   **CONTINUUM OF LEADERSHIP BEHAVIOR**

Autocratic Style						
						Laissez-faire Style
Leader makes decision and announces it.	Leader "sells" decision.	Leader presents ideas and invites questions.	Leader presents tentative decision subject to change.	Leader presents problem, gets suggestions, and makes decision.	Leader defines limits and asks group to make decision.	Leader permits subordinates to function within limits defined by leader.
1	2	3	4	5	6	7

and able the subordinates are to participate, the more freedom of participation should be used, and vice versa.

- *The Situation.* What are the environmental considerations, such as the organization's size, structure, climate, goals, and technology? Upper-level managers also influence leadership styles. For example, if a middle manager uses an autocratic leadership style, the supervisor may tend to use it too. The time available is also another consideration.

As you read about the situational variables, you will realize that they are descriptive; it is difficult to determine which style to use in a situation. The next two leadership styles developed models that tell the leader which style to use in a given situation.

A 1986 follow-up to Tannenbaum and Schmidt's original 1973 article recommends that the leader become a group member when allowing the group to make decisions; that the leader clearly state the style (subordinate's authority) being used; that the leader should not try to trick the followers into thinking they made a decision that was actually made by the leader; and, it's not the number of decisions the followers make, but, rather, their significance that counts.[30]

In the opening case, Mike began the discussion using style 4, in which the leader presents a tentative decision subject to change. Jean did not have to do the report. Mike would have given it to another employee if she did not want to do it. Mike also used style 5, leader presents problem—need for report and what must be included in report—and told Jean he would allow her to select the form, subject to his final decision of approval.

CONNECTIONS

6. What are your views on the leadership continuum? Recall a supervisor you have had. Which of the seven styles did he or she use?

Normative Leadership Theory

Based on empirical research into managerial decision making, Victor Vroom and Philip Yetton attempted to bridge the gap between leadership theory and managerial practice. To do so they developed a model to tell the manager which leadership style to use in a given situation.[31] Vroom conducted research concluding that managers using the style recommended in the model have a 65 percent probability of a successful outcome, whereas those not using the recommended style have only a 29 percent probability of a successful outcome.[32] **Normative leadership theory** *uses a decision tree model that enables the user to select one of fiveleadership styles appropriate for the situation.*

Leadership Styles

Vroom and Yetton identify five leadership styles. Two are autocratic (AI and AII), two are consultative (CI and CII), and one is group oriented (GII).

AI. The leader makes the decision alone using available information.

AII. The leader gets information from subordinates but makes the decision alone. Subordinates may or may not be told what the problem is. They are not asked for input into the decision.

CI. The leader meets individually with subordinates, explains the situation, and gets information and ideas on how to solve the problem. The leader makes the final decision alone. The leader may or may not use the subordinates' input.

CII. The leader meets with subordinates as a group, explains the situation, and gets information and ideas on how to solve the problems. The leader makes the decision alone after the meeting. Leaders may or may not use the subordinates' input.

GII. The leader meets with the subordinates as a group, explains the situation, and allows the group to make the decision.

Determining the Appropriate Leadership Style: To determine the appropriate style for a specific situation, the user answers eight questions. The questions are based on two major variables, quality and acceptance of the decision. Questions 1 through 3 and 8 relate to quality of the decision, and questions 4 through 7 relate to the acceptance of the decision. The questions are sequential and are presented in a decision-tree format similar to the Fiedler model in Exhibit 13–3.

1. Is there a quality requirement such that one solution is likely to be more rational than another?

2. Do I have sufficient information to make a high-quality decision?

3. Is the problem structured?

4. Is acceptance of decision by subordinates critical to effective implementation?

5. If I were to make the decision by myself, is it reasonably certain that it would be accepted by my subordinates?

6. Do subordinates share the organizational goals to be attained in solving the problem?

7. Is conflict among subordinates likely in the preferred solution (not relevant to individual problems)?

8. Do subordinates have sufficient information to make a high-quality decision?

Vroom and Yetton's model is popular in the academic community because it is based on research. However, it is not as popular in the business community because practitioners find it cumbersome to pull out the model and follow an eight-question decision tree every time they have to make a decision. Practitioners

LEARNING
OBJECTIVE

3. Define and contrast the
four contingency leadership
theories.

find situational leadership (discussed next) easier to use on the job. Academic types find situational leadership lacking in research, with inconsistency in its instruments and model.[33]

In the opening case, Mike used the CI consultative individual style. He told Jean that she could select the style subject to his approval. Mike makes the final decision based on Jean's input.

CONNECTIONS

7. What are your views on normative leadership theory? Recall a supervisor you have had. Which of the five styles did the supervisor use?

Situational Leadership

Situational leadership *uses a model for selecting one of four leadership styles that fits the employees' maturity level in a given situation.* Situational supervision, discussed in Chapter 1, was adapted from this model, developed by Hersey and Blanchard.[34] The differences are primarily in the use of terms and application of the model.

V. Situational Supervision and Power

In Chapter 1 you learned about situational supervision and the four leadership styles. In Chapter 6 you learned about two sources and seven bases of power. In this section you will learn the relationship between the two concepts. Power is a person's ability to influence another person's behavior; leadership is the process of influencing employees to work toward the achievement of objectives. Power is not equivalent to leadership, but it is an essential ingredient. Supervisors use power to get what they want done through others. People are not influenced without a reason, and the reason is often the power a leader wields over them. A leader without power is not influential.

When supervisors use the four situational supervisory leadership styles they are also using power bases. Let's review each of the four styles followed by stating the type of power that is used with each style and then matching them together in Exhibit 13–5. (You may want to review this material in Chapters 1 and 6 before reading on.)

EXHIBIT 13–5   **SITUATIONAL SUPERVISION: POWER MATCH**

Laissez-faire S-L	Participative S-P	Consultative S-C	Autocratic S-A
C-4	C-3	C-2	C-1
Expert	Referent	Reward	Coercive
Information	Legitimate	Connection	
←——Personal Power——→		←———Positional Power———→	

The **autocratic style** (S-A) *involves high-directive/low-supportive behavior (HD-LS) and is appropriate when interacting with low-capability employees (C-1)*. When interacting with employees, you, as the supervisor, give very detailed instructions, describing exactly what, when, where, and how to perform the task. You also closely oversee performance. The supportive style is largely absent. Decisions are made by you without input from the employees. When using the autocratic style you are using coercive power, and possibly connection power.

Using the **consultative style** (S-C) *involves high-directive/high-supportive behavior (HD-HS) and is appropriate when interacting with moderate-capability employees (C-2)*. Here, you would give specific instructions, telling employees what, when, where, and how to perform the task, as well as overseeing performance at all major stages through completion. At the same time, you would support the employees by explaining why the task should be performed as requested and answering their questions. You should work on relationships as you "sell" the benefits of completing the task your way. When making decisions, you may consult employees, but you have the final say. Once you make the decision, which can incorporate employees' ideas, you direct and oversee their performance. When using the consultative style you are using reward power possibly with some legitimate, connection power, or both.

The **participative style** (S-P) *is characterized by low-directive/high-supportive behavior (LD-HS) and is appropriate when interacting with employees with high capability (C-3)*. When interacting with employees, you give general directions and spend limited time overseeing performance, letting employees do the task their way while you focus on the result. You should support the employees by encouraging them and building up their self-confidence. If a task needs to be done, don't tell them how to do it; ask them how they will accomplish it. Make decisions together with employees or allow employees to make the decision subject to your limitations and approval. When using the participative style you are primarily using referent power, possibly with some legitimate, information power, or both.

The **laissez-faire style** (S-L) *entails low-directive/low-supportive behavior (LD-LS) and is appropriate when interacting with outstanding employees (C-4)*. When interacting with these employees, you should merely let them know what needs to be done. Answer their questions, but provide little, if any, direction. It is not necessary to oversee performance. These employees are highly motivated and need little or no support. Allow these employees to make their own decisions subject to your limitations although your approval will not be necessary. When using the laissez-faire style you are primarily using expert power, possibly with some information power.

In the opening case, Mike used the participative style with Jean and combined referent, information, and legitimate power. Because Mike had a higher concern for Jean than for the task, he gave Jean more support than directions. Mike gave her the specifics of what had to be included, but he let her decide on the format, subject to his approval.

In general, contingency leadership theories attempt to create a win-win situation by giving the followers the support and direction they need. Overdirecting can frustrate the employee with a need for esteem, growth, and power. Failure to provide enough support can frustrate the employee with a need for social, relatedness, and affiliation achievement.

LEARNING OBJECTIVE

4. Match the four situational supervision styles with the two sources and seven bases of power.

CONNECTIONS

8. What are your views on situational supervision? Recall a supervisor you have had. Which of the four styles and seven bases of power did he or she use? Would you use Model 1–1 on the job?

9. Which of the four supervisory styles and seven bases of power would you like your boss to use with you? Why would you prefer this particular style?

**LEARNING
OBJECTIVES**

5. Describe and contrast
leadership trait theory,
behavioral leadership
theories, and contingency
leadership theories.
6. Describe and contrast
the 11 leadership theories.

VI. Putting the Leadership Theories Together

Eleven different leadership theories have been presented in this chapter. Exhibit 13–6 summarizes the 11 leadership theories. Exhibit 13–7 puts the 11 leadership theories together, converted into four leadership style categories. By reviewing these exhibits, you can better understand the similarities and differences between these leadership theories. There is no one best leadership style. You should develop your leadership skills through this course.

CONNECTIONS

10. Which leadership theory or model do you prefer? Why?

11. Describe the type of leader you want to be.

EXHIBIT 13 – 6   **LEADERSHIP THEORIES**

1. Leadership Trait Theory

Assumes that there are distinctive physical and psychological characteristics accounting for leadership effectiveness.

BEHAVIORAL LEADERSHIP THEORIES

Assume that there are distinctive styles that effective leaders use consistently.

2. Basic Leadership Styles

Autocratic, democratic, laissez-faire.

3. Two-Dimensional Leadership Styles

Structuring/job-centered and consideration/employee-centered styles.

4. Managerial Grid

Blake and Mouton's model identifying the ideal leadership style as having a high concern for both product and people.

5. System 4

Likert's ideal leadership style called participative group.

6. Transformational Leadership

Take the organization through three acts on an ongoing basis.

> Major theories of leadership

CONTINGENCY LEADERSHIP THEORIES

Assume that the appropriate leadership style varies from situation to situation.

7. Contingency Leadership Theory

Fiedler's model used to determine if one's leadership style is task or relationship oriented, and if the situation matches his or her style.

8. Leadership Continuum

Tannenbaum and Schmidt's model that identifies seven leadership styles based on one's use of boss-centered versus employee-centered leadership.

9. Normative Leadership Theory

Vroom and Yetton's decision-tree model that enables the user to select one of five leadership styles that is appropriate for the situation.

10. Situational Leadership

Hersey and Blanchard's model for selecting one of four leadership styles that matches the employee's maturity level in a given situation.

11. Situational Supervision

Lussier's model for selecting one of four leadership styles that matches the employees' capability level in a given situation.

EXHIBIT 13-7   **LEADERSHIP STYLES***

Theory	Four Leadership Style Categories			
Behavioral Leadership Theories				
2. Basic Leadership Styles	Autocratic	Democratic		Laissez-Faire
3. Two-dimensional leadership styles	High structure/ job-centered. Low consideration/ employee-centered.	High structure/ job-centered. High consideration/ employee-centered.	High consideration/ employee-centered. Low structure/ job-centered.	Low consideration/ employee-centered. Low structure/ job-centered.
4. Managerial Grid	High concern for production. Low concern for people. (9,1 sweatshop manager)	High concern for both production and people. (9,9 team manager)	High concern for people. Low concern for production. (1,9 country club manager)	Low to moderate concern for both people and production. (1,1 impoverished + 5,5 organized managers)
5. System 4	1. Exploitative/ authoritative. 2. Benevolent/ authoritative.	3. Consultative.	4. Participative group.	
Contingency Leadership Theories				
7. Contingency Leadership Theory	Task		Relationship	
8. Leadership continuum	1. Make decision and announce it.	2. Sell decision. 3. Present ideas and invite questions.	4. Present tentative decision subject to change. 5. Present problem, get suggestions and make decision.	6. Define limits and ask group to make decision. 7. Permit group to function within limits defined by leader.
9. Normative leadership theory	AI. Make decision alone using available information.	AII. Get information from subordinates, make decision alone.	CI. Meet individually (CII Group) with subordinates explain the situation, get information and ideas on how to solve the problem, make final decision alone.	GII. Meet with subordinates as a group, explain the situation, and allow the group to make decision.
10. Situational leadership	High task Low relationship (Telling)	High task High relationship (Selling)	High relationship Low task (Participating)	Low relationship Low task (Delegating)
11. Situational supervision	High directive Low support (Autocratic)	High directive High support (Consultative)	High support Low directive (Participative)	Low supportive Low directive (Laissez-Faire)

1. Leadership trait theory — based on traits of leader; no actual style

6. Transformational leadership — three acts; no actual style

VII. Substitutes for Leadership

The leadership theories presented assume that some leadership style will be effective in each situation. Kerr and Jermier[35] argue that certain individual, task, and organizational variables prevent leaders from affecting subordinates' attitudes and behaviors. Substitutes for leadership, or characteristics that negate or substitute for leadership influence, are those that structure tasks (directive) for followers or give them positive strokes (support) for their action. Rather than the leader's providing the necessary directive and support, the subordinates, task, or organization may provide these elements.

The following may substitute for leadership by providing directive, support, or both:

I. Characteristics of Subordinates:

- Ability, knowledge, experience, training.
- Need for independence.
- Professional orientation.
- Indifference toward organizational rewards.

II. Characteristics of Task:

- Clarity and routine.
- Invariant methodology.
- Provision of own feedback concerning accomplishment.
- Intrinsic satisfaction.

III. Characteristics of the Organization:

- Formalization (explicit plans, goals, and areas of responsibility).
- Inflexibility (ridged, unbending rules and procedures).
- Highly specified and active advisory and staff functions.
- Closely knit, cohesive work groups.
- Organizational rewards not within the leader's control.
- Spatial distance between superior and subordinates.

LEARNING OBJECTIVE

7. List and discuss the three substitutes for leadership.

These substitutes may replace leadership. A study of nursing work indicated that the staff nurses' education, the cohesion of the nurses, and work technology substituted for the head nurse's leadership behavior in determining the staff nurses' performance.[36]

CONNECTIONS

12. Do you agree that characteristics of subordinates, task, and the organization can substitute for leadership directive and support? Explain your answer.

In this chapter you have learned 11 leadership theories and a theory of leadership substitution. You may select one for use, combine some, or develop your own theory of leadership.

REVIEW

Select one or more methods: (1) fill in the missing key terms from memory; (2) match the key terms from the end of the review with their definitions below; (3) copy the key terms in order from the key terms at the beginning of the chapter.

_____ is the process of influencing employees to work toward the achievement of objectives. Leadership and management are not the same; leadership is one of the five management functions. Leadership, although mediated by a host of intervening variables, does have a causal effect on performance.

_____ assumes that there are distinctive physical and psychological characteristics accounting for leadership effectiveness. The Ghiselli study concluded that there are traits important to effective leadership (supervisory ability being the most important), although not all are necessary for success. Trait theory, although not very popular, is still being studied and written about.

_____ assume that there are distinctive styles that effective leaders use consistently. The three basic leadership styles are autocratic, democratic, and laissez-faire. Two-dimensional leadership styles are called structuring and consideration styles (Ohio State University) and job-centered and employee-centered styles (University of Michigan). The _____ (Blake and Mouton) identifies the ideal leadership style as having a high concern for both production and people. In _____ (Rensis Likert) the ideal leadership style is called participative group. Transformational leaders take the organization through three acts, on an ongoing basis: act 1—recognizing the need for revitalization; act 2—creating a new vision; and act 3—institutionalizing change.

_____ assume that the appropriate leadership style varies from situation to situation. _____ (Fiedler) uses a model to determine whether one's leadership style is task or relationship oriented, and whether one's situation matches one's style. If not, leaders change the situation rather than their style. _____ (Tannenbaum and Schmidt) identifies seven leadership styles based on one's use of boss-centered versus employee-centered leadership. The variables to consider when selecting a style include the manager, subordinates, and the situation. _____ (Vroom and Yetton) uses a decision-tree model that enables the user to select one of five leadership styles that is appropriate for the situation. Its user answers a series of eight questions in a decision tree to determine which style to use. _____

(Hersey and Blanchard) uses a model for selecting one of four leadership styles

that matches the employees' maturity level in a given situation.

The four situational supervision styles (and power matches) are as follows:

_____ , which involves high-directive/low supportive

behavior and is appropriate when interacting with low-capability employees

(coercive power, possibly with connection power); _____ ,

which involves high-directive/high-supportive behavior and is appropriate when

interacting with moderate-capability employees (reward power possibly with

some legitimate or connection power or both); _____ ,

which is characterized by low-directive/high-supportive behavior and is

appropriate when interacting with employees with high capability (referent

power, possibly with some legitimate or information power or both); and

_____ , which entails low-directive/low-supportive

behavior and is appropriate when interacting with outstanding employees

(expert power, possibly with some information power).

It has been proposed that characteristics of subordinates, task, and the

organization can substitute for leadership directive and support.

KEY TERMS

autocratic style

behavioral leadership
   theories

consultative style

contingency leadership
   theories

contingency leadership
   theory

laissez-faire style

leadership

leadership continuum

leadership trait theory

Managerial Grid

normative leadership
   theory

participative style

situational leadership

System 4

REFERENCES

1. Peter Drucker, "Leadership: More Doing than Dash," *The Wall Street Journal,* January 6, 1988, p. 24.

2. R. Bruce McAfee and Betty Ricks, "Leadership by Example: Do As I Do!" *Management Solutions,* August 1986, p. 10.

3. Thomas Licsz, "Supervisory Toolkit," *Supervision,* October 1985, p. 16.

4. James Meindl and Sanford Ehrlich, "The Romance of Leadership and the Evaluation of Performance," *Academy of Management Journal,* March 1987, p. 92; Bernard Bass, *Stogdill's Handbook of Leadership,* rev. ed. (New York: Free Press, 1981).

5. Meindl and Ehrlich, "The Romance of Leadership and the Evaluation of Performance," p. 92.

6. McAfee and Ricks, "Leadership by Example: Do As I Do!" p. 11.

7. Robert Vecchio, "Predicting Employee Turnover from Leader-Member Exchange: A Failure to Replicate," *Academy of Management Journal,* June 1985, p. 479.

8. Abraham Zaleznik, "Managers and Leaders: Are They Different?" *Harvard Business Review,* May–June 1986, p. 54.

9. John Miner, *Organizational Behavior: Performance and Productivity* (New York: Random House, 1988), p. 363.

10. "Leadership Potential," *The Wall Street Journal,* May 19, 1988, p. 1.

11. Nan Weiner and Thomas Mahoney, "A Model of Corporate Performance as a Function of Environmental, Organizational, and Leadership Influences," *Academy of Management Journal* 24 (1981), pp. 453–70.

12. Jonathan Smith, Kenneth Carson, and Ralph Alexander, "Leadership: It Can Make a Difference," *Academy of Management Journal* 27 (1984), pp. 765–76.

13. Bass, *Stogdill's Handbook of Leadership.*

14. Drucker, "Leadership: More Doing than Dash." p. 24.

15. Edwin Ghiselli, *Explorations in Management Talent* (Santa Monica, Calif.: Goodyear Publishing, 1971).

16. "What Does It Take to Be a Successful Supervisor?" *The Wall Street Journal,* November 14, 1980, p. 33.

17. Ted Pollock, "The Qualities of Leadership," *Supervision,* October 1985, pp. 24–26.

18. "Managing," *The Wall Street Journal,* January 15, 1988, p. 21.

19. Robert Blake and Jane Mouton, *The Managerial Grid III: Key to Leadership Excellence* (Houston: Gulf Publishing, 1985), p. 12.

20. Robert Blake and Jane Mouton, "Theory and Research for Developing a Science of Leadership," *Journal of Applied Behavioral Science* 18 (1982), pp. 275–91.

21. Rensis Likert, "From Production- and Employee-Centeredness to Systems 1–4," *Journal of Management,* May 1979, pp. 147–56.

22. Rensis Likert, *New Patterns of Management* (New York: McGraw-Hill, 1961).

23. Rensis Likert, *The Human Organization* (New York: McGraw-Hill, 1967), chapter 2.

24. Ibid., chapter 4.

25. Noel Tichy and Mary Anne Devanna, *The Transformational Leader* (New York: John Wiley & Sons, 1986).

26. "Leadership Potential," p. 1.

27. Fred Fiedler, *A Theory of Leadership Effectiveness* (New York: McGraw-Hill 1967).

28. Fred Fiedler, "When to Lead, When to Stand Back," *Psychology Today,* February 1988, pp. 26–27.

29. Robert Tannenbaum and Warren Schmidt, "How to Choose a Leadership Pattern," *Harvard Business Review,* May–June 1973, p. 166.

30. Robert Tannenbaum and Warren Schmidt, "How to Choose a Leadership Pattern," *Harvard Business Review,* July–August 1986, p. 129.

31. Victor Vroom and Philip Yetton, *Leadership and Decision Making* (Pittsburgh: University of Pittsburgh Press, 1973).

32. Victor Vroom, "Can Leaders Learn to Lead?" *Organizational Dynamics,* Winter 1976, pp. 17–28.

33. Claude Graeff, "The Situational Leadership Theory: A Critical Review," *Academy of Management Review,* August 8, 1983, pp. 285, 290.

34. Paul Hersey and Kenneth Blanchard, *Management of Organizational Behavior: Utilizing Human Resources,* 4th ed. (Englewood Cliffs, N.J.: Prentice-Hall, 1982).

35. S. Kerr and J. M. Jermier, "Substitutes for Leadership: The Meaning and Measurement," *Organizational Behavior and Human Performance* 22 (1978), pp. 375–403.

36. J. E. Sheridan, D. J. Vredenburgh, and M. A. Abelson, "Contextual Model of Leadership Influence in Hospital Units," *Academy of Management Journal* 27 (1984), pp. 57–78.

APPLICATION SITUATIONS

The Managerial Grid®

AS 13–1

Identify the leader's styles in terms of the Managerial Grid (Exhibit 13–2).

a. 1,1 (impoverished)   *c.* 9,1 (sweatshop)   *e.* 9,9 (team manager)

b. 1,9 (country club)   *d.* 5,5 (organized)

_____ 1. The group has very high morale, and they enjoy their work. Productivity in the department is one of the lowest in the company.

_____ 2. The group has adequate morale. They have an average productivity level.

_____ 3. The group is one of the firm's top performers. Group members have high morale.

_____ 4. The group has one of the lowest levels of morale in the organization. The group is one of the firm's top performers.

_____ 5. The group is one of the lowest producers in the organization. The group has a low level of morale.

Contingency Leadership Theory

AS 13–2

Use Exhibit 13–3 to identify the type of situation described and then choose the appropriate leadership style. (Select two answers.)

a. 1   *e.* 5   *a.* task oriented

b. 2   *f.* 6   *b.* relationship oriented

c. 3   *g.* 7

d. 4   *h.* 8

_____ 6. Ben, the supervisor, oversees the assembly of mass-produced containers. He has the power to reward and punish. Ben is viewed as a hard-nosed supervisor.

_____ 7. Jean, the manager, is from the corporate planning staff. She helps the other departments plan. Jean is viewed as being a dreamer; she doesn't understand other departments. People tend to be rude in their dealings with Jean.

_____ 8. Ron, the supervisor, oversees the processing of canceled checks for the bank. He is well liked by the employees. Ron's boss enjoys hiring and evaluating Ron's employees' performance.

_____ 9. Connie, the principal of a school, assigns teachers to classes and has various other duties. She hires and decides on tenure. The school's atmosphere is tense.

_____ 10. Len, the chairman of the committee, is highly regarded by the committee's volunteer members from a variety of departments. They are charged with recommending ways to increase organizational performance.

Leadership Power Match

AS 13–3

Identify the appropriate style and power bases in each situation.

a. autocratic style: coercive power, possibly with some connection power

b. consultative style: reward power, possibly with some legitimate or connection power or both

c. participative style: referent power, possibly with some legitimate or information power or both

d. laissez-faire style: expert power, possibly with some information power

_____ 11. Carl, one of your best workers who needs little direction, has slowed down his production level. You know he has a personal problem.

_____ 12. Your rookie employee, Betty, is developing well; her need for close supervision is diminishing.

_____ 13. Wanda, who needs some direction and encouragement to maintain production, is not working to standard today. She claims to be ill, as she does occasionally.

_____ 14. Jose, one of your best workers, wants a promotion. He has asked you to help prepare him for the opportunity.

_____ 15. Your worst employee has ignored one of your directives again.

_____ 16. The office typewriter needs to be replaced. You're not sure whether you should get a regular typewriter, a memory typewriter, or a word processor. The secretary who uses it is an excellent worker and is in favor of a word processor.

_____ 17. You must select one of your employees for a promotion. Three are qualified. You're not sure, but you think they all would want the new job.

_____ 18. You must lay off 2 of your 15 employees. The organization has a policy.

_____ 19. You have been offered a job with a short deadline. It will require overtime to complete. Employees are not required to work overtime, and you're not sure whether they will want to.

_____ 20. You are writing a report for top management. You need some figures in a hurry. Your employee, Tom, has the figures, but hassles you about your request.

OBJECTIVE CASE 13

The Cleanup Job

Brenda is the head meat cutter in the Big K Supermarket. Brenda hires and has fired meat cutters; she also determines raises. Although it has never been said, she speculates that the all-male meat cutting crew aren't friendly toward her because they resent having a female boss. They are all highly skilled.

Once a month the meat and frozen foods cases are supposed to be cleaned by a meat cutter; they are all equally capable of doing it. It is not any one person's job and no one likes to do it. It's that time of month again, and Brenda has to select someone to clean up. She just happens to see Rif first, so she approaches him.

BRENDA: Rif, I want you to clean the cases this month.

RIF: Why me? I just did it two months ago. Give someone else a turn.

BRENDA: I didn't ask you to tell me when you did it last. I asked you to do it.

RIF: I know, but I'm a meat cutter, not a janitor. Why can't the janitor do it? Or can we start a fairer system?

BRENDA: Do I have to take action against you for not following an order?

RIF: Okay, I'll do it.

Answer the following questions, supporting your answers in the space between questions. (*Note:* Different leadership styles can be role-played in class.)

_____ 1. The basic leadership style Brenda used with Rif was _____ .
  a. autocratic   *b.* democratic   *c.* laissez-faire

_____ 2. With Rif, Brenda used the _____ quadrant leadership style, as described in Exhibit 13–1.
  a. first   *b.* second   *c.* third   *d.* fourth

_____ 3. With Rif, Brenda should have used the _____ quadrant leadership style as described in Exhibit 13–1.
  a. first   *b.* second   *c.* third   *d.* fourth

_____ 4. The Managerial Grid style Brenda used with Rif was _____ , as shown in Exhibit 13–2.
  a. 1,1   *b.* 9,1   *c.* 1,9   *d.* 5,5   *e.* 9,9

_____ 5. The leadership system Brenda should have used to resolve the monthly clean up job is system _____ .
  a. 1   *b.* 2   *c.* 3   *d.* 4

_____ 6. According to Fiedler's contingency theory model, Exhibit 13–3, Brenda is in a _____ situation, and _____ -oriented behavior is appropriate.
  a. 1   *b.* 2   *c.* 3   *d.* 4   *e.* 5   *f.* 6   *g.* 7   *h.* 8
  a. task   *b.* relationship

_____ 7. Brenda used the _____ leader continuum style, Exhibit 13–4.
  a. 1   *b.* 2   *c.* 3   *d.* 4   *e.* 5   *f.* 6   *g.* 7

_____ 8. The appropriate normative leadership style to resolve the monthly cleanup job is _____ .
  a. AI   *b.* AII   *c.* CI   *d.* CII   *e.* GII

_____ 9. The situational supervision style Brenda used with Rif was _____ , Model 1–1.
  a. autocratic *b.* consultative *c.* participative *d.* laissez-faire

_____ 10. The situational supervision style Brenda should use to resolve the monthly cleanup job is _____ , Model 1–1.
  a. autocratic *b.* consultative *c.* participative *d.* laissez-faire

11. In Brenda's position and situation, how would you get the cases cleaned each month?

Leading

SB 13 – 1

1. For this exercise, first select the model you most prefer to use on the job. (It can be a model from this chapter or from the situational supervision model in Chapter 1.)

2. In the space below, write a description of a situation calling for leadership. It may be a situation you were involved in as an employee or supervisor, or you can make up a situation you think you will face as a supervisor. Use as much detail as possible.

3. Using the model you selected, determine the appropriate style for the situation you described.

4. Explain the basic approach you would use in the situation. What would you do and say? Give as much detail as possible.

Leading

SB 13 – 1

Objectives: To select a leadership style you plan to use on the job. To gain experience at applying the style to an actual situation.

Experience: The in-class exercise is discussion oriented.

Material: You will need your completed preparation for this exercise.

Procedure 1
(10–50 minutes)

Option A. Volunteers present their examples to the class. The instructor may lead a class discussion and make concluding remarks following each example.

Option B. Break into groups of five or six and share your examples. Focus on the accurate use of the model. Recommend ways to help members handle their situations.

Option C. Same as option B but the group selects one example to present to the class.

Conclusion: The instructor leads a class discussion and makes concluding remarks.

Application (2–4 minutes): What have I learned from this experience? How will I use this knowledge in the future?

Sharing: Volunteers give their answers to the application section.

IN-CLASS SKILL-BUILDING EXERCISE

Leadership Style

SB 13–2

Procedure 1
(5–10 minutes)

Objectives: To experience leadership in action. To identify the appropriate leadership style and to see how using the appropriate or inappropriate style affects the organization.

Break into groups of 5 or 6 and select the style (autocratic, consultative, participative, or laissez-faire) your group would use in the following situation:

You are an office manager with four subordinates who all do all typing on regular typewriters. You will be receiving a word processor to replace one of the present typewriters. (Everyone knows about it because several salespeople have been in the office.) You must decide who gets the new word processor. Some information about each subordinate follows:

- *Pat* has been with the organization for 20 years, is 50 years old, and presently has a two-year-old typewriter.

- *Chris* has been with the organization for 10 years, is 31 years old, and presently has a year-old typewriter.

- *Fran* has been with the organization for 5 years, is 40 years old, and presently has a three-year-old typewriter. Fran spends the most hours typing.

- *Sandy* has been with the organization for 2 years, is 23 years old, and presently has a five-year-old typewriter. Sandy is the fastest typist.

Procedure 2
(5–10 minutes)

1. Four volunteers from different groups will play the subordinates. While the managers are planning, turn to the end of this exercise and read your role, and the roles of your colleagues. Try to put yourself in the person's position and do and say what the person actually would. No one but the subordinates should read the additional information.

2. The instructor will tell each group which leadership style its manager will use; it may or may not be the one the group selected.

POSSIBLE LEADERSHIP STYLES

S-A
Autocratic

a. Make the decision alone, and then tell each subordinate individually about your decision and how and why you made it.

b. Make the decision alone, then have a group meeting to announce the decision and describe how and why you made it. No discussion is allowed.

S-C
Consultative

a. Before deciding, talk to each subordinate individually to find out whether he or she wants the word processor and why. Then make the decision and announce it to the group.

b. Before deciding, have a group meeting to listen to why each subordinate wants it. Have no discussion among subordinates. Then make the decision and announce it to the group.

S-P
Participative

a. Tentatively decide to whom you want to give it. Then hold a meeting to tell the group your plans, followed with a discussion that can lead to your changing your mind. After the discussion, you make the decision and announce it, explaining the rationale for the selection.

b. Call a group meeting and explain the problem. Lead an open discussion about who should get the word processor. After the discussion, make your decision and explain the rationale for it.

S-L
Laissez-faire

a. Call a meeting and explain the situation. Tell the group that it has X amount of time (5–7 minutes for the exercise) to make the decision. You may or may not stay for the decision. However, if you do stay, you cannot participate.

3. The group selects someone to play the manager and plans who, what, when, where, and how.

Procedure 3
(1–10 minutes)

One manager goes to the front of the class and uses the style assigned to handle the situation.

Procedure 4
(1–5 minutes)

Class members (other than members of the "manager's" group) vote on the style they think the manager used. Then the manager reveals which style it actually was. If several class members didn't think that was the style portrayed, they can discuss why.

Procedure 5
(25–40 minutes)

Continue to repeat procedures 3 and 4 until all managers have their turn or the time runs out.

Procedure 6
(2–3 minutes)

Each class member individually determines the style he or she would use in this situation. The class votes for the style it would use in this situation. The instructor gives his or her recommendation and/or the author's.

Application (2–4 minutes): What did I learn from this experience? How will I apply this knowledge in the future?

Conclusion: The instructor leads a class discussion and makes concluding remarks.

Sharing: Volunteers give their answers to the application section.

ADDITIONAL INFORMATION (FOR PLAYING THE SUBORDINATES' ROLES ONLY)

Pat: You are happy with the way things are now. You do not want to learn how to use a word processor. Be firm and assertive in taking your stand.

Chris: You are bored with your present job. You really want to learn how to run a word processor. Being second in seniority, you plan to be aggressive in trying to get the word processor. You are afraid that the others will complain because you got the last new typewriter, so you have a good idea. You will take the word processor and Sandy can have your typewriter.

Fran: You are interested in having the word processor. You spend more time each day typing than any of the other employees. Therefore, you believe you should get the word processor.

Sandy: You want the word processor. You believe you should get it because you are by far the fastest typist, and you have the oldest typewriter. You do not want a hand-me-down typewriter.

14

Supervising Problem Employees

Learning Objectives

1. Define problem employees and distinguish between the two types of problem employees.
2. Describe the supervisor's role in counseling.
3. List the five steps in the counseling model and use the model.
4. Explain several guidelines for effective discipline.
5. List the five steps in the discipline model and use the model.
6. Describe how to handle the late or absent employee, the substance abuser, and the insubordinate or nonconformist employee.

Key Terms

To achieve our objectives in this chapter, it is important that you understand the following eight key terms. They are presented in the order in which they appear in the chapter. The list of key terms also appears in alphabetical order in the end-of-chapter review.

problem employees	**the counseling model**	**discipline**
supervisory counseling	**employee assistance**	**the discipline**
directive counseling	**programs**	**model**
nondirective counseling		

Al was a model employee for the first six months he was at the State Department of Employment. He was good with clients; he was punctual and neat; and he rarely missed work. No one knows why, but after that, he started becoming surly and difficult with both clients and fellow workers. He was late nearly every day of the week, and several hours late on Mondays.

Sarah, Al's supervisor, was at a loss as to what she should do. Each time he would come in obviously inebriated, she would gently lead him into the coffee room, pour black coffee down his throat, and tell him to stay there "until he started feeling better." Employees resented not only Al's conduct, but also Sarah's. One day, after nearly a year of this, the police came by to report that Al had been found in his garage—an apparent suicide.

The news devastated Sarah. She spent a long time blaming herself for failing to take some action that could have prevented all this. What should Sarah have done?

I. Problem Employees

Who Are Problem Employees?

For our purposes, **problem employees** *are employees who are not performing to expectations.* These expectations may involve job performance, for example, failure to meet quality or quantity standards. Expectations can also involve organization or departmental rules and regulations.

We can distinguish two types of problem employees:

Employees with Problems: This type has problems that affect job performance. The problem may not be related to the job. It is common for personal problems to affect job performance. The employee with problems should be counseled. This is discussed in Section II of this chapter.

Employees Causing Problems: These are problem employees because they choose to break the rules or because they are not willing to make the effort to perform the job to standards. These employees should be disciplined, as discussed in Section III of this chapter.

Exhibit 14–1 lists some problem employees you may encounter as a supervisor. In reviewing the exhibit, you can see that it is not always easy to distinguish between the two types of problem employees. Therefore, it is usually advisable to start with counseling and change to discipline if the problem persists.

Why Solving Employee Problems Is Important

Dealing with the problem employee is important for a variety of reasons:

- Ten percent of the U.S. population has some form of mental or emotional illness that shows up on the job.[1]

- Inappropriate behavior, left unchecked, can impede productivity in far-reaching ways.[2]

- Problem employees cause more work for the supervisor and other employees. They lower employee morale and should be dealt with for the good of all.[3]

- Out of every 10 employees, 3 have personal problems that affect job performance. Personal problems cost firms $44 billion per year—nearly four times the total cost of employee theft, insurance fraud, shoplifting, and arson.[4]

- The annual cost to U.S. companies of alcohol abuse is $10 billion per year.[5]

- The annual cost of drug abuse in lost productivity, reduced product quality, absenteeism, on-the-job injuries, damage to equipment, and theft of company property is more than $100 billion.[6]

EXHIBIT 14–1	**PROBLEM EMPLOYEES**	
	The late employee	The employee who's often away from the workstation
	The absent employee	
	The employee who kids around	The aggressive employee
	The dishonest employee	The insubordinate employee
	The destructive employee	The employee who steals
	The alcoholic employee	The employee using drugs
	The nonconformist	The obscene employee
	The employee with a family problem	The sick employee

- Unwarranted absence, lateness, personal telephone calls, reading, and socializing cost American businesses some $150 billion per year.[7]

As a result of all this, supervisors must be better trained to work directly with the problem employee.[8]

Problem Employees and the Supervisory Functions

How you perform the five functions of supervision, and the supervisory skills you have, will directly affect the number and intensity of problems you will have with employees. Generally, the better the supervisor, the fewer the problems.

The Supervisory Functions: The better the supervisor is at planning the job, the smaller the number of employees who will be frustrated and cause problems. How well the supervisor organizes the department and delegates tasks will affect employee problems. When staffing, the supervisor should be careful not to hire candidates who will become problem employees. The better employees are oriented and trained, the fewer the problems they will have. A poorly done performance appraisal can turn a good employee into a problem employee. The better the leadership provided by the supervisor, the fewer the employee problems. And the supervisor who controls effectively will also have fewer people problems.

The supervisor with good conceptual skills will effectively solve problems and will make decisions that do not result in problems. The supervisor with good human relations and communication skills will be better at handling employees. Good technical skills can also help prevent people problems.

LEARNING OBJECTIVE

1. Define problem employees and distinguish between the two types of problem employees.

CONNECTIONS

1. Describe some of the problem employees you have observed on a job.
2. Describe how a problem employee affected the department's performance.

II. Supervisory Counseling

As mentioned, the first thing a supervisor should do is attempt to help an employee with a problem. This is usually done through counseling. In this section you will learn the supervisor's role in counseling, the benefits of counseling, recognition of employee problems, counseling formats, counseling skills, and actual counseling of employees.

The Supervisor's Role in Counseling

When most people hear the term *counseling*, they think of psychological counseling or psychotherapy. That type of sophisticated help should not be attempted by nonprofessionals such as a supervisor. Instead, **supervisory counseling** *is the process of giving employees guidance on job performance.*

Most supervisors do not like to hear the details of personal problems. Fortunately, this is not a requirement in supervisory counseling. Instead, the supervisor's role is to help employees realize that they have problems and that those problems affect their work. The supervisor is getting the employee back on track.[9] Supervisory counseling involves a one-on-one exchange of thoughts, ideas, and feelings. The employee is given the opportunity to get things off his or her chest. The supervisor should not give advice on how to solve personal problems such as marital difficulty. When professional help is needed, the supervisor can refer the employee to an appropriate professional.[10]

Too often, supervisors choose to ignore problems, hoping that the problems will be solved without their input; or they take the attitude that "it's not my problem." Employee problems *are* the supervisor's problems when they affect work performance. Over the years, while conducting supervisory training programs, a consultant has asked the participants whether ignoring a situation makes things better or worse. Almost every participant stated that ignoring the problem usually makes things worse. Problems don't usually solve themselves.

Benefits of Counseling

Benefits of supervisory counseling include these:

Reduced Anxiety and Fear: A supportive supervisor can help an employee face and deal with anxiety and fear.[11] A supervisor can help develop employee confidence through counseling.

Increased Employee Cooperation and Improved Relationships: The supervisor who takes the time to listen to and to help employees deal with their problems gains their cooperation and better relationships. Often what employees need is a supervisor who shows he or she cares by simply listening.

Counseling Provides Direction: Counseling often gives employees a chance to see things from a different perspective. The supervisor can help point employees in a direction that will help them solve their problems.

Counseling Leads to Growth: With the supervisor's help, employees often realize how problems are affecting their work. Counseling gives employees the opportunity to grow and develop in areas where improvement would help both them and the organization.

Decreased Absenteeism and Turnover: When employees get help in dealing with their problems, they are more likely to come to work rather than trying to escape the workplace. Employees who are helped to handle problems are more likely to stay on the job rather than quit or end up being fired. Organizations realize that it is more economical to counsel an existing employee than it is to recruit, select, orient, and train a new candidate.

Recognizing an Employee with Problems

A supervisor should be aware of changes in employee behavior and try to catch the problem before it becomes serious. The supervisor must realize that behavior is a symptom that a problem exists, but may not be the problem itself. Below are some of the changes that indicate a problem.

Changed Personality: The employee is not the same person. He or she may be moody or irritable. An employee who used to get along well with co-workers is now getting into fights.

Changed Quality and Quantity of Work: The employee who made few mistakes begins to make frequent errors. The productive worker of the past no longer meets the standard level of output.

Increased Time Off: The employee with a good attendance record misses work more frequently. The employee who used to be on time begins to be late. The employee takes longer breaks and lunches and is not at the workstation when he or she should be.

Increases in Errors and Accidents: The employee with a good work or safety record makes errors or has frequent accidents.

Signs of Alcohol or Drug Use: The employee is not as coordinated as he or she was in the past. The employee smells of alcohol or is using something to mask its smell. The employee's appearance has changed. The employee's eyes look different. He or she has less regard for personal appearance.

See Exhibit 14–2 for a review of the signs of problem employees.

Counseling Formats

Suppose you realize that one of your employees does have a problem. How do you go about counseling this person? First, you should choose a format—either directive or nondirective counseling.

Directive Counseling: In **directive counseling** *the supervisor controls the discussion and gives the employee advice on how to solve the problem.* The supervisor asks direct, mostly closed-ended questions to determine what the problem is. Once the problem is determined, the supervisor gives the employee advice on how to solve it. Directive counseling uses the consultative communication style (Chapter 7).

Nondirective Counseling: In **nondirective counseling** *the supervisor helps the employee define and solve his or her problem.* The supervisor asks open-ended questions that enable the employee to define and solve his or her own problem. Employee and supervisor work together. Nondirective counseling involves the participative communication style (Chapter 7). The supervisor uses open elicitation with some initiation and little presentation.

Selecting the Counseling Format

Generally, the nondirective counseling format is preferred because it helps the employee take major responsibility for his or her own problem. The employee gets to fully articulate the problem as he or she likes. Employees derive more satisfaction from and commitment to problem solving when they participate. However, nondirective counseling is not always appropriate. Not all employees are capable of participating. Some employees need to be told what to do; often, they appreciate it.

A good approach is to start with nondirective counseling to determine the employee's level of commitment to solving the problem. With employees who are highly committed to solving the problem and who are capable of participating, use nondirective counseling. With the employee who has a low commitment to solving the problem or who is not capable of participating, use directive counseling.[12]

EXHIBIT 14–2   **SIGNS OF PROBLEM EMPLOYEES**

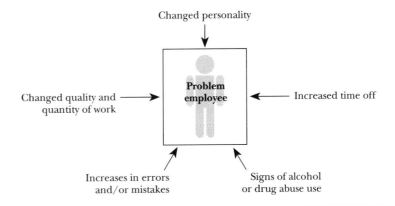

Counseling Skills

It takes a variety of skills to be an effective counselor. Some of these skills have been discussed in previous chapters. The most important skill is communication (Chapter 7); problem-solving and decision-making skills (Chapter 5) and human relations skills (Chapter 6) are also important. The specific communication skills needed were covered in detail in Chapter 7 and are summarized here.

Active Listening: Once he or she realizes that the supervisor is willing to listen, the employee will be more open to changing behavior.[13] Active listening will convey this impression. To actively listen, you must give the employee your undivided attention. Paraphrasing (repeating what the employee said in your own words) helps the supervisor to listen and to ensure mutual understanding.

Dealing with Emotions Empathetically: Counseling often requires that the supervisor help employees deal with their emotions. The supervisor should make the employee realize that emotions are neither good nor bad. Recall that empathic listening is the ability to understand and relate to another's situation and feelings. The supervisor should reflect the employee's feelings so that the employee can become aware of them and deal with them. For example, "It really makes you angry when you have to work overtime, doesn't it?"

Responding: When counseling employees, a supervisor should not use evaluating, confronting, or diverting responses. Appropriate use of probing will help the employee better understand the problem and its causes. Reassuring responses can help build the employee's confidence in solving the problem. Reflective responses can help show your concern and support, and can help the employee solve his or her problem.

Nonverbal Communication: Nonverbal communication such as facial expressions, tone of voice, body movement, gestures, and silence can help or hurt the counseling process. Nonverbal communication must reflect the supervisor's sincere interest in helping the employee.

How to Counsel Employees

The model we will discuss uses the nondirective counseling format. Use this model when the employee has done a good job in the past, but for some reason has changed. The **counseling model** *involves five steps: describing the changed behavior; getting employee comments on the changed behavior and the reason for it; agreeing on a solution; summarizing and getting a commitment to change; and following up.* We will now discuss each step then apply it to a hypothetical situation.

Step 1. Describe the Changed Behavior

In a nonthreatening way, describe the changed behavior. Do not make statements about attitudes or motivation, such as, "You have a bad attitude," or "You don't show much interest in your job."[14] Use only critical incidents that relate to performance. If you make negative evaluative statements, the employee may deny that a problem exists; an argument can develop, and the problem itself gets lost in the shuffle.

Step 2. Get Employee Comments on Changed Behavior and the Reason for It

The employee may become defensive and hostile, blaming others. The supervisor should stay calm and not argue. The employee may not give a reason, or the real reason, for the change. The supervisor should help the employee realize that something is interfering with his or her work. It is not necessary for the supervisor to know what the problem is. It is not advisable to get into all the details of the problem—or to give advice on how to solve personal problems.

M O D E L 1 4 – 1   **THE COUNSELING MODEL**

Step 1. Describe the changed behavior.

Step 2. Get employee comments on the changed behavior and the reason for it.

Step 3. Agree on a solution.

Step 4. Summarize and get a commitment to change.

Step 5. Follow up.

If the employee has a personal problem, the supervisor can suggest professional help. As the supervisor, you should be aware of the services provided through the organization. The human resources department can give you details. Many organizations offer employee assistance programs (EAPs). **Employee assistance programs** *are organization-sponsored professional counseling services.* Some organizations hire their own counselors, and others refer the employee to an outside agency. EAPs have proliferated in the last five years. It is estimated that 10,000 such programs exist and that 70 percent of the large industrial companies in this country have EAPs. In addition, of the employees counseled, 70 percent had problems that involved their families.[15] However, according to a Boston University study, the supervisor is the one most often called on to deal directly with an employee's family crises.[16]

Participation in counseling should be voluntary. However, if performance does not improve, as may be the case with an alcoholic, for example, employees can be given the ultimatum to get help or be terminated.

Step 3.
Agree on a Solution

You are not solving personal problems, nor are you giving advice on how the employee should solve them. You are dealing with a job performance problem. Ask the employee how he or she can solve the problem of performing to standards on the job. You may offer suggestions, but the solution should come from the employee. Be a good listener; let the employee think and talk.[17]

Step 4.
**Summarize and Get
a Commitment
to Change**

Getting a commitment to change is important. Without awareness that a problem exists and a commitment to solve it, behavior and performance will not change.

Step 5. Follow Up

It is important for the employee to know that the supervisor will follow up, and how. Without a follow-up, behavioral changes are less likely.

Although it is not a step in counseling, the supervisor should make a record of the interview in the critical incident file for future reference.

Model 14–1 lists the five counseling steps. Below is an application of the model. Bill is the supervisor and Rhonda is the employee.

Counseling Example

1. BILL: Hi, Rhonda; how's it going?

RHONDA: Okay.

BILL *(continues to develop a rapport by discussing issues not related to the job, and then moves on to job-related issues)*: The major reason I want to talk to you is that I've noticed a change in your work. You never used to be late, but this week you were late on

Monday and Tuesday. You very rarely make mistakes, but on Tuesday you had to retype two letters, and yesterday (Wednesday) you had to make changes on three letters. I am concerned that something is interfering with your job performance.

2. BILL: I'm concerned about your work.

RHONDA: Everyone has an off day or two.

BILL: I agree. I just thought there may be a reason for your having three "off days" in a row. It's never happened before.

RHONDA: Well, there is something bothering me, but it's personal.

BILL: I don't need to know the problem or the details. I want to make you realize that your personal life is interfering with your work. I'm concerned about you. I want you to realize that we do have an EAP available.

RHONDA: Well, I'm having marital problems. Pete is considering a divorce. *(Tears come to her eyes. After a minute of silence, she continues to talk.)* Tell me more about the EAP. I know we have one, but I never paid much attention to it because I never thought I'd need it.

BILL: If you and Pete want to get marriage counseling, it can be arranged at no cost to you, through the company.

RHONDA: Pete won't go.

BILL: You can discuss it with him. If he isn't interested, you can get personal counseling to help you deal with the situation.

RHONDA: Let me talk to Pete about it.

BILL: I think that's a wise decision.

RHONDA: I'll get back to you on it.

3. BILL: Fine, but let me know one way or the other. In the meantime, we still have to get your performance back on track. Is there something you can do to get here on time and improve the quality of your work?

RHONDA *(after thinking for a few minutes)*: Well, being late is easy. I was late because I didn't sleep well and stayed in bed longer than I should have. I'll get some sleeping pills and take them if I need to, and I'll make the effort to get up on time. The quality of work is going to be harder.

BILL: What seems to be the cause of your errors?

RHONDA: I have trouble concentrating. I think about Pete and what we have said to each other, and what I should say to him that night.

BILL: Has thinking about these things helped you to solve your marital problem?

RHONDA: No, but I can't stop thinking about them.

BILL: I understand. What others have done successfully is become aware of their negative thoughts. When they have them, they do not fight and say, "I won't think about it." But they don't entertain the thoughts, either. They replace the negative thoughts with positive thoughts, such as, "Things will work out for the best," "I'll be fine," and so on. With time, they have fewer negative thoughts. It's not easy, but it has worked for others.

RHONDA: I never thought of doing that, I just entertain the thoughts and it makes things worse. I'd like to try using positive thinking instead of negative thinking.

4. RHONDA: Yes, I'll try.

BILL: I believe that you will do better than try; you will succeed. What happened to positive thinking?

RHONDA: You're right; I *will* do it.

5. BILL: One week from today, or sooner if necessary, we will meet at the same time to review how things are going. Let me know if you want counseling. In the meantime, if I can be of help to you, let me know.

RHONDA: Thanks, Bill; I appreciate your concern. I feel better now that we talked.

LEARNING OBJECTIVES

2. Describe the supervisor's role in counseling.

3. List the five steps in the counseling model and use the model.

Get Professional Help

Remember, as shown, the supervisor is not a psychological counselor. Get professional help when needed. Regardless of good intentions, attempting psychological counseling could result in a lawsuit.

CONNECTIONS

3. Recall a time when you or someone else was an employee with a problem, on the job or in school. What were some of the signs a problem existed?

4. In question 3, did your supervisor (coach, teacher) recognize that you or someone else had a problem? Did he or she counsel you or the other person? If so, was it helpful? Why or why not? If counseling did not take place, would counseling have helped? Why or why not?

III. Discipline

Counseling should be the first step in dealing with a problem employee. However, an employee may be unwilling or unable to change. In such cases, discipline is necessary. **Discipline** *is the action taken when employees don't follow standing plans or meet performance requirements.* The major objective of discipline is changing behavior. A secondary objective is to let employees know that action *will* be taken when standing plans or performance requirements are not met.[18]

In this section you will learn the supervisor's role in discipline, guidelines for effective discipline, discipline without punishment, and the process of disciplining employees.

The Supervisor's Role in Discipline

The supervisor is responsible for seeing that employees follow the organization's standing plans and ensuring that employees meet performance standards. When employees do not follow standing plans, it is the supervisor's responsibility to take disciplinary action. Many organizations specify the rules and the penalty for breaking them in writing. An example is given in Exhibit 14–3.

CONNECTIONS

5. Identify some of the rules and penalties for violating them in an organization, preferably one you have worked for.

Guidelines for Effective Discipline

Some guidelines for effective discipline follow.

Understand Your Authority: The supervisor should not exceed his or her authority or the discipline may be overruled. Therefore, a supervisor should be familiar with the organization's discipline system. There may also be union requirements the supervisor must meet.

Understand All the Rules and the Reasons They Are Necessary: If an employee asks why a rule exists or says that it is a dumb rule, the supervisor should be able to give the

E X H I B I T   1 4 – 3   **RULES AND PENALTIES**

	First Offense	Second Offense	Third Offense
Stealing private or company property	Discharge		
Deliberate destruction or abuse of company property	Discharge		
Immoral conduct on company premises	Discharge		
Doing personal work on company time	Written warning	Suspension	Discharge
Conduct dangerous to others	Written warning	Suspension	Discharge
Not working during designated periods	Written warning	Suspension	Discharge
Restricting output or intentional slowdown	Written warning	Suspension	Discharge

rationale for the rule. Work to change rules that are petty, outdated, or simply unnecessary.

Clearly Communicate the Rules to All Employees: Employees must know what is expected of them.[19] The rules and an explanation for them should be a part of the orientation program discussed in Chapter 10.

Do Not Make Negative Comments about the Rules: If you don't like a rule, you are still responsible for enforcing it. Try to change what you don't like, but do so in a constructive way.

Follow the Rules Yourself: Lead by example. You cannot expect employees to follow the rules if you don't.

Get All the Necessary Facts before You Discipline: Do not jump to conclusions. Do not discipline on hearsay evidence. If someone tells you that an employee is breaking a rule, try to catch that employee in the act. Give the employee a chance to explain. Things are not always as they seem. For example, an employee tells the supervisor that Joe is going to steal a tool. The punishment is discharge. The supervisor decides to catch Joe in the act. So he waits and watches Joe leaving with the tool in his pocket. The supervisor stops Joe and says, "I saw you put the tool in your pocket; you're fired." Joe tries to explain, but the supervisor says, "I caught you red-handed; you're fired." Joe goes to the plant manager and explains that the tool room supervisor gave him permission to borrow the tool overnight, but that his supervisor would not listen. As a result of failing to get all the facts, the supervisor hurt relations with employees and was called on the carpet by the plant manager.

Take Action when the Rules Are Broken: The supervisor sets the stage for compliance with the rules.[20] Many new supervisors believe that if they overlook offenses, they will be more popular with employees. However, this is not the case. The supervisor who does not enforce the rules will find that employees who follow the rules will get upset with the supervisor and break the rules, too. Even though few supervisors enjoy it, they must occasionally play the bad guy for the good of all.[21] Remember, employees do what supervisors inspect and enforce, not what supervisors expect.

Discipline in Private and at the End of Work: Normally, no one should see you disciplining an employee. There may be exceptions. For example, it is common for the supervisor's boss to sit in when a repeat offender is disciplined.

Generally, the best time to discipline an employee is at the end of the workday. The advantages are as follows: (1) the supervisor has time to plan; (2) emotions have had time to cool down; (3) the employee has had more time to consider the violation; and (4) there is a minimum of work disruption. If the discipline upsets the employee, which it often does, he or she does not have to face co-workers and explain what happened.

A Typical Discipline Scenario

Tara (who has been warned about lateness) has come in late for work again. Horst, the supervisor, catches her and brings her to his office immediately to discipline her. He is unprepared and upset. Horst yells at Tara and she yells back. She is upset and returns to work. Some of her co-workers come over, one at a time, to find out what happened. The others find out through the grapevine. Horst looks like the bad guy. Some employees believe that he was too soft, and others, too hard. Tara's work for the day is poor and others have disrupted their work to hear what happened.

A Better Discipline Scenario

When Tara arrives late, Horst tells her that they will discuss it 10 minutes before quitting time. Tara was caught in the act and knows she will be disciplined; she does not think she got away with it. At the end of the day, Horst is calm and prepared. The two calmly discuss the situation. Tara, as is normal, is somewhat upset about it. However, she goes directly home after the discipline. Tara does not face co-workers until the next day, when her emotions have settled. Work was somewhat disrupted owing to anticipation of what would happen, but the disruption was minimal.

Document Discipline: It is extremely important to document violations and the action taken. The critical incident file (discussed in Chapter 12) is appropriate for recording what happened. However, it is also advisable to have the employee sign and receive a copy of a written document stating that a warning has been given and why. The document can be handwritten, but preferably should be on company letterhead. It should state the date and time, and the specifics of the violation; briefly report what took place during the discipline session; include a statement of the employee's commitment to change, if given, or reasons for the refusal to change; and describe the penalty for future violations. If the employee disagrees with the written statement, try to get an agreement, making a minor change if necessary. If the employee refuses to sign an accurate document, have a company official, such as your boss, witness the refusal and sign it as proof that the employee was given the warning and refused to sign the statement. Proof that the employee did receive a written warning and was informed of the consequences for future violations will make it difficult for the organization or a court of law to overturn your action.

The Punishment Should Fit the Crime: Punishment for minor offenses should be less severe than for major offenses. This was illustrated in Exhibit 14–3 where some violations result in discharge without warning, whereas others do not.

When the Discipline Is Over, Resume Normal Relations with the Employee: Do not hold a grudge or treat the violator as a criminal. The self-fulfilling prophecy applies: if you treat the employee like a criminal, he or she will probably live up to your expectations and be a repeat offender. If you treat the employee as though it was a one-time mistake which you don't expect to happen again, that will probably be the end of it.

The Hot Stove

The following were primarily developed by Douglas McGregor, who also developed Theory X and Theory Y, and are commonly known as the *hot stove rules.*

Give Advance Warning: The hot stove gives a warning, and so should discipline. The employee must be aware of the rules and know what the consequences are for breaking them. Unfortunately, when you tell some people not to do something, they do it anyway.

Discipline Immediately: When you get burned, you know it right away. Discipline should take place soon after the violation. However, as stated previously, the end of the workday is soon enough. If either the supervisor or the employee is emotional, it is usually better to wait until both calm down.

Discipline Consistently: Everyone who touches the hot stove gets burned in the same manner. The supervisor who enforces sporadically causes frustration and resentment. Employees will make comments such as, "Jose did it yesterday and nothing happened to him."

LEARNING OBJECTIVE

4. Explain several guidelines for effective discipline.

Discipline Impartially: The hot stove does not play favorites; all who touch it get burned in the same manner. They get burned for what they did, not for who they are. The supervisor should focus on the act, not the person.

Exhibit 14–4 summarizes the 15 guidelines for effective discipline.

CONNECTIONS

When answering questions 6 through 8, use a supervisor you have had as an example. Refer to Exhibit 14–4.

6. Review guidelines 1 through 5. Which ones did the supervisor follow and not follow? Explain.

7. Review guidelines 6 through 10. Which ones did the supervisor follow and not follow? Explain.

8. Review guidelines 11 through 15. Which ones did the supervisor follow and not follow? Explain.

EXHIBIT 14–4   **GUIDELINES FOR EFFECTIVE DISCIPLINE**

1. Understand your authority.

2. Understand all the rules and the reasons they are necessary.

3. Clearly communicate the rules to all employees.

4. Do not make negative comments about the rules.

5. Follow the rules yourself.

6. Get all the necessary facts before you discipline.

7. Take action when the rules are broken.

8. Discipline in private and at the end of work.

9. Document discipline.

10. The punishment should fit the crime.

11. When the discipline is over, resume normal relations with the employee.

12. Give advance warning.

13. Discipline immediately.

14. Discipline consistently.

15. Discipline impartially.

Discipline without Punishment

Many people distinguish between discipline and punishment. They view discipline as positive and punishment as negative. Punishment should be avoided because it produces fear, anxiety, and more punishment.[22] Confronting a person during discipline is effective, but punishing the person by criticizing him or her damages work relationships.[23]

These are the major differences between discipline and punishment:

- *Responsibility.* With discipline, the employee is responsible for changing behavior. With punishment, the supervisor is responsible for making the employee obey the rules.
- *Focus.* Discipline focuses on changing future behavior. Punishment focuses on penalizing past violations.
- *The supervisor's role.* The supervisor is a coach when disciplining versus a judge when punishing.

From these distinctions grew the idea of discipline without punishment. This is not a new concept. More than 20 years ago, John Huberman wrote an article on the subject.[24] More recently, Eric Harvey has popularized it through his consulting and writing on the topic.[25]

Harvey and his associates train managers to discipline without punishment. His system it used organizationwide. This nonpunitive discipline involves four steps.[26]

- *Step 1.* The employee is given an oral warning. It focuses on making the employee responsible for changing future behavior.
- *Step 2.* The employee is given a written reminder. If the employee fails to change and repeats the violation after the oral warning, he or she gets a written reminder not to do it again.
- *Step 3.* Decision-making leave. If a third warning is needed, the employee is given a day off, with pay, to determine whether he or she wishes to remain with the organization. If the employee chooses to stay on the job, he or she realizes the need for changing, because a fourth violation will result in termination.
- *Step 4.* Termination. A fourth violation results in the employee's being fired.

Harvey has documented success with this system at organizations including Procter and Gamble, Pennzoil, and Bay Area Rapid Transit.[27] Similar nonpunitive systems have also documented reductions in turnover rate, discipline situations, grievances, and sick leave.[28]

The author agrees with these steps when the situation involves rule violations. However, if performance is below standard, he suggests beginning with a nondisciplinary interview because you should counsel before you discipline.[29] Therefore, your first action would be to use the counseling model (Model 14–1) or the improving performance model (Model 12–1), depending on the situation. Notice that neither of these models involves warning the employee of future consequences, as the discipline systems do.

How to Discipline Employees

The objective of discipline is always the same: to change behavior. However, the severity of the consequences increases if successive discipline sessions are necessary. The steps in the discipline model should be followed each time an employee must be disciplined. What will change is the warning given if the behavior continues.

The **discipline model** *involves five steps: referring to past feedback; describing the lack of change and asking why the behavior did not change; giving the warning; getting a commitment to change; and summarizing and following up.* We will now discuss each step and then apply it to the example of Bill and Rhonda described earlier.

Step 1. Refer to Past Feedback

Begin the interview by refreshing the employee's memory about the previous discussion. The employee should realize that the meeting is a follow-up.

Step 2. Describe the Lack of Change and Ask Why the Behavior Did Not Change

If the behavior had changed, discipline would not be needed. Again, be sure to describe specific critical incidents to support your contention that behavior has not changed at all or has not changed enough to be at standard.

Step 3. Give the Warning

The warning will vary with the number of violations, among other factors. An oral warning should be documented in the critical incidents file, and a written warning should follow the guidelines given earlier.

Step 4. Get a Commitment to Change

Try to get a commitment to change. If the employee will not commit, make note of the fact in the critical incidents file or use the procedures for a written warning. A plan for change may have been developed in the past. If it has, the supervisor may try to get the employee to commit to it again. Develop a new plan, if necessary. A statement such as, "your previous attempt has not worked; there must be a better way," is often helpful.[30]

Step 5. Summarize and Follow Up

State that a warning has been given and describe the commitment or lack of commitment made. Arrange a follow-up method, a meeting, or both.

Model 14–2 summarizes the five steps in the discipline model. Following the model is the continuing application with Bill and Rhonda.

Discipline Example

1. BILL: Rhonda, it's been one week since we last spoke about the personal problem affecting your work. This meeting is a follow-up to review your progress.

RHONDA: The last meeting was helpful.

2. BILL: I'm happy that you have not been late or out sick all week. However, every day during the week you were required to correct errors. Would you like to see a record of them?

RHONDA: No, I remember. You made comments to me throughout the week.

BILL: Why hasn't the quality of your work improved to its normal standard? Have you been following your plan for improving?

MODEL 14–2

THE DISCIPLINE MODEL

Step 1. Refer to past feedback.

Step 2. Describe the lack of change and ask why the behavior did not change.

Step 3. Give the warning.

Step 4. Get a commitment to change.

Step 5. Summarize and follow up.

RHONDA: I've been trying, but it's hard.

BILL: Have you made a decision about counseling? Do you recall that you were supposed to get back to me either way?

RHONDA: Yes, but Pete left me, and I don't feel right about going to counseling.

3. BILL: Because your performance has not been up to standard for two weeks, I am giving you a warning. I will make a record of it in your file.

RHONDA *(emotionally)*: I've been a good employee for 15 years. Now I have a little problem and you won't cut me any slack?

BILL *(calmly)*: I'm sorry you have a problem. I offered to get you professional help. I believe that two weeks of slack is enough. Your performance must change.

RHONDA: Why do you have to record it in the file?

BILL: I keep a record of all performance, good and bad. I've given you examples of good performance during previous appraisals.

4. BILL: Your previous plan to improve performance did not work; can you think of a better way to get back to the regular standard?

RHONDA *(after a few minutes to think about it)*: I didn't realize the problem was so serious. I think counseling will do some good. I'm not myself.

BILL: I think you have made a wise decision. At the end of this meeting I will call Ms. Swanson, the personnel director, to arrange for the counseling.

RHONDA: I'd appreciate that, Bill.

5. BILL: You have been given a warning, and you agree to get counseling and improve you performance. Is that correct, Rhonda?

**LEARNING
OBJECTIVE**

5. List the five steps in the discipline model and use the model.

RHONDA: Yes it is, Bill.

BILL: We will have a follow-up meeting next week at the same time to review your progress. I'll call Ms. Swanson now to tell her about the situation and let you make an appointment to go see her on company time.

IV. Supervising Specific Types of Problem Employees

In this section you will learn tactics for dealing with specific problems: lateness and absence, substance abuse, and insubordination. When dealing with any of these specific types, the supervisor should use the discipline model discussed in the previous section.

The Late or Absent Employee

The average employee is absent seven times a year. If employees are late a few times a month or absent more than seven times per year, action may be needed.[31] Of all absences, 60 percent are due to serious or chronic illness, 20 percent to acute, short-term illnesses such as the flu, 10 percent to minor illness such as headache or cold (attendance is based on the employee's attitude about the job), and 10 percent to faking it to get the day off.[32]

In addition to the direct cost of paying employees for not working, organizations also incur the costs of missed deadlines, overtime, diminished product quality, and customer dissatisfaction, among others.[33] Lateness and absenteeism are resented by other employees who have to do the absent employee's work. This lowers morale and may encourage others to take days off to get even.[34]

Causes of Lateness and Absence

Lateness and absence are symptoms of a problem, rather than the problem itself. Following are some of the actual reasons employees are late or absent.[35]

- *Job dissatisfaction.* Employees who like their jobs are more likely to come to work than those who find their work unstimulating.
- *Attitude toward work.* Some employees come to work even though they are sick, whereas others look for any excuse not to come in.
- *Company culture.* Organizations that accept lateness and absence as a normal practice reinforce the problem.

Tactics to Help Reduce Lateness and Absence

Following are some actions a supervisor can take to overcome the causes of lateness or absence.

- *Make the work interesting.* Use job enrichment (discussed in Chapter 11). Delegate challenging assignments to employees who seem bored. Use flextime. Develop teamwork.
- *Check attendance records.* When hiring a new employee, be sure to check the person's record at previous jobs. If the candidate was chronically absent on the last job, he or she probably will be on your job, too. Try not to hire any problem employees.
- *Attack the problem.* Always confront the employee and ask for the reason he or she was late or absent. Record and track employees' absences and lateness.[36] Look for patterns such as taking long weekends by staying out on Monday or Friday.[37] Calling their home to check on employees can improve their attendance record. They may not have told other people at home that they planned to take the day off. You may catch them in a lie.[38] However, checking up on them may cause problems in your relations with employees. It should only be done with the extremely suspect absence. Offering positive incentives for having a good attendance record is usually more productive.

The Substance Abuser

Since October 1986, when Attorney General Edwin Meese in a press conference described management's responsibility to curb drug abuse in the workplace, and the government began testing, drug abuse has received a lot of attention. Mr. Meese stated that each drug-abusing employee costs employers $7,000 per year. In addition to the cost, employees resent working with substance abusers because abusers are unreliable and do not carry their own load.[39]

Some business and government leaders advocate testing as a means of preventing drug abuse. They believe that when the word gets out that the organization tests for drugs, abusers are less likely to apply for jobs.[40] Others are strongly against testing, claiming that it is not effective; for example, one can actually buy drug-free urine, which allows users to pass the test! Some believe that it is a violation of privacy and thus do not test. According to Jack Gordon, drug testing is a drastic Theory X policy and should not be used.[41] Nonetheless, you may find yourself working for an organization that tests.

Signs of Substance Abuse

Some things the supervisor should look for include the following:

- *Absences.* Absences almost always increase when employees abuse substances. Substance abusers spread absences through the week, and they commonly leave work early. Lateness is not a marked feature.[42] However, the substance abuser has two and a half times more absences than normal.[43]

- *Errors and accidents.* Substance abusers have four times as many accidents as nonabusers.[44]
- *Confrontations.* Substance abusers tend to have an excessive number of confrontations with other workers.[45]
- *Theft.* With the high cost of drugs, abusers often turn to theft from the organization and other employees as a means of paying for their addiction.
- *Erratic performance.* The performance of substance abusers, particularly drug users, fluctuates widely.[46]

Tactics to Help Prevent Substance Abuse

If you suspect substance abuse, take the following steps:

- Do not confront the person when he or she is under the influence. Wait until the person can think straight.
- Do not accuse someone of substance abuse without proof. Substance abuse is classified as a handicap. If the person admits to the problem, help the abuser to get professional help. Adjust the person's work schedule, if necessary.
- Discipline the suspected abuser in the same way as any problem employee, focusing on job performance. According to Ann St. Louis, personnel counselor for Canada's Department of National Revenue, the threat of the loss of a job is the most effective means of convincing a substance abuser to get professional help. It is a more effective threat than the loss of family and friends.

The Insubordinate or Nonconformist Employee

The insubordinate employee intentionally disobeys the supervisor. The nonconformist does not like to follow the rules. For example, if there is a dress code, he or she may ignore it.

Tactics for Dealing with the Insubordinate Employee

LEARNING OBJECTIVE

6. Describe how to handle the late or absent employee, the substance abuser, and the insubordinate or nonconformist employee.

- Do not allow insubordination and nonconformity. Use an autocratic style and confront any employee who doesn't do as you ask, or things will get worse. (This assumes that you are a good leader and make reasonable requests.)
- Do not discuss or debate reasons for insubordination. Make the insubordinate employee realize that action will be taken if the behavior continues.
- Do not allow nonconformity. Confront the employees and make them follow the rules regardless of performance record.[47]

CONNECTIONS

9. Recall a job you have had. Were there any chronically late or absent employees? What seemed to be the causes? What did the supervisor do to stop or prevent this problem? What would you do differently to stop or prevent the problem?

10. Recall a job you have had. Did you suspect any employees of substance abuse? If so, what signs of substance abuse did the employee or employees display on the job? (Do not use actual names of people.) As a supervisor, how will you handle substance abuse?

V. Firing Employees

Perhaps, in spite of your efforts, a problem employee refuses to change. Or there are cutbacks in your department or organization. In either case, you may be faced with firing an employee. In this section you will learn about authority to fire, documenting the reasons for firing, and guidelines for firing employees.

Authority to Fire

Make sure you have the authority to fire employees before you take any action. Even if the responsibility is yours, it is advisable to consult with your boss and get his or her approval to fire the person. It would be very embarrassing and undermine your authority if you fire an employee and have to take him or her back in your department. If you have adequate proof of due cause for firing, authority, and documentation, this should not happen.

Documenting Reasons for Firing

By 1984 more than two-thirds of the nation's courts had overturned the tradition that an employer may hire and fire for any reason or for no reason at all. Organizations including American Express, Aetna Life and Casualty, and Hoffmann-LaRoche have been sued for unlawful termination of employees.[48] One of the courts' major concerns was whether the terminated employees had been made aware of the consequences of their behavior and received adequate warning.[49] If you have proof that an employee violated the rules, a critical incident recorded, and documented reasons for firing (as described in this chapter), you should have a good legal defense for terminating an employee.

Guidelines for Firing Employees

Hopefully, as a supervisor, you will never have to terminate an employee. But if you do, following these guidelines can help you to do it effectively.

Do It Yourself: Do not delegate the task to someone else. If the employee works for you, he or she will probably want to speak to you anyway, so get it over with.

Select the Appropriate Time and Place: Generally, the best time to fire an employee is near the end of the workday. Give the employee enough time to pack up his or her things and leave with the others. Friday is the preferred day. The best place is one where you have control; your office is the better choice. The employee's work area is in his or her control.

Both of You Should Sit Down: This is necessary because the employee may get emotional and cry. (It is easier to gain control when you are seated.) If the terminated employee gets violent, it's also harder to reach you when you're both seated.

Do It Quickly: Firing should not be a surprise. If the employee has been caught violating a rule punishable by termination, or if you have followed the steps in progressive discipline, there is little left to say. The employee knows the reason for termination. Do not argue or give additional chances. Get it over with.

Assign Someone to Help the Fired Employee Pack: Before the employee leaves, get back what belongs to the organization: tools, keys, locks, and so forth. An effective way to do this is to have someone help the employee pack. The person assigned makes sure that the employee does not take company property when he or she leaves.

Don't Tell Co-Workers that the Fired Employee Is Leaving: Your other employees will find out anyway, but if you tell them directly they will want an explanation. There is no reason for you to give them this information. Explaining to your employees can be a no-win situation. Some may think it should have been done sooner, and others will think it should not have been done at all.[50]

The counseling and discipline skills discussed in this chapter should help the supervisor avoid the necessity of firing.

REVIEW

Select one or more methods: (1) fill in the missing key terms from memory; (2) match the key terms from the end of the review with their definitions below; (3) copy the key terms in order from the key terms at the beginning of the chapter.

_____ are employees who are not performing to expectations. We distinguish two types: (1) employees with problems, who need counseling; and (2) employees causing problems, who need discipline. Solving people problems requires skill. The supervisory functions are affected by how well the supervisor handles problem employees.

_____ is the process of giving employees guidance on job performance. Signs that an employee has a problem include changed personality, changed quality and quantity of work, increased time off, increased accidents, and signs of alcohol or drug abuse. There are two major counseling formats: in _____ , the supervisor controls the discussion and gives the employee advice on how to solve the problem; and in _____ , the supervisor helps the employee define and solve his or her own problem. Counseling requires communication skills, problem-solving and decision-making skills, and human-relations skills. The _____ involves five steps: describing the changed behavior; getting employee comments on changed behavior and the reason for it; agreeing on a solution; summarizing and getting a commitment to change; and following up. _____ are organization-sponsored professional counseling services.

_____ is the action taken when employees don't follow standing plans or meet performance requirements. The supervisor is responsible for enforcing the rules and administering discipline. The 15 guidelines for effective discipline are as follows: (1) understand your authority, (2) understand all the rules and the reasons for them, (3) clearly communicate the rules to all employees, (4) do not make negative comments about the rules, (5) follow the rules yourself, (6) get all the facts before you discipline, (7) take action when the rules are broken, (8) discipline in private at the end of work, (9) document discipline, (10) fit the punishment to the crime, (11) when the discipline is over, resume normal relations with the employee, (12) give advance warning, (13) discipline immediately, (14) discipline consistently, and (15) discipline impartially. Discipline is preferred to punishment. The

_____ includes referring to past interviews; describing the lack of change and asking why the behavior did not change; giving the warning; getting a commitment to change; and summarizing and following up.

Some causes of lateness and absence are job dissatisfaction, attitude toward work, and company culture. To help prevent lateness and absenteeism, the supervisor can make the work interesting, check attendance records, and attack the problem. Alcohol and drug abuse is a major problem. Some of the signs of such substance abuse include absences, errors and accidents, confrontations, theft, and erratic performance. Do not confront employees when they are under the influence. Do not accuse them of substance abuse without proof. Discipline the suspected abuser in the same way as any problem employee, focusing on job performance. Do not allow insubordination and nonconformity or things will get worse. Do not discuss or debate reasons for insubordination.

Before firing an employee, be sure you have the authority to do so. Document the reasons for firing. When firing employees, do it yourself, and select an appropriate time and place. Both of you should sit down. Do it quickly; assign someone to help the fired employee pack; and don't tell co-workers that the fired employee is leaving.

KEY TERMS

counseling model

directive counseling

discipline

discipline model

employee assistance programs

nondirective counseling

problem employee

supervisory counseling

REFERENCES

1. Alex Boeder, "What Every Supervisor Should Know but Doesn't," *Supervision,* March 1986, p. 12.

2. H. B. Karp, "The ABCs (Appropriate Behavior Changes) of Effective Management," *Training and Development Journal,* January 1985, p. 32.

3. Marcia Ann Pullich, "What to Do with Incompetent Employees," *Supervisory Management,* March 1986, pp. 10, 13.

4. *The Troubled Employee* (Chicago: Dartnell Publishing, 1987).

5. Jack Gordon, "Drug Testing as a Productivity Booster?" *Training*, March 1987, p. 27.

6. Ibid., p. 26.

7. "Wasted Time at Work Costs Business," *The Wall Street Journal*, November 27, 1984, p. 1.

8. Doris Unger, "Coaching—A Proven Alternative to Employee Termination," *Professional Trainer*, Winter 1986, p. 2.

9. Ibid.

10. Virginia Novarra, "Can a Manager Be a Counselor?" *Personnel Management*, June 1986, p. 50.

11. Ibid., p. 49.

12. Maurice Brown, "Counseling Skills," *SAM Advanced Management Journal*, Winter 1986, p. 33.

13. Karp, "ABCs of Effective Management," p. 33.

14. Ibid.

15. William Miller, "Trouble at Home," *Industry Week*, November 24, 1986, p. 53.

16. Jeanne Saddler, "Job and Family Conflicts Lead Workers to Rely Mostly on Colleagues," *The Wall Street Journal*, August 25, 1987, p. 1.

17. Steve Buckman, "Finding Out Why a Good Performer Went Bad," *Supervisory Management*, August 1984, p. 39.

18. Joseph Seltzer, "Discipline with a Clear Sense of Purpose," *Management Solutions*, February 1987, p. 32.

19. Robert Demers, "What's the Problem?" *Supervision*, April 1985, p. 5.

20. Andre Nelson, "How to Deal with Uncooperative Employees," *Supervision*, March 1986, p. 4.

21. Kenneth Matejka, Neil Ashworth, and Diane Dodd-McCue, "Discipline without Guilt," *Supervisory Management*, May 1986, p. 35.

22. Gene Milbourn, "The Case against Employee Punishment," *Management Solutions*, November 1986, p. 41.

23. Dennis Kinlaw and Donna Christensen, "Confront—Don't Criticize—to Improve Performance," *SAM Advanced Management Journal*, Winter 1984, p. 56.

24. John Huberman, "Discipline without Punishment," *Harvard Business Review*, July–August 1964, p. 62.

25. Bruce Jacobs, "An Apostle of Nonpunitive Discipline," *Industry Week*, November 10, 1986, p. 123.

26. Ibid., pp. 123–26.

27. Eric Harvey, "Discipline versus Punishment," *Management Review*, March 1987, p. 28.

28. David Campbell, R. L. Fleming, and Richard Grote, "Discipline without Punishment—At Last," *Harvard Business Review*, July–August 1985, p. 176.

29. Jill Houser List, "In Defense of Traditional Discipline," *Personnel Administrator*, June 1986, p. 42.

30. "A Little Advice on Giving Advice," *Training*, March 1984, p. 74.

31. Edward Roseman, *Managing the Problem Employee* (New York: AMACOM, 1982), p. 231.

32. P. J. Taylor quoted in Lester Bittel, *What Every Supervisor Should Know* (New York: McGraw-Hill, 1985), p. 237.

33. "How to Reduce the High Cost of Absenteeism," *BNAC Communicator*, Spring 1987, p. 19.

34. Alan Farrant, "Block that Absenteeism," *Supervision*, August 1985, p. 14.

35. "How to Reduce the High Cost of Absenteeism," p. 19.

36. Ibid.

37. Roseman, *Managing the Problem Employee,* p. 232.

38. Farrant, "Block that Absenteeism," p. 15.

39. Jesse Philips, "Enough Talk! What Can Employers Do about Drug Abuse?" *The Wall Street Journal,* November 17, 1986, p. 34.

40. Ibid.

41. Gordon, "Drug Testing as a Productivity Booster?" p. 28.

42. Harrison Trice quoted in Bittel, *What Every Supervisor Should Know,* p. 340.

43. Roseman, *Managing the Problem Employee,* p. 198.

44. Ibid.

45. Phillips, "Enough Talk!" p. 34.

46. Roseman, *Managing the Problem Employee,* p. 198.

47. Ibid., pp. 126, 246.

48. Andrew Kramer, "The Hazards of Firing at Will," *The Wall Street Journal,* March 9, 1987, p. 20.

49. Steve Buckman, "To Fire or Not to Fire," *Supervisory Management,* February 1986, p. 31.

50. Bob Green, "The Boss Needs Advice in Telling Workers to Shove Off," *Chicago Tribune,* April 29, 1982, p. A22.

APPLICATION   SITUATIONS

The Counseling Model

Identify which step in Model 14–1 each statement represents.

AS 14–1

a. 1   *d.* 4

b. 2   *e.* 5

c. 3

_____ 1. "So from now on you will take the bus and be here on time. Is that correct?"

_____ 2. "I've noticed that you've gotten into a lot of arguments with co-workers in the past two weeks."

_____ 3. "I'll be keeping an eye on you to make sure you put the tools back in their proper place."

_____ 4. "I don't think things are any different now than they were last week."

_____ 5. "I think that putting a sign up next to the machine to remind you to log in your time is a good idea. Why don't you do it now?"

Guidelines for Effective Discipline

Identify which guideline in Exhibit 14–4 is being followed, or not being followed, in the statements below.

AS 14–2

a. 1   *e.* 5   *i.* 9   *m.* 13

b. 2   *f.* 6   *j.* 10   *n.* 14

c. 3   *g.* 7   *k.* 11   *o.* 15

d. 4   *h.* 8   *l.* 12

_____ 6. "I think it's a dumb rule, too, but I still have to enforce it."

_____ 7. "The discipline is over; let's get back to normal around here."

_____ 8. "The sign says no smoking, but a lot of employees smoke because the supervisor doesn't mind.

_____ 9. "It's not fair. The supervisor comes back from break late all the time; why can't I?"

_____ 10. "When I leave the place a mess, the supervisor yells at me. When Chris does it, nothing is ever said."

_____ 11. "I got a warning for smoking in a restricted area. I tried to say I don't even smoke, but the supervisor would not listen."

_____ 12. "This is our company handbook. It lists all the standing plans you need to know. I want you to read it now. Then we will go over it."

_____ 13. "I want you to come into my office so that we can discuss the matter."

_____ 14. "You know you should not talk to a supervisor like that. We'll discuss this later when we both are calm."

_____ 15. "The first day I was late, the supervisor gave me a one-day suspension."

The Discipline Model

AS 14–3

Identify which step in Model 14–2 each statement represents.

a. 1   *d.* 4

b. 2   *e.* e

c. 3

_____ 16. "The next time this happens you will be suspended for one day."

_____ 17. "You've been warned not to speed any more. I'll be watching you from now on, so you had better drive slowly around here."

_____ 18. "This is the third time I've called you in to discuss gambling on the job."

_____ 19. "Okay, I won't be late coming back from lunch again."

_____ 20. "You told me that it would not happen again, but it has; what do you have to say about it?"

OBJECTIVE   CASE   14

You're Late

The organization has a progressive discipline program. A first offense gets a reminder, a second offense gets an oral warning, a third offense a written warning, a fourth offense a one-day suspension without pay, and a fifth offense means termination. The following conversation takes place between Bruce, the supervisor, and Helen, the employee:

BRUCE: Helen, come into my office; I want to talk to you.

HELEN: I'm sorry, I'm late.

BRUCE *(in his office)*: This is the fifth time you have been late in three weeks.

HELEN: Yes, I know; I've been having car problems.

BRUCE: I'm not concerned with your personal life. You are expected to be on time for work.

HELEN: I'm sorry; I'll try not to be late any more.

BRUCE: As you know, our discipline policy states that the fifth time you are late you are terminated. I've decided not to terminate you. You are suspended for today without pay. The next time you are late, you will be terminated.

HELEN: What policy are you talking about?

BRUCE: The one in your company handbook. I gave it to you and told you to read it your first day on the job. Didn't you read it?

HELEN: No I haven't. I forgot about it.

BRUCE: That is no excuse.

HELEN: Well, why didn't you say something to me on the other four days I was late? I figured you didn't mind. I was never more than 30 minutes late.

BRUCE: I'm your supervisor, not your mother. You're suspended. You may go now. I'll see you tomorrow.

HELEN: I'm going to the boss. She will agree that you were unfair.

BRUCE: Go ahead, if you want to. Kelly will agree with me. I've documented each of your late days in my file.

HELEN: You haven't heard the last of this.

Answer the following questions, supporting your answers in the space between questions.

_____ 1. Helen appears to be an _____ .
            a. employee with a problem.   *b.* employee causing problems.

_____ 2. Bruce should have begun his first discussion with Helen with _____ .
            a. counseling   *b.* discipline

_____ 3. Bruce used _____ counseling.
            a. directive   *b.* nondirective   *c.* no

_____ 4. Bruce used _____ .
            a. discipline   *b.* punishment

_____ 5. Bruce clearly communicated the rules to Helen.
     a. true   *b.* false

_____ 6. Bruce did an _____ job of documenting this situation.
     a. effective   *b.* ineffective

_____ 7. Helen was given an advance warning or reminder.
     a. true   *b.* false

_____ 8. Bruce used step (or steps) _____ in the discipline model.
     a. 1   *d.* 4
     b. 2   *e.* 5
     c. 3

_____ 9. Bruce _____ attack the problem as suggested in the text under tactics to help reduce lateness and absence.
     a. did   *b.* did not

_____ 10. The boss and a court would most likely agree with _____ .
     a. Bruce   *b.* Helen

11. In Bruce's position, how would you have handled this situation?

PREPARATION FOR IN-CLASS SKILL-BUILDING EXERCISE

Counseling

SB 14–1

1. Recall a work or school situation you are willing to reenact in class, in which counseling would have been beneficial to you. Some of the symptoms of the problem may include a change in personality, a change in the quality or quantity of your work, more time off, increased errors or accidents, and increased use of alcohol or drugs. It may have been a family problem or a problem in a relationship. It may have been the death of a friend or relative. It may have been a time when you broke up with someone you were dating. It may have been a time you had a fight with someone. If you cannot recall a situation, ask someone to describe a situation, or make one up.

2. Below write out a description that will help the person being "counseled" in this situation understand the role. Describe how the person will probably react to counseling.

3. On a separate sheet of paper, make some notes on what you will say to the person you will counsel. Use the counseling model (Model 14–1) to help you. Be sure to cover each step.

IN-CLASS SKILL-BUILDING EXERCISE

Counseling

SB 14–1

Objective: To develop your counseling skills.

Experience: You will counsel, be counseled, and observe counseling using Model 14–1.

Material: You will need your preparation for this exercise.

Procedure 1
(2–4 minutes)

Break into groups of three. Make some groups of two, if necessary. Determine who will be the counselor, the person counseled, and the observer for the first role play.

Procedure 2
(8–15 minutes)

a. Prepare for the role play. The first counselor explains and lets the person to be counseled read his or her role. If the person counseled is not the same sex as the counselor, change the situation so that the person counseled plays his or her own sex. The person counseled should have a feel for the situation that allows him or her to ad-lib. (Keep this preparation to a minute or two.)

b. Role play and observation. Once ready, enact the counseling interview. During the role play, the observer makes notes on the observer form at the end of the exercise. You may not have time to complete the role play. However, groups of two may take extra time because they will do only two role plays, not three.

c. Feedback. The observer leads a discussion on how well the counselor did. Focus on what the counselor did well and how he or she could improve. The person counseled should also give feedback on how he or she felt, and what might have been more effective in getting him or her to change.

Do not go on to the next interview until you are told to do so. If you finish early, wait for the rest of the class.

Procedure 3
(8–15 minutes)

The same as procedure 2, but change roles.

Procedure 4
(8–15 minutes)

The same as procedure 2, but each person plays the role he or she has not played yet.

Conclusion: The instructor may lead a class discussion and make concluding remarks.

Application (2–4 minutes): What did I learn from this experience? How will I use this knowledge in the future?

Sharing: Volunteers give their answers to the application section.

OBSERVER FORM

Try to both make positive comments and to identify areas for improvement. Describe alternative things the counselor could have said to improve the counseling interview.

Step 1. How well did the counselor communicate the changed behavior?

Step 2. How well did the counselor get the person being counseled to comment on the changed behavior and the reason for it?

Step 3. Did they agree on a solution? Will it solve the problem?

Step 4. How well did the counselor summarize? Did he or she get a commitment to change?

Step 5. Did the counselor explain how he or she will follow up?

IN-CLASS SKILL-BUILDING EXERCISE

Discipline

SB 14–2

Objective: To develop your ability to discipline an employee.

Experience: You will discipline, be disciplined, and observe a discipline session using Model 14–2.

Material: It is all in the book. There is no advance preparation.

Procedure 1
(2–4 minutes)

Break into groups of three. Make some groups of two, if necessary. Each member selects one of the three situations from Skill-Building Exercise 12–1. Decide who will discipline employee 1, the clerical worker; employee 2, the ice cream shop server; and employee 3, the auto technician. Also select a different member to play the employee being disciplined.

Procedure 2
(3–7 minutes)

Prepare for the discipline session. Write a basic outline of what you will say to employee 1, 2, or 3; follow the steps in the discipline model below.

Step 1. Refer to past interviews. (Assume that you have discussed the situation before, using the increasing performance model.)

Step 2. Describe the lack of change and ask why the behavior did not change. (The "employee" should make up an excuse for not changing.)

Step 3. Give the warning. (Assume that an oral warning is appropriate.)

Step 4. Get a commitment to change.

Step 5. Summarize and follow up.

Procedure 3
(5–8 minutes)

a. Role play. The supervisor of employee 1, the clerical worker, disciplines him or her as planned. (Use the actual name of the person playing the employee.) Talk; do not read your written plan. Employee 1, put yourself in the worker's position.

You work hard; there is a lot of pressure to work fast. It's easier when you have more than one file. Both the supervisor and employee will need to ad-lib.

The person not playing a role is the observer. He or she makes notes on the observer form at the end of the exercise. Focus on what the supervisor did well and how he or she could improve.

b. Feedback. The observer leads a discussion of how well the supervisor disciplined the employee. The employee should also give feedback on how he or she felt and what might have been more effective in getting him or her to change.

Do not go on to the next interview until you are told to do so. If you finish early, wait until the others finish or the time is up.

Procedure 4
(5–8 minutes)

Same as procedure 3, but change roles so that employee 2, the ice cream server, is disciplined. Employee 2, put yourself in the worker's position. You enjoy talking to your friends, and you're supposed to be friendly to the customers.

Procedure 5
(5–8 minutes)

Same as procedure 3, but change roles so that employee 3, the auto technician, is disciplined. Employee 3, put yourself in the worker's position. You are an excellent technician. Sometimes you forget to put the mat on the floor.

Conclusion: The instructor leads a class discussion and makes concluding remarks.

Application (2–4 minutes): What did I learn from this experience? How will I use this knowledge in the future?

Sharing: Volunteers give their answers to the application section.

OBSERVER FORM

For each of the following steps, try to make a statement about the positive aspects of the discipline and a statement about how the supervisor could have improved. Give alternative things the supervisor could have said to improve the discipline session. Remember, the objective is to change behavior.

Step 1. How well did the supervisor refer to past interviews?

Step 2. How well did the supervisor describe the lack of change and ask for an explanation of why the behavior did not change?

Step 3. How well did the supervisor give the warning?

Step 4. Did the supervisor get a commitment to change? Do you think the employee will change his or her behavior?

Step 5. How well did the supervisor summarize? How effective will the follow-up be?

15

Supervising Groups

Learning Objectives

1. Describe and contrast functional groups, ad hoc committees, and standing committees.
2. Explain the six components of group structure and their effect on group performance.
3. Describe the five stages of group development.
4. Identify each of the four group situational supervisory styles to use with a group, based on its stage of development.
5. Explain how to plan for and conduct effective meetings.
6. Identify the five types of group problem members and explain how to handle them.

Key Terms

To achieve our objectives in this chapter, it is important that you understand the following 13 key terms. They are presented in the order in which they appear in the chapter. The list of key terms also appears in alphabetical order in the end of chapter review.

group	**group structure**	**roles**
participative management	**norms**	**task roles**
functional groups	**group cohesiveness**	**maintenance roles**
ad hoc committees	**status**	**self-interest roles**
standing committees		

Bonnie Sue Swinaski is a machine operator for the Western Pacific Manufacturing Company. In the past she has recommended ways to increase performance, which management utilized. As a result, management appointed Bonnie Sue to lead a group charged to recommend ways to increase performance in her work area. Her group had six members, all from her department, who had volunteered to serve on the committee. The committee has been meeting biweekly now for three weeks for one- to two-hour sessions. The members have grown quite close over the weeks, and participation has been fairly equal. Bonnie Sue, however, has not been very pleased with the group's performance. Only three weeks remain before the report presentation to management. She has been thinking about some of the problems and wondering how to handle them. At first the members came to the meeting really enthusiastic and came up with crazy ideas. But over time they lost some of that enthusiasm, even though they were developing better ideas for improving the performance of the department. During meetings members have been suggesting the need for work to be done outside the meeting, but no one seems to do it. Three of the members cause different kinds of problems in the group. Kirt is destructive—he is constantly putting other people's ideas down, and others have followed his lead. Kirt thinks his way is always better, and he never gives an inch, even when he knows he is wrong. Kirt ends up fighting with members over whose idea is better. Shelby is very pleasant—she tries to keep peace in the group. The problem with Shelby is that she is consistently getting the group off the topic at hand. Carl is the opposite of Shelby — he puts us back on the topic. He doesn't believe in wasting any time, but he's a motor mouth. Carl dominates the air time at meetings. If you were in Bonnie Sue's situation, how would you turn the group into a top performer?

I. The Importance of Groups

For our purposes, a **group** *is two or more people interacting to achieve an objective.* Our definition has three major components: objective, interaction, and performance. The group's objective is what brings members together; the members then interact as the group performs the necessary functions to achieve an objective. As we will see, this is an important concept for any supervisor. Your department will not be composed of separate individuals working in isolation, but of a group or groups of employees interacting. Most people concentrate on supervising individuals rather than a work team.[1] However, those supervisors are evaluated on the results of their departments as a whole. The supervisor's performance is dependent upon the group's performance.[2] As this discussion suggests, it is important to supervise groups.

- Groups are the backbone of organizations.[3] Managers report spending 50 to 90 percent of their time in some form of group activity.

- The current trend is toward participative management. Organizations continue to increase numbers of self-managed autonomous groups. The supervisor of the future will be spending more time as a group facilitator.[4]

- Fran Tarkenton, football quarterback turned management consultant, states that we need people input; technology is useless if people don't feel like part of the team.[5]

- It has long been recognized that group participation in decision making results in better decisions with more commitment to their implementation.[6]

The better you understand groups and their dynamics, the more effective you can be in dealing with groups both as members and leaders.

Why People Join Groups

Each of us belongs to a variety of groups. Yet different people join the same group for different reasons. Often, we have no choice, for example, in choosing our work group. Nonetheless, each group helps us to meet our needs in a variety of ways.

- *Affiliation.* As pointed out in Chapter 11, we all have a need to interact with others. People who like the people they work with have high levels of job satisfaction.

- *Proximity.* We form groups with the people we see often. People who work in same department, live in the same dorm, and so forth hang out together.

- *Attraction.* We are attracted to people who have attitudes, personalities, economic standing, and interests that are similar to ours. We also want to associate with people we find attractive.

- *Activity.* We often join a group because of the activity it performs. This is usually the case at work. The author is a member of the business department (group) because he teaches management classes.

- *Assistance.* We often join groups for the assistance that they provide. This is one of the reasons people join unions. People also join civic groups, like the Rotary Club, in order to develop business contacts.

Teamwork

As mentioned, participative management is becoming increasingly important. **Participative management** *involves the supervisor and employees working together as a team to set objectives and planning how to accomplish them.*

These teams are allowed to be confronting, questioning, and policy making; above all, they are participative. They constantly evaluate those conditions that keep the team from functioning effectively.[7]

The supervisor also uses teamwork to solve problems. Organizations or departments that work together as a team generally outperform others. However, one study found that corporate teamwork is the exception, not the rule.

Nonetheless, there is resistance to participative management. Many managers use the autocratic rather than a participative style, even when the participative style is appropriate.[8] Surprisingly, the greatest resistance to participative management is coming from supervisors. Supervisors don't see the benefits to themselves.[9] They don't realize that leading a team can be more productive than directing individuals. According to one study, supervisors find it hard to decide when to manage participatively.[10] Chapter 5 presented a problem-solving and decision-making model that should help you decide which supervisory style to use in any given situation.

Group Performance

In Chapter 11 the performance formula was presented:

$$performance = ability \times motivation \times resources$$

In that chapter we focused primarily on individual performance. However, the same formula applies to the group or department as a whole. When the department is not performing up to standard, it is much more serious than when the performance of one individual is deficient.[11] Supervisors select employee ability, motivation, or both as the problem when the department performs below standard, but identify resources as the missing component in the performance formula when their own performance level is questioned.

To increase performance, Schermerhorn recommends a performance audit.[12] In the performance audit, the department analyzes how to increase performance by identifying the areas in the performance formula that need to be improved. The department then develops a plan for improving performance. In essence, the supervisor conducts a team-building session (as discussed in Chapter 8) using the performance formula. The supervisor should not be surprised if the group selects resources as the major lack in the performance formula.

In the opening case the group started out being highly motivated with the necessary resources, but it is not performing to Bonnie Sue's expectations. The major component of the performance formula missing is ability. Bonnie Sue is a machine operator. Being a good worker doesn't make an employee a good group leader; it takes training and experience. Management should have trained Bonnie Sue so that she could effectively lead the group. In this chapter you will learn how to be an effective group leader.

CONNECTIONS

1. Why are group leadership skills important to the supervisor?

II. Types of Groups

In this section you will learn about the two types of formal groups—functional groups and task groups.

Functional Groups

Functional groups *are formal groups that perform on an ongoing basis*. Functional groups exist at all levels in the organization. Each work unit or department is a functional group. Each functional group comprises the group's or department's manager, and subordinates reporting to that boss. For example, the marketing, finance, production, and personnel departments are independent functional groups. Each manager in the organization serves as a link between groups. Ideally, all functional groups coordinate their activities through the aid of managers. Rensis Likert calls this the *linking pin role,* as illustrated in Exhibit 15–1.

Functional groups remain in existence indefinitely. The group's objectives and its members may change over time, but its basic functions remain the same. Functional groups tend to deal with routine, recurring tasks.

Thus far our focus has been on functional groups in which the supervisor, with line authority, directs the activities of his or her employees. We will now discuss a different kind of formal group—the task group.

Task Groups

Task groups (or *task forces*) are formal groups sanctioned by the organization to perform a specific function. They are more commonly called *committees.* Task groups have proven to be effective in problem solving.[13] Unlike functional groups, they usually comprise members from different departments. While serving on a task force, members continue to report to their functional groups. Members serve on a task force in addition to their normal work load. They serve until the task is completed or until their time to serve on the committee is ended. Task forces are often created to deal with nonroutine, unique situations, as well as with continuing organizational issues. A task force will either make recommendations to line managers who have the authority to implement the decisions, or the task force is given the authority to implement the decisions. The ad hoc committee and the standing committee are common types of task groups.

Ad Hoc Committees

Ad hoc committees *are temporary task forces formed for a specific purpose.* They are temporary because they exist only until the task is accomplished. Ad hoc committees may be used to select or make recommendations on who to hire (search committees), to select or recommend equipment purchases, or to select or recommend plant locations. Quality circles (Chapter 4) are a form of ad hoc committee. The author served on a budget committee charged with recommending a zero-based budget system to replace the current line-item budget for equipment purchases. Once the committee recommended the system, it was disbanded.

EXHIBIT 15–1   **THE LINKING PIN ROLE**

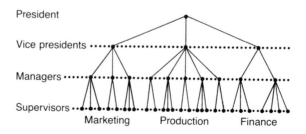

Each triangle represents a functional group, with the manager acting as the linking pin between groups.

With the present trend toward entrepreneurship, venture groups have been increasing in number. *Venture groups* are responsible for planning entry into new profitable business or service areas. They are designed to cut through the red tape inherent in most organizations. Venture groups are composed of a few skilled experts and managers from various functional groups, under one leader. Organizations that use venture groups include Dow Chemical, General Electric, Monsanto, Westinghouse, and Union Carbide; 3M had at least 24 venture groups at one time, and six of its current divisions developed out of these venture groups.

Standing Committees

Standing committees *are permanent groups that exist to deal with continuing organizational issues.* Members often serve a term on such committees. When a term is up, some members are replaced. To keep continuity, committees often replace members on a rotating basis. Corporate boards of directors or trustees are standing committees. They oversee the management of the organization's assets, set or approve policies and objectives, and review progress toward organizational objectives. Many organizations use budget committees to decide or recommend budget allocations. Colleges often have curriculum committees to decide which new courses and majors to offer.

In response to rapid changes in the business environment, over 100 major companies have developed *public policy groups*. These are designed to help management deal more effectively with pressures from the external environment. The role of such groups is to be aware of trends and their effect on the organization while setting policies that will affect the internal environment of the organization.

In the opening case, Bonnie Sue and the members of her group are from the same functional department. However, they are a subgroup of the department and Bonnie Sue is not a supervisor. The group will meet only until the report is complete. Therefore, her group is a task group and an ad hoc committee.

CONNECTIONS

2. Recall a task group you have belonged to. Was it an ad hoc or a standing committee? Give the group's name and purpose.

III. Group Structure

Group structure *is the pattern of interactions that emerge as groups develop.* These interactions are commonly called *group dynamics.* A functional group's structure is heavily influenced by the formal chain of command with leadership clearly defined. Task groups have more influence on how they are structured. Regardless of the type of group, your understanding of group structure and your ability to use this knowledge will affect your ability to manage group performance.

There are six major components of group structure: objectives, size, norms, cohesiveness, status, and roles.

Objectives

To be effective, groups must agree on clear objectives and be committed to achieving them. Although agreement and commitment are separate, they are related. Groups can work on both issues or ignore them simultaneously. As group members participate in defining the objectives, they become committed to attaining them.[14] The leader should allow the group to contribute in setting objectives.[15] The amount of input will depend on the group's capability level. The leader should use the appropriate situational style. Research has shown that acceptance of difficult but specific objectives improves performance.[16]

Implications for Supervisors

Supervisors should be certain that their functional groups have clear objectives and know what the priorities are. As an aid in setting clear objectives, the supervisor should follow the guidelines in Chapter 2 and use Model 2–1. The supervisor must work toward obtaining agreement on and getting a commitment from employees to achieve the group's objectives. One aid in gaining this agreement and commitment from employees is getting the group's input in setting objectives. The extent of participation depends on the group's capability level.

When supervisors serve as committee members rather than leaders, they should try to get the group to set clear objectives that members agree on and are committed to. As a group member, you have an obligation to help the group succeed. If the group begins without setting proper objectives, it will probably not be successful.

Group Size

The ideal group size depends on the group's purpose. For functional groups to work well as a participative team, one expert suggests that the ideal size is 14 or 15.[17] Task groups are often smaller than functional groups. Fact-finding groups can be larger than problem-solving groups. There is no consensus on the ideal size for any group. If the group is too small, it tends to be too cautious; if it is too large, it tends to be too slow.[18]

How Size Affects Group Structure

Group size affects leadership, members, and process. The larger the group, the more formal or autocratic the leadership needs to be to provide direction. Supervisors tend to be more informal and participative when they lead smaller functional groups. Group members are more tolerant of autocratic leadership in large groups. Larger groups tend to inhibit participation. Generally, participation is more equal in groups of around five members. The larger the group, the greater the need for formal standing plans. Groups of 20 or more are too large to get consensus on decisions. Subgroups tend to form at this size.

Implications for Supervisors

Usually supervisors have no say in the size of their functional groups. Nonetheless, the leadership style that is appropriate may depend on group size. Supervisors who chair a committee may be able to select the group size. If so, the chairperson should be sure to get the right people on the committee while trying to keep the size of the group appropriate for the task.

Group Norms

Functional groups generally have standing plans (policies, procedures, and rules) that provide the necessary guidelines for behavior, whereas task groups do not. However, standing plans cannot be complete enough to cover all situations. All groups tend to form their own unwritten rules about how things are done, or norms. Norms are not discussed and agreed upon by the group. If this were to happen they would be standing plans rather than norms. **Norms** *are the group's shared expectations concerning members' behavior.* Norms determine what should or must be done for the group to maintain consistent and desirable behavior.

How Norms Develop

Norms are developed spontaneously as group members interact. All group members have cultural values and past experience. Their beliefs, attitudes, knowledge, and so forth influence the type of norms developed. Norms can change over time to meet the needs of the group. Norms are developed out of the group's routine. Comments such as, "Let's hear everyone's solution to the problem before selecting one," may result in a group norm. The comment becomes a norm only if group members develop a shared expectation that this behavior is desirable. If the group goes along with it, the suggestion becomes a norm.

How Groups Enforce Norms

If a group member does not follow the norms, other members will try to enforce compliance. In the previous example, if a member does not volunteer to give a solution to the problem, other members may directly request a solution. The group may refuse to select a solution until all members have made a suggestion. Other ways groups enforce norms include ridicule, ostracism, and physical abuse. For example, if a group has a norm concerning performance levels and a member breaks it by producing too much or too little, other group members may call the person names, ignore the person, or threaten or actually use physical actions to change the person's production level.

Implications for Supervisors

Group norms can be positive, helping the group meet its objectives, or they can be negative, hindering the group. Supervisors should be aware of their group's norms. They should work at developing and maintaining positive norms while trying to eliminate negative norms. Supervisors should confront groups concerning negative norms and try to work out solutions to the satisfaction of everyone.

Group Cohesiveness

The extent to which a group will abide by and enforce its norms depends upon its degree of cohesiveness. **Group cohesiveness** *is the attractiveness of the group to its members.* The more the group sticks together as a team, the greater its cohesiveness. The more desirable group membership is, the more willing the members are to behave according to the group's norms. For example, some group members take drugs, and the group develops a norm of drug taking. To be accepted by the group, other members will behave in ways they don't really agree with. In this case, the peer pressure to take drugs wins out.

Factors Influencing Cohesiveness

Objectives: The stronger the agreement on and commitment to the achievement of the group's objectives, the greater the cohesiveness of the group.

Size: Generally, the smaller the group, the greater the cohesiveness. The larger the group, the more difficult it becomes to gain a consensus on objectives and norms. Three to nine members seems to be a good size for group cohesiveness.

Homogeneity: Generally, the more similar the group members are, the greater the cohesiveness. People tend to be attracted to others who are similar to themselves.

Participation: Generally, the more equal the level of participation among members, the greater is the group's cohesiveness. Groups dominated by one or a few members tend to be less cohesive.

Competition: Competition may affect cohesiveness in one of two ways. If the group focuses on intragroup competition and everyone tries to outdo each other, there will be little cohesiveness. If the focus is intergroup competition, the members tend to pull together as a team to beat their rivals. It is surprising how much a group can accomplish when no one cares who gets the credit.[19]

Success: The more successful a group is at achieving its objectives, the more cohesive it tends to become. Success tends to breed cohesiveness, which, in turn, breeds more success. People want to be on the winning team.

How Cohesiveness Affects Group Performance

Many studies have concluded that cohesive groups tend to be more successful at achieving their objectives with more satisfaction. Members of cohesive groups tend to miss work less often, are more trusting and cooperative, and have less tension and hostility.

One of the most highly regarded studies of this phenomenon was conducted by S. E. Seashore. Seashore studied the relationship between cohesiveness and productivity in 228 functional groups in a unionized plant that manufactured heavy machinery. He studied each group to determine its degree of cohesiveness and acceptance of management's standards of productivity. The results of Seashore's study, which have recently been substantiated by Robert Keller, reveal that cohesiveness is associated with performance.[20] Groups with the highest level of productivity were highly cohesive and accepted management's standard of productivity. Groups with the lowest levels of productivity were also highly cohesive, but rejected management's standard of productivity. The latter groups set and enforced their own standards. The groups with intermediate levels of productivity were not cohesive, irrespective of their acceptance of management's standards. The widest variance in individual performance was among members of groups with low cohesiveness. These groups tend to be more tolerant of nonconformity with group norms.

Implications for Supervisors

Supervisors should strive to develop cohesive groups that accept management's standards for productivity. Participation helps the group develop cohesiveness while it builds agreement and commitment concerning its objectives. Coaching, discussed in Chapter 12, encourages cohesiveness.[21] Although some intragroup competition may be helpful, supervisors should focus primarily on intergroup competition, which will develop a cohesive winning team and, in turn, motivate the group to higher levels of success.

Status within the Group

As group members interact they develop respect for one another. The more respect, prestige, and influence a group member has, the higher his or her status within the group. **Status** *is a member's rank within the group.*

Status is based on several factors, including a member's job title, wage or salary, seniority, knowledge or expertise, interpersonal skills, appearance, education, race, age, and sex. Status within a group also depends on the group's objectives, norms, and cohesiveness. Members who conform to the group's norms have higher status than members who do not. However, a group is also more willing to overlook it when a member with high status breaks a norm. Members with high status also have more influence on the development of the group's norms. Lower-status members tend to copy the behavior and standards of members with high status.

How Status Affects Group Performance

Members with high status significantly affect the group's performance. In a functional group, the supervisor usually has the highest status. The supervisor's ability to manage affects the group's performance. Employees with high status also affect performance. If these members support positive norms and high productivity, chances are the group will, too. As stated in Chapter 6, the informal leader has a great deal of influence on the group.

Another important factor influencing group performance is status congruence. *Status congruence* is members' acceptance of and satisfaction with their status in the group. Members who are not satisfied with their status may not be active participants in the group. They may physically or mentally escape from the group and not perform to their full potential. Or they may cause group conflict as they fight for higher status. Leadership struggles may go on for long periods and may never be resolved. Regardless of whether the group member who is dissatisfied decides on flight or fight, the end result is the same—lower performance levels for the group.

Implications for Supervisors

To be effective, the supervisor needs to have high status within the functional group. To achieve this, the supervisor must perform the five functions of supervision well and have the skills discussed in this book thus far. The supervisor should also maintain good relations with the group, particularly with the high-status informal leader or leaders to ensure that positive norms and objectives are endorsed. The supervisor should also be aware of conflicts that may be the result of lack of status congruence, and use the conflict management techniques discussed in Chapter 8.

Roles within the Group

As a group works toward achieving its objectives, it has to perform certain functions. In the course of doing this, group members develop roles. **Roles** *are shared expectations of how group members will fulfill the requirements of their position.*

Members develop their roles based on their own expectations, organizational expectations, and the group's expectations. Individuals come to the organization with expectations about how they should fill their positions. They subsequently learn about the organization's expectations through orientation, job descriptions, and managerial supervision. When interacting with the group, the individual learns about the group's expectations of him or her—norms. As employees internalize the expectations of these three sources, they develop their roles.

People often have multiple roles within the same position. For example, a professor may have the roles of teacher, researcher, writer, consultant, adviser, and committee member. Our roles also expand outside the workplace. The professor may also be a family member, belong to professional or civic organizations, and have different circles of friends, all of which may have very different expectations.

Classifying Group Roles

When supervisors interact with the employees, they can use directive behavior, supportive behavior, or both. This is also true of group members as they interact. However, when used to describe groups these interactions are commonly called *task roles* and *maintenance roles.*[22] A third category, *self-interest roles,* is often added.

Task Roles: **Task roles** *are the things members do and say that directly aid in the accomplishment of the group's objectives.* Task roles can be broken down into the following parts:

- Objective clarifiers ensure that everyone understands the objective.
- Planners determine how the objective will be met.
- Organizers assign and coordinate the resources.
- Leaders influence members through direction as the task is performed.
- Controllers take corrective action to ensure that the objective is achieved.

Maintenance Roles: **Maintenance roles** *are the things members do and say to develop and sustain the group structure.* Maintenance roles can be classified as follows:

- Formers get the members involved and committed to the group.
- Consensus seekers get members' input and agreement on group decisions.
- Harmonizers help group members resolve their conflicts so that they do not interfere with group performance.
- Gatekeepers see that appropriate norms are developed and enforced.
- Encouragers are supportive, friendly, and responsive to the needs of the members.
- Compromisers get members to modify their positions in the interest of group cohesiveness.

Self-Interest Roles: **Self-interest roles** *are the things members do and say in order to meet their own needs or objectives at the expense of the group.* Self-interest roles can be classified as follows:

- Aggressors deflate others' status through criticism or by putting members and their ideas down.
- Blockers resist the group's efforts and prevent it from achieving its objectives.
- Recognition seekers try to take credit for the group's accomplishments.
- Withdrawers are physically or mentally involved in personal matters rather than in concerns of the group.

How Roles Affect Group Performance

To be effective, a group must have members who play task roles and maintenance roles while minimizing self-interest roles. Groups that have only task performers will experience performance problems because conflict is not dealt with effectively. On the other hand, groups that do not have members playing task roles will not get the job done. Any group that has self-interest roles being played will not produce to its fullest potential.

Implications for Supervisors

The supervisor should be aware of the roles group members play. If the members are not playing the task or maintenance role required at a given time, the supervisor should play the role. The supervisor should also make the group aware of the need to play these roles and to minimize self-interest roles. In the next section we will discuss group development and the supervisor's use of task and maintenance roles as the group develops.

In the opening case, the objective is fairly clear, group size is adequate, and cohesiveness, status, and roles are not major problems. Kirt has been discrediting others' ideas, and others have followed his lead. A negative norm has developed that needs to be addressed by Bonnie Sue to ensure success of the group. Bonnie Sue can begin the next meeting by stating that the norm has developed and explain how it is destructive to the group. She can interrupt when Kirt and others put ideas down by reminding the group to be positive. The group can also discuss whether there are other negative norms that should be stopped. In addition, they can discuss the development of positive norms that can help the group do a better job. Carl is playing a task role for the group. Shelby is playing a maintenance role for the group. And Kirt is playing a self-interest role. How to handle Kirt, Shelby, and Carl as problem individuals will be discussed near the end of the chapter.

To summarize, effective groups should have clear objectives with agreement and commitment to these objectives by its members, appropriate group size to achieve its objectives, positive norms, cohesiveness, status congruence, and members who play task and maintenance roles while minimizing self-interest roles. Developing effective group dynamics that meets the needs of the individuals and the group or organization creates a win-win situation for all parties. See Exhibit 15–2 for an illustration of the six components of group structure.

LEARNING OBJECTIVE

2. Explain the six components of group structure and their effect on group performance.

EXHIBIT 15–2   **GROUP STRUCTURE COMPONENTS**

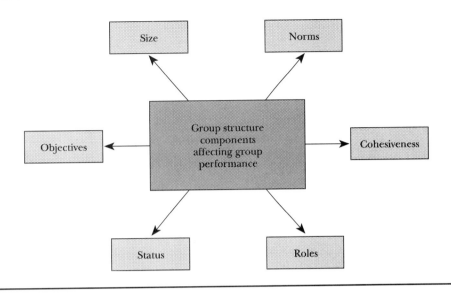

For questions 3 through 9, recall a group you have belonged to. It may be a functional, task, or informal group or team. If you will be doing Skill-Building Exercise 15–1, do not use your group in this class for your example.

3. Did the group members agree on and were they committed to clear objectives? Explain your answer.

4. How large was the group? Should it have been larger or smaller? Why?

5. List at least three of the group's norms. Were they positive or negative? How did the group enforce these norms?

6. Is the group cohesive? How did the factors listed in the text influence cohesiveness? How did the level of cohesiveness affect the group's performance? Explain your answers.

7. Rank each group member, including yourself, in order of status in the group. What are some of the characteristics that gave these people their high or low status?

8. Using your list from question 7, identify the major roles played by each group member, including yourself.

9. What could have been done to improve the group's structure? Explain in detail.

IV. Group Development and Situational Supervision

In this section you will learn about the stages of group development and selection of the appropriate supervisory style to match the group's level of development.

Stages of Group Development

Every group is unique; its dynamics change over time. However, all groups go through the same stages as they grow from a collection of individuals to a smoothly operating, effective team. The stages groups go through as they develop have been the subject of research. One of the most recent and thorough studies was completed by R. B. Lacoursiere. He developed a five-stage model that incorporates most of what is known about group development.[23] The five stages are orientation, dissatisfaction, resolution, production, and termination. Although each stage is described as separate and distinct, we should realize that some elements of most group development stages (GDS) can be found in every other stage.

**Stage 1.
Orientation**

This stage is characterized by low development level (D-1), high commitment, and low competence. When people first form a group, they tend to have a moderate to high commitment to it. However, because members have not worked together, they do not have the competence to achieve the task. When first interacting, members tend to be anxious about how they will fit in, what will be required of them, what the group will be like, what the purpose of the group is, and so forth. When task groups are started, this stage is very apparent. Even though functional groups are rarely composed entirely of new members, some functional groups never go beyond this stage. They never resolve the anxiety issues and progress to the next stage of development. If roles and group objectives are never clearly stated and understood by members, it is difficult to develop as a group.

**Stage 2.
Dissatisfaction**

This stage is characterized by moderate development level (D-2), lower commitment, and some competence. As members work together, they tend to become dissatisfied with the group. They start to ask why they are members, whether the group is going to accomplish anything, why other group members don't do what is expected, and so forth. Often the task is more complex and difficult than anticipated; members become frustrated and feel incompetent. However, the group does develop some competence. Groups in this stage of development are demoralized and have little motivation and low productivity.

**Stage 3.
Resolution**

High development level (D-3), variable commitment, and high competence are characteristic at this stage. With time, members resolve the differences between initial expectations and realities in relation to objectives, tasks, skills, and so forth. As members gain competence, they become more satisfied with the group. Relationships develop that satisfy group members' affiliation needs. Members learn to work together as they develop a group structure with acceptable norms and cohesiveness. Commitment can vary as the group interacts. The group needs to resolve conflict or changes. If the group does not deal effectively with structural issues, it may regress to stage 2, or the group may plateau, fluctuating in commitment and competence. If the group is successful at developing a positive structure, it will move to the next stage.

**Stage 4.
Production**

Outstanding development level (D-4), high commitment, and high competence occur at this stage. Commitment and competence do not fluctuate much. The group works as a team with high levels of satisfaction of affiliation needs. The group maintains a positive structure. Members are very productive, and this helps lead to positive feelings. The group structure may change with time, but the issues are resolved quickly and easily; members are open with each other.

EXHIBIT 15-3   **STAGES OF GROUP DEVELOPMENT**

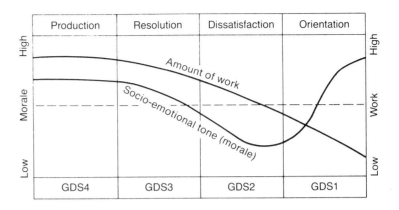

Stage 5.
Termination

In functional groups, the termination stage is not reached unless there is some drastic reorganization. However, it does occur in task groups. During this stage, members experience emotions about leaving the group. If the group has progressed through all four stages of development, the members usually feel sad. However, if the group did not progress through all stages, a feeling of relief is common. The group may talk about its termination over a period of time or only at the last meeting. This varies depending on how meaningful the relationship was and whether members will be seeing each other after the group terminates.

The two key variables identified at each stage of group development are *competence* and *commitment*. The two do not progress in the same manner. Competence increases through each of the first four stages, whereas commitment is high in stage 1, drops in stage 2, and rises through stages 3 and 4. This is illustrated in Exhibit 15–3.

In the opening case, Bonnie Sue's committee is in stage 2, dissatisfaction. The group has had a decrease in commitment and an increase in competence. The group needs to resolve the dissatisfaction to progress to stages 3 and 4 of development. Being an ad hoc committee, the group will go through stage 5, termination, in three weeks. In the next section, you will learn how Bonnie Sue can help the group develop to stages 3 and 4.

LEARNING
OBJECTIVE

3. Describe the five stages of group development.

Situational Supervision of Groups

Situational supervision, discussed in Chapter 1, is designed for use with functional groups. The following section is designed for use with task groups, although the concepts can be used with functional groups as well.

Situational supervision can be applied to the stages of group development.[24] A different supervisory style is needed in order to help the group perform effectively at each stage in its development and progress to the next level.

As stated in the last section, when supervisors interact with their groups, they can perform task roles, maintenance roles, or both. Below, we will specify which role or roles the supervisor should play at the different stages of group development.

- *Group development stage 1, orientation—low development (high commitment/low competence, D-1)—uses the autocratic supervisory style (high task/low maintenance, S-A).* When a task group first comes together, the supervisor needs to help the group clarify its objectives to provide the direction to be sure the group gets off to a good start. Because the members are committed to joining the group, the supervisor needs to help the group develop its competence.

When supervisors work with their functional groups, they must be sure that the group has clear objectives and that members know their roles. If the group does not, or when there are complex changes, the supervisor must provide the appropriate task behavior.

- *Group development stage 2, dissatisfaction—moderate development (lower commitment/ some competence, D-2)—uses the consultative supervisory style (high task/high maintenance, S-C).* When task and functional groups know their objectives and their roles are clear, its members become dissatisfied. When morale drops, the supervisor needs to focus on maintenance roles to encourage members to continue to work toward the objectives. The supervisor should help the members meet their needs as they develop the appropriate group structure. At the same time, the supervisor needs to continue to provide the task behavior necessary to help the group develop its level of competence.

- *Group development stage 3, resolution—high development (variable commitment/high competence, D-3—uses the participative supervisory style (low task/high maintenance, S-P).* When the task and functional group members know their objectives and their roles are clear, there is little need to provide task behavior; they know how to do the job.

  When commitment varies, it is usually due to some problem in the group's dynamics, such as a conflict or a member's losing interest. What the supervisor needs to do is focus on the maintenance behavior to get the group through the issues it faces. If the supervisor continues to provide task directives that are not needed, the group can become dissatisfied and regress or plateau at this level.

  Most supervisors are effective at providing the task roles needed by the group. However, there tends to be a weakness in supervisors' ability to provide the proper maintenance roles. Supervisors tend to be trained to be task oriented, to get the job done. They do not tend to be trained to focus on the process of how the job gets done, and the dynamics that help and hurt the group as it works together. Supervisors who can develop the type of group structure discussed in the first section of this chapter will develop groups to the third or fourth levels. Supervisors who cannot develop an effective group structure will have groups that plateau on the second level of group development. Motivating employees and developing and maintaining human relations is an ongoing process. Using the participative style helps the members to develop their commitment, which, in turn, affects their competence.

- *Group development stage 4, production—outstanding development (high commitment/ high competence, D-4)—uses the laissez-faire supervisory style (low task/low maintenance, S-L).* Groups that develop to this stage have members who play the appropriate task and maintenance roles; the supervisor does not need to play either role, unless there is a problem.

  Outstanding development is more common among task groups than it is among functional groups. Supervisors who develop their functional groups to this level are a small minority. As a supervisor, you should determine your group's level of development and strive to bring it to the next stage of development.

LEARNING OBJECTIVE

4. Identify each of the four group situational supervisory styles to use with a group, based on its stage of development.

In the opening case, Bonnie Sue's committee is in stage 2, dissatisfaction. Bonnie Sue needs to play both task and maintenance roles to help the group progress to stages 3 and 4. Focusing on solving the negative norm of putting each other's ideas down works on both task and maintenance. Bonnie Sue also needs to provide stronger leadership in the areas of completing meeting assignments and making Kirt, Shelby, and Carl more productive. You will learn how in the next section.

Steps 1 through 3 of Model 15–1 are designed for use with Skill-Building Exercise 15–2. The four stages of group development are summarized, along with their appropriate situational supervisory styles.

MODEL 15–1

SITUATIONAL SUPERVISION OF GROUPS

Step 1. For each situation determine the group's level of development. Place the number 1, 2, 3, or 4 on the D _____ lines.

Step 2. Identify each supervisory style of all four alternatives A through D. Place the letters A, C, P, or L on the S _____ lines.

Step 3. Select the appropriate supervisory style for the group's level of development. Circle the letter A, B, C, or D.

Group Development Level (D)

D-1 Low development

High commitment/low competence

Members come to the group committed but they cannot perform with competence.

D-2 Moderate development

Low commitment/some competence

Members have become dissatisfied with the group. They have started to develop competence but are frustrated with results.

D-3 High development

Variable commitment/high competence

Commitment changes over time while production remains relatively constant.

D-4 Outstanding development

High commitment/high competence

Commitment remains constantly high and so does production.

Supervisory Styles or Roles(s)

S-A Autocratic

High task/low maintenance

Provide direction so that the group has clear objectives and members know their roles. Make the decision for the group.

S-C Consultative

High task/high maintenance

Continue to direct the group so that it develops task ability. Provide maintenance to regain commitment as the group structure takes place. Include members' input in decisions.

S-P Participative

Low task/high maintenance

Provide little direction. Focus on developing an effective group structure. Have the group participate in decision making.

S-L Laissez-faire

Low task/low maintenance

Members provide their own task and maintenance roles. The supervisor is a group member. Allow the group to make its own decisions.

CONNECTIONS

10. Using the same group as for questions 3 through 9, identify the group's stage of development and the leader's situational supervisory style. Did the leader use the appropriate style? Explain.

V. Meeting Leadership Skills

One aspect of functioning within a group is meetings. Most supervisors must attend meetings either as a member or a group leader. There are more complaints than favorable comments about meetings. Many consider meetings to be the biggest time waster in their jobs.[25] The most common complaints are that there are too many meetings, they are too long, and they are unproductive.[26] The success or failure of any meeting rests primarily with the leader. Better skills at managing them can lead to more productive meetings. This section is meant to improve your skills in this area.

Planning Meetings

Preparation for any meeting has a direct effect on the outcome. Unprepared leaders conduct unproductive meetings. There are at least five areas where preparation is needed: setting objectives, selecting participants and making assignments, setting the agenda, determining the time and place, and providing leadership. Before the meeting, everyone who will attend should receive a written copy of this plan.

Objectives

What the meeting is meant to accomplish should be determined beforehand.[27] The single greatest mistake made by those who call meetings is that they have no clear idea of the purpose. Leaders should state what they want to have happen as a result of the meeting.[28] Before calling a meeting, you should clearly define its purpose and objective. The only exception is regularly scheduled information dissemination or brainstorming meetings.[29]

Participants and Assignments

Before calling a meeting, the leader should decide who is qualified to attend.[30] Does the full group or department need to be there? Should some specialist from outside be invited to provide input? If controversial issues will be discussed, it may be wise to meet with key members of the group beforehand.

Participants should be told in advance whether they have to prepare for the meeting (read material, do some research, make a report, and so forth). Adequate advance notice should be given.

Agenda

Before the meeting, the leader should tell participants what will take place. The agenda lets the members know what is expected and how the meeting will progress.[31] It is helpful to set a time limit for each item on the agenda.[32]

Agenda items should be placed in order of priority. If the meeting does not cover every item, the least important carry forward. The author has attended too many meetings where the leader puts all the so-called "quick" items first. The group gets bogged down and either rushes through the important items or puts them off until later.

It is helpful to let members give their reports early in the meeting. Otherwise these participants may get anxious and preoccupied about their reports. Once it's over, they are more relaxed and can become more involved in the meeting. It is also frustrating to prepare a report, only to be told, "We'll get to it next time." This sends the message that the member and the report are not important.

Date, Time, and Place

Try to determine which days and times are best for meetings; get members' input. Members tend to be more alert early in the day. The maximum length a meeting should run is 90 minutes.[33] Select an adequate place for the meeting. See to the physical comfort of the group.[34] Be sure seating allows eye contact in small discussion groups, and be sure to allow enough time so that members do not have to rush.[35] If reservations are needed for the meeting place, make them far enough in advance.

With advances in technology, telephone conferences and meetings are becoming quite common. Video conferences are also gaining popularity. These techniques save travel costs and time, and they result in better and quicker decisions. Companies using video conferencing include Arco, Boeing, Aetna, Ford, IBM, TRW, and Xerox.[36]

Leadership

The leader should determine the group's level of development and plan to provide the appropriate task or maintenance behavior. It may even be necessary to handle

EXHIBIT 15–4   **WRITTEN MEETING PLAN**

Time: (date, day, place, beginning and ending times.)

Objectives: (a statement of the objective of the meeting.)

Participants and Assignments: (list each participant's name and assignment, if any. If all members have the same assignment, make one statement describing it.)

Agenda: (list each item to be covered in priority order with the approximate time it will take to cover the item.)

---

each item on the agenda differently. For example, some items may simply call for disseminating information, others will require a discussion, some may require a vote, and some may require a report from a member. An effective way to develop group members' ability is to rotate the role of moderator or leader for each meeting.[37] However, this depends on the group's level of development.

The Written Plan

The leader should distribute copies of the plan to each person who will attend the meeting. Exhibit 15–4 shows the recommended format for this meeting plan.

Conducting Meetings

At the first meeting, the group is in the orientation stage. The leader should use the task role. Members should also be given the opportunity to spend some time getting to know one another. Introductions set the stage for subsequent interactions.[38] If members find that their social needs will not be met, they may quickly become dissatisfied. A simple technique is to start with introductions and then move on to the group's purpose, objectives, and members' roles. A break can be planned that enables members to interact informally.

Once the group is established, meetings should be conducted following the format described. Begin the meetings on time. Waiting for late members penalizes those who are on time and develops a norm for coming late.

The Three Parts of Each Meeting

Each meeting should cover three items:

1. *Objectives.* Review progress to date, the group's objectives, and the purpose/objective of the specific meeting. If minutes from the last meeting were recorded, they should be approved at the beginning of the current meeting. A secretary should be appointed to take minutes.

2. *Agenda.* Cover the items on the agenda. Try to keep to the approximate times, but be flexible. If the discussion is constructive and members need more time, give it to them. If the discussion is more of a distracting argument, move ahead.

3. *Summary and review of assignments.* End the meeting on time. The leader should summarize what took place. Were the meeting's objectives achieved? Review all assignments given during the meeting. Get a commitment from each member concerning his or her assignment. The secretary or leader should make a record of all assignments. If there is no accountability and follow-up on assignments, members may not complete them.

Leadership and Group Structure

As stated in the last section, the leadership needed changes with the group's level of development. The leader must be sure to provide the task or maintenance roles needed.

The leader is responsible for helping the group develop an effective structure. The leader must focus on the group's structure as it performs the task and make the group aware of how its structure affects the performance and commitment of the group. Team building is an effective technique for helping the group develop structure.[39]

CONNECTIONS

11. In the task group selected in question 2, did the leader plan for meetings by stating objectives, identifying participants and their assignments, making an agenda, and stating the time and place of the meeting? Did the leader provide a written meeting plan to the members before the meeting? Explain your answers and state what you would do differently if you were the leader.

12. Recall a meeting you have attended. How would you have conducted the meeting differently to make it more productive? Explain in detail.

Handling Problem Members in a Meeting

As group members work together, personality types emerge, some of which can affect group performance, especially at meetings. The silent, talkative, wandering, bored, and argumentative personality types may prove to be problem members of the groups you supervise.[40]

Silent: To be fully effective, all group members should participate.[41] If a member is silent, the group does not reap the benefits of his or her input.

It is the leader's responsibility to encourage the silent member to participate without being obvious or overdoing it. One technique the leader can use is *rotation*. All members take turns giving their input. This is generally less threatening than directly calling on members. The rotation method is not appropriate all the time. To build up the silent member's confidence, call on this person with questions he or she can easily answer. When you believe silent members have convictions, ask these members to express them.

If you are a silent type, try to participate more often. Know when to stand up for your views. Silent types generally do not make good supervisors.

Talkative: Talkers have something to say about everything. They like to dominate the discussion. However, if they do dominate, the other members do not participate. The talker can cause intragroup problems.

It is the leader's responsibility to slow talkers down, not to shut them up. Do not let them dominate the group. Rotation is also effective with talkers because they have to wait their turn. If you're not using rotation, gently interrupt the talker and present your own ideas or call on other members to present their ideas. Prefacing questions with statements such as, "Let's give those who have not answered yet a chance," can also slow the talker down.

If you tend to be a talker, try to slow down. Give others a chance to speak for themselves. Remember, good supervisors develop their employees' ability.

Wandering: The wanderer will get the group off the agenda. Wanderers often like to complain.

The leader is responsible for keeping the group on track. If the wanderer wants to socialize, cut it off. Be kind, thank the member for his or her contribution, and then throw a question out to the group to get it back on track. However, if the wanderer has a complaint that is legitimate and can be resolved, allow the group to discuss it. Issues involving group structure should be addressed and resolved. If this is not possible, get the group back on track. Griping without resolving anything lessens morale and commitment. If the wanderer complains about issues that can't be resolved, make statements such as, "We may be underpaid, but we have no control over our pay. Complaining will not get us a raise; let's get back to the issue at hand."

If you are a wanderer, try to be aware of your behavior and stay on the subject at hand.

Bored: Your group may have one or more members who are not interested. The bored person may be preoccupied with other issues, and not pay attention to or participate in the meeting. The bored member may also feel superior and wonder why the group is spending so much time on the obvious.

The leader is responsible for keeping members motivated. This is not an easy job. Assign the bored member a task such as recording ideas. Call on bored members; bring them into the group. If you allow them to sit back, things may get worse and others may decide not to participate, either.

If you tend to be bored, try to find ways to motivate yourself. Work at becoming more patient and in control of behavior that can have negative effects on other members.

Argumentative: Like the talker, the arguer likes to be the center of attention. The devil's advocate approach may be helpful for developing and selecting alternative courses of action, but the argumentative employee enjoys arguing for the sake of arguing, rather than for helping the group. They turn things into win-lose situations and cannot stand losing.

The leader should resolve conflict, but not in an argumentative way. Do not get into an argument with arguers; that is exactly what they want to have happen. If an argument starts, bring others into the discussion. If it is personal, cut it off. Personal attacks only hurt the group. Keep the discussion moving on target.

If you tend to be an arguer, strive to convey your views in a debate format, not as an argument. Listen to others' views and be willing to change if they have better ideas.

Whenever you work in a group, do not embarrass, intimidate, or argue with any members, no matter how they provoke you. If you do, the result will make a martyr of them and a bully of you. If you have serious problems with members who do not respond to these techniques, confront them individually, away from the rest of the group. Get them to agree to work in a cooperative way.

In the opening case, Bonnie Sue's meetings lacked specific assignments. She needs to use more directive leadership and assign tasks to specific members to complete outside the meetings. Recall that the problem members in Bonnie Sue's group were Carl, the talker; Shelby, the wanderer; and Kirt, the arguer. Bonnie Sue needs to use her leadership skills to slow Carl down, to keep Shelby on topic, and to keep Kirt from fighting with others and resolve conflicts quickly.

LEARNING OBJECTIVE

6. Identify the five types of group problem members and explain how to handle them.

CONNECTIONS

13. Identify problem members at a meeting you attended. Was the leader effective in handling them? What would you have done to make them more productive members? Explain in detail.

VI. Putting It All Together

When putting it all together, you realize that people join groups to meet their needs. To be more specific, people join groups for affiliation, proximity, attraction, activity, and assistance. The types of groups people join are functional, task, and

EXHIBIT 15–5   **FACTORS INFLUENCING GROUPS**

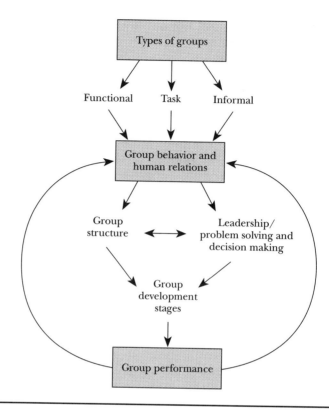

informal. Organizations use groups to meet performance objectives. As the people in a group behave and interact, they develop a group structure. The group structure, leadership, and ability to solve problems and make decisions are major determinants of the group's stage of development. The more effective the group structure, leadership, and ability to solve problems and make decisions, the higher the stage of development. And the higher the stage of development, the greater the level of performance of the group. The group's performance, in turn, affects its behavior and human relations. Have you ever noticed that behavior and human relations of the same group or team changes when it meets objectives (wins), and when it doesn't (loses)?

When you lead groups in a manner that meets the needs of the individuals while attaining the performance objective of the group, you create a win-win situation.

See Exhibit 15–5 for an illustration of how the factors discussed in this chapter influence groups.

When reading Exhibit 15–5, did you understand that the type of group affects behavior, human relations, and performance? The group's behavior and human relations are influenced by the group's structure, leadership, and its problem-solving and decision-making practices as it progresses through stages of development. These, in turn, affect the group's performance. The group's performance also influences group behavior and human relations because the process is an ongoing one; it does not have a clear starting and ending point.

Learning to develop group dynamics, group leadership, and group problem-solving and decision-making skills will help you become a more effective group participant and leader.

REVIEW

Select one or more methods: (1) fill in the missing key terms from memory; (2) match the key terms from the end of the review with their definitions below; (3) copy the key terms in order from the key terms at the beginning of the chapter.

A _____ is two or more people interacting to achieve an objective. The current trend is toward more _____ , which involves the supervisor and employees working together to set objectives and planning how to accomplish them. The performance formula (performance = ability × motivation × resources) also applies to groups. To improve performance, the supervisor can determine which area to work on.

There are two types of formal groups: _____ perform on an ongoing basis; and task groups. Task groups usually comprise members from different functional areas. The two most common task groups are _____ , temporary task forces formed for a specific purpose; and _____ , permanent groups that exist to deal with continuing organizational issues.

_____ is the pattern of interactions that emerge as groups develop. The six components of group structure are objectives, group size, group norms, group cohesiveness, status within the group, and roles within the group. The group should agree on and be committed to clear objectives. The optimal size of a group varies with the group's purpose.

_____ are the group's shared expectations concerning members' behavior. _____ is the attractiveness of the group to its members. Cohesive groups with positive norms tend to have the highest production levels. _____ is a member's rank within the group. _____ are shared expectations of how group members will fulfill the requirements of their position. Group roles can be classified as _____ , the things members do and say that directly aid in the accomplishment of the group's objectives; _____ , the things members do and say to develop and sustain the group structure; and _____ , the things members do and say in order to meet their own needs or objectives at the expense of the group.

The five stages of group development, with the situational supervisory style appropriate to each, are as follows: stage 1, orientation, low development (D-1), autocratic; stage 2, dissatisfaction, moderate development (D-2), consultative; stage 3, resolution, high development (D-3), participative; stage 4, production, outstanding development (D-4), laissez faire; stage 5, termination (this happens in task groups, not usually in functional groups).

Five things should be planned before a meeting: objectives, selection of participants and determination of assignments, agenda, time and place for the meeting, and leadership. Those who will attend should get a copy of the plan before the meeting. Review objectives, go over the agenda items, and summarize and review the assignments at each meeting. The meeting's leader should help the group develop an effective structure and use the leadership style appropriate to the group's level of development. Group leaders may encounter problem members, such as the silent member, whom the leader should get to participate; the talker, whom the leader should slow down; the wanderer, whom the leader should keep on the topic; the bored member, whom the leader should motivate; and the arguer, whom the leader should keep from arguing.

The type of group and its structure, leadership, problem-solving and decision-making ability, and stage of development affect its behavior, human relations, and performance.

KEY TERMS

ad hoc committees

functional groups

group

group cohesiveness

group structure

maintenance roles

norms

participative management

roles

self-interest roles

standing committees

status

task roles

REFERENCES

1. Donald Carew, Eunice Carew, and Kenneth Blanchard, "Group Development and Situational Leadership: A Model for Managing Groups," *Training and Development Journal*, June 1986, p. 46.

2. Karen Brown, "Explaining Group Poor Performance: An Attributional Analysis," *Academy of Management Review*, January 1984, p. 54.

3. Carew, Carew, and Blanchard, "Group Development and Situational Leadership," p. 46.

4. Kenneth Hill, Steven Kerr, and Laurie Broedling, "The First-Line Supervisor: Phasing Out or Here to Stay?" *Academy of Management Review*, January 1986, p. 110.

5. "Tarkenton on Team Building," *Management Solutions*, October 1986, p. 30.

6. Ichak Adizes and Efrain Turban, "An Innovative Approach to Group Decision Making," *Personnel*, April 1985, p. 45.

7. E. M. Parnell, "Self-Examination—The Achilles' Heel of Teams," *Supervision,* February 1987, p. 6.

8. "Corporate Teamwork?" *The Wall Street Journal,* January 20, 1987, p. 1.

9. Janice Klein, "Why Supervisors Resist Employee Involvement," *Harvard Business Review,* September–October 1984, p. 87.

10. W. Matthew Juechter, "The Pros and Cons of Participative Management," *Management Review,* September 1982, p. 47.

11. Brown, "Explaining Group Poor Performance," p. 54.

12. John Schermerhorn, "Team Development for High Performance Management," *Training and Development Journal,* November 1986, p. 40.

13. William Altier, "Task Forces: An Effective Management Tool," *Management Review,* February 1987, p. 52.

14. David Bradford, *Group Dynamics* (Chicago: SRA, 1984), p. 23.

15. "Tarkenton on Team Building," p. 31.

16. Paul Buller and Cecil Bell, "Effects of Team Building on Goal Setting and Productivity: A Field Experiment," *Academy of Management Journal,* June 1986, p. 307.

17. Patricia Galagan, "Work Teams that Work," *Training and Development Journal,* November 1986, p. 34.

18. Altier, "Task Forces," p. 54.

19. "Tarkenton on Team Building," p. 31.

20. Robert Keller, "Predictors of the Performance of Project Groups in R&D Organizations," *Academy of Management Journal,* December 1986, pp. 715–26.

21. Ibid., p. 715.

22. Philip Harris, "Building a High-Performance Team," *Training and Development Journal,* April 1986, p. 28.

23. R. B. Lacoursiere, *The Life Cycle of Groups: Group Development Stage Theory* (New York: Human Service Press, 1980).

24. Carew, Carew, and Blanchard, "Group Development and Situational Leadership," p. 48.

25. Joan Hamann, "Turning Meetings into All-Win Situations," *Personnel Administrator,* June 1986, p. 62.

26. Arthur Miller and Michael Popowniak, "Meetings: How Do Yours Rate?" *Industry Week,* April 6, 1987, p. 38.

27. "Tarkenton on Team Building," p. 30.

28. Hamann, "Turning Meetings into All-Win Situations," p. 63.

29. M. R. Hansen, "Better Supervision from A to W," *Supervisory Management,* August 1985, p. 36.

30. Altier, "Task Forces," p. 56.

31. Colleen Cooper and Mary Ploor, "The Challenges that Make or Break a Group," *Training and Development Journal,* April 1986, p. 31.

32. Miller and Popowniak, "Meetings: How Do Yours Rate?" p. 38.

33. Ibid.

34. Hamann, "Turning Meetings into All-Win Situations," p. 63.

35. Cooper and Ploor, "The Challenges that Make or Break a Group," p. 33.

36. Lad Kuzela, "Communications: Zooming In on Decisions," *Industry Week,* September 2, 1985, p. 46.

37. Robert Reed, "Staff Meetings that Work," *Supervision,* March 1987, p. 3.

38. Cooper and Ploor, "The Challenges that Make or Break a Group," p. 31.

39. Maureen Oberhammer, "Training the Team," *Training and Development Journal,* August 1986, p. 71.

40. "Problem People," *Successful Meetings,* December 1975, p. 6.

41. Reed, "Staff Meetings that Work," p. 3.

APPLICATION SITUATIONS

Types of Groups

AS 15—1

Identify each group as described:

a. a functional group   *b.* an ad hoc committee   *c.* a standing committee

_____ 1. Class groups that meet to discuss application situations, objective cases, and skill-building exercises.

_____ 2. A college group consisting of the heads of departments and the dean. They meet twice per month to discuss a wide variety of items.

_____ 3. A retail group that is meeting to decide on the purchase of (merger with) a clothing manufacturer to supply its clothes.

_____ 4. A group that meets to determine which books will be published. It consists of editors, marketing people, and general administrators.

_____ 5. A group of top executives and personnel people who meet to decide what to offer the union during labor negotiations.

Group Structure

AS 15—2

Identify which aspect of group structure each statement represents.

a. objectives   *d.* cohesiveness

b. size   *e.* status

c. norms   *f.* roles

_____ 6. "I'm a union man. If it wasn't for the union we would not be getting the pay we do. Collective bargaining really works."

_____ 7. "I could use another employee, but there is no work space available."

_____ 8. "I wish the administration would make up its mind. One month we produce one product, and the next month we change to another."

_____ 9. "When you need advice, go see Sharon; she knows the ropes around here better than anyone."

_____ 10. "Conrad, you're late for the meeting. Everyone else was on time, so we started without you."

Roles

AS 15—3

Identify the role each statement represents.

a. task   *b.* maintenance   *c.* self-interest

_____ 11. "Wait, we have not heard Kim's idea yet."

_____ 12. "Could you explain why we are doing this again?"

_____ 13. "We tried that before you came here; it does not work. My idea is much better."

_____ 14. "What does this have to do with the problem? We are getting sidetracked."

_____ 15. "I like that idea better than mine. Let's go with it."

Group Problem People

AS 15-4

Identify the problem type as being one of the following:

a. silent   *d.* bored

b. talkative   *e.* argumentative

c. wanderer

You should also decide what action you would take as the group leader.

_____ 16. "Jesse is always first or second to give his ideas. He is always elaborating on ideas. Because Jesse is so quick to respond, others sometimes make comments to him about it."

_____ 17. "Two of the group members are sitting back quietly today for the first time. The other members are doing all the discussing and volunteering for assignments."

_____ 18. As the group is discussing a problem, a member asks the group if it heard about the vice president and the salesclerk.

_____ 19. Eunice is usually last to give her ideas. When asked to explain her position, Eunice often changes her answers to agree with the group.

_____ 20. Hank enjoys challenging members' ideas. He likes to have the group do things his way. When a group member does not agree with him, Hank makes sardonic comments about the member's prior mistakes.

OBJECTIVE   CASE   15

Group Performance

Through reorganization, Christen has been assigned three additional departments. They all produce the same product. Ted, Jean, and Paul are the supervisors of these departments. Christen would like to increase productivity, so she set up a group to analyze the present situation and recommend ways to increase productivity. The group consists of Christen, the three supervisors, an industrial engineer, and an expert on group work from personnel. The group analyzed the present situation in each department as follows:

Group 1: Ted's department produces at or above standard on a regular basis. It averages between 102 percent and 104 percent of standard on a monthly basis. (Standard is 100 percent.) Members work well together; they often go to lunch together. All members produce at about the same level.

Group 2: Jean's department produces between 95 percent and 105 percent on a monthly basis. It usually produces 100 percent. The members do not seem to interact too often. Part of the reason for the current production level is two employees who consistently produce at 115 percent of standard. Jean will be retiring in six months, and they both want to fill her position. There are three members who consistently produce at 80 percent to 90 percent of standard.

Group 3: Paul's department achieves between 90 percent and 92 percent of standard on a monthly basis. In this department, Betty is a strong informal leader who oversees the production level. She lets members know whether they produce too much or too little. John is the only member in the department who reaches production standards. The rest of the department members do not talk to John. At times, they intentionally keep his level of production down. All other department members produce at about 90 percent of standard.

Answer the following questions, supporting your answers in the space between questions.

_____ 1. Christen, Ted, Jean, and Paul make up a(an) _____ group.
      a. functional   *b.* task   *c.* informal

_____ 2. To increase productivity, Christen set up a(an) _____ group.
      a. functional   *b.* ad hoc committee   *c.* standing committee

_____ 3. Which groups agree and are committed to *its* objectives?
      a. 1   *e.* 1 and 3
      b. 2   *f.* 2 and 3
      c. 3   *g.* 1, 2, and 3
      d. 1 and 2

_____ 4. Which group has objectives (positive norms) that agree with management standards?
      a. 1   *e.* 1 and 3
      b. 2   *f.* 2 and 3
      c. 3   *g.* 1, 2, and 3
      d. 1 and 2

————— 5. Which group is cohesive?
        a. 1   *e.* 1 and 3
        b. 2   *f.* 2 and 3
        c. 3   *g.* 1, 2, and 3
        d. 1 and 2

————— 6. Which group most clearly plays self-interest roles?
        a. 1   *b.* 2   *c.* 3

————— 7. Betty primarily plays a ——————— role for her group.
        a. task   *b.* maintenance   *c.* self-interest

————— 8. Group 1 appears to be in stage ——————— of development.
        a. 1   *d.* 4
        b. 2   *e.* 5
        c. 3

————— 9. Group 2 appears to be in stage ——————— of development.
        a. 1   *d.* 4
        b. 2   *e.* 5
        c. 3

————— 10. Group 3 appears to be in stage ——————— of development.
        a. 1   *d.* 4
        b. 2   *e.* 5
        c. 3

11. What would you recommend doing to increase productivity in each group?

PREPARATION FOR IN-CLASS SKILL-BUILDING EXERCISE

Group Structure

SB 15–1

Note: This exercise is designed for groups that have worked together for some time. (Five or more hours are recommended.)

Answer the following questions as they apply to your group in class.

1. Based on attendance, preparation, and class involvement, identify each member's level of commitment to the group. Include yourself. (Write each member's name on the appropriate line.)
   High commitment _____
   Medium commitment _____
   Low commitment _____

2. Our group is
   _____ too large   _____ too small   _____ okay
   Explain why.

3. List at least five norms your group has developed. Identify each as positive or negative.

   1.

   2.

   3.

   4.

   5.

   What positive norms could the group develop to help it function?

4. Based on the group's commitment, size, homogeneity, equality of participation, intragroup competition, and success, identify its cohesiveness level as
   _____ high   _____ medium   _____ low
   How does cohesiveness affect performance? What can be done to increase cohesiveness?

5. Identify each group member's status, including your own. (Write each group member's name on the appropriate line.)
   high _____
   medium _____
   low _____
   Does the group have status congruence? How can the group improve it?

6. Identify the roles members play. Write the names of each group member who plays each role on the appropriate line. You will most likely use each name several times and have more than one name on each line, but rank them by dominance.
   Task roles
   objective clarifier _____
   planner _____
   organizer _____
   controller _____

Maintenance roles

consensus seeker _____

harmonizer _____

gatekeeper _____

encourager _____

compromiser _____

Self-interest roles (if appropriate)

aggressor _____

blocker _____

recognition seeker _____

withdrawer _____

Which roles should be played more often, and which less, to increase effectiveness? Who should and should not play them?

7. Our group is in the _____ stage of development.

   1. orientation   2. dissatisfaction   3. resolution   4. production

   What can be done to increase the group's level of development?

8. Identify problem people, if any, by putting their names on the appropriate lines.

   silent _____

   talkative _____

   wanderer _____

   bored _____

   argumentative _____

   What can be done to help eliminate problem people? Specifically, who should do what?

9. Review your answers to the questions. In priority order, what should the group do to improve its structure? Specify what each member will do to improve the group's structure.

IN-CLASS SKILL BUILDING EXERCISE

Group Structure

SB 15–1

Note: This exercise is designed for groups that have met for some time. (Five or more hours are recommended.)

Objectives: To gain a better understanding of group structure and how it affects group performance. To improve group structure.

Experience: You will discuss your group's structure and develop plans to improve it.

Materials: You will need your answers to the preparation questions.

Procedure
(10–20 minutes)

Groups get together to discuss their answers to the nine preparation questions. Be sure to fully explain and discuss your answers. Try to come up with some specific ideas on how to improve your group's structure.

Conclusion: The instructor leads a class discussion and makes concluding remarks.

Application (2–4 minutes): What did I learn from this experience? How will I use this knowledge in the future?

Sharing: Volunteers give their answers to the application section.

PREPARATION FOR IN-CLASS SKILL-BUILDING EXERCISE

Situational Supervision of Groups

SB 15–2

Using Model 15–1, identify the group's development stage, the supervisory style each alternative represents, and the appropriate supervisory style for each situation described below. Indicate the stage of development (1, 2, 3, or 4) in the space marked "D." Identify each supervisory style (A, C, P, or L) in the space marked "S." Indicate the appropriate style by circling the letter preceding that alternative.

1. Your group works well together; members are cohesive with positive norms. They maintain a fairly consistent level of production that is above the organizational average, as long as you continue to provide maintenance behavior. You have a new assignment for them. D _____

   a. Explain what needs to be done and tell them how to do it. Oversee them while they perform the task. S _____
   b. Tell the group how pleased you are with their past performance. Explain the new assignment, but let them decide how to do it. Tell them you are available if they need help. S _____
   c. Tell the group what needs to be done. Encourage them to give input on how to do the job. Oversee performance. S _____
   d. Tell the group what needs to be done. S _____

2. You have been promoted to a new position. The group you will supervise appears to have little talent for the job, but they do seem to care about the quality of the work they do. The last supervisor was terminated because of the department's low productivity level. D _____

   a. Tell the group they have a low productivity level, but let them decide how to improve it. S _____
   b. Spend most of your time overseeing group members as they perform their jobs and training them as needed. S _____
   c. Tell the group you would like to work together to improve productivity. Work together as a team. S _____
   d. Describe ways productivity can be improved. Use members' ideas to develop methods and make sure they are implemented. S _____

3. Your department continues to be one of the top performers in the organization. Employees work well as a team. In the past, you generally let them take care of the work on their own. D _____

   a. Go around encouraging group members on a regular basis. S _____

    b. Define members' roles, and spend more time overseeing performance.
       S _____

    c. Continue things the way they are. Leave employees alone. S _____

    d. Hold a meeting. Recommend ways to improve and get members' ideas, as
       well. After agreeing on changes, oversee the group to make sure it
       implements the new ideas and does improve. S _____

4. You have spent much of the past year training your employees. You do not
  need to spend as much of your time overseeing production as you used to.
  However, several group members no longer get along as well as they did in the
  past. You've played referee lately. D _____

    a. Have a group meeting to discuss ways to increase performance. Let the
       group decide what changes to make. Be supportive. S _____

    b. Continue things the way they are now. Supervise them closely and be the
       referee when necessary. S _____

    c. Let the group alone to work things out for themselves. S _____

    d. Continue to supervise closely as needed, but spend more time playing
       maintenance roles; develop a team spirit. S _____

5. Your department has been doing such a great job that it has grown. You were
  surprised at how fast the new employees were integrated. The team continues
  to come up with ways to improve performance on its own. Due to the growth,
  your department will be moving to a new, larger location. D _____

    a. Design the new layout and present it to the group members to see whether
       they can improve upon it. S _____

    b. In essence, become a group member and allow the group to design the new
       layout. S _____

    c. Design the new layout and put a copy on the bulletin board so employees
       know where to report for work after the move. S _____

    d. Hold a meeting to get employee ideas on the layout of the new location.
       After the meeting, think about it and finalize the layout. S _____

6. You were appointed to head a task group. Because of the death of a relative,
  you had to miss the first meeting. At the second meeting, the group seems to
  have developed objectives and some ground rules. Members have already
  volunteered for assignments that had to be completed. D _____

    a. Take over as a strong leader. Change some ground rules and assignments.
       S _____

    b. Review what has been done so far, and keep things as they are. However,
       take charge and provide clear direction from now on. S _____

    c. Take over the leadership, but allow the group to make decisions. Be
       supportive and encourage them. S _____

    d. Seeing that the group is doing so well, leave and do not attend any more
       meetings. S _____

7. Your group was working at, or just below, standard. There has been a conflict
  within the group. As a result, production is behind schedule. D _____

    a. Tell the group how to resolve the conflict. Then closely supervise to make
       sure your advice is followed and production increases. S _____

    b. Let the group work it out. S _____

    c. Hold a meeting to work as a team to come up with a solution. Encourage
       the group to work together. S _____

    d. Hold a meeting to present a way to resolve the conflict. Sell the members
       on its merits, include their input, and follow up. S _____

8. The organization has allowed flextime. Two of your employees have asked
  whether they could change work hours. You are concerned because the

department needs adequate coverage during busy hours, as it has now. The department is very cohesive with positive norms. D _____

   a. Tell the employees things are going well; we'll keep things as they are now. S _____
   b. Tell them you will hold a department meeting to get everyone's input, and then you will reschedule hours. S _____
   c. Tell them you will hold a department meeting to get everyone's input, and then you will reschedule hours on a trial basis. If there is any drop in productivity, you will go back to the old schedule. S _____
   d. Tell them to hold a department meeting. If members agree to have at least three people on the job during the busy hours, they can make changes and give you a copy of the new schedule. S _____

9. You have arrived 10 minutes late for a department meeting. Your employees are discussing the latest assignment. This surprises you because, in the past, you had to provide clear direction and employees rarely would say anything. D _____

   a. Take control immediately and provide your usual direction. S _____
   b. Say nothing; just sit back. S _____
   c. Encourage the group to continue, but also provide direction. S _____
   d. Thank the group for starting without you, and encourage them to continue. Support their efforts. S _____

10. Your department is consistently very productive. However, occasionally, the members fool around and someone has an accident. There has never been a disabling injury. You just heard a noise and went to see what it was. From a distance you could see Sue sitting on the floor, laughing, with a company-made ball in her hand. D _____

   a. Say and do nothing. After all, she's okay and the group is very productive. You don't want to make waves. S _____
   b. Call the group together and ask for suggestions on how to keep accidents from recurring. Tell them you will be checking up on them to make sure it does not continue. S _____
   c. Call the group together and discuss the situation. Encourage them to be more careful in the future. S _____
   d. Tell the group that's it; from now on you will be checking up on them regularly. Bring Sue to your office and discipline her. S _____

11. You are at the first meeting of an ad hoc committee you are leading. Most of the members are second- and third-level managers from the marketing and financial areas. You are the supervisor from production. D _____

   a. Start by working on developing relationships. Get all members to feel as though they know each other before you talk about business. S _____
   b. Start by going over the group's purpose and the authority it has. Provide clear directives. S _____
   c. Start by asking the group to define its purpose. Because most of the members are higher-level managers, let them provide the leadership. S _____
   d. Start by providing both direction and encouragement. Give directives and thank people for their cooperation. S _____

12. Your department has done a great job in the past. It is now getting a new computer, somewhat different from the old one. You were trained to operate the computer and are expected to train your employees to operate it. D _____

    a. Give the group instructions. Then go around and work with them individually, providing direction and encouragement. S _____

    b. Get the group together to decide how they want to get instructions. Be very supportive of their efforts to learn. S _____

    c. Tell them it's a simple system. Give them a copy of the manual and have them study it on their own. S _____

    d. Give the group instructions. Then go around and supervise their work closely, giving additional instructions as needed. S _____

IN-CLASS SKILL-BUILDING EXERCISE

Situational Supervision of Groups

SB 15–2

Objectives: To help you understand the stages of group development. To use the appropriate situational supervision style.

Experience: You will discuss the supervisory styles you selected for the 12 preparation situations, and you will be given feedback on how appropriate your choices were.

Material: You should have completed the 12 preparation situations.

Procedure 1
(3–10 minutes)

The instructor reviews the group situational supervision model and explains how to apply it to situation 1. The instructor states the group's developmental stage (1 through 4), which should be on the line marked "D"; the supervisory style each alternative represents (A, C, P, L), which should be on the "S" line; and the scoring for each alternative (0 to 3).

Procedure 2

Option A (3–5 minutes). The instructor gives the class the recommended answers to situations 2 through 12, as in procedure 1, without any explanation.

Option B (10–30 minutes). Break into teams of two or three and discuss the situations. The instructor will then go over the recommended answers.

Conclusion: The instructor leads a class discussion and makes concluding remarks.

Application (2–4 minutes): What did I learn from this experience? How will I use this knowledge in the future?

Sharing: Volunteers give their answers to the application section.

16

Labor Relations

Learning Objectives   1. Discuss the history of unions, and present and future trends in labor organization.

2. Describe how the Norris-LaGuardia, Wagner, Taft-Hartley, and Landrum-Griffin acts have affected union-management relations.

3. List and explain the five steps of forming a union.

4. Describe the collective bargaining process and the supervisor's role in it.

5. Discuss the supervisor's role in contract administration.

6. List and explain the four steps in handling complaints and use the model.

7. List and explain the five levels of handling grievances.

Key Terms   To achieve our objectives in this chapter, it is important that you understand the following 10 key terms. They are presented in the order in which they appear in the chapter. The list of key terms also appears in alphabetical order in the end-of-chapter review.

labor relations	mediator	complaint
union	arbitrator	grievance
bargaining unit	union steward	complaint model
collective bargaining		